ESSENTIALS of
MARKETING
RESEARCH

Putting Research Into Practice

ESSENTIALS of MARKETING RESEARCH

Putting Research Into Practice

Kenneth E. Clow
University of Louisiana at Monroe

Karen E. James
Louisiana State University, Shreveport

Los Angeles | London | New Delhi
Singapore | Washington DC

Los Angeles | London | New Delhi
Singapore | Washington DC

FOR INFORMATION:

SAGE Publications, Inc.
2455 Teller Road
Thousand Oaks, California 91320
E-mail: order@sagepub.com

SAGE Publications Ltd.
1 Oliver's Yard
55 City Road
London EC1Y 1SP
United Kingdom

SAGE Publications India Pvt. Ltd.
B 1/I 1 Mohan Cooperative Industrial Area
Mathura Road, New Delhi 110 044
India

SAGE Publications Asia-Pacific Pte. Ltd.
3 Church Street
#10-04 Samsung Hub
Singapore 049483

Acquisitions Editor: Patricia Quinlin
Associate Editor: Maggie Stanley
Editorial Assistant: Katie Guarino
Production Editor: Libby Larson
Copy Editor: Melinda Masson
Typesetter: C&M Digitals (P) Ltd.
Proofreader: Dennis W. Webb
Indexer: Judy Hunt
Cover Designer: Karen Hovespian
Marketing Manager: Liz Thornton
Permissions Editor: Adele Hutchinson

Printed in the United States of America

Library of Congress Cataloging-in-Publication Data

Clow, Kenneth E.

Essentials of marketing research : putting research into practice / Kenneth E. Clow, Karen E. James.

p. cm.
Includes bibliographical references and index.

ISBN 978-1-4129-9130-8 (pbk.)

1. Marketing research. I. James, Karen E. II. Title.

HF5415.2.C56 2014
658.8′3—dc23   2012037172

This book is printed on acid-free paper.

12 13 14 15 16 10 9 8 7 6 5 4 3 2 1

Brief Contents

Detailed Contents

Preface

The only thing constant in life is change." This famous quote, largely attributed to French philosopher François de la Rochefoucauld, seems custom-made for marketing research. Clearly the field is changing. New technologies and emerging social trends make marketing research one of the most interesting and possibly volatile career choices possible.

We developed *Essentials of Marketing Research: Putting Research Into Practice* because we concluded that the methods used to teach today's emerging new marketing research need to be different. Further, we believe that the currently available texts do not meet the needs of the majority of students enrolled in the marketing research course required for most marketing majors. Toward that end, this book features four themes that make it distinct from other books and more useful to marketing students. These include:

- Strong emphasis on how to use marketing research to make better management decisions
- Focus on understanding and interpreting marketing research studies
- Application of marketing research to marketing and business situations
- Integration of data analysis, interpretation, application, and decision making throughout the entire text

First, then, as the book title notes, we *put research into practice* in every chapter. The goal is to show students how research is used by marketing professionals to make more informed decisions. While uncertainty cannot be eliminated, marketing research can reduce the uncertainty managers face in the decision-making process.

Second, the book has a *focus on understanding and interpreting marketing research studies*. While statistics and analytical techniques are presented in the text and are important, the focus of this text is on how to understand those findings and more importantly how to interpret the findings in a practical manner. Data analysis may show something to be significantly different, but what does that mean? How can it be interpreted, and is it of managerial significance? These types of questions are answered in every chapter of the text in a way that allows students to see how marketing research is used by businesses in the 21st century.

Third, this text focuses on the *application of marketing research to marketing and business situations*. The marketing situations faced by businesses today are different from what businesses faced even 10 years ago. Social media especially have revolutionized the way consumers communicate and how businesses market their brands. These changes have also impacted marketing research, especially in terms of data collection. But, they have also impacted reporting of results and the role marketing researchers have in the development of marketing strategies.

KEY FEATURES

This textbook was designed to help students learn, understand, and apply the concepts and theories of marketing research. A variety of methods are used to reach this goal. Each has a special purpose that addresses a component of learning.

Chapter Openings

Each chapter begins by describing the results of a research study that apply to the topics being presented in that chapter. These are taken from a variety of industries, with a greater emphasis on social media and the Internet. This approach allows students to better understand how firms use marketing research to make decisions. It also exposes students to research findings of practical value. Thus students not only benefit from a better understanding of how research results guide decision making, but their understanding of marketing tactics and marketing decision making is also enhanced.

Statistics Review

Beginning with Chapter 2, each chapter has a "Statistics Review" section that reviews basic principles of statistics. Rather than focusing on theory and formulas (as is common in statistical textbooks), the "Statistics Review" section of this text emphasizes the practical interpretation and application of the statistical principle being reviewed. Because many students take statistics two to four semesters prior to the marketing research class, this content provides a necessary and helpful refresher of statistical topics. Furthermore, the section addresses a common problem among undergraduate students in that many suffer from a disconnect between statistical theory, as explained in statistics courses, and practical application and usage of statistics, as required in marketing research courses.

Dealing With Data

As with the "Statistics Review," each chapter has a feature called "Dealing With Data." Most marketing research textbooks wait until the final few chapters to present data analysis and interpretation. Starting with Chapter 2, this text provides students with multiple opportunities to practice how to interpret and apply results to marketing decisions throughout the entire semester. When the section is used on a regular basis, repetition helps students to internalize the information, allowing for true learning to occur. Because students begin dealing with data in Chapter 2 and continue through the rest of the book, they develop a superior understanding of how to interpret and apply research results. Multiple SPSS data sets are provided at the textbook's accompanying website for instructor/student use. These data sets can be used for the purposes outlined in each chapter's "Dealing With Data" section or can be adapted by the instructor for use with additional assignments. For instructors who do not want to spend time teaching SPSS during class, step-by-step instructions for running analyses in SPSS are available at the textbook website. These instructions can also be used by students for review of the analytical process.

Continuing Case Study: Lakeside Grill

The "Lakeside Grill" is a comprehensive case and is positioned at the end of each chapter. The unique feature of this case is that it was conducted by students and as such can be a valuable teaching tool in a number of ways. While the team of students made some very good decisions in the research process, they also made some decisions that were not optimal. Questions follow each chapter segment of the case. These can be used for class discussion, in-class group work, or individual assignments. Because it is a continued case, it shows potential trade-offs, difficulties, and flaws that often occur during the implementation of a research project. Students can critically evaluate the decisions made, as well as how they were implemented, and suggest improvement. When assigned on a regular basis, this section is useful for reinforcing the chapter material, and very helpful in terms of developing students' critical thinking and analytical reasoning skills.

Glossary of Key Terms

Terms presented in bold are defined at the end of each chapter. This helps students to both review the chapter and reexamine the terms to make sure they understand them.

Presentation of Research Findings

This text has an emphasis on the presentation of research results. Graphs, tables, and figures are used extensively to present research findings. Early exposure to the use of graphing to present findings allows students to better understand when and how different types of charts or graphs should be used, as well as the necessity of using legends and meaningful titles. Plus, Chapter 14 discusses the most current presentation practices used by research practitioners, which differ radically from those of the past that are discussed by most textbooks. The applied focus in Chapter 14 helps students understand not only what information should be presented, but how it can be done most effectively.

Critical Thinking Exercises

These are not review questions. These critical thinking exercises are applied in nature, and emphasize key chapter concepts as well as understanding marketing research results and how they can be applied to decision making. They require students to utilize critical thinking and analytical skills. These exercises can easily be incorporated into class discussion, or assigned on a daily basis as homework. They may also be used as exam questions for those who prefer short-answer or problem-oriented testing.

Marketing Research Portfolio

The "Marketing Research Portfolio" section provides more challenging opportunities for students to apply chapter knowledge on an in-depth basis, and thus "learn by doing." A summary of each "Marketing Research Portfolio" is offered at the end of each chapter. The full "Marketing

Research Portfolio," containing expanded client information, key facts, tasks to be performed, and questions to be answered, is available on the open-access companion website: www.sagepub .com/clowess. With the exception of the final two chapters, each "Marketing Research Portfolio" can function as a stand-alone assignment, though some may incorporate tasks that span multiple chapters. These assignments challenge students to apply text material in an advanced fashion; critical thinking and secondary research skills can be honed in this manner. The "Marketing Research Portfolio" assignments can be used as individual or group assignments, in-class group tasks, or testing. If used extensively, the student will develop a portfolio of work that could be helpful when interviewing for jobs in the research industry.

Global Concerns

Firms competing in the global arena now more than ever need accurate information to enhance their decision making. Conducting research in foreign countries involves some unique challenges that are highlighted in each of the chapters of this text.

RESOURCES FOR STUDENTS

Several resources are available to students via the www.sagepub.com/clowess student website:

"Dealing With Data" Resources: Students have access to the "Dealing With Data" SPSS data sets, data collection instruments that accompany the data sets, and an expanded set of the SPSS instructions with embedded screenshots that will facilitate students' understanding of SPSS and various data analysis techniques.

SAGE Journal Articles: A "Learning From SAGE Journal Articles" feature provides access to recent, relevant full-text articles from SAGE's leading research journals. Each article supports and expands on the concepts presented in the chapter. This feature also provides discussion questions to focus and guide student interpretation.

Web Resources: These links to relevant websites direct both instructors and students to additional resources for further research on important chapter topics.

eFlashcards: These study tools reinforce students' understanding of key terms and concepts that have been outlined in the chapters.

Web Quizzes: Flexible self-quizzes allow students to independently assess their progress in learning course material.

RESOURCES FOR PROFESSORS

One of our goals in creating this textbook is to make sure professors can augment what is written in each chapter with additional teaching resources available at the textbook website, www.sagepub.com/clowess. The total package for this book includes the following.

Test Bank (Word®): This Word test bank offers a diverse set of test questions and answers for each chapter of the book. Multiple-choice, true/false, short-answer, and essay questions for every chapter help instructors assess students' progress and understanding.

PowerPoint® Slides: Chapter-specific slide presentations offer assistance with lecture and review preparation by highlighting essential content, features, and artwork from the book.

Lecture Notes: These lecture notes summarize key concepts on a chapter-by-chapter basis to help instructors prepare for lectures and class discussions. Chapter objectives and an outline of each chapter's material are also provided.

Sample Syllabi: Two sample syllabi—for semester and quarter courses—are provided to help professors structure their course.

Data Sets: Data files are provided that relate to the Lakeside Grill questions in the text. Data sets used in the "Statistics Review," certain critical thinking questions, and a "Marketing Research Portfolio" exercise are also available for instructor download and usage. Questionnaires accompanying the larger data sets are also provided.

SAGE Journal Articles: A "Learning From SAGE Journal Articles" feature provides access to recent, relevant full-text articles from SAGE's leading research journals. Each article supports and expands on the concepts presented in the chapter. This feature also provides discussion questions to focus and guide student interpretation.

Web Resources: These links to relevant websites direct both instructors and students to additional resources for further research on important chapter topics.

Answers to In-Text Questions: Answers to the in-text critical thinking questions are provided to help instructors with lectures and grading.

Marketing Research Portfolio: An expanded version of the "Marketing Research Portfolio" case is available to instructors.

ACKNOWLEDGMENTS

There are many persons who have assisted us in the development of this textbook.

We would like to thank the following individuals who assisted in the preparation of the manuscript through their careful and thoughtful reviews.

Gary J. Bamossy
Georgetown University

Hyejeung Cho
University of Texas at
San Antonio

David Crockett
Moore School of Business at
the University of South Carolina

Ronald E. Goldsmith
The Florida State University

James S. Gould
Pace University

Dr. Pola B. Gupta
Wright State University

Jared M. Hansen, PhD
University of North Carolina at Charlotte

Bill Hauser, PhD
Department of Marketing &
International Business
The University of Akron

Joel Herche
University of the Pacific

Alexandra Hutto
Metropolitan State College of Denver

Gauri Kulkarni
Loyola University Maryland

Vaidotas Lukosius
Tennessee State University

Sanjay S. Mehta
Sam Houston State University

Camelia Micu
Fairfield University

Mark S. Nagel
University of South Carolina

Tom Reilly
Virginia Polytechnic Institute and
State University

Srivatsa Seshadri
University of Nebraska Kearney

Chris Y. Shao
Midwestern State University

Ross B. Steinman
Widener University

Gail Tom
College of Business Administration
California State University,
Sacramento

Boonghee Yoo
Hofstra University

Finally, Kenneth Clow would like to thank many of the individuals at the University of Louisiana at Monroe. They continue to provide an exciting and accommodating work environment. He would also like to thank his sons Dallas, Wes, Tim, and Roy, who offer continuing encouragement and support.

Karen James would like to thank Douglas Bible and the management and marketing faculty at LSU Shreveport for their support. She also wishes to thank and acknowledge many former students, who served as "guinea pigs" for critical thinking and dealing with data exercises.

We would like to especially thank our spouses, Susan Clow and Marc James, for being patient and understanding during those times when the work seemed monumental. They have been enthusiastic and supportive for many, many years.

SECTION 1

Introduction to Marketing Research

CHAPTER 1

The Role of Marketing Research

LEARNING OBJECTIVES

After reading this chapter, you should be able to

1. Discuss the basic types and functions of marketing research.
2. Identify marketing research studies that can be used in making marketing decisions.
3. Discuss how marketing research has evolved since 1879.
4. Describe the marketing research industry as it exists today.
5. Discuss the emerging trends in marketing research.

■ Objective 1.1:
Discuss the
basic types
and functions
of marketing
research.

INTRODUCTION

Social media sites such as Facebook, Twitter, YouTube, and LinkedIn have changed the way people communicate. Accessing social media sites is now the number-one activity on the web. Facebook has over 500 million active users. The average Facebook user has 130 friends; is connected to 80 pages, groups, or events; and spends 55 minutes per day on Facebook. In 2011, marketers wanting to take advantage of this activity posted over 1 trillion display ads on Facebook alone.

Facebook is not the only social media site being used by consumers. LinkedIn now has over 100 million users worldwide. YouTube has exceeded 2 billion views per day, and more videos are posted on YouTube in 60 days than were created by the three major television networks in the last 60 years. Twitter now has over 190 million users, and 600 million–plus searches are done every day on Twitter.[1]

Social networks and communication venues such as Facebook and Twitter are where consumers are increasingly spending their time, so companies are anxious to have their voice heard through these venues. But, getting consumers to become a fan or agree to receive e-mails is only half of the battle. Engaging them with the brand and encouraging them to become active followers through these social media tactics is equally, if not more, difficult. While consumers join a company's Facebook page, or agree to receive e-mails and tweets, many are also opting out after a short time. For companies using social media, understanding why individuals opt out after agreeing to be a fan is important information. To gather this information, ExactTarget CoTweet surveyed 1,561 online users in the United States.[2] Figure 1.1 shows the results of the survey.

The top reason consumers quit being a brand fan on Facebook is because the company authors too many posts, which in turn clutters the recipients' wall with marketing information. The fact that messages tend to be repetitive, boring, and irrelevant, and are perceived by many fans as being overly promotional, is also an important factor in influencing fans to quit a brand's Facebook page. Companies can use these results to modify their marketing approach and how they author Facebook posts.

This type of information is provided by marketing research, which is defined as the systematic gathering and analysis of marketing-related data to produce information that can be used in decision making. Marketing research involves following a systematic sequence of steps that will produce reliable and valid data. Through analysis and interpretation the data are transformed into information suitable for decision-making purposes by managers. Typically, data alone are simply not usable. It is the analysis and interpretation of the data that makes them useful to managers.

Figure 1.1   Top Reasons Consumer Quit Brands on Facebook

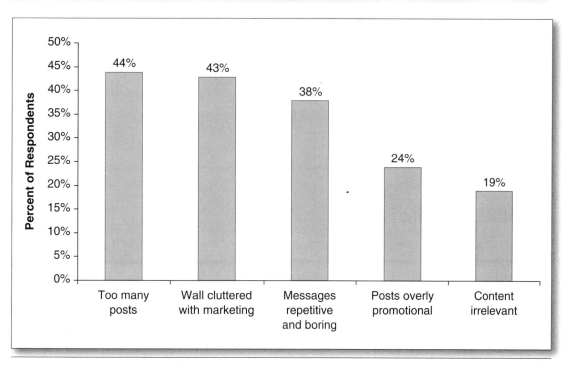

Source: Author-created with data from "The Social Break-up," Report #8, *ExactTarget CoTweet,* 2011, http://www.exacttarget.com/Resources/SFF8.pdf (retrieved June 9, 2012).

Figure 1.2 provides an example of marketing researchers turning data into useful information.[3] In this situation, consumers were asked the question, "In a typical week, how many hours do you spend with each of the following media?" The marketing researcher took the raw data, which was the number of hours spent with each type of media, and converted it into the percentage of time spent with each type of media. This allowed marketers to see that consumers now spend almost as much time with the Internet as they do with television. Further, almost 70% of consumer media time is spent either with television or with the Internet.

Figure 1.2   Percent of Time Consumers Spend With Each Media

Source: Author-created with data from Shar VanBoskirk, "US Interactive Marketing Forecast, 2009 to 2014," *Forrester Research Inc.*, July 6, 2009 (updated July 20, 2009).

―――――――――――――― ∞ ――――――――――――――

MARKETING RESEARCH

Marketing research may be conducted internally by the firm's marketing department or performed externally by a marketing research firm. The information gathered is then used to make decisions related to the marketing mix or other marketing functions. The **marketing mix** is the specific combination of product, pricing, promotional, and distribution decisions made for the purpose of targeting a particular group of consumers. Some of the more common marketing uses of research information include market segmentation, identifying specific target markets and their media habits, analyzing consumer behavior and needs, tracking customer satisfaction, developing new products, and evaluating various forms of advertising executions and pricing tactics. But, the use of marketing research information is not limited to just the marketing department. It can be used by all levels of management to make decisions that impact other aspects of a firm's operation. It can guide top management in making strategic decisions about acquisitions, divestitures, and expansion. It can be used by middle managers to develop production schedules, purchase raw materials, develop departmental budgets, and determine appropriate staffing levels.

Functions of Marketing Research

As shown in Figure 1.3, marketing research serves four primary functions within an organization. The **exploratory function** of marketing research occurs when researchers have a limited understanding or no knowledge at all about a marketing situation or a particular outcome. For example, a company may be losing customers or sales may be declining, but managers are not sure why. Marketing research can be used to explore some of the possible causes of lost sales or customers. Alternatively, a firm may be considering offering a new product in a category with which it has little experience. In this case, marketing research could be used to delve deep into a consumer's mind to uncover some of the hidden reasons or thought processes that go into making a purchase decision for the type of good being considered.

Figure 1.3   Functions of Marketing Research

- Exploratory
- Descriptive
- Diagnostic
- Predictive

Marketing research often serves a **descriptive function**, which refers to the gathering and presentation of information about a marketing phenomenon or situation. For example, marketing research can be used to describe the primary consumer of a product, such as a Panasonic HDTV or a John Deere tractor. It can be used to describe the process a customer uses in deciding on a restaurant for dinner, such as Romano's Macaroni Grill or Outback Steakhouse. Figure 1.4 illustrates the descriptive function of marketing research since it shows the primary reason individuals watch the Super Bowl football game. While the majority, 55%, are mostly interested in the football game, some watch it specifically to see the commercials (15%), and others watch for the social aspect of being with family and friends (27%).[4]

The **diagnostic function** of marketing research is particularly helpful in many situations. Here, data analysis techniques are used to investigate relationships and phenomena within data that have been gathered through marketing research. The analysis may show that females eat at Olive Garden more frequently than males. It may show the reasons individuals opt out of subscribing to a Facebook brand page, as was shown in Figure 1.1. Further analysis of the data may show different reasons for opting out of a Twitter feed and an e-mail permission program. The diagnostic function is important to marketers because it allows marketers to discover interrelationships with data.

The **predictive function** of marketing research allows data to be used to predict or forecast the results of a marketing decision or consumer action. Retailers use predictive research to determine what items a consumer is likely to purchase together so suggestive selling can be used. Barnes & Noble utilizes this technique when website customers select a particular book and the software then suggests other books they might also want to purchase. Marketing research can be used to estimate the impact of a coupon or another sales promotional offer. It is often used to estimate the market share of a brand extension or new product introduction.

Figure 1.4   Primary Reason Individuals Watch the Super Bowl

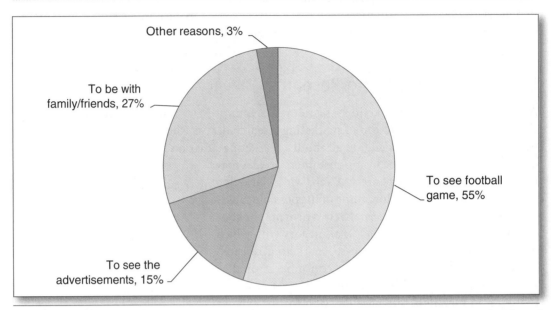

Source: Author-created with data from "Super Bowl Sunday Consumer Survey," Super Bowl XLV (January 2011), *Lightspeed Research*, p. 17.

Applied Versus Basic Research

Marketing research can be either applied or basic. **Applied marketing research** is designed to solve a specific marketing problem, to investigate a particular marketing phenomenon, or to understand the results of previous decisions. The previous research investigating why consumers opt out of a brand's Facebook page and why individuals watch the Super Bowl are examples of applied research. Most commercial marketing research and research conducted internally by research departments is applied research since companies are seeking solutions to problems or information that can help them exploit potential opportunities. Marketing research should provide information that will allow managers to make better marketing decisions.

Understanding why individuals watch the Super Bowl football game is an example of applied research.

Basic marketing research is more theoretical in nature and is conducted to advance marketing knowledge in general or to verify a proposed marketing theory or concept. Findings from basic research studies cannot be implemented by managers in the short run. This is because basic research is typically not conducted in the context of a particular brand or firm, or for the purpose of solving a specific marketing problem or exploiting an opportunity facing a given brand or firm.

Most basic marketing research is conducted by academicians in an effort to advance our knowledge of marketing. For instance, many research studies use questions to assess how consumers claim they will act when confronted with a given situation. A recent basic research study evaluated four different methods by which *consumers' willingness to pay* for an item is commonly measured in consumer research studies, and compared the results with actual purchase data in an effort to ferret out the relative strengths and weaknesses of each measurement technique.[5] The results of this study cannot be immediately applied to any *particular* problem facing a firm, but rather serve to advance our knowledge of marketing research practices. However, in the future, the results of the study may influence the types of questions asked as part of an applied research study commissioned by a firm that needs to investigate consumers' willingness to pay for their product as part of a larger research study.

The Philosophy of Science

The philosophy of science underlies researchers' efforts to make sense of the world and its various activities and events in a wide variety of disciplines. The philosophy of science assumes that for a given event or activity, causes or "antecedents" can be identified, meaning that things don't just happen; they happen for a reason. Thus, scientific research seeks rational and logical explanations for activities or events that are true the vast majority of the time. Most marketing researchers desire to be 95% confident that the results of their research efforts are accurate and unlikely to have occurred by chance. The philosophy of science also tends to value a more general understanding of events or phenomena (i.e., why Facebook fans quit "liking" brands), as opposed to understanding of a particular event (i.e., why Facebook fans of Diet Coke quit "liking" the brand). This is because such knowledge is useful in forming theories and because it allows a scientific law to be generalized, meaning it can be applied to a larger group of activities or events. By contrast, the reasons why Diet Coke Facebook fans "quit" liking the brand may be unique to Coca-Cola, and though this information would be helpful to the firm from a broad scientific standpoint, the information would be not at all useful in the formulation of theory or scientific law.

Another characteristic inherent in the philosophy of science is that science, by its very nature, is empirically verifiable, meaning that the theories and laws created can be tested through the collection and analysis of data. The nature of science and empirical testing is such that we can never totally prove a theory to be true; however, the more a theory is subjected to testing under different conditions, and the more empirical testing fails to disprove the theory, the more confident researchers can be in the validity, or truthfulness, of the results. So part of the research process is to also investigate the specific conditions under which a law or theory could be disproved.

Finally, the philosophy of science requires that researchers remain open to the possibility of change and modification. It is common for a scientific theory to be tested over time and eventually disproven in too many circumstances, ultimately leading to better theories with greater explanatory value.[6]

The Scientific Method

In conducting marketing research, it is important that researchers follow the scientific method shown in Figure 1.5. The research process begins with a thorough investigation of current knowledge. Whether applied or basic research, marketing researchers should examine current knowledge on the topic and review prior research. This typically involves examining past research studies, academic articles, news articles, and facts, figures, and statistics from a variety of sources. From this state of current knowledge, researchers can develop a theory that explains the nature of what is being studied, followed by one or more hypotheses. The next step is to design a study and then collect the data to test the hypothesis. It is important to state the hypothesis prior to collecting data to prevent the data from biasing the hypothesis in any way. From the data, the researcher can draw conclusions, advance theories, and create new knowledge that can be used for future research. The cycle then begins again.

Figure 1.5   The Scientific Method

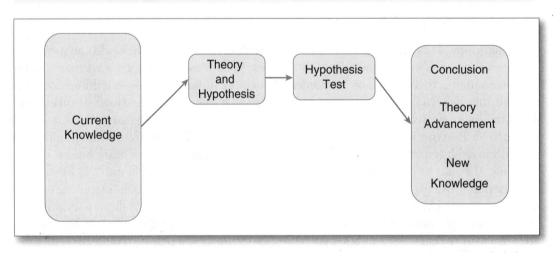

■ Objective 1.2: Identify marketing research studies that can be used in making marketing decisions.

MARKETING RESEARCH AND DECISION MAKING

The primary objective of conducting marketing research is to support marketing decisions. Managers will never have perfect knowledge, and as a result there will always be some uncertainty in choosing a course of action. But, through marketing research, the amount of uncertainty can be reduced, allowing the manager to be more confident the correct or best decision is being made. Marketing research plays a role in a number of marketing areas, as shown in Figure 1.6.

Segmentation and Targeting

Marketing research provides essential information for decisions on segmentation and targeting. Benefit and lifestyle studies examine the similarities and differences consumers seek in products and how these

Figure 1.6   Marketing Research and Marketing Decisions

- Segmentation and targeting
- Product development
- Marketing communications and media selection
- Market and competitive analysis
- Pricing and sales potential/forecast studies
- Site selection and distribution studies

benefits fit into particular lifestyles. This information is then coupled with **target market analysis,** which provides basic demographic, geographic, psychographic, and behavioral information about specific target markets. From these research studies, marketers can decide which segments best match the features of their brands. Details such as usage patterns, attitudes, preferences, and lifestyles will allow a company to make better segmentation and targeting decisions.

Product Development

Marketing research is used in all stages of product development. Research can be used in the concept stage to gather customer input on ideas for a new product or modifications of a current product. **Product testing studies** identify how a product fits the needs of consumers and what changes need to be made to the product to make it more attractive. **Test markets** can be conducted to provide information on how well a new product or product modification will do before the product is launched. Modifications and decisions that will increase the probability that the new product will be successful can be made based on the results of the test market.

Marketing Communications and Media Selection

Marketing research can provide valuable information concerning marketing communications (MarCom) and media selection. **Advertising effectiveness research** examines the effectiveness of advertising and marketing communications. These studies can be conducted on a continuous basis and compared to a benchmark, previous ad campaigns, or competitive advertising. Input from these research studies allows marketers to develop more effective advertising and marketing communications. It also can identify when consumers are not paying attention any longer and allows for detection of when an ad is wearing out. **Media studies** are used to identify the most appropriate media to reach a specific target market. In addition to the best media, media studies will also identify the best vehicles, such as the best magazines or the best television shows to use.

Market and Competitive Analyses

A **market analysis study** will examine the current marketing situation faced by a company or brand and then identify potential markets. While market analysis studies are especially important for new products or entry into new markets, the studies are also important for current products, as market dynamics change. Companies can lose market share quickly if they do not stay in touch with current consumer behavior trends. Just like market analysis studies, **competitive analysis studies** should be conducted regularly to ensure market share is not lost to competitors. Many organizations will use a marketing information system to gather market and competitive information on a continuous basis.

Pricing and Forecasting

Pricing is an important determinant in buying decisions, so **pricing studies** can be used to evaluate the elasticity of a brand's price and the impact pricing changes will have on demand.

Part of a pricing study is to examine competitors' prices and determine how consumers (or businesses) evaluate price relative to other product features. Additional studies, such as **sales forecasts** and **sales potential studies,** are used to estimate future sales. These studies are often used for budgeting, production, and staffing decisions.

Site Selection and Distribution

Finally, **site selection** studies help retailers determine the best locations for their stores. Other research studies can help determine whether a single- or multichannel distribution system will be most effective, which channels a manufacturer should use, how logistics can be improved, and so forth.

Marketing research is an essential input into marketing management decisions. The studies previously cited are just a few examples of the types of information marketing research can provide. Because of the impact marketing decisions make on a firm's income and profit generation, obtaining good information through marketing research has become more critical.

■ Objective 1.3: Discuss how marketing research has evolved since 1879.

BRIEF HISTORY OF MARKETING RESEARCH

The first documented instance of marketing research was in 1879 and was conducted by the advertising agency N. W. Ayer. The company surveyed state and local officials about expected levels of grain production. This information was used by a manufacturer of farm equipment in the preparation of an advertising schedule. From that first beginning marketing research slowly evolved. The basic foundation of marketing research was developed during the first 30 years of the 20th century. The first textbook on marketing research was published in 1921, and the first marketing research courses taught on college campuses occurred in the 1930s.[7]

The early years of marketing research focused on methods of sampling, collecting data, and analytical techniques. Researchers also focused on ways to measure concepts such as opinions, perceptions, preferences, attitudes, personalities, and lifestyles. The primary goal of marketing research at that time was to measure marketing phenomena and consumer characteristics. Raw data were converted to information, which was then passed on to managers to make decisions.

The period of the 1970s and 1980s is often referred to as the "golden age of consumer research." During this time marketing research techniques became more scientific. Computing power made collecting and analyzing data faster, easier, cheaper, and more accurate. Companies invested substantial dollars into marketing research to better understand the market, the consumer, and the decision process. Few decisions were made that were not supported by marketing research. Research study results became the support or rationale for choosing particular marketing strategies and marketing tactics.[8]

During the late 1990s and early 2000s a cultural shift in marketing research began to occur. Decision makers wanted more than support for marketing decisions. They wanted marketing researchers to offer insights into what the data meant. Simply describing potential markets, characteristics of consumers, and the decision process was no longer sufficient. Decision makers wanted insights into why particular choices were made by consumers and how the results of a marketing research study could provide a better understanding of the best strategies and tactics. Marketing researchers were no longer just data providers. They were to assist in providing insights into marketing situations.

Some marketing researchers believe we are now beginning to enter another, newer phase of marketing research—the consultative stage. Just providing insights may no longer be enough. Managers want marketing researchers to be part of the solution, to provide input and direction into marketing decisions. For traditional marketing researchers, this is a challenge. They were trained and educated in data analysis. Now, they are being asked to assist in developing marketing strategy. It means not only do the researchers need a thorough understanding of marketing research; they must also have a thorough understanding of marketing and especially marketing planning and strategy. Figure 1.7 highlights these various stages.

Figure 1.7 Historical Stages of Marketing Research

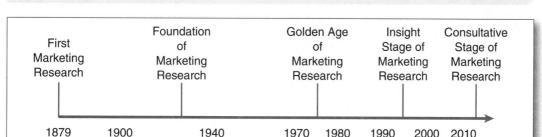

THE MARKETING RESEARCH INDUSTRY TODAY

Major catalysts of the significant changes in marketing research in the last two decades are (1) the rise of international competition and (2) the explosion of communications and computer technology. Figure 1.8 provides a pictorial illustration of the marketing research industry as it exists today.[9] While it looks complicated, it is not. But, it does illustrate how interrelated the components of marketing research have become and how a research project often involves multiple entities.

The client companies illustrated in the figure are numerous firms such as Nike, Kraft Foods, Home Depot, Toyota, and Sony. These companies are called client companies because they are the ones seeking information for making decisions through marketing research. Chapter 2 will provide an overview of the research process and the request for proposal (RFP) that is issued by client companies.

Conducting Research In-House Versus Outsourcing

When the decision has been made to conduct marketing research, client companies have two alternatives: (1) They can conduct the research study themselves, or (2) they can hire a marketing research firm. If the company is large and has a research division, then the marketing research study may be conducted internally within the firm. Even though a company has a research division, it may not conduct all of the studies that are needed. The department may be overloaded and need to commission a research firm to conduct particular studies. Or, it may want an independent research firm to conduct a particular study to prevent internal bias from impacting the outcome. Also, when commercially available research studies could provide the

■ Objective 1.4: Describe the marketing research industry as it exists today.

Figure 1.8   Marketing Research Industry Today

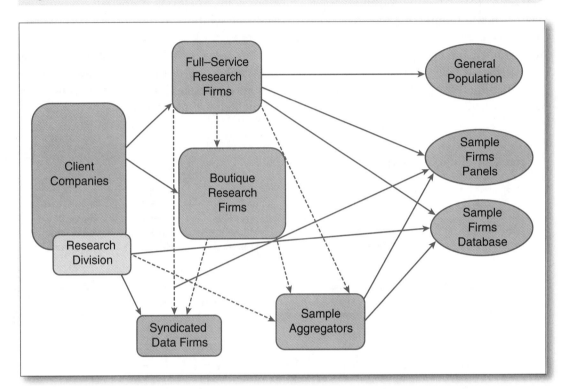

information needed to solve the research problem, the research division may simply purchase this information from a commercial syndicated data firm. Many full-service market research firms also subscribe to a wide variety of syndicated data sources.

The decision to conduct research in-house versus hiring a marketing research firm rests on many factors. Generally, it is less expensive to conduct research in-house, so the budget available for a given study is one factor. The level of specialization required for the study is also a critical factor. It would make sense to hire a firm that specializes in Hispanic marketing research, such as ThinkNow Research, than it would to attempt such research in-house. But, in other cases, in-house corporate research departments are chosen over external suppliers when a full-service firm lacks the business or technical knowledge necessary to truly understand the industry or problems facing the firm. The current workload of those employed by the firm's internal research division might also be important. However, while one might reasonably assume that outsourced research projects free up time for the in-house research staff, surprisingly, a recent online survey of 197 corporate researchers found that making more time available for the firm's internal research staff was not a factor in determining whether or not research duties were outsourced. The study conducted by Research Innovation and ROI in partnership with *Quirk's Marketing Research Review* divided corporate researchers who responded to the survey into three groups: those whose corporate research departments relied primarily on full-service firms to conduct their research, those that relied primarily on their own internal efforts for research, and those that split research duties fairly evenly between external suppliers and their own in-house research department. Corporate research respondents were asked to indicate the importance of each factor in the decision to conduct the research in-house or outsource the study to an external entity.[10] The results of this survey are shown in Figure 1.9.

Figure 1.9   Pros and Cons of In-House Versus Outsourced Research

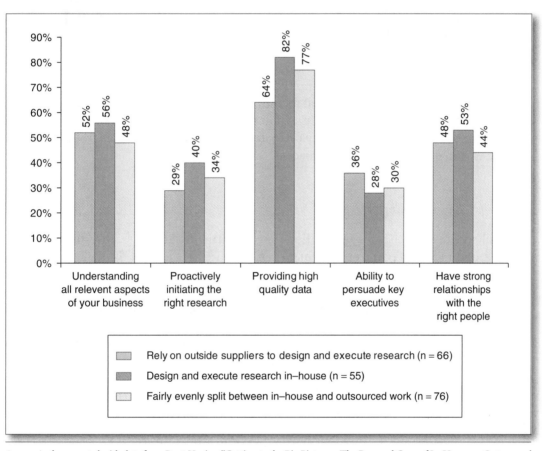

Source: Author-created with data from Brett Hagins, "Getting to the Big Picture—The Pros and Cons of In-House vs. Outsourced Research," *Quirk's Marketing Research Review* (May 24, 2011).

The most important factor for all three types of corporate researchers was the quality of data, though the importance level varied by group. While 82% of those designing and executing research in-house indicated this factor was important, quality was of lesser importance (64%) to firms that relied on an outside supplier. When hiring an external supplier, the client firm has no control over the data collection process. Thus, if high-quality data is an important factor, then often the decision is to conduct the study in-house because the firms have more control over the integrity of the data. The least important factors influencing the decision to go in-house or outsource were the ability of the marketing researcher to persuade key executives concerning the findings of the research and proactively initiating the right research.

Full-Service and Boutique Market Research Firms

If the decision is made to hire a marketing research firm, a company has a wide array of choices from small boutique firms to full-service research agencies. Full-service agencies, called "full-servs" within the industry, have the capability of conducting all types of research, including focus groups, individual interviews, telephone surveys, mail surveys, Internet surveys, and more. These companies start with the research objectives the client firms want to accomplish. The full-serv will then design the study, collect data, analyze the data, and make a report.

While full-service research firms offer a full array of services, boutique firms specialize in either a particular type of research or a particular type of audience. For instance, ThinkNow Research focuses only on Hispanic respondents and firms that want to research the Hispanic market. EC Insights is a boutique research agency that specializes in providing meaningful insights and strategic guidance for a brand throughout its life cycle. The Realise Group is a boutique marketing research agency that focuses on mystery shopping in the retail sector providing retailers with a full measurement and evaluation of customer experiences. Axion is a boutique agency that specializes in creative research methods that utilize focus groups, in-depth interviews, and other one-on-one approaches.

Sample Aggregators

Both full-service research firms and boutique research firms design the research study, interpret the data, and make a report to the client. When it comes to collecting the data, the research firm has three basic choices. First, it can use the general population and one of the sampling techniques that will be discussed in Chapter 8 of this text. The second option is to use one of the many companies that specialize in providing samples and collecting data. Third, the research agency can go to a **sample aggregator,** which is a firm that collects data through utilizing multiple sample companies. While some full-serv and boutique agencies will collect their own data using the general population, most are moving away from doing their own data collection and are using companies that specialize in sampling.

Research firms are shifting the sample selection and data collection to independent companies for two primary reasons: cost and time. It is more cost effective to use sampling firms that already have sample panels (groups of individuals who have agreed in advance to participate in research studies) or databases. It is also more time efficient. Both are important as client companies push for faster, but lower cost, results.

A new player in the research industry is the sample aggregator. This is a company that knows the sample and data collection industry and can work with either a client company or a marketing research firm to expedite the data collection process and at the same time provide a better quality, more valid sample. For instance, if a company wants to survey decision makers related to the purchase of computer software in medium to large companies internationally, a sample aggregator such as ReRez can identify various sample firms that have these types of respondents. It is unlikely any one sample provider will have enough people within its panel or database to fill the quota desired by the client. Thus, ReRez can contract with a number of different sampling firms throughout the countries specified by the client. Furthermore, extensive experience with various sampling firms allows the sample aggregator to limit its selection to only those firms that practice strong quality control practices. As you will learn later, the quality of the sample—particularly when it is Internet based—is extremely important in assuring that the information provided to the client is accurate and meaningful. Thus, an aggregator such as ReRez can better ensure that the responses are valid and truly represent software decision makers. Finally, through the firm's expertise, the data can be collected accurately, and in a timely and cost-effective manner.

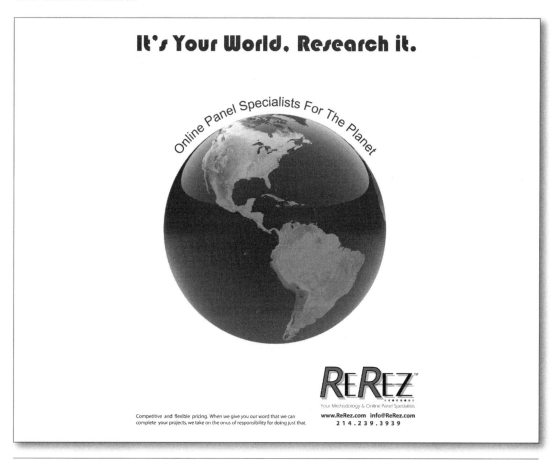

Source: ReRez.

EMERGING TRENDS IN MARKETING RESEARCH

For many years marketing research relied on landline telephones and mail surveys to conduct research. While other methods were used, these were the mainstay; then came the dawn of the 21st century. A number of significant changes occurred that have had and will continue to have a profound effect on marketing research. Some of these changes are still occurring, and the full-service marketing research firms have to adapt quickly or be left behind by smaller, more nimble start-up research agencies that can see what is occurring. The major factors influencing the changes are listed in Figure 1.10. While these factors are listed separately and discussed separately, they are all interrelated, which has created a synergistic impact that is having a profound effect on the way marketing research is being conducted now and how it will be conducted in the future.[11]

■ Objective 1.5: Discuss the emerging trends in marketing research.

Figure 1.10   Factors Impacting
the Marketing
Research Industry

- Telecommunications technology
- Economics
- Competition

Telecommunications Technology

Advances in telecommunications, primarily social media and smartphones, have impacted consumers all over the world and created a significant change in the way individuals communicate with each other, with brands, and with companies. Social media and smartphones have not just changed the way people communicate, but have created cultural changes as well. Individuals now can communicate with one another through social media, such as Facebook, or through Twitter, instead of talking in person or even calling on the phone. An individual in Maine can communicate with someone in California or even in Spain or Japan at a fraction of the cost that talking via phones would incur. Smartphones allow these individuals to take the Internet with them, which means they don't even have to telephone someone to talk. They can use text messages, or access the Internet and correspond through e-mail, Skype, or some type of social media platform.

This technology has changed the way brands and firms are influenced by word-of-mouth communication. If consumers have a bad experience with a brand, they are not limited to telling just a few of their friends and family members verbally. They can now use social media and Twitter and be "heard" by thousands of consumers all over the world within hours and many times within minutes. The potential for negative word-of-mouth can be devastating to a brand. On a positive note, this same technology can be used to engage consumers and stimulate positive endorsements.

The cultural shift in communications is now beginning to impact the marketing research industry. Marketing researchers have for decades relied on surveys to gather information. That approach is quickly shifting to social media. According to Joan Lewis, global consumer

Cell phones, especially smartphones, have changed the way people communicate and as a result have impacted the way marketing research is conducted.

and marketing knowledge officer of Procter & Gamble, the marketing research industry should get away from "believing a method, particularly survey research, will be the solution to everything. We need to be methodology agnostic. Social-media listening isn't only replacing some survey research but also making it harder to do by changing consumer behavior and expectations." Taking this thought further, she says, "The more people see two-way engagement and being able to interact with people all over the world, I think the less they want to be involved in structured research. If I have something to say to that company now, there are lots of ways to say it."[12]

As a result, companies are now monitoring social media. They are listening to what consumers are saying and responding. They see social media as a means of engaging consumers in two-way communication. For marketing research firms, it is a new avenue for collecting data and monitoring consumers' conversations about brands. Smartphones now make the process of collecting data and monitoring possible 24/7 regardless of where the consumer is located. This makes data collection faster and easier as it is no longer necessary to reach consumers at their home or place of business.

Economics

The financial crisis that hit the world in the beginning of the 21st century produced significant changes in the marketing research industry. It was stressful for traditional marketing research firms but an opportunity for start-up companies and traditional full-service agencies that recognized changes were about to occur. Business as usual had vaporized. Tighter corporate budgets meant finding firms that could produce more results for less money, more quickly than research had been completed in the past. Faced with these demands from clients, marketing research firms had two choices: (1) earn less revenue and less profit or (2) find a cheaper and faster way of conducting marketing research. The solution: both!

Marketing research firms had to do what the rest of the business, private, and governmental sector experienced—tighten their costs and learn to operate on lower revenues and lower profits, yet produce the same or higher levels of results. Unfortunately, as a result of this experience, client companies realized they could get the same research done at lower costs and that huge sums of money were not necessary to fund research studies, an attitude that prevails today, despite the fact that the economy has recovered somewhat.

Research firms were forced to look for cheaper ways to conduct research. A solution was to utilize online marketing research via e-mail, Internet survey websites, and online panels and databases. The cost of conducting a survey online versus in person or by telephone is considerably cheaper and typically faster. Another advantage is that, with smartphones, consumers can be reached anywhere, anytime. Of course, the survey methodology needs to be changed, but research firms knew that could be done!

Competition

While tighter client budgets and online research techniques were prompted by changes in the economic environment, competition sparked two additional changes in marketing research—accelerated timelines and an increased focus on international research. Because of global competition, firms are increasingly seeking to conduct research internationally.

If a brand is distributed in 14 countries, then in most cases, research should be conducted in all 14 countries. If a company is planning to expand into a new region of the world, then research should be conducted in that region and within each country or province of that region.

Coupled with the need to do research in multiple countries, research firms faced a compression of the timeline. Instead of having months to complete a marketing research study, many companies now expect the entire project to be completed within 6–8 weeks.[13] For this to happen, the data collection component of the research needed to be streamlined. This time compression for research studies contributed to an increased reliance on firms specializing in sample provision, primarily with online samples. In almost all cases, online data collection can occur considerably faster than other methods such as telephone, mail, or in person.

OVERVIEW OF THE TEXT

The textbook is divided into four sections. Section 1 introduces marketing research by providing an overview of marketing research and an explanation of the marketing research process. Section 2 reviews the various types of marketing research, including secondary research, qualitative research, observation research, experimental research, and survey research. The third section explains how data are obtained via sampling and measured using scales and survey questions. Questionnaire design considerations are also addressed. Finally, Section 4 describes how data are analyzed using fundamental and more advanced statistical methods, and how they are reported.

Global Concerns

Because of the increase in global competition and due to the elimination of geographic barriers and lower costs provided by the Internet, marketing research is now being conducted on a broader scale that involves multiple countries. Compared to the past, fewer studies by major firms are limited to the United States or just one country. Expanding research into additional countries involves some unique challenges that will be highlighted in each of the chapters of this text.

A primary challenge, of course, is the translation of surveys into various languages. English is a very rich language, and sometimes there is not an equivalent word available in a foreign language, forcing the question to be reworded to ensure a similar meaning. But, more problematic is the difference in cultures. What is appropriate to ask in one country may be deemed to be inappropriate in another. For instance, interviewing females in Western countries is perfectly acceptable. But, to do so in many Middle Eastern countries is not as acceptable unless a male is present. Furthermore, in most cases it needs to be a female-female surveyor and respondent relationship.

In some countries like the United States, getting individuals to participate in studies is difficult. That is one reason for the increased usage of online panels and databases. But, in some of the developing countries, individuals are eager to participate in studies. It is novel and new to them. Of course, this raises questions of how representative the samples are in both situations, in the United States where participation is difficult to obtain and in other countries where individuals are eager to participate.

STATISTICS REVIEW

Statistics are important in marketing research because any data that are obtained must be analyzed and then converted to useful information. Most courses in marketing research have statistics as a prerequisite. The ideal would be if students took the course in statistics immediately prior to the course in marketing research. Seldom does this occur. It may have been one or even two years since the statistics course was taken.

For this reason, rather than wait until the data analysis chapter of this text to discuss statistics, a "Statistics Review" section has been incorporated into each chapter. The material presented in this section should not be new. However, it may appear new depending upon when the statistics course was taken and how well the concepts were learned. Reviewing these topics in smaller chunks on a chapter-by-chapter basis will make it easier to relearn the statistical concepts than cramming the entire content into one or two chapters near the end of the marketing research course.

 DEALING WITH DATA

Data are central to marketing research. While some marketing research involves collection of information that is not in the form of data, most marketing research has some type of data. These data must be examined, analyzed, and converted to information that is useful to managers for decision making. Rather than wait until the end of this text to discuss data analysis, each chapter contains a "Dealing With Data" section. The concepts presented and the exercises shown are designed to allow students to apply the "Statistics Review" section to marketing research data. Exercises and information in this section should not be new, but as with the "Statistics Review" they may appear new depending on how long ago the statistics course was taken and how well the material was learned. The majority of the data sets are provided in SPSS format. SPSS is an advanced statistical analysis program used by many universities, large corporations, and marketing research firms. Limited instructions for using SPSS will be incorporated into the "Dealing With Data" section. More detailed step-by-step instructions for using SPSS can be found on the textbook's companion website at www.sagepub.com/clowess.

SUMMARY

Objective 1: Discuss the basic types and functions of marketing research.

Marketing research studies can perform one or more of the following functions: exploratory, descriptive, diagnostic, and predictive. Most commercial marketing research studies are applied research, while basic marketing research is typically conducted in university settings. The philosophy of science and scientific method guides the marketing research process.

Objective 2: Identify marketing research studies that can be used in making marketing decisions.

Segmentation and targeting decisions often rest on data obtained via benefit and lifestyle studies and target market analysis. Product testing studies and test markets provide essential information as part of the new product development process. Existing brands benefit from market analysis and competitive analysis studies, which allow decision makers to understand changes in the dynamic marketplace and how their brands will be affected. Marketing communication decisions are enhanced by data stemming from advertising effectiveness research and media studies. Pricing studies evaluate the impact that pricing changes have on demand, and studies of sales potential and sales forecasting efforts are used by many departments within the firm.

Objective 3: Discuss how marketing research has evolved since 1879.

The first documented instance of marketing research occurred in 1879 with the basic foundation of marketing research being developed during the first 30 years of the 20th century. The early years of marketing research focused on methods of sampling, collecting data, and analytical techniques. The primary goal of marketing research was to measure marketing phenomena and consumer characteristics. During the "golden age of consumer research" (1970s and 1980s) marketing research techniques become more scientific, and computing power made collecting and analyzing data faster, easier, cheaper, and more accurate. Marketing research became the support, the rationale for choosing particular marketing strategies and marketing tactics. During the late 1990s and early 2000s a cultural shift resulted in researchers being asked to provide insights into what the data meant and to assist in providing insights into marketing situations. The current stage of marketing research is "the consultative stage." Now, marketing researchers are being asked to assist in developing marketing strategy.

Objective 4: Describe the marketing research industry as it exists today.

Client firms conduct research in-house or hire full-serv or boutique marketing research firms to provide information needed for decision making. Data collection can be undertaken with the general population, or a firm may be hired to provide a sample from its panel or database. Research agencies are increasingly relying upon sample aggregators to obtain more representative, reliable samples.

Objective 5: Discuss the emerging trends in marketing research.

Advances in telecommunications technology have changed the ways that consumers interact with each other, companies, and brands. Marketing researchers now monitor social media as a result. Economic constraints have tightened client budgets, while competitive pressures have compressed deadlines and forced research firms to embrace the Internet as a faster, more cost-effective method of data collection. Furthermore, the globalization of business has resulted in a greater need for multicountry marketing research efforts.

GLOSSARY OF KEY TERMS

Advertising effectiveness research: research that examines the effectiveness of advertising and marketing communications

Applied marketing research: research designed to solve a specific marketing problem, to investigate a particular marketing phenomenon, or to understand the results of previous decisions

Basic marketing research: research conducted to advance marketing knowledge in general or to verify a proposed marketing theory or concept

Benefit and lifestyle studies: research that examines the similarities and differences consumers seek in products and how these benefits fit into particular lifestyles

Competitive analysis studies: research that examines competitors within a market industry

Descriptive function: gathering and presentation of information about a marketing phenomena or situation

Diagnostic function: data analysis techniques used to investigate relationships and phenomena within data that have been gathered through marketing research

Exploratory function: occurs when researchers have a limited understanding or no knowledge at all about a marketing situation or a particular outcome

Market analysis study: research that examines the current marketing situation faced by a company or brand and then identifies potential markets

Marketing mix: specific combination of product, pricing, promotional, and distribution decisions made for the purpose of targeting a particular group of consumers

Marketing research: systematic gathering and analysis of marketing-related data to produce information that can be used in decision making

Media studies: research that identifies the most appropriate media to reach a specific target market

Predictive function: marketing research used to predict or forecast the results of a marketing decision or consumer action

Pricing studies: research that evaluates the elasticity of a brand's price and the impact pricing changes will have on demand

Product testing studies: research that identifies how a product fits the needs of consumers and what changes need to be made to the product to make it more attractive

Sales forecasts: research that estimates future sales for a company or brand

Sales potential studies: research that estimates potential sales for a product industry

Sample aggregator: firm that collects data through utilizing multiple sample companies

Site selection: research study to help retailers determine the best locations for retail outlets

Target market analysis: research that provides basic demographic, psychographic, and behavioral information about specific target markets

Test markets: research that provides information on how well a new product or product modification will do in a limited market before a national or international launch

CRITICAL THINKING EXERCISES

1. Have you ever participated in a marketing research study? If so, describe how the research was conducted. Was the study exploratory, descriptive, diagnostic, or predictive in nature? Justify your answer.

2. What impact do you think social media and smartphones and other forms of emerging technology will have on the way companies conduct marketing research in the future?

3. Think about the place where you currently work, or a place you have worked in the past. Describe how marketing research could be used to gather information that would be beneficial to the business or organization.

4. Interview a professor at your school other than your instructor. Ask the professor about the types of research he or she conducts. Is it applied or basic research? Show the individual the diagram in Figure 1.5. Ask if that process applies to his or her research process.

5. A research study investigated the factors that influence and determine a firm's reputation. The study included 150 firms from a variety of industries, and several factors that influence or determine firm reputation under various conditions were identified. Is this an example of applied research or basic research?

6. Find an article in each of the following journals: *Services Marketing Quarterly, Journal of Services Marketing, Business Communication Quarterly, Journal of Health Care Marketing,* and *Journal of Advertising.* Identify whether the research is applied or basic in each article. For applied research studies, briefly describe how the data were collected. If you classified an article as basic research, explain the theory or concept that was proposed or tested.

7. A student bookstore conducted a series of group interviews with several groups of students in order to try to understand why textbook sales were declining, despite the fact that enrollment had increased during the same semester. Which function of research does this illustrate?

8. Give an example of how a health club, fashion retailer, or manufacturer of fishing boats might conduct four separate studies that exemplify each of the types of research: exploratory, descriptive, diagnostic, and predictive.

9. Have social media and smartphones changed culture? Explain. Have they changed the way humans communicate with each other? Explain.

10. Do you use Twitter? Why do you use it? If so, how has it impacted your life? Have you ever used Twitter to communicate with a company or brand? What happened as a result? If you have not used Twitter, why not?

11. Are you a Facebook fan of one or more brands? If so, which ones? Why did you join? If you have stopped being a fan of a brand, which of the reasons shown in Figure 1.1 explain why? Did any other factors influence you to quit being a fan of a brand?

12. Interview five individuals of different ages ranging from young teenagers to a senior. Ask them about their use of social media, cell phones, and smartphones. Write a short report contrasting the differences and how age impacts the use of modern technology.

CONTINUING CASE STUDY: LAKESIDE GRILL

As part of their annual service project, five students of the American Marketing Association student chapter have agreed to conduct marketing research for a local business—Lakeside Grill.

This "Lakeside Grill (Continuing Case Study)" section provides a summary of how these students used the information in each chapter for their research project. Because it is a continuous project that flows throughout the entire text, it will be possible to see a research project from beginning to end. However, being students, the team does not always make the most optimal decisions. Following a description of their actions, questions will encourage a critique of the decisions made by the student team. This section allows a glimpse of a marketing research project conducted by a team of students from inception to completion.

Critique Questions:

1. How important is it for students to conduct a real-world project while taking a course in marketing research? What are the pros and cons of doing this?

2. What could a local business realistically expect from a student team conducting a research project?

3. How much guidance or direction should a faculty member or an instructor of the course provide for the student team? Explain.

4. If you were part of a student team conducting research for a local business or nonprofit, what type of business or nonprofit organization would provide the best learning experience? Why?

5. Is it fair to the local marketing research firms for a business to use a student team to conduct research rather than hiring the marketing research firm? Justify your answer.

MARKETING RESEARCH PORTFOLIO

The "Marketing Research Portfolio" mini-cases emphasize "learning by doing," and provide an excellent method by which students can practice and apply the skills learned in each chapter. Beginning with Chapter 2, each mini-case will present relevant client background information, and then list specific questions to be answered or tasks to be performed. Although some chapters use the same client and project, most chapters (with the exception of 13 and 14) can be treated as independent assignments, suitable for either individual or group work. The marketing research portfolio cases and supplemental files can be found online at www .sagepub.com/clowess.

STUDENT STUDY SITE

Visit the Student Study Site at www.sagepub.com/clowess to access the following additional materials:

- eFlashcards
- Web Quizzes
- SAGE Journal Articles
- Web Resources

The Marketing Research Process

After reading this chapter, you should be able to

1. Compare and contrast the three types of research design.
2. Explain the marketing research process.
3. Describe the components of a request for proposal (RFP) and a research proposal.
4. Provide an overview of qualitative and quantitative research.
5. Recite the ethical considerations in designing research studies.

INTRODUCTION

In recent years, marketing managers have become concerned that the millennial generation (individuals born between 1981 and 2000) is influenced less by advertising than older generations. Often characterized as "stimulation junkies," members of this generation are the first to grow up with computers, have known the Internet and cell phones all of their lives, and are used to technology. The group consists of 79 million consumers and has an estimated annual purchasing power of $178 billion. Reaching these consumers has become a high priority of marketing managers, especially for products geared to the millennial generation.

A major goal of marketing research is to provide information that managers can use to make better decisions. In this particular case, research can be used to gain a better understanding of how advertising influences the millennial generation and what can be done to increase advertising's effectiveness. A recent study examined the recall rate of four generations from millennials to seniors. Results are shown in Figure 2.1. An examination of the graph shows that millennials have

Figure 2.1   Ad Recall for Four Generations

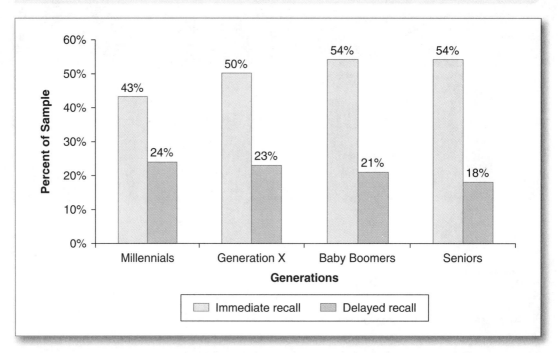

Source: Author-created with data from Laurie Sullivan, "Millennials Remain Difficult to Reach," *Online Media Daily,* January 24, 2012, www.mediapost.com/publications/article/166427 (accessed June 15, 2012).

the lowest immediate recall rate of any generation. They are not paying attention to ads. They may be involved in multitasking, or it could just be that they do not care about ads. However, their delayed recall is slightly higher than that of the other generations.[1]

While the information in Figure 2.1 is good and of interest, it just verifies what marketing managers already suspected. It does not provide any information that can be used to increase the effectiveness of advertising to the millennial generation. If the study would have ended at that point, then the dollars spent and the time involved in conducting the study would have been seen as a waste. But, the study explored deeper into several facets of advertising among the generations. Based on additional results, the researchers who conducted the study suggested that to reach the millennials companies should "show the product longer in ads, make the brand name more visible, and make more mentions [of the product and the brand] throughout the ad campaign."[2]

This chapter explores the different types of research and the research process that can be used to obtain information similar to what has just been discussed. Following a detailed research process allowed the researchers to go beyond collecting data to providing insights that can be utilized by individuals advertising to the millennial generation. The chapter discusses the two primary types of research: qualitative and quantitative. Both were used in the previously cited study. Finally, the chapter concludes with a discussion of ethics and where unethical conduct may creep into marketing research studies.

TYPES OF RESEARCH DESIGN

As has already been stated, the purpose of marketing research is to help managers make better decisions. While it is impossible to remove all uncertainty, information can help managers understand the problem being faced and the possible ramifications of decision options. For example, many companies are struggling with what to do about providing online reviews of products. Recent research found that 50% of online shoppers conduct research online for at least half of their purchases. Further, 64% of online shoppers said they read online reviews prior to making product decisions.[3] Based on these findings, it would appear that companies should offer some type of online review on their websites. But, what type of reviews? And, if reviews are provided, how and where should they be posted? An even more pertinent question is revealed by examining who responded to this particular survey. The study stated online shoppers were interviewed, which begs the question "Who were the online shoppers, and are they different from consumers who shop primarily in retail stores?"

While research can provide information, managers must be able to interpret that information and relate it to the problem they are facing and the decisions that need to be made. This process requires an understanding of the basic types of research design, shown in Figure 2.2.

■ Learning Objective 1.1: Compare and contrast the three types of research design.

Exploratory Research

As the name implies, **exploratory research** involves a preliminary examination of a problem or situation to identify parameters to be studied further and in some cases to even define the problem itself. Researchers will often launch exploratory research when the problem they are facing is not clear. They have symptoms, such as declining sales or a decrease in market share, but do not fully understand what is causing the sales or market share to decline. The goal of exploratory research in such cases is to help researchers understand the situation, the problem being faced, and perhaps even some possible solutions. Exploratory research is not definitive. It is designed to be used by managers not for making decisions, but rather to guide the development of future research projects or to better understand a situation.

Exploratory research is often used in the first stage of a more comprehensive research study. In addition to shedding light on the problem, exploratory research can provide clues as to the variables that should be studied. Additional types of research can then be used to determine the relationships among variables and any cause-and-effect relationships that may exist.

Exploratory research can provide information that can be used to develop hypotheses. A **research hypothesis** states an expected research outcome relevant to one or more variables that seems reasonable in light of existing information. In simpler terms, research hypotheses represent educated guesses with respect to what the researcher expects to find after analyzing the

Figure 2.2 Types of Research Design

Exploratory Research	Descriptive Research	Causal Research

research data. For example, if a marketing researcher wished to explore the impact of consumers' online shopping behavior in greater detail, he or she might develop the following hypothesis after reading the article about how consumers use online reviews, ratings, and searches.

> Hypothesis: When researching branded products online prior to purchasing, 50% or more of consumers will start with a search engine.

Methods of exploratory research include secondary research, focus groups, in-depth interviews, case studies, and even pilot studies. With the widespread availability of the Internet and easy access to large article databases, conducting secondary research can be done rather quickly and inexpensively. After all, someone else may have faced a similar problem. Articles relating to the situation may provide useful information and understanding, and possibly help lead to hypothesis development. Internally, the firm can review previous research studies that may shed some light on the issue at hand.

Focus groups and in-depth interviews will be discussed in more detail in a later chapter, but both methods allow researchers to gather information from individuals. With the focus group, researchers talk with a small group of individuals about a specific topic, exploring their thoughts and ideas in detail. With in-depth interviews, the researcher is talking to individuals one-on-one to explore a particular topic in greater depth or to better understand the thinking behind an individual's actions or behaviors. Both forms of research can provide rich, detailed information and consumer insights that can help researchers to better understand important aspects of a current situation.

Occasionally, a researcher will launch a **pilot study,** which is an abbreviated study with a limited number of respondents designed to provide information to the researcher in developing a larger, more definitive study. A researcher may not know exactly what questions to ask. A pilot study can be helpful, especially by asking open-ended questions. Suppose a researcher wants to study the impact of various factors on the consumer decision process that is used in determining whether online reviews will be consulted before purchasing a product. A pilot study might be used and respondents asked to identify what factors influence whether they conduct an online search for information prior to making a purchase decision. Pilot studies are also useful in testing aspects of research methodology, such as sampling and data collection procedures.

Descriptive Research

As the name implies, **descriptive research** answers the questions who, what, when, where, and how in describing the characteristics of consumers, brands, and other marketing phenomena. In contrast to exploratory research, marketers who use descriptive research already have a good understanding of the marketing problem or situation. They are just seeking additional information in order to make a more informed decision.

Consider the example of descriptive research findings presented in Figure 2.3. Respondents were asked to "select the top 3 places where you typically research products online." Notice that 65% of the individuals who answered the question indicated they use retail sites to research products online. The least used were social media sites at 6%.[4]

Descriptive research can be used for a large number of research situations and is the most frequently used type of research. In most cases, descriptive studies use numbers, which allows for statistical and mathematical relationships to be examined. Caution should be undertaken

Figure 2.3   Top Places Where Products Are Typically Researched Online

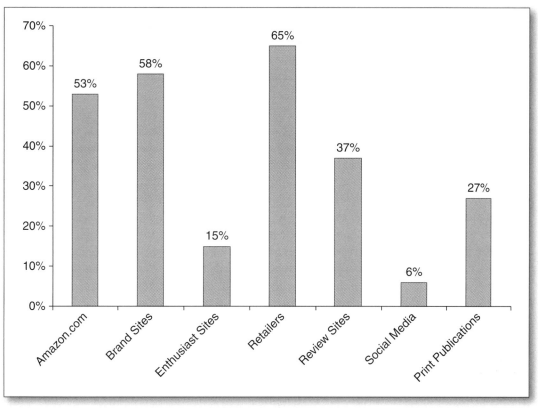

Source: Author-created with data from "Online Shoppers Value Reviews, Ratings, Search," April 23, 2010, http://www.marketing profs.com/charts/2010/3563/online-shoppers-value-reviews-ratings-search (accessed June 15, 2012).

when interpreting these relationships, as descriptive research findings cannot be used to prove causality. For instance, descriptive research may show that there is a relationship between online product reviews and purchase intentions, but this fact alone does not prove that one causes the other. It is merely a description of the relationship.

Causal Research

To determine if one variable causes another, researchers utilize **causal research.** Most causal research designs involve experimentation, which is the topic of Chapter 7. Care has to be taken to ensure that the relationship is truly cause-and-effect and not just a coincidence, or **spurious association.** Spurious association occurs when two variables appear to be related in such a way that the first variable appears to be causing something to happen to the second variable, but in fact the observed change is due to other factors. For instance, a hardware store may run a special advertising campaign on snow shovels. Over the weekend, sales triple. It would appear that the increase in the sale of the snow shovels was caused by the advertising campaign. However, the more likely cause is the 14 inches of snow that fell at the beginning of the weekend. The goal of causal research is to control or eliminate all other possible causes of an effect except the one being studied.

In determining cause and effect, two conditions must be met. The first, called **temporal sequence,** is related to timing issues and simply means that the cause must precede or occur at the same time as the effect. In the case of the hardware store, the ad campaign must precede or occur simultaneously with the increase in the sales of snow shovels. In the case of understanding the impact of online customer reviews on purchase decisions, the viewing of the review by the shopper must occur prior to or at the time of the purchase and not after the purchase. Assuming that such behavior is the norm would be dangerous; many individuals will in fact read product reviews after making a purchase, as one method of alleviating buyer's remorse (also called cognitive dissonance).

The second condition for establishing causality is **concomitant variation**, which means the two items thought to be part of a causal relationship vary or change together and in the direction hypothesized. In the case of the hardware store, if the researcher wants to show a cause-and-effect relationship between the ad campaign and the sale of snow shovels, then an increase in ad spending should result in an increase in the sales of snow shovels, rather than no sales increase or, even worse, a decrease in sales. Correspondingly, a decrease in ad expenditures would be expected to create a decline in the sales of snow shovels, though perhaps not immediately, due to advertising's carryover or lag effect. From this example, it can be seen that to show a cause-and-effect relationship between advertising and sales is difficult. While marketers believe there is a strong relationship, they also understand there are a large number of other factors that impact sales beyond an advertising campaign.

■ Learning Objective 2.2: Explain the marketing research process.

OVERVIEW OF THE MARKETING RESEARCH PROCESS

Figure 2.4 illustrates the typical research process. It starts with understanding the research purpose, which stems from a need to understand a situation, an opportunity, or a particular problem being experienced by a firm or brand. Managers often confuse symptoms with

Figure 2.4 The Marketing Research Process

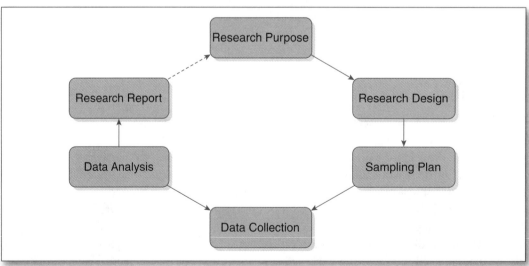

problems, so it is up to the market researcher to persistently investigate or question management until the true problem is understood and the research purpose is clearly identified. Sometimes, it will require exploratory research because the manager may not know why a particular symptom, such as slumping sales or declining market share, is occurring.

Research Purpose

Market research is conducted with a specific purpose in mind. The **research purpose** might be to gain a better understanding of a situation or phenomenon, to investigate an opportunity, or to understand or address one or more problems that may be negatively impacting the firm. As Figure 2.5 illustrates, defining the research purpose is a multitiered process in which the research purpose statement serves as a springboard for developing research questions and hypotheses. Although it is not an easy task, its importance cannot be overstated as the research purpose impacts every area of the research design.

Symptoms or Problems. The task is particularly challenging when the purpose of the research relates to a problem being experienced by the firm or brand. Too often management's preconceived notions of the problem are incorrect, which may result in research that isn't helpful because it doesn't collect the proper data. This can occur when symptoms are confused with the problems, or the true underlying cause of the problem is not properly identified. The difference between symptoms and problems can be illustrated by the *iceberg principle*. With an iceberg, typically only about 20% of the iceberg is visible above the water. The portion below the water is much larger, and poses a much greater risk to ships. Most managers see the part above the water, such as loss of sales. It is the task of the marketing researcher to discover the part under the water, the problem or cause of the symptoms.

Figure 2.5   Defining the Research Purpose

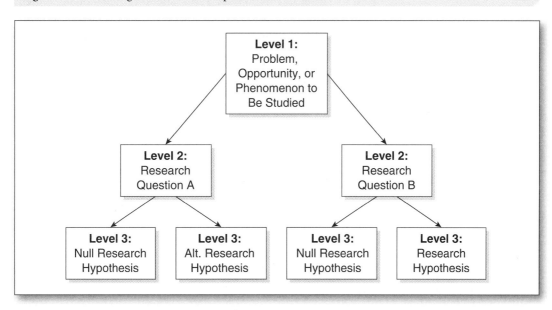

Sales may be lost due to declining levels of customer satisfaction. But the decline in customer satisfaction may in turn have been caused by something else—perceptions of inferior product quality, poor performance, unsatisfactory customer service, a price that is too high for the benefits received, and so forth. Determining the true problem is akin to peeling an onion—researchers much continually ask "What caused that?" as they strip away each layer in an attempt to uncover the root cause.

Some typical research problems that may trigger research studies are shown as part of Figure 2.6. The symptom for each of the research problems identified in the figure may have been declines in key marketing metrics related to the problem, slumping sales, or declining market share. But, the problems causing the symptom are vastly different. In terms of research design, a study examining poor brand image will be conducted differently than one examining a poor distribution system or poor customer service.

Exploiting Opportunities. Research studies are also conducted for the purpose of exploiting an opportunity. A few examples also appear in Figure 2.6. Site selection research is conducted for the purpose of determining the best location to open a new retail store or restaurant. Similarly, with millions of dollars at risk, consumer goods firms often invest in a great deal of research when developing a new product. Research conducted during the new product development process typically includes concept testing in the early stages to ascertain whether the idea is even feasible. Later stages of research will involve a variety of studies geared toward optimizing the package design and many aspects of the marketing mix, such as price and marketing communications. In some instances, research culminates in a test market, where the product is introduced on a limited basis in an actual store and promoted via the initial marketing communications campaign.

Investigating Phenomena. Not all research studies involve a marketing or business problem. Researchers or managers may be seeking a better understanding of a situation or phenomenon. For instance, in the study referred to earlier in this chapter, researchers wanted a better understanding of how consumers value product reviews, ratings, and online searches. In another example, the Reputation Institute conducts a survey every year to determine the top 100 global brands in terms of each company's reputation. Nielsen Online conducted a survey to investigate how pervasive social media are in the lives of Americans. In all three of these situations,

Figure 2.6   Typical Research Purposes

Investigating problems that may cause symptoms	Investigating opportunities
• Poor brand image • Lower-quality products • High pricing • Poor distribution • Poor customer service • New competition	• New product or service development • Site selection for store • Shifts in consumer wants **Investigating phenomena** • Top 100 advertisers • Endorser ratings

marketers were seeking a better understanding of the marketplace and consumers in order to develop more effective marketing strategies.

Research Questions. Once the research purpose and the related problem, opportunity, or situation to be studied has been clearly identified, research questions and hypotheses are formed. Typically, multiple research questions are formed for a particular research purpose. Research questions should not be confused with survey questions. **Research questions** specify the *type of information* needed in order to successfully fulfill the research purpose and make important managerial decisions. As such, they should be clearly written and stated as specifically as possible in order to help guide the research process down the line. A research question that asks "What is the profile of the credit union's target market?" would not be as helpful in guiding survey development as one that asks "What is the demographic, geographic, and psychographic profile of the credit unions' depositors, investors, and mortgage holders?" Some researchers prefer forming research objectives. The only difference between these two concepts is that one is phrased as a question, while the other is phrased as a statement. Figure 2.7 illustrates how the same information can be phrased as a research question or a research objective.

Figure 2.7   Research Questions Versus Research Objectives

Research question	Research objective
• What is the demographic, geographic, and psychographic profile of the credit unions' depositors, investors, and mortgage holders?	• To determine the demographic, geographic, and psychographic profile of the credit unions' depositors, investors, and mortgage holders.
• Which of three test package designs has the greatest impact on consumer attitudes and purchase intentions?	• To identify which of three test package designs has the greatest impact on consumer attitudes and purchase intentions.

Research Hypotheses. Research hypotheses are included only when the researcher has reason to suspect, or "conjecture," an answer to a particular research question. Sources of potential hypotheses include secondary research, focus group results, other exploratory research findings, and theory.

Suppose the purpose of a research study is to investigate how consumer perceptions influence brand sales. If exploratory research results suggest that a decline in sales may be due to consumer perceptions of product quality, one potential research question might be written as "How do consumers perceive the quality of Bell Electronics' products relative to the competition?" Correspondingly, a related research hypothesis might be written as "Consumers view digital cameras sold by Bell Electronics as being of lower quality than leading brands." Alternatively, the research hypothesis might state "Consumers rate our brand superior to most competing brands, except for Nikon and Sony" or even "Consumers rate our brand third best among digital camera manufacturers." Additional research questions might address consumer perceptions of pricing, promotion, or distribution decisions, if these were identified as potential causes of lower sales in exploratory research. Figure 2.8 demonstrates the relationship between a research problem, research questions, and research hypotheses.

Figure 2.8   Research Purpose, Questions, and Hypotheses

Research Purpose

- To understand how consumers value product reviews, ratings, and online searches.

Research Questions and Hypotheses

- What criteria do consumers use to determine which online search engine they will use for product research?
    - H_0: Search engine toolbars installed in the browser influence the choice of search engines used in product research.
    - H_0: Previous experience with search engines influences the choice of search engines used in product research.
- How do consumers feel about our brand, compared to our competitors?
    - H_0: Customers rate our brand second only to Nikon.
- What is the profile of customers who spend at least $300 a year with our firm?
    - H_0: Average household income exceeds $50,000 a year.
    - H_0: Time spent online averages 10+ hours a week.

Research Design

The **research design** is the plan that will be used to address the research problem, question, and/or hypothesis. It guides the research process and outlines how data will be collected. The specific design chosen will vary depending on the problem being studied and the constraints imposed by management. Typical constraint issues that impact the design include time, costs, and quality of information. If time to conduct the study is short, then the researcher must look for quicker methods of collecting data, which often drives up costs and may impact the quality of the information obtained in a negative manner. If management wants a high level of information quality, it will normally lengthen the time for the study and, again, increase the budget to accommodate the correspondingly higher costs. If management is concerned about costs, then it limits the researcher's options, which then usually has an inverse impact on the quality of data. Therefore, management and the researcher must come to an agreement on the desired level of precision of the information needed in light of costs and time constraints.

Descriptive or Causal Approach. The first research design decision involves whether to use a descriptive or causal approach. As described earlier, both designs assume the researcher has a good grasp on the problem or question to be studied. If not, then further exploratory research needs to be conducted. If the researcher is looking for an understanding of specific variables or relationships among variables, then a descriptive approach is appropriate. For example, suppose a credit union was interested in profiling the characteristics of its current mortgage holders. In this instance, the credit union is looking to describe the relationship between those who hold home mortgages with the credit union and factors such as gender, marital status, type and number of other accounts held within the credit union, income, and so forth. If the purpose of the study is to prove a cause-and-effect relationship, then a causal design works better. So if the credit union was interested in learning whether a $50 savings bond, $25 gift card, or free dinner for two at Red Lobster was the most effective incentive for enticing new customers to open an account, causal research could be used. In making the decision, time, costs, and quality of information must be considered. While causal research will normally provide a higher level of information, it tends to take longer, and costs are higher. For most marketing decisions, descriptive research provides ample information for managers to make decisions.

The second component of research design is how the data will be collected. As shown in Figure 2.9, researchers have three basic methods of collecting data. For descriptive research, the most common approaches are surveys and observation. For causal research, the typical approach is to use an experiment.

Figure 2.9   Methods of Collecting Data

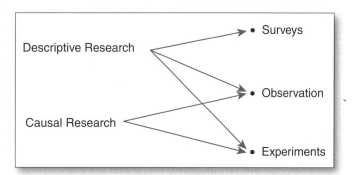

Survey Research. **Survey research** can be conducted in a number of ways, but the overall methodology involves a researcher asking individuals a series of questions about the topic under study. It can be done one-on-one with an interviewer asking individuals questions. It can be done through distributing a questionnaire to individuals. Today, a large number of surveys are distributed via the Internet and e-mail. Survey research can also include interaction with a group of individuals who meet to discuss a particular topic. Surveys are a primary method of conducting descriptive research since the typical who, when, where, what, and how questions can be asked of participants.

Observation Research. Instead of asking individuals a series of questions, researchers can observe their behaviors or observe the result of their behaviors in the **observation approach.** Researchers can watch individuals interact with a point-of-purchase display at a retail store or watch children playing with a new toy. This approach can even involve giving children money to spend at a toy store and watching how they go about deciding which toy to purchase. It may be watching how an adult buys groceries. In all of these examples, the researcher observes, but does not interact with the subject being studied. If the researcher believes his presence may influence the subject's behaviors, then the observation is normally done through a two-way mirror or recorded with a video camera and watched later.

Instead of watching the behavior, a common approach is to observe the results of behavior. Technology, especially retail scanners, has increased the desirability of this approach. Instead of actually watching shoppers at a point-of-purchase display, scanner data from the store's cash register system can identify how many individuals purchased the items on display. If the store has loyalty cards, even who made the purchases can be identified. This information can then be tied into an individual's demographic information and past purchase history for richer information.

The Internet offers a wealth of observation data. Through cookies, a company can track individuals who visit a website. Data such as how long they stay on a page, what links they click on, and where they go on the page can all be tracked. This type of data is very useful in studying the impact of banner ads and other forms of Internet advertising.

Observation can be used in descriptive research since the actions of individuals can be described and measured. It can also be used in causal research, but requires more controls to ensure there is truly a cause-and-effect situation. When used for causal research, most marketers would use the results of behavior rather than observing the behavior itself. Scanner data and Internet tracking data can be used in more tightly controlled situations and can possibly show cause and effect.

Experimental Research. The last method of collecting data is **experiments,** which involves a research study where all variables are held constant except the one under study. Most experiments are conducted in tightly controlled environments, such as laboratories. In advertising, it might take place in a movie theater where individuals are shown a documentary or new television show with ads as would normally be in a television show. Embedded among the ads is one the researchers are studying. Questions asked before and after can provide information on any impact the target ad may have had on the participants in the study.

Another approach is what is called a **field experiment,** which involves conducting an experiment in a real-world setting. Controlling all of the variables except the one under study becomes much more difficult because a number of other extraneous factors could have an impact on the results. A company such as Tyson could create a study examining three different package designs for its fajita chicken. Price and location of the product is the same in all of the stores. The only difference is the package design. Sales could then be examined to see if the package design impacted the purchase decision. The challenge is ensuring that any change in sales was due to the package design and not some other factor, such as one of the stores having a special sale on a competing brand or complementary product, such as fajita steak.

Because researchers strive to control all of the variables in an experiment but the one being manipulated, it is ideal for causal research. Experiments can be used for descriptive studies in situations where it is difficult to control all of the extraneous variables, such as field studies. When relationships are found through descriptive research, then a subsequent study can be designed that uses a causal research approach to verify cause and effect.

Sample Selection

Because of time and cost constraints, researchers in most studies will select a sample, or subset of individuals to study, rather than the entire population being studied. The sample selection process begins by defining the **population,** which is the group that a researcher wants to study. It can be as small as the students at a university or as large as the entire population of the United States. It can be broadly defined such as online shoppers or narrowly defined such as women who have given birth to a child within the last six months. Once the population of study has been defined, then the researcher designs a method for selecting a sample from the population. Chapter 8 describes the process of sample selection in greater detail. Most critical to the selection process is the assurance that the sample is representative of the population. If it is, then conclusions and findings of the research obtained from the sample can be applied

The population is the group the researcher wants to study, such as students at a particular college.

to the population being studied. If it is not, then regardless of how large the sample and how detailed the information, inference cannot be made to the population.

Suppose JPMorgan Chase conducted a survey of 500 randomly selected individuals who accessed their financial account information (mortgage, credit card, checking, savings, etc.) online during the month of April. If the purpose of the study is to assess customer satisfaction of checking account holders, then the population for this study should include all Chase customers who have a checking account with the financial institution. Unfortunately, in the situation described above, the survey administration and resulting sample is flawed because it is restricted to online users only, as those individuals who do not use online banking (or who did not access their account information online in April) have no opportunity to participate in the study. As certain demographics might be associated with those unlikely to use online services (older, financially disadvantaged), the study results would clearly not be representative of the population, and satisfaction levels could realistically differ between users and nonusers of online services. An additional problem stems from the fact that many of Chase's online account information users may not have checking accounts with the bank, but instead use the online service to track or pay credit card bills. If such an individual were randomly selected to participate in the study, his or her ratings of checking account services would "confound" the data, meaning that the information provided would not be relevant because the checking services being rated were not those offered by Chase.

Data Collection

For a marketing researcher, now the fun begins! It is time to collect the data. How the data are collected depends on the research design process. If survey research is used, then it can be collected through personal interviews, telephone interviews, mail surveys, or online using a website or e-mail. Surveys can be distributed at a mall, passed out in a class at a university, or stuffed in a credit card bill. The method that is chosen goes back to the three criteria already identified— time, costs, and quality of information. Chapter 6 provides more in-depth discussion of these topics as well as relative advantages of various methods of survey research.

For observation research, multiple methods are available. It can be done in person or with a video camera. Scanner data from cash registers can be used. Internet metrics can be utilized through cookie information for online observations. Again, time, costs, and quality of information will impact the decision. Methods involving human observation are almost always more expensive and take longer.

Data collection can vary widely for experimental research. It can take the form of questionnaires given at the end of an experiment that assess attitudes, thoughts, feelings, or intentions. It can be observation of human behavior, such as electronic tracking of eye movement when viewing a print ad, or results of human actions. With experiments, the type of experiment that is conducted will have the most impact on how the data are collected.

Regardless of the method used to collect data, the goal should be to produce data that are free of errors. This requires identifying ways errors can possibly occur and then designing methods of reducing the probability. For instance, an interviewer's facial expression or tone of voice in asking someone questions may influence the respondent's answers, creating error. This type of error can be reduced by proper training of interviewers or by switching to a self-administered questionnaire. Errors can occur in recording of data or in selecting the sample. While every study will have some random error, the goal of the researcher is to minimize error as much as possible. The various types of errors and more specific methods of reducing them will be discussed in future chapters, especially Chapter 6. For now, it is important to understand that in collecting data, errors should be minimized, and steps should be taken in the design of the research to reduce errors.

Data Analysis

Once the data have been collected, it is time for the analysis. The purpose of the analysis is to make sense of the data and turn raw numbers into meaningful information that management can use to make informed decisions. In some studies, simple procedures such as frequency counts and averages are sufficient. In other studies, more complex analyses are needed to understand the relationships among variables. This is especially true for causal research.

Listed in Figure 2.10 are the results of an analysis concerning trust in online consumer reviews. Over 1,000 consumers were interviewed. The researcher who analyzed the data had a computer count how many respondents indicated each of the answers, then converted that number to a percentage of the total sample. Thus, out of all of the online shoppers who answered this particular question, 57% said they trust customer reviews but only to corroborate other information, 35% said they think the customer reviews may be biased, and only 6% trust the reviews completely more than any other source of product information. The next question in the survey asked individuals what factors degraded their trust in the online product reviews. Notice the reasons given and the percentage who gave each reason.

Analyses do not always need to be complex to be of value. The results presented in Figure 2.10 provide valuable and useful information to marketers about consumer trust in online product reviews. But, a deeper analysis may provide additional information that will allow a marketer to make better decisions. For instance, statistical tests can be run that will show if there is a difference between males and females in how they use customer reviews. Another analysis that might be valuable is how much money a person spends online to see if that impacts his or her usage

Figure 2.10   Results of an Analysis Concerning Trust in Online Consumer Reviews

Question 1

- Trust customer reviews, but only to corroborate other information (57%)
- Customer reviews may be biased (35%)
- Trust reviews completely, more than other sources (6%)

Question 2

- Not enough reviews (50%)
- Doubts they are written by real customers (39%)
- Lack of negative reviews (38%)
- Positive reviews always positioned first (25%)
- Lack of information about reviewers (23%)

Source: Author-created from "Online Shoppers Value Reviews, Ratings, Search," April 23, 2010, http://www.marketingprofs.com/charts/2010/3563/online-shoppers-value-reviews-ratings-search (accessed June 15, 2012).

and view of online reviews. Alternatively, consumers' level of knowledge of the product they are purchasing may have a significant influence on using online product reviews.

Research Report

Once the analysis is complete, it is time to write the research report. The purpose of the report is to present the research findings. But, in preparing the report, the intended audience of the report should guide how it is prepared. Executives tend to be extremely busy and do not have time to read long, lengthy reports. They prefer reports that summarize the findings of the research and have clear, succinct conclusions and recommendations.

The report should begin by stating the research purpose, problems, questions, or hypotheses. This should be followed by a description of the methodology that includes how the sample was chosen and then how the data were collected. Seldom will executives or managers care about how the data were analyzed. They just want to see results. Using graphs and charts provides pictures that are easier and quicker to read than having results listed in a table or in the written part of the report. Notice the column graph in Figure 2.11. Compare it to the results listed for Question 2 in Figure 2.10. A business executive can look at the graph in Figure 2.11 and quickly see what factors lead online shoppers to degrade trust in online product reviews. It is easier to read and provides a picture of responses rather than just a list. For oral presentations, graphs are especially good to use.

In reporting the results, it is easy to overwhelm executives with a large number of graphs, charts, and tables. Not everything has to be reported. The report should focus on the research purpose and identify the portion of the analysis that answers the research questions and supports the findings of the research. Additional information can be put in an appendix for reference.

While researchers love to talk about results, executives want to know the conclusions and the corresponding recommendations. As discussed in Chapter 1, executives now are looking to researchers to supply insights and to be consultants in the decision process. Just supplying the

Figure 2.11   Factors That Degrade Trust in Reviews

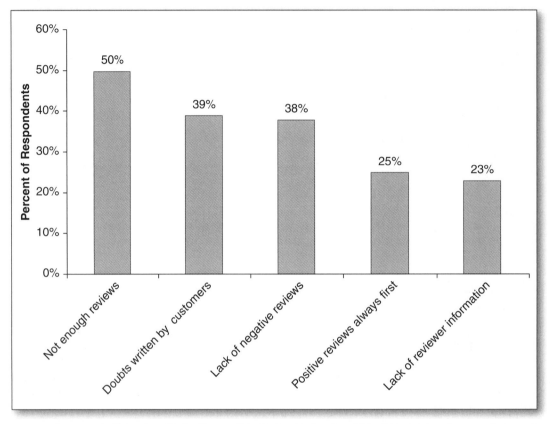

Source: Author-created with data from "Online Shoppers Value Reviews, Ratings, Search," April 23, 2010, http://www.marketingprofs .com/charts/2010/3563/online-shoppers-value-reviews-ratings-search (accessed June 15, 2012).

results is insufficient. How do those results impact the company, and how do they impact the decision that management needs to make? More information about the content of the report and how it is written is provided in Chapter 14.

■ Learning Objective 2.3: Describe the components of a request for proposal (RFP) and the research proposal.

PREPARING THE RESEARCH PROPOSAL

The research process typically starts with some type of **request for proposal (RFP)**, which is a request soliciting proposals from research companies. This document is especially important for firms seeking to hire an external research firm. But, it can also be part of the research process for companies that house an internal research department. In such situations, companies will often have more requests than can be funded by the company so the RFP can be an internal approval process in which research projects move forward.

Typically, an RFP will provide a background for the research request to justify why the study is needed. The research objective or question will be stated as well as the population of the study. While the RFP typically does not specify the exact methods of sample selection and data collection, it may contain information on what is expected and an approximate sample size since these two criteria are big determinants of cost. It makes a difference whether a company wants to use an online data collection methodology with a desired sample size of 500 or face-to-face personal interviews of 300 people. Most RFPs will close with a time frame when the study needs to be completed.

The **research proposal** is prepared by a marketing research firm in response to an RFP. It can also be developed by internal marketing research staff for executives within the company. In either situation, the research proposal is a document that provides basic information about the research process that will be used. Figure 2.12 identifies the primary components of a research proposal. The depth of information within each section will depend primarily on the cost and complexity of the study.

The research proposal begins by providing a background of the study and any issues that may have prompted the research or that are pertinent to the research situation. Next, the research objectives or questions are stated. While this may have been stated in the RFP, it is important to restate it in the proposal because the proposal then becomes a contract or an agreement between management and whoever is conducting the research.

The research design identifies if the research will be exploratory, descriptive, or causal. The target population is defined, because it is from the target population that the sample will be drawn. Sample size and method of selection should be stated with the goal of ensuring the sample will be representative of the target population. As stated earlier, the size of the sample has a significant impact on the cost and time frame of the study as does the method of collecting the data.

Figure 2.12   Components of a Research Proposal

- Introduction and background information
- Research objectives or questions
- Research design
- Target population
- Sample size and selection method
- Data collection methodology
- Cost and time frame for study

The last part of the proposal is the cost of the study and the time frame. Certainly for hiring an external firm this information is critical to the decision process. But, it is also as important for firms using an internal research department. In addition to using the research proposal to make decisions about which studies to approve, it provides information for budgeting.

QUALITATIVE AND QUANTITATIVE RESEARCH

Another facet of marketing research is examining the difference between qualitative and quantitative research. These differences are highlighted in Figure 2.13. **Quantitative research** involves structured data collection methods that provide results that can be converted to numbers and analyzed through statistical procedures. On the other hand, **qualitative research** involves unstructured data collection methods that provide results that are subjectively interpreted.

■ Learning Objective 2.4: Provide an overview of qualitative and quantitative research.

Qualitative Research

Qualitative research is typically used for exploratory research. But, it can also be used after a descriptive study to explore deeper into the minds of consumers or whoever the research participants may be. A major advantage of qualitative research is that it is unstructured. The

Figure 2.13   Comparison of Qualitative and Quantitative Research

Feature	Qualitative	Quantitative
Type of research	Exploratory	Descriptive/causal
Sample size	Small	Large
Types of questions	Unstructured	Structured
Type of analysis	Subjective	Objective, statistical
Generalizability	Limited	High
Costs (Typically)	Lower	More expensive
Time frame (Typically)	Shorter	Longer

researcher will normally follow a guide sheet to ensure all of the study topics are covered, but the researcher is free to depart from it in order to ask probing questions to better understand the respondent's thoughts, feelings, behaviors, or ideas.

Most qualitative research is conducted with a small sample. Interviews can be with individuals, or they can be with a small group ranging from just 3 or 4 to as many as 10 or 12. When groups become too large, then it is difficult to probe individual thoughts, and the advantages of group dynamics begin to disappear.

Since qualitative research involves probing via open-ended questions, the results become subjective. That makes generalizing the findings to a larger population or other consumers more difficult. Also, business executives are reluctant to make major decisions on the thoughts of just a few individuals, and most data obtained by qualitative methods are subjected to verification using larger samples that allow for quantitative analysis.

However, Dave Snell of The Richards Group states "that you should never underestimate the power of qualitative data." The Richards Group is an advertising firm in Dallas, Texas, and has clients such as Motel 6, Bridgestone, Home Depot, and Chick-fil-A. The agency regularly tests print and broadcast ads through Millward Brown, a marketing research firm. In addition to quantitative measures such as awareness, level of interest, and liking, Millward Brown solicits open-ended thoughts from test participants about the ads they are viewing. Dave Snell says, "These verbatim remarks are extremely valuable. It provides clues into what people are thinking, and how they see the ad, and how they feel about it." Typically, Millward Brown will use a sample of about 150 people. According to Snell, "When you read all of the comments and see some patterns or a number [of people] that speak about a certain aspect of the commercial, then you know you've got to go back and look at that ad again or you've hit the sweet spot that really speaks to people." While the qualitative data will not tell The Richards Group what to do or exactly what worked, it does provide valuable insight into ads the agency produces.[5]

The approach used by Millward Brown in evaluating ads for The Richards Group is growing in popularity with researchers. This type of qualitative research is less costly and normally can be conducted in a shorter time frame since it is part of a quantitative study. More importantly, it can add richness and depth to quantitative studies.

Quantitative Research

Because of the issue of accountability that managers and business executives face, they prefer research that can provide numbers. Quantitative research is a structured approach that is used for descriptive and causal research. It is objective, and because of its numerical data format, it is subject to statistical tests and procedures.

Nielsen IAG and the Advertising Research Foundation (ARF) wanted to compare recall and likability for online ads and television ads. The study examined 238 different brands, 412 products, and 951 ad executions. A total of 14,000 surveys were obtained. Figure 2.14 shows the overall results of this study.[6] Notice for all four measures, online ads scored higher than television ads. This research would provide strong support for a marketing manager who is trying to justify increasing the company's online advertising budget.

The Nielsen IAG and ARF study illustrates some of the other aspects of quantitative research. This study involved 14,000 surveys. While this number is larger than typical quantitative studies, it does illustrate that the sample size for quantitative research is significantly higher than for qualitative studies. The larger sample size means most quantitative studies are more expensive and require a longer time to execute. The trade-off to the higher cost and longer time frame is that results are more objective and can normally be generalized to a larger population.

Figure 2.14   Recall and Likability for Online Versus Television

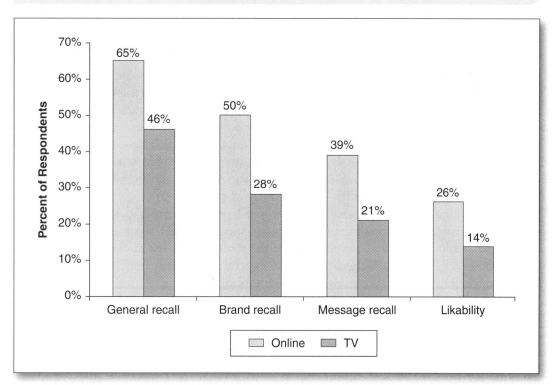

Source: Author-created with data from Wayne Friedman, "Online Ads Surpass TV Ads in Recall, Likability," *Media Daily News*, April 22, 2010, http://www.mediapost.com/publications/article/126671/online-ads-surpass-tv-ads-in-recall-likability.html (accessed June 15, 2012).

Because 14,000 individuals were surveyed by Nielsen IAG and ARF, it is rather safe to say that consumers as a whole tend to recall online ads better than they do television ads.

As with any study, individuals reading these results would want to know why online ads have a higher general recall, a higher brand recall, a higher message recall, and greater likability. Dave Kaplan, senior vice president of product leadership at Nielsen IAG, and Beth Uyenco, director of global research at ARF, offer the following insights[7]:

- Internet viewers are more engaged with the medium than TV viewers.
- Online videos are a new medium compared to TV, so curiosity is a factor.
- Viewers cannot skip online videos like they can with TV (about one third of Americans are able to fast-forward through TV commercials).
- There is reduced advertising clutter online (4 minutes per hour for online versus 15 minutes per hour for TV).

Social Media: An Illustration of the Marketing Research Process

To illustrate the marketing research process, consider a study examining the role of social media today in the United States. The research process began with an RFP by BlogHer and iVillage, two websites targeted toward women. The research had two main objectives: (1) to determine the number of bloggers and compare media usage patterns across gender, generations, blogging focus, and media channel preference and (2) to describe the purchasing behavior of social media users across bloggers, social networks, online versus offline media consumption, and online versus offline influence.[8]

Nielsen Online was contracted to do the research and served as a cosponsor along with Ketchum. The research design involved a descriptive study using an online survey. The study used two samples. The first sample was the Nielsen Online panel, which was carefully weighted to be representative of the U.S. population in terms of demographic characteristics. The second sample contained individuals from the BlogHer network and was chosen across 2,500 different blogs with approximately 20 million participants. The total sample consisted of 3,155 women and 379 men. Approximately 1,700 of them were from the Nielsen Online panel, and the remaining were participants in the BlogHer network sample. Although 87% of the sample is female, that is OK since the study's objective focused on females.

Nielsen found that 73% of the sample engaged in social media at least once a week. Engagement was defined as reading a blog, visiting a social network, or commenting on a message board. Because it was a quantitative study, the results can be extrapolated to the general online audience. Therefore, Nielsen Online estimated that approximately 127 million people in the United States are engaged in some way with social media.

When investigating Facebook in particular, Nielsen found that 47% of the sample visit Facebook daily. To be able to see how this compares to other media, Nielsen's survey also asked about television, radio, and newspapers. The results are shown in Figure 2.15. Facebook almost matches television in daily viewing and clearly outperforms both radio and newspapers. In interpreting the results, however, it is critically important to go back to the sample. It is online users. It would be expected, therefore, that their viewing of Facebook would be higher than that of the U.S. population in general. It is also highly likely that online users spend less time with other media such as television, radio, and newspapers because they spend more time online.

Figure 2.15   Daily Viewing of Major Media and Facebook by Online Users

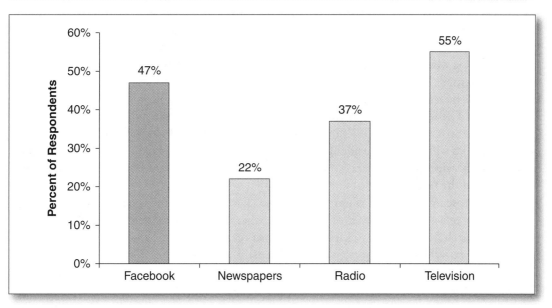

Source: Author-created with data from Brian Morrissey, "Social Media Use Becomes Pervasive," *Adweek*, April 15, 2010, http://www .adweek.com/news/technology/social-media-use-becomes-pervasive-102092 (accessed June 15, 2012).

Would these sample percentages hold true for the population in general? It is very unlikely, which means these results can be generalized to online users, but not to the U.S. population as a whole.

A component of the research objective was to determine if there was a difference in how women use social media versus men. By having quantitative data, Nielsen Online is able to use statistical procedures to determine if there is a significant difference. The research study found little difference between males and females in terms of social media adoption. The company did find that women are slightly more likely to tweet and blog than men, while men tend to watch more videos than women.

The Nielsen Online research study illustrates the power of marketing research and how companies can obtain valuable information to make important marketing decisions. While part of this study is public, many details are owned by BlogHer and iVillage, who paid for the study.

ETHICAL CONSIDERATIONS IN DESIGNING RESEARCH STUDIES

A number of potential ethical situations could occur when requesting, designing, and conducting research studies. Honesty and integrity should be the guiding principles of marketing research firms, individuals conducting the research, and client companies. Unethical situations can arise easily due to competitive pressures among firms and the desire for companies to succeed in the marketplace, whether it is a research firm or a client. Within companies, individuals have a desire to succeed to obtain promotions and bonuses and can be tempted to engage in unethical behaviors.

■ Learning Objective 2.5: Recite the ethical considerations in designing research studies.

Ethics and the RFP

Most research firms will spend time, effort, and money on preparing a research proposal in response to an RFP. These companies expect the RFP to be accurate, honest, and truthful. In the vast majority of situations, this is true. However, there are opportunities for unethical behavior.

The first is when a company sends out an RFP to various companies, but the decision has already been made about who will do the research. Some companies have policies requiring that multiple bids be secured, especially when the research project is projected to cost over a certain dollar value. The RFPs are sent to various companies in order to satisfy this policy.

A second instance in which RFPs may be sent despite the fact that a firm has already been selected occurs when a vice president or another business executive requests additional bids to cover his or her decision in case anyone questions why a particular research agency was selected. Regardless of the reason, it is not fair to request that companies spend time, effort, and money preparing a research proposal when they have no chance of winning the contract.

A closely related ethical situation may occur when the company sending out the RFP has a favored research firm it wants to hire, for whatever reason. It may be due to a personal friendship or past experiences that were positive. To ensure the favored company gets the contract, information from the other proposal bids is shared with the favored company. This allows the favored company to then modify its proposal to ensure selection.

A third potentially ethical situation occurs when a firm sends out RFPs with no intention of hiring any of the applicants. The firm is seeking information on how to do the study. It may even ask for additional details on questionnaire design or sample selection with the guise of wanting to make sure the objectives will be met. The company then hires freelancers to conduct the study, completes the study using its own employees, or goes to a data collection firm to just collect the data rather than design the entire study.

A fourth ethical consideration is when a firm makes false promises to a marketing research firm with the goal of enticing its researchers to conduct a study at a lower price in exchange for future studies. The future studies never come, or if they do, they have been modified drastically. A firm may say "we have a number of large studies we want to conduct that will involve extensive research designs and large samples of several thousand." The marketing research firm is told that if it will do this "first study at a substantially lower price," then it will be given the larger studies, without further bidding.

Ethics and the Research Proposal

Similarly, firms that prepare the research proposals will sometimes engage in unethical behavior. The two most common ethical situations that can occur with the research proposal are lowball pricing and bait-and-switch. **Lowball pricing** is submitting a bid with an extremely low price in order to get the contract, when in fact the firm has no intention of doing the work at the quoted price. Once the contract is obtained, then the research company identifies some means of increasing the price. For instance, the client company may be told that the fee for the respondents was not included in the bid price, or that interviewer expenses were not included. The research company identifies some fee that was not included in the bid price and of course must be added to the bill.

The second unethical situation is bait-and-switch. With this approach the marketing research firm submits a price that is legitimate. But, once the contract is signed and the researchers start working on the study, the research firm identifies some means of upgrading the study. Instead of 250 respondents, the research firm convinces the client that to obtain reliable results it needs to interview 400 respondents. Instead of the basic questions that are on the current survey, the research firm convinces the client it needs to add more questions or a supplemental research study of an additional topic to better validate the results the client is seeking. With the bait-and-switch tactic, the original bid is legitimate, but often only addresses a stripped-down version of what should be done. While the research company could perform the original bid contract, its goal was always to get the contract, then convince the client to switch to a more expensive research design.

Ethics and the Research Process

When it comes to the research process itself, a number of potential ethical situations can occur. Some are easy to identify; others are more difficult. As shown in Figure 2.16, ethical issues that may occur include advocacy research, biased or unrepresentative sample selection, distorted data collection procedures, data falsification, improper statistical manipulations, and confidentiality issues with proprietary studies.

Advocacy research occurs more often with internal marketing research projects than it does with outside research agencies. **Advocacy research** is designed to advocate or support a company's position. Perhaps a company wants to justify a buzz marketing campaign or a direct response campaign. The company is looking specifically to find statistical evidence that the decision already made or the decision it wants to make is the

Figure 2.16   Ethics and Marketing Research Process

- Advocacy research
- Biased or unrepresentative sample selection
- Distorted data collection procedures
- Data falsification
- Improper statistical manipulations
- Confidentiality issues with proprietary studies

best course of action. Thus, the research is clearly to prove a particular point of view or decision. The research is then designed and carried out to increase the probability the results the company wants are obtained. The manager can then wave the research report to superiors as support for the decision.

Obtaining a sample that is representative of the target population can be a challenge for a marketing research firm. Once the company has the contract, to cut costs the company may look for alternative or more convenient methods of identifying the sample participants. For instance, the sampling plan may call for a mall intercept survey, and every 12th person who walks into the mall is supposed to be interviewed. Instead, researchers just pick individuals who they think will complete the survey, or they may go to the bookstore in the mall and ask individuals who are reading a book or having coffee to complete the survey. Either process violates the procedure for selecting the sample that was outlined in the sampling plan, detracting from the quality of data gathered.

Similarly, rather than solicit respondents in the population, a research firm may use professional research respondents who have agreed to participate in research studies or use respondents from a previous study. In both cases, the respondents are easy to identify and have experience in participating in research studies. In such situations, it is very likely the respondents do not match the target sample of the study, or if they do, because they have participated in other studies, they may not be representative of consumers in general. It is very tempting for a research firm to look at alternative ways of selecting a sample in an effort to control costs while disguising the fact that these individuals may not match the target sample.

To reduce data collection errors, it is important for the research firm and researchers not to intervene or influence the respondents in any way. Data collection distortion can occur in a number of ways. For instance, when conducting personal interviews the interviewer's tone of voice can influence the option selected by the respondents or inhibit the degree to which they respond to open-ended questions. In a telephone survey, the interviewer may skip some of the answer options under a question to save time, or tell the respondents to tell him or her when they come to a response that matches their feelings, thus not reading the entire list of options. Data collection distortion is very difficult to detect unless the client company actually observes the data collection process.

A more serious data collection problem is falsification of data. Companies rely on accurate data to make decisions. Any type of falsification is a very serious ethical and potentially legal problem. In order to produce the sample size a client wants, a research company may be tempted to manufacture or duplicate data to reach the required number of responses. This can be particularly true in telephone surveying if data recorders are contract employees who are paid on a per-completed-survey basis rather than an hourly wage. It may also be tempting for data recorders to "fill in" answers to partially completed surveys that the respondent terminates midway through, or even particular questions that the respondent refuses to answer. For example, many individuals resist answering questions about their race, age, or income. In recording survey responses, the data recorder may be unclear about which answer a respondent selected, and arbitrarily choose one rather than clarify the answer with the respondent or leave the answer to a particular question blank.

Improper statistical manipulations occur most often in advocacy studies. When researchers are requested to provide a particular type of support, then the temptation is to use statistical procedures or manipulate the data to ensure the predetermined results are obtained. For example, suppose a significance level of .05 was stipulated prior to data collection, but results indicate a significance level of .0598. While technically it is not significant, the researcher could just leave off the last two decimal points and not round up, indicating it was significant at the .05 level.

A more serious data manipulation may occur when researchers leave out part of the sample in the analysis in order to obtain significant results. Suppose that in analyzing the differences between business travelers and leisure travelers, researchers find no significant difference in how much money they spend on merchandise in the *SkyMall* magazine. But, when business travelers who make fewer than 10 trips per year are left out of the analysis, there is a significant difference, and this result is ultimately reported in the study. Such an action would be highly unethical if in the report nothing is said about the data manipulation, as the difference is actually only between business travelers who make more than 10 trips per year and leisure travelers, rather than business travelers in general.

The last ethical issue in terms of the research process is the confidentiality of propriety studies. When companies hire marketing research firms to conduct studies, in most cases the results are confidential and are the property of the client. Without the client's approval, nothing from the research studies can be made public or used in other studies. But, it is very easy for a company conducting research for another company to go back and pull data or results from a prior study to include in the current study.

In every aspect of marketing research, there is the potential for unethical conduct. Some behaviors are clearly wrong. Others are more difficult to judge. Each person working in marketing research must keep an eye open to potential ethical situations and strive to always perform work that is of the highest integrity.

Ethics and Respondents

Marketing research firms also have ethical responsibilities toward research participants. ESOMAR (www.esomar.org) is a global organization serving the marketing research industry. Among its many contributions, ESOMAR developed a guide to ethical research practices that is currently in use in more than 100 countries worldwide.[9] Several of the provisions outlined in ESOMAR's code of standards address respondent issues, and are shown in Figure 2.17.

Treating respondents ethically means respecting their rights. According to ESOMAR, respondents have the right "not to participate in a market research project; to withdraw from the market research interview at any time; to require that their personal data are not made available to others; and to delete or to rectify incorrect personal data" obtained by the researcher.[10]

It is important to be honest and not abuse the trust of respondents in the process of conducting the research. Respondents should not be misled as to the purpose of the research. It is also imperative to ensure respondents will not be harmed in any way, or experience any negative reactions to the research.

Researchers should explain how the data will be collected and fully inform respondents of the recording and observation techniques being used. For instance, participants of a focus group should understand that the session is being videotaped and will be analyzed later. In **cognitive neuroscience**, which is a brain-image measurement process that tracks brain activity, researchers need to explain to participants how the process works and how it is used.

This principle does not apply, however, to observation techniques in public places if the respondent's identity or information about the respondent is not in any way tied to the results. For instance, in studying respondent behavior at a point-of-purchase display in a retail store, individuals do not need to be informed they are part of the study. If later some of the individuals are recognized and the researcher wants to append the research entry to include any personal information about the person, then consent from the respondent would have to be obtained.

Figure 2.17   Ethical Responsibilities to Research Respondents

- Respondents have the right not to participate.
- Respondents have the right to stop participating in a research study at any time.
- Respondents have the right to require that their information remain confidential.
- Respondents have the right to require that personal information be deleted after use.
- Respondents have the right to the expectation of safety and freedom from harm.

Source: Author-created from "ICC/ESOMAR International Code on Social Science and Market Research," http://www.esomar .org/uploads/public/knowledge-and-standards/codes-and-guidelines/ICCESOMAR_Code_English_.pdf (accessed June 21, 2010).

Confidentiality is absolutely critical, especially if there is any way the respondent can be identified through personal information. Researchers have the responsibility to guard carefully research results to ensure that no one can tie data to specific respondents.

Corollary to confidentially is the protection of a respondent's identity. It is common for demographic and even psychographic and behavioral information to be part of the data collection process or appended to the research results at a later time. If this is done, then researchers have the obligation to protect respondents' privacy and ensure information about respondents remains confidential.

Global Concerns

Conducting global marketing research involves a number of concerns and potential ethical situations, which makes planning the research process even more critical. Differences in language and cultures across countries can easily lead to poor market research results and embarrassing situations. To prevent costly errors, companies may have to invest in more exploratory research that not only aids in identifying the problem to be studied, but provides relevant information about the target population to be studied.

For instance, while qualitative studies in the United States are being used to enrich descriptive studies, quantitative analysis tends to be more dominant in other parts of the world, especially in Central and Eastern Europe. Between 70% and 85% of all research in Europe involves quantitative data collection methods with face-to-face interviews the most frequently used. Telephone research has grown in recent years, as has online research. The challenge in many countries with online research, however, is the dependability of Internet connections and bandwidth to handle visuals that may accompany a research study.[11]

Another area of concern in global marketing research is ethical standards and conduct. Ethical beliefs vary widely across the world and even within countries with different cultures and subcultures. In the United States, bribes are considered unethical as well as illegal. In other countries it is a standard business practice and even permitted as a tax write-off. Obtaining a marketing research contract may require paying a bribe to government officials or to the RFP issuing company. Gift giving can also be an accepted practice during the business negotiations, and even how negotiations are conducted will vary widely from Eastern cultures to Western cultures.

To avoid potential pitfalls, companies will often engage local marketing research firms or international firms with experience in various countries. Alternatively, nationals from the country where the research is to be conducted can be contracted to provide valuable insights into the dos and don'ts of that country or culture.

 STATISTICS REVIEW

The research hypothesis, null hypothesis, and alternative hypothesis are related concepts, which often cause a great deal of confusion. As stated earlier, a research hypothesis states an expected research outcome relevant to one or more variables that seems reasonable in light of existing information. Research hypotheses are linked to specific research questions or objectives, and typically describe the anticipated nature of a variable or the expected relationship between two variables.

Suppose the purpose of a research study was to introduce a new type of snowmobile. Several research questions must be answered in order to fulfill the research purpose, including "How does demand for snowmobiles vary by region of the country?" The research hypothesis, "Demand for snowmobiles will be lower in the southeastern area of the country than in the northwestern area of the country," seems reasonable in light of average temperature and average annual snowfall data for various regions of the United States. Research hypotheses aren't always developed in response to research questions, but are useful in guiding the data analysis process when sufficient information exists to create logical hypotheses.

Taking the time to create well-written research hypotheses is time well spent. Well-designed research hypotheses should be as specific as possible, yet restricted to a single sentence. Hypotheses should also be concise; thus words that add little to the meaning of the sentence should be deleted. Since data analysis is only accurate within a determined margin of error, the word *prove* should never be included as part of a research hypothesis, as error exists in all market research studies. A research hypothesis should clearly indicate the phenomenon or variable to be studied, without referencing possible implications of the research or making other improper statements. A research hypothesis that states "Tobacco advertising is bad for society" is judgmental and does not specify the variable to be investigated. Conversely, one that proposes that "Greater exposure to tobacco advertising increases the likelihood of smoking" indicates the variables to be investigated (level of tobacco advertising exposure, likelihood of smoking) and their expected relationship, without passing judgment or jumping ahead to implications. Research hypotheses that compare groups (users vs. nonusers, males vs. females, etc.) should be stated in the plural form, and the subgroups to be compared specifically identified. Furthermore, when the hypothesis features a stated comparison (lower, higher, more, less, etc.), the variables being compared should be explicitly referenced, using consistent terminology. Finally, the word *significant* should not be incorporated in the research hypothesis, since it is understood that tests of significance will be used during hypothesis testing.[12]

The concept of null and alternative hypotheses is a basic statistics principle, although often confusing. Represented by the symbol H_0, the null hypothesis is a statement or claim that can be statistically tested. When the subject of a research hypothesis is a single variable, the null hypothesis is stated in terms of equality. For instance, a research hypothesis might propose that "Individuals most likely to purchase a yacht for personal use have an average annual income of $5 million or more." This research hypothesis would be rephrased into the following null hypothesis: "Individuals most likely to purchase a yacht for personal use have an average annual income equal to $5 million."

The alternative hypothesis, designated as H_A, states that which must be true when the null hypothesis is false. In the example above, H_A would be designated as "Individuals most likely to purchase a yacht for personal use have an average annual income not equal to $5 million." Or, two separate alternative hypotheses specifying income levels of less than $5 million and greater than $5 million, respectively, could be created (so long as both were included).

In the case of group comparisons, the null hypothesis is sometimes called the status quo hypothesis, as it essentially states that no differences exist between the groups. The snowmobile

(Continued)

(Continued)

research hypothesis conjectured that "Demand for snowmobiles will be lower in the southeastern area of the country than in the northwestern area of the country." Prior to data analysis, the null hypothesis would be phrased as "Demand for snowmobiles does not vary by region of the country," and the research hypothesis can be listed as one of several potential alternative hypotheses. The process of hypothesis testing would then be used to determine whether or not sufficient evidence exists—based on the results of the study—to reject the null hypothesis. Recall that the null hypothesis is only rejected when the study results are unlikely to have occurred by chance, as determined by the appropriate significance test.

DEALING WITH DATA

SPSS is a software application used by many research professionals and university professors to analyze data. SPSS allows users to perform a variety of analyses, ranging from simple procedures such as basic descriptive statistics and nonparametric tests such as chi-square analyses to more involved and complex processes such as regression, ANOVA, time series analysis, classification analysis, correlation analysis, and more. SPSS also provides extensive charting capabilities and export options to facilitate the creation of research reports.

The purpose of this exercise is for you to become acquainted with SPSS. You will need to download the following two files that are on the student website for this textbook at www.sagepub .com/clowess:

- Chapter 02 Dealing with Data (SPSS file)
- Chapter 02 Dealing with Data Survey (Word file)

The first file is the actual data file that contains the results obtained from a student research project. The second file is the questionnaire composed by the student. If you are not familiar with

This female indicated she spends on the average between $50-$74 on clothes per shopping trip.

SPSS, detailed step-by-step instructions are provided for each chapter's exercise on the student website for the textbook.

Open the questionnaire. It may be helpful to print the one-page questionnaire so you can refer to it as you complete this exercise. Open the SPSS data file and save it to your hard drive or a flash drive. Go through the following steps to become acquainted with SPSS.

1. Notice SPSS has two views or sheets. The first contains the raw data numbers; the second is the variable view that provides information about each variable.

2. On the sheet that contains the raw data, change the view so you can see the actual data that were entered. This is called "value labels." With this view instead of numbers, it will show the actual answer the respondent indicated, such as "two or three times a month" for Question 1 and "$50–$74" for Question 2.

3. Go to the variable view and examine each column. Compare it to the questionnaire.

4. Write a short description of each column. For instance, the first column is the name of the variable. It is a short, abbreviated name with no spaces and identifies the question number to easily identify which question it is in the questionnaire. It is also beneficial to click on each column to examine the different options available.

5. Two columns that are especially important for you to examine closely are the columns titled "Label" and "Values." Why do you think these are important?

SUMMARY

Objective 1: Compare and contrast the three types of research design.

Exploratory, descriptive, and causal research designs are each appropriate under certain conditions. Exploratory research uses focus groups, one-on-one interviews, secondary research, and/or pilot studies to develop a better understanding of a particular problem or situation that may otherwise be ambiguous. An exploratory study might seek to define the marketing research problem, identify parameters or variables to be studied further, or generate potential research hypotheses for testing. Descriptive research studies are the most common form of marketing research and typically seek to describe existing characteristics, attributes, or behaviors of people, brands, organizations, or other objects. Survey and observation research form the bulk of descriptive research studies. Causal research is appropriate when attempting to investigate whether a change in one item causes a change to occur in another. Establishing causality requires both a temporal sequence and concomitant variation. Carefully controlled laboratory experiments and field experiments are used in the determination of causality.

Objective 2: Explain the marketing research process.

The marketing research process is often organized into six key steps: (1) defining the research problem, (2) developing the research design, (3) determining the sampling plan, (4) implementing data collection procedures, (5) analyzing the data, and (6) preparing and sharing the research report. Defining the research problem starts by establishing the research purpose. Next is the development of research questions or objectives that outline the scope of the research project and guide the development of the research design, followed by the creation of hypotheses. Research design decisions include determining the nature of the approach (descriptive or casual) and selecting the method of data collection (survey, observation, or experimentation). The sampling plan begins with a determination of the population to be studied, then describes the process by which the sample group of study participants will be selected. During data analysis, researchers apply mathematical and statistical processes to raw numbers for the purpose of providing meaningful information that can assist managers in making decisions. The final stage of the research process involves writing and presenting the research report to include a set of actionable recommendations.

Objective 3: Describe the components of a request for proposal (RFP) and a research proposal.

Requests for research proposals, commonly referred to as RFPs, are created by firms commissioning a research study. RFPs typically include background information; an overview of the research purpose, problem, or question; and a description of the target audience for the study. Important expectations that influence the cost of the study should be provided, such as desired sample size, data collection methodology, and the time frame for the study. A research proposal is prepared by firms who wish to bid on RFPs and contain the following information: (1) introduction and background to the RFP, (2) research questions, (3) research design, (4) target population, (5) sample size and method, (6) data collection methodology, and (7) cost and time schedule for the study.

Objective 4: Provide an overview of qualitative and quantitative research.

Qualitative research involves the use of small-sample, unstructured data collection methods, such as focus groups, personal interviews, case studies, and other techniques. It is subjective and exploratory in nature, and results should not be interpreted as providing definitive answers. In contrast, quantitative research is a more structured process in which data are collected objectively using larger, more representative samples. Research designs allow for data to be represented numerically, which permits statistical tests and analyses. Results are more definitive and can be generalized to the population. Quantitative research is most commonly associated with descriptive and causal studies.

Objective 5: Recite the ethical considerations in designing research studies.

Ethical considerations impact research decisions as well as various entities involved in the research industry. Firms seeking to commission research studies may behave unethically if RFPs are issued that are not sincere requests for bids. Marketing research suppliers who submit research proposals in response to RFPs behave unethically when engaging in lowball pricing or bait-and-switch tactics. Numerous opportunities for unethical behavior exist throughout the research process and include, but are not limited to, purposively engaging in advocacy research, biasing the sample selection, distorting the data collected, falsifying data, improperly analyzing data or manipulating statistics, and violating the confidentiality of proprietary studies. Respondents' rights to confidentiality and safety should be protected, as should their rights to withdraw their participation from the study and to correct inaccurate information.

GLOSSARY OF KEY TERMS

Advocacy research: research that is purposively designed to advocate or support a particular position

Causal research: research used to determine cause-and-effect relationships between variables

Cognitive neuroscience: a research process involving brain-image measurements through the tracking of brain activity

Concomitant variation: condition for causality in which the two items thought to be linked in a causal relationship vary or change together and in the direction hypothesized

Descriptive research: answers the questions who, what, when, where, and how in describing the characteristics of consumers, brands, and other marketing phenomena

Experiment: a research study where all variables are held constant except the one under study

Exploratory research: preliminary examination of a problem or situation to identify parameters to be studied further or to define the research problem itself

Field experiment: an experiment in a real-world setting

Lowball pricing: submitting an extremely low-priced bid in response to an RFP simply for the purpose of getting the contract, with no intention of doing the work at the quoted price

Observation approach: research in which the behaviors of those being studied or the results of their behaviors are observed by researchers

Pilot study: an abbreviated study with a limited number of respondents designed to provide information to the researcher useful in developing a larger, more definitive study

Population: the group that is being studied from which samples are drawn

Qualitative research: unstructured data collection methods that provide results that are subjectively interpreted

Quantitative research: structured data collection methods that provide results that can be converted to numbers and analyzed through statistical procedures

Request for proposal (RFP): a written document containing an official request for a research proposal (also referred to as an "invitation to bid")

Research hypothesis: expected research outcome that seems reasonable in light of existing information

Research design: a plan to address the research problem, question, and/or hypothesis

Research proposal: a written document prepared in response to an RFP that provides basic information about the research process that will be used

Research purpose: statement that broadly specifies the situation, phenomenon, opportunity, or problem to be investigated, and guides the creation of research questions and hypotheses

Research question (research objective): specifies the type of information needed to fulfill the research purpose and make managerial decisions

Spurious association: apparent cause-and-effect relationship between two variables that is actually caused by other factors

Survey research: research in which individuals are asked a series of questions about the topic under study

Temporal sequence: condition for causality in which the cause precedes the effect

CRITICAL THINKING EXERCISES

1. Visit http://www.harrisinteractive.com and locate past research studies. Select a recent time frame and choose either the "Marketplace" or "Social and Lifestyle Issues" category. Review the titles of the various articles available. Select a study that has implications for marketers and is of interest to you. Summarize the results of the study. Is this an example of exploratory, descriptive, or causal research? Was it gathered via observation, survey, or experimental methods? What type of businesses could make use of this information, and how could it be useful?

2. Is it ethical for churches, charities, governmental organizations, or other not-for-profit organizations to request pro bono or discounted rates in their RFP? Why or why not?

3. Critique the following research hypotheses. What is wrong with each one? Rewrite each to address the problems noted following the principles outlined in this chapter. Write both a null and an alternative hypothesis.

   a. Demand for new technology products will be higher among students.
   b. All drivers should purchase automobile insurance.
   c. Coupon redemption rates vary significantly by income.
   d. Among brand-loyal consumers, those who have higher levels of brand loyalty will be more willing to pay higher prices while brand-loyal consumers who have moderate levels of brand loyalty will be less willing to pay higher prices.
   e. Search engine advertising will be proven to be more effective than banner advertising.

4. A veterinarian has commissioned a research study to investigate whether or not selling specialty dog food, cat food, and other pet products at her clinic would be profitable for business. You have been

working as a receptionist at the clinic for the past six months, and she has asked for your help in creating research questions that will provide the information necessary to make the correct business decision. Develop a minimum of three research questions or objectives that can help to achieve the purpose of the study.

5. Review the American Marketing Association's Statement of Ethics found at http://www.marketingpower .com. Do any of the items discussed in this document apply specifically to marketing research? Can the existing ethical standards be generalized to marketing research? If so, explain. Contrast the AMA's code of ethics to the Code of Standards of the Council of American Survey Research Organizations (CASRO) found at http://www.casro.org. Which ethical code is more useful for the marketing research profession? Does the CASRO code apply to all forms of marketing research? If not, what forms are missing?

6. Requests for proposal (also called invitations to bid) are commonly listed on the website of the issuing firm and sent directly to research entities the firm hopes will submit a bid. Using the search engine of your choice, search either or both of the following terms: *request for proposal market research* and *invitations to bid market research*. Review the search results until you find an actual RFP document. Read through the document, and prepare a one- to two-page report that answers the following questions:

   a. Based on your understanding of the RFP, will the research project be primarily qualitative or quantitative in nature, or will both forms of research be required? Explain.
   b. Would you classify the research likely to result from the RFP as exploratory, descriptive, or casual?
   c. Are surveys, observations, experiments, or some other form of data collection likely to be involved? Explain.
   d. Does the RFP contain all of the components of an RFP discussed in this chapter? Is it clearly written, or are some portions of the RFP ambiguous? Would you feel comfortable responding to the RFP based on the information provided?
   e. What ethical concerns might be raised by the RFP?

   Your report should be accompanied by a link to the RFP, a hard copy of the RFP, or an electronic copy of the RFP.

7. A mystery shopper visits a Chick-fil-A restaurant and places an order for a sandwich at the counter. After leaving the restaurant, the mystery shopper submits a report that lists the following items:

   - The amount of time he stood in line waiting to place his order
   - Whether or not the order taker smiled when taking the order, suggested the purchase of a drink or fries with the sandwich, and thanked the shopper for placing an order
   - The amount of time that it took to receive the food after placing the order
   - Whether the order was filled correctly
   - Whether or not the tables within the restaurant, the windows, the floor, the countertops, and the restrooms were clean

   Is this research study an example of qualitative or quantitative research? Would you describe the research as exploratory, descriptive, or casual? Does the research method described in this scenario reflect survey, observation, or experimental research? Are there any other factors that might be added to those evaluated by the mystery shopper? Justify your answers.

CONTINUING CASE STUDY: LAKESIDE GRILL

Students Brooke, Alexa, Juan, Destiny, and Zach began their research proposal by outlining the background for the study and specifying the research problem and research objectives. According to the group, "The purpose of this research study is to determine why sales at Lakeside Grill are declining, and what changes to the marketing mix are needed in order to improve sales and profitability." Based on the research purpose, the group wrote the following research questions:

1. What is the current level of customer satisfaction with various operational aspects of Lakeside Grill, such as the menu, hours of operation, atmosphere, quality of service, and quality of food?

2. Why have customers reduced their level of patronage at Lakeside Grill?

3. How has the addition of a new competitor down the street impacted Lakeside Grill's customer base?

4. Would changing Lakeside Grill's menu, prices, advertising, and/or promotional practices increase sales and profitability?

In terms of type of research, Juan explained, "We will conduct descriptive research and collect primarily quantitative data. We really don't need to conduct any exploratory research because Mr. Zito [owner of Lakeside Grill] has provided us with information about the restaurant's background and the situation that he is facing now."

Critique Questions:

1. Evaluate the research purpose. Is it clear? Should "determine why sales are declining" be part of the research purpose, or is it a symptom? What about "changes in the marketing mix?" Is this a strategy, or can this be a legitimate purpose for the study?

2. Based on information provided in this chapter, improve and rewrite the research purpose statement for the student group.

3. Are the research questions appropriate for the research purpose you wrote in response to Question 2, or do they need to be rewritten also? If the latter, please rewrite the research questions to match your new research purpose.

4. Would you agree with Juan's statement that the best approach is descriptive research and quantitative data? Why or why not?

5. Would you agree with Juan's statement that "we really don't need to conduct any exploratory research because Mr. Zito [owner of Lakeside Grill] has provided us with information?" Why or why not?

6. What ethical issues could arise with the AMA student team conducting this research project? What steps should the students and faculty advisor take to ensure no unethical behaviors occur?

MARKETING RESEARCH PORTFOLIO

The "Marketing Research Portfolio" provides an excellent example of a comprehensive RFP. After reviewing the RFP issued by the Wiley Botanical Gardens and Zoo, students apply chapter material by answering a series of questions related to the nature of the research, the type of research projects to be used, the population and sample, data collection, and ethical considerations. The answers to these questions can then be used to guide students in the preparation of a research proposal. The RFP and assignment questions can be found online at www.sagepub.com/clowess.

STUDENT STUDY SITE

Visit the Student Study Site at www.sagepub.com/clowess to access the following additional materials:

- eFlashcards
- Web Quizzes
- SAGE Journal Articles
- Web Resources

SECTION 2
Types of Marketing Research

CHAPTER 3

Secondary Data and Research

LEARNING OBJECTIVES

After reading this chapter, you should be able to

1. Discuss the advantages and disadvantages of secondary data.

2. Identify key uses of secondary data.

3. Explain how internal sources of data can be used for secondary research.

4. Describe the open access sources of secondary data.

5. Summarize the primary differences among the bibliographic digital databases.

6. Identify and explain the types of data available from syndicated sources.

INTRODUCTION

The NPD Group is a leading global provider of consumer and retail market research information. Data are collected on a regular basis, analyzed, and then sold to clients and other interested businesses. It is cheaper for firms to purchase data from the NPD Group than for each company to collect its own data. One area of concern to retailers is online sales. The NPD Group collects online sales data on a continuous basis. Figure 3.1 shows the percentage of consumers who have made a purchase in various categories within the last 12 months.[1]

The leading category is books, stationery, and office supplies with 48% of consumers saying they made a purchase within that category within the last 12 months. But almost equal are the categories of apparel and electronics, each at 46%. The last two categories are footwear at 34% and fashion accessories at 24%. This type of information is very useful to online retailers and manufacturers who sell through online retail outlets. It can be used by online retailers in modifying

Figure 3.1   Online Purchases in Select Retail Categories Within Last 12 Months

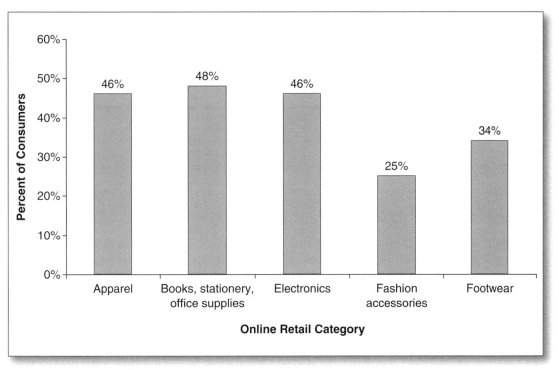

Source: Author-created with data from "NPD Reports on E-Commerce: A Look at Consumers' Cross-Category Online Shopping Behavior," *NPD Group Press Release,* January 24, 2012, https://www.npd.com/wps/portal/npd/us/news/pressreleases/pr_120124#. UAc1zzFSRDQ (accessed July 18, 2012).

websites or the merchandise mix to better meet the needs of consumers. Companies do not always have to collect their own data to make good marketing decisions. Often, data can be purchased from another source, such as the NPD Group.

IT ALL BEGINS WITH SECONDARY DATA

Data previously collected for purposes other than the current study at hand are **secondary data.** By contrast, **primary research** may involve new focus groups, questionnaires, experiments, or observation studies specifically developed to help answer the research questions currently being investigated. While both types of research are often necessary to fulfill the research purpose, studies should always begin with secondary data research. While this type of research may not answer all of the questions being posed by the researcher, gathering secondary data is almost always a useful exercise that can produce a number of benefits. It is well worth the time and effort and in some cases can provide adequate information that can be used by management for making more informed decisions. The primary advantages and disadvantages of using secondary data are listed in Figure 3.2.

■ Learning Objective 3.1: Discuss the advantages and disadvantages of secondary data.

Figure 3.2   Advantages and Disadvantages of Secondary Data

Advantages	**Disadvantages**
• Accessibility	• Not available
• Cost savings	• Relevancy
• Time savings	• Insufficient

Advantages of Secondary Data

The major advantage of secondary data is their accessibility, which in turn produces cost and time savings. From the Internet, the library, syndicated data sources, or internal company sources, a marketing researcher may be able to locate useful information. If so, the amount of time it takes to acquire the information will be considerably less than if primary research is undertaken. The information also will be much less costly to acquire for several reasons. First, internal data and many forms of high-quality secondary data are available free of charge (such as census data from the government). Secondly, even data that are purchased from syndicated sources cost less, because the overall study expense is shared among multiple subscribers, making each individual purchaser's cost a fraction of the whole. A **syndicated research service** is a marketing research firm that supplies standardized information to a number of clients, such as the NPD Group in the Introduction. Finally, collecting secondary data will cost less and take less time than collecting primary data because all of the steps outlined in Chapter 2 for the primary research process will not have to be followed.

Consider a company that needs to make a decision on how much, if any, of its advertising budget should go toward mobile advertising. The proposed media change might be based on the belief that since so many individuals have mobile phones, the probability of the ad being seen on a cell phone is greater than the probability of it being seen via television or one of the other traditional media. Faced with this decision, management may request a research study to determine if some of the advertising budget should be allocated for mobile phone advertising.

In conducting secondary research, the researcher may locate the study by Lightspeed Research published in the *Marketing News*. In a survey of 1,170 individuals, Lightspeed Research found that only 9% were receptive to personalized mobile advertising. Further reading of the study, however, highlights that 32% of individuals 18–34 were receptive, compared to only 6% of individuals 55 and older. A statement by Ralph Risk, marketing director for Lightspeed Research, provides additional insight. Risk stated, "You have to get the right message across, make it something that is of value to them and educate them on the benefits of it in order for it to be successful."[2] Thus, if the company wants to spend money on mobile phone advertising, it must examine the target audience and the message it will promote. While primary research may provide more specific information, the secondary research may be sufficient for management to make a decision on how much money to allocate for mobile advertising. If so, the company has saved considerable time and money since the information may have been obtained within a few hours compared to the several weeks or months required when conducting a primary research study.

Disadvantages of Secondary Data

A number of disadvantages are associated with secondary data. First, the exact information needed *may not be available.* This occurs when the information management is seeking has not been studied by someone else. For example, a company such as John Deere may want information about how consumers and commercial customers feel about its line of lawn mowers with a hydrostatic transmission, and if there is a difference in attitudes between consumers who purchase the lawn mower and commercial customers such as golf courses, school districts, hospitals, and parks. A study identified via secondary research may rank the various brands of lawn mowers. Another study may have examined consumer preferences in terms of the desirability of lawn mower features. But, neither secondary study tells John Deere what consumers and commercial customers think of their lawn mower featuring the hydrostatic transmission. Such is often the case with new products that have just been introduced to the market. Some primary research would be needed to answer questions such as this.

Unfortunately, a great deal of secondary data will be *irrelevant* to the research purpose. Carefully crafted search phrases can limit the degree to which superfluous information is found when searching electronic databases or the Internet. A major source of frustration for many marketers occurs when secondary data are found that are "close" to what is being searched for, but that use irrelevant units of measure in defining the target market or other variables of interest.

A researcher may be seeking information on the number of unique (separate) individuals who use mass transportation in an average month. Suppose a secondary research study was found that listed the number of fares collected each month by type of public transportation. Unfortunately, this information would be irrelevant; the number of fares collected cannot be used as a proxy for the number of unique riders. Fares are collected each time a rider—any rider—uses the bus or city train system. Thus, a commuter who takes the bus to work each day would log 10 fares in a single week. Using fares as a proxy for riders would overstate the number of individual people using the transportation system.

Secondary data may be available and relevant to the current research topic, but still *insufficient* to answer the question. Suppose three years ago John Deere conducted a study that examined how customers felt about its line of lawn mowers and the various features that it offered. The study may have even compared the John Deere brand to other brands. But, the study did not survey commercial customers. Thus, the secondary data are not sufficient to answer the current research question and provide information to John Deere if the feature was desired by its commercial customers.

Evaluating the Accuracy of Secondary Data

In using secondary data, it is important to assess their accuracy. As shown in Figure 3.3, a number of issues need to be examined. Data may be easily accessible and save a company money and time, but if the data are inaccurate, then flawed decisions will be made that could cost the firm more than if it had conducted primary research initially.

Figure 3.3   Issues in Examining Accuracy of Secondary Data

- Data source
- Purpose of study
- Sample selection
- Data collection process
- Data analysis
- Data interpretation

Data Source. Evaluating the accuracy of secondary data begins with determining the source of the data. With the Internet, secondary data are readily available. It is not, however, always easy to determine who produced the data. Websites do not always clearly identify the company or organization behind the site or the data. This is especially true with microsites that companies have developed for specific purposes. It is also true of sites hosted by individuals. The researcher must be very careful not to mistake statements of opinion for statements of fact. Anyone can say anything on a website. Without insight into the source of the data, the sample studied, and the methodology used to collect and analyze data, taking results on blind faith can be dangerous and result in poor decision making.

Sources of data that tend to be accurate include government organizations, major syndicated data providers, custom research firms, trade organizations, and educational institutions. The federal, state, and even local governments produce a large number of data sets that are publicly available free of charge to individuals and companies. Syndicated data providers exist for the sole purpose of gathering, analyzing, and packaging standardized data to multiple subscribers. Thus, the data they provide must be of high quality in order to keep their subscriber base strong. Custom research firms are also actively involved in collecting data. Similar to syndicated data, some data collected by these research firms may be available for businesses to purchase at a price that is typically much lower than that for collecting the same data through primary research. However, much of the data collected by custom research firms is proprietary and belongs to the client who paid for the study.

Fortunately, custom research firms will sometimes publish the results of studies for free. The rationale usually for publishing this information is to show the research firm's expertise and to encourage additional business from companies interested in the topic. Care should be taken, though, because published studies of this nature—though accurate at the time of data collection—can be out of date. Furthermore, it would be erroneous to assume that the quality and accuracy of data gathered by custom research firms are always inherently strong. Unlike syndicated firms, which rely on repeat business in the form of subscriptions, custom research firms are more dependent upon new business. Bidding low to secure a research project may result in cutting corners during study implementation or simply failing to pay attention to detail, either of which may damage the accuracy of the information collected. Furthermore, the marketing research profession does not currently require that those who call themselves professionals be licensed or certified. Thus, the quality and accuracy of data provided by custom research firms may be highly variable. The expertise and training of the staff assigned to a project can be a major contributing factor. Suffice it to say that reputable firms will disclose the methodology of their studies in detail when asked, maintain strict quality control measures, and adhere to proper sampling practices. If, upon reviewing the methodology, certain practices or procedures are not adequately described, the quality of data may be suspect.

Trade organizations will collect data unique to the industry and make that information available to firms within the industry. Some of the data will be used as the basis for articles posted in the trade journal and on the trade organization's website. Other data can be purchased by firms within the industry.

The last source of secondary information is educational institutions. Most of these data are free and collected as a public service. Many universities have centers for economic research that study issues affecting the local workforce and economy.

Purpose of Study. Accuracy of secondary data is affected by the purpose of the study. Studies are sometimes conducted to justify a particular position (advocacy research). In such cases the results may be biased, or at least the methodology will be suspect since the goal was to arrive at a predetermined result. An advertisement for a particular type of toothpaste or toothbrush that states 7 out of 10 dentists recommend the brand is likely an advocacy study.

Often it is difficult to determine the purpose of the study. In such cases it is important to look at the source of the study, why it was conducted, and the sample used. Consider the results shown in Figure 3.4 for a study conducted by BlogHer Inc. Respondents indicated they spend more time reading blogs than they do watching TV, listening to radio, or reading print media. The sample was primarily individuals from the BlogHer network, which provides a valuable clue as to the results found. Since the respondents are members of the BlogHer network, they like reading, commenting on, and writing blogs, which explains the results. While the purpose of the study is not fully known, the sample and the source of the study show a bias to individuals, very likely females, who like blogging. It would be difficult for any company other than BlogHer to use these data to make management decisions. Certainly it would be inappropriate for another firm to conclude that *all women* like blogging; doing so

Figure 3.4   Results of a Survey by BlogHer

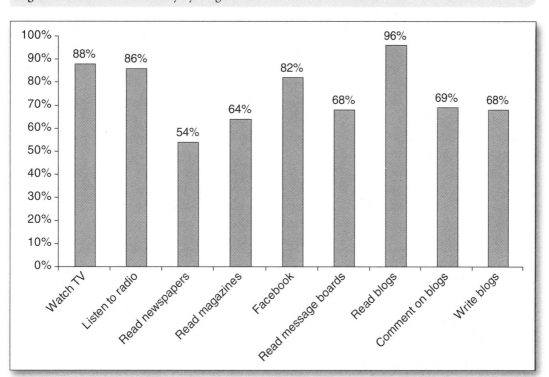

Source: Author-created with data from *Social Media Matters 2010*, BlogHer Inc., BlogHer network sample, $N = 1,550$.

may lead to added and unnecessary expense should the firm then decide to create blogs on product websites that primarily cater to women.

Sample Selection. Who the sample is and how it is selected are critically important in determining the accuracy of secondary data. Referring back to Figure 3.4, note that the sample not only is part of the BlogHer network but is limited to *active* social media users. By sampling active social media users it is not surprising to see that 96% read blogs "weekly or more." If occasional social media users or even nonsocial media users were surveyed, the results would be quite different. Similarly, if Ford surveyed only individuals with incomes of $75,000 or more concerning their attitudes toward the Ford F-150 series pickup trucks, the results would be different than if all consumers, regardless of income, were surveyed.

With secondary research how the sample was selected may not be stated or otherwise be evident. But, it is important because the sample needs to represent the population being studied. If a company wants to use the results of a secondary research study to support a management decision, then the sample needs to represent the company's population or target market for which the decision will be made. For instance, the sample used by BlogHer was predominantly female. It would not be representative of the population as a whole. As mentioned earlier, it isn't even representative of all females, but rather represents just those who are actively engaged with social media and who are members of the BlogHer network.

Data Collection Process. Even harder to determine when evaluating the quality of secondary data is when the study was undertaken, how the data were collected, what type of analysis was conducted, and how the analysis was interpreted. All of these facets of the research process are important in determining the accuracy of the data. A study examining what people do on the Internet would be of little value today if conducted five years ago. Too much has changed; blogging and social networking opportunities have grown exponentially, while new alternatives—such as watching entire television episodes online—have been made possible by enhancements in technology.

Seldom would the research methodology details be provided within a published report. The information can be obtained, however, if the secondary data are purchased from a marketing research firm. If the source is government data, such information may be contained in footnotes or available upon request.

Consider a study from the Council for Research Excellence on the viewing habits of individuals before, during, and after television commercials. According to the study, only 14% of viewers switch channels during the commercial break compared to 11% who change channels during the four minutes before the commercials and 13% who change channels in the four minutes after the break. The study was designed to support the concept that the majority, 86% of viewers, watch television commercials. The sample consisted of 375 adults, and the study tracked live TV consumption across 750,000 minutes of television broadcasting.[3]

Under deeper scrutiny, it can be seen that the study examined only live television watching, not DVR viewing. While the study appears to support the idea that individuals watch television commercials, there is no record of how the sample was selected and if the 376 people are representative of the U.S. population. Also, the report does not tell how the data were collected and if the viewers were actually watching the commercials, or if they had left the TV to go to the kitchen or bathroom or to do something else. For the researcher to be able to use these secondary data, it would be important to have more information about the sample selection,

Research by the Council of Research Excellence found that most people do not switch TV channels during commercial breaks.

the data collection process, and analysis of the data. The results may be legitimate, but not enough details are provided to know for sure.

Data Analysis. The accuracy of the data can be greatly influenced by the type of analysis performed and the degree of error that the researcher finds acceptable. Determining whether the data were properly analyzed can be quite difficult since access to the questionnaire or data collection instrument, the full data analyses results, and the data set used in analyses is rarely, if ever, available. Furthermore, a strong working knowledge of statistics and the properties of different types of data yielded by the types of questions or data collection methods is essential to understanding whether the analyses undertaken were appropriate. These topics are discussed in greater detail in later chapters, but the following simplistic illustration will help make the point. Suppose a survey question asked respondents to indicate their age by checking a category from among the following choices: less than 18, 18–24, 25–34, 35–44, 45–54, 55 and older. An analysis that reported an "average" age of 35, based on these data, would be inaccurate because means cannot be computed on the basis of categorical data. Only counts and percentages would be appropriate to report.

The degree of error allowed by the researcher is also critically important in judging the accuracy of the research. A survey that is purported to be accurate to within "plus or minus 10%" indicates a high tolerance of error. Suppose the survey found that 64% of the population was in favor of stricter political advertising regulations. In reality, the "true" attitude of the population could be anywhere between 54% and 74% in favor of stricter control, which is quite a difference!

Data Interpretation. Interpretation of some forms of data, such as the various forms of qualitative data that will be discussed in Chapter 4, is highly subjective. When subjectivity is introduced into the data interpretation process, the accuracy of the results may vary considerably depending on who interprets the results. For example, one form of qualitative data asks consumers to tell stories about products or consumption situations. Two psychologists trained in different schools of thought could realistically interpret the same story as having different meanings.

■ Learning
Objective 3.2:
Identify
key uses of
secondary data.

Key Uses of Secondary Data

Despite the disadvantages just cited, secondary data are important and useful to companies. They provide information that sometimes is impossible for a company to collect itself. Collecting secondary data can also save thousands of dollars and provide quality information sooner than conducting primary research. At times, secondary research may even be superior to data a company can collect through primary research. Figure 3.5 identifies the key uses for secondary data.

Figure 3.5 Key Uses of Secondary Data

- Exploratory research
- Preparation for primary research
- Identifying consumer trends
- Industry information
- Estimating demand
- Selecting target markets, trade areas, and sites
- Measuring advertising exposure
- Database marketing
- Data mining

Exploratory Research and Preparing Primary Research. As presented in Chapter 2, secondary data are often used for exploratory research and as preparation for primary research. When a company doesn't really know the problem it is facing, or needs additional information to determine the problem, exploratory research and secondary data can be helpful. Even in preparing a primary research study, secondary data can provide excellent background information and guide the primary research process. They can help the researcher decide the best research design, determine how to word questions, or suggest potential sampling sources (databases, panels, lists, etc.). Rather than create an entirely new research design or questionnaire, researchers would do well to review secondary data for information on how previous research was conducted and to understand where improvements need to be made.

Identifying Consumer Trends. Secondary data are excellent for identifying consumer trends. Consider the data in the restaurant industry report produced by the Small Business and Technology Development Center of North Carolina. The most frequently cited circumstance for the last visit to a casual dining restaurant was "fun evening with friends." "Special occasion" and "Didn't want to cook" were the second and third most popular reasons given.[4] The entire list is shown in Figure 3.6. This secondary information can be used by a restaurant to design advertising campaigns or special offers to attract customers. An entire campaign can be built about how much fun it is dine at a particular restaurant with friends.

A more comprehensive study of restaurant trends was conducted by Joseph Baum and Michael Whiteman Co., Inc. (JBMW). In addition to overall industry trends, the research also investigated menu and flavor trends.[5] This information can be used by restaurant managers

Figure 3.6   Reasons for Last Visit to Casual Dine-In Restaurant

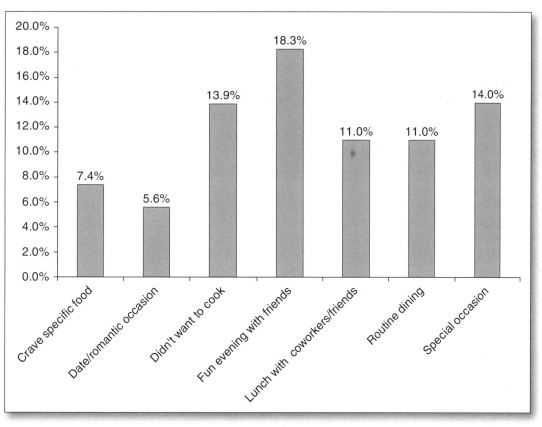

Source: Author-created with data from *NC SBTCD Restaurant Industry Study*, Small Business & Technology Development Center, 2005.

to guide their operations as well as marketing programs. The following trends were identified by JBMW:

- Restaurants are catering to kids with children's menus and promotions that encourage patronage by families with kids.
- Increased emphasis is being placed on fresh, local, and handmade menu items that customers feel are safer and better.
- Restaurants are losing control of what is being said about them. It is now in the hands of bloggers, texters, tweeters, and Facebook users. Consumers control the buzz.
- Menu churn, where restaurants are stealing successful menu items from competitors by creating an imitation, is common. This trend is even occurring across categories, such as fast-food restaurants offering dine-in and specialty items, and the reverse.

When it comes to menu trends, the JBMW study found that consumers want breakfast foods available all the time (24/7), at both full-scale and limited-scale restaurants. Another menu trend is the increase in demand for Korean, Indonesian, and Southeast Asian food. Sweet potatoes are becoming known as the new functional food due to their rich dietary fiber content, vitamins C and B6, and beta-carotene.

Obtain Industry Information. Another use of secondary data is to obtain industry information such as sales, market share, and competitive position. The JBMW restaurant study contains considerable industry information that can be useful. It provides industry sales by type of restaurant, sales growth over the last 10 years, sales by different types of restaurants (i.e., Asian, family-style, Mexican, and seafood) and sales by size of restaurant chains or units. Some data that are especially useful for operations are industry averages for restaurant expenditures. A restaurant can compare its expenditures to industry averages to see where improvement should be made, or where it is doing well.

Competitive information is also available. The report shows the sales increases or decreases for the major restaurant brands. The sales figures are even broken down by corporate-owned versus franchise units. For example, same-store sales for Buffalo Wild Wings Grill and Bar increased 6.8% for corporate restaurants versus 2.1% for franchised operations. Figure 3.7 shows changes in same-store sales for some of the well-known quick-service restaurants. Notice that McDonald's had the largest increase at 5.0% while Arby's had the sharpest decline at 7.2%. Such information is valuable, especially to those chains that lost sales.

Other industry information that a company could use includes the top growth chains and the chains opening the most new restaurants. The top three chains in terms of sales growth

Figure 3.7   Changes in Same-Store Sales for Quick-Service Restaurants

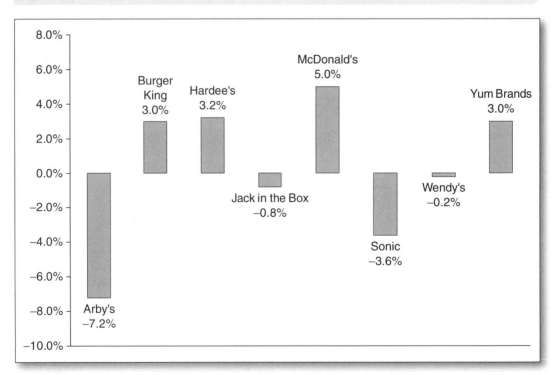

Source: Author-created with data from Ciji A. Tlapa, Richard K. Miller, and Kelli Washington, "Restaurant & Hotel Food Trends," *Restaurant, Food & Beverage Market Research Handbook* (2010), p. 28.

were Five Guys Burgers and Fries (grew 50%), Tim Hortons (grew 23%), and Buffalo Wild Wings Grill and Bar (grew 22%). In terms of new restaurant chains, WingStreet added 913 new locations, Dunkin' Donuts 645, and Little Caesars 299. Obtaining this type of information from secondary sources is quick, easy, and often free. More detailed information can also be obtained, usually for a fee from marketing research firms that track industry trends and gather industry information.

Estimating Demand. Secondary data are often used to estimate demand. Demographic information from government sources such as the U.S. Census Bureau can provide raw numbers in terms of population. Coupled with sales data from a company's own database, estimates of future demand can be forecasted. This information is then used to set production schedules, determine staffing, and set operating budgets. Many trade associations also provide data on sales, market share, and even market potential. For instance, the *Restaurant, Food & Beverage Market Research Handbook* provides sales data for various types of restaurants and the changes in sales during the last year and over the last 10 years. This information can be used by a company to estimate its demand for the upcoming year. *Sales & Marketing Management*'s Survey of Buying Power provides subscribers with statistics, such as effective buying income (EBI) and the buying power index (BPI), for counties and media markets located throughout the United States. Purchasing data, rankings, and demographics are also provided.

Selection of Target Markets, Trade Areas, and Facility Locations. Secondary data are beneficial in the selection of target markets, trade areas, and facility location sites. Not only can companies obtain population figures, they can also obtain maps with population densities shown. A number of companies specialize in **geocoding,** which involves combining geographic information with demographic and psychographic information. This can be extremely valuable for companies wanting to locate the right customer base for a retail outlet or even for developing an advertising or direct mail campaign.

A popular geocoding segmentation system is called PRIZM and was developed by Claritas, and later purchased by Nielsen. For each zip code in the United States, PRIZM identifies the primary cluster segments. Claritas has identified a total of 62 different clusters or segments, each with its own characteristics. For instance, in Denver, Colorado, the zip code 80205 consists of clusters called American Dreams, Big City Blues, City Roots, Close-In Couples, and Multi-Culti Mosaic. The American Dreams segment is described as an ethnically diverse population with about half of the residents being Hispanic, Asian, or African American. One in 10 speak a language other than English. The median income is $56,982. Ages range from 35 to 54, and those in this segment tend to be college graduates and work in white-collar jobs. About 2.15% of the U.S. population fits into the "American Dreams" geosegment.[6]

In locating fast-food restaurants and other retail establishments, traffic counts can be obtained for major streets or highways. These data will tell a business how many and what types of vehicles pass certain points on a road. For downtown locations, pedestrian traffic counts may be important. Companies rely heavily on secondary data from transportation departments at the state and local level in choosing site locations.

Measuring Ad Exposure. Advertising agencies and companies use secondary data to measure ad exposure. The most well-known source is Nielsen Media Research, which produces weekly ratings for television. The ratings tell companies how many people were tuned into a specific TV program and thus how many potentially saw the advertisement. Nielsen ratings are also used to determine advertising rates. The higher the Nielsen rating, the more it will cost to advertise on the program since more individuals are exposed to the ad. Nielsen also produces ratings for the Internet. Similar figures can be obtained from other agencies for magazines (Starch Research, www.starchresearch.com) and radio (Arbitron, www.arbitron.com). Mediamark Research provides comprehensive information on magazine, cable, and Internet website media usage for specific brands, activities, and usage situations.

Database Marketing and Data Mining. Database marketing programs utilize secondary data. This information can be internal data from a company's own database, or it may be purchased through one of the database marketing firms. For example, to receive a player card, casino patrons must first complete a questionnaire in which they provide contact information and demographic characteristics and answer questions related to lifestyle interests. Patrons present this card whenever they play at the casino, and the player card system tracks and stores records of individual player behaviors related to the type of gaming activity, the amount wagered, the amount of time spent playing, and related activities (dining on premises, use of casino hotel, etc.). Using various computer programs, the data can be parsed to include only individuals who fit a specific target profile or meet some other criteria. A casino may want to target "high rollers" who like country-and-western music with an offer of a free hotel room and complimentary tickets to a Garth Brooks concert to entice them to "stay and play."

Lastly, secondary data are used for **data mining,** which is the process of scanning and analyzing data to uncover patterns or trends. Many companies now have large databases of customers with millions of records. These can be mined in various ways. They can provide a profile of a firm's best customers. They can indicate which products people tend to purchase together. For retail stores, the data can provide information on what merchandise to stock and when it is usually sold. For example, Amazon.com suggests products purchased by other users who also purchased items being considered by those who search its website. This is based on data mining of internal information, in this case past sales data.

In conducting marketing research, secondary data should never be overlooked. Collecting secondary data is an excellent place to start the research project. It is cheaper and quicker. It often can provide the information that is needed. If not, secondary data can provide clues or information on how best to conduct additional research.

■ Learning Objective 3.3: Explain how internal sources of data can be used for secondary research.

SOURCES OF SECONDARY DATA

Secondary data can be obtained from a number of different sources and with the Internet are often readily accessible. The primary source categories of secondary data are shown in Figure 3.8. The best source depends on the type of information needed, how quickly the information is needed, and if the firm has a budget to purchase secondary data.

Internal Sources of Secondary Data

Keep in mind that any internal data that have been collected for a purpose other than the current study are secondary data. Even a primary research project that involved data collection just a month ago is secondary data if it was not specifically collected for the current research agenda.

Past marketing decisions, sales data, cost data, customer data from the company's database, and internal accounting system data are all secondary data.

Many research studies are undertaken for the purpose of deciding how best to market a good or service. An important form of internal secondary data to be examined in such cases relates to past marketing decisions. Budget allocations by media type, advertising campaign themes, sales force quotas, allocation of sales forces across geographic territories, and the like are just some of the factors that might be examined, particularly when considered in conjunction with the outcomes resulting from these decisions.

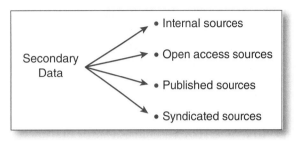

Figure 3.8 Primary Source Categories of Secondary Data

Rather than conduct primary research or hire a marketing research firm, a number of marketing and management questions can be answered with a company's sales data. If collected and stored correctly, sales data can be used to do the following:

- Build a profile of a firm's customer base or its best customers.
- Determine the profile of customers who purchase a particular product.
- Geographically locate particular types of customers for a variety of marketing programs, such as billboard locations, radio advertising campaigns, or a sampling campaign.
- Identify the best prospects for cross-selling of other products.
- Determine the best channel of communication with customers, or the best channel of distribution.
- Determine the most profitable segments of customers to pursue.

For retail stores, sales data obtained through their own checkout scanners can provide considerable information that can be used for marketing and merchandising decisions. If the store has loyalty cards where the data can be tied to specific customers, it becomes even more valuable. Retailers can use the information to determine what products are often purchased together, and then use cross-promotions to encourage purchases. The store can also place items close together that tend to be purchased within the same shopping trip. Special promotions and point-of-purchase displays can be tested for effectiveness. For retail chains, a number of marketing programs can be tested in various stores and then compared to stores that used a different or no marketing program.

Companies that maintain a customer marketing database have an advantage when it comes to secondary internal data. A marketing database is different from an accounting database. An **accounting database** contains a record of customer transactions, follows the rules of accounting, and is used for accounting purposes. A **marketing database** contains records of customers that involve communication interactions, demographic profiles, and any other information that a company has collected or purchased from an independent marketing data research firm.

Marketing databases allow researchers to investigate a number of additional questions not possible with accounting data only. A company can examine the various methods customers use to interact with the firm. These can be analyzed further to determine the best channels of communication for various target segments. Demographic profiles, and if it is in the database, even psychographic, behavioral, and attitudinal information can be tied together to create a much richer description of a firm's market segments. How much can be done with a firm's marketing database is determined, of course, by the amount of data it contains.

Tying the accounting and marketing databases together allows a researcher to identify various characteristics of market segments based on actual purchases. Rather than arbitrarily selecting the "best" marketing segment for a product, a firm can use the marketing database to systematically determine who is purchasing the product and the characteristics of those buyers. This profile can be valuable for advertising purposes as it will allow advertising agencies and individuals designing ads to better understand the type of consumer who is purchasing the product.

A primary advantage of using internal data first is that they are readily and easily accessible. More importantly, they provide information about a firm's own customers. If the research agenda involves comparisons with noncustomers, then it will be necessary to go beyond a firm's own internal sources. It may, however, be possible to use the firm's internal data for its customers, and then purchase data of noncustomers to match and compare.

Open Access Sources of Secondary Data

■ Objective 3.4: Describe the open access sources of secondary data.

As shown in Figure 3.9, open access sources of secondary data include government sources, online blogs, social networks, Twitter, website analytics, and independent websites. Most of this information is free and available to the public. A few, however, charge a subscription fee to access the data, or at least for some of the more detailed data.

Figure 3.9   Open Access Sources of Secondary Data

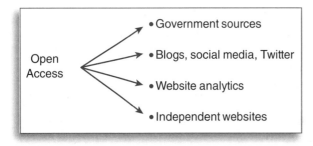

Government Sources. The federal government produces volumes of data and secondary information. State, county, and local governments also have data that can be accessed. The most well-known and used data are the various census and economic data. Every 10 years the United States takes a census of the population and aggregates the data at www.census.gov. The data can be examined and sorted on the website in various ways and also downloaded into Excel spreadsheet files. This demographic information is valuable in developing sales potential forecasts and looking at market size. In addition to population demographics, the Census Bureau also contains business information. This type of information is useful for business-to-business operations.

An excellent starting point for secondary research into government data, reports, and information is USASearch.gov at www.fedworld.gov. It is operated by the U.S. Department of Commerce and is the gateway to government publications and data. Researchers can search over 30 million government webpages through www.fedworld.gov, which eliminates the need to search individual federal government agency pages. If desired, individuals can gain access to key agencies and federal topic sites through the USASearch.gov website. Any data, report, or information that is made publicly available at a federal agency can be accessed in some way through this site.

Blogs, Social Media, and Twitter. Blogs, social media, and Twitter are a second major source of open access secondary data and information. The Internet provides a wealth of information. The challenge is shifting through it to locate data that are relevant and useful.

Blogs are simply online musings, or discussions. But, researchers should not be too quick to dismiss them as personal opinions and, therefore, unreliable sources of information. The usefulness of a blog is partly determined by who posted it and how it is run. Blogs may be the thoughts of a single individual on a particular topic, or they can be maintained by a company. Some blogs allow browsers to post comments, add files, and add links. For others, only the administrator can post.

The first task in determining the viability of a blog is to determine who posted it and why. Blogs sponsored by companies tend to be more viable than blogs written by individuals. Blogs that allow browsers to post usually are there to seek input and as such often can provide more useful information. The second task is to determine if the information in the blog is that of a single individual (or company) or if it can be supported in some scientific or statistical manner.

Suppose a marketing researcher wants to collect secondary information on the effectiveness of e-mail and direct marketing for a financial service firm. In conducting research on the Internet, a blog is found about e-mail and direct marketing written by Ed Lee. In his blog, he states that a plain e-mail campaign can anticipate response rates of 20% to 40% in terms of opening the e-mail, and click-through rates of 6%.[7]

Can the researcher use these data to support a decision to use an e-mail marketing campaign? Further investigation of the site determines Mr. Lee is an employee of Radar DDB Toronto, which is a public relations and online marketing firm in Toronto. The statistics he states certainly support a decision to use an e-mail marketing campaign. That is one of the services his company offers. No citation or information is given in the blog about the origin of the statistics. Was the information collected by Radar DDB Toronto, or was it collected by an independent third party? Without further information, it would be difficult to rely on this information since the writer of the blog has a personal incentive in showing e-mail is an effective online marketing tool. It may very well be valid, but there is no way to know.

In contrast, consider a blog from DIRECT, posted by the Chief Marketer Network, a trade association. DIRECT's mission is to be the "authoritative resource for direct marketing professionals." Its goal is to provide information, trends, and issues to direct marketing professionals. In a blog on the Chief Marketer Network website is a posting about a study of direct e-mail effectiveness. The blog states the study was conducted by Bigfoot Interactive, an independent research firm not connected with DIRECT. For financial services, the blog states the average click-through rate was 9.5%.[8] No details are given about how the data were collected or how the study was conducted, except it was done prior to 2003. The study does seem to support the first blog written by Ed Lee, but since it is over 10 years old the results may not be valid today.

When using blogs, it is important to evaluate them carefully. Using multiple blogs as in this example is one way to ensure that information given is valid and not just the opinion of individuals. The date of the posting must also be taken into consideration. If a marketing researcher wanted to increase confidence in the effectiveness of an e-mail campaign, further research could be conducted using other types of sources, such as articles from journals. Certainly, more recent information should be gathered beyond these two blogs.

Social media and especially Twitter can be used to gather secondary information, although it will typically be qualitative in nature. Some quantitative data may be available. For instance, one of the fast-food restaurants, such as KFC or Burger King, could look at the volume of mentions on Twitter and social media sites following the launch of a new sandwich or menu item. However, the extent to which useful information can be obtained for research purposes via Twitter is debatable, and may vary by brand or industry. A six-month study published by 360i found that only 12% of consumer tweets actually mentioned a specific brand name. Twitter, Apple branded products, and Google were the three most mentioned brand names, and over 50% of tweets involving brand names related to technology (17%), entertainment (17%), or social networks (22%)[9]. Thus, marketers of consumer goods would most likely not benefit from tracking consumer tweets related to their brands.

Some companies now hire individuals to monitor the Internet, especially social media pages and Twitter, to see what consumers are saying about their brand. Web-scanning software allows researchers to follow conversations on the Internet and to be alerted every time a company's name or particular brand name is mentioned. These can be tabulated if a company just wants to know the volume of online chatter. Reading and categorizing the comments will provide more detailed information on what individuals are saying and how they feel about a particular company or brand.

Harrah's, a gaming and hospitality company, used this methodology to collect secondary data on people's thoughts about casinos, hotels, and spas. Ogilvy, an advertising agency, was hired to do the research. Ogilvy scanned travelers' reviews and comments made at TripAdvisor.com and on social network sites, such as Facebook and Twitter. Common chatter themes were about the view from the hotel room, such as the view of the Las Vegas Strip from Paris Las Vegas Hotel & Casino, and hotel amenities, including the size of the room, menu offerings, and other services. Using this secondary information, Harrah's changed the primary photo on the Paris Las Vegas Hotel website to the Las Vegas Strip. Information and photos on rooms, menus, and other services were also provided on the website. These changes resulted in a notable increase in sales. In addition, Harrah's developed a TV, print, radio, and web advertising campaign based on what was learned from web chatter.[10]

Website Analytics. Another important open access source of secondary data is **web analytics,** which are various data collected from a website. The primary website analytic used by companies

Through secondary data, Harrah's found people on Facebook and Twitter chatted about the view of the Las Vegas strip.

is the **click-through,** which is a measure of how many people see an online ad, click on it, and go to the ad sponsor's website. Once at the website, other metrics that are used include length of engagement, dwell rate, dwell time, redemption and response rates, and sales. Redemption rates and response rates occur when visitors to the site take an action. Sales occur when the individual makes the purchase online. **Dwell rate** measures the percentage of ad impressions that resulted in a user engaging with the ad, such as clicking on it or just mousing over it, rather than just being on the page where the ad was located. **Dwell time** measures the amount of time users engage with a particular advertisement or website page. **Length of engagement** is a newer metric that measures how long the person stays at a website and may even include how many pages were viewed in total within the website. It is an indicator of how much interest a person has in the product and site being visited.

A number of tools have been developed to measure website activity. For instance, Adknowledge introduced an online management tool called MarketMatch Planner to evaluate Internet advertising campaigns. MarketMatch Planner software includes two components: Campaign Manager and Administrator. Campaign Manager records traffic to a site and performs postbuy analysis to determine what activities the individual engaged in prior to the purchase, such as dwell time, dwell rate, and length of engagement. Additional measures of what products were examined and which pages were visited are also part of the analysis. Administrator integrates web ad-buy data and performance analysis with the firm's accounting and billing systems. In addition, MarketMatch Planner has the capability of integrating third-party data, from sources such as Media Metrix (basic demographics), Nielsen (GRP and other ratings instruments), Strategic Business Insights (psychographic data), and BPA Worldwide Interactive (web traffic audit data).

Website analytics can provide valuable information about web traffic at company or brand website. The data can be aggregated to determine number of visitors and unique visitors, or they can be analyzed in more detail to determine where visitors go on the site, how long they stay, and what they do.

Google offers an advanced web analytics solution that is free to users. With the simple insertion of HTML code on each page of the website, Google Analytics provides rich insight into who's visiting the website and the effectiveness of various marketing initiatives. The easy-to-use interface makes Google Analytics practical for even small business owners with little website expertise.

Independent Websites. The last open access source of secondary data is independent websites. Researchers can access literally thousands of independent websites. Most will not be of value. Some, however, can provide extremely valuable information. As with blogs, it is important to determine whose website it is, why it is up, and if the information on the site is viable. An advertising agency that specializes in guerrilla marketing will probably have information about the effectiveness of guerrilla marketing and how it is superior to using traditional marketing channels. How that information is conveyed is important to its usefulness and viability. If the site quotes statistics based on its own research and its own guerrilla marketing campaigns, then it is highly likely the data will be biased. If, however, the site has information from independent sources and associations, then the viability increases sharply. A company using third-party support for its brand, product, or service is seen as more credible than one that touts itself.

Search engines, such as Google, Bing, and Yahoo, allow researchers to search the Internet. Each search engine uses a slightly different algorithm to locate sites. Since about 80% of web traffic begins with a search engine, companies strive to have their name on the first page or at least near the beginning of the results.[11] The process of increasing the probability of a particular company's website emerging from a search is called **search engine optimization (SEO)**. SEO occurs in one of four ways. First, a *paid search insertion* comes up when certain products or information are sought. Companies can speed this process by registering with various search engines in order to have the site indexed and also by paying a higher placement fee for top positions. The placement of the ad on a search page depends on the price the company pays and the algorithm a search engine uses to determine the advertisement's relevance to a particular search word or phrase.

Sponsored link ads are similar to paid search insertions. Sponsored link ads appear as text messages or small display ads when phrases searched by the consumer match keywords on which the marketer has bid. Other factors, such as the degree to which the webpage content at the destination URL or the ad content itself matches the search phrase, determine how likely it is the ad will display toward the top of the list. The amount that a marketer is willing to pay per click also impacts the position in which the ad appears.

The third method of optimization is a *natural* or *organic emergence* of the site. This method involves developing efficient and effective organic results that arise from a natural search process. Each search engine uses a slightly different set of algorithms to identify key phrases that match what was typed into the search box. To be listed first in an organic search requires time and effort. When a website is first launched, it will not emerge at the top of the organic search results. It takes time for the search engine to locate the site.

The last optimization method is *paid search ads.* These ads are small text boxes that pop up when a particular word is typed in, or they can be paid link boxes at the top or side of a search result.

Published Sources of Secondary Data

■ Objective 3.5: Summarize the primary differences among the bibliographic digital databases.

In the past when searching published sources of secondary data, it was assumed that published sources were print sources. However, the majority of published sources are now available in digital formats. Searching through digital publications is much easier and quicker as thousands of published works can be searched within seconds by powerful computer search engines. As a result, libraries are moving away from print journals to digital databases that archive thousands of journals and can be searched through a single search engine.

The primary source for secondary data at libraries now is **bibliographic databases,** which are databases that provide references to magazine, journal, and newspaper articles. In addition to the title and author of the article, most bibliographic databases provide summaries or abstracts. With increased computer storage capabilities and financial arrangements with journals and magazines, full-text articles are now more common. Figure 3.10 identifies some of the major bibliographic databases. Because of the high cost, libraries tend to purchase subscriptions to the databases used most frequently by their patrons rather than subscribe to all of these services.

For business information, ABI/INFORM has been a reliable source. It contains full text, abstracts, and citations of more than 1,800 academic and general business publications. LexisNexis is an interdisciplinary database with full-text articles from over 18,000 newspapers, journals, wire services, newsletters, company reports, SEC filings, case law, government

Figure 3.10   Bibliographic Digital Databases

- **ABI/INFORM** – Full text, abstracts, and citations of more than 1,800 academic and general business publications.
- **LexisNexis** – Interdisciplinary, full-text database of over 18,000 newspapers, journals, wire services, newsletters, company reports, SEC filings, case law, government documents, and broadcast transcripts.
- **EBSCO** – Aggregator of full-text content from over 300 different databases, which includes journals, magazines, books, monographs, reports, and other publications.
- **ProQuest** – Archives of newspapers, periodicals, dissertations, and aggregated databases. Contains 125 billion digital pages.

documents, and transcripts of broadcasts. EBSCO is not a database, but an aggregator of full-text content. EBSCO searches over 300 different databases, which include journals, magazines, books, monographs, reports, and other publications. ProQuest is another digital database with over 125 billion digital pages from newspapers, periodicals, dissertations, and aggregated databases. Similarly, the specialized Scholar search available through Google provides access to a variety of academic journal articles, patents, and legal opinions. Using the search function is free, but full-text articles must be purchased.

The key to using bibliographic databases effectively is to develop an understanding of the search process. Each database searches by key words that are typed in by the user. It is important to remember that terminology will vary in articles and with different bibliographic search engines. Using different words or phrases will provide varying results. It is also helpful to pay attention to key words that are listed for articles of interest. These key words can be used to obtain additional related articles on the same topic. The phrasing of key words in a bibliographic database may be different from what the researcher is using. The search syntax specific to a particular database will also influence results.

Syndicated Sources of Secondary Data

■ Objective 3.6: Identify and explain the types of data available from syndicated sources.

A major source of marketing information is syndicated research services. As mentioned previously, a syndicated service supplies standardized information to a number of clients. Much of the research conducted by syndicated firms is too expensive for a single company to purchase. The syndicated research company can conduct the study or track the information and then sell it to a number of companies within the industry since it is more generic in nature. At the same time, the firm can collect company-specific information that is supplied only to clients that pay an additional charge.

For instance, J. D. Power and Associates collects data on an annual basis from consumers who have a home mortgage. These data are then sold to firms such as Chase Home Mortgage and other home mortgage companies. The data are standardized and apply to all home mortgage companies. During the process of collecting the data, J. D. Power will identify the company that holds each individual's home mortgage. By doing this, J. D. Power can provide company-specific information, which can be compared to competitors. It is extremely valuable information to companies in the home mortgage business like Chase because the firm can see how it ranks compared to competing firms overall and on specific attributes. Purchasing these data from J. D. Power and Associates is much cheaper for Chase than if the firm hired a research company to conduct a primary study.

Syndicated services will often issue press releases that contain a nugget of information from a study or an executive summary with the primary purpose of encouraging companies to purchase the full report. Recently, the NPD Group released information from a study of do-it-yourself (DIY) auto products customers.[12] As part of the research of the company's ongoing survey of tracking consumers' automotive parts purchases, the NPD Group examined factors that contribute to overall satisfaction and future purchase intentions. Using its Car Care Track system of consumer ratings of 12 different attributes, NPD determined that the lowest price was the most significant driver of customer satisfaction, cited by 55% of the sample. Other key drivers of customer satisfaction are shown in Figure 3.11.

Figure 3.11   Key Drivers of Customer Satisfaction With DIY Auto Products Customers

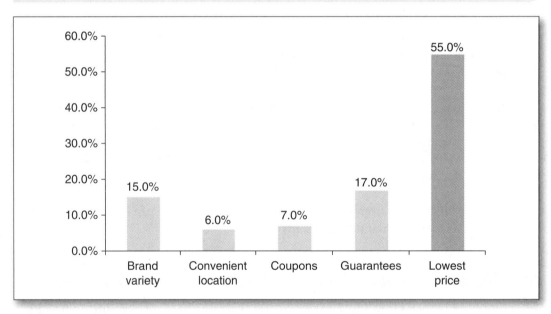

Source: Author-created with data from Kim McLynn, "Lowest Prices, Guarantees, and Brand Variety Are the Top Customer Satisfaction Drivers in the DIY Market, Reports NPD," June 7, 2010, http://www.npd.com/press/releases/press_100607.html (accessed July 18, 2012).

The last paragraph of the press release contains the sentence "Automotive product manufacturers can add greatly to this understanding [drivers of satisfaction and future purchase intentions] by further examining the specific nuances of consumers of their categories and brands." To receive this information, the manufacturer would need to purchase this report from NPD.

Various types of syndicated data are available to companies. Some require a subscription service, and data are provided a routine basis. Others are studies performed ad hoc or periodically and provided to companies for a charge. Figure 3.12 identifies the major categories of syndicated sources of secondary data. Because of space limitation, only a few of the primary providers will be discussed in the following sections.

Sources of Business and Corporate Information. The best source for business and corporate information is Dun & Bradstreet, often referred to as D&B. One of the primary uses of the Dun & Bradstreet Business Information Report is credit information on businesses and corporations. But, the report has a number of other pieces of information that can be valuable:

- Industry statistics
- Financials of the business or corporation (sales, net worth, cash, etc.)
- Company history
- Mailing addresses
- Product and industry descriptors
- Number of employees

Figure 3.12   Types of Syndicated Sources of Secondary Data

- Sources of business and corporate information
- Sales tracking sources
- Consumer data sources
  - Satisfaction and product quality
  - Consumer behavior
- Media audience measurement sources
  - Traditional media
  - Online environment

In addition to demographic information about a company, the Dun & Bradstreet report can be used to locate potential customers since it produces sector-based information that can be compared and contrasted with similar industries on a local, state, or regional basis. Federal agencies and the European Union have endorsed the D&B Business Information Report as the primary identification system for international business assessment and validation throughout the world.

Sales Tracking Sources. A number of research companies offer sales tracking data. The most well-known syndicated sources are the NPD Group and SymphonyIRI Group. Sales tracking is done on a continuous basis by both research firms and primarily uses scanner data from retail outlets.

The major supplier of retail sales tracking data is the NPD Group. The company was founded in 1967 and has become the leading global provider of retail tracking services at the point of sale (POS). The company has partnerships with over 850 retailers representing more than 125,000 retail outlets worldwide. Each store provides the NDP Group with its POS data. The data are used to generate various sales reports. Other key measures include market share, pricing, and sell-through at the item level. In exchange for providing POS information, retailers can use NPD's retail market research information to guide assortment planning, merchandising, and pricing. For subscribers, NPD can provide store-level information and tracking that can be used to compare the store's performance against various benchmarks.

From the data collected through POS systems, NPD produces more than 100 special market research reports that can be purchased by clients. These reports are written by NPD research analysts with in-depth knowledge of their industries and covers subjects such as the following:

- Category/market performance
- Trend analysis in consumer purchasing and consumption
- Consumer behavior and demographics

- Category profiles
- Retail industry trends
- Market share and segment analyses
- Brand analyses

SymphonyIRI Group also provides sales tracking data. SymphonyIRI Group provides clients with consumer, shopper, and retail market intelligence and analysis for the consumer packaged goods (CPG) industry. The firm operates in 58 different countries and represents 95% of the Fortune Global 500 CPG companies.

SymphonyIRI's sales tracking service is called InfoScan. Each week several thousand grocery stores, department stores, discount stores, and drugstores provide InfoScan with POS data on consumer packaged goods. SymphonyIRI sorts, analyzes, and verifies product price and volume and then delivers to clients sales data for the week.

Consumer Data Sources. In terms of measuring consumer satisfaction and product quality, the most well-known syndicated service is J. D. Power and Associates. Founded in 1968, the company now conducts surveys of customer satisfaction, product quality, and buyer behavior for several industries, ranging from automobiles to electronics to travel. The company became famous for its customer-satisfaction research on new cars and then expanded into other industries, including home mortgages as discussed at the beginning of this section. The company develops customer surveys and collects data from several thousand participants within each industry. The data are tabulated and then sold to clients.

Several other syndicated research firms collect consumer behavior data. In addition to retail sales tracking, the NPD Group also has a consumer panel. The NPD consumer panel has 1.8 million registered adults and teens who have agreed to let NPD track their purchases via POS systems. This allows NPD to provide its clients with information on trends, purchasing, consumption, ownership, and usage by various demographic profiles. The online panel also provides customer satisfaction information that can be tied to specific brands.

Experian Simmons conducts ongoing consumer behavior studies. Data collected include media usage, product purchases, and attitudes about various issues. The National Consumer Study has over 60,000 data variables, usage behavior from 450 product categories and 8,000 brands, and in-depth demographic, psychographic, lifestyle, and attitudinal insights. The data are collected from 25,000 adults on a continuous basis and reported quarterly.

Experian Simmons has also developed a syndicated National Hispanic Consumer Study that surveys over 8,000 Hispanics living in the United States. Similar data to what are found in the National Consumer Study are collected. Experian Simmons has recently expanded its samples to include a database on the lesbian, gay, bisexual, and transgender population. Then twice a year, Experian Simmons produces a study of teen (ages 12–17) consumption behavior and attitudes.

The NPD Group is just one of the syndicated research firms that collects data on consumers' shopping behavior.

Mediamark is another syndicated provider of consumer behavior information. The company has been conducting consumer research since 1979. The Survey of the American Consumer measures consumer attitudes, product consumption, and media usage. The research process begins with a group of randomly selected individuals who are asked to participate. Each individual who is recruited for the consumer panel is then interviewed personally by researchers from Mediamark. The personal interviews increase response rates and accuracy of information gathered.

Mediamark collects information from each respondent on usage of various media, such as magazines, television, radio, the Internet, national and local newspapers, and yellow pages. Demographic, lifestyle, and psychographic data are obtained along with consumer attitudes. All of this information is then collated with the consumer's usage data for over 6,000 brands and 500 product categories.

Media Audience Measurement Sources. The primary provider of audience measurement data for both traditional and online media is Nielsen Media Research. The company has become the standard for audience measurement, and its statistics are used by numerous companies and media outlets. The company is most famous for its Nielsen ratings of television shows. But in addition to television, Nielsen also measures audiences for radio, mobile phones, and the Internet.

The two most common television ratings are the Nielsen rating points and share, which is typically reported as "rating points/share." A single Nielsen rating point currently is equivalent to approximately 1,149,000 households. This represents 1% of the total number of households in the United States with televisions. Each week the Nielsen ratings/shares are reported on the firm's website as well as other websites such as Yahoo TV. If a television show received a rating/share of 12.3/19.7, it would mean that 12.3% of the households in the United States were tuned to that particular television show. To find the actual number of households, the 12.3 would be multiplied by the 1,149,000 to arrive at a total of 14,132,700. The 19.7% share figure indicates that of the televisions that were turned on at that particular time, 19.7% of them were tuned into that program. Not every household in the United States will be watching television at any particular time. Nielsen Media Research also provides demographic information of the viewers of each television show since the Nielsen ratings influence advertising rates. The higher the Nielsen rating, the more a show's producer can charge advertisers.

Nielsen also measures radio audiences. The company surveys a sample of the population in each of the 51 Nielsen radio markets, tracking their radio listening. It has recently moved into mobile phone audience measures collecting measurements on mobile consumer behaviors, attitudes, and experiences. Nielsen has become the industry standard for metrics such as market share, customer satisfaction, device share, service quality, revenue share, and advertising effectiveness. These data are collected through mobile subscriber counts, phone bill data, panels of consumers who agree to have their mobile activity monitored, and online surveys.

Nielsen offers a number of online measurement metrics. Similar to Nielsen TV ratings is Nielsen Online, which monitors and measures more than 90% of Internet activities. Measurements include audience demographics, advertising, video, e-commerce, and consumer behavior.

In addition to Nielsen Online, Nielsen offers Nielsen BuzzMetrics. Nielsen BuzzMetrics monitors online chatter from 100 million blogs, social networks, groups, boards, and other consumer-generated media.

One of the unique products offered by Nielsen is *Data Fusion,* which is the matching of two or more Nielsen databases at the respondent level to create a unified database. The matching utilizes information common to both databases and then fuses the data together. The result is a unique data set that can then be mined for relationships, or examined along a particular variable. Data Fusion provides clients with unique opportunities to learn about their target market.

Although not as well-known as Nielsen, Mediamark does provide media audience measures through its data collection process. The results are not as robust as Nielsen's since the sample size is much smaller. But, it is unique in that it includes a number of different measures in all of the major media (magazines, television, radio, Internet, newspapers, and yellow pages). Combined with demographic, psychographic, and lifestyle information, Mediamark is able to provide a rich view of consumer media consumption and how it relates to purchase behavior. A compilation of website links to open access and syndicated data sources can be found at www.sagepub.com/clowess.

GLOBAL CONCERNS

Secondary data are an important source of information in international marketing research. They are often readily available at a low cost. They can provide valuable background information relating to various countries and cultures that can be used in preparing primary research. Collecting secondary data is especially important for individuals conducting research in countries that are not native to those performing the research.

When collecting secondary data in international markets, researchers need to be aware of two key issues. First, databases in other countries often do not have the detail of databases in the United States. This is especially true of government databases. The federal government in the United States collects and disseminates much more information than do governments in other countries. Second, many databases are not available in English. While many are, researchers must be aware that if they utilize only English databases they may be missing extremely valuable information.[13]

In respect to publicly available data from government sources, it is not unusual for data to be distorted or reported in such a way as to make the country look favorable to others. Data that reflect negatively on a country may be left out and only positively related data reported. At other times the information may be modified or collected in such a way as to make it more attractive.

Also, other countries may not collect the same types of information as the United States, and if they do, it may not have the same relevancy. For instance, in some countries individuals do not report their actual income because of fear of increased taxation by the government. In other countries, they do not report it to protect themselves from criminals and extortionists.[14]

To obtain good secondary data requires an understanding of each country's culture. It also may require the expertise of someone from that country who understands what information is valuable, what is not, and what has been modified or distorted. But, despite these cautions, secondary data are extremely important in conducting global marketing or international studies.

STATISTICS REVIEW

Index numbers are often used to make comparisons between periods of time, places, industries, or market segment characteristics. Index numbers offer an easy point of comparison, as they express "the difference between two measurements by designating one number as the 'base,' giving it the value 100, and then expressing the second number as a percentage of the first."[15]

Suppose the population of your hometown was 50,000 according to the 2000 census. Following the 2010 census, you find that the population size has increased to 53,000. Using the year 2000 as your time period base, its index number would be 100. Dividing the 2010 population size by the 2000 population figure shows that as of 2010, the size of your town is 106% of the population size in 2000, and thus the index number would be 106.

It is critical to understand what index numbers mean. If the price index for HDTVs rose to 110 relative to the base year, while the price index for milk increased to 120, it simply means that the price of milk has increased twice as much in *percentage* terms as did the price for HDTVs. It does not mean that milk is more expensive, or that the absolute dollar amount of the increase was greater than the dollar increase in the price of HDTVs.

Index numbers are commonly included in many forms of marketing-related secondary research as they allow users to quickly compare a characteristic of some type to its base. Consider the hypothetical data in Figure 3.13. Frequent diners for this illustration are defined as individuals who dine out at least once per week. The figure shows the total population of the United States is 225,900,000. Out of the total population, 27,100,000 are frequent diners. Dividing the 27.1 million by the 225.9 million shows that 12.0% of the population are frequent diners. This 12.0% becomes the base to calculate the index for each of the educational demographic groups.

Figure 3.13   Educational Index Numbers for Frequent Diners

	Total U.S. Population (000s)	Frequent Diners (000s)	Freq. Diners % of Total Pop.	Index
Did not graduate HS	32,300	1,650	5.1%	43
Graduated HS	69,800	6,300	9.0%	75
Attended college	63,000	8,650	13.7%	114
College degree	40,600	6,800	16.7%	140
Postcollege degree	20,200	3,700	18.3%	153
Total	225,900	27,100	12.0%	100

The fourth column in the table labeled "Freq. Diners % of Total Pop." is calculated by dividing the number of frequent diners in each row by the respective total U.S. population. Thus, for "Did not graduate HS [high school]" the 1,650 is divided by 32,300 to arrive at 5.1%. This means that 5.1% of

(Continued)

(Continued)

individuals who did not graduate from high school are considered frequent diners. The corresponding index value is then calculated by dividing the 5.1 by the base of 12.0. This same process is then used for every row of the table.

From these data, it appears that frequent diners are 40% more likely to have a college degree and 53% more likely to have obtained a postgraduate degree than the population in general. In contrast, frequent diners are 57% less likely to have not graduated from high school.

The essence of target marketing is to identify the characteristics that best describe the target and, more importantly, separate the target from other segments. The higher the index number, the more likely it is that people in the segment share that trait, compared to the population as a whole. Thus, incorporating the trait into the segment profile, and customizing a marketing campaign to such individuals, should lead to more efficient and effective campaigns. Figure 3.14 lists a few magazines and hypothetical readership for those who dine out at least once per week.

Figure 3.14   Selected Magazine Readership Habits of Frequent Diners

	Total U.S. Population (000s)	Frequent Diners (000s)	Freq. Diners % of Total Pop.	Index
Total	225,900	27,100	12.0%	100
BusinessWeek	39,000	5,300	13.6%	113
Cosmopolitan	4,600	870	18.9%	158
Fitness	6,200	890	14.4%	120
Money	7,700	1,300	16.9%	141
Outdoor Life	5,500	550	10.0%	83
Reader's Digest	31,200	4,200	13.5%	112
TV Guide	17,000	1,500	8.8%	74

Notice the highest index number from this list of magazines is for *Cosmopolitan,* indicating frequent diners are 58% more likely to read this magazine than is the nation as a whole. Advertising in *Cosmopolitan* would be an efficient way to reach a portion of the target market while resulting in less wasted coverage. In addition to the index, it is also important to examine the number of individuals, which in the case of *Cosmopolitan* magazine would only be 870,000 individuals. It is dangerous to focus exclusively on index numbers without properly considering the size of the population involved and the costs to place ads. In this case, the readership of *Cosmopolitan* is a fraction of the size of that of *BusinessWeek* and *Reader's Digest.* Many individuals within the frequent diner cluster who don't care about fashion would be missed if the media selection was restricted to this publication, or one of the other smaller publications. On the other hand, *BusinessWeek* and *Reader's Digest* boast a much larger circulation base. However, cost considerations and potential audience duplication must be considered when selecting the best media schedule.

DEALING WITH DATA

Before data can be entered into the SPSS spreadsheet, it is necessary to build the variable list. Chapter 2 reviewed the basic structure of a SPSS data file and the components of the variable portion of the data file. In this "Dealing With Data" exercise, the goal is to develop the variable portion of the spreadsheet so data can be entered. It may be helpful to compare the questionnaire from Chapter 2 with the SPSS data file that corresponds to the questionnaire.

Download from the textbook student website (www.sagepub.com/clowess) the file titled "Chapter 03 Dealing with Data Survey." Your task is to create a SPSS spreadsheet for each of the questions on the questionnaire with a variable name, variable label, and variable values. Note that the variable name cannot have spaces and should be a shortened version of the question. The variable label can have spaces and be an abbreviated version of the question that makes sense. For instance, for Question 2 the variable name may be "Q2MealsWeek" and the variable label may be "Average number of meals per week eaten at fast-food restaurants."

The variable values would list the codes for the various answers. For example, for Question 1 a code of "1" would be used to represent "less than 10%" and a code of "2" would be "10% to 19%." Questions 2 and 3 will not have value labels since respondents are asked to write in a number. The individual recording the data will then transcribe the number on the survey sheet to the spreadsheet.

SUMMARY

Objective 1: Discuss the advantages and disadvantages of secondary data.

Secondary research is less costly and less time-consuming than conducting primary research. The ease with which information can be accessed either internally from the firm or externally from bibliographic databases, open access sources such as the government, or even syndicated data firms is another key advantage, and one that helps to explain why secondary research is always completed prior to initiating a primary research study. Despite these obvious advantages, secondary data are often not available or, if available, can be irrelevant to the study purpose or insufficient to answer the research question. It is critical that marketers carefully evaluate the quality of secondary data by examining the data source, study purpose, sample, and overall methodology, data collection, analysis process, and interpretation.

Objective 2: Identify key uses of secondary data.

Secondary research has many uses. It complements exploratory efforts when additional insight into the research problem is needed. When designing a primary research study, a number of decisions can be influenced by relevant secondary data, including sampling procedures, data collection procedures, and measurement instruments. Secondary data are the key source of background information that can be included in both the RFP and the final research report. Secondary data are helpful to researchers seeking to identify consumer trends and industry information. In some cases, these data can even be used to solve the research problem, or to answer one of the research questions. Secondary data are often instrumental in estimating demand, and can be highly beneficial when defining or selecting target markets, trade areas, or locations. Advertising agencies and other media users rely on secondary data when selecting media for marketing campaigns, and in evaluating advertising exposure via major media, such as television. Furthermore, secondary data are used to build databases that can be used in direct marketing programs. Finally, secondary data are helpful in data mining efforts, as marketers seek to discover patterns and trends in data files.

Objective 3: Explain how internal sources of data can be used for secondary research.

While past marketing decisions provide information helpful when developing new campaigns, sales data are one of the most useful forms of internal information if collected and stored correctly. Sales data are helpful in profiling various customer groups, making geographic targeting decisions, and determining the best channel of communication or distribution to reach customers. Retail sales data stemming from scanners or loyalty cards help retailers develop cross-promotions, arrange items in the store, evaluate the effectiveness of point-of-purchase displays, and test marketing programs. Both accounting and marketing databases can provide useful internal information, though marketing databases typically are superior due to the large amount of consumer information that they contain.

Objective 4: Describe the open access sources of secondary data.

Open access sources of secondary data include governmental sources, blogs, social media, twitter, web analytics, and independent websites. Governmental sources are particularly valuable due to their high data quality, and because they are free. Key governmental websites include census. gov and fedworld.gov. Many marketers tap into what consumers are saying about products or the competition by monitoring blogs, social media, and Twitter posts on a regular basis. Greater effort is required to weed out irrelevant information from these sources. Using multiple blogs is superior to relying on a single forum, and blogs sponsored by companies tend to be more viable than blogs written by individuals. Website analytics provide valuable information regarding consumers' behavior in response to online ads. Click-through rates, dwell rates, dwell time, and length of engagement can be used to gauge the amount of interest a consumer has in the product or website visited. Independent websites, though by far the most prevalent source of secondary data, are rarely relevant and must be carefully scrutinized to ascertain whether the information provided is valid.

Objective 5: Summarize the primary differences among the bibliographic digital databases.

Bibliographic databases are the primary source of published information for libraries. Some databases provide citation information along with article abstracts; others, such as ABI/ INFORM, contain full-text articles from academic and business publications. EBSCO is an excellent reference tool as it aggregates full-text content from over 300 different databases covering journals, magazines, industry publications, books, monographs, and reports. Similarly, ProQuest provides access to newspaper archives, dissertations, periodicals, and aggregated databases. While content overlaps between many of these databases, each usually has access to content that is unique and different from that of the others.

Objective 6: Identify and explain the types of data available from syndicated sources.

Syndicated data firms collect high-quality data by product category, industry, media, or consumer market and sell it to data subscribers. While more costly than other forms of secondary data discussed in this chapter, standardized information is still less expensive than it would be for the firm to engage in primary research. The added time savings and high-quality of the data make syndicated information a strong choice for many marketers. Various forms of syndicated data exist, and each form is characterized by multiple providers. Business and corporate information sources are found in Dun & Bradstreet. The NPD Group and SymphonyIRI Group sell point-of-sale information gathered via in-store checkout scanners. While a variety of consumer data sources exist, NPD and J. D. Power and Associates are among the best known and respected firms. Finally, Nielsen remains king of the media audience measurement sources.

GLOSSARY OF KEY TERMS

Accounting database: contains a record of customer transactions that follows the rules of accounting, and is used for accounting purposes

Blogs: online musings or discussions

Bibliographic databases: digital databases that provide references to magazine and journal articles

Click-through: a primary website analytic measuring how many individuals see an online ad, click on it, and go to the ad sponsor's website

Data mining: the process of scanning and analyzing data to uncover patterns or trends

Dwell rate: a web analytic measuring the percentage of ad impressions that resulted in a user engaging with the ad, such as clicking on it or mousing over it

Dwell time: a web analytic measuring the amount of time users spend engaged with a particular advertisement or website page

Geocoding: a secondary data compilation process that involves combining geographic information with demographic and psychographic information

Length of engagement: a web analytic measuring how long an individual stays at a website and may include how many pages were viewed in total

Marketing database: contains records of customers that involve communication interactions, demographic profiles, and any other information that a company has collected or purchased from an independent marketing data research firm

Primary research: new research studies specifically developed to help fulfill the research purpose currently being investigated

Search engine optimization (SEO): a process of increasing the probability of a particular company's website emerging from a search

Secondary data: data collected previously for purposes other than for the current study at hand

Syndicated research service: a marketing research firm that supplies standardized information to a number of clients

Web analytics: various data collected from a website

CRITICAL THINKING EXERCISES

1. Suppose that the U.S. census revealed the following data about the racial profile of a zip code in North Carolina. Compute the index numbers for each line of data by comparing the zip code % to the U.S. % for each row. What conclusions can you draw from this information?

	Number	Zip Code %	U.S. %	Index
One Race	30,533	98.3%	97.6%	
Two or more races	527	1.7%	2.4%	
One Race				
White	22,063	71.0%	75.1%	
Black or African American	7,418	23.9%	12.3%	
Hispanic or Latino (of any race)	993	3.2%	12.5%	
American Indian and Alaska Native	169	0.5%	0.9%	
Asian	518	1.7%	3.6%	
Native Hawaiian and Other Pacific Islander	19	0.1%	0.1%	
Some other race	346	1.1%	5.5%	

2. Visit the U.S. Census website at www.census.gov to investigate the profile of your zip code. Report on the gender, age, race, and income characteristics of your zip code. Compare the index numbers of the various demographics. In what way is the population in your zip code different from the U.S. population?

3. Consider your university. What specific forms of internal secondary data are likely to be available? As you formulate your answer, think about the types of information that might be tracked related to recruiting, the current student body, alumni, and fund-raising.

4. Visit Google.com and locate the "Google Scholar." Access this specialized search engine, and use it to research a topic of your choice. Conduct the same search using the same key words in the main Google window. Compare the results obtained through Scholar to the search from the main Google window. What similarities and differences did you see?

5. Using your preferred search engine, locate the blog search function. Pick some type of marketing topic. Search the web for blogs on that topic. Critically evaluate at least three blogs, applying the criteria for assessing blog viability discussed in this chapter.

6. Locate the "Google Analytics" page on the Google website. Take the "Product Tour" or follow appropriate links to learn more about this service. Report on what you learned. Under what circumstances would this information be considered secondary data, as opposed to primary data? Be specific.

7. Visit http://www.nielsen.com/us/en.html and mouse over the "News and Insights" tab on the home page. Select one of the subtopics from the dropdown menu. Find a topic that interests you, and report on your findings.

8. Visit http://www.trendwatching.com/ and select the current "Trend Briefing." Prepare a one-page report on the nature of the trend, and its impact for brand marketing.

9. Pick one of the following topics and conduct secondary research using one or more of the bibliographic digital databases available at your school's library. Find at least four articles that provide information about the topic. Summarize your findings.

   a. Advertising to teenagers
   b. Mobile phone advertising
   c. Online advertising
   d. Student recruiting at colleges or universities
   e. Marketing in France

10. Pick one of the following topics or products. Conduct secondary research. Locate at least three articles from your library's bibliographic digital database, three articles or sites on the Internet in general that discuss the topic, and three blogs that provide information. Summarize your findings. Remember to cite the references in your paper and include all of your sources in a reference list at the end of your paper.

    a. Advertising to children
    b. Print advertising (magazines and newspapers)
    c. Search engine optimization (SEO)
    d. Marketing (and advertising) of educational institutions, such as colleges and universities
    e. Marketing in Japan

CONTINUING CASE STUDY: LAKESIDE GRILL

The student team of Brooke, Alexa, Juan, Destiny, and Zach collected the following information:

- Lakeside Grill sales data for the last three years aggregated by the month.
- Amount of money spent on hourly labor and food by Lakeside Grill and the number of customers for the past three years, by month.
- Comment cards from customers spanning the last three years. The comment cards are placed in a box by diners as they leave the restaurant.
- "Restaurant and Hotel Food Trends" from this year's *Restaurant, Food & Beverage Market Research Handbook.*
- Census data for the zip code in which the restaurant is located.
- Two articles from EBSCO on trends in restaurant patronage and desired attributes of restaurants.
- A blog written by a restaurant owner in San Diego that discusses various marketing techniques that she has used for her seafood restaurant.

(Continued)

(Continued)

Critique Questions:

1. Evaluate the types of internal data obtained by the team. What other data would the owner of Lakeside Grill be likely to have in his database that could be useful for this research project?

2. How useful are comment cards? Who tends to respond to comment cards? How can the group use this information?

3. How useful will the trend information from the *Restaurant, Food & Beverage Market Research Handbook* be to the group?

4. What can the group learn from the census data of the zip code where the restaurant is located? Is the one zip code enough? Why or why not?

5. In addition to the two articles found on EBSCO, what other topics might be of interest? Generate a list of key terms that the group could use to search for additional articles.

6. How useful is the blog information? Can blogs provide good secondary data? What is the best way to locate a blog that would be useful to the team?

7. Overall, how would you evaluate the effort of this group in locating secondary data for their Lakeside Grill project?

MARKETING RESEARCH PORTFOLIO

The ability to locate high-quality secondary data is a useful skill for all marketing students, regardless of whether they pursue a career in marketing research or another discipline. This chapter's "Marketing Research Portfolio" mini-case, found at www.sagepub.com/clowess requires students to gather external secondary data for a client facing a particular scenario. A short description of three potential "clients" and their situations is provided. Instructors may wish to assign students to simply gather the data, or to gather data and write a report based on the information found. A more challenging option would require the students not only to collect and report secondary data, but also to make use of these data in drafting a proposed research purpose and research questions for the chosen scenario.

STUDENT STUDY SITE

Visit the Student Study Site at www.sagepub.com/clowess to access the following additional materials:

- eFlashcards
- Web Quizzes
- SAGE Journal Articles
- Web Resources

Qualitative Research

INTRODUCTION

When they think of AARP, most people think of individuals who are retired and over 60. But, recently AARP has added a new target market—individuals 25 to 34. The organization found through research that AARP members wished they had started thinking about retirement when they were 20, not when they turned 50. Through preliminary research AARP found that offering financial advice was the best way to reach this new target market. From this finding, AARP developed a new website called LifeTurner. But, to build the website AARP needed a better understanding of the younger target market. To gather this information, AARP turned to qualitative research provider Beacon Research.[1]

The qualitative study was conducted in three phases. The first phase was to investigate the concept of the LifeTurner website and if the name would resonate with the new target market. The research involved 29 in-depth interviews one-on-one with people in their 20s. About 75% of the interviews were conducted via webcams so the sample would have representation across the entire United States. The webcam approach allowed for in-depth feedback related to the preliminary website design. It also measured the interviewees' blink reactions to the AARP brand logo and placement of the logo.

The second phase involved 208 personal interviews. Each interview lasted two days and consisted of both closed- and open-ended questions. The purpose of the interviews was to provide more specific feedback on the website design and functionality. Three different website designs were tested using a variety of usability tests. Based on feedback from the second phase, Beacon Research moved into the last stage of the qualitative study. The research company tested early versions of two different tools: a credit card tool and a retirement tool.

This chapter examines various qualitative tools that are used by marketing research firms, like Beacon Research. Focus groups and in-depth interviews are the two primary qualitative methods. But, other methods exist, such as projective techniques that can be valuable in certain situations. As with other forms of marketing research, a sizeable portion of qualitative research studies is shifting to online methodologies.

THE ROLE OF QUALITATIVE RESEARCH

■ Learning Objective 4.1: Explain the role of qualitative research.

Companies often face situations that need information that cannot be sufficiently supplied through secondary research. In these situations, qualitative research may meet the need. It is not always necessary to collect quantitative data, which typically takes longer and is more expensive than collecting qualitative data. Figure 4.1 identifies the primary ways qualitative research can be used.

As explained in Chapter 2, **qualitative research involves unstructured data collection methods that provide results that are subjectively interpreted.** Therefore, it is an excellent means of conducting exploratory research. When companies do not understand the problem fully or wish to have additional information about an opportunity or a situation, qualitative research can be used to provide valuable insight. Focus groups can be especially helpful.

Qualitative research is often used as a precursor to quantitative studies, questionnaire construction, and development of the research design. Qualitative research can clarify information that is needed to execute quantitative studies. For instance, through qualitative research a company such as Garmin may be able to uncover what benefits consumers seek in a GPS and also how and when consumers use it. To verify these findings, this information can then be used to develop survey questions for a larger quantitative study. It can also be helpful in identifying the sample that should be used, and to refine the research design process to ensure that the primary study objectives are met.

In the past, qualitative research was perceived as inferior to quantitative studies and was used only prior to quantitative research. Now, companies use qualitative data at every

Figure 4.1   Ways Qualitative Research Can Be Used

- Exploratory research
- Background for quantitative studies
- Questionnaire or research design
- Deeper understanding of consumer thinking
- Explore subconscious of consumers
- Add richness to quantitative studies

stage of the research process. It is used to explore the subconscious of consumers to uncover why consumers act in the manner they do, as consumers are often unwilling or unable to articulate reasons for their behavior. It can provide a deeper understanding into consumer thoughts and decision making. All of this can add richness to quantitative studies, and provide important input into management decisions.

The Richards Group uses quantitative research and tracking studies to measure the effectiveness of advertising the agency creates for various clients. But, the company also uses qualitative research to understand what consumers think about the ads and how the ads are processed. A quantitative study can provide data on how an ad is doing in the marketplace, but it cannot tell the agency how the ad is being mentally processed and what is working and what is not working within the mind of the consumer. "When we read the actual comments of 150 consumers who view a particular advertisement, we get a good feel for what is going on in their minds," says Dave Snell, of The Richards Group.[2]

Figure 4.2 identifies the primary methods of conducting qualitative research. Traditionally, qualitative research was conducted through face-to-face interactions with the market researcher or moderator. In recent years, however, companies have shifted to more online techniques.

Figure 4.2   Qualitative Research Methods

- Focus groups
- Online methodologies
- In-depth interviews
- Projective techniques

FOCUS GROUPS

A widely used qualitative research method is the focus group. Typical **focus groups** consist of 8 to 12 individuals who are brought together to discuss a particular topic led by a focus group **moderator**. The primary idea behind the focus group is that the group will discuss ideas and produce thoughts that individuals interviewed singularly may not consider. One person will feed off of a comment from another participant, generating new thoughts and ideas. Indeed, consideration of whether or not group dynamics will add to the findings is often one of the key factors considered by research professionals when determining whether to use the focus group or individual in-depth interview technique.[3]

■ Learning Objective 4.2: Describe the traditional focus group process.

The Richards Group used focus groups as the basis for developing the Motel 6 campaign when the company first obtained the account.[4] Travelers were solicited to participate. These individuals were strangers to one another but shared two key characteristics: They traveled frequently, and they stayed in motels. The participants were selected to participate in the focus group studies specifically because they had stayed at a Motel 6. But the purpose of this study was disguised, meaning that no one knew the reason for his or her selection or that Motel 6 was the client behind the focus groups.

In the first focus group, participants were asked to indicate what hotel they used on their last trip and why. Around the room, various brands were mentioned, but no one mentioned Motel 6. After some discussion of how a particular hotel is chosen, the moderator asked the individual participants to again identify specific hotels they had patronized during recent travels other than the one they mentioned the first time. Even during the second round Motel 6 was not mentioned, which was surprising, given that all focus group participants had stayed at a Motel 6. Then, finally, one individual rather sheepishly said, "If it is really late at night, then I will stay at a Motel 6." Others in the group then admitted they had stayed at a Motel 6. Another individual stated that "with the money I had saved by staying at a Motel 6 I was able to purchase a present for my kid." Someone else mentioned, "I was able to buy a nice dinner with what I saved." The discussion then shifted to why Motel 6 was chosen.

Through that initial focus group and supplemental focus groups, it became clear to The Richards Group that while Motel 6 may not have been the first choice of travelers in lodging, participants boasted and were proud of the money they had saved and how they used the money for other things. During one of the focus groups a participant commented, "You know when the lights are turned out, price doesn't make a difference—all of the motels look the same." The input from the focus groups and this key consumer insight were the genesis for the Motel 6 campaign.

In working with Motel 6, The Richards Group used a traditional focus group. Traditional focus groups are conducted in person at the agency's place of business, or at a neutral location. The facility in which the interview takes place should be comfortable, and seating arrangements should be considered carefully. Professional moderator Raúl Pérez notes that even the table shape can influence group dynamics "by altering distance among respondents, proximity of respondents to the moderator, respondents' ability to make eye contact with each other and the moderator's ability to visually follow respondents."[5] Similarly, the clients' ability to view focus group participants is also affected by the table design. By conducting the focus group in person, the agency is able to observe body language of participants in addition to their verbal comments. This is important, because body language cues can be used to identify when a participant may disagree with something that is being said. A good moderator will capitalize upon this opportunity by actively encouraging the participant to share his or her thoughts. Differing points of view can stimulate the discussion and provide valuable information.

Figure 4.3   Steps in Conducting Focus Group Interviews

1. Develop study parameters
2. Compose interview questions
3. Select participants
4. Conduct focus group interview
5. Debrief the client
6. Write the report

Successful focus groups are the result of careful planning. Figure 4.3 identifies the major steps in conducting a focus group.

Develop Study Parameters

The focus group interview begins by developing the study parameters. The person or agency that is conducting the focus groups needs to meet with the client to determine the study purpose and research questions, which were likely determined as part of the problem definition process. It is essential that the agency or person conducting the study understand what information is needed, what types of decisions will be made from the information, and how the results will be used. Answers to these questions will guide the focus group process.

Other study parameters that need to be decided include the timeline for conducting the interviews, the number of focus groups, the budget, participant stipends, and whether or not client observers wish to be present. Most companies use multiple focus groups, especially when seeking input from different groups (users vs. nonusers, for example), and when the results will be used for management decisions or input into the development of marketing strategies and tactics. The number of focus group interviews will then impact the timeline and budget needed.

Participants in focus group interviews receive some type of remuneration for their efforts. While it can be in cash, it is often in merchandise, vouchers, or certificates. Participants for a focus group about airlines may receive an airline voucher while participants for a clothing manufacturer may receive a certificate for free clothes. Beverages and snacks are often provided to participants as sessions typically last between one and a half and three hours. To ensure unbiased results, the sponsor of the focus group is not revealed until the end of the session.

The final decision to be made includes which and how many client observers will be present. Focus groups are typically recorded, but observers are also often present behind a one-way mirror. They can observe what is being said and the body language of the participants. As a result of these observations, the client will sometimes send the interviewer a discreet message asking that a particular answer be explored in more detail, or that an additional question be addressed by the participants before the focus group concludes their activities. Clients can gain valuable insights into what consumers think of their brand. But, they also must be willing to calmly listen if individuals criticize their brand. Such was the case with Domino's as focus groups revealed people's thoughts about the brand's poor quality and cardboard-like taste. While it was difficult for Domino's leadership to hear, it provided extremely valuable insight into consumer thoughts about the brand and its pizza. As a result, Domino's made changes in its products and marketing approach.[6] Company leaders even used the results in an advertising campaign to inform consumers they listened and as a result modified their product.

Compose Interview Questions

Preparation of the **discussion guide** requires that the researcher and client work closely together to identify the series of questions that will be asked of participants during the focus group interview. Thus, interview questions should be composed in advance, with the caveat that the moderator can modify questions and explore thoughts as the interview proceeds. In

Dominos gained valuable insights through focus groups with consumers.

general, questions within the discussion guide are arranged so that more general questions are asked first, and then are followed by more specific questions. By asking general questions first, the moderator is able to encourage participants to become involved in the discussion, build rapport within the group, and stimulate in-group discussions. Then as the session progresses the moderator is able to ask more specific questions to guide the conversation toward fulfilling the research purpose.

Questions should probe into the thoughts and even the subconscious of participants. To do so requires open-ended questions that individuals feel free and comfortable to answer and that do not have a right or wrong response. Once the flow of information begins, additional questions can be used to probe deeper by asking "What else?" or asking other participants how they feel. It is helpful to write some good probing questions in advance of the focus group to ensure the discussion goes beyond surface answers.

Questions should never imply an answer or even hint at what the answer should be. Such questioning quickly squelches open discussion. More importantly, it may cause participants to guard their responses and look for the "accepted" thoughts the moderator is seeking. For instance, asking participants to discuss "the impact of eating at fast-food restaurants on people's health" implies fast foods are not healthy while asking them to "tell me your thoughts about fast foods" allows participants to freely discuss positive or negative thoughts.

Select Participants

The validity of results is highly dependent upon the selection of the focus group participants. In the situation with The Richards Group and Motel 6, both leisure and business travelers were chosen who had stayed at a Motel 6 sometime during the past year. Notice they had also stayed at other hotels, which was important for exploring the decision-making process and thoughts about Motel 6 in comparison to other motels. In most cases, participants are recruited who have used the brand or at least been exposed to it. However, a company may want to explore the thoughts of individuals who have never used a brand to see why it has never been chosen, though these individuals would most likely be included in a separate focus group. It is rare to mix users and nonusers together in a single group. Sometimes separate focus groups are also developed for different genders, ages, or other demographic variables that have important links to attitudes or purchasing behaviors.

In most instances, marketing research professionals, employees of the parent company or competing firms, and individuals who have participated in a focus group study of any type within the last six months (or longer) are not recruited as participants. Participants should be strangers. Thus, recruiting from churches, work sites, or other entities in which multiple participants may have come in contact with one another can negatively impact the dynamics and results of a focus group.

The remaining criteria used for participant selection must be related to the objectives of the study. In a focus group conducted for a small regional airport, one of the research questions sought to understand why individuals chose to drive two hours to a regional airport instead of using the local facility. In order to explore this component of the interview, it was important that the participants had used the regional airport on at least one trip during the previous year and also used the local airport during the same time period. Different focus groups were used for leisure and business travelers in order to discuss topics of interest for each segment, as these interests did not always coincide.

Recruiting focus group participants is not an easy task, as professional respondents are a growing problem in all forms of qualitative research, including focus groups. **Professional respondents** are individuals who belong to multiple research panels for the purpose of participating in multiple research studies, sometimes deceitfully, in order to obtain financial rewards or gifts. Professional respondents may establish false identities to participate multiple times in the same study or to qualify for studies on various topics. They may lie about their qualifications (such as product ownership) in order to be eligible to take a survey. Professional respondents damage the quality of the data collected, as their lack of knowledge on certain topics often forces them to make up answers. Some professional respondents randomly select answers or barely consider the question in order to complete the study as quickly as possible.

According to Mark Goodin, president of the Aaron-Abrams Field Support Services, the prevalence of professional respondents may be growing. Goodin points to both an unwillingness on the part of professional research firms and recruiters to address the problem (as doing so would increase both the time and the cost of participant recruiting), and the ease of access that Craigslist and search engine sites provide to individuals who wish to mass-register with multiple studies and recruiting firm websites. While professional respondents are certainly problematic, the Qualitative Research Consultants Association (QRCA) in conjunction with the Marketing Research Association has published best-practice papers and other guidelines that are helpful in managing professional respondents via the organizations' websites (www .qrca.org and www.marketingresearch.org). A sampling of the tactics that can help to eliminate professional respondents from qualitative research studies[7] is summarized in Figure 4.4.

Figure 4.4   Tactics for Minimizing Professional Respondents

1. Delete online registration forms and require phone registration to better screen potential participants.

2. Discontinue participant recruiting ads on Craigslist and similar sites.

3. Delete respondent databases with a history of professional respondents; start a new database from scratch.

4. Return to old-school respondent sources, such as telephone books, directories, and lists provided by clients or other sources.

5. Verify identities with background checks or Internet searches.

6. Implement high-tech respondent verification techniques, including picture IDs.

7. Demand proof of product or service ownership when this represents a criterion for participation.

8. Alter payment practices to eliminate both instant payments and payments to professional participants (cheaters) or nonqualified respondents during or after the research study.

9. Initiate legal action against individuals who lie about their qualifications to participate in the study and who are compensated for their participation in a research study.

10. Establish and support a professional industry organization whose mission would be to combat professional respondents globally.

Adapted from Mark Goodin, "No More Mr. Nice Guy: Professional Respondents in Qualitative Research," *Quirk's Marketing Research Review,* December 2009, Article ID: 20091225–2, https://www.quirks.com/articles/2009/20091225-2.aspx?searchID=115593271&msg=3 (accessed September 6, 2010).

The Focus Group Session

The actual focus group interview has four distinct stages, shown in Figure 4.5. While each step is important, the bulk of information obtained will occur during the discussion phase.

Introduction. During the introduction stage, the focus group participants become acquainted with each other and with the moderator. This step is important since no one in the room should have met prior to the focus group. The participants also learn more about the purpose of the focus group and any basic rules of courtesy that are expected, such as not interrupting individuals who are talking, allowing everyone to express their opinion, not talking to each other while someone else is speaking, not criticizing or making fun of a participant's response, and not being offended should the moderator need to interrupt a respondent in order to move the conversation along. Laying a good foundation for the study ensures a smooth-running focus group and one that produces beneficial insights for the client.

Participants should be carefully briefed on the purpose of the focus group so the research is not compromised. For instance, if participants in the airport focus group were told at the beginning that the purpose of the focus group is to determine why individuals drive two hours to the regional airport, free flow of information may be hindered, and questions not related to that objective would seem irrelevant. Instead, participants may be told that the purpose of the focus group is to discuss their thoughts about flying and usage of airports in general. This vagueness allows the group to explore multiple issues related to the selection of an airport and flying in general that may impact that decision. For instance, it is possible that some may drive the two hours because they don't feel comfortable (or safe) in small planes and want to fly in large jets. Their reasons for driving to a regional airport may have nothing to do with cost savings.

During the introduction, the sponsor of the focus group is rarely identified because it can easily bias responses. If The Richards Group had told participants that the focus group was sponsored by Motel 6, then that name would have come up during the first round of questioning, and participants would not have freely shared their thoughts about the hotel chain. It would have especially restricted negative thoughts about the brand.

Rapport building. As the focus group moves to the rapport-building stage, the moderator asks general questions to encourage participants to talk. The questions should be easy to answer and ones that everyone can answer. For example, it was easy for members of the motel focus group to identify what hotels they had patronized since all were selected because they had stayed in more than one hotel brand. Similarly, for the airport focus group individuals could talk about

Figure 4.5   Stages of the Focus Group Interview

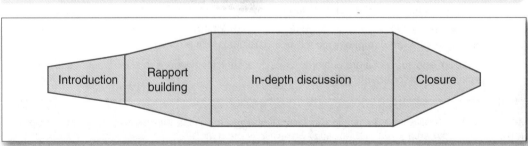

the various airports they had used since all had flown out of more airports than just the local facility. They could also talk about what they liked and disliked about the local airport as well as other airports.

In-depth discussion. Once the group members have been put at ease and become comfortable with each other, the moderator can guide the conversation using the questions developed for the discussion guide. It is typical for moderators to also ask probing questions that require deep thought on the part of participants. **Probing questions** respond to participant comments by asking "Why?" "What?" "How?" "Please explain," or "Tell me more." These types of questions lead to deeper thinking. During the discussion stage it is also helpful if participants begin responding to each other and not just to the moderator. Group dynamics come in to play when this free flow of information causes participants to feed off of each other's comments, which often provides valuable information. The moderator's role is to monitor the discussion and bring it back on topic if it strays too far away.

In addition to answering questions, focus group participants may be asked to work in teams to brainstorm ideas, to view visual stimuli (ads, package designs, etc.) and provide responses, or to perform other research tasks, such as sentence completion exercises.

Closure. As the focus group session nears the end, the moderator should bring the interview to closure by asking participants if they have any final thoughts on the topic. It may be appropriate at this time to reveal the sponsor or provide more information about the purpose of the study with the caveat of asking respondents to provide any additional thoughts.

Moderator characteristics. The success of focus groups is highly dependent on the ability of the moderator to manage the interview process. Managing a group of 8 to 12 individuals within an interview is not an easy task. It requires training and experience. It is also helpful if respondents can relate to the moderator. "It makes sense when doing a fashion-related group of overweight, 18–28 year-old women that the moderator be female, that the moderator not be a size two and that the moderator be able to empathize with this segment."[8]

Perhaps the most important characteristic of a good moderator is that he or she is completely open to participant feedback, be it positive or negative. Listening in a nonjudgmental manner is critical so that participants believe that there is not a right or wrong answer. Moderators must also carefully control their own body language, particularly facial expressions, as a grimace can cue respondents that the information being provided is unwelcome in some fashion, which in turn could potentially cut short the flow of valuable information. Coaxing respondent feedback from those less likely to participate and preventing overly talkative group members from dominating the conversation are also among the most important skills possessed by experienced moderators. Figure 4.6 summarizes the key responsibilities of moderators.

Debriefing

When the focus group is over, all of the observers and the moderator should meet to discuss what just occurred. This debriefing allows each observer and the moderator to indicate what they saw and heard. While everyone witnessed the same focus group interview, the interpretation of what was seen is likely to vary considerably. It is similar to eyewitnesses of an auto accident.

Figure 4.6 Tasks of the Moderator During the Focus Group

- Establish and maintain rapport
- Maintain eye contact
- Actively listen
- Probe for clarity and in-depth thoughts
- Solicit input from quiet members
- Manage dominant, talkative members
- Guide interviews to stay on topic
- Manage time to ensure all topics are covered
- Provide positive feedback and encouragement
- Allow and manage silence

Source: Author-created from "Two Maxims for Moderators," *Marketing Research*, Vol. 21, No. 2 (Summer 2009), pp. 26–27.

Each person has a different account of what happened. But, new insights are often gained that are not readily evident to the moderator. Some questions that might be asked of the observers include[9]:

- What did you hear that was a surprise—that you did not expect?
- What did you hear that confirmed what you expected?
- What new thoughts were generated by the focus group?
- How will you use the insights from the focus group?

Wyeth (now part of Pfizer), which is a producer of health care and pharmaceutical products such as Advil, ChapStick, and Robitussin, finds debriefing extremely valuable. The company uses focus groups regularly to explore innovation opportunities and evaluations of marketing messages, and as a precursor to quantitative research. According to Tony DiMiceli, Wyeth's vice president of marketing, "The fact that we're all together in the back room is important because it is a way to get everyone on the same page, to make sure the qualitative learning that is taking place is being interpreted properly."[10]

Focus group debriefing provided valuable insight for Denny's and resulted in a change in the company's advertising approach and positioning strategy. The participants in the focus groups did not refer to Denny's as a family restaurant. According to Frances Allen, chief marketing officer at Denny's, "People think of the brand as a diner, with great comfort food at a great price, and they feel that incredible warmth and incredible connection to the servers. There's a soul to a diner that is very authentic, very warm, and very accepting." Using the information from the focus group, Denny's was repositioned as a diner, not a family restaurant, with a new slogan. "America's diner is always open."[11]

Written Report

Once the series of focus group interviews is complete, the client will want a report. Although the sessions are recorded and can be reviewed, the moderator should capture major ideas from each session immediately upon finishing. This can be done by writing down "hot notes" that capture the ideas and thoughts that shout the loudest and stand out.[12] The idea is to capture these impressions immediately before they are gone. Even conversations that support the ideas can be noted, with exact wording located on the transcripts later.

The actual report should refer back to the research purpose and specific research questions investigated by the focus group interviews. A summary of the findings should then be written in the context of these research questions. Using the hot notes, support for the various findings can then be provided. Most reports will conclude with recommendations that are based on the findings of the qualitative research.

Disadvantages of Focus Groups

The primary disadvantage of focus groups is that each represents the opinion of only a few individuals. Even with multiple focus groups, it is still only the view of a small number of individuals in comparison to the thousands or millions of consumers who may purchase a particular product. Thus, a key disadvantage of focus groups is that the results may not represent the larger population of consumers.

Second, as focus groups are qualitative in nature, the results are highly subjective to the interpretation of the moderator and marketing researchers involved in the interviews. The client participants observing the sessions can also affect the results through the debriefing process and observing what they want to see rather than what actually occurred.

Groupthink is another often cited disadvantage of focus group interviews. **Groupthink** occurs when individuals within the group come to a consensus on a thought or an idea through the informal leadership of one or two individuals. Rather than disagree or talk about their true feelings, individuals may be swept along with the majority of consumers. It is difficult to speak up in a focus group and say "I disagree; I think . . ." when the majority of the group has expressed a different opinion. This is especially true for individuals who may be more introverted or too timid to talk in a group setting.

Restaurant operators have regularly used focus groups to solicit input on new menu items. But in recent years, restaurants have moved away from focus groups because they believe groupthink tended to dictate what consumers thought of new menu items. When one or two disliked it, others would agree rather than stand alone in their thoughts. Another disadvantage to these focus groups according to Andy Stefanovich, a senior partner at Prophet (a marketing consulting firm), "is that consumers can only react to what they're fed, and not propose something new."[13]

Executives at Quiznos, however, are strong believers in focus groups, but use them in a unique way to test new menu items. They use a speed-dining approach with as many as 25 focus groups in back-to-back sessions. The company reworks recipes based on focus group input; then it resubmits the recipes to the original as well as new focus groups. This process allows Quiznos to find the right ingredients, portion sizes, and prices that consumers want.[14]

ONLINE QUALITATIVE RESEARCH

■ Learning Objective 4.3: Discuss the various types of online qualitative research being used by companies.

In developing the concept for Burger Studio at colleges and universities, Aramark conducted online focus groups and sponsored chat rooms. The goal was to capture student thoughts about all of the elements of operation of the Burger Studio from conception to final delivery. Even the name was the result of an online contest with over 1,200 names being submitted.[15]

The qualitative research methods used by Aramark illustrate the recent trend by a number of companies and research firms that are relying more on online methodologies. As shown in Figure 4.7, this trend is due to a number of reasons. Reduced costs and quicker results are the primary reasons for this switch. With tighter marketing, advertising, and research budgets, lower costs are a very attractive reason for using online methodologies. Just as important is the need for quicker information to make management decisions.

Advances in online and cell phone technologies have provided researchers with a number of different ways of engaging individuals in online research. Focus groups can be held via text

Figure 4.7   Reasons for Conducting Qualitative Research Online

- Lower costs
- Quicker results
- Advancements in technology
- Availability of geographically dispersed sample
- Engagement of more individuals
- Convenient for participants, clients, and researchers
- Current trend in consumer communication

messaging, videoconferencing, or audio conferencing. It can be synchronous (done in real time) or asynchronous (spread out over longer periods of time with different people participating at different times). Discussion boards, chat rooms, and social media sites can be used.

Online methodologies allow for geographically dispersed individuals to participate in the same research. While 8 to 12 individuals are optimal for in-person focus groups, online focus groups can accommodate more individuals using various formats for discussion. Since travel is not involved, it is more convenient for participants, especially if asynchronous discussions are used. Lastly, the Internet has become a primary method of communication for individuals. They share ideas and thoughts online now, so using it for qualitative research is a natural extension of this current method of communication.

Online Focus Groups

Focus group interviews can be conducted online during real time just like traditional focus groups. Online focus groups can be text-based or video-based. Moderators are able to guide the discussion just as they would if the participants were in a physical room. Early attempts at online focus groups were criticized as being overly biased toward articulate respondents who could type quickly, and since body language could not be observed in text-based sessions the results were not considered to be the same. However, technology has improved to the point where such concerns are now minor. High-speed Internet, webcam technology, and greater bandwidth availability have led to a greater prevalence of video-based focus groups, such as those hosted by the firm Channel M2. Furthermore, client observation is often easier, and suggestions, questions, or probes offered by the client can be more readily and easily incorporated when an online format is used, particularly when focus groups are asynchronous.

The trend in online focus groups, however, is moving away from real-time to asynchronous communication. With this format focus groups tend to run over a few days to as long as two weeks. Respondents log on at their convenience, make comments, reply to questions or queries, and interact with other respondents. While asynchronous online focus groups share the benefits common to all online methodologies, groupthink and other negative personality influences associated with traditional focus groups are often minimized under this format. According to Katie Harris of Zebra Research, "You're providing respondents with a relatively safe and anonymous environment, conducive to deep thought and honesty. You're giving them thinking time. You're giving them air time. It's a level playing field where everyone looks the same. [Online focus groups] mirror the way people voice opinions and communicate with each other, including corporations, in the real world."[16]

The market research firm Decision Analyst (www.decisionanalyst.com) uses a bulletin board format for its asynchronous online focus groups, which the firm labels "Time-Extended™ Online Discussion Forums." Moderators facilitate discussions among 12 to 15 participants who have been recruited for a specific study. Follow-up questions encouraging detailed, thoughtful responses are posted by the moderator targeting either the group as a whole or a specific individual. The result is very rich, highly detailed information. Decision Analyst believes that this key benefit of the extended format stems from the fact that "the extra time available to the moderator (and to the clients) allows them to ask more reflective and insightful follow-up questions than what would be practical in other types of qualitative research."[17]

J. C. Penney recently used an online focus group to investigate cross-channel shopping behaviors. The study began with an online survey that asked broad questions about shopping behaviors and attitudes. Heavy cross-channel shoppers were gleaned from the survey participants for an online focus group. Each participant was given $50 to go shopping. The shoppers were asked then to share via the online focus group venue what they purchased, where they purchased it, their feelings about the shopping experience, and why they bought what they did. As J. C. Penney observed the interactions among the

A female participating in an online focus group.

participants, the company was surprised that cross-channel shopping was not limited to a specific demographic group, age, or income. The company also learned that shopping can begin with any of the three channels—the physical store, online store, or catalog.[18]

Discussion Boards, Online Communities, and Chat Rooms

Another online approach is to recruit a large number of individuals and utilize discussion boards and chat rooms. For example, Roxy is a manufacturer of footwear that strives to stay in touch with the latest fashion happenings of the teen and immediate post-teen market. To do so, Roxy has established an online focus group called the Style Squad, which consists of thousands of girls from across the United States. Birgit Klett, designer for Roxy, posts questions and styles online to get Style Squad members' reactions and feedback. Since feedback is quick and anonymous, Klett is able to obtain input much quicker than through traditional focus groups. She is also able to obtain feedback from a much larger sample. While it is still subjective information, it does provide input into what styles of shoes are "in" and what will be acceptable to her target market.[19]

Online communities and chat rooms offer an excellent way to obtain quick, gut-level feelings about a topic, an issue, or a concept. Data can usually be collected in a few hours, especially through panels of preestablished participants. One method of data collection occurs when a researcher joins a community or chat room and monitors conversations without participating. Actively participating in the community or chat room by posing questions or asking for feedback can also elicit interesting information. However, the ethical researcher should follow the Word of Mouth Marketing Association's guidelines, and not misrepresent themselves as regular consumers, but instead identify their company affiliation. It also common in this type of research to set up in advance of the study a panel or group of individuals who have already agreed to participate. Individuals meeting certain demographic profiles or other criteria can be parsed out of the larger group to participate in particular studies on an as-needed basis.

While live chat rooms are still being used for data collection, a more common approach is to use message boards or blogs. It is a more relaxed method for both respondents and researchers to collect qualitative data. Data are collected over a few days, rather than a few hours as with chat rooms, but the message boards allow for deeper thinking and participation at the respondent's convenience. Questions are posed by the moderator to the group, and participants are asked to comment. Interaction among participants is quick to develop, especially since each person is anonymous.

Additional versions of online qualitative research have developed as technologies have advanced. For instance, a marketing researcher can now post a question via a text message to an individual's phone. The participant then uses his or her phone to post a reply to a message board. Software is available that can schedule text messages at specific times, such as at 5 p.m. asking about dinner plans, then at 9 p.m. asking about television viewing or other activities the individual may be engaged in. Because questions are posed in real time of the respondent's life, memory (or lack thereof) is not a factor into the behaviors and thoughts that are recorded by participants. It can also spur interactions among participants as they see what others have posted. Rather than post to a message board, the text message could encourage participants to log into a live chat room, prompt a webcam to record activities, or leave a phone message.

The Internet provides ample opportunity for qualitative research. The challenge to marketers is to understand how to use it to obtain quality data that can be used by management to enhance decision making. The lower costs and speed of data collection make it an attractive medium to use for this type of research.

IN-DEPTH INTERVIEWS

■ Learning Objective 4.4: Explain the process of using in-depth interviews to conduct qualitative research.

Focus groups are excellent at probing into the thoughts of individuals, as a group. But, it sometimes results in groupthink where one or two individuals control the conversation or at least the direction of the discussion. Also, some participants are reluctant to speak out in a group. Others may give what they perceive as socially acceptable answers rather than reveal their true feelings. To avoid these potential pitfalls the researcher may conduct an **in-depth interview**, which is a qualitative research method involving one-on-one interviews conducted by a marketing professional. The goal of the in-depth interview is to probe deeply into an individual's thoughts and ideas in order to better understand a person's mental activities and behaviors.

Just like with the focus group, the marketing researcher will develop a list of questions for the in-depth interview. Based on input from the client, specific goals will be set that will form the basis for the questions. Probing questions or cues should also be planned, though the researcher may ask unplanned questions as needed to better understand the participants' responses. But, with the in-depth interview, the researcher has an opportunity to dig deep into the thoughts and ideas of individuals in a way that is not possible with a focus group. Because it is one-to-one, individuals often feel more comfortable talking, especially about deep-seated beliefs, thoughts, and ideas.

BMW Motorcycles used in-depth interviews to investigate why individuals like riding motorcycles. In addition to men, the researchers interviewed women, especially wives of male bikers. From the interviews the company learned that men enjoy motorcycles because riding them provides a feeling of freedom. As one man stated, "It's like you are a cowboy out on the open road, free to roam and go wherever you want. No one or no thing can stand in your

In-depth interviews provide researchers with opportunities to probe deeply into thoughts and ideas of consumers.

way." "It's the last American frontier," another person stated. BMW also learned that what the wife thinks is highly significant. As one man stated, "If she ain't happy, no one is happy!" This sentiment was reinforced in the interviews with the females. From these in-depth interviews, BMW developed a marketing and advertising campaign directed toward women talking about the comfort of the passenger seat and the feel they would get from the motorcycle adventure.[20]

The typical in-depth interview lasts one to two hours, which provides ample opportunity for probing deep thoughts. It also allows the researcher and the participant to become comfortable with each other so more intimate and personal reflections can be shared. Thoughts and ideas that would never be said in a group can be made to an individual, especially knowing that results of the interview will remain anonymous.

Because in-depth interviews involve one-on-one interaction, it is highly subjective. The researcher not only controls the interpretation of what occurred, but also has great control over the interview itself. Stronger interviewer rapport with the subject is critical to encouraging honest, thoughtful responses. Similar to focus group moderators, interviewers must also be careful not to bias the respondents' replies via words or actions. Respondents may think they are "helping" an interviewer whom they like by giving responses they think that person desires to hear, rather than sharing the thoughts, feelings, and beliefs that they truly hold. Because of the length of time involved in the interview and the reporting of each interview, in-depth interviews tend to be costly to conduct, and as a result only a small set of interviews is usually conducted.

Sarah Stanley, of the University of Wisconsin Oshkosh, used in-depth interviews to better understand why brand communities form. She attended two Jeep Jamborees and interviewed people about the Jamborees and why they attended. Through the in-depth interviews she found that the Jeep brand had a strong meaning to the participants. Many had developed relationships with their vehicles. For instance, one person said "his Jeep was overworked that weekend and 'she' needed to go home and rest for a couple of days." Statements of personality or persona given to their vehicles were common during the interviews. Individuals felt their Jeeps stood for freedom, being able to "go anywhere—through streams and over rocks." Through storytelling and communicating with other Jeep owners, individuals developed an even stronger bond with the brand and each other.[21]

In-depth interviews can be used by marketing researchers to learn about a topic or an issue prior to conducting a quantitative study. For instance, before conducting a quantitative study about digital versus traditional newspaper readership, a pair of marketing researchers conducted in-depth interviews. From these interviews they found four primary reasons individuals read newspapers: (1) to search for specific information, (2) to get updated news, (3) for leisure, and (4) as a habit. This information then served as the foundation for conducting structured quantitative research.[22]

In-depth interviews can be conducted online. It can be a text-based interview or a video interview. Online further reduces the costs since no travel is required. It is a good way to conduct interviews of sensitive topics that may be embarrassing to individuals. This is especially true for the text-only approaches where the interviewer cannot see the respondent. While online in-depth interviews may be as short as 30 minutes, research firm Decision Analyst (www .decisionanalyst.com) offers a time-extended version of the in-depth interview, which varies in length from as little as two days to as long as one week. Key advantages of the time-extended format include (1) richer content and deeper, more meaningful consumer insights; (2) real-time transcript viewing by clients, and a correspondingly greater opportunity for clients to interact with the facilitator; and (3) the ability to ask more detailed, insightful follow-up questions, compared to other forms of qualitative research.[23]

Focus groups and in-depth interviews each have their place in the research process. Ultimately, the study purpose and research questions need to be considered when determining whether a focus group or an in-depth interview is the appropriate methodology. More specific factors influencing the choice of focus groups versus in-depth interview methodology are summarized in Figure 4.8.

Figure 4.8   Factors Influencing the Choice of In-Depth Interview Versus Focus Group

Use in-depth interviews when:	Use focus groups when:
• Research questions are directly related to specific respondent segments and individual behavior.	• Research questions seek to explore disparate views via consensus or debate.
• In-depth interviews reach the population of interest easier (such as in the case of small, geographically dispersed populations).	• Group dynamics are helpful in discovering information.
• The cost-benefit ratio favors in-depth interviews.	• Topics are broad, and participants need help generating or sharing ideas.
• Groupthink/group dynamics might be a problem.	• Participant interaction is desired and helpful in stimulating discussion and discovering underlying issues.
• Usability testing of a device or process is sought.	• Teamwork is desired.
• Subject matter is highly sensitive.	• Exploring common trends.
	• Client interaction is desirable.

Source: Author-created from Carey V. Azzara, "Qualitatively Speaking: The Focus Group vs. In-Depth Interview Debate," *Quirks Marketing Research Review*, June 2010, Article ID 20100601, p. 16. http://www.quirks.com/articles/2010/20100601.aspx?searchID =116421703&sort=4&pg=1 (accessed September 6, 2010).

PROJECTIVE TECHNIQUES

Researchers, especially psychologists, believe that respondents tend to give answers they believe the researcher wants to hear and that are socially acceptable. Too often, respondents are unwilling to offer negative answers, and respondents typically avoid giving any responses that might reflect negatively on their own behavior, beliefs, attitudes, or values. In some situations, respondents may not consciously even understand the reasons or motivations behind their actions and thoughts, and thus are prevented from articulating those reasons with researchers. Because of these theories, psychologists have developed alternative approaches that allow respondents to project beliefs and ideas outside of themselves. These **projective techniques** are indirect methods of qualitative research using ambiguous stimuli that allow respondents to project their emotions, feelings, thoughts, attitudes, and beliefs onto third parties or inanimate objects.

Projective techniques work especially well in situations where respondents cannot or will not respond truthfully to direct questioning. Projective techniques are based on the principle of free association as respondents are not asked questions that in any way limit or inhibit their reactions. Instead individuals are asked to share immediate thoughts that are generated by stimuli provided by a researcher. Quite often the goal is to stimulate the subconscious and to uncover emotions, feelings, and thoughts that respondents may not even consciously be aware of, but that become evident to a trained psychologist. The most common projective techniques are shown in Figure 4.9 and are based on the concept of free association.

Sentence Completion

With **sentence completion,** respondents are given a partial sentence and asked to complete it with the first thoughts that come to mind. For a study about motorcycles, some examples may be:

- People who ride motorcycles are . . .
- When I ride a motorcycle, I feel . . .
- Women who ride motorcycles are . . .
- Men who ride motorcycles are . . .
- Women who own their own motorcycle are . . .

Figure 4.9   Projective Techniques

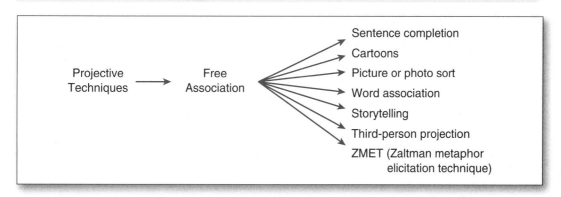

■ Learning Objective 4.5: Enumerate the various projective techniques.

The purpose of the sentence completion projective technique is to solicit individuals' thoughts without inhibiting their answers. Responses are recorded word for word and later analyzed in conjunction with the individuals' other answers and in comparison to those of other respondents. While qualitative research involves subjective interpretations, sentence completion is less subjective than some of the other techniques. Consider the following responses from three different respondents to the first question:

- People who ride motorcycles are scary and are usually criminals or at least in some type of gang or something.
- People who ride motorcycles are free, independent people who enjoy the outdoors and doing things.
- People who ride motorcycles are a lot of times professionals, like lawyers, doctors, and business-people, not people you would normally think of as being bikers.

The way each person answered the question provides a rich insight into that person's thoughts about motorcycles and the types of individuals who ride motorcycles. As the person answers additional questions, researchers gain a deeper insight into the respondent's thoughts and attitudes.

In developing questions, researchers have to be careful not to guide the individual's answers or convey the purpose of the study. Suppose the purpose of the above study was to better understand why women ride motorcycles, both as a passenger and as a driver. If only questions about women were asked, the purpose of the study would become obvious and as a result may influence the response patterns. Similarly, careful attention must be paid with respect to the order in which sentences appear so that information contained in one sentence doesn't serve as a cue that in turn influences responses to sentences asked later.

Cartoon Tests

Cartoon tests are very similar to sentence completion tasks and serve much the same purpose. **Cartoon tests** show a cartoon illustration in which one or more characters are present. At least one of the characters has an empty dialogue bubble. The respondent is asked to project his or her feelings and thoughts by filling in the character dialogue. A cartoon test might show a man and a woman in a car dealership showroom examining a motorcycle. The man's character may be shown as saying, "What do you think?" while the female's dialogue bubble is left empty for the respondent to fill in.

Picture or Photo Sorts

Photo sorts require that participants sort through a stack of cards or photos, and select those that are representative of the topic of interest. Respondents in a motorcycle study may be given a stack of cards featuring photos of individuals from all walks of life. Gender, age, ethnicity, and dress would vary by photo. The photos selected by the participant as representative of Harley-Davidson riders might still reflect the leather-clad, tough, long-haired, bearded biker image that was long their norm, though as a group this portion of Harley-Davidson's market is relatively small today. Alternatively, the same individual may select photos of young men in casual clothes or business apparel as indicative of Honda riders. Photo sorts may be combined with in-depth interviews or focus groups.

Word Association

Word association is a qualitative projective research technique where respondents are read a series of words and asked to respond with the first word that comes to mind. In developing the list of words, the researcher will often add neutral words that have nothing to do with the study in order to disguise the study's purpose. For the study on motorcycles, stimulus words that might be given are *motorcycles, biker, bike, leather jacket,* and *Harley-Davidson.* Neutral words mixed in might include *food, blue jeans, red,* and *shopping.* Word association can be very helpful in understanding the various associations (positive or negative) that people form toward brand names, retail stores, product categories, ad slogans, or spokespeople.

As with sentence completion, responses are recorded word for word, and the length of time between the question and the answer is recorded. Analysis identifies what types of associations the person makes with each of the words being studied. The goal is to dig into the subconscious or at least the attitudes that might be below the surface. Also, with a topic such as females and motorcycles, individuals may try to hide their true feelings and thoughts about female bikers because they feel they may be perceived as being prejudiced. Projective techniques are designed to uncover a person's true feelings without them realizing it.

When analyzing word associations, researchers tend to look at three things. First, the researcher examines the frequency with which a particular word is given by different respondents or even by the same respondent to different stimulus words. When a stimulus word reflects a product category, and a large proportion of responses reflect a particular brand name, the results reflect strong top-of-the-mind awareness of that brand. Similarly, if a stimulus word is a brand name, high-frequency responses reflecting key benefits such as "low prices" indicate that marketing communications are successful in portraying this benefit.

Second, the amount of time that lapses before a response is given indicates whether it is a top-of-mind response, or if the individual is thinking about a response perhaps because he or she does not want to state the first word that comes to mind. For instance, when responding to the word *biker* the first thought by a female respondent may be *rape*. But, the respondent doesn't want to say that because it may appear she has a negative attitude or is fearful of bikers, so she pauses to think of a different word. This pause is an indicator that the individual may be hiding some underlying thoughts or attitudes.

Lastly, researchers will look at words where individuals did not give a response within the stated amount of time, usually three seconds. Again, this can be an indicator of hidden thoughts, but it can also indicate a neutral position or weakly held beliefs and attitudes, which make it difficult for the respondent to think of anything to say.

In developing the study, the selection of stimulus words and neutral words is critically important. Also, the order of words can impact the responses. Even with neutral filler words, respondents may see a pattern that reflects sequential thinking. For example, if *Harley-Davidson* preceded the word *motorcycle,*

Word association may allow researchers the opportunity to understand consumers' true feelings about topics such as females and motorcycles.

responses to the second stimulus word may be colored by perceptions of Harley-Davidson, specifically. Depending on the purpose of the research, this may not always be a negative aspect of the study, but the order of stimulus words should always be reviewed for potential problems, which may cause bias.

Compared to sentence completion, word association is more difficult for the researcher to analyze. It involves more subjective analysis since the researcher has to piece together the responses to understand the individual's thoughts. But, it also has the potential to reveal deeper hidden attitudes and beliefs.

Storytelling

The **storytelling** approach involves showing respondents a picture or series of pictures and asking them to tell a story about what they see. Instead of pictures, researchers can use cartoons or cartoon-type characters. With the storytelling approach, respondents may be shown a picture of a couple riding a motorcycle through the mountains and be asked to describe what they see or who they are—in other words—to tell a story about the picture. Additional pictures can be shown that display specific elements of a study to gather more details and understanding. For example, the couple may be shown stopped at a gas station, with a service bay in the background. Stories may reveal thoughts about gas mileage, comfort, or even the reliability of the motorcycle brand.

Like the other methods, this projective technique allows respondents to convey their thoughts without any type of restriction. While deep-seated, hidden beliefs and attitudes may surface, it is more difficult to get at these because the respondent can provide a story about a single picture that is socially acceptable. Thus, by using a series of pictures a researcher is better able to uncover a person's real thoughts about the topic. It is more likely he or she will make statements that reflect inner thoughts rather than the socially acceptable answer.

Third-Person Technique

We as individuals are very protective of our self-image and especially the image of ourselves we want other people to see. We guard this image by attempting to control the environment around us, including the words we speak. This defense mechanism may make it difficult for the researcher to gather accurate information from respondents, especially about sensitive subjects that in some way may negatively impact a person's image or be seen as socially unacceptable. To get around this defense, researchers can use a **third-person technique**, which involves asking individuals how someone else (a third person) would react to the situation, or what his or her attitude, beliefs, and actions may be.

To understand how this technique is used and the importance of it, consider a college educator who wants to examine student cheating on homework. When asked directly about cheating, almost all students would deny they have cheated and become defensive about the topic. But, with the third-person technique, the student may freely talk about cheating, why students cheat, how it is done, the ethical views of students who cheat, and even the ethics of society in general. When students project all of their thoughts to a third person, defensive self-protection mechanisms are bypassed.

The challenge for the researcher is interpreting the results. Are these individuals expressing their own thoughts about cheating, or are they expressions from conversations with other students and projections on why they think others cheat? To separate these two, researchers will watch the respondent's body language closely. While not a foolproof indicator, it does provide some indication of which it may be. A better technique is to ask probing questions and keep the individual talking. The more the respondent talks, the more likely the person will reveal his or her own thoughts about cheating.

ZMET (Zaltman Metaphor Elicitation Technique)

The last projective technique is called the **ZMET,** which stands for Zaltman metaphor elicitation technique. ZMET is a qualitative projective technique that uses an in-depth interview to uncover emotions and subconscious beliefs and attitudes. The technique was developed and patented by Olson Zaltman Associates. Gerald Zaltman explains, "Consumers can't tell you what they think because they just don't know. Their deepest thoughts, the ones that account for their behavior in the marketplace, are unconscious."[24]

With the ZMET method, participants are told the topic of the study, such as motorcycle riding, or it can even be more specific such as females and motorcycles. Respondents are then asked to collect 10–15 pictures or images that in some way reflect the topic. During the in-depth interview respondents are asked to talk about each picture. They are also asked to project what else the picture might contain if it could be enlarged. Once participants have talked about all of the pictures, they are asked to string them together in a mini-movie discussing the sequence and how they all fit together. At the end of the interview, respondents are asked to summarize their feelings about the topic.

A major advantage of the ZMET methodology is that it allows individuals time, usually one to two weeks, to think about a topic and collect images or photographs that reflect their thoughts. Coupled with the in-depth interview, the ZMET method elicits thoughts that often are not part of a typical in-depth interview and may not surface using one of the other projective techniques. It is a good method of extracting deep-seated thoughts that individuals may not have even realized they possessed.[25]

Global Concerns

Understanding the various cultures throughout the world is important for conducting qualitative research. For instance, in Western cultures individualism tends to be dominant, which allows for greater freedom to discuss opinions and ideas in focus groups and in-depth interviews. But, in Eastern cultures collectivism tends to be dominant. **Collectivism** refers to the extent an individual's life is intertwined with the life of others and society. Individuals living in these societies see their life as part of a larger group and the needs of society as being more important than the needs of individuals. Thus, in focus groups and in-depth interviews they tend not to express opinions that will differ from those of others or what they believe the moderator is seeking.

Another facet of Eastern cultures is that they tend to take a long-term orientation versus the short-term orientation found in Western cultures. With a long-term orientation, it is important for individuals to take time to become acquainted with each other before consummating any type of business transaction, or before engaging in marketing research. Long-term orientation also puts a higher priority on future rewards over short-term rewards and values thriftiness and perseverance toward goals. In contrast, societies with a short-term orientation place emphasis on the now and present. As a result, they are very time-conscious and want to move immediately into the research and get it finished so they can move on to other things. Taking time to become acquainted first is not necessary, and often viewed as a waste of time and money.

Projective techniques are also more challenging in other countries. In addition to the reasons already discussed, not all cultures have the same level of independence and freedom for individuals to express themselves as in the United States. In some cultures, the need to be part of the group (collectivism) encourages individuals to provide socially acceptable answers rather than true feelings. Even with projective techniques it is difficult to get below the surface of an individual's thoughts and feelings.

 STATISTICS REVIEW

Frequency distributions are perhaps the most simplistic method of compiling and presenting data. *Frequencies* are computed by counting the number of times a particular response is recorded for a particular variable. *Frequency tables* compile these data. Percentages are normally computed to make the data easier to understand. Frequency tables, similar to the one shown in Figure 4.10, may be included within the body of a research report, or within the appendix of the study.

Figure 4.10   Frequency Table

Table 1: Respondent's Age

		Frequency	Percent	Valid Percent	Cumulative Percent
Valid	18–22	37	43.5	53.6	53.6
	23–29	23	27.1	33.3	87.0
	30–49	6	7.1	8.7	95.7
	50+	3	3.5	4.3	100.0
	Total	69	81.2	100.0	
Missing	System	16	18.8		
	Total	85	100.0		

Interpreting Frequency Table Information

The last row of the table shows a total frequency of 85, which in this case represents the total number of research subjects who were asked this question. Unfortunately, age is one of the more sensitive demographic questions, and 16 people, representing 18.8% of the sample, did not supply an answer.

These numbers can be found in the "Missing" row, under the "Frequency" and "Percent" columns. The remaining frequency counts are specific to those individuals who did answer the question. Of these 69 individuals who responded, 37 were between the ages of 18 and 22, 23 were between 23 and 29, 6 were 30 to 39 years of age, and 3 were 50 or older.

The last three columns show percentages. The key to understanding the difference between the three columns is to understand what number was used as the denominator in the percentage calculation. The denominator used in computing the "Percent" column figures includes both people who did (69) and did not (16) answer the question. The "Valid Percent" column and the "Cumulative Percent" column calculate percentages on the basis of those who provided a response. In examining the 23–29 age bracket, 27.1% of the total sample was this age. Of those who provided a response to the age question, 33.3% were 23 to 29. For the cumulative percent, 87% of the respondents were 18 to 29 years old. Note the cumulative percentage grows progressively larger for each row of data, as each successive line in the table adds the valid percent for that row to the cumulative percent shown on the previous line.

Measures of Central Tendency

Measures of central tendency include the mean, median, and mode. *Means* are frequently calculated in marketing research when numerical data representing actual quantities are collected. For example, a fill-in-the-blank question may ask respondents to indicate the number of radio ads they could actually recall hearing during their drive to work, the number of times they ate at a particular restaurant during the last week, or the number of jeans they purchased on their last shopping trip. For this type of data, calculating a mean would be appropriate.

For the purpose of reviewing measures of central tendency, suppose 10 individuals answered the question about hearing radio ads as shown below:

0, 0, 0, 1, 1, 1, 2, 2, 3, 9

The number of ads recalled by different respondents could be averaged, meaning that the values would first be summed, and then divided by the number of respondents answering the question. In this instance, the sum of these responses (19) was divided by the number of responses (10) to compute a mean of 1.9. Notice three people could not recall a single ad, although they had been listening to the radio, thus the value of zero. If the respondent had left the question blank, the researcher could not assume the response was zero. It must be recorded as a missing value.

It is important to remember that means should not be calculated for all data. For instance, the values 1 through 4 are used in the data file to represent the ages of respondents in Figure 4.10. These numbers in and of themselves do not represent quantities—they are used strictly for classification purposes. Therefore, averages cannot be calculated since the values do not represent actual ages.

The *median* is the value within a frequency distribution that marks the midway point in an ordered frequency distribution, in that half of the observations within the frequency distribution fall below the median value and half are above the median value. Review of the cumulative percentage column can often help to identify this value. While the use of median data is inappropriate for classification variables such as age and gender, it can be used with other types of data. The median is particularly

(Continued)

(Continued)

helpful in better understanding the central tendency of a variable when extreme observations, called outliers, are present. For the radio ad data, the median is 1. The median in this case offers a better understanding of the central tendency for this variable than does the mean, as the mean was artificially inflated by the outlier value of 9.

The final measure of central tendency is called the *mode,* a term used to describe the value that occurs most frequently. The mode is the only measure of central tendency that can be used with classification data. Reviewing the "age" frequency table presented in Figure 4.10 shows the highest frequency is 37, for the 18–22 age bracket. On the other hand, the radio recall data do not demonstrate a single mode, as both 0 and 3 occur three times. However, with larger samples as is common in most research studies, a single mode usually emerges.

DEALING WITH DATA

The SPSS software simplifies the process of preparing frequency tables. It also makes it possible to recode existing data into new variables. For this exercise you will need to download the SPSS word association data titled "Chapter 4 Dealing with Data" found at the student website, www.sagepub.com/clowess. This data file was created from a word association exercise. Students viewed a word and were told to write down the first word that came to mind. A total of 85 students completed the word association exercise within the specified time limit, four seconds for each stimulus word. (Detailed step-by-step instructions for using the SPSS software are provided at the textbook student website.)

Exercise 1: Frequency Counts

Using SPSS, run a frequency count of all of the variables except the first variable, which is just the code number for each case. Based on the output, answer the following questions. The frequency command is located under the descriptive statistics menu button.

1. For each of the 12 stimulus words from *insurance* through *money*, identify the top five responses with the frequency and valid percent for each.

2. Identify the demographic profile of the sample by providing the frequency, percent, and valid percent for gender and race. How many individuals did not provide their gender or race?

3. What is the mode for each of the 12 stimulus words from *insurance* through *money*?

4. What is the median for student credit hours completed and age?

5. Use the valid percentage values to create a column chart for each of the following variables. Graph only the top five responses. Be sure to provide a title for each graph and titles for the x-axis and y-axis. It is also helpful to place values above each of the bars so they can be read easily by managers.

   a. Fast-food restaurant
   b. Geico
   c. Soft drink

6. For gender, create a pie chart. Include the percentage of females, males, and missing values (i.e., the percent of no responses). Be sure to provide a title for the graph and label each section of the pie with the variable name and value.

Exercise 2: Mean

Use SPSS to calculate a mean for student credit hours and age. The mean command is found under the "Descriptive" menu in SPSS. What is the mean for each of the variables: student credit hours and age?

Exercise 3: Recoding

Researchers will sometimes want to recode variables either for reporting purposes or to conduct additional analysis. For this exercise recode the "student credit hours completed" variable into a new variable using the following categories. It is always wise to use a new variable when recoding so you never lose the original data.

Category 1: 0–29

Category 2: 30–59

Category 3: 60–89

Category 4: 90+

Now recode the age variable into a new variable using the following categories.

Category 1: 19–20

Category 2: 21–22

Category 3: 23+

Once the two variables are recoded, run a frequency count of your new variables. Answer the following questions using the output file of these two variables.

1. What is the frequency count and valid percent for each of the two variables?

2. What is the mode for each of the two variables?

SUMMARY

Objective 1: Explain the role of qualitative research.

Qualitative research provides valuable insights into consumer motives, attitudes, and feelings. Commonly used in exploratory studies, findings from qualitative research can be used to refine research questions, aid in questionnaire or research design, and develop background information for quantitative studies. Furthermore, the deep understanding of consumer behavior made possible via qualitative research provides richness to quantitative studies. Qualitative research is particularly helpful in exploring consumers' subconscious when they cannot or will not answer direct questions.

Objective 2: Describe the traditional focus group process.

Focus groups are useful when group dynamics can produce new insights or thoughts that might not otherwise be discovered via in-depth interviews. The focus group process begins with the development of the study parameters during which decisions related to the research questions, study timeline, number of focus groups, budget, stipends, and level of client participation are made. The interview questions and probes are developed next for the discussion guide. Prior to recruiting participants, criteria for participant selection should be developed. Care should be taken to avoid professional respondents. The moderator conducts the focus group in four stages: (1) introduction, (2) rapport building, (3) in-depth discussion, and (4) closure. Immediately following each focus group session, the observers and moderators meet to debrief. Once all sessions have been conducted, the moderator writes and submits a written report to the client. While focus groups are very popular, they suffer from three disadvantages: (1) Results are not definitive and cannot be generalized to the population, (2) results are highly subjective, and (3) group think may intimidate some respondents and prevent them from sharing their opinions.

Objective 3: Discuss the various types of online qualitative research being used by companies.

Online qualitative research offers reduced costs and quicker results leading to widespread adoption of online techniques. Focus groups can be held using chat rooms, discussion boards, social media sites, websites, videoconferencing, or even text messaging. The trend toward asynchronous communication methods maximizes participant convenience, and often results in better probing and richer responses.

Objective 4: Explain the process of using in-depth interviews to conduct qualitative research.

In-depth interviews conducted one-on-one probe deeply into an individual's thoughts, ideas, and motives using a prepared list of questions asked by a professional interviewer. Often, interviews are conducted prior to a quantitative study. Respondents normally feel more comfortable discussing sensitive issues or deep-seated beliefs in a one-on-one scenario. Richer data are gathered, compared to focus groups. Interpretation is highly subjective and entirely dependent upon the interviewer, as unlike during focus groups, clients do not observe in-depth interviews. In-depth interviews can also be conducted online, in text, or in video format. Online interviews are especially useful when the subject is sensitive or potentially embarrassing to the respondent.

Objective 5: Enumerate the various projective research techniques.

Respondents are often unwilling to respond truthfully to direct questions regarding sensitive issues or behaviors, and at other times are unable to articulate their motives or why they behaved in a given fashion. Projective techniques use indirect motives to discover feelings, thoughts, attitudes, and the motives that underlie respondent behavior. Based on the principle of free association, projective techniques include word association, sentence completion, cartoon tests, picture and photo sorts, storytelling, third-person techniques, and ZMET.

GLOSSARY OF KEY TERMS

Cartoon test: projective technique using cartoon illustrations in which one or more characters are present, at least one of whom has an empty dialogue bubble, and the respondent is asked to project his or her feelings and thoughts by filling in the character dialogue

Collectivism: the extent an individual's life is intertwined with the life of others and society

Discussion guide: series of questions that will be asked of participants by the moderator during the focus group interview

Focus groups: qualitative research method in which 8 to 12 individuals unknown to each other are brought together to discuss a particular topic

Groupthink: phenomenon that occurs when individuals within the group come to a consensus on a thought or an idea through the informal leadership of one or two individuals

In-depth interviews: qualitative research method involving one-on-one interviews for the purpose of probing deeply into an individual's thoughts and ideas to better understand a person's mental activities and behaviors

Moderator: trained interviewer who guides the focus group discussion, encourages respondent participation, and prepares the client report

Photo sort: projective technique requiring that participants sort through a stack of cards or photos, and select those that are representative of the topic of interest

Probing questions: "why," "what," "how," "please explain," or "tell me more" types of questions that will lead to deeper thinking

Professional respondents: individuals who belong to multiple research panels for the purpose of participating in multiple research studies, often deceitfully, in order to obtain financial rewards or gifts

Projective techniques: indirect methods of qualitative research using ambiguous stimuli that allow respondents to project their emotions, feelings, thoughts, attitudes, and beliefs onto third-party or inanimate objects

Sentence completion: projective technique in which respondents are given a partial sentence and asked to complete it with the first thoughts that come to mind

Storytelling: qualitative projective approach that involves showing respondents a picture, cartoon, or series of pictures and asking them to tell a story about what they see

Third-person technique: qualitative projective technique that involves asking individuals how someone else (a third person) would react to the situation, or what his or her attitude, beliefs, and actions may be

Word association: qualitative projective research technique where respondents are given a series of words and asked to respond with the first word that comes to mind

ZMET: qualitative projective technique that uses an in-depth interview to uncover emotional and subconscious beliefs and attitudes, over a two- or three-week period of time

CRITICAL THINKING EXERCISES

1. You have been asked to investigate college students' attitudes toward and usage of various social media, as well as their thoughts about the use of social media for marketing purposes. What type of qualitative research technique would you use, and would it be appropriate to combine multiple techniques? Justify your recommendations.

2. Visit www.decisionanalyst.com and review the information related to Time-Extended™ Online Discussion Forums, which should be found within the qualitative research section of the research services menu. A short demo video of their online qualitative service may also be available for viewing. Next, visit www.channelm2.com and watch the demo video. For what specific types of research tasks would a researcher be better off using the Time-Extended™ Online Discussion Forum instead of an online focus group? Would the nature of the product or service make a difference as to the appropriateness of one format or the other? Why or why not?

3. A snack food company that markets various types and flavors of chips is interested in better understanding consumer attitudes toward snack foods, including how and when snack foods are consumed, and positive and negative perceptions of snack foods. Develop a focus group discussion guide to investigate this topic.

4. Develop a set of stimulus (test) words and neutral words for a client, such as Chick-fil-A restaurant. Your list should contain a minimum of five stimulus words. Administer your word association test to 10 students not enrolled in your class, and summarize the results.

5. Develop a series of 10 sentence completion exercises, for the purpose of investigating college students' attitudes toward and usage of various social media, as well as businesses' use of social media for marketing purposes. Administer your sentence completion exercises to 10 college students who are not currently enrolled in your research class. Take care to select an equal number of males and females. Summarize the results, being careful to note any common themes that emerge, as well differences that appear to be gender specific.

6. Develop a series of 10 sentence completion exercises, for the purpose of investigating college students' attitudes toward and usage of credit cards. Administer your sentence completion exercises to 10 college students who are not currently enrolled in your research class. Take care to select an equal number of males and females. Summarize the results, being careful to note any common themes that emerge, as well as differences that appear to be gender specific.

7. Using the following series of questions and probes, interview three people who are not enrolled in your marketing research class. Summarize your findings.

   a. Describe a typical morning from the time you get out of bed until the time you leave the house and arrive at either work or school.

      i. Probe: Explain how breakfast fits into your morning routine.
      ii. Probe: Does your breakfast routine vary on those days you don't leave your residence in the morning for school or work? If so, how?

   b. What type of food do you eat for breakfast?

      i. Probe: Under what circumstances are you likely to eat breakfast out at a fast-food restaurant? At a sit-down restaurant?

   c. Tell me your thoughts about cereal.

     i. Probe: What cereals do you like or dislike? Why?

     ii. Probe: Do you eat cereal at any time other than breakfast, or use it as an ingredient when cooking something else? Explain.

8. Using the following series of questions and probes, conduct a mini–focus group with four or five people who are not enrolled in your marketing research course. Summarize your findings.

   a. Describe a typical morning from the time you get out of bed until the time you leave the house and arrive at either work or school.

     i. Probe: Explain how breakfast fits into your morning routine.

     ii. Probe: Does your breakfast routine vary on those days you don't leave your residence in the morning for school or work? If so, how?

   b. What type of food do you eat for breakfast?

     i. Probe: Under what circumstances are you likely to eat breakfast out at a fast-food restaurant? At a sit-down restaurant?

   c. Tell me your thoughts about cereal.

     i. Probe: What cereals do you like or dislike? Why?

     ii. Probe: Do you eat cereal at any time other than breakfast, or use it as an ingredient when cooking something else? Explain.

9. Conduct a 30-minute in-depth interview on the topic of your choice. Submit a copy of your questions and probes, as well as a summary of your results.

10. Suppose you have been assigned the task of determining which brands are perceived as being trendy and "in" (e.g., "cool") by teenagers. Could a photo sort exercise be used for this purpose? Explain. What other type of qualitative research method could be used? Explain why.

CONTINUING CASE STUDY: LAKESIDE GRILL

The AMA student team held a focus group at the university in a meeting room that had a two-way mirror along one side of the room. Lakeside Grill owner Mr. Zito supplied free beverages and appetizers to the participants and observed from behind the mirror along with the members of the student project group. The focus group was moderated by one of the college professors with experience in focus group research, and was assisted by Brooke, one of the student team members. Prior to the focus group, the team composed the following interview questions:

1. How often do you eat at a dine-in restaurant?

2. What are some of the dine-in restaurants you have patronized in the last two weeks?

3. Suppose you were going to eat out tonight. How would you decide on the restaurant?

4. What criteria are important in selecting a restaurant?

   Probe → What is the one most important thing? Why?

(Continued)

(Continued)

5. In terms of the food, what is the most important to you? Quality, variety, something else?

6. What about service? How important is it?

    Probe → What constitutes good service? What constitutes bad service?

7. Let's go back to some of the restaurants you have mentioned. How many have been to [pick a restaurant that several have already mentioned, but not Lakeside Grill]? Tell me about your experience.

    Probe → What did you like? What did you not like? Why?

8. OK, let's talk about another restaurant, Lakeside Grill. How many have been there? Tell me about the last time you were there.

    Probe → What did you like? What did you not like? Why?

9. Let's think about a restaurant that you have patronized, but for some reason have never gone back. What happened?

    Probe → Why have you never gone back?

10. OK, let's think about one of your favorite restaurants. One that you really enjoy going to. Why is it your favorite? What makes it different?

11. Let's suppose that your significant other or someone close to you said, "You know, let's eat out tonight. What about going to Lakeside Grill or [pick a restaurant that has been mentioned by several people]?" Which would you pick?

    Probe → Why?

12. As we close our focus group, is there anything you would like to add to our discussion about eating at dine-in restaurants?

The local Chamber of Commerce assisted the group in locating participants for the focus group. An e-mail was sent to the chamber's membership asking the recipients at each business to pass the e-mail invitation to participate on to their employees. The e-mail contained a link to a qualifying questionnaire that asked for demographic information and a qualifying question that listed 20 local restaurants that were randomly selected each time a different person logged on to the online questionnaire. For each restaurant, participants were asked if they had eaten at the restaurant and, if so, approximately when was the last time. From the 42 replies received, 10 were selected randomly.

While Brooke assisted with the focus group, Alexa and another marketing faculty member conducted four in-depth interviews. To provide consistency, the same set of questions used in the focus group was also used for the in-depth interviews.

Since the Chamber of Commerce had received 42 replies to its e-mail, Juan decided to utilize a sentence completion exercise with the 28 individuals who were not selected for the focus group or for the in-depth interviews. The 28 individuals were sent an e-mail and asked to go to a survey website to complete the exercise. Detailed instructions were given before they began. The following sentence completion exercise was developed with the help of the other group members:

- Lakeside Grill is _____
- My favorite place to eat seafood is _____
- People who eat at Lakeside Grill are _____
- The service at Lakeside Grill is _____
- The food at Lakeside Grill is _____
- Eating out is _____
- The restaurant that is most like Lakeside Grill is _____
- Lakeside Grill's menu is _____
- The reason I eat at Lakeside Grill is _____
- I would eat at Lakeside Grill more often if _____
- If Lakeside Grill was a person, I would describe it as _____

Critique Questions:

1. Evaluate the list of questions and the sequence in which they are used for the focus group. What changes would you suggest? Does the list allow for a free flow of information?

2. Critique the process the group used to obtain focus group participants—what did the students do well, and what did they do poorly? How could it be improved?

3. Is selecting participants randomly the best process, or should some type of approach be used to ensure gender, age, income, and ethnic diversity?

4. From the 42 replies, 7 had never eaten at Lakeside Grill. Should these be eliminated from the pool of potential focus group participants? Why or why not?

5. Should the same questions be used for the focus group as for the in-depth interviews? Why or why not?

6. Evaluate the sentence completion exercise the group designed. Which statements should the group eliminate? Why? What additional statements should be added? Should the order in which these statements are presented be changed, and if so, how?

7. Evaluate Juan's decision to contact the 28 remaining individuals from the Chamber of Commerce via an e-mail request for the sentence completion exercise.

8. What are the pros and cons of conducting the sentence completion exercise online?

MARKETING RESEARCH PORTFOLIO

The research portfolio mini-case for Chapter 4 combines the task of conducting secondary research with the development of topics and questions suitable for online in-depth interviews. It can be used as an alternative to the research portfolio case presented in Chapter 3, and reinforces the fact that secondary data should be conducted prior to implementing primary research.

Students are first asked to select and conduct external secondary research either on certificate training programs or executive MBA programs. The information gathered by students should form the basis for their recommendations regarding the topics to be addressed in the online in-depth interview. Students will also be responsible for developing a series of questions that would be posted to the discussion board, as well as probing questions designed to elicit more information.

STUDENT STUDY SITE

Visit the Student Study Site at www.sagepub.com/clowess to access the following additional materials:

- eFlashcards
- Web Quizzes
- SAGE Journal Articles
- Web Resources

CHAPTER 5

Observation Research

LEARNING OBJECTIVES

After reading this chapter, you should be able to

1. Identify the conditions for observation research.
2. Describe the dimensions of observation research.
3. Discuss the various human observation methods.
4. Describe the various online observation methods.
5. Elaborate on how mechanical devices can be used for observation research.

INTRODUCTION

The previous chapter highlighted qualitative methods of conducting research. Rather than investigate subconscious thoughts, ideas, and beliefs, researchers may choose to study actual behavior. The idea behind this approach is that the ultimate goal of marketing is to influence actions, primarily purchases. Thus, rather than study what people think, it is sometimes better to just observe their actions in the marketplace.

This chapter will present three primary methods of observation: human observation, mechanical observation, and online observation. Human observation involves people watching people. Mechanical observation uses various devices to track human actions and behavior. Online observation utilizes web metrics and other online tracking devices to map human movement on the web and within a particular website.

To illustrate the last method of observation, consider the pharmaceutical companies that are now investing millions of dollars in direct-to-consumer advertising. The objective is to encourage patients to ask their physicians about specific brands of medicines. A critical component of this advertising strategy is the drugs' websites and encouraging patients to visit those sites for additional information. To determine how successful the advertising is at driving consumers to websites, one of the metrics that can be used is the average number of page views per visit. Figure 5.1 highlights this online metric for seven newly marketed drugs. Notice that, on the average, visitors to the Herceptin site visit 7.92 pages. That is in sharp contrast to the Lipitor website where visitors only visit an average of 2.10 pages.[1]

Figure 5.1 Pages Visited on Prescription Drug Websites

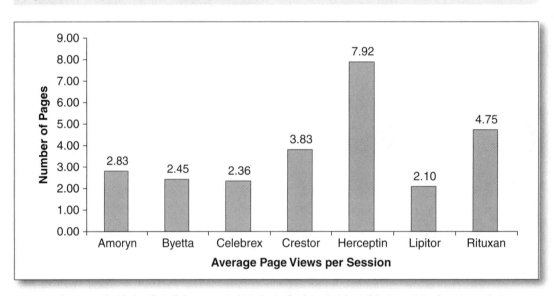

Source: Author-created with data from "Pharmaceutical Marketing," *Ad Age Insights,* White Paper (October 17, 2011), p. 10.

OBSERVATION RESEARCH CONDITIONS

■ Learning Objective 5.1: Identify the conditions for observation research.

Baby animals learn from watching adult animals. Children learn from watching adults and other children. Considerable learning occurs from simply observing the actions of human beings as well as animals, and even objects such as a car engine or an airplane in flight. It is not surprising then that marketing researchers use observation as a means of collecting data. Within the context of marketing research, **observation research** is defined as the systematic process of recording the behaviors or the results of behaviors of people, objects, and occurrences.

Observation research can be used to collect data about behaviors and results of behaviors. It cannot be used to explain consumers' motivations, attitudes, or reasoning behind the behaviors. At the same time, while respondents can lie or just not reveal their inner thoughts on a survey or in focus groups, deceit is less likely when actual actions can be recorded via observation research. Individuals may say that sex in advertising does not impact them at all, but eye-tracking devices or brain waves may indicate otherwise, as well as products that are actually purchased. While understanding motivations, attitudes, and thoughts is important to marketers, equally important are the actions of consumers. Thinking about purchasing a product or even liking a particular brand does not generate revenue. Only the actual purchase of the product produces sales.

Figure 5.2 highlights conditions where observation research can be used to collect data. First, the action or behavior must be observable, or the results (such as product packages thrown in the trash) must be observable. Individuals shopping in a mall or examining a point-of-purchase display are observable. So are the facial expressions and verbal

- Action or behavior is observable or results are observable
- Action or behavior must be repetitive or frequent
- Action or behavior must be of short duration

comments made to employees in a retail store. The number of visits to a micro-website listed on an advertisement can be measured. However, what occurs in the privacy of a home is typically not observable; nor could marketers ethically or legally observe behavior in store dressing rooms.

The second condition for observation research is that the behavior or action must be repetitive or frequent in nature. Observing pedestrians walking down the street to see how many look at a store display or stop and read a sign is repetitive in nature and occurs frequently enough to produce usable results. However, observing how many times a particular individual looks at new cars on a car dealer lot or showroom during nonbusiness hours before coming to talk to a salesperson is difficult because the actions are not frequent and repetitive. The individual may look more than once, but it may be several weeks apart.

Actions or behaviors need to be of a short duration. Observing a consumer's browser and mouse movements on a company website is of short duration and can be easily measured. So can the reactions of children to a new toy. But, more difficult would be the changes in how children play with a toy over a year or the impact of a new over-the-counter drug to reduce the signs of aging on skin. Shorter-duration behaviors are necessary in order to complete research projects in a timely manner and to minimize the cost of conducting the research.

DIMENSIONS OF OBSERVATION RESEARCH

■ Learning Objective 5.2: Describe the dimensions of observation research.

In using observation research, marketers have a number of options created by the various dimensions of the research procedure. Figure 5.3 identifies five dimensions that must be considered. Each dimension has its own set of advantages and disadvantages. The best approach is dependent on the objectives of the research and the types of decisions management must make. The quality of data needed and the budget available will also impact the choice of observation method.

Natural Versus Contrived

Researchers can observe consumers in a natural setting or in a contrived situation. With **natural setting observation,** individuals are observed in their natural environment. They may or may not know they are being observed. With **contrived setting observation,** individuals are studied in a controlled setting or in a laboratory. With this approach, subjects know they are being observed and have agreed to participate in the research study.

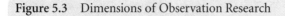

Figure 5.3   Dimensions of Observation Research

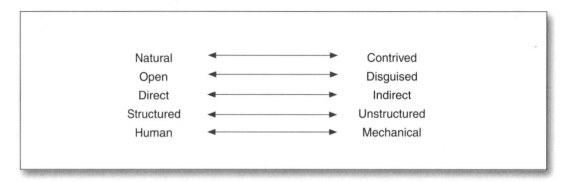

A company such as Hallmark could use a natural-setting approach to observe how customers use an in-store kiosk to create a personalized greeting card. A fast-food restaurant could watch customers' reactions to a new menu display board, condiment station, or point-of-purchase display. The primary advantage of using a natural setting is that researchers do not interfere with customers and thus observations are natural reactions. Even if consumers know they are being watched, they will still tend to act more naturally than they may in a laboratory or contrived setting.

The major disadvantage is that researchers must wait until the behavior occurs. Also, other factors may impact the consumer's behavior. For example, if researchers are measuring the amount of time customers at a fast-food restaurant look at the menu display before making a decision, a friend walking in may distract the customer, and they spend time talking. It would then be difficult to know exactly how long the customer examined the menu before making a decision because he or she may look at it several times in the process of carrying on a conversation with the other person.

To control for such extraneous variables impacting, or confounding, the results, researchers can use a contrived environment. An approach used by consumer packaged goods manufacturers is simulated supermarkets. Researchers can observe consumers as they interact with the supermarket, displays, and other items placed in the simulated store. Recently, Frito-Lay created a 15,000-square-foot facility to study how different merchandising tactics influence shopper behavior, particularly impulse purchasing. According to Rob Clancy, then group manager of consumer strategy and insights with Frito-Lay North America, "The key thing we struggled with in the past was how shoppers would react when they were actually in that environment. You can observe them in stores, but this was the first time we could do it on our own. We could create whatever we wanted to. We could change the merchandising, the product, or whatever we wanted."[2]

An alternative to using a physical facility or lab is conducting the research online using computer simulations and virtual displays or virtual reality store simulations. While the participant knows he or she is being studied, researchers have the advantage of being able to control the setting to prevent extraneous variables. In a natural setting, extraneous variables such as competitive coupon offerings, in-store circulars, and other factors can complicate the consumer's decision-making process and potentially interfere with accomplishing the research purpose. Such factors can be controlled in both simulated and virtual environments.

Firms such as Vision Critical (www.visioncritical.com) offer clients the opportunity to test product packaging, product pricing, shelf placement, in-store signage, and point-of-purchase displays. Researchers can also manipulate specific variables in virtual shopping and note the impact of these changes on shopping behavior. Because researchers carefully design the environment, data can be collected faster and at a potentially lower cost. Virtual reality shopping research via the Internet is becoming increasingly popular due to lower costs, especially for new product tests that might otherwise cost millions in a test market study. By comparison, virtual reality store simulations may cost anywhere from $30,000 to $1 million. Technological enhancements resulting in higher-quality simulations and greater emphasis on in-store marketing tactics have also influenced the popularity of virtual reality simulations.[3]

The primary disadvantage of a contrived environment is that it is artificial. Participants may act differently than they would in a natural setting. As a result, the results may not be applicable to real-world situations. But, this may not be a significant problem depending on the research purpose. Often it is used as a precursor to a quantitative study or to more fully understand the results obtained from a previously conducted quantitative study.

Open Versus Disguised

In **open observation** (or undisguised observation), individuals know they are being observed. In the Hallmark kiosk example, the researcher would ask the customer for permission to observe and then encourage the individual to interact with the kiosk as he or she normally would. The same may be true of an observation study undertaken in a fast-food restaurant, except in that setting the customer may not know exactly what the researcher is observing, just that he or she is being watched. This approach may help encourage the customer to act normally and not be affected by the researcher's presence, though some individuals may alter their behavior or choices specifically because they know they are being watched. An alternative for open observation in the retail and service sector is to inform customers as they enter the facility that researchers are observing customers, and encourage them to go ahead and shop as they normally would. Unless researchers walk around in a suit with a clipboard, customers may not notice the researchers and quickly forget they are being observed.

With the **disguised observation** approach, participants do not know they are being observed. This can be done through video cameras, one-way mirrors, electronic measures such as website cookies, or even human observers who look and act like another customer or perhaps one of the employees. The major advantage of the disguised approach is that the participants' behaviors are not affected by knowledge of being observed. They also are not affected by the physical presence of a researcher. Having a researcher standing close to customers using a kiosk may impact how they use it, make them more nervous, or even cause them to use it in a way they believe the researcher wants.

A major disadvantage of the disguised observation approach is that researchers cannot gather any demographic or additional information about the participants. While they can see the person's gender and may be able to approximate the individual's age or race, that is about all they know about the individual. If the open observation method is used, the researcher can request demographic information from each of the participants. Additional information could even be gathered that might relate to the study. For example, with the

With disguised observation shoppers do not know they are being observed.

fast-food study the researcher could find out what other fast-food restaurants participants have visited, how often they visit the one being studied, and even what other menu items they have purchased in the past.

Direct Versus Indirect

Most observation research is **direct observation,** which involves researchers watching participants as the behavior is taking place. This approach allows researchers to observe not only the behavior, but also any words spoken and even body language. **Indirect observation** involves observing the results of consumer actions rather than the action itself. Online observations often fall into this category since the research examines the results of the behavior rather than actually watching the behavior itself. The same would be true for using point-of-sale data to measure the impact of an endcap at a retail store.

Unstructured Versus Structured

Unstructured observation research involves researchers watching participants and recording behaviors they feel are relevant to the study being conducted. Observers have considerable latitude and freedom on what to record and how it is recorded. As such, the data are subjective in nature. This research method is better suited for exploratory research where the research problem is not clearly understood. Unstructured observation can provide information as to what the problem may be, which can later be framed as a hypothesis and tested using quantitative research methods.

The primary advantage of unstructured observation lies in the freedom to observe and record whatever data the researcher believes to be important. Essentially, the researcher can note anything that is relevant or may appear to be relevant. For exploratory studies, this advantage can be instrumental in understanding problems a company or brand may be facing.

The disadvantage is that not all relevant behaviors may be recorded, or adequately categorized, because the observer is watching too much to be able to notice fine details. This problem would especially surface if more than one individual was being observed simultaneously. It could even occur when only one person is being observed if that person is with other individuals. Furthermore, when multiple observers are involved in the same study, each observer may actually judge different behaviors as important. Thus, behaviors deemed important by one observer may be ignored entirely by another.

With **structured observation research** the problem has been sufficiently defined, which allows researchers to know beforehand what behaviors they can expect and even the various categories or options within each behavior to be tracked. Data collection usually involves the use of a checklist form, which tells the researcher exactly which actions should be recorded. All other behaviors are ignored. Structured observations work well with descriptive research studies because researchers have specific objectives they want to accomplish and may even have hypotheses related to the behaviors expected.

Referring back to the fast-food example, with structured observation the researcher would have the menu categories listed on his or her data collection form and would check the one that is ordered. There could be a place to record the number of seconds or minutes the customer looked at the menu board or special display, the time it took for the counter worker to greet the customer, or whatever else is being studied. The researcher could even record the number of times the customer looks away, then back at the menu, which may indicate indecisiveness. With structured observation, the checklist form is prepared in advance, and the researcher simply checks off or records the behaviors under study.

As observation research often relies upon multiple individuals to collect data, structured observation studies offer the advantage of being more objective, which increases the reliability of the findings. Less bias is introduced since the researcher checks or records behaviors that have been specified prior to the undertaking the observation research. Each observer is not placed in the position of deciding what is and is not important enough to record. In many cases this allows for comparisons and parametric analysis procedures since it produces more objective quantitative-type data.

Human Versus Mechanical

The last dimension that differentiates observation methods is whether the observation is undertaken by humans or some type of mechanical device. Humans have the advantage of being able to observe another person's entire repertoire of behaviors from actions to body language to words spoken. Significant data could be missed if a mechanical device were used. However, that ability to fully observe could also result in failure to accurately notice various behaviors if the actions occur too rapidly or the researcher is distracted by another person, the environment, or even the subject's actions that are not part of the study. In addition, human observation tends to be subjective in nature, which may be OK for exploratory research but would not be as appropriate for more quantitative-type studies, unless a structured observation method was also used.

Mechanical devices used in observation research can vary from scanner data at retail stores to web tracking data to eye-tracking devices. A major advantage of mechanical devices is data accuracy. Unless the machine is malfunctioning or out of proper calibration, it will measure the phenomena being studied accurately. Imagine the difficulty that a human observer might have in counting the number of vehicles traveling through an intersection during rush hour.

Human observation allows a researcher to observe a person's entire repertoire of behaviors.

Mechanical traffic counters aren't subject to fatigue or other factors that may detract from a human observer's accuracy, and can easily be used 24 hours a day. On the other hand, additional behaviors that may provide valuable information can be missed since the machine is programmed to measure a specific set of often limited behaviors or results of behaviors.

OVERVIEW OF OBSERVATION RESEARCH

Observing actual behavior is often more accurate than data obtained from surveys that ask people to report what they did. A scanner record of customer purchases will be more accurate than asking consumers what they purchased on their last trip to the store as consumers often have difficulty recalling information. There may be no intention of being deceptive or untruthful. They may not have paid attention to their purchases, or they may simply have forgotten. This is particularly true for shopping trips involving the purchase of routine items or those in which many items were purchased. Furthermore, the likelihood of forgetting increases as the time between the study and the shopping trip lengthens.

Similarly, watching how long a customer looks at various brands of packaged goods will be more accurate than asking individuals how much time they spent examining the available brands. This fact is particularly important for customer service studies, as participants almost universally overestimate the amount of time they spend waiting to be seated, or acknowledged by a server, for instance.

Another factor must also be considered. Sometimes survey participants may be reluctant to share specific information related to particular types of purchases or behaviors. For instance, in a study about gambling, individuals may not want to admit they gamble or go to casinos. If they do, they will almost always underestimate the amount of money gambled in order not to look bad in front of the researcher, or appear to be a habitual gambler.

Children are often studied through observation research methods not only due to accuracy issues, but also because children lack reasoning skills, and are typically not capable of answering questions on a survey. A 3-year-old child cannot explain why he or she chose a particular toy, or played with a toy in a certain manner. But, through observation, researchers can often attain this type of information.

The primary disadvantage of observation research is that only observed behaviors or observed characteristics can be reported. Researchers are not able to discern motives, attitudes, beliefs, or feelings of the participants. They may learn what the person did, but not why the individual acted in a particular manner. This is a serious disadvantage, as understanding why certain actions were taken is often more important than learning what was done. In addition, current actions may not be a good predictor of future behaviors. Thus, observation research may be part of a larger research study that also includes focus groups, in-depth interviews, or some other type of qualitative research technique that is helpful in understanding consumer motivations.

A second disadvantage is that only public or observable behaviors or results of behaviors can be researched. What occurs in private, before or after the observation session, cannot be seen. The before actions may be important in explaining a participant's behavior. For instance, researchers watching individuals shop for clothes may notice that a number of participants spend little time walking around the store and looking at clothes. They find the item quickly and then move to the checkout. The reason for such quick purchase behavior may be that they were on the Internet and had already picked out the clothes they wanted, or they may have been at the store the day before and later decided to come back and purchase the items.

As shown in Figure 5.4, observation research can be divided into three main categories: human observation, online observation, and mechanical observation. While these three often overlap in terms of characteristics and design, for the sake of studying observation research it is useful to think along these three categories.

Figure 5.4   Observation Research Categories

HUMAN OBSERVATION

Human observation provides the opportunity to watch the behaviors of people. A tremendous amount of learning can take place from careful observation. Figure 5.5 identifies the four primary methods researchers use for human observation.

■ Learning Objective 5.3: Discuss the various human observation methods.

In-Person Observation

Using humans to observe consumers is a form of ethnographic research discussed later in this chapter. The difference is that with traditional "in-person" observation research, no interaction takes place with the participants during the observation period. The researcher may ask for demographic and other types of information at the conclusion of the observation, but does not interact with the person being studied in any way as the behavior being recorded takes place.

Moniek Buijzen and Patti Valkenburg used human observation to study parent-child communication as it related to purchasing behavior.[4] They wanted to observe the actual

Figure 5.5   Human Observation Research Techniques

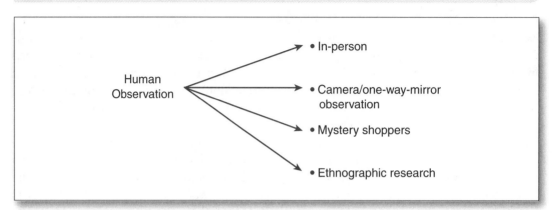

communication as it occurred in real, everyday life and not rely on memory recall. They also felt that direct observation would be more accurate in determining how parents and children communicated during the purchase process in the retail store.

The study was conducted in 10 supermarkets and 5 toy stores in the Netherlands. A total of 269 parent-child dyads were observed. The children ranged from ages of less than a year to 12 years old. The parent-child dyad was observed from the time they entered the store until after they passed through the checkout having made their purchase. The researchers wrote down all of the behaviors they observed as well as the interactions between the children and parents. After the purchase was made and the individuals were leaving the store, the researchers approached them and told them about the study and asked for their permission to use the data they had just collected through observation. The parent was then asked to fill out a questionnaire that asked for demographic information, the child's television viewing habits, and family communication patterns.

While the researchers were free to write down any behavior or interaction they thought was relevant, the researchers had also developed a coding sheet that required looking for specific behaviors and interactions. By structuring the majority of the observation cues in advance, they were more diligent in looking for specific behaviors and communication interactions. This allowed the two researchers to work independently observing different parent-child dyads, yet producing data that were compatible.

In the study by Buijzen and Valkenburg, the observers did not identify themselves until the parents had left the store. By using this procedure, the individuals acted normally since they had no idea someone was watching them. Some researchers feel this approach borders on being unethical and an invasion of privacy, so they stop individuals prior to entering the store to solicit permission to watch them. The danger of this approach is that the individuals being watched may not act normally, but act instead in a way they think the researcher wants. However, companies that use this approach say that most consumers forget within minutes they are being watched and soon act normally.

Camera/One-Way-Mirror Observation

In situations where in-person observation may bias the behaviors of the participants, researchers can observe via cameras or one-way mirrors. Most retail stores have security cameras that can be used for observation research. Participants can be studied as they interact with special displays or shop for merchandise. The primary concern with using cameras is that it may be considered an invasion of privacy. However, if consumers are asked for permission, then the rationale for using cameras is defeated.

Research firms such as Envirosell (www.envirosell.com) use both in-person and video observations to capture store traffic patterns as well as other behaviors. One advantage of videotaping activity in-store is that researchers have multiple opportunities to observe and code behavior, as the tape can be reviewed multiple times. Envirosell also offers a hybrid form of research called the "Videotaped Shop-Along Interview." This methodology combines open observation of willing subjects with attitudinal research gained via personal interviews. Researchers accompany a shopper throughout the store, videotaping his or her activities, and interviewing the shopper about his or her behaviors as they take place. For example, when a subject picks up an item, the interviewer may ask, "What are you looking at on the package?"

One-way mirrors are often used for observing children. Companies, such as Mattel, have playrooms where children can play with toys. Researchers can watch from behind glass to see which toys the children choose and how they play with them. Having an adult in the room taking notes may change the children's behavior. Children often want to please adults or let them see what they are doing, so the actions may not be natural without the use of a one-way mirror.

Mystery Shoppers

Mystery shoppers are used by a large number of companies, and are particularly popular in the retail and restaurant industries. Mystery shoppers are typically used to evaluate customer service. But, mystery shoppers can also be used to investigate the appearance of a retail store, the cleanliness of a facility, and other elements of business décor or customer amenities. Some

One-way mirrors are an effective way to watch children play with toys.

companies will have mystery shoppers visit the competition in order to make benchmark comparisons.

While companies strive to gather feedback from customers via 1-800 numbers, e-mail, or website comment forms, such feedback tends to be bipolar. The good customers are happy to talk about the great service, the great products, or the wonderful employees. The unhappy customers are often even more eager to be heard. Unfortunately, it is the group of consumers in between these two extremes that is usually not heard from, which is troubling as this group makes up the largest percentage of a firm's customer base. For this reason, mystery shoppers are used to provide a better gauge of how all customers see a firm.

According to Marshal Cohen of market research firm NPD Group, "It [using mystery shoppers] doesn't just help you understand how customers see the display of merchandise and determine the case of finding product; it can also measure employees' willingness to give help within the store. Is the shopper treated as a guest or the enemy? Are employees more interested in cleaning the store than they are in saying hello to the customer? Service is very much a part of the value equation today, and mystery shopping lets you gauge it more effectively than many other channels."[5]

While mystery shoppers are trained to observe and record whatever they see, they also typically use a structured, specific code sheet to record information. The code sheet is based on the company's operational standards and goals. For instance, a mystery shopper at a restaurant would note the time it takes to be seated, the time it takes the waiter to bring a menu or ask for a drink order, the time it takes to get the food, and the appearance of the food when it arrives. The shopper would also take notes on the waiter's appearance, demeanor, and quality of service. Other elements that may be recorded are type of music playing, loudness of music, and cleanliness of the facility. By posing as a customer, a mystery shopper is able to obtain very detailed information about a firm's operation. This information can be used for training programs, staff motivational programs, communication and sales strategies, and branch or site evaluations.

CiCi's Pizza needed concrete data to develop new policies and standards. The company used multiple methods of collecting data, one of which was mystery shoppers. Unlike management or customers, the mystery shopper had no vested interest in the performance evaluation of any location. The mystery shopping was conducted by Corporate Research International (CRI) of Findlay, Ohio. The mystery shoppers resembled typical guests, but were trained to assess specific corporate standards and expectations. Mystery shoppers were randomly assigned to various CiCi's locations and reported the data within 24 hours after visiting the CiCi's site. Through these data, CiCi's was able to gather information on how well the various locations were following corporate standards.[6]

Mystery shopping studies vary in complexity. Some studies involve minimal interaction with employees, while others are designed to test the depth and accuracy of employee knowledge. Mystery shopping does not have to be conducted in person at a physical facility. Datamonitor used mystery shopping to investigate how well banks with central offices in the United Kingdom handled customer inquiries. The researchers posed as prospective customers and contacted banks via the Internet, e-mail, and the telephone asking about various products and services. A total of 133 banks were contacted in 15 European countries. The results were startling to management. The mystery shopping research found that 93% of the inquiries were not treated as potential sales opportunities. Questions were answered, but no attempt was made to cross-sell any additional products. In 86% of the instances, no record was even made of the inquiry for future use or for follow-up. An astounding 28% were not even acknowledged and did not receive any type of response from a bank.[7]

Another component of mystery shopping programs is a competitive audit. With competitive audits, mystery shoppers visit competitors. It provides an opportunity to collect comparative data. A firm can see how well it performs in relation to its competitors. In addition, the data can serve as a benchmark against a company's own performance levels. The value in the data is that they are from the customer's perspective since the mystery shopper is posing as a customer. This type of mystery shopping provides more accurate information than would be obtained from interviewing actual customers from competing firms. Depending on the level of loyalty to the brand, customers of competing firms tend to be biased toward their favorite brands, which makes it difficult to objectively compare brands.

Ethnographic Research

Ethnographic research involves observing individuals in their natural settings using a combination of direct observation and video and/or audio recordings. Adopted from the field of anthropology, ethnographic research allows researchers to study individuals through observing their behaviors, emotions, and responses to the environment where they live. Instead of asking consumers how they use various products as part of a focus group, ethnographers can observe the products being used in their home and interact with individuals during the consumption process. Many researchers believe that people will be more open in their home than in a focus group facility, and that richer insights can be obtained regarding things such as how and where products are stored, and how consumers interact with packaging.[8]

Icon Health and Fitness decided to use ethnographic research to examine how consumers used treadmills for exercising. The researcher observed individuals using treadmills in their homes as well as in fitness centers. The company noticed that individuals came to the treadmill with a variety of personal items such as towels, water bottles, keys, cell phones, magazines, and books. They would search the floor for a place to put items or try to find something to put on the treadmill to hold their items, especially the magazines and books. It might be some old plastic piece, an old magazine rack, something that they could wedge or tie or hang onto the treadmill so they could read while walking. During the workout the individuals would slide the reading material to the side to see their time or read other measurements on the display. During a typical workout they would use the display panel for 5 minutes, but then use it as a magazine or book holder the remaining 25 minutes. Through observation and video recording of these sessions, the company realized it needed to redesign its treadmill so it would be able to accommodate how individuals used it.[9]

Ethnographic research can be used in a wide variety of situations. In addition to product design, it can be used to study how and when consumers use products. On-Site Research used ethnography to understand how consumers use technology in their homes. The company sent teams out to observe 150 Americans using technology in their homes. They found that dining rooms are rarely used for dining. Instead computers are moving into the dining room out of the home office, and additional technology is being added, such as television screens. One reason for this move is that Americans of all ages are multitasking, and while on the computer they also are watching TV. One family who had moved all of their computers to the living room said, "I want to be able to watch my shows, check my stocks, and do work on my computer. So I have had to move my computers into the area where my media center is, and that's the bar area." Another family explained they wanted to monitor their children's online activities, so having multiple technologies in one room made that possible.[10] Gaining this type of knowledge would have been very difficult using other types of research, but was relatively easy through ethnography.

Icon Health and Fitness used ethnography to study how individuals used treadmills.

Typically, ethnographic research involves the researcher working primarily from the background as an observer with little interaction with the consumer being studied. An alternative is to become engaged with the consumer and become his or her "instant" friend. This process may produce insights with the consumer talking about things he or she does and explaining the reason for behaviors. The concept behind this approach is that in addition to the observation, the ethnographic researcher is gaining valuable understandings of motivations through the trust and friendship that has been built.[11]

Traditional ethnographic research is quite time-consuming and very expensive. Rarely can researchers afford to study more than one or two geographic areas. A relatively new variation on ethnographic research combines video diaries and in-person interviews. Prescreened participants are sent video cameras with instructions or a checklist on what to film. For example, the instructions might read, "Please film the preparation and consumption of a typical weekday evening meal in your home. Please film the interior of your freezer, each shelf of your refrigerator, and any other storage area where food is kept." Completed videos are returned to the research firm for review. Follow-up interviews are conducted in person to uncover the reasons behind key behaviors identified by researchers who viewed the video.[12]

■ Learning
Objective 5.4:
Describe the
various online
observation
methods.

ONLINE OBSERVATION

With consumers spending more time online and making greater use of the Internet in the purchase decision process, it is important for marketing researchers to examine ways of studying online behavior. Online observation research offers a number of advantages and disadvantages,[13] as shown in Figure 5.6.

Because of the large number of people on the Internet, the number of potential participants for research studies is almost limitless. Many have higher levels of education and have been using the Internet for a number of years. This easier access to participants means costs are lower and collecting data is faster than with conventional human observation methods of research. Participants do not have to travel to a central site, a retail store, or another location. The same is true for the researchers. They can conduct the study from their office or company headquarters.

Computers leave a digital trail, so research can be conducted more accurately. Researchers can also go back and track data. They can use the computer to tally and track activities and movement on the Internet. The research is not dependent on humans carefully observing behavior and trying to accurately record everything that occurs, when it occurs. This digital trail also means there is greater flexibility in the types of research that can be conducted.

Figure 5.6   Advantages and Disadvantages of Online Observation

- Advantages
  - Access to large group of potential participants
  - Lower costs
  - Faster data collection
  - Digital trail
  - Greater flexibility in observation methods
- Disadvantages
  - Lack of auditory and visual cues
  - Lack of respondent authenticity
  - Rambling and unfocused content complicate task
  - Profile of online users may not be representative

On the downside, online researchers cannot see any visual cues, such as facial expressions and body language of the person at the computer. They cannot hear verbal tones or inflections. The same words can be written online by two individuals, yet have totally different meanings based on auditory cues or body language. It is not always easy to interpret what is meant by individuals from written communications.

Researchers cannot always be sure the individual on the Internet is who he or she purports to be. There is no way to authenticate identity. With anonymous observation, authentication is virtually impossible. Someone who appears to be an adult female may actually be an underage person or even a male.

Blogs, chat rooms, and even websites can provide valuable opportunities for online research, but may also contain considerable rambling and unfocused content. With a focus group or an interview, individuals can be kept on track. With human observations, participants tend to stay on task. That does not always occur online. Individuals tend to vent emotions, share ideas, and just share thoughts. Some may be of value; others may not. Researchers may have to sort out what is relevant and what is not.

Lastly, online users may not always be representative of the population. Low-income and undereducated individuals tend not to have computers and online access. If they do use a public-access computer at a library or another facility, the individuals are less likely to be part of chat rooms or blogs.

A major concern facing online observation research is the issue of privacy. Consumers are concerned that the technology companies have can track their movements and online activities. Congress and other government entities have discussed this issue and are considering legislation that may restrict what companies can and cannot do in terms of web tracking. Such legislation would have an impact on how online research is conducted, especially in situations where individuals are being studied without their knowledge.

Marketing researchers have a number of online observation research methods that can be used (see Figure 5.7). The best method will depend on the research problem and research objectives. It will also depend on the information that is needed and the location of those data on the web.

Social Media Monitoring

The rise in the popularity of social media has provided market researchers with an opportunity to study a wide variety of topics. Marketing researchers can observe online chatter, communications, and postings without participants ever knowing they are present, which allows them to capture real thoughts of individuals in natural online settings. Even in situations where researchers identify themselves, the online environment offers participants a high level of confidentiality, and they may not be identified at all. Participants often feel more comfortable sharing thoughts online than they do in focus groups or personal interviews.

In social media observation, researchers utilize a variety of online sources such as social media sites, Twitter, blogs, chat rooms, bulletin boards, newsgroups, and even websites. Most information will be written, but a number of blogs and websites will also contain videos. These videos can be as insightful as written material, but may be more difficult to interpret. The choice of online sources will depend on the research purpose and research questions being addressed. Locating postings about topics of interest may not be the researcher's greatest challenge. Devoting the time necessary to read through all of the postings and determining which are relevant is the largest drawback of this technique.

Unlike human observation, researchers can download text from the Internet and take more time to analyze what is written. The information is almost always asynchronous, except for live chat rooms. By downloading the textual information, researchers can use computer programs to locate key words. They can also pull out postings by a single individual and study changes in communication and/or behavior over time.

Researchers can study communication by, between, and among individuals. Actual behaviors cannot be seen, but can be inferred by written words. Nevertheless, actual behaviors may not always translate from intentions and communicated words. On the other side, however, typical observation research involves studying behaviors without the ability to understand

Figure 5.7   Online Observation Research Techniques

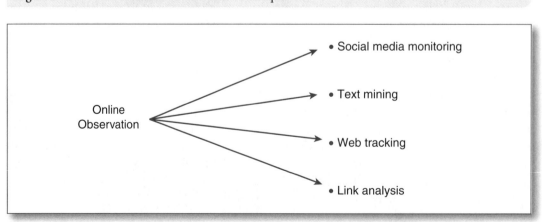

the thoughts, motivations, ideas, and feelings behind actions. With social media monitoring, these mental activities are evident. The challenge is being able to correctly infer the emotions and feelings that may be behind words that are written on a blog or on a social media website.

Social media research can be used in a number of ways by companies. It can be used for exploratory research to gain a better understanding of a particular topic or to investigate potential problems a company or brand may be facing. It is an excellent method of learning what consumers think about a brand and what they are telling others. While it is not a true assessment of word-of-mouth communications, it is a good gauge of what consumers are telling others about the brand. Social media research can be used in conjunction with descriptive research to provide a better understanding of particular findings and provide personal insights into thoughts and feelings of consumers.

Because of their large size and easy access, social media sites can be used as research samples. In addition to monitoring chatter, researchers can post questions on social media sites, on blogs, on Twitter, and in newsrooms. Responses come almost instantaneously. If the research is carefully crafted, important information can be gathered. But, it is important to remember that the sample being used is not likely to be representative of the population being studied. The results, therefore, are not likely to be applicable to the population as whole. Despite this disadvantage, using social media as a sample for marketing research can provide useful data.

During the last Super Bowl, Twitter was monitored to measure people's opinions and to rank the brands being advertised according to the Twitter chatter that was measured. The first step was to tally the number of tweets for each brand. A sentiment score was calculated by subtracting the number of negative tweets from the number of positive tweets, then dividing that result by the total number of tweets. To rank the brands the following formula was used:

(Positive tweets + neutral tweets − negative tweets) / total tweets for all brands = Rank

This type of data provides advertisers with an idea of what individuals who watched the Super Bowl thought about the ads. It also indicates how a particular brand's ads compared to other brands. Since the tweets occurred during and immediately after the game, it was a quick, easy, and inexpensive way to evaluate the impact of Super Bowl ads and to measure the buzz created by the ads.[14]

Text Mining

It is impossible for marketing managers to keep up with the huge volume of information now on the Internet. In addition to websites, brands and companies are being talked about on blogs, bulletin boards, Twitter, and social media sites. This information can be useful in making a number of marketing decisions.

For instance, Stephanie Hoppe, senior marketing director for 7-Eleven, knew the market for iced coffee was very competitive. Before making a decision on launching an iced coffee product, 7-Eleven wanted to investigate what was driving the demand. Digital Anthropology, text-mining software produced by Omicron Group, was used to mine conversations on blogs, Twitter, and social media sites to identify emotional aspects and reasons behind the demand. According to Hoppe, "It's not in a focus group setting so we were getting explicit and authentic data. It helped us create an effective campaign that was a little out of the norm for us in that it was sassy."[15]

Figure 5.8   Text-Mining Technologies

- Information extraction
- Topic tracking
- Summarization
- Clustering
- Duo-mining

Based on Weiguo Fan, Linda Wallace, Stephanie Rich, and Zhonju Zhang, "Tapping the Power of Text Mining," *Communications of the ACM*, Vol. 49, No. 9 (September 2006), pp. 77–82.

Computer and software technologies have recently been developed that allow advanced forms of text mining. Figure 5.8 identifies text-mining technologies that are now being used by marketing research firms.[16] While text mining is used in other disciplines, such as medicine, government, and education, the most promise is in the field of business. It is being used to research competitors and a firm's own customers, and to develop marketing and advertising strategies.

Most text-mining research begins with information extraction. **Information extraction** looks for predefined sequences in text through analyzing unstructured text and identifying key phrases and relationships. For example, when studying iced coffee, the software would look for text that would mention *iced coffee* and other key words such as *purchase, buy,* and *like*. The key to its use is defining the key words and phrases to be analyzed.

Topic tracking develops a user profile based on the documents a user views, then attempts to predict other documents that would be of interest. It is the same technology that is used by companies such as Amazon.com to recommend additional books based on the book searches a customer does or the books that are purchased. It can also utilize information from other customers on similar searches and purchases to make recommendations. In terms of marketing research, topic tracking can be used to monitor competitive actions and to monitor the Internet on specific marketing topics.

A more advanced technology is **summarization text mining,** which attempts to summarize long-text articles. It allows researchers to determine if an article is relevant to the topic being studied. It uses sentence analysis algorithms and key phrase words, such as *in conclusion*, to determine weight for sentences and then summarizes the material.

Clustering involves grouping similar documents together. The software looks for phrases or words or groups of words that are similar and puts them into groups or categories. A researcher can look at the clustering words that tie articles together and determine which clusters of articles are of value.

The future trend in text mining is to combine it with data mining in a single software analysis tool, knowing as **duo-mining.** This method of research is now being used by banks and credit card companies to better understand their customers. In addition to analyzing the financial data of a customer, the software will analyze call and e-mail logs associated with each customer. It can also reach into the Internet and locate web chatter, blogs, social media, and other places where customers may be talking. These text-mining analyses can be combined with financial data analysis to look at such things as spending patterns and best-customer profiles.

Web Tracking

Web tracking involves studying human actions and movement on the Internet. It can be performed using historical data generated by computer tracking software, or it can be observed live as it is happening. In both cases, the research can take place anonymously in the background without participants knowing it is occurring. This procedure prevents any potential changes in behavior due to the subject knowing he or she is being watched.

Web tracking observation research is valuable in assessing website traffic and the effectiveness of web content. Web tracking can be used to identify the page where individuals enter a website, the referring site visited directly before they entered the site, where they go and how long they stay on the site, and what they do. Even activities such as mousing over a button can be detected. Often researchers will begin with a specific action or result of the visit (e.g., adding an item to the online shopping cart) and track backward to see where individuals have been on the site, perhaps what drove the action, and how they entered the website. Researchers can even trace prior activity to see what other sites the individuals visited and if they used a search engine to initiate the process.

An extremely important research agenda for web tracking is to detect "leaky" or "drop-off" points. These are the places were web visitors leave a website. In addition to identifying the place where the person leaves, researchers are able to construct the clickstream that occurred prior to the person leaving. This type of research is valuable in identifying potential negative points in the website, though additional research may be required to learn why people abandoned their shopping cart or did not place an order.

Because of cookies that uniquely identify visitors to a website, it is possible to track the activities of individuals over time. This can be valuable especially in terms of discerning what drives various activities, such as making a purchase, signing up for a newsletter, or requesting additional information. One danger of tracking visitors over multiple visits is that the cookie is tied to a particular computer. It is possible that different members of the family may be using the computer, and thus the web tracking that is done may be confounded and not provide an accurate picture of a single individual. Alternatively, many households now have multiple computers, and some consumers shop online at lunch from work. Thus, it is equally possible that a given individual may initiate some activities on one computer, but finish the transaction on another.

As with human observation, web tracking research does not have to be disguised. Valuable information can be gained from recruiting individuals to participate in a study, then watching their online actions. Honda UK used this approach to better understand how consumers interact with a used-car website. Participants were recruited then given a single or set of online tasks to perform using their home computers. With software downloaded by the participants, researchers were able to watch them as they carried out the tasks on Honda's used-car website. Watching how participants carried out the tasks provided information to Honda UK on how to redesign the website to make it more user-friendly and meet the needs of customers.[17]

Link Analysis

To understand how researchers use link analysis in marketing research, it is helpful to first see how search engine firms use this technique. Link analysis is used by search engines as part of their algorithms to determine the organic listing of websites for searches. Most search engines use links to analyze the viability of websites for particular topics because it is harder to fake good links to a site than it is to fake key words at a particular site. Thus, to improve a company's organic listing to a particular search word, it is important to have links from other sites. But, quantity is not the key. Quality of links is also important. Search engines analyze key words at link sites to determine the fit and importance of various links.[18]

Consumers will often post links on blogs, on discussion boards, in chat rooms, and on websites. Link analysis examines these links to determine who is behind the link and why the link is posted. Someone who is willing to post a link to a brand or company website is in effect generating a positive word-of-mouth recommendation—although at times links are also provided by individuals who dislike a brand or company.

As with the other forms of observation research, link analysis needs to be tied to the research purpose and research questions. It is an effective means of exploratory research and can also provide some additional information to descriptive studies. A challenge with link analysis is to determine who exactly is behind the link posting and why it was posted. Such information may not be clear, especially if it is posted on a blog or other type of online open communication forum.

■ Learning Objective 5.5: Elaborate on how mechanical devices can be used for observation research.

MECHANICAL OBSERVATION

Marketing research can be conducted using some type of mechanical device, as shown in Figure 5.9. The most common mechanical forms of observation are market basket analysis, radio and television monitoring, and eye tracking. The newest technique, which is rapidly gaining adherents because of its potential, is cognitive neuroscience. The physiological measures are still being used, but less frequently as the accuracy of the other methods increases.

Figure 5.9   Mechanical Observation Research Techniques

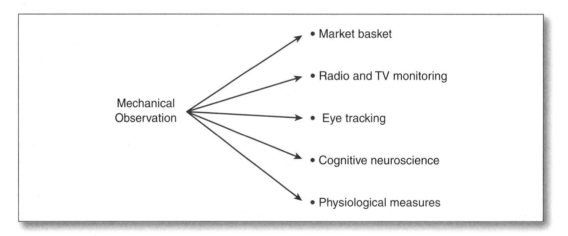

Market Basket Analysis

Using scanner-generated data, **market basket analysis** involves analysis and modeling of items purchased by households on shopping trips to retail stores. The research typically utilizes frequent shopping cards to tie purchases to demographic profiles. Market basket analysis can be used in a number of ways by various members of the distribution channel to enhance marketing decisions.

Market basket analysis begins by analyzing the various items that are purchased by a consumer on shopping trips. Through this analysis, companies can identify:

- How often consumers purchase a product
- How much of it they purchase per trip

- Where they purchase the item
- What other products they purchase with the item
- Whether they used coupons in the purchase of the item

This information can be used for cross-promotions by a manufacturer or in-store product placement by a retailer. It makes sense if two items are typically purchased together to place the items in close proximity to encourage purchasing both products. The importance of promotions, such as coupons, in the purchase decision process can also be determined, particularly when household behaviors are tracked over time.

Because most basket analysis uses loyalty cards, researchers can tie demographic profiles to the basket analysis. Retail stores, casinos, and other businesses that use electronic loyalty cards require that consumers fill out an application to secure the card. Demographic and psychographic data are collected in this manner. When these data are combined with behavioral data, marketers can identify the consumer profile of users of a product. Regular users can be identified and compared to occasional users to see if there is a difference in their profiles. Marketers can also see if there is a difference in the basket composition of occasional versus heavy or regular users of a product.

Researchers can look for differences in the content of a market basket between stores, regions, and types of retailers. These differences may be just as important as commonalities. As market basket analysis will not typically tell researchers why there is a difference, further research may be needed. If it is a difference between retail stores within the same retail chain, for instance, store audits or observation research may be needed to uncover what is causing the difference. It could be the types of customers at each store, the appearance of the stores, or even the type of customer service being offered to customers.

Radio and Television Monitoring

Syndicated data research firms such as Arbitron and Nielsen historically relied upon research subjects to self-report their radio station listening and television viewing habits via media "diaries." Diary data were used by Arbitron to compile ratings of radio stations in various markets; similarly, data provided by Nielsen families historically served as the basis of television program ratings, and ultimately influenced the advertising prices charged to marketers. Concerns about the accuracy of the data have led both firms to implement mechanical observation methods on a limited basis.

In 2010, Arbitron finished rolling out its Portable People Meter (PPM™) to the top 50 U.S. markets.[19] The PPM is about the size of a cell phone, and is worn by consumers throughout the day. The device recognizes unique identification codes that are embedded in broadcast transmissions that are "heard" by the consumer in the home, the car, the workplace, or other locations. At the end of the day, the consumer syncs the PPM to its base station, which sends the data collected by the device to the household hub. The hub collects the codes from all of the base stations corresponding to family members' PPMs, and transmits the data back to Arbitron.[20] This methodology allows Arbitron to issue reports on a monthly basis, as opposed to the previous quarterly delivery system in use with diary methods.

Nielsen uses a similar system to garner television ratings from its national panel to supplement the 1.6 million paper diaries collected during sweep periods. A boxlike device—Nielsen's version of the People Meter—is attached to each television in the home for the purpose of observing and recording the length of viewing time that each channel is watched. The unit senses as people enter and exit the room. Lights flash on the meter unit, reminding family members to click their assigned "personal" button on the people meter remote to ensure that their gender and age are matched to their viewing habits. Local People Meters (LPMs) are used to measure ratings specifically within the top 25 markets nationwide.[21]

While many believe that mechanical observation methods of assessing television ratings offer substantial improvement over the diary method, critics contend that accuracy is still a problem. Unlike Arbitron's passive PPM, Nielsen's device requires that panel members actively "sign in and out" when entering and exiting the room. Too often, panel members become bored and stop participating, forget to sign in or out, or refuse to do so, especially when leaving the room for only a few minutes.

Eye Tracking

Eye-tracking analysis involves analyzing the movement of the eye. Most eye tracking uses infrared technology to show where the pupil is by reflecting off of the eye's retina. The sensors can be placed in a computer monitor, headgear that is worn by the participant, or a special eyeglass apparatus. Eye-tracking research is being used to study advertising in various forms such as print, television, outdoor, and Internet. It is used to study package design and in-store signage and shelving.

Eye-tracking studies are beneficial because they show the spots in an advertisement or a marketing piece where people focus. For television ads, it will show this focus through sequential scenes in the advertisement. When the results from multiple consumers are placed on a perceptual-type map, it gives advertisers a good picture of what individuals notice in an ad, potential hot spots that attract a lot of attention, and areas that tend to be ignored.

In eye-tracking studies, it is important to realize that catching a person's attention may not always be positive. A negative visceral reaction can grab attention, but not enhance the selling of a product or a consumer's attitude toward the advertisement being studied. Thus, with eye-tracking research it is always a good idea to include other types of observation, quantitative research, or qualitative research.

Seattle-based research firm Global Market Insite used eye tracking to examine website usability and online advertising. Some of the major findings of the research include[22]:

- Ads in the top and left portion of a website receive the most eye fixations. Ads in the right column are seen less, and ads at the bottom are seldom noticed.
- On the average, text-based ads were seen for about seven seconds compared to two seconds for visual or display ads.
- Larger ads and images hold eye attention longer than smaller ads or images.
- Clean, clear faces in an image attract more eye fixations.
- Shorter paragraphs received more attention than longer paragraphs.
- When first accessing a website, eyes fixate in the upper left of the page first and then will move down going from left to right.

Prudential uses eye-tracking research regularly to examine its website, its advertising, and even its forms. One form that was analyzed by eye tracking dealt with an endowment policy. Eye tracking found that people focused most on the area of the form that mentioned the sum of money and not on the instructions for returning the form for further processing. The form was modified, and the result was that it saved Prudential about $130,000 in telephone calls and follow-up mailings.[23]

Cognitive Neuroscience

The most recent and scientifically advanced form of mechanical observation research is **cognitive neuroscience,** which is a brain-image measurement process that tracks the flow and movement of electrical currents in the brain. Cognitive neuroscience was used to verify a preference for Coke or Pepsi. According to Justine Meaux, a neuroscientist, "Preference has measurable correlates in the brain; you can see it." Another neuroscientist, Richard Silberstein from Australia, was able to show through brain activity that successful ads tend to generate higher levels of emotional engagement and long-term memory coding.[24]

In terms of marketing research, cognitive neuroscience is being used in advertising to measure consumer reactions to various advertisements. With certain ads, such as ones that may contain sexually provocative material, individuals may not be honest about how it affects them using standard survey testing procedures. Members of a focus group may cover up their true feelings and reactions to the ad by stating that the ad is sexist and inappropriate. This is more likely to occur if someone in the focus group has already expressed a negative opinion of the ad, or if individuals detect the moderator feels that way. The negative stigma attached to sex in advertising often affects self-reported reactions. Such reactions cannot be faked using cognitive neuroscience. Many marketing researchers believe physiological tests that measure body reactions or brain activity are more accurate than self-report tests, because physiological reactions cannot be easily faked.[25]

Researchers can use cognitive neuroscience to track brain waves as an individual watches a television advertisement.

Companies such as EmSense, NeuroFocus, OTX, and Sands Research are using portable devices that measure both brain waves and biologic data. This research methodology was used by Coca-Cola to select ads to run on the Super Bowl from a dozen that were produced. EmSense measured brain waves and monitored breathing, heart rate, blinking of the eyes, and skin temperature of participants as they watched the ads. Through these physiological measurements, researchers were able to determine which ads to use during the Super Bowl and how to modify the ads to produce higher levels of emotions.[26]

Frito-Lay used neuroscience research to test product packaging. The company discovered that matte beige bags of potato chips picturing potatoes and other healthier ingredients did not trigger guilt feelings as much as shiny potato chip bags. Ann Mukherjee, Frito-Lay's chief marketing officer, said, "Brain-imaging tests can be more accurate than focus groups." A Cheetos advertisement that was rejected by a focus group for its "mean-spirited" content was tested using neuroscience. The neuroscience test showed women loved the commercial.[27]

The power of cognitive neuroscience is that it reveals physiological reactions to a message. It shows where brain activity occurs and to a certain degree the level of that activity. It can identify times when a test subject becomes enthralled with a marketing message. It also indicates when the person merely focuses on the logo, an attractive person, or some other component of the commercial. The methodology identifies positive and negative emotions and the intensity of the emotions by the amount of neurons that are firing. This research method allows marketers to better understand how marketing messages are being processed, where they are processed in the brain, and how the individual reacts to an ad or marketing piece. Although still in its infancy, cognitive neuroscience offers great potential for evaluating advertising and marketing.

Physiological Measures

Cognitive neuroscience and eye-tracking techniques are replacing, or supplementing, long-standing physiological measures such as voice-pitch analysis, the galvanometer, and the pupilometer. **Voice-pitch analysis** focuses on subtle, involuntary physiological changes and anomalies in respondents' voice as these changes are believed to reflect various emotions, stress, truth, or deception. Channel M2's Voice Analysis service uses specialized software to analyze responses to open-ended questions either live or via recording. Each subject answers several warm-up questions that the software uses for calibration purposes, and as a point of comparison when analyzing responses to open-ended questions. Voice analysis can serve as a supplemental technique when researching brands, customer satisfaction, customer motives, consumers' evaluations of package designs, or responses to advertisements, and may also be helpful in analyzing ethnographic information. According to Channel M2, its technology produces accuracy levels of 90% or greater in the identification of emotions.[28]

Galvanometers measure changes in the electrical resistance in the skin in response to a subject's exposure to stimuli, such as a television commercial. The resulting galvanic skin responses (GSRs) were originally deemed important to marketers because GSR is strongly linked to emotions. Unfortunately, in and of itself, the GSR measure is of limited use to researchers, as these measures cannot identify what emotion has been stimulated or changed.

Pupilometers measure pupil dilation, as cognitive activity will cause pupils to change in response to visual stimuli when other factors are held constant. While the device can note changes in the size of the pupil, similar to the galvanometer, the pupilometer cannot identify the reason behind pupil changes, although it is able to identify rather accurately if the emotion is positive or negative. Anger or negative emotion typically causes the pupil to get smaller, while positive or pleasurable scenes cause the pupil to get larger.

Global Concerns

Compared to other forms of marketing research, observation research can be used in global markets with fewer problems. The method of observation may be altered somewhat due to local customs and culture, but the overall techniques can be used. Human observation, online observation, and mechanical observation are all viable methods of research throughout the world. As with other forms of research, hiring a local native of the country to assist in the planning and execution of observation reach is important. Major problems can be easily prevented.

Open human observation in some cultures may yield biased results since individuals may alter their behavior in an effort to please the observing researcher. In some countries, such as those in the Middle East, the gender of the observer is very important. It would be unacceptable for a male researcher to observe or interact with a female consumer without the husband's presence. In fact, observing females in general is more difficult because of their role within the culture.

For observation research to be successful, researchers must understand the culture being studied. The demand for ethnographic research of Hispanics has recently increased as more companies focus marketing efforts on this ethnic group. But, to be successful, researcher companies need to understand the importance of the family to Hispanics and allow extra time to become acquainted with the Hispanic subjects. It is important to be conscious of their customs and beliefs. In general, Hispanics are less forthcoming with information than the general population. They also tend to be more positive about companies or brands. Again, these differences highlight the need for having someone who fully understands the culture of the group being studied.[29]

 STATISTICS REVIEW

Cross-tabulations are used to describe the relationship between two variables when one or more of these variables is a classification variable. Classification variables contain category data, meaning that the numbers that represent information in a data set are only used to group together respondents who share a particular characteristic. Examples are gender (male and female), race (Caucasian, African American, and Hispanic), brands (Ford, Chevrolet, Toyota, Nissan, Dodge, etc.), and day of the week (Sunday through Saturday).

In examining the impact of various types of display racks for blue jeans, cross-tabulation analyses could provide insight into the relationship between the type of display table or rack and demographic variables such as gender, age, and income. The most basic form of cross-tabulation analysis shows data counts. Thus, cross-tabs combine frequency tables of two or more variables when displaying data. As shown in Figure 5.10, the dependent variable of interest (in this case type of rack/table) is displayed in rows, and the classification variable of gender is displayed in columns. The output shows a total of 72 people were observed, 25 males and 47 females. Of the 47 females, 25 stopped at the display table first, 11 stopped at the sales rack first, 6 went to the featured brand rack first, and 5 went to the regular jeans rack first.

Figure 5.10   Cross-tabulation of "First Rack/Display Approached" and Gender

		Gender		
		Male	Female	Total
First rack/display approached	Display Table	6	25	31
	Sales Rack	5	11	16
	Featured Brand Rack	7	6	13
	Regular Jeans Rack/Area	7	5	12
Total		25	47	72

(Continued)

(Continued)

Usually, marketers find it more beneficial to display data as percentages, rather than counts in the cross-tabulation. Figure 5.11 includes the percentages of males and females and which table or rack they went to first. It is normally easier to make comparisons when using percentages rather than raw numbers. For instance, when examining the raw numbers for the featured brand rack, 7 males went there first compared to 6 females. It would appear there is not much of a difference. But, when looking at the percent, 28% of the males went to the featured brand rack first compared to only 12.8% of the females. Rather than putting these data into a table, a researcher may want to show it graphically, as shown in Figure 5.12.

Figure 5.11   Cross-tabulation of "First Rack/Display Approached" and Gender Showing Counts and Percentages

			Gender		Total
			Male	Female	
First rack/display approached	Display Table	Count	6	25	31
		% Within Gender	24.0%	53.2%	43.1%
	Sales Rack	Count	5	11	16
		% Within Gender	20.0%	23.4%	22.2%
	Featured Brand Rack	Count	7	6	13
		% Within Gender	28.0%	12.8%	18.1%
	Regular Jeans Rack/Area	Count	7	5	12
		% Within Gender	28.0%	10.6%	16.7%
Total		Count	25	47	72
		% Within Gender	100.0%	100.0%	100.0%

Note that cross-tabulations cannot be used to prove causality. The only statistical test appropriate for cross-tabulation data is the chi-square, which tests the goodness of fit of the observed data with that which would be expected under the null hypothesis of no difference. SPSS provides for a chi-square test. Figure 5.13 shows the chi-square test for the cross-tabulation of the first rack/display approached and the respondent's gender.

The Pearson Chi-Square value is 8.364 with 3 degrees of freedom. The significance level (or p-value) is .039. If the statistical test was being conducted at the 95% confidence level, then any p-value below .05 would indicate a rejection of the null hypothesis. Recall from Chapter 2 that a null hypothesis would state there is "no significant differences in which table/rack is approached first based on the respondent's gender." Since the p-value is .039, which is less than the .05 test p-value, the null hypothesis would be rejected. Therefore, we can assume there is a significant difference between males and females in which table/rack is approached first upon entering the store. The chi-square value does not tell us where the difference is, but tells us only that there is a difference. Examination of the table in Figure 5.11 and the graph in Figure 5.12 would show that females

Figure 5.12 Graphical Presentation of the "First Rack/Display Approached" by Gender

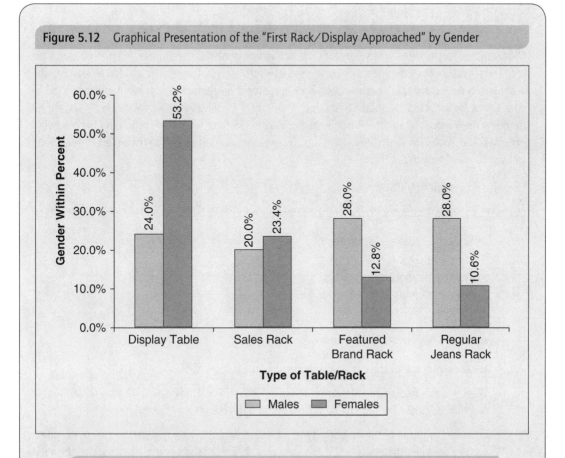

Figure 5.13 Chi-Square Test Results

	Value	df	Asymp. Sig. (2-sided)
Pearson Chi-Square	8.364	3	.039
Likelihood Ratio	8.400	3	.038
Linear-by-Linear Association	7.933	1	.005
N of Valid Cases	72		

are more likely to go to the display first than males and less likely to go to the featured brand rack or the regular brand rack first.

Another way to look at the p-value is to think about it as a percent, or probability. In this case, the probability of the researcher being wrong in stating there is a difference between males and females in which table they approached first is only 3.9%. Alternatively, the researcher is 96.1% (100 – 3.8) confident there is a significant difference based on gender.

DEALING WITH DATA

Observation data are often well suited for cross-tabulation analysis. The data set "Chapter 05 Dealing with Data" was generated at a retail clothing store by an observer. The retailer wanted to examine the difference between a display table, a sales rack, a featured brand rack, and a regular jeans rack. The data that were collected are shown in the file "Chapter 05 Dealing with Data Variables." It is helpful to review the various data that were collected and the SPSS data file before beginning the following exercises. The data files and step-by-step instructions for using SPSS are available on the textbook website (www.sagepub.com/clowess).

Exercise 1: Frequency Counts

Using SPSS, generate frequency counts for all of the following variables that deal with the display table.

- Did customer stop at display table?
  - Time at display table
  - Number of jeans examined
  - Number of jeans tried on
  - Number of jeans purchased

Based on the output, answer the following questions.

1. What percentage of the customers stopped at the *display table?*

2. What was the median and mode for each of the four subvariables: *time at display table, number of jeans examined, number of jeans tried on,* and *number of jeans purchased?*

3. Create a bar graph of the *number of jeans tried on* from the *display table.* Be sure to provide a graph title, label the x-axis and y-axis, and provide value labels above the bars. Use the valid percent for the graph.

Exercise 2: Means

Using SPSS, calculate the mean for each of the following variables under each of the types of racks or displays. That is, obtain a mean for *number of jeans examined* under the *display table* variable, the *sales rack* variable, the *featured brand rack* variable, and the *regular jeans rack* variable. Do the same for *number of jeans tried on* and *number of jeans purchased.*

- Number of jeans examined
- Number of jeans tried on
- Number of jeans purchased

Use the SPSS output file to create three different bar graphs. For the first bar graph, graph the means obtained for *number of jeans examined* for each of the four types of racks or displays. Create graphs for each of the other two variables. Based on the graphs and output, answer the following questions.

1. At which table or display do customers appear to examine the most jeans?

2. At which table or display do customers appear to try on the most jeans?

3. At which table or display do customers appear to purchase the most jeans?

Exercise 3: Compare First Table Approached to
the Respondent's Age

An important question posed by the retailer was "Did the respondent's age impact what table/rack
the customer approached first?" Perform a cross-tabulation using the SPSS variable *first rack/display
approached* for the row variable and *age* as the column variable. In order to better understand the
results, ask for column percentages and run the chi-square test. Based on the chi-square results at
a 95% confidence level, did the respondent's age make any difference on which table/rack was
approached first? If it did, explain what differences you observed.

SUMMARY

Objective 1: Identify the conditions for observation research.

Observation research is useful when researchers are interested in tracking behaviors, but cannot
be used to explain why people behave the way they do. Observation research is only appropriate
when the behavior or action (1) is observable, or the results are observable; (2) occurs frequently
or is repetitive in nature; and (3) is of short duration.

Objective 2: Describe the dimensions of observation research.

Approaches to observation research vary across five key dimensions, each of which has its distinct advantages or disadvantages. Observation research can (1) occur in a natural or contrived
setting; (2) be openly conducted or disguised so subjects are unaware; (3) directly observe the
behavior, or instead use indirect observation to assess the results of the behavior; (4) rely on the
observer to record important actions in an unstructured manner, or require that all observers
look for the same behavior in a structured fashion; and (5) use humans or machines to observe
the behavior as it takes place.

Objective 3: Discuss the various human observation methods.

Human observation of behavior may take place in-person, through one-way mirrors, or
remotely, by viewing surveillance video footage. Mystery shoppers are frequently used in the
service industries to gauge employee knowledge, friendliness, and a host of other factors. While
most mystery shopping occurs in-person, mystery shopping telephone calls are also useful.
Ethnographic researchers watch consumers in their home or whatever setting is natural for
the use of the product under study, and supplement observation data with in-depth interviews
designed to reveal deeper consumer insights.

Objective 4: Describe the various online observation methods.

Social media monitoring of tweets, blogs, online community postings, and other venues is one of the fastest-growing forms of online observation. Text mining of online conversations is a specific form of social media monitoring, but can also involve other online postings. Computer software can track web traffic patterns within websites, as well as between sites, while link analysis assists marketers in determining where links are being posted and by whom.

Objective 5: Elaborate on how mechanical devices can be used for observation research.

Scanner data provide the mechanism for advanced market basket studies that tie consumer purchases to shopper card data files. Arbitron and Nielsen use metering technology as a supplement to their traditional diary methods of audience measurement. Mechanical devices also measure physiological responses to stimuli via eye tracking, cognitive neuroscience, and voice-pitch analysis. Cognitive neuroscience and eye-tracking technology are replacing traditional physiological measures, such as the galvanometer and pupilometer.

GLOSSARY OF KEY TERMS

Clustering: form of text mining that groups similar documents together

Cognitive neuroscience: brain-image measurement process that tracks the flow and movement of electrical currents in the brain

Contrived setting observation: individuals are studied in a controlled or laboratory setting where they know they are being observed

Direct observation: researchers watch participants as the behavior takes place

Disguised observation: participants do not know they are being observed

Duo-mining: software analysis tool combining text mining with data mining analysis

Ethnographic research: observing individuals in their natural settings using a combination of direct observation and video and/or audio recordings

Eye-tracking analysis: infrared technology that shows where the pupil is tracking by reflecting off of the eye's retina

Galvanometer: measures changes in the electric resistance in the skin that results from a subject's exposure to stimuli

Indirect observation: observing the results of consumer actions rather than the action itself

Information extraction: form of text mining that looks for predefined sequences in text through analyzing unstructured text and identifying key phrases and relationships

Market basket analysis: analysis and modeling of items purchased by households on shopping trips

Natural setting observation: individuals are observed in their natural environment where they may or may not know they are being observed

Observation research: systematic process of recording the behaviors or the results of behaviors of people, objects, and occurrences

Open (or undisguised) observation: individuals know they are being observed

Pupilometer: measures the degree of pupil dilation that occurs in response to stimuli

Structured observation research: researchers know beforehand what behaviors to expect and even the various categories or options within each behavior that should be recorded

Summarization text mining: uses sentence analysis algorithms and key phrase words to determine if an article is relevant to the topic being studied

Topic tracking: form of text mining that develops a user profile based on the documents a user views, then attempts to predict other documents that would be of interest

Unstructured observation research: Researchers watch participants and record behaviors they feel are relevant to the study being conducted

Voice-pitch analysis: focuses on subtle, involuntary physiological changes and anomalies in respondents' voice to reflect various emotions, stress, truth, or deception

CRITICAL THINKING EXERCISES

1. Access the Nielsen website at http://en-us.nielsen.com. Under the "Measurement" tab, access the information about television measurement. Summarize the information that is presented. Would you be willing to serve as a Nielsen ratings subject? Why or why not?

2. Access the Nielsen website at http://en-us.nielsen.com. Under the "Measurement" tab, access information about one of the items listed other than television. Summarize the information that is presented. How could a marketer use this information to market his or her company or product?

3. Why are diary methods of recording radio listening behavior less accurate than information collected via the Portable People Meter? Explain.

4. Access Vision Critical at www.visioncritical.com. Under "Vision Critical University," locate two areas that look interesting. Read the material found and watch any videos that are posted. Write a summary of your findings.

5. Del Monte has commissioned an observation research study for the purpose of better understanding the actions undertaken by consumers when buying canned fruit. Explain how you would implement the study. Would you recommend a virtual shopping observation study, or a study conducted within the actual grocery store? Should human or mechanical observers be used? Should the observation be open or disguised? Structured or unstructured? Justify your decisions.

6. While Twitter is commonly used to build relationships with business clients, it can also be used as a research tool to track conversations about brands, companies, ads, and celebrity endorsers in real time. Visit http://search.twitter.com and search for tweets on (1) a company that has recently made news and (2) a well-advertised brand that has recently introduced a new advertising campaign. Review a minimum of 50 tweets for each. Summarize the relevant findings.

7. Visit www.google.com/analytics. What type of measurement tools are available through Google Analytics? How could a florist located in Arkansas, who sells in the retail store, over the phone, and online, use this information? What types of information can be tracked?

8. A consumer goods manufacturer is interested in learning more about meal preparation in the homes of dual-career couples. Specific topics to be investigated include factors influencing the choice and usage of fresh ingredients versus those that are frozen, canned, or freeze dried; the relative importance of nutrition and healthy food factors versus convenience; and the situations or factors that influence whether meals are cooked and consumed at home, picked up from restaurants and eaten at home, or eaten out at restaurants. What type of observation research study would you recommend? Why? List the specific actions, behaviors, questions, and so on that you would investigate, and how this information would be recorded.

9. LeapFrog, a manufacturer of educational toys, is interested in seeing how 5- to 8-year-old children react to and play with several new toy prototypes. What type of observation research technique would you recommend? Why?

10. Design a mystery shopper observation form to evaluate facility and signage aspects of a retail store environment. Do not include observations related to employees, such as customer service interactions.

CONTINUING CASE STUDY: LAKESIDE GRILL

The student team of Alexa, Brooke, Zach, Juan, and Destiny decided to use human observation to study Lakeside Grill. The following decisions were made in regard to the dimensions:

- Natural setting
- Disguised format
- Direct observation
- Structured observation form
- Human observers

Each member of the team participated in the observation. Since Lakeside Grill was open for two meals, each student observed a lunch meal and a dinner meal over a two-week period. "Because the employees had seen all of us in there," Zach explained, "we got a copy of Mr. Zito's financial report and would pretend to be working on tabulating it. We thought if the waitstaff knew we were observing that it would alter their behavior." Before conducting the research, the group developed the observation form shown below.

Lakeside Grill Observation Research Form

Observer name: _____ Date: _____

1. Meal: Lunch _____ Dinner _____

2. Time of arrival: _____

Upon arrival

3. Number of tables with customers: _____

4. Number of total customers: _____

5. Number of waitstaff: _____

6. Table number where you sat: _____

Observation (**Complete for each table you observe**)

7. Number of people at the table: _____

8. Time between being seated and server greeting: _____

9. Demeanor of waitperson: unhappy ____|____|____|____|____|____ cheerful

10. Demeanor of customers: unhappy ____|____|____|____|____|____ cheerful

11. Time between taking drink order and bringing drinks: _____

12. Was drink order correct? Yes:_____ No:_____

13. If no, why not? _____

14. Did customers place order when drinks arrived? Yes: _____ No:_____

15. If no, time between waitstaff leaving and returning to take order: _____

16. Time between placing food order and arrival of food: _____

17. Number of times waitstaff checked on customers between order and arrival of food: _____

18. Was food prepared correctly? Yes: _____ No:_____

19. If no, what was wrong? _____

20. Response of waitstaff: _____

21. Number of times waitstaff checked on customers from delivering food to leaving ticket: _____

22. Time between customers finishing food and arrival of ticket: _____

23. Time between customers leaving payment and waiter picking up ticket: _____

24. Time between picking up payment and return of ticket: _____

25. Relevant comments made by customers during the time waitstaff was present.

26. Relevant comments made by customers when waitstaff was not present.

(Continued)

(Continued)

Critique Questions:

1. For this study, do you think the dimensions of the human observation were the best choice? Why or why not? Explain.

2. Consider Zach's comment, "we got a copy of Mr. Zito's financial report and would pretend to be working on tabulating it. We thought if the waitstaff knew we were observing that it would alter their behavior." Do you agree with this statement? Why or why not?

3. Do you think it is likely the waitstaff figured out they were being observed anyway? Why or why not? How could the group use human observation and be sure that their observation did not change the waitstaff behavior?

4. Although the group obtained some good observation data, the students do not know anything about the customers and whether they were satisfied. Brooke had suggested waiting for customers to finish the meal, then going to their table, introducing themselves, explaining their research project, and asking the customers questions about the food, service, and level of satisfaction. Is this a good idea or not? What are the pros and cons?

5. What about using mystery shoppers? What would have been the pros and cons? How would the students obtain mystery shoppers since they had an extremely small budget for the research project?

6. Critique the observation form. What suggestions would you make?

MARKETING RESEARCH PORTFOLIO

The mini-case for Chapter 5 instructs students to use the five dimensions of observation research as a basis for developing and justifying multiple observation research studies for a bank. Key aspects to be studied include employee-customer interactions conducted face-to-face, by phone, and over the web; product knowledge assessment of specific services offered by the bank; and customer usage of the bank's website and online banking services. The assignment instructions and case information can be found at www.sagepub.com/clowess.

STUDENT STUDY SITE

Visit the Student Study Site at www.sagepub.com/clowess to access the following additional materials:

- eFlashcards
- Web Quizzes
- SAGE Journal Articles
- Web Resources

CHAPTER 6

Survey Research

INTRODUCTION

Social media consultants from companies such as the Marketing Zen Group often hear clients discuss the need to be on Facebook and other social media sites. Many companies feel the need to post on Twitter. But, as Shama Kabani of the Marketing Zen Group has advised, "You need a strategy and a purpose. Just being there won't get you more customers."[1] With all of this hype surrounding social media, Econsultancy surveyed 1,400 individuals in the United States about their use of social media. Although it seems like everyone is using social media, the survey revealed that 37% of consumers do not use social networking at all, and those consumers who actually become a fan or friend of a company or brand are still in the minority. When respondents were asked how they prefer notification of sales and special deals, the largest percentage, 42%, said they prefer e-mail notification, and 33% said they prefer a phone call. Only 3% said they prefer seeing this type of information on a social media site, such as Facebook, and only 1% chose Twitter. Figure 6.1 shows the complete results of this survey question.[2]

Figure 6.1   What is the Best Way to Receive Ads for Sales and Specials?

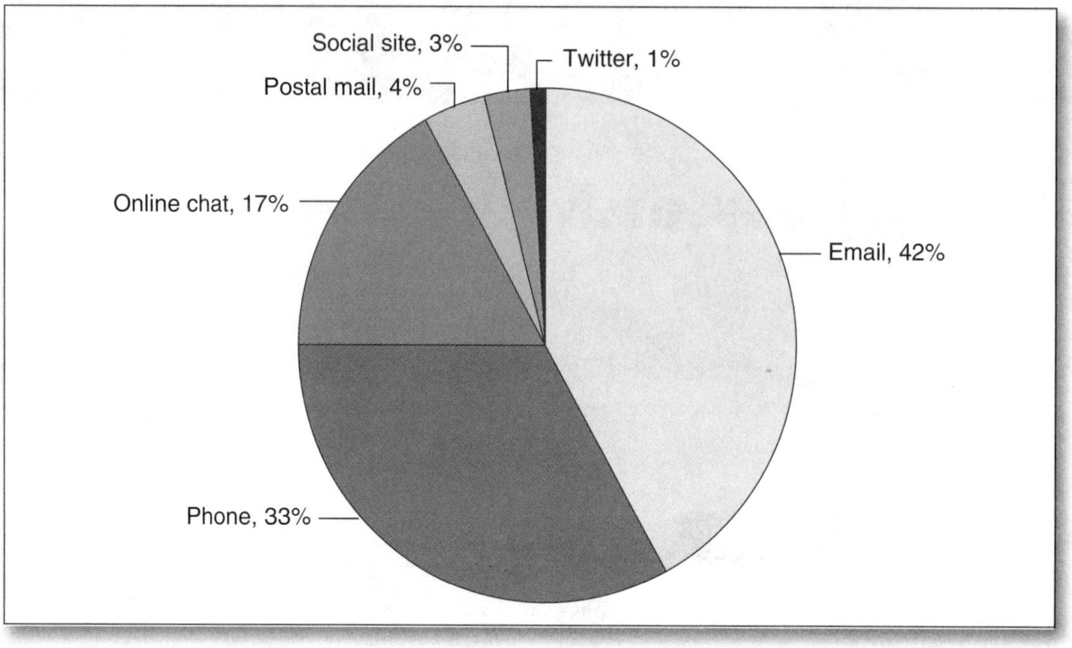

Source: Author-created with data from Diana Alison, "Email Beats Social Media for Grabbing Consumers' Attention," *Information-Week,* July 30, 2010, www.informationweek.com/story/showArticle.jhtml?articleID=226400046 (accessed July 28, 2012).

For companies wanting to make a decision on the best method of contacting their customers about sales and special deals, the findings of this study are extremely valuable. Econsultancy collected other pertinent information in addition to what was reported in Figure 6.1. The survey examined how consumers use customer reviews, the impact such reviews have on their purchases, and how consumers feel about e-mails and other methods companies use to keep in touch with customers. This type of information is useful to marketing managers developing marketing programs, especially if they want to utilize social media.

This chapter presents information about survey research and various data collection methods such as telephone, mail, personal interview, and online. Types of errors, and how errors can be measured and minimized in survey research, are highlighted. The chapter concludes with a discussion of the criteria marketing managers need to consider in selecting the appropriate survey method.

— ∞ —

WHY USE SURVEY RESEARCH

■ Learning Objective 6.1: Discuss why survey research is used.

Survey research remains one of the most popular forms of marketing research. Through surveys companies can gather the information that is needed to make good business decisions. Survey research tends to be used for descriptive purposes. The results can be used to describe situations, target markets, and other phenomena. Survey research is an effective means of providing answers to the "W questions"—who, when, where, what, and why. The information is very important in making optimal marketing decisions because it tends to be quantitative in nature. While qualitative questions may be part of survey research, it tends to be a minor component and used more for exploration purposes or in the early stages of questionnaire development as part of the survey instrument pretest.

Over recent years the methods of collecting survey information have changed with the increased usage of digital media and digital communications. While the traditional methods of telephone and mail data collection are still used, they are being quickly replaced by cheaper and faster methods of surveying individuals and businesses.

Get a reason to get up
Hug

SURVEY RESEARCH TIME FRAME

■ Learning Objective 6.2: Identify the two time frames for survey research.

Survey research can be conducted using two different time frames: cross-sectional and longitudinal. Cross-sectional studies are conducted at a single point in time and thus provide a snapshot of the subject or topic being studied at that particular time. The study by Econsultancy on the use of social media was a cross-sectional study. Most marketing research survey studies are cross-sectional in nature as marketing mangers seek information to solve a particular problem or to develop specific marketing strategies.

An alternative to cross-sectional studies is a longitudinal study, which is a study that asks the same questions at multiple points in time. Typically, a longitudinal study will involve retaining the same respondents, although it is not absolutely necessary. Longitudinal studies are an excellent method of identifying and tracking trends, as a key purpose of longitudinal studies is to examine the change or continuity of responses over time. If the same respondents are used, then it is easier to verify whether a behavior or response has actually changed. If different respondents are used, then there is a possibility that any differences found may be due to differences in the sample respondents (old vs. new) rather than due to true changes in behaviors, attitudes, opinions, or whatever is being measured.

Cost too much.

The Gallup polls that are used during political seasons are a type of longitudinal study. Gallup polls tend to measure voter reactions to issues and candidates through the weeks leading up to the election. Different respondents are identified for each polling period, but comparisons are made since the Gallup organization uses very strict sampling procedures.

Within marketing, tracking studies are a type of longitudinal study. Marketing research firms such as Nielsen IAG use tracking studies to measure the impact of advertising and branding campaigns over time. Through the data collected, Nielsen IAG is able to determine when an advertising campaign takes off or connects with the intended audience, or, conversely, when it begins to wear out and needs to be changed.

Another source for longitudinal studies is the consumer panel; that is, individuals who have been recruited by a marketing research firm to participate in various studies over time. Nielsen uses a consumer panel to determine television viewership and, thus, the Nielsen television ratings. Other firms, such as Experian Simmons, use consumer panels to study consumer behavior and consumer attitudes. An advantage of using these panels is that the research firm is not always seeking new study participants each time a study is conducted. But, since the studies ask the same questions and seek the same information, using a panel allows companies like Experian Simmons to measure changes that occur over time. These data can be examined by marketing researchers to identify trends and in some cases predict the future or at least theorize about what may happen in the future.

■ Learning
Objective 6.3:
Describe the
various types
of errors that
can occur with
survey research.

TYPES OF ERRORS IN SURVEY RESEARCH

The goal of marketing research is to collect useful, accurate information that is free of errors. In reality, however, that is extremely unlikely. Errors will occur that can impact the quality of the data gathered. As shown in Figure 6.2, research errors can be divided into two broad groups: random error and systematic error. Random error results from chance variation between the subjects surveyed and the population, or group, they are chosen to represent. As will be discussed in Chapter 8 on sampling, researchers can reduce random error simply by increasing the sample size. Generally speaking, the more people who are surveyed, the less impact random error will have on the data. The only way to eliminate random error entirely is to survey every single member of the population. For the vast majority of studies, this would be impossible.

Figure 6.2   Types of Errors

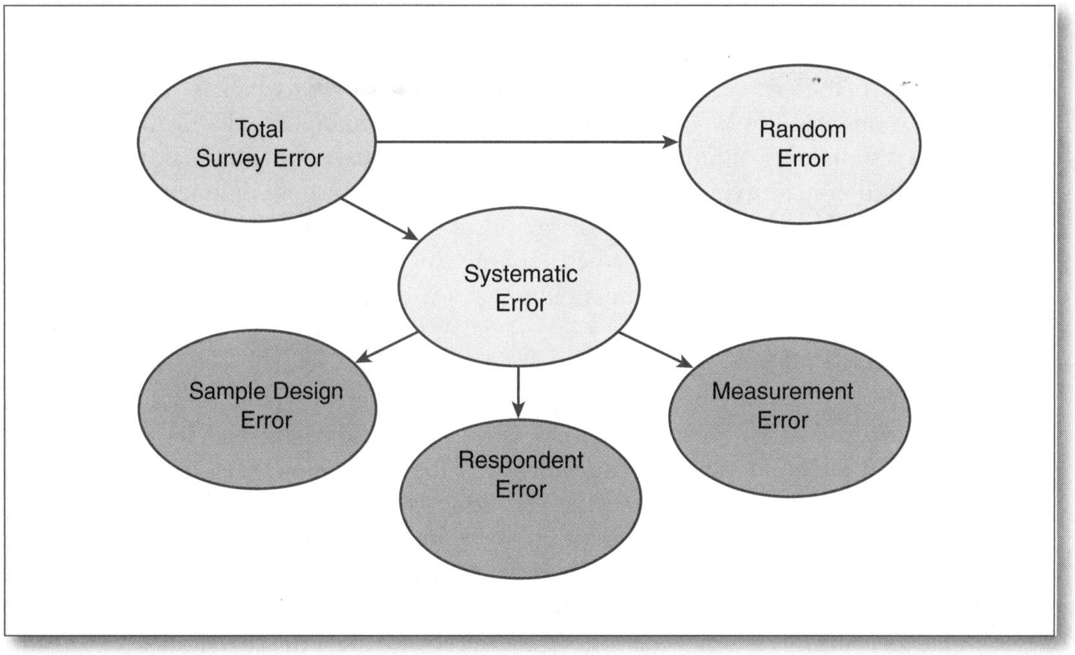

Systematic error results from a mistake or problem in the research design or the research process. For example, suppose on a questionnaire respondents were asked if they were:

1. Single

2. Married

3. Single, but living with someone

Option 3 is unclear. Does it mean living with a roommate or a significant other, or does it mean living with one's family? Thus, when a 3 is recorded in the data, the researcher has no idea which situation best fits the respondent. In this case, increasing the sample size may compound the systematic error that has resulted from a problem in the measurement process.

While reducing random error is important, systematic error is of greater concern. By careful attention to the research design and the research process, the occurrence of systematic error can be significantly reduced. As was shown in Figure 6.2, there are three broad categories of systematic errors: sample design error, respondent error, and measurement error.

Sample Design Error

It is rare that in a research study every person in the study population can be surveyed, so marketing researchers will typically select, or "sample," individuals within the population to complete the survey. In this process several different types of systematic error may occur. These include population specification error, frame error, and selection error (see Figure 6.3).

The initial step in the sample design process is to specify the population, or group of subjects, that is to be studied. Most populations are composed of individuals, though sometimes stores or companies may form the population. **Population specification error** occurs when the population is incorrectly identified. Suppose a company defines the population as all users of Facebook. The study is conducted. Then, in meeting with the client, the client mentions that the population should have been

Figure 6.3   Sample Design Error

- Population specification error
- Frame error
- Selection error

all individuals who use social media. The population was incorrectly specified, as individuals who use social media sites other than Facebook did not participate in the study. This creates error in the data if the responses of the individuals who were missed were different from the responses of Facebook users. A study flawed in this manner would yield results that cannot be extrapolated, or generalized, to the larger category of social media users. It would be applicable to Facebook users only. Minimizing this error requires that the researcher sit down with the client and carefully explain the specific characteristics that describe the population that will be studied, as well as any characteristics that will cause potential respondents to be excluded from the study. It is also helpful if the researcher puts things into perspective for the client. This particular population specification could have been avoided had the researcher said, "So you understand that any results we gather from this study can only be inferred to Facebook users, and not to users of LinkedIn, Twitter, or other social media?"

If the population is defined correctly, then a second type of error that can occur relates to the choice of sample frame. The **sample frame** is the list of population members or elements from which the sample will be selected. **Frame error** occurs when an incorrect or incomplete sample frame is used to choose study participants. Suppose a bank such as JPMorgan Chase wanted to survey its customers and defined the population as all of its customers. Now suppose that all credit card and/or checking account holders were used as the sample frame. Has frame error occurred? Almost certainly! Chase most likely has customers who have neither type of account, but instead maintain a savings account, a Christmas club account, a home equity line of credit, a vehicle loan, or a home mortgage with the bank. Frame error occurs because these individuals did not have the opportunity to participate in the study because they were not even included in the sample frame. The results of the study could be misleading if the opinions of those who were not part of the sample frame differ significantly from the opinions of those who were. Minimizing frame error requires diligence on the part of the researcher. As will be discussed in Chapter 8, building a sample frame often requires seeking, combining, and purging for duplication multiple lists related to the population in question.

The last type of sample design error occurs as part of the selection process. Selection error occurs when the sampling procedures are not followed or are not clearly defined. Suppose interviewers in using a mall intercept approach are told to interview every 14th person. If an interviewer counts off and sees a 14th person, but decides that individual looks too busy, and instead just skips to the 15th or 16th person, then selection error has occurred. This error becomes worse if the interviewer continues self-selecting respondents based on looks or what is perceived to be willingness to participate based on appearance. Minimizing this type of selection error requires that interviewers be properly trained and supervised in the field. Careless mistakes, in which an individual simply miscounts, can only be avoided by proper attention to detail.

Selection error can also result from incomplete instructions. Going back to the mall intercept study, suppose the 14th individual happens to be a child 13 years old, and the study requires all participants to be 21. What should the interviewer do? Should he or she go to the next person, the 15th, or count off another 14? What if the 14th person is identified, but declines to participate in the study? Should the interviewer choose the very next person, or count off another 14? To ensure consistency among interviewers and to prevent selection errors, it is important to have clear instructions on how to handle these situations as well as others that may occur.

Respondent Error

As shown in Figure 6.4, respondent errors fall into two categories: nonresponse bias (or error) and response bias (or error). Nonresponse bias occurs when there is a difference between the responses of those who participate in a study and those who do not. Suppose a survey is sent out over Twitter concerning the use of coupons offered by businesses through Twitter. It would be a logical way of conducting the survey since the purpose of the study is to examine how effective coupon issuance is with Twitter users. Suppose 300 people respond to the survey. The question in terms of nonresponse bias would be whether there is a significant difference in the attitudes of the 300 who responded and the attitudes of individuals who did not respond. Is it possible that the 300 who responded are heavy users of coupons and actively watch for coupons issued through Twitter? If so, their attitudes are likely to be more favorable than are the attitudes of those who make little or no use of coupons. It is very likely that if those who did not respond to the original survey were contacted and questioned, their responses to the survey question would be quite different.

Figure 6.4   Respondent Error

- Nonresponse bias
- Response error or bias
  - Deliberate falsification
  - Unconscious error, omission, or bias

The response rate of a study gives some indication of the potential for nonresponse bias. The response rate is simply the percentage of individuals who complete a study from among those who are contacted and asked to participate. For example, the response rate to a mail study may be 1.7%, meaning that 98.3% of those contacted did not respond.

Individuals do not respond to surveys for three primary reasons. First, the individual cannot be contacted at the particular time of the study. Suppose a bank identifies

500 of its customers randomly to receive a mail survey. If a particular customer happens to be out of the country for an extended period of time, then he or she may not be available to participate in the study. Alternatively, an individual may be away from home or engaged in outdoor activities when called to participate in a telephone survey.

The second situation occurs when the individual is contacted but cannot participate in the study at that particular time. He or she may be ill, be involved in a complex business deal, or have another reason for not being able to participate at the particular time the study is being conducted. Again, telephone surveys that interrupt an evening meal, putting children to bed, or watching a favorite television program may suffer from this form of nonresponse bias.

Minimizing nonresponse bias in either of the first two cases may require sending multiple survey mailings, making multiple attempts to call the household at different times, or sending reminders designed to encourage the individual to complete the survey.

The final type of nonresponse bias occurs when individuals are contacted but just refuse to participate. They are not interested. This reason for not participating, unfortunately, has become more common and may have the greatest impact on nonresponse bias. Since they refuse to participate, it is difficult to know if these individuals' responses would have been different from the responses of those who did participate. Incentives such as cash, the chance to win prizes, or other inducements can help to minimize outright refusals somewhat. However, there will always be a portion of the sample that refuses to participate in the study.

The only way to measure nonresponse bias is to conduct a second wave, which involves sending the survey to those who did not respond the first time. With the second wave, it is highly likely that individuals from the first two groups will respond—those who could not be contacted and those who were unable to participate. But, individuals in the third group will still likely refuse to participate. By comparing the responses of the first wave and second wave, it is possible to get a feel for any type of nonresponse bias. Unfortunately, it will never be possible to compare the answers of the respondents to the group of individuals who refuse to participate.

Response bias (or error) can occur under two circumstances: deliberate falsification and unconscious error. **Deliberate falsification** occurs when an individual provides false answers, purposely. There may be a number of different reasons why individuals are not truthful. If a question is potentially embarrassing or makes a person look foolish or bad, particularly in personal interview situations, then the respondent may provide a false answer. If a question is too personal and the respondent doesn't want to answer, then he or she may lie rather than not respond. Also, the respondent may want to appear intelligent or frugal, or display some other desirable characteristic, and thus provide a false answer. Sometimes respondents are in a hurry and provide the answer they think will end the survey most quickly. Other times they offer the interviewer the answer they think that individual wants to hear.

In cases where respondents are not truthful due to privacy concerns, instructions that explain why the data are needed, how the data will be reported, and whether responses will be confidential and anonymous can deter some people from providing false answers. Also, rotating the order in which questions appear on the survey can help to statistically "even out" such biases, especially when due to fatigue or time pressure.

The second type of response bias is an unintentional error. It may be placing a checkmark by the third response item when the respondent meant to check the second item in the list. It may be due to a faulty memory. When asked how many times an individual accessed a particular website over the last month, the respondent may respond it was four when it was actually five. The response was not intentionally false. The person just could not remember accurately. Shortening the recall period from a month to a week, or even from a week to "yesterday," can minimize memory errors and improve the quality of data.

Measurement Error

Figure 6.5 identifies three types of measurement errors: processing error, interviewer error or bias, and measurement instrument error or bias. **Measurement error** is the difference between the responses that are obtained and the true responses that were sought. By paying close attention to the design of the survey instrument, the measurement process, and the data entry procedure, measurement error can be reduced.

Figure 6.5   Measurement Error

- Processing error
- Interviewer error or bias
- Measurement instrument error or bias

Process errors occur when data from a survey instrument are either incorrectly coded or incorrectly entered into the computer program that is being used to tally the data and to analyze results. If humans are coding data on a paper survey, different response categories are represented by a particular number. An employee coding gender as 1 to represent a male respondent when males are supposed to be coded as 2 is one type of processing error. In transferring data from a paper survey sheet into Excel or SPSS, processing errors occur when the wrong number or information is typed. For instance, the survey response was 23, but the data-processing person mistakenly typed 32 or accidentally hit a 4 instead of a 3, resulting in 24 instead of 23. If the survey is being machine scored, the machine may be out of calibration or the response sheet may not be clearly marked, so the machine may not be able to pick up the answer.

To check for process errors, researchers can randomly select 10% of the surveys and proofread the coding process and data entry process. If a large number of errors are found in the coding process, all surveys may be proofread for errors. Frequency tables and double data entry can be used to identify process errors resulting from the data input process as well. A frequency table that shows a value above or below the legitimate range for a variable indicates process error. In double data entry, one individual enters the data for the study. A separate set of variables that mimic those entered is created, and a second individual reenters the data into this new set. Correlation analysis between the first and second data sets will identify any discrepancies when a particular variable does not have 100% correlation. The researcher can then examine the original survey data and both data entries to see which is correct.

Interviewer error or bias occurs when an interviewer influences a respondent to give erroneous answers, either intentionally or unintentionally. Respondents who like an interviewer may provide the answer they think the interviewer wants to hear. The tone of voice or the way an interviewer asks a question can influence a respondent's answer. Body language of the interviewer can have an effect on the respondent. For example, an interviewer who refuses to make eye contact and who speaks in a quick, clipped tone of voice may receive short, nondescriptive answers from study participants. In addition, such things as the interviewer's age, his or her gender, and even what he or she is wearing can impact how respondents answer. To reduce interviewer errors it is important that all interviewers be properly trained so they do not have any impact on how respondents answer questions. It is also important that the interviewers follow instructions and are monitored to ensure interviewer errors are kept to a minimum. Mystery shoppers might be used to evaluate interviewer quality.

Measurement instrument error or bias occurs with the questionnaire itself. A large portion of Chapter 11 is devoted to questionnaire development and issues that may impact the quality of data. Researchers must be careful about how questions are worded to avoid leading respondents or confusing them as to what is being asked. Response categories should be mutually exclusive, meaning respondents fit into only one category, and categorically exhaustive, meaning every respondent has a category into which he or she fits. Questions that are clear to a researcher may not be clear to individuals responding to the survey. By paying careful attention to the design of the questionnaire and pretesting the survey instrument with individuals who are similar to the survey sample, potential problems can be detected and corrected before data collection begins, thus minimizing this form of error.

While systematic error cannot be completely eliminated, it can be reduced by paying close attention to the research design and the research process. It is also helpful to know the types of errors that can occur and thus guard against them. Therefore, it is important to take steps to reduce systematic errors when designing the research and also during the survey collection process.

DATA COLLECTION ALTERNATIVES

Figure 6.6 identifies the various data collection alternatives for survey research. Each method has its own set of advantages and disadvantages. The traditional methods of telephone and mail surveys have been steadily declining in usage in favor of online methods and mixed modes. Cost and speed of response have been major reasons behind the shift, but other factors such as response rates and changes in technology have influenced the shift as well.

■ Learning Objective 6.4: Discuss the advantages and disadvantages of each of the data collection alternatives.

Telephone Surveys

Before the 1990s and the rise in popularity of cell phones, landline telephone research was the most popular method of conducting survey research. It was less costly than other methods, had a higher response rate, and was a quick way to collect data. It was an efficient method for conducting research and provided usable, valuable data.

Telephone interviewing became especially effective with the development of random digit dialing. Researchers no longer had to rely on telephone directories. Homes could be dialed randomly, producing a good sample and, in most cases, a sample with a relatively high response rate. The technology allowed for the elimination of business phones so only residences were contacted.

Telephone survey research is still used today for a large number of studies. For instance, Opinion Research Corporation conducted a telephone survey of 1,008 adults over a four-day period concerning health care issues. The subjects were carefully

Figure 6.6   Data Collection Alternatives

- Telephone
- Mail
- Personal interviews/intercept
- Internet
  - E-mail
  - Online
  - Mobile
  - Twitter
- Mixed modes

selected based on age, sex, geographic region, and race to ensure the sample would accurately reflect the adult U.S. population. Among the research findings was that Americans spend twice as much time researching information for major household purchases, such as a car, appliances, furniture, and real estate, as they do for a family physician or health care insurance. When asked how likely they would be to shop around for medical services if information on quality and price was made available, only 10% said extremely likely and 29% said very likely. The full results of the question are shown in Figure 6.7.[3] By carefully selecting the sample for the telephone survey, the research company was able to obtain useful results since the sample was representative of the total population.

Figure 6.7   How Likely Individuals Would Be to Shop Around for Medical Service if Given Price and Quality Information

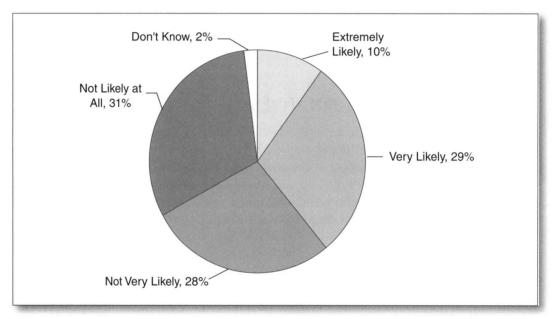

Source: Author-created with data from Reba L. Kieke, "Report Shows Americans Do Not Do Their Homework When It Comes to Health Care," *Managed Care Outlook*, Vol. 19, No. 16 (August 15, 2006), pp. 1–6.

The advantages and disadvantages of using landline telephones for research are identified in Figure 6.8. As can be seen, about the only advantages of telephone research today are low cost and speed of collecting data. However, with the rise of online research, these two advantages are not nearly as strong as in the past.

The types of research information that can be collected by telephone are limited to respondent behaviors, attitudes, and opinions about topics that do not require visualization. Respondents cannot be shown an advertisement, a marketing brochure, or even a product. It is difficult to ask certain questions over the phone, such as those that require respondents to choose from a set of set of scaled responses such as *very satisfied, satisfied, somewhat satisfied, somewhat dissatisfied, dissatisfied,* and *very dissatisfied.* As these response options would need to be read for each question using these categories, the number of questions that could be

Figure 6.8   Advantages and Disadvantages of Telephone Research

Advantages	Disadvantages
• Low cost • Fast	• Type of information that can be collected • Screening devices • Declining number of landlines • Declining response rate • Sample distortion

asked on the survey would be limited. Furthermore, some respondents may become impatient and terminate the survey early. In general, telephone surveys are most suitable for shorter surveys. But, even with these limitations, a large number of topics can be researched through telephone surveys.

The last four disadvantages are interrelated and have occurred almost simultaneously. Consumers increasingly started using answering machines and caller ID to screen calls, initially to screen out telemarketers. With increased screening came a declining response rate and a higher level of refusals to participate, even when individuals could be reached. The rise in the popularity of cell phones reduced the number of landlines. Many households now do not even possess a landline. They rely totally on cell phones. This trend, however, is not equal across all demographic groups. It is primarily the younger consumers who have moved to cell-only phones while older consumers who own their homes and have higher incomes have maintained landlines. Taken together, these factors create a distorted sample frame for telephone research, which contributes to sample design error.

For companies who want to utilize telephone surveys, mailing a letter in advance increases the response rate significantly. This alerts potential respondents that a phone call survey will be coming and solicits their support. Research has shown that the advance letter will increase the response rate about 8% to 10% over no advance letters.[4]

Using an advance letter requires identification of the sample in advance, so random digit dialing cannot be used. This in turn means that households whose phone numbers are unlisted are not included, resulting in higher levels of frame error. But, for certain types of research, this is acceptable. For instance, suppose a company such as Toyota wants to survey individuals who have purchased a new car within the last year. Sending a letter to a sample of these customers will make them more likely to participate in the telephone survey even though it is likely that Toyota will use a marketing research firm to do the actual data collection.

Cell Phones. The rise in the use of cell phones has spurred an interest in using them as a means of conducting survey research. Currently, about 75% of households in the United States have a cell phone compared to about 85% in Europe. In the United States, current estimates are that more than 40% of adults 30 years of age and under have only cell phones, compared to only 5% of adults 65 and older. As this trend continues, researchers will have to consider using cell phones for research rather than landlines. The difficulty, currently, is that either approach alone produces a biased sample of adults. To create a representative sample of the U.S. population using telephone research would involve sampling from both landlines and cell phones.[5]

One caveat to cell phone research is that many consumers who have cell phones now have smartphones with Internet capabilities. This feature allows researchers to conduct online research. It really makes little difference if the online research is answered via a smartphone or a computer. This feature also means that as quickly as cell phone survey research rises in use, it may also decline in favor of online survey methodologies as more consumers move to smartphones.

In examining cell phone survey research that does not involve smartphones, a number of factors must be considered. These factors are listed in Figure 6.9. Unlike landline phones, there is not a directory or listing of cell phones. Also, because of the transitory nature of individuals with phones, the phone number does not indicate where the person lives. The individual can be anywhere in the United States. For national studies, this would be OK. But for any type of study limited to a specific geographic area, it would be a problem.

Figure 6.9   Factors in Cell Phone Survey Research

- No cell phone list
- Legal restrictions
- Cell phone user or owner
- Location of respondent
- Length of survey
- Cost of phone call

Currently, there are legal restrictions that apply to cell phones that do not apply to landlines. Specifically, research companies cannot use random digit dialer technology to contact a cell phone user without the individual's prior consent. To obtain such consent is costly, time consuming, and practically impossible. Therefore, each number has to be dialed individually by the researcher, which increases the costs and time needed to complete the study. Also, because cell phones are viewed as personal, many individuals feel that receiving a phone call from a research company is an invasion of their privacy.

The owner and the user of a cell phone may be two different individuals. Many cell phones are used by children, but owned by parents. With a landline, researchers know that there will be an adult in the home, even if a child answers the phone. Such is not the case with cell phones.

Another challenge with cell phones is that the person answering the phone may be anywhere and engaged in any number of activities. The person may be at work, at a restaurant, shopping, or driving a vehicle. These circumstances may prevent the subject from completing a survey. Even if he or she consents to the survey, it may be a distraction, especially if the survey is longer than the respondent anticipated.

In most cases, surveys using cell phones must be shorter than those using a traditional landline phone, for a number of reasons. First, the location of the respondents may dictate they cannot or should not spend very much time on the phone. Second, many individuals see a phone call to their cell phone as invasive and thus may answer a few questions, but do not want to participate in a lengthy survey. Third, the individual may be engaged in activities, such as driving or working, or using smartphone apps. As a result, the subject may not fully concentrate on the questions, or may give hurried answers, incomplete answers, or wrong answers, or just discontinue the survey prior to completion.

The last issue relates to the cost of the phone call. With landlines, the research company absorbs all costs. With cell phones, plans vary widely. For many individuals now, there are no additional costs for incoming calls. But, this not true for all cell phone users.

Cell phones offer a number of opportunities not found with landline telephones. For instance, researchers may be able to send and receive pictures and videos as answers to questions. In addition to multiple-choice questions, open-ended and rating questions can be used.

Time and date stamps with cell phones allows for tracking of results and tracking when each question was answered. Researchers can use GPS to identify the location of the respondent, if the respondent grants permission. While responses are confidential, respondents can choose to be anonymous by hiding their personal cell phone data in the results database. If respondents do not respond, a reminder can be sent via a text message or phone call.[6]

Currently, one of the major advantages of cell phone research is speed of responses. Tests by Lightspeed Research with its mobile panel found that 60% of the usable, completed surveys were returned within 15 minutes of distribution and 90% were returned within an hour. FlyResearch had similar response rates. Approximately 85% of surveys are completed and returned within two hours with its mobile panel of 18- to 25-year-olds.[7]

Another unique aspect of mobile research is that individuals are more likely to respond to "private, personal" questions on a cell phone than in telephone or personal interviews. They are also happy to send photographs or videos of themselves, brands, events, advertisements, in-store displays, and other phenomena. Because they view their cell phones as a personal device, consumers are willing to provide these more intimate thoughts and views of personal situations, which allows researchers a deeper understanding of consumer behavior than is possible with the other survey methods.[8]

Mail Surveys

Mail survey research has been around a long time, but just like telephone research has declined in recent years due to a variety of reasons. As shown in Figure 6.10, mail survey research can be divided into three types. Ad hoc surveys are sent to individuals at random or through some type of selection process from a database. The individuals have not been notified in advance.

Figure 6.10   Mail Survey Research

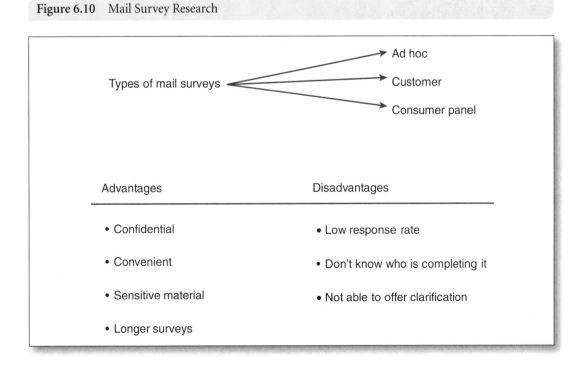

They may have been selected from a marketing research database based on a demographic or psychographic profile requested by the client. Other than meeting the predetermined criteria, nothing else is known about the individual receiving the survey.

Marketing Systems Group used an ad hoc mail survey approach to investigate consumers' attitudes toward advertising by optometrists. The company mailed out 4,000 surveys and had 382 respond. Because consumers in the past looked negatively upon advertising by professional services, the research company wanted to investigate current attitudes as professional services advertising has escalated in recent years. The results indicated that consumers tend to have a good image of optometrists, and advertising does not lower that image. Consumers felt it was useful for optometrists to provide information about their services, especially any specialties they provide. One piece of information that advertisers should not provide, according to the research, is price. Consumers indicated that ads focused on price indicated a lower-quality service and the possibility of deceptive pricing. They felt that the price advertised would not be the price charged once they were at the optometrist.[9]

The second type of mail survey is with a firm's customers. Normally, these surveys are sent by marketing research firms, but they are mailed to specific individuals who have purchased a product. Companies like to use surveys to follow up on purchases to learn more about who purchased the product and why. They may also survey individuals one, two, or even more years after the initial purchase to gauge the level of satisfaction and to evaluate any difficulties with the product or need for repair. This information is especially important in making product changes and discovering weak parts or defective areas. It also serves as a reminder that it may be time to make another purchase or trade the old product in for a new one.

The last type of mail survey is sent to consumer panels. These are individuals who have agreed to participate in research studies. Either they are paid a small gratuity for participating, or their names are put into a lottery for a gift card or some other prize that is given to participants on a random basis. Consumer panels vary across research firms, but participating in three or four studies per year is common.

As indicated in Figure 6.10, mail survey research has some specific advantages and disadvantages. A major advantage is confidentiality. Respondents can answer questions in the privacy of their homes and without any interviewers present in person, or on the telephone. This allows for survey questions involving sensitive or potentially embarrassing topics that individuals would otherwise find difficult to answer in the presence of an interviewer. Because the respondent can complete the survey anytime that is convenient, it allows for longer surveys. Unlike telephone surveys, visuals can be sent in the mail or placed on a website that individuals can view before or during the survey.

The major disadvantage of mail surveys is the low response rate, especially for ad hoc studies. The response rate tends to be a little higher for customer surveys. The challenge, however, with customer surveys is that customers at the two extremes are the most likely to respond while those in the middle tend to ignore the survey. Customers who have had a positive experience and those who have had a negative experience will be most likely to complete the survey. Since the product or experience was neither good nor bad, those who are neutral often feel they have nothing really worthwhile to report in a survey. Figure 6.11 offers a number of suggestions for improving the response rate to mail surveys. While these suggestions can improve the response rate, it still remains extremely low, often around 1% for ad hoc studies, and a little higher for customer surveys. As panel participants have agreed in advance to participate in surveys, the response rate for this type of mail survey is the highest.

Figure 6.11   Suggestions for Improving Mail Surveys

- Teaser on the outside of the envelope to encourage individuals to open the letter
- Prenotification letter before the survey
- Incentives
  - Unconditional incentive regardless of whether survey is completed (based on reciprocity and guilt)
  - Nonmonetary incentives such as prizes through a lottery
- Provide opportunity to see results (online)
- Send second copy of questionnaire to nonrespondents
- University or nonprofit sponsorship of the survey
- Use of a stamped return envelope

Source: Author-created from Neil G. Connon, "Improving Postal Questionnaire Response Rates," *The Marketing Review*, Vol. 8, No. 2 (2008), pp. 113–134.

Another problem with mail surveys is that you don't really know who is completing them, even if they're addressed to a specific person. A spouse, a significant other, a roommate, or even a child may complete the survey and mail it back. Researchers have to rely on the honesty of individuals that the demographic information provided and the responses given are indeed the responses of the individual and not of someone else.

Lastly, mail surveys offer no opportunity for clarification of a question. With telephone and personal interview surveys, explanations can be given. While doing so can possibly bias the response, it is often better than individuals guessing at what they think a question means. In instances where the question is not understood, instrument error or bias occurs, but the researchers have no idea it is present. They assume, if a question has a response, that the respondent fully understood what was being asked.

Personal Interviews and Intercept Studies

Personal interviews can be used to conduct survey research. The questionnaire may be given to the respondent to complete with the interviewer standing by ready to answer questions or provide information, or the interviewer can read the questions and record the respondent's answers. In addition, the personal interview can occur in the respondents' homes, at their businesses, or at some neutral location. When the latter is used, quite often research companies will use an intercept approach where they intercept individuals at random or according to a sampling plan. A common location for intercept studies is a shopping mall, but other locations can be used such as county fairs, sporting events, and tourist sites.

The advantages and disadvantages of personal interview and intercept studies are shown in Figure 6.12. Because the interviewer is present when the questionnaire is completed, there is an opportunity to clarify questions or instructions. This can occur even when respondents are completing the questionnaire on their own. Interviewer presence can also reduce nonresponse to particular questions by offering explanations or clarifications of the question, or relating why it is important. With self-administered questionnaires, the interviewer can examine the completed questionnaire prior to the respondent leaving to ensure all of

Figure 6.12   Advantages and Disadvantages of Personal Interviews

Advantages	Disadvantages
• Question clarification • Lower item nonresponse • More complete answers • Longer interviews • Visual aids • Higher participation	• Lack of respondent anonymity • Poor for sensitive topics • Interviewer bias • Higher costs

the questions have been answered. As a result, personal interviews and intercept surveys tend to have the highest percentage of completed answers.

In most cases, personal interviews allow for longer surveys than would be possible with the telephone, the web, and other modes. The only possible exception may be mail surveys. But, the problem with mail surveys is that if the respondents think a survey is too long, they are likely to quit and never finish. With personal interviews, respondents can often be encouraged to answer just a few more questions.

Visual aids can be used. It may be something as simple as a print advertisement, or as large as an automobile. It is even possible to have short demonstrations or to show a short video or television commercial. Personal interviews offer the researcher considerable latitude in the types of visuals that can be used.

Because the interviewer asks individuals to participate, the response rate is higher. It is more difficult for people to say "no" when they are confronted in person by the interviewer than when contacted by phone or mail. The one exception may be at malls where individuals are busy shopping and do not want to take time for a survey, especially a lengthy survey.

A primary drawback of personal interviews is that the respondents are not anonymous. The interviewer knows who they are. While answers can be confidential, respondents may not feel comfortable providing answers to all of the questions on the survey. This happens more for surveys that are read by the interviewer than for those that are self-administered. Sensitive topics or potentially embarrassing questions are difficult to administer with personal interviews. Individuals will either become embarrassed or give socially acceptable answers rather than their true feelings.

Another concern that has already been discussed is interviewer bias, especially if the interviewer conducts the survey. Tone of voice, body language, and other characteristics of the interviewer can influence a respondent's answers. Even with training and supervision, it is difficult for the interviewer not to display reactions to respondent answers. Self-administered surveys that the interviewer collects and reviews are less subject to interviewer influence.

The last disadvantage of personal interviews and intercept studies is costs. Individuals must be hired and trained to conduct the research. Because of the personal nature of the interviews, only one interview can be conducted at a time, and if the interviewer reads the questions, it normally takes longer than if it is self-administered.

Internet Surveys

Online survey research is now the leading survey research methodology, primarily because it is faster and cheaper than any of the other alternatives. Approximately 77% of the U.S. population now has access to the Internet,[10] and about 40% of cell phones are now smartphones with Internet access.[11] Consumers and businesses are now readily accessible, and the population of online survey respondents is not that much different from the general U.S. population.

Online surveys can be conducted in a variety of ways, as indicated in Figure 6.13. The survey can be placed on a website, and visitors to the site can be asked to complete it. Surveys can be sent through an e-mail, or a web link can be provided in an e-mail that will take individuals to the survey website. Social networking sites and Twitter can also be used to conduct research. Lastly, survey research can be conducted through smartphones, which allow researchers to utilize voice and texting in addition to a web link.

Figure 6.13   Types of Online Surveys

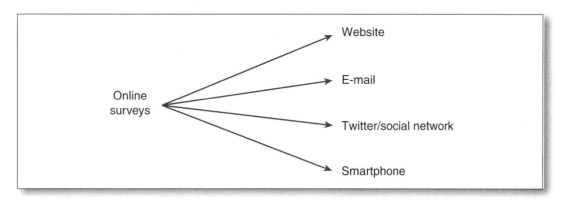

Online research has a number of advantages and disadvantages, as shown in Figure 6.14. As cited earlier, individuals enjoy a high level of accessibility to the Internet, and that number continues to grow each year. Speed and costs are major considerations. Thousands of e-mail surveys can be sent to potential respondents simultaneously. Surveys can be completed in just days or even hours in some cases at a very low cost. Results are almost in real time. Researchers do not have to wait until all of the surveys are received to tabulate results. Specialized survey software instantly transforms responses into spreadsheets and graphs so at any time researchers can examine the results. Survey software also minimizes item nonresponse by forcing subjects to answer key questions before they can go to the next question.

It is possible to personalize surveys to increase the response rate. Through branching, questions can even be worded to match a person's purchase behavior, gender, or other characteristics.

Figure 6.14   Advantages and Disadvantages of Online Research

Advantages	Disadvantages
• High level of accessibility	• Location of respondent
• Speed	• Sample representativeness
• Lower costs	• Data quality
• Real-time results	• Spam and clutter
• Personalization	• Hardware/software capabilities
• More sophisticated surveys	
• Use of visuals	

At the same time, respondents can be assured their responses will be confidential and tabulated with other responses to obtain an overall picture of consumer behavior.

The web allows for more sophisticated surveys as well as the use of visuals. Videos, 3D images, and virtual illustrations can be used with online surveys. Realistic and complex visuals can illustrate various features of a product or marketing materials. Tasks that would be difficult to do with other survey modes can be programmed into an online survey. Piping occurs when the answer to one question is incorporated into the text of sequential questions. For example, a question may ask respondents to select their favorite restaurant from a dropdown menu. If Denny's is selected, that answer can be piped into a subsequent question, such as "How would you rate Denny's restaurant on the following characteristics?"

Although online research offers a number of advantages and is growing in popularity, it does have some disadvantages. First is in identifying the location of the respondent. If the respondent is using a computer, the location can be identified through the IP address. However, if a smartphone is being used, it becomes more difficult. In addition, the person may live in Ohio, but be in Florida attending college, working, or just on vacation when the survey is completed.

There is some concern about how representative online survey respondents are of the population in general. This concern has diminished in recent years as more people gain access to the Internet. But, another concern has arisen as many online researchers rely on volunteers to complete the survey, or they utilize an online panel. While the general population is becoming less willing to complete online surveys, a small percentage of individuals have become "professional respondents" completing surveys for a number of different research firms and organizations. Because these individuals are paid or rewarded in some manner for completing surveys, they may complete as many as 15 to 20 a month. These professional respondents are not like the general population. They are more likely to be White, educated, and either young or old, but not middle-aged.[12]

It should be pointed out that not all professional respondents are bad. Some individuals like giving their opinion. They are thoughtful and take time to answer questions carefully. They only respond to surveys on topics in which they are knowledgeable. While these individuals may be called professional respondents because they participate in multiple surveys, their motivation is different. It is not to earn credits, prizes, or money. It is to share their opinion on various topics. They also tend to answer fewer surveys than other professional respondents, perhaps only one or two per month.[13]

The speed of data collection and the rise of the negative professional respondents have led to another concern—data quality. The less time individuals spend in completing a survey, usually the poorer the data quality. Respondents will answer questions without thoroughly reading the question and without spending time thinking about the best response. The rate of honest or random errors will also increase when respondents mark the wrong answer not on purpose but because they rush through the survey. For those negative professional respondents who do 15 to 20 surveys a month, quality of data is a major concern as the individual's goal often is to complete the survey, not to provide valuable data for the research study.

Research companies and data collection firms, such as Research Now and ReRez, have methods in place to check data quality. Computer programs can check for "straight liners." These are individuals who just go down a survey and answer C or some other response for all of the questions. The program also checks for "speeders," or individuals who take only 5 minutes to answer a survey that should take 30. Leaving the survey open for 30 minutes just to make it appear that it took that long when the person only spent 5 minutes checking responses can also be detected because the program will look at actual time spent between clicking various responses. Questionnaires will also have feedback or check questions that have obvious wrong answers and may have nothing to do with the survey to see if the person is even reading the question. Most research panels have a policy of "three strikes and you're out" in an attempt to eliminate the bad professional respondent.[14]

Despite concerns about data quality, research studies have shown that qualitative data obtained through online surveys are comparable to data obtained from telephone and mail surveys.[15] Similar studies have validated the quality of quantitative data.[16] Obtaining quality data requires careful attention to research design, the research process, and the sample selection. Doing so will increase costs, but greatly increases the usability of the data.

Spam and online clutter have increased, which has had a negative impact on people participating in ad hoc online survey research. Just as with the other survey alternatives, it is becoming more difficult to obtain a good sample of respondents from the general population. As a result, companies are increasingly using research panels and firms that have built large consumer and business-to-business research panels.

Because of smartphones and various forms of computer Internet connections, hardware and software capabilities vary widely. Some individuals have high-speed Internet connections; others must rely on satellite or phone connections. Also, software and hardware vary widely. If videos, visuals, and other more sophisticated aids are used, not all Internet users will be able to view the materials due to having older computers that lack memory or video cards.

Mixed Modes

For some research studies, using multiple modes provides better results. For instance, using both landline telephones and cell phones can increase the response rate and ensure the sample is more representative of the U.S. population. With online research, multiple forms may be used, combining the posting of a survey on a firm's website with e-mailing it to individuals in its database.

Coca-Cola utilized a mixed-mode approach to track emotional responses to its products in retail stores and its advertisements. The first stage of the research involved online questionnaires designed to understand individuals' relationships with various brands. The second stage used mobile phones. Individuals were asked to text whenever they came into contact with one of the brands indicated in the first stage of the research. The individuals were to text where they saw the brand, how they felt about the venue or medium where it was displayed, and how it influenced their purchase decision. By using cell phones, Coca-Cola was able to collect data in real time, at the touch point when it occurred. Respondents did not have to rely on memory. Many of the respondents attached photos to their messages, and GPS technology allowed the researchers to identify the location where the interaction occurred.

SURVEY SELECTION CONSIDERATIONS

A number of factors must be considered when deciding which survey alternative to use. These factors are highlighted in Figure 6.15. In discussing these factors, it is important to know that they are interrelated, and a decision on one factor will impact other factors. None can be considered in isolation.

■ Objective 6.5: Discuss each of the survey selection considerations as they apply to the various data collection alternatives.

Figure 6.15   Survey Selection Considerations

- Cost
- Time frame
- Level of precision or accuracy
- Questionnaire length
- Questionnaire structure
- Incidence rate
- Sample characteristics

Budget, Time Frame, and Precision

The level of data precision or accuracy that is desired is inversely related to the research budget and the time frame. The greater the desired precision, the more costly the research, and the longer it will take to collect the data. If a company is in a time crunch to make a decision and needs data quickly, it will almost always sacrifice precision and accuracy. The type of decision to be made and the monetary value connected with that decision will largely determine the level of precision that is needed. Decisions involving millions of dollars will require much greater accuracy than decisions that involve thousands of dollars.

In terms of the survey research methods, the level of precision or accuracy is determined more by research design, costs, time frame, and the research process than it is by the data collection method. All of the alternatives, from the telephone to the Internet, can provide high-quality data if careful attention is paid to the research design and its implementation. Alternatively, poor-quality data are often obtained when corners are cut to save money and time, or the research design is poorly developed or not followed.

Because companies have finite budgets for research, cost is an important consideration. Costs can vary widely within each data collection alternative depending on the depth of the research design, the desired sample size, and the time frame for the study. Increasing sample size increases costs and also lengthens the time frame for the study. So does developing a comprehensive research design that has a large number of steps to ensure low systematic error.

Of the different modes for survey data collection, the least costly tends to be online research, especially online panels. The major costs for an online survey are hosting the survey questionnaire, survey design, and data tabulation. Sending out thousands of e-mails with a survey attachment or link is no more costly than sending out hundreds.

The most expensive methodology is personal interviews and intercepts. Interviewers can do only one interview at a time, which limits the number of interviews that a single individual can do within a specified time frame. Most research involving personal interviews and intercepts will have multiple interviews. So, in addition to the cost of the interviewers, there are costs for training, supervision, and travel. The costs are only slightly reduced if the questionnaires are given to respondents for self-administration.

Telephone and mail interviews tend to fall in the middle in terms of costs. With landline survey research, interviewers are required to read the questions. However, the system is computerized, and automatic dialing increases the number of interviews that can be conducted per hour. Data are automatically recorded into the computer, eliminating the data-recording process required for personal interviews and mail surveys.

Costs for cell phone research vary depending on how it is conducted and the length of the survey questionnaire. Text surveys can be pretyped and sent to potential respondents, thousands at a time, very much like e-mail. Additional costs may be incurred if visuals, videos, or photos are used as part of the research study. Personal interviewing via cell phone would require the same costs as landline telephone surveys, with the exception of travel.

Mail surveys tend to be more costly than telephone primarily because of the high nonresponse rate. Each survey questionnaire has to be mailed, which requires postage. Often, survey names are purchased from a database research firm, which adds to the costs. Also, either return postage is prepaid, or stamps are placed on return envelopes. Plus labor costs are incurred in the envelope-stuffing process.

The time frame allotted for a study can impact which type of survey is used. Cell phone, and especially text message, surveys tend to have very quick response rates. Online surveys also have a fast response with most responses coming with 48 hours of posting either online or in an e-mail. The slowest method is mail since research firms have no control over when individuals complete the survey and mail it back. Responses will often trickle in for weeks after the initial mailing. In addition, firms often send a follow-up letter or second-wave mailing to individuals who have not responded, which lengthens the amount of time to complete the study.

With telephone and personal interview methods, the amount of time to complete a study is directly related to the number of responses desired. A study requiring 4,000 responses will take considerably longer than a study involving 1,000 or 500 responses. For this reason, telephone and personal interview studies tend to have smaller samples than online, mail, or cell phone studies.

Questionnaire Length and Structure

Questionnaire length and structure are important considerations when choosing the best survey method. Mail surveys are good for long questionnaires. In some cases, personal interviews can also work well for long questionnaires. Telephone surveys cannot be as long, and cell phone surveys typically are even shorter, especially text surveys. Online surveys can vary greatly in length depending on the sample and how it is administered. However, if online surveys are too long, respondents either stop reading the questionnaire thoroughly and just quickly fill in answers, or quit taking the survey altogether. One advantage to online surveys is that responses can be saved so that individuals who leave a survey before finishing it can return to the exact location where they left off.

Online surveys provide the greatest flexibility in terms of questionnaire structure. Simple multiple-choice questions can be used, as can choice modeling that involves complex programming. Videos, photos, and other visuals can be used as part of the study. Other modes, such as mail and telephone, are much more limiting. However, cell phones do allow for some of the same capabilities of online.

Incidence Rate

Another important factor is the **incidence** rate, which is the percentage of individuals, households, or businesses in the population that would be qualified as potential respondents in a particular study. Not everyone meets the criteria for a study. Thus, researchers must search the population for individuals that meet the criteria set forth in the research design. Mail surveys typically have a high incidence rate since individuals are prescreened, and only individuals who meet the criteria are sent the questionnaire. The same can be true for telephone and cell phone research, though not always.

The incidence rate for personal interviews and intercepts can be quite low depending on the method of selection. Using a shopping mall is convenient, but may not exactly meet the sample selection criteria for the study. To increase the incidence rate for personal interviews, prescreening can be done. But, this process also increases the **search cost,** which is the cost to locate individuals who meet the sample criteria for a study.

The incidence rate for online research tends to be higher because respondents can be pre-screened through cookies, tracking software, or a series of qualifying questions. Cookies and tracking software can quickly exclude individuals who do not meet the requirements for the study. If these technologies cannot be used or are not available, then individuals can be asked questions prior to the research to determine if they qualify. If individuals are part of a research panel, then their profile can be used as means of selecting the correct respondents and those who meet the research sample criteria.

Sample Characteristics

The selection of the survey method may be impacted by the characteristics of the desired sample. For example, recently a company approached ReRez about surveying decision makers for land-scaping tools.[17] The company wanted to conduct the research online since it would be less costly. ReRez pointed out two potential problems with this approach. First, individuals who use landscap-ing tools may not be online and thus may not be part of a research panel, and those who are online are very likely a minority of the population. Second, many individuals who perform landscaping are of Hispanic decent and cannot be reached online. Thus, an online survey method would pro-duce biased results. Instead, telephone or personal interviews were suggested because they would ensure reaching a larger and more representative sample of individuals who purchase landscaping tools. Thus, in making a decision about the survey method, researchers must look at the sample characteristics and choose the method that will produce the most representative sample.

Global Concerns

Because of culture and language differences, systematic error is a greater concern with inter-national marketing research. It is important to carefully plan the research to reduce sample design error, respondent error, and measurement error. Using native speakers and translators is essential. Although an individual may be able to speak multiple languages, he or she is not likely to understand the nuances of the various cultures and common idioms used by each nationality and culture. For example, someone from Mexico can speak Spanish, but it is not the same Spanish that is spoken in Puerto Rico, Cuba, or Brazil. Idioms and meanings of words will vary, just as they do in English-speaking countries such as the United States and England.

In conducting a telephone or personal interview in the United States it is customary to use an assumptive approach. After saying hello, the interviewer will normally launch directly into the study's introduction and then move on to the first question. In some cultures, this approach would be considered rude and unacceptable. After saying hello, the interviewer is expected to engage in small talk before asking the interviewee for his or her cooperation.[18]

In Middle Eastern countries, it is important to understand the differences in status between men and women, especially married women. Before interviewing a female, the interviewer must ask permission from the husband. It is also not unusual that to be granted permission the interviewer must also be female. For orthodox Arabs, it would be unacceptable for a male interviewer to conduct an interview with a female respondent, especially a personal interview. It is also common for the male to be present during the interview process.

The types of visuals that can be used and even the types of questions that can be asked will vary across cultures. Again, in Middle Eastern countries visuals that display any type of sexual situation or even show affection between males and females would not be acceptable. Discussing personal sexual situations and products related to sex or personal hygiene is often taboo.

 STATISTICS REVIEW

Understanding the margin of error, confidence intervals, and the confidence level associated with research studies is critical to understanding the accuracy of the results based on sample data. Many organizations use public opinion polls or surveys with "yes" and "no" or "approve" and "disapprove" type answers to track attitudes toward various issues. Gallup may track the percentage of people who approve or disapprove of the U.S. president's job performance on a weekly basis using a random telephone sample of over 3,500 adults. A recent Gallup report stated that compared to the previous week, the president's job approval rating had declined from 50% to 46%. The article explained, "For results based on the total sample of national adults, one can say with 95% confidence that the maximum margin of sampling error is ± 2 percentage points."[19]

Margin of Error

The margin of error determines how close the results obtained from your sample are compared to what you might find if you surveyed the entire population. In the case of the president's job approval rating, this means that the real approval rating of the U.S. population as a whole could have fallen anywhere between 44% (46% − 2% margin of error) and as high as 48% (46% + 2% margin of error) during the second week. As the same margin of error characterizes all of Gallup's presidential job approval polls, it also means that the president's job approval rating may not have slipped at all! The 50% rating reported during the first week may have been 2% higher than what would have been found if Gallup had surveyed the entire population, while the 46% rating found during the second week (using a different random sample) might have underestimated the population's approval of the president by 2%.

Minimizing the level of sampling error associated with a research study can be critical, especially in instances in which opinions are fairly evenly divided. On the other hand, if a survey found that 85% of a sample answered "yes" to a question while only 15% answered "no" or "undecided," a higher level of sampling error, such as ± 5%, or even ± 10%, could still provide useful information.

Confidence Levels

Referring back to Gallup's statement that "one can say with 95% confidence that the maximum margin of sampling error is ± 2 percentage points,"[20] confidence levels are best explained in the following manner. Suppose Gallup conducted a new study to determine the approval ratings (in percentage terms) of the president pertaining to his handling of 20 specific issues, such as the deficit, higher education funding, the economy, and so forth. At the 95% confidence level, one would expect that for 1 of the 20 questions (5% of the data), the percent of people who answered "yes" to that question would be *more* than the margin of error *away* from the true answer, which would be found if the entire population was surveyed. Thus, the confidence level simply indicates the degree to which the researcher can

(Continued)

be assured that the results obtained from sample data are truly representative of the population, and not due to random chance.

Confidence Intervals

Confidence intervals estimate the range of values that are likely to include the true population value for a particular variable, at a given confidence level. In this regard, they are very similar to the margin of error. The difference is that confidence intervals are calculated for means, rather than proportions.

Suppose a local retailer was considering buying an ad package through the Fox affiliate for the upcoming National Football League (NFL) season. Though expensive, this would allow the retailer to run a 30-second commercial in the local market during each NFL game broadcast by Fox. However, the retailer is not willing to commit to the deal unless the population, on average, watches at least 14 NFL games a year. Figure 6.16 shows the results of a one-sample t-test using sample data gathered from shoppers in the local market.

Figure 6.16   Results of One-Sample t-Test

One-Sample Statistics

	N	Mean	Std. Deviation	Std. Error Mean
Number of professional football games watched in a year	573	12.0052	18.23281	.76169

One-Sample Test

	Test Value = 14					
					95% Confidence Interval of the Difference	
	t	df	Sig. (2-tailed)	Mean Difference	Lower	Upper
Number of professional football games watched in a year	-2.619	572	.009	-1.99476	-3.4908	-.4987

The first table in Figure 6.16 demonstrates that the average number of professional football games watched in a year by the sample is 12.0052. The second table shows the results of the one-sample t-test using a 95% confidence level. The null hypothesis being tested is that the population watches, on average, 14 NFL games a year. The number found under the Sig. (2-tailed) column indicates that the exact probability that the mean of the sample (12.00052) is equal to 14 is .009, which is less than the alpha value of .05. The null hypothesis should be rejected. As a result, the retailer can be 95% confident that the true number of games watched by the population is fewer than 14.

But what is the actual confidence interval? While SPSS does not provide the confidence interval, it can be computed by using the "Lower" and "Upper" columns of the 95% confidence interval of the difference. The difference between the test value of 14 and the sample mean of 12.0052 is −1.99476. The lower boundary of difference is −3.4908, and the upper boundary of difference is −0.4987. Subtracting these values from the test value of 14, respectively, yields a lower boundary of 10.5092 and an upper boundary of 13.5013. Thus, the researcher can be 95% confident the actual number of professional games watched is between 10.5 and 13.5, which is lower than the 14 that was stated in the hypothesis. Again, the null hypothesis can be rejected.

Realizing that gender may well be related to the number of NFL games watched, a researcher can utilize an analysis of variance (ANOVA). Gender is designated as the grouping variable. The results of this analysis are shown in Figure 6.17.

Figure 6.17   Results of ANOVA Analysis

Descriptives

Number of professional football games watched in a year

| | N | Mean | Std. Deviation | Std. Error | 95% Confidence Interval for Mean | | Minimum | Maximum |
					Lower Boundary	Upper Boundary		
Female	321	6.8255	9.42043	.52580	5.7911	7.8600	.00	100.00
Male	249	18.6426	23.88946	1.51393	15.6608	21.6244	.00	250.00
Total	570	11.9877	18.25011	.76441	10.4863	13.4891	.00	250.00

ANOVA

Number of professional football games watched in a year

	Sum of Squares	df	Mean Square	F	Sig.
Between Groups	19581.495	1	19581.495	65.451	.000
Within Groups	169933.419	568	299.179		
Total	189514.914	569			

The null hypothesis being tested is that the mean number of NFL games watched by women is equal to the mean number of NFL games watched by men. The tables shown in Figure 6.17 suggest that this is not the case, as the p-value found in the Sig. column of the second table is less than .05, indicating that the null hypothesis should be rejected. Of greater importance to the retailer, though, are the numbers shown under the "Lower Boundary" and "Upper Boundary" columns of the 95% confidence interval of the mean. Unlike the one-sample t-test, which listed the confidence interval of the difference (between the mean and the test value), the column in the ANOVA table shows the actual confidence interval. Using this information, the retailer now realizes that he can be 95% confident that the true number of games watched by men in the population actually exceeds 14, and falls instead within the range of 15.6608 to 21.6244. When confidence intervals are desired for the means of different groups, ANOVA can be used.

⊘ DEALING WITH DATA

Visit the textbook website and download the files needed to complete this exercise. The questionnaire is titled "Chapter 06 Dealing with Data Survey," and the data file is titled "Chapter 06 Dealing with Data." The files and step-by-step instructions are also available on the textbook website, www.sagepub.com/clowess.

A local businesswoman is considering purchasing a package of television spots, which will run during college football game broadcasts during the upcoming season. However, she is not willing to invest in this marketing effort unless the population watches, on average, at least 15 college football games a year.

1. Run one-sample t-tests at the .90, .95, and .99 level. Compute confidence levels for each analysis. Report the results of the analysis. Based on these data, would you recommend that she invest in the college football advertising package?

2. Suppose the majority of her clientele are African Americans. Perform an ANOVA using race as the grouping variable. Based on this analysis, do you still believe she should invest in the college football advertising package? Why or why not? Justify your decision based on the results of the analysis.

SUMMARY

Objective 1: Discuss why survey research is used.

The results of survey research are used to describe situations, target-market profiles, and attitudes toward brands, endorsers, and ads, as well as other phenomena. Survey research provides answers to who-, when-, where-, what-, and why-type questions.

Objective 2: Identify the two time frames for survey research.

Cross-sectional research studies provide a snapshot of the subject being investigated because they take place at a single point in time. Longitudinal studies are effective for tracking trends, as they ask the same question, to essentially the same respondents, at multiple points in time. Longitudinal studies are typically conducted by syndicated research firms, and often make use of consumer panels to track branding campaigns, media consumption, and advertising impact.

Objective 3: Describe the various types of errors that can occur with survey research.

Random error is unavoidable, and can only be reduced by increasing sample size. Systematic error results from problems in the research process related to the sample design, measurement process, or respondents. Sample design error may result from population specification error, frame error, or selection error. Measurement error may occur as a result of interviewer error or bias, measurement instrument error or bias, or processing error. Respondent error takes the form of nonresponse bias, and response error or bias that occurs deliberately or unconsciously. Various strategies exist for minimizing each type of error.

Objective 4: Discuss the advantages and disadvantages of each of the data collection alternatives.

While data collection via telephone can be completed quickly and at a low cost, only limited information can be collected, and visuals cannot be used. Answering machines, sample distortion, and declines in both the number of households that have landlines and response rates are key disadvantages of phone surveys. Other issues apply to cell phone survey research. Mail surveys suffer from low response rates, an inability to clarify questions that respondents may have about the survey, and lack of knowledge as to who is completing the questionnaire. However, mail surveys are good for sensitive material and longer surveys, and offer greater convenience to respondents along with confidentiality. Personal interviews allow the researcher to clarify questions respondents may have, and stimulate more complete answers, lower item nonresponse, and higher participation. Personal interviews are useful for longer interviews and those requiring the use of visual aids. Disadvantages include lack of respondent anonymity, interviewer bias, higher per-respondent costs, and poorer data quality for sensitive topics. The advantages of online research are many and include fast, real-time results; lower costs; the ability to personalize and use more sophisticated surveys that may include visuals; and a high level of access. Disadvantages exist related to respondent locations, sample representativeness, data quality, spam and clutter, and hardware/software capabilities.

Objective 5: Discuss each of the survey selection considerations as it applies to the various data collection alternatives.

When selecting a data collection method, researchers must consider a number of factors, including the level of precision or accuracy desired, cost, time frame available to complete the study, questionnaire length and structure, the incidence rate, and sample characteristics. The level of precision is influenced more by the research design, budget available and projected costs, time frame, and research process than it is by the data collection method. Online data collection is the least costly while personal interviews and intercepts cost the most. Online surveys and those targeting cell phone users have higher response rates, while mail surveys may take weeks to collect. Personal interviews, mail surveys, and some types of online surveys are appropriate for long questionnaires, while telephone surveys must be shorter and are among the least flexible with respect to questionnaire structure. Online surveys provide the greatest flexibility in this area.

GLOSSARY OF KEY TERMS

Cross-sectional study: research conducted at a single point in time that provides a snapshot of the subject or topic being studied at that particular time

Deliberate falsification: error that occurs when an individual provides false answers on purpose

Frame error: use of an incorrect sample frame

Incidence: percentage of individuals, households, or businesses in the population that would be qualified as potential respondents in a particular study

Interviewer error or bias: error that occurs when an interviewer influences a respondent to give erroneous answers, either intentionally or unintentionally

Longitudinal study: research study over time in which the same questions are asked at different points in time

Measurement error: difference between the responses that are obtained and the true responses that were sought

Measurement instrument error or bias: error caused by the questionnaire or instrument being used for measurement

Nonresponse bias: difference between the responses of those who participate in a study and those who do not participate in the study

Population specification error: error that occurs when population is incorrectly identified

Process error: error that occurs when data from a survey instrument are incorrectly entered into the computer program being used to tally and analyze the data

Random error: error that is the result of chance and occurs accidentally throughout the research process

Response rate: percentage of individuals who complete a study from among those who are contacted and asked to participate

Sample frame: list of population members or elements from which the sample will be selected

Search cost: cost associated with locating individuals who meet the sample criteria for a study

Selection error: error that occurs when sampling procedures are not followed or are not clearly defined

Systematic error: error resulting from a mistake or problem in the research design or the research process

CRITICAL THINKING EXERCISES

1. Identify the type of error found in each of the following scenarios and discuss what actions could be taken to minimize future errors of this type:
   a. An interviewer frowns and blinks her eyes rapidly upon hearing the response offered by a study participant.
   b. The researcher in charge of programming the random digit dialer for a telephone survey forgets to enter two area codes for the population being studied.

c. The data entry clerk's finger slips, and he enters a 2 for a variable coded as 3.

d. An individual forgets to fill out a mail survey by the due date.

2. A local heating and air-conditioning (AC) firm that traditionally targeted the construction trade needs to look for other revenue sources, as the faltering economy has led to a sharp decline in new housing construction. While the firm provides maintenance for some business and residential AC/heating units, it must expand its presence within these markets if the business is to survive. The firm is willing to invest in marketing research and is in the process of developing a questionnaire. Specifically, the firm wants to learn how important the AC/heating unit brand name is to business owners and residential consumers when purchasing a replacement unit. The firm also wants to know what criteria both groups use when selecting an AC/heating firm to provide maintenance for existing units. Finally, it wants to understand how aware consumers and businesses are of the firm, and how its image is perceived by each group. What survey method would you recommend to gather these data? Why? Should the same data collection method be used for residential consumers and businesses? Why or why not?

3. A minor league baseball team has developed a questionnaire that will be administered to people who attend the game scheduled on July 4. The purpose of the survey is to determine how satisfied attendees are with the park, in terms of parking, food service, and other amenities. Is this an effective method of data collection? Why or why not? How can it be improved? How can the baseball team get feedback from fans who visited the park and watched a game in the past, but never returned?

4. Suppose a bank is considering surveying its customers to determine their awareness of a new service that was recently introduced. Compare and contrast the pros and cons of surveying via cell phones versus landlines versus mail surveys. Evaluate each method against the selection criteria discussed in the text. Which method would you recommend? Why?

5. A fast-food franchise with multiple restaurant locations throughout the designated market area has chosen the mall intercept approach to collect data. What types of systematic error are to be expected with this technique? Give examples to clarify your answer. What steps can the researchers take to minimize systematic error in the mall intercept study?

6. The state congressman for your area has chosen to survey constituents via telephone to better understand their views toward higher education funding. What types of systematic error are to be expected with this technique? Give examples to clarify your answer. What steps can the researchers take to minimize systematic error when data are collected via telephone?

7. A national music store chain has chosen an online survey methodology to collect data regarding attitudes toward purchasing music online compared to purchasing it in the store. The chain also wants to understand consumer perceptions of its strengths and weaknesses. What types of systematic error are to be expected with this technique? Give examples to clarify your answer. What steps can the researchers take to minimize systematic error when data are collected online?

8. A university researcher is using mail surveys to study the type of business-to-business marketing techniques employed by firms within a variety of industries. What types of systematic error are to be expected with this technique? Give examples to clarify your answer. What steps can the researchers take to minimize systematic error when data are collected by mail?

9. Create a table in which the method of data collection is listed at the head of each column. List a different type of systematic error at the beginning of each row. For each data collection method and error type combination, identify whether the error type is a major concern, a minor concern, or of no concern by filling in the table with the appropriate label.

CONTINUING CASE STUDY: LAKESIDE GRILL

The students studying Lakeside Grill chose an intercept approach for the survey component of their research. As Juan explains, "Since we were dealing with a local restaurant that most people had either been to or at least heard about, we thought an intercept approach would work well." To ensure a more "unbiased sample" the team conducted the intercept in two places. First, the students surveyed customers in Lakeside Grill as they waited for their food. Second, they surveyed people at the local mall on two different weekends. That was to reach people who hadn't eaten at Lakeside Grill or hadn't eaten there lately for some reason, such as maybe having a bad experience.

The group spent a long time debating whether or not to read the questions to participants. The alternative being considered was to give the survey questionnaire to individuals, let them fill it out on their own, and just collect it later when they were finished. The group chose the latter. "Especially since people may be eating, we didn't feel like it would be appropriate to sit down and ask them the questions," Brooke explains. "Also, we thought people would be more honest if they wrote down their answers themselves instead of giving them to us. It completely eliminates any interviewer error!"

Not everyone in the group was in agreement with the survey approach used. According to Zach, "using telephones and cell phones would have been better. We had a lot of refusals, especially at the mall because people were busy shopping and didn't want to complete the survey. I really think the nonresponse bias would have been lower with a telephone survey, and I also think response error would have been less because you don't have somebody watching you fill out the questionnaire. People tend to be more honest on the phone than in person."

Critique Questions:

1. How would you evaluate the approach the student team used? Do you think it was the best survey approach? Why or why not?

2. What about Zach's statement that "people tend to be more honest on the phone than in person"? Do you agree or disagree? Why?

3. Do you agree or disagree with Zach's statement that "nonresponse bias would have been lower with a telephone survey" than the intercept approach that was used? Why?

4. Consider Brooke's statement "We thought people would be more honest if they wrote down their answers themselves instead of giving them to us." Do you agree or disagree? Why?

5. Brooke made the statement that by having respondents complete the survey themselves, "it completely eliminates any interviewer error." Do you agree or disagree with this statement? Why?

6. What types of systematic errors would be a concern with the intercept approach used by the students?

7. Instead of an intercept approach, what other survey method could the team have used? How would it compare to the intercept approach that was used in terms of systematic error? What about the survey selection considerations listed in the chapter? How would the selection factors compare?

MARKETING RESEARCH PORTFOLIO

The Chapter 6 mini-case underscores the importance of considering multiple factors when selecting a data collection method. The client, an eye clinic specializing in laser surgery, wishes to survey only individuals who meet certain criteria. Students are asked to evaluate the pros and cons of each data collection method with regard to the client's needs, and to make use of the survey selection factors discussed in the chapter when recommending the most optimal data collection method. The assignment instructions and case information can be found at www.sagepub.com/clowess.

STUDENT STUDY SITE

Visit the Student Study Site at www.sagepub.com/clowess to access the following additional materials:

- eFlashcards
- Web Quizzes
- SAGE Journal Articles
- Web Resources

Experimental Research

After reading this chapter, you should be able to

1. Identify the three conditions that must be present to prove causation.

2. Name and define the basic terms and notation used in experimental design.

3. Discuss the extraneous factors that can affect internal and external validity.

4. Describe the various types of preexperimental designs.

5. Describe the various types of true experimental designs.

6. Describe the various types of quasi-experimental designs.

7. Discuss the concept of test markets.

INTRODUCTION

DTech Canada wanted to explore new market opportunities for remanufactured diesel engine parts. DTech's traditional market is diesel engine repair shops. Two other potential markets the company wanted to explore were gasoline repair shops and independent parts distributors. To determine the feasibility of these markets and the best approach, DTech hired Hep Communications to conduct a test market. The agency selected 20,000 shops and distributors for its test market. Each company was sent a sealed, printed, folded postcard encouraging the prospect to visit a website to learn more about DTech and to register for a discount on an initial parts stock order.

The companies that visited the website and registered for the discount on the initial order were divided into four equal test markets for the follow-up. Companies in Test Market 1 were sent a follow-up postcard, companies in Test Market 2 were sent a follow-up fax, companies in Test Market 3 received an outbound telephone call, and companies in Test Market 4 received a follow-up e-mail. The response rates of the four test markets were compared. The highest response rate was 19.8% for those in the last test market.[1] By using test markets, DTech Canada was able to determine the best approach to use to follow up on its leads.

In addition to test markets, Chapter 7 explores the topic of experimental research. Various experimental designs can be used by marketing researchers. Because of its high cost and the need to have tight controls on the variables being studied, experimental design is not used as much in the commercial marketing research industry as other forms of research. But, it is important to understand how experimental research is conducted and how it can be used.

NATURE OF CAUSAL RESEARCH

- Objective 7.1: Identify the three conditions that must be present to prove causation.

Experimental research is conducted by marketing researchers because it is the only type of research that can actually prove cause and effect. Thus, experimental research is often referred to as causal research. Many people make the mistake of thinking that descriptive research, which can be used to determine if two variables vary (or correlate) together, provides proof of causation. For instance, an increase in a firm's advertising budget might be followed by an increase in sales for the item that was advertised. While it may appear that advertising was the cause of the increase in sales, descriptive research of this nature cannot prove that it actually was the cause. A number of other factors may have also contributed to the increase in sales, such as a price drop by the manufacturer (or a price increase by a competitor), issuance of coupons, changes in the economy, changes in product-quality perceptions, or a lack of competition. The only way to prove a cause-and-effect relationship between advertising and sales is to conduct some type of experimental research in which these other alternative explanations are either eliminated or held constant. To demonstrate a causal relationship, three conditions must be met: concomitant variation, time order of occurrence, and elimination of extraneous factors (see Figure 7.1).

In examining causation, it is important to understand the current, popular view held by most marketing researchers and the scientific view. When conducting causal research, the popular view is that if X causes Y, then the relationship always holds true, and changes in X will always cause corresponding changes in Y. The scientific view holds that one can never prove beyond a shadow of doubt that X causes Y. There is always a possibility that an extraneous variable is present that contributes to the change in Y, and because of this possibility, all researchers can do is infer that X causes Y. Further, the relationship between X and Y is not perpetual. However,

Figure 7.1   Conditions for Causal Relationships

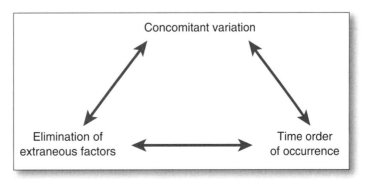

one can reasonably infer the relationship exists and that there is a high probability that any changes in X will cause corresponding changes in Y.

Concomitant Variation

The first condition that must be met for causation is **concomitant variation,** which means two variables are correlated and will vary together in a predictable manner. The correlation can be positive or inverse. With a positive correlation, as X increases, Y increases. The reverse is also true in that decreases in X correlate with decreases in Y. With an inverse correlation, the opposite occurs, meaning that as X increases, Y decreases, and as X decreases, Y increases.

The second component of concomitant variation is the *predictable manner.* This means that if the correlation between X and Y is such that for every 1-unit increase in X there is a corresponding 3-unit increase in Y, then a 2-unit increase in X should produce a 6-unit increase in Y.

It is also important to realize that just because two variables are correlated it does not mean a true causal relationship exists. The correlation between these variables can be spurious—that is, coincidental. For instance, the number of snow shovels and snow blowers sold is highly correlated (inversely) with the average winter temperature of a region. More snow shovels and snow blowers are sold in states with lower average winter temperatures, such as Minnesota and New York, than in states with higher average winter temperatures, such as Florida and Texas. But, it is not the temperature that makes the difference. It is the amount of snow. New York receives more snow than Texas, and as a result more snow equipment is sold in New York than in Texas. While the temperature is a factor, it is not the cause. People buy snow shovels and snow blowers to remove snow, and what they buy is directly related to the level of snow they anticipate. Thus, correlation alone does not prove causation; though necessary for causation to occur, the presence of a predictable correlation alone is insufficient. Demonstrating a true cause-and-effect relationship requires that two other conditions be satisfied as well.

Time Order of Occurrence

For causation to be present, X must occur before or simultaneously with Y. To say issuing coupons caused an increase in sales means the coupons must have been issued before or as sales increased. If the coupons were issued after the increase in sales, then the condition does not meet the time order of occurrence condition.

Just as mentioned with concomitant variation, meeting the time order of occurrence does not prove a cause-and-effect relationship. Coupons for pizza may have been distributed just before the Super Bowl football game, and during the evening of the game sales of pizza may have doubled or tripled. But, the large increase is more likely due to the Super Bowl game and not the issuance of coupons, especially if competitors also issued coupons or other promotional deals.

Elimination of Extraneous Factors

The most difficult condition for a causal relationship is the elimination of extraneous factors. To meet all three conditions, researchers often use experiments where variables can be controlled, meaning that they are kept the same as different treatments are administered and measured, and only the variable that is under study is manipulated to see if it has an impact. To prove that

X indeed causes Y, a researcher must eliminate all other variables that could possibly have an impact on Y. For that reason, most experimental research studies are conducted in a laboratory or tightly controlled environment where everything but the variable under study can be controlled.

While field studies can be used for causal research, it is much more difficult to control extraneous variables, and results are not as conclusive as those obtained in a lab setting. Referring back to some of the examples that have been used, most marketers would agree that advertising, hiring new salespeople, and issuing coupons have an impact on sales. But, to show cause and effect during a field study, it would be necessary to isolate all of the variables but the one being studied. Such a task would be impossible in an actual marketplace (field) setting!

BASIC ELEMENTS OF EXPERIMENTAL DESIGN

Before discussing experimental designs, it is necessary to define certain terms and develop a notation to represent those terms and various design approaches. The three basic components of experiments are the dependent variable, independent variables, and treatment. The **dependent variable** is the outcome variable of the experiment, which the researcher measures and is most interested in studying—this is the *effect* component of the cause-and-effect relationship being studied. **Independent variables** are those variables that are manipulated, or changed, in the experiment in order to observe the impact they may have on the dependent variable. They are the *cause* element in the cause-and-effect relationship.

To ensure causality, researchers will manipulate only one variable at a time and hold the other independent variables constant. The manipulation of the independent variable is called the **treatment.** For example, in studying the impact of age of the model in print advertising on attitudes toward advertising, the researcher created a number of identical ads. Since age of model was the treatment variable, the only difference in the ads was the age of the model; the size of the ad as well as the headline, copy, layout, and background shown in the ad remained the same. While different models of various ages were used, the gender and ethnicity of the model were held constant to ensure that if differences in attitude toward the ad did occur, they were due to the age of the model and not to some other factor.

This type of experimental research would be valuable for a marketer targeting individuals in the 50- to 70-year age group. Past research has shown that these individuals are getting older but don't want to admit it. They are reluctant to "act their age" and often will purchase sports cars and engage in activities to make themselves appear young. So the question advertisers face is whether they should use models in the 50- to 70-year age category, or younger models. To test this, a researcher may use four different treatments, in which four different-aged models (20s, 30s, 40s, and 50s) are portrayed, one to each treatment. The experimental material being presented, in this case the ad, is called the stimulus, while those who participate in an experiment are referred to as **subjects,** rather than respondents. Different subject groups would be used in each treatment, and measurements would be taken at various points in time, depending on the type of experiment being used.

Experimental Notation

A standard system of notation has been developed for experiments consisting of X and O, with subscripts included to note the time period. X denotes the application of a treatment

■ Objective 7.2: Name and define the basic terms and notation used in experimental design.

to a variable or group of participants. O represents a measurement of a variable or group of participants, also called an **observation.** When written in a horizontal line, these notations represent different periods of time. Consider the following example:

$$O_1 \quad X \quad O_2$$

The notation can be interpreted in the following fashion. The experiment began with an observation or measurement of the dependent variable(s). The experiment took place with some type of treatment. Then a second observation or measurement of the dependent variable took place. This type of experiment includes pre- and posttests. To illustrate, suppose a company wants to test the impact of a product placement in a movie. Subjects are recruited and asked, before seeing the movie, to complete a survey on their attitude toward various brands (O_1). They watch the movie, which is the treatment (X). Then, at the end, they take the same survey again (O_2). The attitude toward the test brand before the movie is compared to the attitude toward the test brand after the movie to see if the product placement had any effect (or change) on the subjects' attitude toward the target brand. This impact, known as the experimental effect, is calculated by means of this simple formula: $O_2 - O_1$. In order for researchers to repeat the survey without the subjects being suspicious, they are typically told that a brand(s) was inadvertently left out of the original survey, so the subjects are requested to take the survey again.

There are times that a researcher will have more than one test group of subjects, each of which receives a different type of treatment. In the above example, one group may see the primary actor using the brand and mentioning the brand's name in the movie. The second group may see the brand being used by the actor, but the brand name itself is not mentioned. Assuming a pre- and postsurvey, the notation for this experiment would appear as follows:

$$(R) \quad O_1 \quad X_1 \quad O_2$$
$$(R) \quad O_3 \quad X_2 \quad O_4$$

X_1 would denote the first treatment group, the one where the actor used and also mentioned the brand name. X_2 would denote the second treatment group that saw the product being used by the actor but heard no verbal mention of the brand name. The symbol R means that subjects have been randomly assigned to either the first or the second treatment condition, a process called **randomization.**

Control and Treatment Groups

To prove causation, the three conditions mentioned earlier all must occur. To be certain the results are from the treatment and not some other extraneous variable, researchers will use a control group. The control group receives the same measurement process as the test subjects, but is not exposed to any treatment. For the product placement in the movie, the control group would be surveyed before and after the movie just as the treatment group would. But, the movie watched by the control group would not contain the product placement at all. Thus, the control subjects' attitude toward the brand should not change. By comparing the results of the experiment of the test group with those found in the control group, researchers would be able to determine if the product placement did indeed have an impact on attitude toward the brand. If the test subjects indicated a more positive attitude and the control group showed no change in attitude, then researchers could assert that product placement does have an impact on consumer attitudes toward brands since that was the only difference in the movies being watched by the two groups. Alternatively, when researchers are considering changing a marketing communication vehicle, the control group may be shown the existing point-of-purchase display, while the experimental group views the redesigned display. In this case, the researcher is trying to ascertain that the new display is superior to the old, on the basis of whatever dependent measures are observed.

In terms of notation, this type of experiment would be denoted in the following manner:

$$O_1 \quad X_1 \quad O_2$$
$$O_3 \quad O_4$$

The first line denotes the treatment group, and X_1 is the product placement episode in the movie. The second line is the control group. Notice the control experiences both measurement processes, but is not exposed to the product placement. Keep in mind that the treatment is the product placement, not the movie. The movie is just the vehicle researchers use for the experiment.

Ethics in Experimentation

Administering an experiment requires careful attention to detail and ethical conduct by the researcher (see Figure 7.2). First and foremost, participants should never be put at risk of physical or mental harm. Experimental subjects should always be informed of their right to withdraw from the experiment at any time for any reason. Subjects also have the right to know how the data will be used, and whether the information they provide is confidential and anonymous. Normally this information is provided in an "informed consent" document that researchers may ask participants to sign.

The purpose of the experiment or the exact nature of the experimental treatment itself is often disguised by the researcher in order to minimize bias on the part of the respondent. When a disguise of some type is used, the ethical researcher should debrief participants once the experiment is concluded. **Debriefing** entails explaining the true purpose of the study, what variables were being manipulated, and why.

Figure 7.2 Ethical Considerations in Experimental Research

- No physical or mental risk
- Right to withdraw
- Knowledge of how data will be used
- Information confidential or anonymous
- Debriefing

Internal and External Validity

A major reason researchers conduct experiments is the potential for a higher degree of validity. **Validity** refers to the degree to which an experiment (or research study) measures what it is supposed to measure. An experiment designed to measure brand image has a high degree of validity if indeed brand image is being measured and not something else, such as product attractiveness, attitude toward an ad, or even brand preference.

Validity consists of both internal and external validity. **Internal validity** is the extent to which a particular treatment in an experiment produces the sole effect on the dependent variable. Obtaining a high level of internal validity requires ruling out any other possible extraneous effect that may contribute to the change in the dependent variable. Otherwise, these extraneous effects represent competing explanations for the dependent variable change that confound, or call into question, the results of the study.

External validity refers to the extent the findings of an experiment (or research study) can be generalized to the population as whole or to the specific population being studied. External validity depends on how well the sample selected for the study represents the population to which it is projected. If the population under study is college students, then to obtain external validity the sample needs to be representative of college students in terms of characteristics such as major, class status, age, gender, and race.

■ Objective 7.3: Discuss the extraneous factors that can affect internal and external validity.

EXTRANEOUS VARIABLES

To prove causation or even to assert causation, it is important to control for any extraneous variables that may have an impact on the dependent variable, because the presence of extraneous variables provides an alternative reason, or competing explanation, for any changes observed in the dependent variable. Controlling for these extraneous factors is much easier in a laboratory setting than in field studies. Figure 7.3 identifies the primary extraneous variables or factors that can impact experimental research.[2] Controlling for these factors increases the validity of an experiment. The elimination of competing explanations for the study findings allows the researcher to have confidence in asserting that the change in the dependent variable is due to the treatment, and not to the presence of one or more extraneous variables.

Figure 7.3   Extraneous Factors in Experimental Research

- History
- Maturation
- Testing
- Instrumentation
- Selection
- Attrition

History

History effect occurs when some external event occurs between the beginning and the end of an experiment that changes the outcome of the event. Internal validity is impacted by history effect since the change in the dependent variable is due to something other than the treatment. In field studies, a large number of events can impact the results, such as actions by competitors, changes in the economy, and a catastrophic event such as a tornado or hurricane. The longer the experiment lasts, the more likely history will impact the results. Conducting experiments in a laboratory reduces the chances of history effect, especially if there is a short time between the beginning and the end of the experiment. Minimizing changes to the lighting, the room location, the noise level, the people administering the experiment, or other extraneous factors within the laboratory setting can also help to minimize history effect.

Maturation

While the history effect involves some event that changes the results of an experiment, **maturation** involves changes in the subject over time that can impact the results of the experiment. Time series studies, which take place over weeks, months, or sometimes even years, are particularly prone to this effect. Maturation often occurs when subjects become fatigued or tired or hungry, or simply as a result of maturing (i.e., "growing up") over time.

If an experiment lasts several hours, subjects may get tired or hungry, and hurriedly answer questions after the treatment without paying much attention to what they are reading, or without thinking through the answer. In this case, the results that are attributed to the experiment may be caused by the subject's fatigue or hunger, rather than exposure to the treatment. Experiments that last several weeks or months are often affected by subject maturation. The person just gets older; with age comes greater life experiences, different priorities, and physical changes to the mind and body. The subject's mood can also vary from one time period to the next. As a result of any or all of these factors, the subject's views may change, which in turn affects the results, and damages the internal validity of the experiment. The longer an experiment runs, the more likely maturation effects will occur.

Randomly assigning subjects to treatment and control groups is one method by which researchers can control for history effects. By randomly assigning subjects, the laws of probability allow the researcher to assume that uncontrolled effects will be evenly spread between treatment conditions. This is an important assumption, as it means that the negative impact due to maturation effects will in fact "cancel out" in the final analysis, because what affects one group affects all equally.[3]

Testing

Testing effect occurs when subjects become sensitized to the measurement instrument or experiment through the pretest in a way that affects the results of the experiment. Testing effect occurs in one of two ways. First, when subjects receive the posttest after the experiment, they have already seen the questions, so they know how to answer. Some subjects choose to answer the same as they did on the pretest to demonstrate consistency, regardless of whether or not their actual attitudes or reactions have changed. Others will provide different answers to the posttest based on what they think the researcher wants them to say, rather than how they really feel, because exposure to the pretest and experiment has given them a clue as to the topic being studied.

The second way testing effect occurs is to sensitize the subjects to the experiment. They pay closer attention than normal. For instance, a common experiment in advertising research begins with a pretest in which subjects are asked their thoughts about several brands. Questions that are not relevant to the true purpose of the study are also interspersed throughout the survey to disguise the researcher's intent. The subjects then watch a documentary or some other television show with ads or product placements embedded. When it is over, they are asked about the brands again, though the purpose of the posttest is disguised in some fashion. The researcher might claim to have accidentally left one or more brands off the list, or the researcher may state that he or she is interested in respondents' reactions to the television show they have just viewed. But, the process of participating in the experiment may cause the subjects to pay more attention to the ads and product placements than they would in "real life." Suppose Coca-Cola is one of the brands. When the subject sees the actor drinking the Coke, it is noticed, where in normal circumstances the subject may never have noticed it.

Several methods are often used to reduce testing effect with the measurement component of an experiment. Random assignment of subjects is often used, and as mentioned previously, the purpose of the study is typically disguised in some fashion. Claiming the intent of the study is to assess attitudes toward the TV show, rather than toward the ad, is not

Subjects involved in an experiment in a movie theater.

unethical, unless the researcher fails to debrief participants afterward. Including multiple ads for different brands in addition to the test ad(s) helps to disguise which brand is being studied. Furthermore, researchers will often modify the measurement process by changing (1) the order of the questions, (2) the names of brands that have been added to disguise the true brand being studied, or (3) the wording of the questions themselves. Finally, the posttest often includes a question asking subjects to identify the purpose of the study. If the subject answers in a way that indicates knowledge of the specific topic and brand, the researcher often chooses to exclude that individual from the sample.

Instrumentation

It was just mentioned that researchers will often modify the measurement process to reduce the impact of testing effect. Doing so, however, creates the possibility of **instrumentation effect,** which is caused by a change in the measurement instrument, its calibration, or other procedures used to measure the dependent variable.

Changing the wording of questions used on the posttest is one way of reducing testing effect. But, changing the wording raises the possibility of instrumentation effect since the change in the dependent variable may be due to the way the posttest questions were worded and not to the experiment itself. So researchers have to be careful when they use pretests and posttests to ensure any changes between the two testing instruments are not due to the instrument itself.

If human interviewers are used, then instrumentation effect can occur in two ways. First, if different interviewers are used for the pretests and posttests, then the effect on the dependent variable may be due to the differences in the interviewer and not the experiment. If the same interviewer is used and he or she asks the questions in a different way, with different words, different body language, and a different tone of voice, then instrumentation error can occur.

So researchers face a dilemma. To reduce testing effect, the researcher wants to modify the posttest from the pretest. But, in so doing, it increases the likelihood of instrumentation effect. The solution is to find a method that is least likely to produce error and as a result will increase internal validity.

Selection

Selection effect occurs when the sample selected for a study is not representative of the population being studied or the samples selected for different groups within the study are not statistically the same. If the study sample is not representative of the population being studied, then external validity is threatened since the results of the experiment cannot be generalized to the population.

If the samples within the study differ, then the internal validity of the experiment is threatened. For instance, if an experiment uses a control group and a treatment group, then both samples need to be similar, and both need to be representative of the population being studied. If the control or treatment sample is different, then any results obtained in the experiment may be due to the differences in the two samples rather than the treatment. For example, if the treatment group has statistically more females than are present in the control group, then the results may be due to the larger percentage of females in the treatment group rather than the treatment itself. While it is possible to "match" samples between groups on one or possibly two important characteristics, researchers typically rely on two methods of controlling for selection effect. First, subjects who match the population's characteristics are randomly assigned to treatment or control conditions. Second, during the data analysis stage, various statistical techniques can be used to control for the influence of important characteristics, such as gender in the example above, which may not otherwise be evenly distributed among treatment conditions, even when randomly assigned.

Attrition

Sample **attrition,** also called mortality, is the loss of subjects during the time the experiment is being conducted. As would be expected, the longer the experiment lasts, the more likely it is that individuals will drop out of the study. The impact of attrition depends on the size of the sample. If the sample size is sufficiently large and only a few drop out of the study, it may not affect the overall results of the study. But, if a larger number drop out of the study, then there is concern that those who drop out may in some way be different from those who complete the experiment, resulting in a nonresponse bias. Thus, the results would be impacted by attrition.

Controlling for attrition is difficult. The ethical marketing researcher must respect the subject's right to terminate participation in an experiment at any time, for any reason. Forcing subjects to complete an experiment via coercion, or "guilt-tripping," is unethical and should not be used.

Randomly assigning subjects to treatment conditions is again recommended as a means of "evening out" the influence of attrition between experimental and control groups. Alerting subjects ahead of time to the amount of time needed to complete the study may help to stave off some attrition. Providing incentives for participation, which are given only to those who complete the experiment, may also be helpful. Recruiting participants from research panels may result in a sample that is less subject to attrition than one recruited by the researcher via other means. Of course, the shorter the experiment, the less likely attrition will occur, so the pretest and posttest measurement instrument should be kept as short as possible, while still accommodating "dummy" questions that help to disguise the research purpose.

It is important for marketing researchers to be aware of all six extraneous factors that can impact both internal and external validity. While completely eliminating these factors may not be possible, being aware of each one can help researchers reduce their impact. But, at the same time, researchers must be aware of the potential tradeoffs between internal and external validity. By tightening experimental controls, researchers can increase the internal validity of the findings. But, in so doing, they may decrease the realism of the study and detract from the findings' external validity. Such an outcome would defeat the real purpose of the study—being able to generalize the findings to the population.[4]

■ Objective 7.4: Describe the various types of preexperimental designs.

PREEXPERIMENTAL DESIGNS

As shown in Figure 7.4, experimental designs can be divided into three broad groups: preexperimental designs, true experimental designs, and quasi-experimental designs. The difference in the designs is based on the way researchers handle the treatment, extraneous variables, and the presence of a control group.

Figure 7.4   Types of Experimental Designs

- Preexperimental designs
- True experimental designs
- Quasi-experimental designs

Preexperimental designs are characterized by little or no control over extraneous variables and no randomization of subjects (see Figure 7.5). Preexperimental designs tend to be used in field tests where the researcher has no or little control over factors that may impact the dependent variable. Thus, preexperimental designs lack both internal and external validity.

Figure 7.5   Pre-Experimental Designs

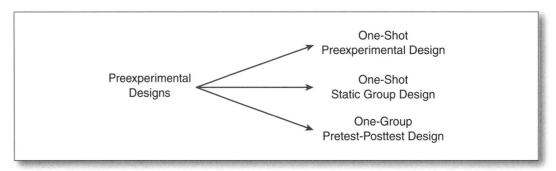

Preexperimental Designs
- One-Shot Preexperimental Design
- One-Shot Static Group Design
- One-Group Pretest-Posttest Design

One-Shot Preexperimental Design

With the **one-shot preexperimental design** test subjects are exposed to a treatment variable followed by a measurement of the dependent variable. It does not have any type of control group, nor is there a pretest prior to exposure to the treatment variable. In terms of experimental notation, it would be shown as follows:

$$X \quad O_1$$

Because there is no control group, researchers cannot say with any degree of certainty that a change in the dependent variable was due to the treatment effect. Further, with no pretest, it is impossible to determine whether or not a change actually occurred. Thus, the one-shot preexperimental design lacks both internal and external validity.

The one-short experimental approach is often used with the introduction of new products. No past data exist, so there is no way a company can obtain pretest measures. Thus, the new product is placed in select markets, featured in select stores, or offered on a company's website only. After a prespecified time, sales are measured to determine if the new product has potential and should be launched nationally.

Komal Nagar used the one-shot preexperimental design to examine the effect of deceptive advertising on claim recall. Respondents in the experiment were told the study was concerned with the effectiveness of advertising in print media. Each was then given a print ad of a fictitious brand of oral antiseptic that had both true claims and deceptive claims (the treatment, X). After the participants had time to look at and study the ad, it was returned to the researcher. The participants were then asked to recall as many of the claims as possible and to list them on a blank sheet of paper (the measurement, O). It was found that true claims were recalled with a higher frequency than deceptive claims.[5]

One-Shot Static Group Design

With the **one-shot static group design** measurements are also taken after the experiment. However, this design differs from the one-shot preexperimental design in that it includes a control group for comparison purposes. However, it does not include any pretesting of subjects. In terms of notation, the one-shot static group design would be written as follows:

$$X \quad O_1$$
$$O_2$$

The first row indicates the treatment group and contains the treatment and observation. The second row is the control group that consists of only a measurement. The experimental effect is calculated by subtracting the measurement of the treatment group from the posttest results of the control group, $O_2 - O_1$.

The major validity problem with this design is the comparison of the two groups: the experimental group and the control group. For the results to be valid, the two groups must have been equal prior to the experiment. Since no pretest was conducted and subjects were not randomly assigned to conditions, researchers have no way of knowing if the two groups were indeed equal. It is possible that the difference in regard to the dependent variable was already present prior to the experiment and that the experiment itself did not cause any change in the test group.

The one-shot static group design is sometimes used in the testing of new products. For instance, a company may conduct an experiment to test a new software program that allows salespeople to track their activities. Suppose the software is distributed to half of the salespeople in a company. After using the software, the research company measures satisfaction of the salespeople with the software they used. Half used the new software (the experiment); the other half continued using the old software (the control). By comparing the two groups, the research company can determine if there is a higher level of satisfaction with the new software.

While the results provide an indication of how effective the software was in increasing satisfaction, two problems exist. First, it is possible there were differences already between the two groups and that the new software had nothing to do with the treatment group's higher scores. Second, since no pretest was taken, the researcher has no idea if there was a change in satisfaction. It's even possible that the level of satisfaction with the old software was higher and that using the new software resulted in a decrease in satisfaction.

One-Group Pretest-Posttest Design

With the **one-group pretest-posttest design** observation measurements are taken prior to the experiment and again after the experiment. Taking a pretest measurement is certainly an advantage over the one-shot design, but still lacks a control group. In terms of notation, it would be

$$O_1 \quad X \quad O_2$$

To measure the impact of the treatment, researchers calculate the experimental effect by $O_2 - O_1$, which is the difference between the posttest results and the pretest measurement.

This approach would measure subjects prior to the experiment and then after the experiment to see if any differences occurred. Kraft may want to test the impact of a new digital end-of-aisle display with its Planters breakfast bars. The company has weekly sales data for the breakfast bars already. Suppose the company obtains the cooperation of 25 different grocery stores to test the new digital display for four weeks. Kraft is able to access its database for the exact sales for each of the 25 stores, which is the pretest score. Kraft can monitor the sales of Planters breakfast bars that are placed on the display at the 25 stores and, after the four-week period, compare sales for the four-week period with the digital display to sales for the four weeks prior to the special display.

While it seems that the one-group pretest-posttest design is an excellent research method, it suffers from some internal validity issues. The history effect is especially a problem with field studies, such as the one with the breakfast bars. If sales increased in the stores with the digital display, it is conceivable that the increase was due to other factors, such as actions by competitors, advertising, and promotions.

■ Objective 7.5: Describe the various types of true experimental designs.

TRUE EXPERIMENTAL DESIGNS

With **true experimental designs,** subjects are randomly assigned from a pool of subjects. The sample size needed for each cell (treatment or control group) can be influenced by a variety of factors. For instance, in pricing research it is common to have sample sizes that range from 200 to as many as 400 subjects per group. Variables that influence the exact sample size per cell may include the number of brands involved in the study or the number of price points being tested.[6] Whereas in preexperimental designs subjects were not randomized, randomization is a key component shared by all true experimental designs. Randomizing reduces the selection effect since probability theory tells us that groups within an experimental design should not differ due to the individual assignment of members to the groups. Figure 7.6 identifies the two primary experimental designs.

Figure 7.6   True Experimental Designs

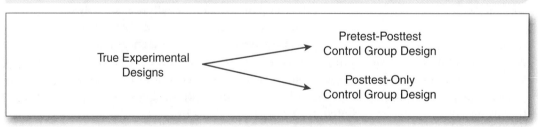

Pretest-Posttest Control Group Design

In the **pretest-posttest control group design** subjects are randomly assigned to an experimental group and a control group. Both groups are then pretested. The experiment is conducted with only the experimental group being exposed to the treatment. Once the treatment is over, both the experimental and the control group are measured again, which is the posttest. The notation used for the pretest-posttest control group design is

$$(R) \quad O_1 \quad X \quad O_2$$

$$(R) \quad O_3 \quad O_4$$

Suppose advertising researchers want to test an advertisement that has been developed for the Super Bowl. Assume 400 individuals are recruited to participate in the study. They are not told the purpose of the research, but are told only that they will be watching a new television show with advertisements as it would appear on television during sweeps week. The subjects are randomly assigned with half being selected for the experimental group and the other half being selected for the control group. During the television show, both groups see 10 different ads. The experimental group is exposed to the newly designed Super Bowl ad, and the control group is not. Pretest measures are taken by both groups before watching the television show and again after the show is over.

To determine the experimental effect, or impact of the experiment, it is necessary to subtract the pretest scores from the posttest scores and then compare the treatment group difference to the control group difference. In notation language, it would be written as follows:

$$(O_2 - O_1) - (O_4 - O_3)$$

To illustrate, suppose the treatment variable is brand awareness. Before the experiment, 42% of the experimental group was aware of the brand compared to 40% awareness among the control group. After the experiment, awareness of the brand in the experimental group, whose members were shown the new Super Bowl ad, rose to 54%, compared to 43% for the control group. The difference in the experimental group was 12% (54 − 42), and the difference in the control group was 3% (43 − 40). Thus, the treatment effect was 11% (14 − 3).

The benefit of a true experimental design is that the extraneous variables discussed earlier would have the same effect on both the experimental and the control group. Therefore, these factors would not impact the validity of the research. It is the randomization process that allows researchers to make this claim. History, maturation, instrumentation, selection, and attrition, if present, would have the same impact on both the treatment and the control group.

The one extraneous variable that may decrease internal validity is testing effect. Asked to identify their awareness before the experiment, the subjects may become more sensitized to watching ads during the television show. No matter how the posttest questionnaire is worded, the results of the posttest could be biased because the subjects have already been exposed to the questionnaire or survey before the television show. In the preceding example, the increase in brand awareness of the test brand in the control group may be an indicator that testing effect was present. Theoretically, the difference in awareness should have been zero.

Posttest-Only Control Group Design

The **posttest-only control group design** looks very similar to the one-shot static group preexperimental design. The only difference is the randomization of the subjects, which makes the design a true experiment rather than a preexperimental design. The notation would be

$$(R) \quad X \quad O_1$$

$$(R) \quad O_2$$

Subjects are randomly assigned to either the experimental or the control group. The experimental group is exposed to the treatment variable. Then both groups are tested. The treatment effect is the difference between the control group posttest score and the experimental group posttest score, $O_2 - O_1$.

The posttest-only control group design is often used to study the effect of new products. Suppose Skin So Soft developed a new skin lotion with a medicated compound that is designed to help soothe the itch in dermatitis. Subjects selected for the study are randomly assigned to the treatment group and the control group. The treatment group receives the skin solution with the new anti-itch compound, and the control group receives the product without the anti-itch compound. Both groups use the lotion and are then asked a series of questions about the itch of the dermatitis. If the treatment group indicates less itching when using the new product than the control group, then it would indicate that the decline in itching is likely due to the anti-itch compound.

Because only a posttest is used, the potential for testing and instrumentation effect is eliminated. The other extraneous variables, history, maturation, selection, and attrition, are not factors since the subjects were randomly assigned to the two groups.

QUASI-EXPERIMENTAL DESIGNS

■ Objective 7.6: Describe the various types of quasi-experimental designs.

While true experimental designs can be used for marketing research, the use of these designs requires an appropriate laboratory setting, and time, which is often a scarce commodity. More often, marketing research is conducted using either one of the preexperimental designs or one of the quasi-experimental designs. With **quasi-experimental designs,** researchers lack control of when the treatment occurs or cannot randomly assign subjects to groups. Quasi-experimental designs work well for field studies where marketers have limited control of the environment. Figure 7.7 identifies the two primary quasi-experimental designs.

Figure 7.7   Quasi-Experimental Designs

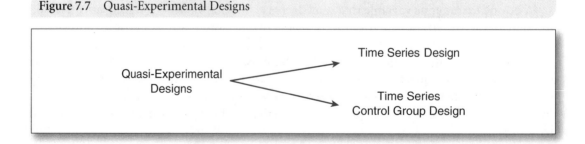

Time Series Design

While individual Super Bowl ads can be tested in a laboratory setting, the impact of an actual Super Bowl ad is a different situation. One method that marketing researchers can use is a **time series design**. Notation for the time series design might be

$$O_1 \quad O_2 \quad O_3 \quad X \quad O_4 \quad O_5 \quad O_6$$

In studying Super Bowl ads, researchers cannot have a control group since they cannot control who watches the Super Bowl and who does not. Also, they cannot control which ads individuals watch and which ads they do not see due to extraneous factors such as snack breaks and conversations with friends.

Because advertising tends to have a lag effect, researchers can use multiple measures to measure any trend that may occur. Suppose Bridgestone wants to measure the impact of being the Super Bowl half-time sponsor and its corresponding Super Bowl ads. A single pretest on awareness of Bridgestone or even attitudes toward Bridgestone may not be accurate. So researchers may choose to measure Bridgestone awareness, attitude, and image several times prior to the Super Bowl, and several times after the Super Bowl.

By comparing before and after scores, Bridgestone can determine how much of an impact the Super Bowl half-time sponsorship and ads may have had on consumers. They can also see if any trends exist and how long the Super Bowl advertising carried over. A single measurement of the dependent variable(s) before and after the Super Bowl would not be as accurate as multiple measurements. It also helps to offset the fact that the researchers are not able to have much control on the extraneous variables that affect validity of the study.

Time Series Control Group Design

Researchers can improve the validity of time series studies through adding a control group. However, not all time series situations allow for a control group. The notation for the **time series control group design** is

$$\text{Treatment Group:} \quad O_1 \quad O_2 \quad O_3 \quad X \quad O_4 \quad O_5 \quad O_6$$

$$\text{Control Group:} \quad O_1 \quad O_2 \quad O_3 \quad O_4 \quad O_5 \quad O_6$$

With this quasi-experimental design, researchers have no control over whether the subjects are part of the treatment or the control group. In some situations individuals may self-select to be part of the treatment; in other situations it may be a random event.

Consider a study to measure the impact of a new advertising campaign. Instead of launching the ad campaign nationally, the advertising agency may launch the campaign in a selected city, such as New York City or Chicago, or in a specific region, such as the northeastern or southwestern part of the United States. In either situation, sporadic measures of the brand, such as awareness, image, and attitude, can be obtained prior to the campaign from individuals in the area where the campaign will be launched and in the area where it will not be launched. Measures can then be taken again after the campaign. Scores for the treatment group can then be compared to the control group.

■ Objective 7.7:
Discuss the
concept of test
markets.

TEST MARKETS

Marketing researchers will often use test markets to study various facets of marketing. **Test marketing** involves using preexperimental or quasi-experimental designs to test new product introductions and aspects of the marketing mix. Advertising, promotions, pricing, products, and distribution can all be examined in test markets. While it is common to think of test markets as being appropriate for consumer goods typically sold in grocery or mass merchandise stores, test marketing is also used by service providers, restaurant chains, and business-to-business firms such as DTech mentioned in the opening of the chapter.

Test markets serve two primary functions. First, test markets allow a company to introduce a new product or modify elements in the marketing mix of a current product on a small scale rather than at a national level. Based on the results of the test market, national estimates can be made in terms of sales and marketing costs. These estimates also allow the manufacturer to kill a brand that fails its test market before incurring the enormous expense of a national launch. Second, test markets allow a firm to make corrections in the marketing mix before a national launch. Again, making those corrections on a small scale is less costly and less damaging to the brand's image than doing it at a national level. Test markets provide managers with valuable information that can be used in making better marketing decisions.

Challenges of Test Markets

As shown in Figure 7.8, there are a number of challenges to conducting a test market. Cost and time are the two major challenges. It took Chick-fil-A six years of test marketing before the company deemed its char-grilled barbecue chicken sandwich ready for a national rollout.[7] It is also costly to set up a test market. Testing a new product or modified current product may require setting up a new distribution system or making arrangements with the current distribution system members to stock the new product. Then new promotional materials may have to be prepared. This may include point-of-purchase materials, advertising, promotions, and, of course, packaging. The idea behind a test market is that the product and the marketing communications should resemble that which will be used in the national market as much as possible. Thus, all of the costs that go into marketing a national product are incurred, but on a smaller scale for the test market. It is not unusual for a test market to cost in the millions of dollars. Because of the costs involved, managers must weigh the benefit of a test market against the costs.

In terms of experimentation, a major challenge of test markets is controlling extraneous variables, which affect the validity of the test market. Almost all of the extraneous variables discussed earlier can impact a test market. Since test markets are conducted in the real world, researchers have little control of events that may impact the results. The advantage, however, is that it is in the real world and marketers can gauge the reactions of consumers to the new product or a change in the marketing mix. If done correctly, the test market can be an accurate predictor of what would occur on a larger,

Figure 7.8   Challenges of Test Markets

- Cost
- Time
- Controlling extraneous variables
- Competitive reactions
- Measuring results
- Novel versus normal behavior

national scale. It is more difficult to expand the findings to an international scope because of differences in culture and consumers throughout the world.

Measuring the results of a test market can offer challenges. It is easy to measure sales, but other measures may be more difficult. Measures such as consumer awareness, brand and product image, and consumer attitude offer greater challenges. These measures are important because they will provide additional information for marketing managers to make good decisions. Researchers will often use one of the quasi-experimental methods to obtain these measurements. Not only does it provide multiple measures, but it will also provide trend results. Marketers need to know if purchases are because of the novelty of the item and if repeat purchases occur. One-time trial purchases are important, but will those purchases continue? That is a very important measurement.

The length of the test market is a major decision that has ramifications, good and bad. The longer the test market, the more it will cost. Longer test markets also give competitors more time to develop their own new brands, if desired. But, on the positive side, longer test markets provide more reliable and accurate results, resulting in greater predictive power. Managers must carefully weigh the advantages of test marketing against the disadvantages to determine how long they want to run the test market.

Competitive Reactions

One of the primary disadvantages of test markets is competitive knowledge of what a company is doing. Most companies are engaged in collecting competitive information on a continual basis. If the test market runs long enough to obtain multiple measures and to obtain information that is valuable, the competitors will learn about it. Competitors can react in a number of ways, as identified in Figure 7.9.

An immediate reaction competitors can take is to offer consumer promotions on their own brands. Coupons, premiums, and price-offs are the easiest and quickest to offer. Such offers can alter consumer actions in a test market and can easily skew sales figures. Procter & Gamble test marketed a new color-safe, low-temperature bleach named Vibrant in Portland, Maine. Clorox learned of the test market, and went to the extreme length of giving every household in Portland a free gallon of Clorox bleach. Vibrant never went to market, as the competitive actions undertaken by Clorox trumped P&G's advertising, couponing, and sampling efforts during the test market.[8] If the test market is about pricing, promotions, or some other component of the marketing mix, competitors offering special deals are still likely to affect the test market results.

For longer test markets, competitors can alter their advertising budget and even the content of their advertising. Competitors are not likely to take this approach unless they feel that whatever is being test marketed can have a significant impact on their market share. Competitors do not want to lose customers and do not want to lose any of their market share, so advertising is a long-term approach to their protection. This strategy

Figure 7.9   Competitive Reactions in Test Markets

- Offer consumer promotions
- Increase advertising
- Do nothing
- Reverse engineer a new product
- Develop a competitive version
- Prepare a national counter campaign

can also be taken if a company believes that whatever is being test marketed will be launched nationally. Rather than wait on the national launch, competitors can be one step ahead with an advertising campaign aimed at countering the national launch even before it happens.

Competitors may choose to do nothing. This approach is used for two reasons, primarily. First, competitors do not believe whatever is being test marketed will succeed in the marketplace. So by doing nothing competitors are saving resources, but also it may give the test market a false hope. That is, the test market results will look good for the company conducting it, and the company will go ahead with the national launch only to have the new product or change in marketing mix fail.

The second reason competitors may do nothing is just the opposite. They believe the new product or whatever is being test marketed is a major threat. Rather than combat it in the test market, resources are gathered, and a marketing plan is developed to counter the national launch. The longer the test market lasts, the more time it gives competitors to build a counter marketing campaign.

For new products, companies will certainly pursue reverse engineering. They will purchase the new product and tear it apart, trying to find out exactly how it is made. Competitors will then take this information and look at ways of improving their own products. Thus, by the time the test market is finished and a national launch is made of the new product, competitors may have already developed a competitive version. The longer the test market, again, the more time competitors have to develop their own version of the new product with identical or similar features. This in turn enhances the likelihood that competitors will counter the launch with a national advertising campaign of their own.

The challenge for planners of test markets is to properly interpret competitive reactions. If competitors react during the test market, marketing managers have to decide if these reactions would be consistent with a national launch. If so, then the test market results would be a good predictor of future sales potential and consumer reactions. If marketing managers feel that competitors have intentionally reacted to sabotage the test market, then the results of the test market are much more difficult to interpret.

Novel Versus Normal Behavior

Another facet of test markets that researchers must consider is novel versus normal behavior. For a new product, individuals may make an initial purchase because of its novelty. The same can occur with a test market involving advertising, special promotion, pricing, or other marketing test variables. The novelty or uniqueness may trigger a purchase by a consumer. But, will the consumer purchase the product once the novelty is gone?

Marketers must be able to distinguish between novel and normal behavior. Novelty can result in initial signs of success, but spell doom in a national launch. To ensure long-term success it is critical that normal behavior occurs during the test market. One way of ensuring this occurs is to lengthen the time for the test market. Doing so, however, invites competitor reactions that further complicate the situation.

Test Market Opportunities

Test markets offer a number of opportunities for companies because of the wide range of marketing phenomena that can be manipulated in a test market. Figure 7.10 provides an idea of some of the marketing elements than can be part of a test market. New products are a natural opportunity for test markets and have already been discussed. So are brand extensions. A new flavor of oatmeal, a new type of potato chip, and a new cosmetic extension can be tested to gauge consumer reactions.

A major advantage of test marketing a brand extension is to measure the level of cannibalization. The primary goal of a brand extension is to gain new customers. But, instead, what may happen is that current customers switch to the new extension. So the firm does not gain new customers. The brand

Figure 7.10   Marketing Elements That Can Be Test Marketed

- New products
- Brand extensions
- Consumer promotions
- Pricing
- Advertising and communications
- Distribution elements

extension just cannibalizes sales from current versions of the product. If this occurs, launching the brand extension will increase costs but not sales. The only way a company should go ahead with the brand extension is to counter competitive actions. If a competitor is introducing a similar brand extension or is anticipated to introduce it, then moving ahead with the extension is a good decision.

Test markets can be used for a variety of consumer promotions and pricing points. A company can develop a special coupon offer and have it distributed in the test market. Using the code on the coupon, researchers can easily measure the redemption rate in the test market. It is possible to have multiple markets, each with a different type of coupon or a coupon with varying face values. Test markets can be used to examine different pricing points. The ideal would be to have one test market at a special price point and then compare the results to markets with the standard price. However, to save money and time, marketers may develop several test markets each with a different price point.

Advertising and communications programs can be evaluated through test markets. The challenge with advertising and communications campaigns is the lag effect in marketing communications, meaning that advertising does not usually have an immediate impact. So to measure the impact it is necessary to run the test market for several months and maybe even up to a year. During that time a number of the extraneous variables can alter the treatment effects.

Test markets can be used for a number of distribution decisions. Various retail displays, shelf locations, and even channels of distribution can be evaluated with test markets. Before developing an entire distribution channel, a company can use a test market to see how a product would sell first. The restaurant chain El Pollo Loco used test marketing when it participated in the 10-day Taste of Chicago festival in order to gauge consumer acceptance and demand of its menu items before going to the expense of building an actual restaurant. At that point no locations existed in the Chicago area.[9]

Issues in Selecting a Test Market

Projecting results from a test market to the national level requires careful consideration of which market should be selected for the test. Figure 7.11 identifies the primary issues that are to be considered when selecting a test market. Foremost are the population characteristics. It must be of sufficient size to obtain reasonable results. If the area is too large, it drives up costs and often does not provide any better results than a smaller test market. However, if the test market is too small, then it is difficult to generalize any results to the population as whole.

Figure 7.11   Issues in Selecting Test
Markets

- Population
  - Size
  - Demographic composition
- Market situation
- Media options
- Distribution options

In addition to size, the test market population needs to represent the population as a whole, or at least the target market of the product that is being tested. Test markets should be "a microcosm that matches the larger market. The two should be functionally equivalent on all variables that might affect the criterion measure."[10] Thus, demographic composition in terms of gender, age, income, ethnicity, and education should be representative of the population. It is also helpful if the psychographic profile matches the population. For most national products, the test market population should resemble the U.S. population. However, if a product in the test market has a target market that consists primarily of senior citizens, then test marketing in areas that have a high density of seniors, such as locations in Florida or Arizona, may be appropriate.

In light of these characteristics, it may be somewhat surprising to learn that some test markets have recently taken place in Montreal, Canada. "The rationale is that Quebec's relative cultural isolation—its language barrier prevents much outside media from seeping in, and vice-versa—makes it an ideal place for U.S.-based marketers to experiment with new ideas and approaches before rolling them out to wider audiences."[11] While such an approach has the advantage of limiting competitive knowledge of the test market, careful consideration of the factors discussed in the previous paragraph should ultimately govern the ultimate choice of test market.

The market situation in the test market needs to match as closely as possible the marketing situation the company will face when the product is launched. Especially important are competitors. The test market needs to represent the same situation that consumers will face with the national launch in terms of choosing among competing brands. If the test market is done where the primary brands are only part of the brands that are available, the test market will not provide accurate results.

Media options are important if any type of advertising or marketing communications is part of the test market. But, it is also important that the media do not cover an area that is exceptionally larger than the target market. For example, suppose Dallas, Texas, is chosen as a test market location. If television and radio stations in Dallas cover an area much larger than Dallas, then not only is money wasted since the product is not available in areas outside of Dallas, but it may also affect the results of the study.

For new products, a more difficult issue is distribution. What options does a company have in moving the product to the test area? If the test market lasts several weeks (or months), the company must ensure there is a distribution channel to handle it. For companies with an established distribution channel, this is not an issue normally. But, it can add extra costs to the test market.

Global Concerns

Experimental design becomes more challenging in global markets, especially as it transcends countries and cultures. It involves more than just translating languages. It requires understanding the culture of the region so the experiment can be designed properly to accomplish the intended objectives. Unfortunately, results obtained in one country or region are not always transferrable to other regions of the world.

Researchers have to pay close attention to nonverbal communication aspects of experimental design, such as concept of time, mannerisms, body language, space, etiquette, and relationships. For instance, in most Western countries time is important and an experiment set for 2:00 is expected to start right at 2:00. However, in some countries, especially in Spanish-speaking countries, time is not so formal. Also, afternoon siestas are part of the culture. Personal space is another issue. Some individuals and cultures feel uncomfortable if another person is too close to them. In other cultures it is acceptable. Etiquette varies greatly between countries. In countries such as Japan, etiquette, especially toward elders, is more formal than in the United States. Because of these types of differences, it is important to hire a research company that understands the customs and culture of a region, or to involve someone who has this level of understanding to assist in designing experiments.

Test marketing presents a unique challenge for global companies. The greatest challenge relates to deciding where the product should first be introduced, as results in one country may not be indicative of whether the product will succeed or fail if marketed globally. Recently, Coca-Cola used New Zealand to test a raspberry version of its Coca-Cola. The decision to launch or not launch the flavor globally was based on the results of the New Zealand test market.[12] In deciding where to test market a new product or brand extensions, marketers have to think about which country would be most like the global markets it is seeking for expansion.

 STATISTICS REVIEW

With an experiment, researchers want to see if the treatment creates a significant difference in the dependent variable. Depending on the type of experiment, two popular statistical tests that can be used are the independent sample t-test and a paired sample t-test.

Independent Sample t-Test

To review these statistical procedures, suppose an advertising agency interested in evaluating the effectiveness of a TV ad conducted an experiment using 300 subjects. Half of the respondents were in the control group and did not see the new test ad while the other half did. After the experiment, individuals were asked about their attitude toward the brand and purchase intentions, both using a 5-point scale. Suppose the ad agency wants to be 95% confident that the brand attitude and purchase intention effects were truly indicative of real differences and so would likely occur among the population if the ad was used in an actual campaign. To determine if it was significant, an independent t-test was used. Results are shown in Figure 7.12. The difference in means for attitude toward the brand was .707, and for purchase intentions it was .173.

The column of data titled "Sig. (2-tailed)" shows the probability of the difference in means (i.e., the effect) occurring due to chance. In the case of brand attitudes, the independent t-test revealed that there is a $p < .000$ chance of the .71 increase in attitudes being due to random luck (where p stands for probability). Note also that the $p < .000$ means that the actual probability is *not* zero, but is smaller than .000.

Based on the data shown in this table, the advertising agency would conclude that the test ad significantly increased attitudes toward the brand in a positive manner. However, the same cannot be

(Continued)

(Continued)

Figure 7.12   Independent Sample t-Test Results

		Levene's Test for Equality of Variances		T-Test for Equality of Means					95% Confidence Interval of the Difference	
		F	Sig.	t	df	Sig. (2-tailed)	Mean Difference	Std. Error Difference	Lower	Upper
Attitude toward the brand	Equal variances assumed	1.696E1	.000	-5.575	298	.000	-.707	.127	-.956	-.457
	Equal variances not assumed			-5.575	286.614	.000	-.707	.127	-.956	-.457
Purchase intentions	Equal variances assumed	2.859E1	.000	-1.350	298	.178	-.233	.173	-.573	.107
	Equal variances not assumed			-1.350	284.552	.178	-.233	.173	-.573	.107

said for purchase intentions. Since the p-value of .178 is higher than the .05 cutoff value, the researcher cannot be 95% confident that purchase intentions toward the brand would also increase if this ad were used as part of an actual campaign.

Paired Sample t-Test

A different type of statistical test would be needed in a one-group pretest-posttest design due to the lack of control group and the nature of the observations. Since pretest and posttest measures of the dependent variable are taken from the sample group of subjects, the data set will actually contain two separate variables. The paired comparison test for differences compares the mean of one variable to the mean of a second variable, and analyzes the difference. Consider the results shown in Figure 7.13

Figure 7.13   Mean for Purchase Intentions: Pretest and Posttest

Paired Samples Statistics					
		Mean	N	Std. Deviation	Std. Error Mean
Pair 1	Pretest purchase intentions	3.34	150	1.389	.113
	Posttest purchase intentions	3.75	150	1.112	.091

of a different experiment, which sought to determine whether a magazine ad would positively impact purchase intentions. The mean for the pretest purchase intentions was 3.34 and for the posttest was 3.75.

The experimental effect can be calculated by using a paired t-test, shown in Figure 7.14. In this experiment, the likelihood of purchase intentions increased by .407 as a result of exposure to the test advertisement. The results shown under the "Sig. (2-tailed)" column are significant, and indicate that purchase intentions are highly likely to increase due to the magazine advertisement.

Figure 7.14   Paired t-Test Results for Magazine Ad

Paired Samples Test

		Paired Differences							
					95% Confidence Interval of the Difference				
		Mean	Std. Deviation	Std. Error Mean	Lower	Upper	t	df	Sig. (2–tailed)
Pair 1	Pretest purchase intentions – Posttest purchase intentions	.407	.977	.080	.564	.249	5.098	149	.000

DEALING WITH DATA

A retail chain is interested in determining whether a digital point-of-purchase display would stimulate higher sales for an advertised brand than would a standard point-of-purchase (POP) display. To test this, a one-shot static group design experiment was conducted over a four-week period in 100 different stores. Sales were measured at the end of the four weeks for both the control group (standard display) and the experimental group (digital display). The data are in the SPSS file titled "Chapter 07 Dealing with Data 1" (www.sagepub .com/clowess). Compare the sales of the control group (standard POP) to those of the experimental group (digital POP) using an independent sample t-test. Based on your output, answer the following questions.

1. What were the average sales for the standard POP display (control group)? What about the digital display (experimental group)?

2. What is the mean difference in sales between the experimental group and the control group?

(Continued)

(Continued)

3. At a 95% confidence level, was the difference significant? Explain why or why not.

4. Should the manager of the retail chain install new digital displays? Justify your answer. What other factors should the manager consider?

Another retail outlet tested a digital POP display using a one-group pretest-posttest design. The data are in the file "Chapter 07 Dealing with Data 2" (www.sagepub.com/clowess). With this experiment, the retailer measured the sales of a regular POP display for four weeks prior to the experiment. The standard POP display was replaced with the digital display in 59 stores, and sales were measured after another four weeks. Use a paired sample t-test to compare sales before and after the new digital display. Based on your output, answer the following questions.

1. What were the average sales for the four weeks prior to the experiment?

2. What were the sales during the four weeks when the stores used the digital display?

3. What is the mean difference in sales?

4. At a 95% significance level, was the difference significant? Explain why or why not.

5. Should the manager of the retail chain install new digital displays? Justify your answer.

SUMMARY

Objective 1: Identify the three conditions that must be present to prove causation.

Experimental research, also known as causal research, is the form of research that can actually prove cause and effect. Proving causation requires that three conditions be met: (1) concomitant variation between X and Y; (2) time order of occurrence, in that X occurs prior (or simultaneously) to Y; and (3) elimination or control of extraneous factors, which might otherwise be responsible for causing a change in Y. Most experiments take place in a laboratory setting instead of the field, in order to control for the influence of extraneous factors.

Objective 2: Name and define the basic terms and notation used in experimental design.

Three notation symbols are used to identify actions undertaken within control groups or treatments. The notion R is used to designate the fact that subjects have been randomly assigned to a group. Exposure to the treatment, or experimental stimuli, is designated by the X notation. Observations, during which measurements of the subject groups are undertaken, are denoted by the symbol O. Observations occurring at different times or among different treatments and multiple treatments are followed by a subscript number.

Objective 3: Discuss the extraneous factors that can affect internal and external validity.

Extraneous factors may confound the results of an experiment by offering a competing explanation for any changes noted in the dependent variable(s). This damages the internal and external validity of the experimental results. Extraneous factors include (1) history effect, (2) maturation, (3) testing effect, (4) instrumentation, (5) selection effect, and (6) attrition.

Objective 4: Describe the various types of preexperimental designs.

Preexperimental designs have low internal and external validity, as they do not randomly assign subjects to groups, and offer little or no control over extraneous variables. The one-shot preexperimental design exposes subjects to the treatment, then measures the dependent variable. The one-shot static group design expands this design to include a control group. The one-group pretest-posttest design has the advantage of measuring the dependent variable before the treatment occurs, as well as after, though no control group is used.

Objective 5: Describe the various types of true experimental designs.

True experimental designs are characterized by the randomization of subjects, which controls for the influence of extraneous variables, thereby resulting in greater internal validity. True experimental designs include the pretest-posttest control group design and the posttest-only control group design.

Objective 6: Describe the various types of quasi-experimental designs.

Quasi-experimental designs lack internal validity because they do not allow for subject randomization. They tend to be used in field studies that limit the researcher's control over extraneous variables and when the treatment actually occurs. To compensate for these weaknesses, both the time series design and the time series control design take multiple measurements of the dependent variable before and after the treatment occurs.

Objective 7: Discuss the concept of test markets.

Marketers use test markets to evaluate new products and aspects of the marketing mix. Test markets are time-consuming and costly, and it is difficult to control for extraneous variables. Furthermore, competitive reactions can interfere with the test market or the national rollout of a product that passes this test. Selecting a test market requires consideration of the population, market situation, media options, and distribution options. Global test markets present a special challenge.

GLOSSARY OF KEY TERMS

Attrition: the loss of subjects during the time the experiment is being conducted (also called mortality)

Concomitant variation: condition for causality in which two variables are either positively or inversely correlated and vary together in a predictable manner

Debriefing: explains the true purpose of a disguised experiment

Dependent variable: outcome variable of the experiment that the independent variable seeks to influence, the *effect* component of a cause-and-effect relationship

External validity: the extent to which the findings of an experiment (or research study) can be generalized to the population as whole, or to the particular population being studied

History effect: occurs when some external event takes place between the beginning and the end of an experiment that changes the outcome of the event

Independent variables: variables that are manipulated, or changed, in order to observe the effect on the dependent variable, the *cause* element in the cause-and-effect relationship

Instrumentation effect: occurs when a change in the measurement instrument or other procedures used to measure the dependent variable cause an unwarranted change in the dependent variable

Internal validity: the extent to which a particular treatment in an experiment produces the sole effect observed in the dependent variable

Maturation: changes in the subject over time that modify the results of the experiment

Observation: measurement of a variable or group of participants during an experiment

One-group pretest-posttest design: preexperimental design in which measurements of the dependent variable are taken prior to the experiment and again after the experiment

One-shot preexperimental design: preexperimental design that exposes test subjects to a treatment variable, which is then followed by a measurement of the dependent variable

One-shot static group design: preexperimental design that uses a control group for comparison purposes and takes measurements after the experimental treatment

Posttest-only control group design: experimental design in which subjects are randomly assigned to experimental and control groups, followed by exposure to the treatment in the experimental group, after which both groups are posttested, with no pretest

Preexperimental design: offers little or no control over extraneous variables and no randomization of subjects

Pretest-posttest control group design: true experimental design in which subjects who have been randomly assigned to experimental and control groups are pretested, followed by exposure to the treatment in the experimental group, after which both groups are posttested

Quasi-experimental design: type of research design in which researchers are unable to randomly assign subjects to the group or lack control of when the treatment occurs

Randomization: process by which subjects are randomly assigned to treatment and control groups

Selection effect: occurs when the sample selected for a study is not representative of the population being studied or the samples selected for different groups within the study are not statistically the same

Subjects: participants in an experimental research study

Test marketing: uses preexperimental or quasi-experimental designs to test new product introductions and various aspects of the marketing mix

Testing effect: occurs when exposure to a pretest sensitizes subjects to the test or experiment in a manner that affects the results of the experiment

Time series control group design: time series design that includes a control group that is pretested and posttested at the same intervals as the treatment group

Time series design: quasi-experimental design in which several pretests are conducted over time prior to exposure to the treatment, followed by several posttests over time

Treatment: change or manipulation in the independent variable

True experimental design: experiment in which subjects are randomly assigned to treatment conditions from a pool of subjects

Validity: refers to the degree to which an experiment (or research study) measures what it is supposed to measure

CRITICAL THINKING EXERCISES

1. A consumer goods manufacturer recently conducted an experiment in which coupon formats were tested in different variations, classified as "high," "moderate," or "low" value. The face values of the high-, medium-, and low-value cents-off coupon treatments were 75 cents, 50 cents, and 25 cents, respectively. Similarly, "buy one get one free," "buy two get one free," and "buy three get one free" treatments were classified as high-, moderate-, and low-value treatment conditions for the second coupon type. Redemption rates for each coupon treatment are shown in the table below:

Type of Coupon	COUPON REDEMPTION RATE		
	High Value	**Moderate Value**	**Low Value**
Cents-off	1.5%	2%	1.5%
Buy X, Get One Free	4%	2%	0.5%

Do the results shown in this table provide evidence of concomitant variation? Why or why not? Interpret these results. What conclusions can be drawn regarding the relationship between the type of coupon and the coupon redemption rate in this experiment? What other factors should be considered when interpreting the data?

2. Suppose your supervisor is interested in determining whether or not a sweepstakes program should be used to promote your brand. Identify potential independent variables, dependent variables, and treatments. What would you recommend? Why?

3. Knowing that you are a college student majoring in marketing at the local university, your supervisor at the local pizza parlor has asked for your input regarding a research study. She wants to determine which of three new pizza toppings should be added to the menu: broccoli, spam, or pineapple. She plans on promoting broccoli in February, Spam in March, and pineapple in April, and using the

number of pizzas ordered with each topping to make her decision. List and briefly describe the extraneous factors that may interfere with the results of her study.

4. A researcher was trying to determine the impact that placing a product in a movie has on brand attitudes. In the pretest (O_1) and posttest (O_2) measurement process, a single question is used to assess attitude toward the brand that asks respondents to rate how favorable their attitude is by selecting one of seven responses: very unfavorable (1), unfavorable (2), neutral (3), favorable (4), and very favorable (5). In between the pretest and posttest measurements, subjects watch a movie in which the hero conspicuously consumes the product while commenting favorably on its attributes. In both the pre- and posttests, subjects' responses to each question are assigned the value shown in parentheses above. These values are averaged across all subjects for the pretest and averaged again for the posttest. The results are as follows: pretest: 2.57; posttest: 4.21. What is the experimental effect? How would you interpret this information? What does it mean?

5. A researcher has designed an experiment in which three groups of subjects are first surveyed regarding their attitudes toward various brands of snack food in general, and potato chips in particular. The subjects are then told to "shop" for products they would purchase for a Super Bowl party if they were hosting such an event. Shopping takes place in a simulated supermarket environment controlled by the researcher, which is designed to mimic an actual grocery store. In the chip aisle, two of the three subject groups walk past a point-of-purchase display for Frito products, though the display shown differs for each group. Everything else in the store is the same. After completing the shopping exercise, the group is told that a brand was inadvertently left off of the survey, and the subjects are asked to complete it again. Identify the following: (1) independent variable(s), (2) dependent variable(s), (3) treatment, (4) experimental notation depicting this experiment, and (5) the formula for calculating the experimental effect.

6. Suppose Procter & Gamble is interested in updating the package design for one of its laundry detergents. Design an experiment to help with this task, clearly identifying the dependent variable(s), the independent variable, and the treatment(s) and how the experiment should be administered. Defend your choice of experimental design.

7. A manufacturer of plug-in air fresheners is curious to learn whether consumers rely more on brand name or the scent of the air freshener when making their purchase decision. Design an experiment to help with this task, clearly identifying the dependent variable(s), the independent variable, and the treatment(s) and the experimental design that should be used. Justify your choice of experimental design.

8. Suppose a brewery was considering introducing a new packaging alternative—plastic bottles. Would experimentation designed to test consumers' preference of packaging materials be the first step undertaken by the company in researching this potential opportunity? Why or why not? Justify your answer.

9. As a student worker in the marketing department, one of your professors has assigned you the task of randomly assigning members of a sample to either the control group or one of two treatment conditions. Explain the process and tactics you would use in completing this assignment.

10. Suppose that the mass merchandiser Target wanted to test a digital point-of-purchase display. How should Target choose the stores to be part of the test market? What type of experimental design would you recommend? Why? What treatments should be used? What dependent variables would be measured? Explain and justify your answer.

CONTINUING CASE STUDY: LAKESIDE GRILL

Making a decision about experimental research was challenging for the student team researching Lakeside Grill. While ideas were generated, there were doubts if experiments could be conducted with the restaurant. The students felt the inability to control extraneous variables would dilute any results that might be obtained. Here are some of the ideas that were generated by the group.

- Some of the other area restaurants served bread or chips and dip to customers while they waited for their meal. Destiny suggested using a one-shot preexperimental design where a free loaf of bread would be given to guests for a two-week time period. Overall restaurant sales would be measured to see if the bread caused an increase in sales. Alexa suggested a different dependent variable. She thought customers should be surveyed to see if the free bread would impact their decision to return.

- In comparing Lakeside Grill's menu with other restaurants' menus and the results of the focus group, Juan suggested the restaurant offer three new appetizers not currently on the menu. A new menu would be printed containing the three new appetizers, but otherwise it would look identical to the current menu. Half of the customers would receive the new menu with the new appetizers, and the other half would receive the old menu and serve as the control group. (Everyone in a party at a table would receive the same menu.) This one-shot static group design would allow the student team to see if adding new appetizers would impact the number of orders for appetizers by comparing the control group orders with the experimental group orders.

- The last suggestion dealt with waitstaff. Approximately three quarters of the waitstaff were male. However, the focus group results suggested that having more females might enhance the image of the restaurant. Brooke suggested scheduling more females to work over a three-week period so the ratio was closer to 50:50, and that waitstaff be randomly assigned to customers. At the conclusion of the meal all customers would be given a card asking them to rate the quality of service and the likelihood of their return. For the control group, Zach suggested that during the next three weeks the group keep the 75:25 ratio of male-to-female waiters and again use the feedback card. The results of the control group could then be compared to the experimental group. "Comparing males and females is not a one-shot static group design," he added.

Critique Questions:

1. Evaluate the three experimental design suggestions. Do they fit the criteria for preexperimental designs?

2. Is Zach's statement correct that "comparing males and females is not a one-shot static group design"?

3. For the free bread experiment, what extraneous variables would be of concern? What can be done to control for each of the extraneous variables?

(Continued)

(Continued)

4. For the free bread experiment, which observation variable is the best, sales or future purchase intentions? Why?

5. For the second experiment, the three new appetizers, what extraneous variables would be of concern? What can be done to control for each of the extraneous variables?

6. For the third experiment, the new male/female staff ratio, what extraneous variables would be of concern? What can be done to control for each of the extraneous variables?

7. Which experimental design would you recommend? Why?

8. Do you have any other suggestions in terms of experiments or different ways of designing the ones suggested? Elaborate.

MARKETING RESEARCH PORTFOLIO

The mini-case for Chapter 7 challenges students to design an experiment. Students identify the independent and dependent variables to be studied, justify the research design proposed, and discuss the potential influence of extraneous variables and how they can best be minimized or controlled. The assignment instructions and case information can be found at www.sagepub.com/clowess.

STUDENT STUDY SITE

Visit the Student Study Site at www.sagepub.com/clowess to access the following additional materials:

- eFlashcards
- Web Quizzes
- SAGE Journal Articles
- Web Resources

SECTION 3

Sampling and Measurement

CHAPTER 8

Sampling Procedures

LEARNING OBJECTIVES

After reading this chapter, you should be able to

1. Explain the difference between a population and a sample.

2. Discuss the steps involved in selecting a sample.

3. Identify and describe the four nonprobability sampling methods.

4. Identify and describe the four probability sampling methods.

5. Describe the various methods of determining sample size.

6. Discuss the benefits and issues related to online research panels.

INTRODUCTION

A mobile marketing survey was conducted by Hipcricket using a national sample of 607 respondents. The survey was conducted by e-mail using a company called Zoomerang. Respondents in the survey were cell phone users and were

- distributed across five age categories (18–24, 25–30, 31–35, 36–40, and 41–45);
- distributed across the United States with 30% from the Northeast, 25% from the Midwest, 26% from the South, and 19% from the West; and
- 51% female and 49% male.

The survey examined a number of issues related to mobile marketing. One of the questions asked respondents why they visited a retailer's mobile website. Responses are shown in Figure 8.1. The

Figure 8.1 Why Individuals Visited a Retailer's Mobile Website

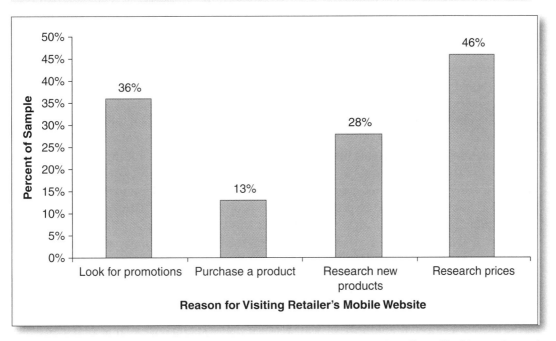

Source: Author-created with data from "Hipcricket: 2011 Mobile Marketing Survey Research Brief," **www.hipcricket.com** (accessed February 12, 2012).

number-one reason was to research prices, indicated by 46% of the respondents. Other reasons included looking for promotions, researching new products, and to purchase a product.[1]

The study by Hipcricket contained a number of findings related to mobile marketing. By using a sample that was carefully selected, Hipcricket was able to project its findings to the U.S. population of mobile phone users. This chapter examines the procedure companies such as Hipcricket would use in selecting a sample to survey. Probability and nonprobability sampling methods are discussed as well as methods of determining the size of the sample. The chapter concludes with a discussion of online research panels since they have become such a prominent means of soliciting respondents for marketing studies.

INTRODUCTION TO SAMPLING

In the previous chapter, the various methods of survey research were presented. Most involved surveying individuals in some manner. The process of choosing the group of individuals to survey is called sampling, and the group of individuals chosen is the **sample.** It is important to keep in mind that a sample can also refer to objects, such as retail stores, websites, and products. Sampling does not always have to involve people, although it is the most common form of sampling used in marketing.

The group from which the sample is drawn is called the **population.** The population can vary widely. It can be all of the individuals in the United States, all of the individuals in

■ Objective 8.1: Explain the difference between a population and a sample.

a specific state, all of the employees of a company such as Kraft, or all of the individuals in a small, private college graduating class. It can also be all individuals who own a certain type of product or who suffer from a particular medical condition. It can range from millions of people or objects to just a few.

Sampling is used because in most cases it is not practical to survey an entire population, unless the population size is small. Surveying all of the parents of seventh-grade students at a local school that has 75 children is feasible. Surveying all the members in a local advertising club or Lions organization makes sense. A business-to-business firm that has only 40 clients can survey all of its customers. When the entire population is surveyed, then it is called a **census**.

In most cases, sampling an entire population is not practical, for two reasons. First, if the population is large, the cost and time to conduct the survey would be prohibitive. For instance, to survey all women ages 18 to 34 about their use of Facebook would be impossible. So Lightspeed Research selected a sample of women ages 18 to 34 and found that 40% admit to being "Facebook addicts" and 57% say they talk to people more often online than face-to-face. Lucid Marketing surveyed moms who described themselves as "hooked on Twitter" and found that 54% of Twitter-addict moms check their feeds 10 or more times a day and 15% said they check it "every waking moment." In contrast, 13% said they check it once a day or less. While this information is interesting, more important from a marketing standpoint are the reasons moms follow businesses on Twitter. According to the Lucid Marketing survey, 67% follow businesses on Twitter to learn about a company's products, 67% follow because they are a customer of the business, and 60% follow to get special deals.[2] Thus, surveying a sample of females ages 18 to 34 can provide marketers and businesses with considerable information for a fraction of the cost that surveying the entire population would require.

The second reason to use surveys rather than a census is accuracy. If a sample of a population is properly selected, the survey can provide results that accurately reflect the entire population within an acceptable degree of error. In some cases, the sample may even be more accurate. It would be extremely difficult to locate everyone in a population, much less ensure everyone's participation, which leads to the possibility of nonresponse bias. In addition, surveying an entire population would require a large staff of individuals to conduct the surveys, which compounds the likelihood of interviewer error. It is not necessary to survey an entire population as long as the sample adequately represents the population.

■ Objective 8.2: Discuss the steps involved in selecting a sample.

THE SAMPLING PROCESS

Obtaining a good sample does not happen by accident. It takes careful planning and execution. Figure 8.2 outlines the steps involved in selecting a sample.

Define the Population

The first step is to define the target population. While it sounds easy to do, for many marketing studies it can be a challenge. In addition to defining the individuals to include, limitations or boundaries of exclusion must be part of the definition. Keep in mind that a population can be stores, businesses, households, institutions, and even purchase transactions.

StrongMail Systems is a provider of marketing solutions for businesses seeking assistance in e-mail and social media marketing. Recently, the company joined with the Relevancy Group to conduct research in the travel and hospitality industry. Before selecting a sample, the researchers had to define the target market of the research. The company defined the population as marketing executives in the United States and in the United Kingdom within three industries—retail, travel, and media/publishing. The definition also contained an exclusion or boundary. Companies that sent fewer than 1 million e-mail messages per month were excluded.[3] By carefully defining the population, StrongMail Systems and the Relevancy Group were able to locate e-mail marketers that met the criteria to be part of their sample.

Figure 8.2   Steps in Selecting a Sample

1. Define the population.
2. Identify the sample frame.
3. Choose a sampling procedure.
4. Decide on the sample size.
5. Select the sample.

The simpler the population definition, the higher the incidence and the less costly it will be to locate an appropriate sample. Recall from Chapter 6 that incidence refers to the percentage of individuals, households, or businesses in the population that would be qualified as potential respondents in a particular study. Incidence is important because it provides clues to the level of effort that will be required to find eligible respondents. The more restrictions or exclusions that are included, the more difficult it will be to locate sample respondents because a lower percentage of the population will meet all of the criteria. Consider a population defined as males ages 20 to 40 with incomes between $50,000 and $100,000. If further restrictions are added, such as *married with at least one child* and *spouse does not work*, then incidence is reduced, which means a smaller percentage of the population now qualifies. These additional criteria require that screening questions related to the number of children, marital status, and spousal employment be included in the survey to determine eligibility.

A similar situation occurs for studies involving objects, such as retail stores. If the population is defined as individual retail clothing stores with sales of $2 million or more, the population is rather simple and broadly defined. A large number of stores would meet this definition. If the researcher wants to examine only stores that sell female clothing and that are not part of a major retail chain, then the definition becomes more complex, and incidence will be reduced. Notice to define the population, the term *major retail chain* will also have to be defined. Does it mean a company with more than 50 stores, 100 stores, or even 500 stores? Defining *major retail chain* has a significant impact on the size of the population and the incidence.

Identify the Sample Frame

Once the population has been defined, the next challenge is to identify the sample frame, which is the listing of people or objects from which the sample will be drawn. In some cases identifying the sample frame is rather easy, but in other situations it is very difficult. For example, suppose a business wanted to survey its customers. If it is a business-to-business firm, it is very likely the company has a listing of every customer who has made a purchase. Thus, the sample frame would be drawn from the customer database. But, if a company such as Reebok wanted to survey its customers, there is no listing of all individuals who have purchased Reebok shoes. Identifying a sample frame would be more challenging.

Suppose a researcher wanted a sample drawn from the city of Atlanta. In the past, a telephone directory could be used since it contained most individuals who had a telephone. Now, a large number of individuals have unlisted phone numbers. An even greater and growing problem is that many individuals no longer even have a landline. Cell phones have replaced landlines in many households, and no directory exists for cell phones. An alternative to the phone book for a telephone survey is to use random digit dialing. While this works for landlines, the law currently prevents using a random digit dialer for cell phones, so while the sample will include unlisted numbers, it is still not completely representative of the entire Atlanta population.

Richard Vioksy and Todd Shupe wanted to investigate the attitude of manufacturers of children's playground equipment toward using treated wood. The sample frame for their study was a census of all 188 manufacturers of children's playground equipment. The source for developing the sample frame was the U.S. census. The actual names and addresses for the mail survey were purchased from Best Lists, a national survey list company. The researchers sent a prenotification letter to the 188 manufacturers, alerting them that they would soon receive a survey in a separate mailing, a cover letter explaining the study, and the questionnaire. A follow-up postcard was sent later to remind the manufacturers to complete the survey, followed by a second letter with a second questionnaire. This process resulted in 52 usable responses.[4]

Seldom will a sample frame match a target population perfectly. Therefore, the researcher's goal is to develop a sample frame that will include most elements of a population and be representative of the population. For Reebok, a sample frame may consist of individuals who have logged into the company's website during the last 90 days, who "like" Reebok on Facebook, and who follow Reebok on Twitter. This sample frame would exclude the part of the population that had purchased Reebok shoes, but did not engage in any of the online activities mentioned. An alternative sample frame would be to obtain customer information from stores that sold Reebok shoes and obtain a listing of individuals who had purchased Reebok shoes within the last year. This approach would work for credit card customers, loyalty card holders, and others

The sample frame for a study about playground equipment was the 188 manufacturers.

who were in the stores' databases. It would not include cash customers since no information about the individuals would be in the retailers' databases.

As can be seen, identifying a sample frame is difficult, and researchers have to use a process that would include the largest percentage of a target population. Sometimes this includes combining multiple sources and purging duplicate entries. Magazine subscription lists can be used as part of the sampling frame when the magazines in question feature a lifestyle activity that is related to the purpose of the study or the manufacturer's brand. For example, Reebok might have included subscribers to *Runner's World, Running Times, Fitness,* and *Men's Fitness* magazines. As some households may subscribe to more than one of these publications, duplicates would need to be eliminated from the sample frame list. Of course, Reebok manufactures more than just running shoes, so other magazines may be appropriate as well. If magazine subscriptions are to be part of the sampling frame, the most efficient method of selection would be to require access to the syndicated data provided by Mediamark. As discussed in Chapter 3, Mediamark provides brand-specific information related to the demographics and media habits of product users. Thus, Reebok could select magazine titles with the highest index numbers to add to their sample frame.

In terms of national or even regional U.S. household samples, telephone surveys were the staple approach in the past. With random digit dialing, fairly robust samples of households could historically be generated. But in recent years the rise of cell phones and the decrease in willingness of consumers to respond to telephone surveys have caused a number of research companies to shift to address-based mail sampling. The United States Postal Service (USPS) maintains a computerized delivery sequence file (DSF) that contains every delivery point in the United States. The second-generation database (DSF2) is the most comprehensive list of addresses available with over 135 million addresses. The USPS also offers validation and completion of address services allowing a research firm to maintain accurate mailing addresses. About 85% of the addresses in the DSF2 can be name-matched, and about 60% can be linked to a land phone. This makes the DSF2 a feasible sample frame for national surveys.[5]

In recent years there has been a shift to using online samples and online research panels. Both of these topics are discussed later in this chapter. The online sample has dramatically changed the way samples are built and even the way companies conduct research. The online methodologies allow companies to obtain samples quicker and cheaper than other, traditional methods.

Choose a Sampling Procedure

Choosing a sampling procedure is closely related to identifying the sample frame. Typically, both decisions are made at the same time. The next section discusses the various sampling methods and approaches that can be used, but researchers have two broad categories from which to choose: probability and nonprobability samples. With a **probability sample** each member of the target population has a known and nonzero chance of being selected. The probability of each member being selected may not be equal, but the probability for each member is known. The exact probability is determined by the process used to select the sample. A key advantage of using a probability sample is that sampling error can be computed, allowing the researcher to determine the degree of accuracy of his or her results. **Sampling error** refers to the amount of error that the researcher is willing to accept as a result of the sampling process. This allows the results of the study to be generalized to the larger population with some degree of confidence.

With a **nonprobability sample** the probability or chance of someone being selected is not known and cannot be determined. Nonprobability samples rely on the judgment of the researcher. For instance, a researcher may identify the students at the University of Arkansas as the target population. Suppose the researcher staged individuals at three different points on campus to intercept students as they walked by. The chance of a particular student of the university being selected is not known and cannot be determined. Only students who are on campus the day the research is being conducted, and only those who happen to go past one of the three researchers, have a chance of being selected. Thus, only a portion of the university student body has a chance of being selected. There is no guarantee that those who are selected to participate are representative of those who are not. Technically, this means that the results of such studies should not be generalized to the population, as sampling error cannot be computed, and the researcher has no way of knowing how much confidence can be placed in these results.

Decide on the Sample Size

The next step in the process is to decide on the sample size needed. Statistical methods for determining sample size are discussed later in this chapter. But, what is statistically desired and what the budget will allow may not coincide. The marketing research project must be conducted within the time frame and budget that is allocated. Unfortunately, this may require using a smaller sample than is statistically desirable. Caution must be exercised, however, for if the sample is too small, then the research project may not reach any conclusions, and the funds that are spent will have been wasted. Figure 8.3 identifies some principles of sample size that are important to consider.

First, and most important, is to understand that using the correct sample size does not guarantee that the findings of the research will accurately reflect the target population. It does, however, increase the probability. The sample has to be large enough to reveal important patterns in the data. If the sample is too small, patterns may not appear. If the study involves comparing various segments of the population, then the sample must be large enough to show if significant differences are present. The more segments that are being compared, the larger the sample that is needed. Lastly, the method for obtaining the sample is just as important as the sample size.[6]

Most research projects use a **fixed sample,** which means the sample size is determined prior to conducting the research. Occasionally, researchers will use a **sequential sample,** which involves surveying a sample, and if enough respondents are obtained, then the research moves

Figure 8.3   Considerations on Deciding the Sample Size

- The correct sample size increases the probability the findings will accurately reflect the target population.
- The sample should be large enough to reveal important patterns.
- The sample should be large enough to show significant differences between segments being studied.
- The method for obtaining the sample is as important as the sample size.

Source: Author-created from Bonnie W. Eisenfeld, "Qualitatively Speaking: Sampling for Qualitative Researchers," *Quirk's Marketing Research Review,* March 2007, Article 20070308, www.quirks.com/articles/2007/0308.aspx (accessed January 4, 2011).

into the analysis stage. If there are not enough respondents or the evidence is not conclusive to draw any inferences, then another set of elements is chosen for a second round of research. The sequential sampling is also used in situations where obtaining samples is very expensive, or an object being evaluated by study participants is destroyed or used up in the process of conducting the research study.

Surveying CEOs or vice presidents of corporations using personal interviews would be very costly. In addition to the costs of the interviewer's time, a substantial incentive may need to be given to these corporate executives in order to help garner their participation. A research firm may select a sample of 50 to survey. If a sufficient number did not respond or refused to participate, then another sample of 50 may be selected. The sequential process would continue until the research firm had enough responses to meet its client's needs.

Select the Sample

The last step in the process is the actual selection of the sample. The next section of the chapter presents methods that can be used. In selecting the sample, the goal is to have a sample that represents the target population. Thus, if the target population is females in the 18- to 34-year age group, then the sample needs to consist of females ages 18 to 34.

NONPROBABILITY SAMPLING METHODS

With nonprobability samples, the probability of being selected for the sample is unknown, and not all members of the population have an equal or known chance of being selected. The process of selecting the sample is based on the judgment of the researcher. Figure 8.4 identifies four methods that can be used.

■ Objective 8.3: Identify and describe the four nonprobability sampling methods.

Convenience Sample

As the name implies, **convenience samples** are individuals or objects that are convenient for the researcher to survey. It can also involve individuals self-selecting to be part of a research project (for example, clicking on a link on a website to take a survey). The challenge with either method is collecting a representative sample. It is much more difficult with self-selection than when the researcher selects the sample. But, even when the researcher selects the sample, the convenience sample is seldom representative of the target population. The convenience sampling method is more appropriate for exploratory research or the early stages of a descriptive study than for more definitive studies.

To understand challenges with a convenience sample, suppose a minor league baseball team wanted to conduct a survey of fans. A convenience sample may be individuals who attended games over a two-week period. Each person 18 and over who entered the park would be given a survey and asked to complete it and then drop if off at a number of drop boxes throughout the baseball stadium. This method raises several questions concerning validity of the sample. First, are the views of those who complete the survey the

Figure 8.4   Nonprobability Sampling Methods

- Convenience sample
- Judgment sample
- Quota sample
- Snowball sample

same as those who do not? Often individuals who like the stadium and those who have complaints complete surveys. Individuals whose feelings are somewhat in the middle or neutral tend to neglect the request. If this happens, management may think there is a significant dislike of an amenity, such as concessions, when in fact it is only a small minority who hold that opinion. To illustrate, suppose 1,200 out of the 2,750 surveys received rate concessions as poor or extremely poor. It would appear that 44% of the respondents had a negative opinion of concessions and that management needs to make some changes. But, what about the 12,000 fans who did not complete the survey? If only 1,200 out of the 12,000 felt concessions were bad, that is around 8% (1,200/14,750), not 44%. Alternatively, perhaps those who did not answer the survey shared the opinion that concessions are bad. In this worst-case scenario, as much as 89% (13,200/14,750) could believe that the concessions are poor. Which is correct? We just don't know. The problem is that the researcher has no way of estimating the confidence level for the results found.

A second factor that must be considered with this example is how representative the sample is during the two weeks the survey is distributed. Are they the same as the individuals who attended games the rest of the minor league baseball season? Without conducting some type of spot or random check with fans at other times during the season, it would be difficult for management to know.

When using convenience samples, researchers should strive to make it representative of the target population. Careful planning and careful execution of the sampling process can aid in producing a good convenience sample.

Judgment Sample

With a **judgment sample,** researchers use their personal judgment to select a sample they believe can provide useful information or reflects the population being studied. Suppose someone in education wanted to survey the student population at a university about their attitudes toward online education versus traditional classroom education. In using a judgment sample approach, the researcher could go through the list of online classes offered by the university and handpick the classes the researcher thinks would provide valuable input and be representative of the student population. The same process could be followed for the traditional classroom portion of the sample. This approach produces a judgment sample since the classes selected were based on the judgment of the researcher conducting the study.

The key to using a judgment sample is to choose individuals or objects that will mirror the population being studied. In the case above, if the demographic profile of the sample reflects the makeup of the university student population, then it can be a good sample for the study.

Unfortunately, though, judgment samples often are not representative. A mall interceptor may decide not to select an individual to interview who otherwise fits the qualifications for the study because he or she thinks the individual "looks" scary, mean, stupid, too smart, impatient, unlikely to participate, or any one of a number of factors that may in fact not be true. When personal bias gets in the way of collecting data, the information obtained will not be representative of the population.

Quota Sample

In order to produce a nonprobability sample that is more representative of the population being studied, researchers will often use a **quota sample.** The concept behind the quota sample is to ensure that the sample contains the same proportion of characteristics specified by the researcher as is evident in the population being examined.

Suppose a medical facility hired a research firm to survey patients about their level of satisfaction with the medical care received and the effectiveness of treatment. Figure 8.5 shows the demographic composition of the patients who have used the facility during the last two years broken down by gender, age, and primary physician. The fourth column indicates the percent within each category. For instance, 56.9% of the patients are females, and 43.1% are males. In terms of age, 8.6% of the patients are 18 to 24, 12.2% are 25 to 34, and so forth. The last few rows show the number of patients for each attending physician.

The last three columns indicate how many individuals would need to be interviewed to create a quota sample of 200, 400, and 600 individuals. For a quota sample of 200, the sample would need to contain 114 females and 86 males. For a quota sample of 400, then it would be necessary to interview 228 female patients and 172 male patients. Looking further down the table at the sample of 600, the sample needs to include 108 patients from Dr. Cook, 130 from Dr. Dempster, 118 from Dr. Millwood, and so on.

Suppose to conduct the study, the research firm sent interviewers to the medical facility to talk to patients as they waited for their appointment to see their primary care physician. Each interviewer would be given a quota. For example, Andrea may be sent to the clinic and told to interview the following 20 individuals:

- 12 females and 8 males
- 5 patients 18–24, 5 patients 25 to 34, 5 patients 35 to 44, and 5 patients 45 to 54
- 10 patients of Dr. Cook and 10 patients of Dr. Dempster

Notice that Andrea's quota does not match the quota percents shown in Figure 8.5. Andrea is not going to interview patients of Millwood, Rogers, or Sanchez. It is not necessary for each

Figure 8.5   Quota Sample for Medical Facility

Demographic Variable		Number	Percent	Sample Size		
				200	400	600
Gender	Female	4,332	56.9%	114	228	342
	Male	3,275	43.1%	86	172	258
Age	18–24	653	8.6%	17	34	52
	25–34	926	12.2%	24	49	73
	35–44	1,638	21.5%	43	86	129
	45–54	1,145	15.1%	30	60	90
	55–65	1,814	23.8%	48	95	143
	66+	1,431	18.8%	38	75	113
Physician	Cook	1,363	17.9%	36	72	108
	Dempster	1,647	21.7%	43	87	130
	Millwood	1,502	19.7%	39	79	118
	Rogers	1,755	23.1%	46	92	138
	Sanchez	1,340	17.6%	35	70	106
Total number of patients		7,607	100.0%			

interviewer to have a quota that matches the overall sample quota as long as the total sample matches the population characteristics specified in the quota plan.

The quota sampling method is a nonprobability approach since not every patient has a known chance of being selected. It is really up to the judgment of the interviewer. Andrea can pick any of the patients in the waiting room who fit her quota. As a result, the sample may not truly reflect the opinion of all patients. Andrea may look around the room and pick patients who look like they would be willing to answer questions. Thus, her sample may be biased toward patients who have a positive attitude toward the medical facility. Other interviewers may use a different approach to select patients to meet their quotas, but it could also produce a biased sample. Also, once a particular quota is filled, say males aged 18–24, no other individuals exhibiting these characteristics will be interviewed regardless of who their physician might be. Using a quota sample does not guarantee a sample that truly reflects the opinion of the population. What it does do is produce a sample that more closely mirrors the population based on the demographic or behavioral characteristics identified by the researcher.

Snowball Sample

A unique nonprobability sampling technique is the **snowball sample.** The research begins with one or a few individuals who have been identified as good subjects for the research. Then each of these individuals is asked for names of others who would be good candidates for the study. This approach is used in situations where it is difficult to identify individuals who meet specific criteria needed for the research project, such as those characterized by low incidence.

The snowball sample approach might be used by companies such as Legendary Whitetails, Danner, or Wolverine that sell equipment and supplies to avid deer hunters. While other sampling approaches may work, the snowball approach could be used to locate avid deer hunters who spend considerable time and money on the sport. Hunters often hunt together and know other avid deer hunters. Starting with a few names, a researcher would be able to get contact information for other avid hunters. The personal reference from a friend who hunts would increase the probability of each hunter participating in the research. A sequential approach could be used until the research company obtained a sufficient sample size.

The disadvantage of the snowball approach is that the views of the sample obtained may not truly represent all avid deer hunters. The researcher has little control over the composition of the sample since he or she is relying on hunters to provide names of other hunters. It's possible the sample may be largely composed of individuals who hunt using rifles. Hunters who use a bow and arrow may be vastly underrepresented in the final sample as the season for bow hunting occurs at a different time of year than that for rifle hunting, reducing the likelihood that rifle and bow hunters may know one another. Furthermore, hunters who hunt with a rifle may subconsciously forget to provide the names of those who bow hunt to the researcher due to their differing technique. The advantage, however, to snowball sampling is that most who are contacted are likely to participate in the study, so the cost and time involved in obtaining the sample are reduced.

Earlier, it was mentioned that the results of nonprobability studies should not be generalized to the population because nonprobability samples typically do not represent the population and because it is not possible to ascertain a confidence interval for the results that would allow the user to understand the margin of error associated with the results. In actual practice, however, researchers may make inferences to the population on the basis of data drawn from nonprobability samples. They often justify their actions by incorporating some element of random selection into the sampling process. For example, many studies make use of online samples and randomly select participants from online panels to participate in the research. The random selection of participants doesn't negate the fact that not all members of the population are part of the panel, even if the population is defined as broadly as individuals who have online access. Thus, the data are in effect drawn from a convenience sample.

Given that firms may draw inferences from nonprobability data, it is absolutely critical that researchers strive to ensure that the sample accurately reflects the target population as much as possible. The more the sample reflects the makeup of the target population, the higher the generalizability of the results to the population being studied.

PROBABILITY SAMPLING METHODS

With a probability sample, every person or object in the population has a known and nonzero chance of being selected. Researchers can actually calculate what that probability is since subjects are selected objectively and not subjectively by individuals. Because of the objective nature of selection, it is possible to determine the reliability of the sample and the amount of sampling error that is likely to occur. Probability sampling does not guarantee the sample will be representative of the population. It is highly likely to be, but there is no guarantee. It is possible, although unlikely, that a nonprobability sample may produce a more representative sample than a probability sample. Researchers have several options for probability sampling, as shown in Figure 8.6.

■ Objective 8.4: Identify and describe the four probability sampling methods.

Simple Random Sample

With a **simple random sample** each element in the population has a known and equal chance of being selected. If a small business has 5,000 customers and wants a sample of 500, then with simple random sampling each customer would have a 10% chance of being selected for the sample (500/5,000). By using a random process, such as a random number generator on a computer, every customer has the same chance of being selected.

Generating a simple random sample begins with numbering every element in the population. Students at a university, members of a nonprofit organization, stores in a retail chain, and employees of an organization can all be listed and given numbers since each is known and can be identified. The next step is to use a random number generator or random number table to generate a list of random numbers. The elements of the population that correspond to those random numbers are then selected to be part of the sample.

Figure 8.6   Probability Sampling Methods

A simple random sample is ideal for marketing research because every element has a known and equal chance of being selected. However, for many studies it is not possible to use the simple random approach because not every element can be identified. For example, suppose a firm wanted to study males ages 20 to 50 in the city of

- Simple random sample
- Systematic random sample
- Stratified sample
- Cluster sample

Detroit. There is no way to generate a list of every male who lives in Detroit in that age group. Whatever sample frame is suggested would leave some males out. For this reason, researchers tend to use one of the other methods of generating a sample.

Systematic Random Sample

The difference between the systematic random sample and a simple random sample is the process of how the elements are selected. With both sampling methods, members of the population have an equal and known chance of being selected. Rather than using a random number generator or table, a **systematic random sample** uses some type of systematic process to select participants.

With the systematic random sample approach individuals in the population must be arranged in some type of order or list. A random starting point is selected. Then every "nth" element is chosen. To determine the "nth" number, the total population is divided by the number of elements desired in the sample. The resulting number is called the skip interval. So if a sample of 300 is desired out of a population of 4,800, then every 16th element would be selected. The process would begin by generating a random number between 1 and 16. Suppose it was 4. The 4th element would then be chosen for the sample followed by the 20th element, the 36th element, the 52nd element, and so forth.

Systematic random sampling is used often in direct marketing campaigns for testing direct offers. Almost all direct mail, database, and CRM (customer relationship management) software has capabilities to sort based on a systematic random sample. The problem is that many researchers mistakenly began with the first record, which means that the sample selection is no longer random. To be random, it is critical that the first element be chosen through a random process using either a random number table or random number generator.[7]

Stratified Sample

A simple or systematic random sample works best for studies involving one population. It does not work best in situations where researchers want to make comparisons between segments of a population. For instance, researchers may want to test a new type of digital point-of-purchase (POP) retail display and want to compare stores with the new display to those without the new display. Alternatively, a company may want to compare the sales of a particular brand of a product at discount stores versus department or specialty stores. It may even be a case where a university wants to evaluate the attitude of students concerning online classes and compare the traditional students to the nontraditional students. In all of these cases, a simple or systematic random sample will probably not produce a sample that will represent both or multiple groups equally or proportionately.

The **stratified sample** involves dividing the population into mutually exclusive and categorically exhaustive groups that are related to the behavior (or variables) of interest, then randomly selecting elements independently from within each group. In the case with the new digital POP display, stores would be divided into two groups, those that were using the new digital display and those that were not. Then from each group a random sample would be chosen either using the simple random sample approach or the systematic sample approach. This process ensures the researcher will have sufficient subjects in each group to make valid comparisons. The same process would be used for comparing discount, department, and specialty stores and in comparing traditional and nontraditional students.

The criteria used to divide the population into groups are based on the research objectives of the study and the discretion of the researcher. The key, however, is it must meet the two criteria. Every member of the population must be in one of the groups, and no member can be in two or more groups. The division must be mutually exclusive and collectively exhaustive.

On occasions, stratified sampling is confused with quota sampling. With both approaches, the population is divided into groups. The key difference is in how the subjects are selected for the sample. With the stratified sample, some type of random process is used. With the quota sample, subjects are chosen based on the judgment of the researcher. In the example of the medical facility discussed in the section on quota sampling, recall that interviewers were given quotas, but they could use their personal judgment in selecting who to interview. With a stratified sample approach, the patients would be divided into mutually exclusive and exhaustive groups, then selected randomly.

Cluster Sample

Cluster samples are very similar to stratified samples. With a **cluster sample** the population is divided into mutually exclusive and exhaustive groups, or subsets, called clusters. Each cluster is assumed to be representative of the population as a whole rather than homogenous groups based on some criterion as with the stratified sample approach. Once the clusters are formed, then elements can be chosen through some type of random approach or through surveying all the elements within a cluster, which then is a census.

To illustrate, suppose a state board of higher education wanted to interview faculty at its state-supported universities about impending legislation concerning higher education in the state. With the cluster approach, each of the state's universities would be considered a cluster. Suppose there are 18 universities in the state. With a **one-stage cluster sample** a certain number of universities are selected, such as 2 or 3 or 4, and then all of the faculty members at the selected universities are interviewed. To be random, the selection of the universities must be chosen through a random process. Instead of interviewing all faculty members at the chosen universities, a **two-stage cluster sample** could be used, which involves randomly selecting faculty within the universities that were chosen in the first stage of the sample selection process.

A popular form of cluster sampling that is used by research firms is area sampling. A research company may want to study the marketing efforts of independent retail clothing stores. It could use a cluster sample since obtaining a listing of all independent retail clothing stores for the United States would be difficult. If it was obtained, the cost of sending interviewers to retail stores all over the United States would be quite high. Costs and time can be greatly reduced by using a cluster approach.

The research firm could begin with the U.S. Census Bureau data and create clusters based on the 366 metropolitan statistical areas (MSAs). From the 366 MSAs, the research firm could choose a specific number of MSAs. The number chosen would likely depend on whether a one-stage or two-stage approach is used. With the one-stage approach, the research firm may choose 10 MSAs, then interview managers/owners of all of the independent retail clothing stores within each chosen MSA. For large MSAs such as New York, Houston, and Chicago, that may be quite cumbersome. So instead of the one-stage approach, the firm may use a two-stage approach and select 30 MSAs. Then within each MSA the research firm could select 10 independent retail clothing stores. To be a cluster sample approach the MSAs must be chosen randomly, and with the two-stage approach the retail clothing stores must also be chosen randomly.

From a cost and time perspective, sending research personnel to 10 or even 30 MSAs would be considerably cheaper than sending staff to 300 different retail clothing stores scattered throughout the United States. Also, it requires obtaining a listing of independent retail clothing stores for only a few MSAs rather than for the entire United States. If conducted properly, the cluster approach will yield results that would be as valid as a simple random sample, at a much lower cost.

With increased pressure from clients and marketing research firms to obtain results quickly and as inexpensively as possible, researchers can be tempted to reduce the number of clusters and increase the sample size within each cluster to maintain the same overall sample size. Doing so risks losing precision and statistical reliability. It is better to increase the number of clusters and reduce the sample size within each cluster.[8] From the previous example, surveying 30 stores in 10 MSAs will yield a sample of 300. But, depending on how those 10 MSAs are chosen, it could be a very biased sample. To increase precision and reliability of the study, it would be better to survey 10 stores in 30 MSAs. Even 30 MSAs out of 366 is a very small percentage of MSAs being represented. It would increase costs, but surveying 5 stores out of 60 MSAs would increase the reliability and precision of the study and ensure it does accurately reflect what is happening in all 366 MSAs.

DETERMINING THE SAMPLE SIZE

■ Objective 8.5: Describe the four methods of determining sample size.

Sample size is an important issue because clients would like large samples to ensure results are accurate in order to make important decisions. But, as sample size increases, so does the costs to conduct the research. So in every research project, there is a balance between the desired or adequate sample size and costs. Figure 8.7 lists the most common methods for determining sample size.

General Practice

In practice, most companies consider a sample of 1,000 to 2,000 respondents to be sufficient for national surveys. For example, Arbitron interviewed 1,753 people in a study about Americans' use of digital platforms and new media. The annual Social Shopping Survey conducted by the E-tailing Group and PowerReviews surveyed 1,000 consumers who shop at least four times per year and spend at minimum of $250 per year online. Nielsen Online surveyed 1,700 individuals about their use of social media.[9] The key to such a small sample being interpreted as the view of the general population is obtaining a sample that is representative of the population. If it is not representative of the target market, then sample size doesn't mean anything. Sampling 50,000 would still not yield results that could be generalized to the target population.

Figure 8.7   Methods of Determining Sample Size

- General practice
- Previous studies
- Statistical formula
- Sample size calculator
- Sample size table

Previous Studies

Another approach to sample size is looking at previous studies that are similar to the one being proposed. If a previous study sampled 800 respondents, then the current study could sample the same number, assuming similarities exist between the population being studied and the number of groups being compared. The primary motivation behind using this approach is often cost. The client requesting the study often has a limited budget and may request the same sample size as a previously completed study to ensure costs are close to the same. If a previous study was utilized for decision making and the results were positive, there is not an urgent need on the part of management to increase the sample size. However, if the new study requires comparing a greater number of subgroups, the sample size will likely need to be increased. Furthermore, if the recommendations garnered from the previous study were implemented and failed, the new study may benefit from a larger sample size.

Statistical Formula

From a statistical standpoint, the necessary sample size can be calculated if a probability sampling approach is used. If one of the nonprobability sampling approaches is used to obtain a sample, then sample size cannot be statistically calculated. One of the other methods would have to be used instead.

Sample size can be calculated in a number of ways. Each will yield a slightly different sample size. One of the simplest methods is to calculate the sample size using a formula based on the desired level of confidence, the allowable or acceptable margin of error, and the variability of the population characteristic being studied. The more variability that is present in a population characteristic, the larger the sample that will be needed. The formula for calculating sample size using these three variables is

$$\text{Sample size} = Z^2 \, pq \, / \, e^2.$$

The value for Z is based on the level of confidence, or accuracy, that is desired. For example, a 95% confidence level is often assumed, which means the researcher is willing to tolerate only a 5% chance that the confidence interval for a variable does not include the true value of the population. Z values for various confidence levels are obtained from a Z-table. If a 95% confidence level is desired, then the Z value would be 1.96. For a 99% confidence level, $Z = 2.58$, and for the 90% confidence level, $Z = 1.64$. The estimated proportion of an attribute that is present in a population is designated in the formula as p. In most studies, p is not known; therefore researchers will often use a value of $p = 0.5$. That means there is a 50/50 chance that the population will have the characteristic being studied, which is the maximum level of variability within a population. The value q is equal to $1 - p$. The last value e is the margin of error that the researcher is willing to accept. For example, .03 would indicate a plus or minus ($\pm$) 3% margin of error. Margin of error determines the level of precision that the study results provide. Margin of error, confidence levels, and confidence intervals were discussed in greater detail as part of the "Statistics Review" section of Chapter 6.

Suppose a researcher wanted to know the sample size needed at the 95% confidence level, the variability of the population is unknown, and the desired precision is at ± 3%. The sample size needed would be 1,067. The calculation would be

$$\text{Sample size} = \frac{(1.96)^2 (.5 \times .5)}{(.03)^2} = \frac{(3.8416)\ (.25)}{(.0009)} = \frac{.9604}{.0009} = 1,067.$$

If the researcher wanted a higher level of precision, meaning a lower margin of error, or a higher level of confidence in the results, then a larger sample would be needed. If the confidence level was increased to 99%, then sample size would have to be increased to 1,849. If instead the researcher wanted a lower margin of error, such as ± 2%, then a sample size of 2,401 would be necessary to yield a 95% confidence level when $p = 0.5$.

Assigning p a value of 0.5 always results in the most generous estimate of sample size for a given confidence level and margin of error, ensuring that the sample size is adequate. If p is any other value, the sample that is needed would be less. Consider a situation where in a previous study the percentage of youth who used social media was 78%. Suppose that researchers want to see if this percentage has changed since the original study was conducted. Assuming a 95% confidence level, a relatively high precision level featuring a margin of error of ± 3%, and a p value of = 0.78, then $q = 0.22$. When the numbers are plugged into the formula, the size of the sample needed would be 732, instead of 1,067.

Sample Size Calculators

A number of online sample size calculators are available for researchers. Usually, all that is needed is to type in the level of confidence desired, the precision (or margin of error) desired, and the variability. The calculator will provide the necessary sample size. Some calculators make adjustments based on the size of the population. These adjustments are necessary when a smaller sized population exists (for example, if surveying organizations that belong to a particular trade association). More advanced calculators take into account the anticipated survey response rate so that the researcher knows how many people must be contacted in order to achieve the desired number of completed surveys. Sample size calculators are convenient when a client requests the necessary sample size for various levels of confidence, precision, or variability, and when other factors, such as small population sizes and response rates, come into play.

Sample Size Tables

The formula and simple calculator methods of determining sample size assume an infinite or a large population, such as that of a country like the United States. For a finite population, the formula has to be corrected slightly. While some sample size calculators can be used for this purpose, a number of tables also exist that can be used, such as the one displayed in Figure 8.8. This table provides sample sizes for finite populations for a confidence level of 95% and precision levels of ± 5%, ± 3%, and ± 1%.

Notice that for a population of 100, it would take a sample of 80 for a precision level of ± 5% and a sample size of 99 if the precision level was increased to ± 1%. For a small population, researchers often will conduct a census and attempt to survey everyone in the population. For a precision of ± 5%, it would take 357 for a population of 5,000, but only 384 for a population of 1 million. Notice after a population reaches 50,000, the sample size does not change much.

Earlier, it was stated that for national samples the general practice was to survey 1,000 to 2,000 individuals. Notice that surveying slightly over 1,000 individuals would produce a 95% confidence level and a precision of ± 3%. The general practice that a sample of at least 1,000 is needed was actually based on tables such as this and calculations illustrated in the previous section.

Figure 8.8   Table for Determining Sample Size

Population Size	Confidence Level of 95%		
	5%	3%	1%
100	80	92	99
300	169	234	291
500	217	341	475
1,000	278	516	906
5,000	357	866	3,288
10,000	370	964	4,899
50,000	381	1,056	8,056
100,000	383	1,064	8,762
500,000	384	1,065	9,423
1,000,000	384	1,066	9,512

ONLINE RESEARCH PANELS

■ Objective 8.6: Discuss the benefits and issues related to online research panels.

A number of firms provide research panels for the purpose of conducting research. Most are online panels. For instance, Research Now has a worldwide research consumer panel of 6.5 million people and worldwide business-to-business panel of 2.3 million. The company has panels in 37 countries. In the United States, the company's panel consists of 3.6 million consumers, and for business-to-business the panel size is 1.8 million.[10]

Recruiting members for a research panel is done in a number of ways. A common method is to obtain names from partnering firms such as Best Buy, British Airways, Hilton HHonors program, and Pizza Hut. Based on demographic characteristics that are needed for the panel, individuals are sent an e-mail or a letter with a request to be a part of the research panel. Other companies, such as SurveySpot, publicly solicit participants through their website and allow individuals to sign up to be part of the panel. J. D. Power and Associates uses a combination of the two, inviting to be part of its panel individuals who fit a demographic profile, and offering membership to others who request it.

The number of surveys each panelist will complete varies by company and each person's profile. Most research firms that use panels will send one to two surveys per month to panelists on topics in which they have knowledge, experience, or interest and who fit the demographic profile requested by the researching company. A few firms allow panelists to select surveys they want to complete. Typically, panelists will receive points for each survey they complete. These points can be accumulated and used for prizes, cash payments, or entries into sweepstakes for gift cards and other merchandise.

Panelists are monitored. Individuals who do not respond to surveys or who submit surveys that are not properly completed are dropped from panels. Individuals can also opt out of the panel at any time. For most panels, the annual attrition rate is between 10% and 50%.

In using a panel for research, clients should request some basic validation metrics to ensure quality. Some basic metrics that can be supplied by companies are listed in Figure 8.9. The percentage of panelists who have verified or updated their profile within the last month, three months, or six months provides an indication of the currency of a research firm's panel. People move, change jobs, and change other aspects in their personal lives. To ensure the sample selected meets the client's demographic and even psychographic profiles, updating of profile information on a regular basis is important.

The attrition rate provides an idea of why people join a particular panel and how the research firm handles the panel. A panel with a high attrition rate would indicate potential problems in either recruiting legitimate members or maintaining their interest in completing surveys. Inability to maintain members can be due to a low reward structure, lack of interest in survey topics, insufficient number for surveys to hold their interest, or even being sent too many surveys.

The panelist activity rates refer to the range and mean number of surveys completed by panelists within the last month, or three months, or six months. A wide range may indicate some members are being overused while others are not being used enough. A high mean may indicate individuals are in the panel just for the rewards and not because they have an interest in providing their opinions. Too many surveys can result in people just filling in answers and not taking time to read or think about the information being requested.

Figure 8.9   Validation Metrics for Sample Panels

- Percentage of panelists who have verified or updated their profile
- Monthly or annual dropout rate
- Panelist response rates
- Panelist activity rates

Figure 8.10   Benefits of Online Research Panels

- Faster data collection
- Cost-effective
- More efficient targeting of low-incidence groups
- Use of graphics, videos, and audio
- Longer and more detailed questionnaires
- Automated data entry
- Automated data validation

Benefits of Online Research Panels

Online panels provide researchers with a number of benefits, listed in Figure 8.10. Collecting data is faster and more cost-effective since the panels already exist. Estimates are that using an online research panel can save up to 40% on a research project compared to traditional sampling methods.[11] Selecting a sample that meets a client's demographic target can be done quickly and easily. For groups that have a low-incidence rate, a sufficient sample can usually be selected since many of these panels consist of a million or more individuals.

Being online, researchers can use graphics, videos, and audio with the survey. It also allows for more detailed and longer questionnaires since panelists are recruited for the specific purpose of conducting research. The online feature allows for automated data entry into a spreadsheet, reducing data entry errors that can occur when employees transfer a paper survey to a computer spreadsheet. Online surveys can also have some automated data validation procedures that ensure people are reading the questions and that the panelists are completing the survey and not someone else. For instance, the same question worded differently at two different spots on the survey can be automated to check to see if the person provides the same reply, or if he or she is just filling in blanks.

Concerns With Online Research Panels

A major concern with online research panels is the recruitment process. Recruitment can occur through "invitation only" or through "open recruitment." One of the greatest challenges facing researchers is finding a qualified sample that meets the target population characteristics. Once identified, then it is even more challenging to gain the recruits' cooperation to complete a survey or participate in a research study. Using online research panels simplifies this process.

"Open source" recruitment allows individuals to self-select to be on a research panel. They may see an advertisement on a search engine or on the Internet and respond, search for sample firms that offer open enrollment, or hear from a friend about the research panel. Which method is used is not the issue. The issue is that the individual has chosen to be part of the research panel.

The danger of open-source recruiting is that it is likely to produce a biased sample. While it can result in millions joining the panel, it can create a sample that is biased toward Internet-savvy people who like giving their opinion, who respond to online ads, or who want to earn money or rewards. In many cases these individuals participate in a number of online panels and complete large amounts of surveys. These individuals are known in the industry as "professional respondents." As presented in Chapter 6, not all professional respondents are bad. There are some who enjoy giving their opinion, take the survey seriously, and take their time in answering the questions.

The danger with most professional respondents is that they tend to give false and misleading information in order to qualify for surveys or to complete surveys quickly. They may read questions, but will give little thought to the answers. They may even use different profiles and e-mail addresses in order to take the same survey several times, thus saving time and effort. They often are members of multiple online research panels.

The presence of negative professional respondents is more pronounced with international samples. For instance, in India companies offer seminars to individuals on how they can locate research panels and how to complete surveys. For these individuals, completing surveys is a way of living. They are often a member of multiple online research panels and may even do so under a number of different profiles. They may be a 25-year-old college graduate working for an international firm for one survey and a 40-year-old female homemaker for another. While companies strive to locate and eliminate these individuals from their research panels, they are difficult to identify.[12]

A study by comScore found that 30% of all online surveys were completed by less than 1% of the population. The study also found that professional respondents took an average of 80 surveys over a three-month period. Some individuals completed several surveys a day.[13]

"Invitation only" recruiting is a closed system where individuals are requested to be part of the online research panels. Most often, these panels are developed through purchasing rights to a large company's database, such as Hilton Hotels or Best Buy. Individuals are then selected based on their demographic profile. Individuals are sent a request to participate in the research panel. Using this type of method allows a research company to have much tighter control over who becomes a member of the panel. While it does not eliminate the professional respondent it greatly reduces the number that will be on the panel. The attempt is made to recruit individuals who truly want to share their opinions as opposed to those whose sole goal is to earn money or prizes.

Another problem with online research, in general, is the representativeness of the sample. While more and more people use the Internet and have access to it, Internet users still tend to be a little different from the general population. Internet users tend to be younger and more educated, and have higher incomes than non–Internet users. While this may not be a problem for some products, such as electronics, it can pose a problem for others, such as food products and their manufacturers.

Global Concerns

Issues that concern marketing researchers in the United States regarding samples are present in other countries as well. In addition, issues with translation and cultural differences add to the challenge of conducting global studies. While survey questions can be translated into a different language, the meaning may still be different depending on the culture of that region.

Research panels can be used, but it creates unique problems in terms of global research. While the differences between online users and non-online users in the United States are not that great, in other countries the differences can be much larger. It may be that only a small part of the country's population has access to the Internet. For instance, only 11.7% of the billion individuals living in Africa use the Internet.[14] By contrast, 90.2% of the population of Greenland uses the Internet.[15] The differences in income and education between Internet users and nonusers can be much greater, especially in third world countries.

Most people would think that online studies in China and India would closely resemble online studies conducted in the United States. Such is not the case. While the number of Internet users is high, the composition is skewed toward urban areas and large cities. In countries such as the United Arab Emirates the floating population is high, which means the profiles of locals versus expatriates vary greatly. For these countries, updating profiles on a regular basis is important. Respondents in Japan and France are very sensitive to how they are treated, so survey quality is highly dependent on effective communications with panel members.[16]

Another facet of global samples is that in Western countries, such as the United States, many individuals do not want to be part of a research panel. Even for invitation-only panels, the refusal rate to participate is high. But, in other countries where the Internet is new and online survey research is in its infancy, being part of a research panel is exciting and novel. It can even be a status symbol for those who participate. As a result, the views of people in these countries may differ considerably from the views in a world where it is difficult to recruit panel members.

 STATISTICS REVIEW

To be able to make inferences to a population, the sample needs to be representative of the population being studied. A statistical method to check for representativeness is the chi-square test. The test can be used to compare sample characteristics to population characteristics to see if they are statistically the same.

Consider Figure 8.11, which compares the gender of the sample to the gender of a target population. In this situation the target population consists of 50% males and 50% females. Thus, the 1,054 responses should be split equally between males and females. The sample, however, has 563 females and 491 males, a ratio of 53.4% to 46.6%. The question that must be considered is whether the difference in gender between the population and the sample is significant at the 95% confidence level. For this to be true, the p-value of the chi-square test must be below .05. If it is, then it would indicate a significant difference between the population and the sample. As a result, the sample would not be truly representative of the population, at least with respect to gender.

Before examining the chi-square test statistic, examine the table in the bottom left titled "Demographic: Gender." Since the target population is split equally between males and females, in the

Figure 8.11   Chi-Square Test—Gender

Demographic: Gender

		Frequency	Percent	Valid Percent	Cumulative Percent
Valid	Female	563	52.8	53.4	53.4
	Male	491	46.1	46.6	100.0
	Total	1,054	98.9	100.0	
Missing	System	12	1.1		
Total		1,066	100.0		

Demographic: Gender

	Observed N	Expected N	Residual
Female	563	527.0	36.0
Male	491	527.0	-36.0
Total	1,054		

Test Statistics

	Demographic: Gender
Chi-square	4.918[a]
df	1
Asymp. Sig.	.027

a. 0 cells (.0%) have expected frequencies less than 5. The minimum expected cell frequency is 527.0.

sample of 1,054 the chi-square test assumes an expected frequency of 527 females and 527 males. The "Observed N" is 563 females and 491 females. The residual shows the sample has 36 more females than it should (563 − 527) and has 36 fewer males than expected (527 − 491).

The table on the bottom right shows the chi-square value is 4.918. The p-value, or significance level, is designated as "Asymp. Sig." in the table, and shows a p-value of .027. This is below the test value of .05, which means there is a significant difference between the gender makeup of the sample and what was expected for the population. Thus, the sample is not representative of the population in terms of gender. It has too many females and not enough males.

Figure 8.12 shows a chi-square test for age. The top left table shows the target population's age composition. In the target population, 68% are ages 18–22, 25% are 23–29, 5% are 30–39, and the remaining 2% are 40 or older. The top right table shows the sample's age breakdown. Does the sample adequately represent the target population? The bottom left table shows the "Observed N" from the sample, the "Expected N" calculated from the sample characteristics, and the residual difference. The chi-square test in the bottom right table shows a chi-square value of 2.674 and a p-value of 0.445. Since the p-value is greater than .05, there is not a significant difference between the age composition of the sample and the age composition of the target population. Thus, in terms of age, the sample is representative of the population for this research study.

The greatest difficulty in determining the representativeness of the sample is locating the appropriate target population parameters. Data from the U.S. census can be helpful when surveys attempt to represent the population of the United States as a whole, or a particular state, city, or zip code. Marketing studies may sample college students at a particular university. Characteristics of a university's student population are usually made available by the institutional research department, and can typically be found on the university's website. Customer databases that include demographic profiles can be compared

(Continued)

(Continued)

Figure 8.12   Chi-Square Test—Age

<table>
<tr><td colspan="2" align="center">Population: Age</td></tr>
<tr><td>18 – 22</td><td>68%</td></tr>
<tr><td>23 – 29</td><td>25%</td></tr>
<tr><td>30 – 39</td><td>5%</td></tr>
<tr><td>40+</td><td>2%</td></tr>
</table>

		Frequency	Percent	Valid Percent	Cumulative Percent
Valid	18–22	723	67.8	68.3	68.3
	23–29	274	25.7	25.9	94.2
	30–39	44	4.1	4.2	98.4
	40+	17	1.6	1.6	100.0
	Total	1,058	99.2	100.0	
Missing	System	8	.8		
Total		1,066	100.0		

Demographic: Age

	Observed N	Expected N	Residual
18–22	723	719.4	3.6
23–29	274	264.5	9.5
30–39	44	52.9	-8.9
40+	17	21.2	-4.2
Total	1,058		

Test Statistics

	Demographic: Age
Chi-square	2.674 [a]
df	3
Asymp. Sig.	.445

a 0 cells (.0%) have expected frequencies less than 5. The minimum expected cell frequency is 21.2.

against those of the sample when satisfaction or other studies targeting current customers are used. In situations in which no customer database is present, an alternative source that approximates these characteristics may have to be used. If Reebok conducted a survey drawn from the population of individuals who purchased athletic shoes in the last six months, the company could use the demographic characteristics contained in the data available from syndicated research firms such as Mediamark. Of course, Mediamark's data are also based on a sampling procedure, but at least it is a large national sample and as such would likely be very close to the population of Reebok purchasers.

DEALING WITH DATA

A marketing professor has surveyed the students at her university concerning the use of PowerPoint slides. To be able to make inferences to the entire student body, the sample drawn needs to represent the university's student population. Figure 8.13 shows five student demographic variables. The professor found the breakdown of the overall student population along the five dimensions in the university's fact book posted online.

The questionnaire used for this study is located at www.sagepub.com/clowess and is titled "Chapter 08 Dealing with Data Survey." The SPSS data file is titled "Chapter 08 Dealing with

Figure 8.13 Population Characteristics

Variable	Category	Population Percent
Gender	Female	64%
	Male	36%
Traditional/Nontraditional	Traditional	66%
	Nontraditional	20%
	Other	14%
Race/Ethnicity	African American	25%
	Caucasian	66%
	Other	9%
Full-Time/Part-Time	Full-Time	63%
	Part-Time	37%
College	Arts and Sciences	34%
	Business	25%
	Education	26%
	Heath Sciences	15%

Data." Use the chi-square test found under the nonparametric menu button in SPSS. Test the sample demographics against the population percentages shown in Figure 8.13. Remember, each variable will have to be tested separately. After running the five chi-square tests, answer the following questions:

1. Based on the chi-square test, which sample variables adequately represent the population? Support your answer by providing the p-value of the chi-square test and explaining what it means.

2. Based on the chi-square test, which sample variables do not adequately represent the university's student population? Explain why by providing the p-value of the chi-square test. How does the professor need to adjust the sample (i.e., which categories have too many respondents, and which ones do not have enough)?

3. Based on the five chi-square tests, is this sample representative of the student population? Why or why not? Can the professor make inferences to the student population about the use of PowerPoint slides by students? Why or why not?

4. Can the professor make inferences to college students in general (i.e., for all college students in the United States)? Why or why not?

5. Are any important population characteristics missing from this study? If so, what are they? Why do you feel that they would be relevant?

SUMMARY

Objective 1: Explain the difference between a population and a sample.

A population is the set of people, websites, stores, or other objects the researcher wants to study and from whom the researcher wishes to collect data. A sample is a subset of the population that should provide a representative cross-section of the people, stores, websites, or objects that exist in the population.

Objective 2: Discuss the steps involved in selecting a sample.

The sample selection process begins with a definition of the characteristics that describe the sample, as well as characteristics that should exclude participants from being part of the sample. Next, the sample frame is identified and developed. Sometimes multiple sources are used in this process. The next step requires that the researcher make a choice between probability sampling and nonprobability sampling. This step is followed by determination of the sample size. Finally, the specific sampling technique used to select sample elements is selected.

Objective 3: Identify and describe the four nonprobability sampling methods.

Convenience samples choose sample elements based on convenience factors, such as ease of access or availability during the surveying period. The personal judgment of the researcher determines who is and is not selected to be a member of a judgment sample.

Quota samples attempt to ensure some level of representativeness of the population in the sample based on one or more characteristics of the target population, or some other factor specified by the researcher. Most appropriate for populations with low incidence rates, snowball samples are formed when a few respondents who initially participate in a study agree to provide the researcher with the names of additional individuals who share some key characteristic.

Objective 4: Identify and describe the four probability sampling methods.

Random sample elements are randomly selected from a numbered list using a random number generator or some other random selection process. A skip interval is used to select members of a systematic random sample, following the random selection of a starting place on an ordered list of sample frame elements. Stratified samples first create mutually exclusive and exhaustive groups for one of the characteristics of the sample or behavior of interest to the study. Subjects are randomly selected from within each group to ensure that the population is adequately represented. Cluster samples divide populations into mutually exclusive and exhaustive groups, or clusters where each cluster is assumed to be representative of the population as a whole. One-stage cluster samples randomly select clusters, then survey all elements within the cluster.

Two-stage cluster samples begin by randomly selecting clusters, then randomly selecting elements within the clusters to be part of the sample.

Objective 5: Describe the various methods of determining sample size.

Methods of determining sample size include using general practice rules of thumb, sample sizes found in previous studies, the sample size statistical formula, sample size calculators found on the web, and sample size tables.

Objective 6: Discuss the benefits and issues related to online research panels.

Online research panels allow data to be collected faster and in a more cost-effective manner. It can be especially beneficial in targeting low-incidence populations. Online panels allow for longer, more detailed questionnaires as well as for graphic, video, and audio stimuli. Data quality is enhanced by the automated data entry and validation aspects associated with online software. Open recruitment practices and professional respondents damage the quality of data available via online panels. Furthermore, online panels are not truly representative of the general population. But, as more individuals gain access to the Internet, online panels are becoming more representative.

GLOSSARY OF KEY TERMS

Census: survey of the entire population

Cluster sample: probability sample method that involves dividing the population into mutually exclusive and exhaustive groups or subsets where each group or subset is assumed to be representative of the population, then randomly selecting elements from within each group or subset

Convenience sample: nonprobability sample method where individuals or objects are chosen based on convenience

Fixed sample: sample size is determined prior to conducting the research

Judgment sample: nonprobability sample method where researchers use personal judgment to select the sample

Nonprobability sample: chance or probability of someone being selected within a target population is not known and cannot be determined

One-stage cluster sample: probability cluster sample method that involves randomly selecting clusters, then surveying all of the elements within the clusters that are selected

Population: group from which a sample is drawn and which is the target of the research study

Probability sample: each member of the target population has a known and nonzero chance of being selected

Quota sample: nonprobability sample method of selecting a sample based on the target population's characteristics or criteria specified by the researcher

Sample: group of individuals chosen to survey

Sampling error: refers to the amount of error that the researcher is willing to accept as a result of the sampling process

Sequential sample: sample is selected in stages or sequences stopping when sample size is sufficient for research purpose

Simple random sample: probability sample method where each element of the population has a known and equal chance of being selected

Snowball sample: nonprobability sample method of selecting a few respondents to participate in a study, then asking each respondent for names of additional individuals to participate

Stratified sample: probability sample method that requires dividing the population into mutually exclusive and exhaustive groups related to the behavior or variables of interest, then randomly selecting elements independently from within each group

Systematic random sample: probability sample method that involves randomly selecting the first respondent, then selecting each nth element of the population

Two-stage cluster sample: probability cluster sample method that involves randomly selecting clusters, then randomly selecting elements within the clusters that were selected

CRITICAL THINKING EXERCISES

1. Topol is a whitening toothpaste that is known for its ability to clean tough stains while controlling tartar and fighting plaque. Suppose the manufacturers of Topol were interested in surveying both current consumers of the product and those who don't use it but who would benefit from its superior whitening ability. Define the population characteristics for the study. Remember to include exclusionary factors that are relevant.

2. Your employer would like to sample people who participate in fishing activities on a regular basis. Define the population characteristics in greater detail. Assume that you have been tasked with building a sampling frame list of individuals who are part of this population. What sources would you use to build this list? Your goal is to develop a sampling frame that is as representative as is possible.

3. Under what circumstances would a stratified sample be preferable to a random sample? Explain. List one or more products or services where stratification would be especially helpful. Why do you feel that a stratified sample would be best?

4. Identify the type of sampling technique used in the following studies:

   a. A telephone surveyor calls people listed in the phone book in alphabetical order. The survey is administered to the first 100 African American men and 100 African American women who agree to participate.
   b. A pest control company uses a random number generator to select 100 current customers from its customer database to survey regarding their satisfaction with the firm's services.
   c. The state of Texas randomly selects 10 school districts in the state, then randomly selects 5 middle schools within each district to participate in a survey.

5. You have been asked to conduct a study of students who attend your university. Unfortunately, you are restricted to using one of the nonprobability sampling techniques discussed in this chapter. Which would you choose? Why? Explain how you would implement your sampling plan and the tactics you would use to try to make your sample as representative of the student population as you can.

6. Describe the differences between systematic samples, cluster samples, and stratified samples. Give examples of each that differ from those described in the textbook.

7. Calculate the skip interval to be used in a systematic random sample if the population size is 5,000 and a sample of 350 individuals is required to provide the desired confidence level and margin of error.

8. Suppose a researcher wanted to know the sample size needed at the 99% confidence level for a pharmaceutical drug study in which the variability of the population is unknown and the acceptable margin of error is ± 1%. Use the statistical formula discussed earlier in this chapter to calculate the sample size needed. What if the researcher was willing to drop the confidence level to 95%? What sample size would be needed under these conditions? Show your work for both sets of calculations.

9. A trade association with 3,500 members needs to know how many members should be sent e-mail invitations to participate in a study. The variability of the population is unknown, and the trade association wants to be 95% confident that the sample results fall within a margin of error of ± 3%. Find an online sample calculator that takes into account the population size and response rate in addition to confidence level, variability of the population, and margin of error. Calculate the sample size needed and provide the URL of the sample size calculator used.

10. Go to your university's website and locate the page or document that describes the population characteristics of the student body. This information may be listed in a document titled "Fact Book," "Fast Facts," "Student Profiles," or something similar. Typically the information is provided by the division or department of institutional research, so search there first. Some universities provide access to this information from webpages that target parents or families, community members or media, or new students. This information should be publicly available, so if you don't find it on the website, visit your university's library and speak to a reference librarian. Once you have located the population characteristics, prepare a report of what you've found. Make certain that you paraphrase the information (don't cut and paste directly from the website), and cite your source appropriately.

CONTINUING CASE STUDY: LAKESIDE GRILL

After considerable discussion, Brooke, Alexa, Juan, Destiny, and Zach arrived at a sampling plan, shown in Figure 8.14. Based on information from the owner of Lakeside Grill, secondary research, and the focus group work, the team defined the population as individuals who live or work within a 5-mile radius of the grill. They believed that most patrons of the restaurant come from within that distance. A couple of the group members, Juan and Brooke, had argued that a 5-mile radius was too far and that they should concentrate on a 2- or 3-mile radius.

Since the target population was defined as households within a 5-mile radius, the sampling frame was designated as all homes, apartments, and businesses within that area. That decision was easy. The liveliest discussion occurred over the sampling procedure. The group finally decided on a four-prong approach.

(1) survey customers at Lakeside Grill while eating

(2) send e-mails to Chamber of Commerce business members and request they be distributed to employees

(Continued)

(Continued)

(3) mall intercept

(4) ask students in 3 different marketing classes to send the survey to friends and relatives who live in the area

Critique Questions:

1. Do you agree with the group's definition of the target population? Why or why not?

2. Is the sampling frame defined properly? Why or why not?

3. What is your evaluation of the four-prong approach? Is it a convenience sample? Justify your answer.

4. What other methods of sampling could the group use? What would be the pros and cons?

5. Go through each method of sampling and discuss its feasibility for the research project with Lakeside Grill.

6. The group decided on a sample size of 300. Is this enough? Is this realistic?

Figure 8.14   Sampling Plan for Lakeside Grill

- Population: Individuals who live and work within 5 miles
- Sampling frame: homes apartments and businesses within 5-mile radius
- Sampling procedure: convenience
- Sample size: 300

MARKETING RESEARCH PORTFOLIO

The quality of data in a primary research study is highly dependent upon the degree to which a sample represents the population. The Marketing Research Portfolio mini-case for Chapter 8 focuses students' attention on this issue and challenges students to develop a sampling plan for the featured client. Students are expected to define the population (including exclusionary factors), identify and justify sources that could be used to build a sampling frame, recommend a sample size for the study, justify the specific choice of probability or nonprobability sampling technique to be used, and describe how the sample selection process will be implemented. The assignment instructions and case information can be found at www.sagepub.com/clowess.

STUDENT STUDY SITE

Visit the Student Study Site at www.sagepub.com/clowess to access the following additional materials:

- eFlashcards
- Web Quizzes
- SAGE Journal Articles
- Web Resources

CHAPTER 9

Measurement Methods

After reading this chapter, you should be able to

1. Explain the concept of measurement.
2. Describe the characteristics and give examples of nominal scales.
3. Describe the characteristics and give examples of ordinal scales.
4. Describe the characteristics and give examples of interval scales.
5. Describe the characteristics and give examples of ratio scales.
6. Discuss methods for assessing reliability.
7. Elaborate on methods of evaluating validity.

INTRODUCTION

The smartphone has been both a blessing and a curse to brick-and-mortar retail stores. The smart phone allows shoppers to use a coupon at checkout and to access the store's app. But, the smartphone also allows shoppers to search for better prices from other retailers and to scan the bar code to find the product online. Figure 9.1 identifies the different ways consumers utilize their smartphones while shopping. More importantly, the bar graph shows the percentage for each category. At the top of the list is searching for a better price (32%), searching reviews (27%), and scanning bar codes (26%).[1]

This chapter addresses the concept of measurement and how marketers can determine if the measures are reliable and valid. For instance, with the use of smartphones, researchers have several

Figure 9.1   Smartphone Usage While Shopping

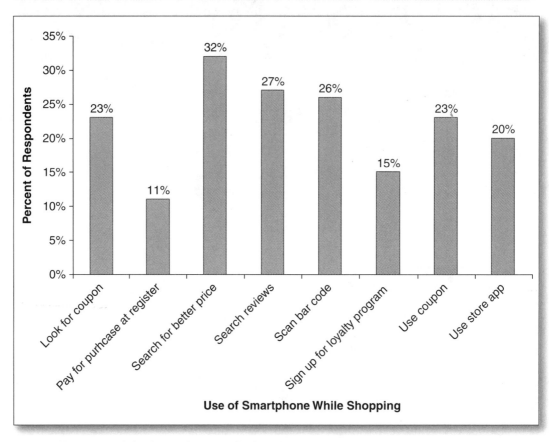

Source: Author-created with data from Carl Marcucci, "Mobile Advertising Up Dramatically," *Radio & Television Business Report*, November 28, 2011, http://rbr.com/mobile-advertising-up-dramatically/ (accessed August 6, 2012).

options. They can provide the list of options shown in Figure 9.1 and ask respondents to check all that apply, which was done in this case. Alternatively, they could provide the list and ask respondents to rank the options in various ways such as by importance, by usage, or even by level of benefit. The researchers could have provided the list and asked which option or options respondents used on their last shopping trip. The bottom line is that researchers have a number of ways of asking a question. Each way could yield a different type of data that will in turn impact the ways the data can be analyzed. This chapter begins with a discussion of the four types of scales, then provides information about how to decide on the best scale to use.

The last part of the chapter examines the issues of reliability and validity. Obtaining responses to questions is only part of the researcher's task. The marketing research must also ensure that the responses accurately measure what they are supposed to measure. In addition, the researcher must take steps to minimize errors from adversely affecting the results of the marketing study.

THE CONCEPT OF MEASUREMENT

■ Objective 9.1:
Explain the
concept of
measurement.

Managers seek information from marketing research in order to make intelligent decisions. To obtain the necessary information, marketers are often engaged in measuring various phenomena or characteristics of a respondent or an entity. These might include demographic characteristics, product ownership characteristics, and attitudes toward various things. **Measurement** is the process of assigning numbers or labels to those phenomena or characteristics. It can be individuals, objects, or events.

The numbers must be assigned according to specific rules or guidelines to ensure the numbers are meaningful and consistent. Figure 9.2 provides several examples. For instance, the number 1 may be assigned to females and the number 2 to males. Numbers can also be assigned to more abstract concepts such as brand attitude or brand loyalty. Researchers could use a range of numbers from 1 to 5 to indicate the strength and direction of a person's attitude. A 5 may represent a very positive attitude and 1 a very negative attitude. A 3 might be a neutral attitude with 4 being slightly positive and 2 being slightly negative. The key to measurement is to specify the rule and/or process for assigning numbers to whatever is being measured.

The process of measurement involves two important concepts. First, it is not the person, object, or event that is being measured. It is an attribute or a characteristic, such as the income of an individual, sales produced by an advertising campaign, or degree of willingness of a person to purchase a product. Second, the numbers are assigned by rules and/or process specified by the researcher. While the way the numbers are assigned can impact the types of analyses that can be done, the process of assigning values is determined by the researcher. For instance, the number 1

Figure 9.2   The Process of Measurement

Respondent or Entity	Characteristic/Phenomena	Measurement Designations
Survey Respondent	Gender	1 = Female 2 = Male
	Attitude Toward Brand	1 = Very Unfavorable 2 = Unfavorable 3 = Neutral 4 = Favorable 5 = Very Favorable
	Brand Usage	1 = Current User of Brand 2 = Former User of Brand 3 – Never Used Brand
Store	Type	1 = Convenience 2 = Grocery or Supermarket 3 = Mass Merchandise 4 = Discount 5 = Department Store 6 = Boutique 7 = Other

Figure 9.3   Types of
Measurement Scales

- Nominal scales
- Ordinal scales
- Interval scales
- Ratio scales

does not have to be assigned to females and 2 to males. It can be the reverse—1 could be males and 2 could be females—or the numbers 33 and 45 can be used, or whatever numbers the researcher designates, because these numbers do nothing other than group respondents with similar characteristics together. So long as all females are designated by the same number, and that number differs from the one assigned to males, the actual numbers used are irrelevant.

Researchers have four different types of scales that can be used for measurements: nominal, ordinal, interval, and ratio (see Figure 9.3). The characteristics of each scale determine the types of data analyses that can be performed. Nominal scales are considered to be the lowest or most restrictive type of scale and ratio the highest-order scale.

■ Objective 9.2: Describe the characteristics and give examples of nominal scales.

Nominal Scales

With **nominal scales** numbers are assigned to objects or sets of objects for the purpose of identification and classification. It is the lowest order of the four scales since the numbers have no meaning other than identifying a particular characteristic. The number used for each object or set is entirely up to the discretion of the researcher. Examples of nominal scales are:

Gender: (1) Female (2) Male

Preferred Fast Food: (1) McDonald's (2) Burger King (3) Wendy's (4) Taco Bell (5) KFC

How did you hear about our business? (Check all that apply):

____ Yellow pages

____ Radio

____ TV

____ Newspaper

____ Internet

____ Friend or relative

____ Other (please specify): _____

Notice the numbers assigned in the first two examples have no real meaning other than they provide a process for coding each respondent's answer and grouping together those with similar characteristics. No numbers are provided in the third example. Instead, respondents are asked to check the blank next to each answer that applies. While this may be confusing at first glance, this type of question does collect nominal data. Each potential response (yellow pages, radio, etc.) is treated as an individual question or variable, the responses to which would be coded as 0 = no (*not checked*) and 1 = yes (*checked*). Thus, the response options implied by the "Friend or relative" variable are "Yes, I heard of the business [from a friend or relative]" and "No, I did not hear of the business [from a friend or relative]."

In developing nominal scales, it is highly desirable for the scale choices to be **mutually exclusive** and **collectively exhaustive**. Mutually exclusive means that each response is uniquely different from other possible responses. Thus, respondents fit into either one category or another, but cannot belong to multiple categories. This is why the third question creates separate variables for each possible checked response. **Categorically exhaustive** means that all possible responses are included in the answer categories. With gender, that is evident. But, for the fast-food preference, suppose an individual wanted to select Carl's Jr. restaurant. It is not listed, so while the scale is mutually exclusive it is not collectively exhaustive. In case a choice was left out, researchers often include as the last item "Other" and allow the respondents to write in their own response. These "Other" responses can then be coded later in the spreadsheet being used for the analysis, or if it is a small number of responses the researcher may leave it as "Other." When preferences or consumption habits are being surveyed, researchers may also wish to include additional categories, such as "No preference" or "Do not eat fast food." Doing so would avoid forcing respondents to make a selection that otherwise would introduce error into the data.

The nominal scale is considered the lowest scale form since the only analysis that can be conducted is to obtain a frequency count or percentage of responses. For instance, researchers can count how many males and females were in a sample and even assign a percentage, such as 63% females and 37% males. For the fast-food item, it is possible to count how many respondents indicated each choice and then calculate a percentage. Figure 9.4 shows the type of results that may be obtained from the fast-food item. The figure shows 74 individuals preferred McDonald's, which was 21.7% of the sample. The least preferred fast food was Taco Bell with 44 respondents, or 12.9%. The figure indicates 17 individuals, or 4.88%, checked "Other." These 17 could be listed in the figure if the researcher deemed it was important. Otherwise, they could be left in the "Other" category since they made up only about 5% of the responses.

Ordinal Scales

With **ordinal scales** numbers are assigned for the purpose of identification, but also have the property of being arranged in some type of array or order. As with nominal scales, response options should be mutually exclusive and categorically exhaustive. The sequence of numbers means something in terms of one response category being larger or better than another.

■ Objective 9.3: Describe the characteristics and give examples of ordinal scales.

Figure 9.4   Results From Using a Nominal Scale

Preferred Restaurant	Number of Respondents	Percent of Total
McDonald's	74	21.70%
Burger King	82	24.05%
Wendy's	51	14.95%
Taco Bell	44	12.90%
KFC	68	19.94%
Other	17	4.99%
None/Don't Eat Fast Food	5	1.47%
Total	341	100%

However, the basic mathematical functions of adding, subtracting, multiplying, and dividing cannot be used with ordinal scales. Consider the following examples of ordinal scales administered to people aged 18 and older:

Age: (1) 18–24 (2) 25–34 (3) 35–44 (4) 45–54 (5) 55+

Number of websites visited: (0) None (1) 1 or 2 (2) 3 to 5 (3) 6 to 9 (4) 10 or more

Please rank the following search engines in terms of your personal preference with 1 indicating your first choice, 2 indicating your second choice, 3 indicating your third choice, and 4 indicating your fourth choice.

Bing: _____

Google: _____

WebCrawler: _____

Yahoo:_____

Notice with the first ordinal scale, age, the values given range from 1 for individuals 18 to 24 to 5 for individuals 55 and over. The reason ordinal scales are used for age is that many individuals will not write down their age if asked directly, but will normally check one of the brackets to indicate their age group. There is an order to the sequence in which numbers are assigned to categories. Specifically, the larger the number used to represent a response category, the older the respondent. However, ordinal scales do not allow the researcher to compare numbers using mathematical operations. You cannot say that individuals in the fourth category are twice as old as those in the second category, or four times older than those in the first category. All the numbers can be used to indicate is the category to which the respondent belongs and whether a given respondent is older or younger than other respondents.

The same properties hold true for the second ordinal item dealing with the number of websites visited. In this case, the researcher chose to use 0 to represent an answer of "None." The researcher could actually have used any number for this response as well as any other response. The only stipulation is that whatever numbers are chosen, an ascending order must be maintained. Instead of using codes of 0 through 4, the researcher could have chosen 10, 20, 30, 40, and 50 or even 5, 22, 36, 41, and 99. Ordinal scales do not imply the existence of equal intervals, as the last example makes clear.

The last ordinal item asks respondents to rank four search engines based on their personal preferences with 1 indicating their first choice, 2 their second choice, 3 their third choice, and 4 their last choice. Order is still maintained with numbers from 1 to 4. But, with this coding, the lower the number, the more preferred the search engine is among the respondents who were interviewed. There is no rule that says the greater the quantity, the higher the code number must be. It is common to do so, but not absolutely necessary. More often, ranking questions use the format of 1 for the first choice, 2 for the second choice, and so on. This is common because that is the way consumers would think when asked to indicate their preferences for restaurants.

Figure 9.5 shows one method for reporting the age variable. The pie chart can be used since the categories are mutually exclusive and collectively exhaustive as only those 18 years of age or older were surveyed. The graph shows that the largest category of respondents is the 25- to 44-year-old age category. It consists of 144 respondents, or 40% of the sample.

Figure 9.5 Ordinal Scale—Age

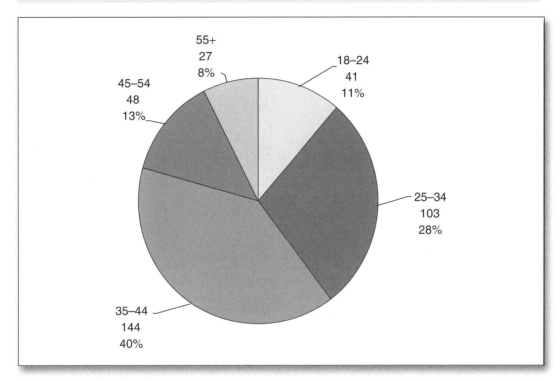

Figure 9.6 provides another way for reporting ordinal data. The 3D column chart shows the number of respondents who indicated each answer. The raw numbers are presented in this graph. The researcher could have reported the percentages instead, or reported both numbers. Most people (218) visited 3 to 5 websites.

Figure 9.7 reports the results of the last question, the ranking of the four search engines. Notice for this figure the researcher has chosen to report the percentages for each category. Google was ranked first choice by 48% of the respondents, Bing was ranked first by 31%, Yahoo was ranked first by 17%, and WebCrawler was ranked first by only 4%. The mode, or most frequently occurring number, could also be reported.

It would be tempting to calculate a mean for the ranking question to determine a relative ranking among the four search engines. While some researchers may do this, such a calculation violates the characteristics of an ordinal scale. Recall that with ordinal scales, numbers signify order but do not possess mathematical properties. The numbers merely indicate group membership or classification. Instead of using numbers 1 through 4, the researcher could have used the numbers 1, 3, 6, and 10, or any other numbers.

To understand ordinal scales and why mathematical operations such as means are inappropriate, it also helps to consider how different individuals may go through the process of ranking the four search engines. Suppose Chelsea ranks Google as her first choice, but has a really difficult time because she also likes to use Bing just about as much. But, she finally decides to rank Google first and Bing second, and for her Yahoo is a distant third. She doesn't like WebCrawler and so gives it a 4, but in her mind it wouldn't even rank in her choice of

Figure 9.6   Ordinal Scale—Number of Websites Visited

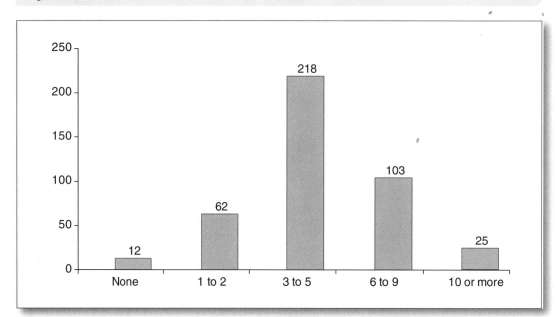

Figure 9.7   Ordinal Scale–Ranking of Search Engines

Search Engine	First Choice	Second Choice	Third Choice	Fourth Choice
Bing	31%	36%	22%	11%
Google	48%	33%	15%	4%
WebCrawler	4%	13%	23%	60%
Yahoo	17%	18%	40%	25%

search engines. Furthermore, one of her favorite search engines isn't shown on the list. Now consider Codie who has the same order for the four search engines. But, Google is his first and *only* choice as the other three aren't even a consideration. Instead, he has a hard time ranking the second, third, and fourth choices as in his mind those three search engines are about equal. While Chelsea and Codie rank the engines in the same order, the distance or interval between the rankings is quite different in their minds. For Chelsea first and second are very close. For Codie they are not close at all.

Unlike nominal scales, ordinal scales that ask respondents to rank order items cannot include an "Other" option. For the data to have meaning, all respondents must rank the same items. Allowing people to enter an "Other" choice would result in different people potentially ranking different search engines since Person A may enter AltaVista in the "Other" category while Person B may enter Lycos. This is further complicated by the fact that Person C's rankings may have differed if either AltaVista or Lycos had been originally listed as part of the ranking question.

Interval Scales

■ Objective 9.4:
Describe the
characteristics
and give
examples of
interval scales.

With **interval scales** the distance, or space between the numbers assigned to objects or sets of objects, is considered to be equal. So if a scale from 1 to 5 is being used, then the distance between 1 and 2 is the same as between 2 and 3 as well as any other set of consecutive numbers that is chosen. Interval scales subsume the properties of both the nominal and ordinal scales in that numbers are assigned to objects or sets of objects and the numbers chosen represent an ordered progression. The difference between the ordinal and interval scales is that the distance between scale points cannot be assumed to be equal with ordinal scales, while with interval scales this assumption does hold true. While an ordinal ranking question can tell us that something is ranked more favorably than something else, we don't know by how much. The advantage of interval scales is that they allow us to determine the degree to which something is preferred, or the level of agreement that is being expressed via calculations of means and standard deviations. For this reason, interval scales are the scale of choice when measuring attitudes. The following are examples of interval scales:

Please evaluate each of the following appetizers served at the Riverfront Grill on a scale of 1 to 5 according to how well you like the appetizer.

Cheese sticks Dislike a lot	__1___|__2___|__3___|__4___|__5___	Like a lot
Coconut shrimp Dislike a lot	__1___|__2___|__3___|__4___|__5___	Like a lot
Chicken fingers Dislike a lot	__1___|__2___|__3___|__4___|__5___	Like a lot
Potato skins Dislike a lot	__1___|__2___|__3___|__4___|__5___	Like a lot
Egg rolls Dislike a lot	__1___|__2___|__3___|__4___|__5___	Like a lot

Please indicate your level of agreement with the following statements.

I like to eat Mexican food. Strongly Disagree	__1___|__2___|__3___|__4___|__5___	Strongly Agree
I eat only healthy food. Strongly Disagree	__1___|__2___|__3___|__4___|__5___	Strongly Agree
The quality of service is excellent. Strongly Disagree	__1___|__2___|__3___|__4___|__5___	Strongly Agree

Both scales use 5 intervals or **points,** but the number of points used on an interval scale is up to the researcher. It could be 3 points, 4 points, 7 points, or any number that the researcher feels would be the best for collecting the information needed. Because the distance between the scale points is equal, it is possible to calculate a mean and standard deviation and to compare differences among the items within each question using more advanced statistical techniques. Figure 9.8 shows a common method of reporting the results from interval scales.

For each item, the mean or average is computed. The results show that potato skins are the most liked, followed by chicken fingers. The least liked appetizer is egg rolls. In terms of agreement or disagreement with the statements, the statement "The quality of service is excellent" shows a rather high level of agreement while the statement "I eat only healthy food" shows a lower level of agreement.

Because interval scales do not have an **absolute zero point,** in which 0 indicates a total absence of the property being measured, you cannot compare means and say that one is twice as much as another. For instance, if the mean for one appetizer is 4.0 and the mean for another

Figure 9.8   Interval Scale–Sample Report

Appetizer	Mean
Cheese sticks	3.79*
Coconut shrimp	3.11*
Chicken fingers	4.13*
Potato skins	4.27*
Egg rolls	3.37*
Statement	**Mean**
I like to eat Mexican food.	3.88**
I eat only healthy food.	2.75**
The quality of service is excellent.	4.03**

* Items were evaluated on a scale of 1 to 5, where 1 = dislike a lot and 5 = like a lot.

** Items were evaluated on a scale of 1 to 5, where 1 = strongly disagree and 5 = strongly agree.

one is 2.0, you can't say that one appetizer is liked twice as much as the other. While the distances on an interval scale are assumed to be equal, the absence of an absolute zero prevents such comparisons.

Comparisons of means between various groups can also be conducted. Suppose the researcher would like to see if there is a difference between males and females in terms of how much they like the various appetizers. Figure 9.9 shows this comparison in graphical form.

From the graph of this survey, it would appear that males like chicken fingers and potato skins more than females while females like egg rolls and coconut shrimp more than males. There is not much difference between males and females in regard to cheese sticks.

In addition to calculating a mean, interval scales allow researchers to conduct more advanced tests such as t-tests and analysis of variance (ANOVA). These tests can help to determine if the difference in preference for potato skins or any other appetizer is significant, or "real," or merely due to random error. In addition to gender, the researcher could see if there were any differences based on other factors, such as age or whether the person was a college student or not.

■ Objective 9.5: Describe the characteristics and give examples of ratio scales.

Ratio Scales

The highest-order scale is a **ratio scale.** It has all of the properties of the interval scale plus the attribute of having an absolute zero point. The numbers entered as data represent actual quantities of the variable in question. Examples would be open-ended questions asking for income or distance travelled. A zero would signify none, or absence of the variable in question. Zero income means no income, and zero distance means no distance. The presence of the absolute zero point allows the numbers to have ratio properties, meaning that numbers can be divided, multiplied, subtracted, or added. An income of $50,000 is twice as much as an income of $25,000

Figure 9.9 Interval Scales—Differences Between Males and Females

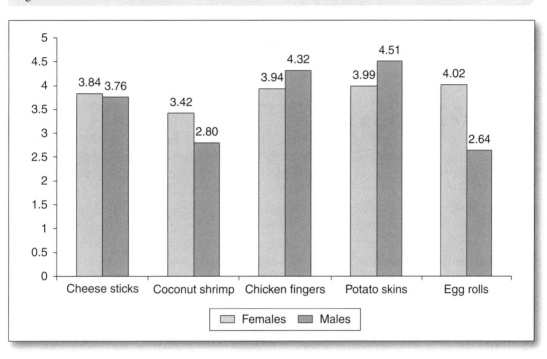

and 5 times greater than an income of $10,000. A distance of 20 feet is half the distance of 40 feet and one-fifth the distance of 100 feet. Examples of ratio scales follow:

> For each of the following quick-service restaurants, indicate how many times you have eaten there during the last month.
>
> McDonald's:_____
>
> Burger King:_____
>
> Wendy's:_____
>
> Taco Bell:_____
>
> KFC:_____
>
> On the average, how much do you spend dining out each month at all types of restaurants? _____
>
> What year were you born? _____

Notice that no coding scale is indicated on the questions because the respondent will write in his or her response. For instance, Tim may record the following answers:

> For each of the following quick-service restaurants, indicate how many times you have eaten there during the last month.
>
> McDonald's:____3____
>
> Burger King:____6____
>
> Wendy's:____2____

Taco Bell:____2____

KFC:____0____

On the average, how much do you spend dining out each month at all types of restaurants? $125

What year were you born? ____1990_____

Notice the answers have ratio properties. Ratio scales have an absolute zero indicating an absence of a characteristic. We can say Tim has not eaten at KFC during the last month. We can also say that he has eaten at Burger King 3 times more than he has at Taco Bell. In terms of average expenditures dining out, Tim's answer of $125 can be compared to the answers of other individuals, or males can be compared to females. Comparisons can be made based on age and any other variable the researcher feels may impact the amount of money spent on dining out.

The last item asks for the year the respondent was born. People are often reluctant to provide how old they are on a survey and will often leave it blank. Researchers can use a scale, like the one that was under the ordinal scale discussion, or they can ask for the year of birth. Amazingly, people who will not write down their age will often give their year of birth. All a researcher has to do then is to subtract it from the current year to obtain the person's age. As with the other questions, someone who is 40 is twice as old as someone 20.

Results from the ratio scales are shown in Figure 9.10. Of the quick-service restaurants listed, respondents eat at Taco Bell the most, an average of 4.82 times per month. That is over twice as much as for KFC (2.06) and Wendy's (1.78). In terms of how much money is spent each month dining out at all types of establishments, the mean or average was $147.16. The average age of the sample was 26.45. Note that age collected as ratio data can always be recoded into categories by creating a new variable, thus allowing for pie charts or frequency tables, if desired.

Figure 9.11 is a graph of dining out at Taco Bell based on the respondent's age. Notice that for individuals 18–24, the average was 6.27 times per month compared to only 1.22 for individuals 55 and over. From the graph it is easy to see that as individuals get older they eat at Taco Bell less.

Figure 9.10   Ratio Scale—Sample Report

Fast-Food Restaurant	Mean Response
McDonald's	3.21
Burger King	2.95
Wendy's	1.78
Taco Bell	4.82
KFC	2.06
Variable	**Mean**
Expenditures per month dining out	$147.16
Average age	26.45

Deciding Which Scale to Use

In some situations, researchers do not have a choice on which scale can be used. For instance, gender will always be a nominal scale. So will ethnicity and the college or university you are now attending. But, for other questions, researchers may have a choice. When they do, it is advisable to use higher-order scales to increase the types of analyses that can be conducted.

Suppose a researcher wants to investigate consumer use of coupons. Figure 9.12 shows four ways researchers could ask a question about coupon usage, each using a different type of scale. With the nominal scale, all the researcher can determine is what percentage of the sample has used coupons within the last 30 days. No information about frequency or quantity is available. With the ordinal scale, the researcher can determine what percentage of the sample does not use coupons at all, what percent uses them occasionally, what percent uses them sometimes, and what percent uses them frequently. Thus, the ordinal scale provides more information than the nominal scale in terms of coupon usage.

Figure 9.11   Differences in Dining Out at Taco Bell Based on Age

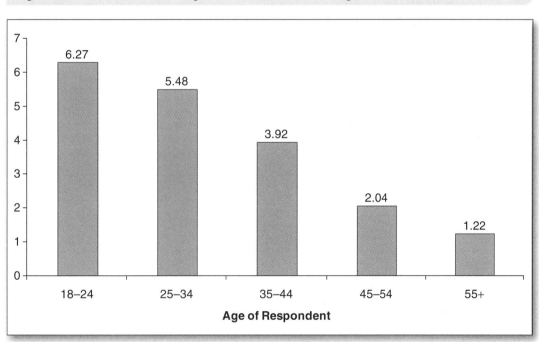

Figure 9.12   Coupon Usage and the Four Types of Scales

Nominal ———▸ Have you used coupons within the last 30 days?   Yes_____ No_____
Ordinal ———▸ In the last 30 days, how often have you used coupons?
            Not at all_____ Occasionally_____ Sometimes _____Frequently_____
Interval ———▸ In the last 30 days, how frequently did you use coupons?
            Very infrequently _____|_____|_____|_____|_____ Very frequently
Ratio ———▸ In the last 30 days, approximately how many coupons have you used? _____

With the interval scale, a mean can be calculated that provides researchers with an indication of how frequently consumers use coupons. Comparisons can also be made among different types of consumers by comparing the means of each group, which gives the research more analytical options. With the ratio question, researchers can determine how many coupons are redeemed and not have to rely on the concept of frequency. The problem with using the scale indicator of "Frequently" is that one respondent may have used five coupons and considered that "Frequently," while another may have used the same quantity but marked it "Sometimes." They may also have checked different boxes in the interval scale. Because frequently has different meanings to people, the results are not as accurate as having the actual number that is produced with the ratio scale. Also, the ratio scale allows for the highest-order data analysis.

When developing questions for a survey, it is advisable to use the highest scale possible. This allows for higher-order analyses. It also provides more in-depth information. Data can be reduced to lower levels, but cannot be increased. For instance, the responses from the ratio scale data in Figure 9.13 can be grouped to provide additional information beyond the mean. The mean response was 4.6. However, Figure 9.13 indicates that more than 28% of the respondents did not use coupons within the last 30 days and that 31% used only 1 to 4 coupons. Only about 10% of the sample appears to be heavy users of coupons using 10 or more during the last 30 days. However, having the mean also allows for better comparisons among groups. For instance, the mean for males was 3.15 while the mean for females was 6.04.

Figure 9.13   Coupon Usage

Coupons Used	Number of Respondents	Percent of Total
None	98	28.74%
1 to 4	106	31.09%
5 to 9	64	18.77%
10 to 19	33	9.68%
20 or more	11	3.23%
Total	312	

VALIDITY AND RELIABILITY

The purpose of marketing research is to provide decision makers with information. If that information is correct, timely, and accurate, then more intelligent decisions can be made. The challenge for researchers is to collect data that are both correct and accurate. The difficulty is that errors creep into the measurement process. Recall from Chapter 6 that two types of errors were identified: systematic error and random error. Both can impact the accuracy and correctness of the measurement process. Random error can be reduced by increasing the sample size and by paying careful attention to the research process. Systematic error, however, increases with sample size, so researchers need to carefully guard against any type of systematic error that will have a significant impact on the results. While systematic error cannot be completely eliminated, it can be reduced to where its impact is minimal.

Validity and reliability address the issues of measurement and error. Validity deals with systematic error while reliability deals with random error. Both approaches are important to ensure the lowest possible total error.

RELIABILITY

A measurement instrument that provides the same results time and time again is said to be reliable. Scales that show an object weighs 150 pounds are said to be reliable if every time the object is weighed on the scale it indicates it is 150 pounds. One reason researchers like to use mechanical measuring instruments is that they tend to be more accurate, and also more reliable, than human measurements. But, with most marketing research, nonmechanical methods have to be used, such as questionnaires and observation. So from a marketing perspective, **reliability** is defined as the degree to which a measurement is free from error and provides consistent results over time. Reliability can be evaluated using three different approaches: test-retest, equivalent forms, and internal consistency (see Figure 9.14).

■ Objective 9.6: Discuss methods for assessing reliability.

Figure 9.14 Methods of Assessing Reliability

- Test-retest
- Equivalent forms
- Internal consistency

Test-Retest Reliability

One method to evaluate reliability is to repeat the measurement process with the same instrument with the same set of subjects, which is called **test-retest reliability.** For instance, suppose a survey is administered to a group of retail store managers. Then four weeks later the same survey is administered to the same set of store managers. Scores for the two surveys are then compared. If there is a high level of correlation (or similarity) between the two, then the survey is believed to have a high level of reliability. Since the same measurement instrument was used with the same subjects, the answers should be the same. Differences should be due to random error and not to deficiencies in the testing instrument.

Using the test-retest reliability method poses three potential problems, as indicated in Figure 9.15. As discussed in the chapter on experimentation, exposing individuals to the survey or measurement instrument during the first measurement may have an impact on their responses to the second survey. The longer the researcher waits between the first and second administrations, the less likely it is that testing effects will occur. But, from a practical standpoint, researchers have a limited time and budget to prepare a measurement instrument and collect the data.

The second problem is changes in the environment that can alter the responses of the subjects. It can be personal factors, such as mood or health. It can be a wide range of external factors depending on the type of measurements. For retail stores, sales may be

Figure 9.15 Potential Problems With Test-Retest Reliability

- Testing effects
- Environmental changes
- Locating same subjects

down, the weather could be poor, or the manager could have been extremely busy and rushed through the survey. Any number of environmental factors could impact the responses given.

The third potential problem may be in locating the same subjects. If it is retail store managers, this would not be a major concern. There may have been some attrition, but most will still be in their positions and available for the second survey. But, if the subjects were consumers, then locating each one would be more difficult.

Equivalent Form Reliability

With **equivalent form reliability** a second measurement instrument is developed that is equivalent to the first and then administered to the same subjects. Suppose researchers wanted to measure brand attitude toward soft drinks. Two separate surveys would be developed with questions that are similar and believed to measure the same thing. The first survey would be given, then at a later time the second would be given, just as was done with the test-retest approach. Sometimes both are given at the same time because of difficulty in locating the same set of subjects. But, researchers feel giving the two tests at the same time is not as reliable as using two different time periods.

Some of the same problems occur with the equivalent form reliability approach, such as environmental changes and locating the same subjects. However, testing effects are not present since the survey or measurement instruments are different. The challenge is in creating a second survey using different questions that will produce the same results. Some believe it is impossible to do. Others see it as extremely difficult and not worth the time and money required to do so.

Internal Consistency Reliability

Internal consistency reliability involves using one measuring instrument and assessing its reliability through using different samples or different items within each scale. This method eliminates the problems that can occur with a second administration of a survey instrument. The internal consistency reliability method is used more frequently than test-retest or equivalent forms techniques, and can be assessed in three different ways.

The first is to administer the survey to a group of test subjects. The subjects are then randomly split into two groups. If the instrument is reliable, then the scores between each group should be highly correlated. This approach is used in judging Olympic events and beauty pageants with multiple judges. The idea is that a more reliable score should be obtained when several judges evaluate the same performance since they are looking at the same set of criteria.

The second approach is called the **split-half technique** and is used with scales that have multiple measures. For example, to measure brand loyalty a researcher may have a set of 8 questions, or to measure attitude toward a brand a set of 10 questions may be used. The items are randomly split into two groups. If the items are measuring the same construct, then there should be a high correlation between the two groups or sets of questions. In practice, though, reliability may vary considerably depending upon which items are assigned to each group. This occurs because each item is supposed to measure a part of the overall construct that is uniquely different in some way from the other items.

The most popular internal consistency reliability method is to use a test called **Cronbach's alpha,** which produces a reliability coefficient for all possible combinations of a set of items within a scale. The higher the Cronbach's alpha score, the more reliable the measure. A major advantage of the Cronbach's alpha procedure is that if one of the items within the construct is not a good measure, it will have a low correlation with the other items. Researchers can then discard the item and retest the construct for reliability. This is particularly helpful when researchers are creating a new measurement scale, though Cronbach's alpha is also frequently calculated with scales that exist and have been used in prior research.

The internal consistency reliability method avoids the problems discussed with the other two approaches since it is not administered at two different times or with two different measuring instruments. But, it does have a potentially serious problem. It measures reliability with just one exposure. There is no guarantee if a different set of subjects is used or if the instrument is used at a future point in time with the same subjects that the same results will occur. Thus, many researchers review the literature for the purpose of identifying prior studies where the measure may have been used. This allows the researcher to see whether the Cronbach's alpha achieved in the current study is consistent with those reported in other research studies.

VALIDITY

■ Objective 9.7: Elaborate on methods of evaluating validity.

Validity refers to the ability of a measurement scale to measure what it proposes to measure and the degree to which it is free of both systematic and random error. Thus, for a measurement to be valid, it must be reliable. However, the opposite is not true. A measurement instrument may be reliable yet still not be valid if it does not measure what it is supposed to measure. For example, it may be designed to measure customer satisfaction, but instead measures customer loyalty reliably, time after time. In such cases the results are erroneous and if used to make a decision may result in a poor or even incorrect decision. Researchers have four ways to evaluate validity, identified in Figure 9.16.

Face Validity

Face validity is present when it is the opinion of the researcher or experts that an instrument measures what it is intended to measure. It is the weakest form of validity since it is the subjective opinion of the individual designing the instrument or of other experts in marketing research. Some items on a survey are easy to evaluate as being valid, such as requesting demographic information like gender, age, income, and ethnicity. Even for the following questions, marketing researchers would agree they are valid questions and measure what is intended.

Figure 9.16 Methods of Assessing Validity

- Face validity
- Content validity
- Predictive validity
- Construct validity

Have you purchased a new lawn mower within the last six months?

How much did you spend on your last trip to purchase groceries?

Which brand of computer do you currently own?

Many concepts marketers want to measure are more complicated and cannot be easily measured, such as brand attitude, brand loyalty, brand image, service quality, and purchase intentions. Since these concepts are more abstract, researchers often develop a series of questions to measure the construct, or idea. On the surface (i.e., in terms of face validity), the questions may appear to be measuring the construct that is intended. But, it also may be measuring something else. That is why researchers look to one of the other forms of validity to assess a survey instrument.

Content Validity

With **content validity** researchers use a systematic process to assess the adequacy of the items used to measure a concept or construct. The steps involved in the process are identified in Figure 9.17. The process begins with a literature review to identify how other marketing researchers measured the concept. If brand image is being measured, then researching how other people measured brand image will identify questions, phrases, or words that have been used. A list is compiled that includes all items that have been used with notation of those that have been used the most frequently. The second step then involves using a panel of marketing research experts to assess the list of items, eliminating items that may not fit with what is being measured and adding new items that may not have been identified with the literature review.

The third step is to pretest the instrument using all of the items that have been identified in the first two steps by administering the instrument to a sample similar to the intended target audience. In addition, an open-ended question is added allowing the respondent to identify any idea or concept that should be included that was not. Sometimes study participants are also asked questions related to item phrasing and their comprehension of various items. The last step is to reduce the number of items through data analysis to determine which items have a high correlation with each other. This can be done through a process called factor analysis and through the reliability measure of Cronbach's alpha. When the process is finished, the researcher should have a smaller number of questions, phrases, or words that can be used to measure the construct that has a high level of correlation, and thus has content validity.

With this process a researcher may start with a list of 15 items to measure brand image of a company such as Shell Oil or Delta Air Lines. After the literature review, another 10 to 15 items may be added. Then in the second step the panel of experts may either add more items or delete some from the list that do not appear to be relevant for the current study. The list of items is then pretested with a sample similar to the target audience with an open-ended question at the end in case the respondent thought of an item that was not included. If a number of new items are identified with the open-ended question, then they would be added to the list, and another pretest would be conducted. Changes in phrasing would also be considered based on participant feedback. The next step would be to do a factor analysis to reduce the items to a smaller subset of highly correlated items. These items would then be tested using Cronbach's alpha to determine their level of intercorrelations. Those achieving intercorrelations of 0.7 or higher are generally retained within the scale. The end result will be a smaller list of items that can be used to measure the company image of Shell Oil or Delta Air Lines.

Figure 9.17 Steps in Developing Content Validity

1. Literature review

2. Panel of experts

3. Pretest with open-ended question

4. Scale reduction through data analysis

Predictive Validity

Predictive validity assesses how well a measurement can predict future actions or behavior. For instance, attitude toward an advertisement should influence attitude toward the brand being advertised, and the attitude toward the brand should influence purchase intentions and purchase behavior. If this occurs, then each of the scales is said to have predictive validity. Another example would be the SAT that everyone takes to enter college. It is believed to be a predictor of how well an individual will do in college and the person's potential to learn.

Construct Validity

Construct validity is the most difficult to achieve and exists more in theory than it does in actual practice with marketing research companies. **Construct validity** assesses how well the measurement captures the construct or concept under consideration and how well it logically connects to underlying theories. In addition to the measuring instrument capturing the construct it is supposed to measure, it also must be based on theories that are accepted by research experts. While such discussions are part of the academic world, construct validity is seldom addressed in the practical business world of marketing research.

Construct validity can be demonstrated by finding that a measure has both convergent validity and discriminant validity. Both apply to constructs that have multiple dimensions, such as the SERVQUAL measure developed by Parasuraman, Zeithaml, and Berry,[2] as well as unidimensional scales comprising multiple items. **Convergent validity** refers to the degree of correlation among constructs, and tests whether constructs that should be related are related. For example, a great deal of academic research has demonstrated that attitude toward an ad should influence brand attitudes, which in turn should influence purchase intentions. There should be a high level of correlation among these constructs as determined by theory and prior research.

Discriminant validity means the items designed to measure one construct, such as attitude toward an ad, have a low correlation with items that measure a different construct that should be unrelated to the first, such as social desirability bias. While the statistical techniques used to assess convergent and discriminant validity are beyond the scope of an introductory marketing research textbook, using valid measures is a key consideration in research. For this reason, many researchers choose to use existing measures that have been validated by previous researchers. Many classic measures still useful for consumer behavior and advertising research can be found in the various editions of the *Marketing Scales Handbook,* along with a history of the scale usage, reliabilities reported in previous studies, and the manner in which scale validity was assessed.[3]

RELATIONSHIP OF VALIDITY AND RELIABILITY

Figure 9.18 highlights the relationship between validity and reliability. An analogy that has often been used is target practice with a gun or pistol. The figure on the left illustrates an instrument that has neither validity nor reliability. The shots (or data points in this case) are all over the target. A loose sight on a gun that moves every time the gun is fired would produce these types of results even if the person firing the gun always aimed at the center of the target.

Figure 9.18   Relationship Between Validity and Reliability

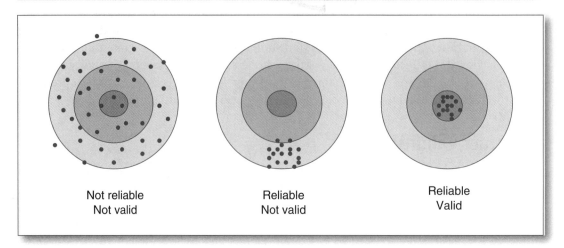

Not reliable
Not valid

Reliable
Not valid

Reliable
Valid

The middle picture shows what happens when the sight on the gun is adjusted improperly. The person firing the gun is aiming at the center of the target, but the bullet always lands below the center. It is very reliable because it always hits in the same area, but is not valid since it does not hit in the center. This would be a good representation of survey results achieved when a great deal of systematic error is present. The only way a measurement can be valid is for the instrument to measure what it is supposed to measure. For a gun, that means when you aim at the center of the target, the bullet hits the center of the target, not above, below, or to one of the sides. Similarly, a research instrument can be reliable, in that it consistently measures something, but not valid if the construct being measured is not what the researcher is trying to measure. However, a research instrument can never be valid if it isn't also reliable.

The last picture shows the gunshots hitting the center of the target. The sight on the gun is properly adjusted and hitting where it is supposed to hit. In terms of marketing research, it is measuring what the instrument proposes to measure and is doing so in a reliable manner. It is both valid and reliable.

Global Concerns

While the four types of scales are universal, how they are used will vary depending on the culture of a particular region. People in Pacific Rim countries such as Japan tend to be more modest, which may reflect the way scales are developed. Instead of using a ratio scale to reveal their absolute level of income, Japanese respondents may be more comfortable responding to an ordinal scale that lists income in ascending categories.

Scale responses are often influenced by cultural norms. In the Philippines, respondents tend to give positive answers rather than negative answers. One research study found that using more scale points helped to mitigate this skewing effect. Instead of using the more traditional 5-point scale, this cross-cultural segmentation study adopted a 10-point scale, which ultimately yielded nine segments after the data were analyzed.[4]

STATISTICS REVIEW

Understanding the type of data that survey questions will yield is important because it determines both the type of descriptive measure that is needed as well as the type of analyses that can be performed on the data for each question. Figure 9.19 summarizes the type of descriptive measures that can be used with each type of scale and the type of analyses that would be used to test for differences in means or in frequency counts.

Figure 9.19   Descriptive and Difference Tests and Type of Scale

Type of Scale	Descriptive Measure	Difference Test
Nominal	Frequency	Chi-Square
Ordinal	Frequency	Chi-Square
Interval	Mean Standard Deviation	t-Test, z-Test, or ANOVA
Ratio	Mean Standard Deviation	t-Test, z-Test, or ANOVA

With both nominal and ordinal scales, the appropriate descriptive measure is a frequency count. The appropriate test for differences would be a chi-square test. For interval and ratio scales, the appropriate descriptive measure is the mean and standard deviation. The standard deviation is a measure of dispersion indicating how variable, or spread out, the data points are around the mean. Suppose the following statements were evaluated using a 5-point scale where 1 = strongly disagree and 5 = strongly agree.

	Mean	Standard Deviation
Fast food is convenient.	3.82	.55
Fast food tastes great.	3.75	1.63

While the means are quite similar, the standard deviations vary widely. In the case of the first statement, the majority of respondents rated the convenience aspect of fast food similarly, as evidenced by the small standard deviation, or spread, in the data. In fact, a frequency analysis would reveal that most respondents answered 3 or 4 to this question. However, opinions related to the taste of fast food were much more diverse, as evidenced by the large standard deviation. Frequency counts in this instance would show more people answering toward the extreme ends of the scale (e.g., 1 or 5) than in the case of the first statement. In fact, the mean alone may be misleading as the large standard deviation suggests that the taste of fast food may be a subject on which people's opinions are polarized.

The tests that can be used for differences with mean data would be a t-test, a z-test, or ANOVA depending on the number of categories in the grouping variable and the sample size in each cell.

(Continued)

(Continued)

If the analysis involves only two categories, such as gender, then the t-test would be used if the sample contained fewer than 30 subjects of each gender, while the z-test would be appropriate if 30 or more subjects represented each gender. Programs such as SPSS automatically adjust the testing procedure to reflect the proper technique, even though users choose the t-test option. If a test for difference in means involved three or more categories, then the ANOVA can be used so long as each cell, or category, contains at least 30 subjects. All tests assume that the data were drawn from a normal population.

 DEALING WITH DATA

Data were collected from 184 individuals concerning their patronage and attitudes toward fast-food restaurants, and five fast-food restaurants in particular. The data are in the SPSS file "Chapter 09 Dealing with Data." The corresponding questionnaire that was used is titled "Chapter 09 Dealing with Data Survey." Both files can be downloaded from the textbook's companion website (www.sagepub .com/clowess).

Create a table similar to Figure 9.20. Identify the type of scale for each question, and then determine the appropriate descriptive measure and difference tests. Once your table has been completed, use SPSS to run the appropriate frequency count or mean. Answer the following questions or create the appropriate graph.

Figure 9.20   Sample Table for Dealing with Data Exercise

Question	Type of Scale	Descriptive Measure	Difference Test
Q1	Ratio	Mean, Standard Deviation	t-Test, z-Test, or ANOVA
Q2			
Q3			
Q4			
Q5			
Q6			
Q7			
Q8			
Q9			
Q10			

1. What percent of the respondents ranked Arby's (Q4) as the most desirable?

2. What percent of the sample ranked Burger King (Q4) as the most desirable?

3. Create a column graph showing the ranking of McDonald's (Q4).

4. Based on the frequency counts of Question 4, which fast food was ranked the most desirable by the most people? Which fast food was ranked the least desirable by the most people?

5. What was the average number of times respondents ate at fast-food restaurants in a typical week (Q1)?

6. Examine the means for the statements in Question 3. Which one had the highest level of agreement? What was the mean? Which one had the lowest level of agreement? What was the mean?

7. Examine the standard deviations for the statements in Question 3. Which one had the highest variability of responses? What was the standard deviation? Which one had the least variability in responses? What was the standard deviation?

8. For Question 5, which fast-food restaurant had the highest mean? What was the mean?

9. For Question 6, which fast-food restaurant had the highest level of customer service? What was the mean response? Which restaurant had the lowest level of customer service? What was the mean? Which fast-food restaurant had the greatest variability in responses? What was the standard deviation?

Using the table you created for this exercise and SPSS, run either a t-test or ANOVA for Questions 1 and 2 based on the respondent's gender, age, income, and race. Answer the following questions or create the appropriate graph.

1. At the 95% confidence level, did gender have an impact on either Question 1 or Question 2? If so, what was the mean and standard deviation for each gender?

2. At the 95% confidence level, did age have an impact on either Question 1 or Question 2? If so, what was the mean and standard deviation for each age group?

3. Create a column graph showing the results from SPSS for Question 2 by the respondent's age. Which age group had the highest percentage of dollars spent at fast-food restaurants? Which age group had the lowest percentage?

4. At the 95% confidence level, did income have an impact on either how many times a fast-food restaurant was patronized (Question 1) or the percentage of money spent dining out that is allocated to fast-food restaurants (Question 2)? If so, what was the mean and standard deviation for Question 1 or 2 for each income bracket?

5. At the 95% confidence level, did race have an impact on either Question 1 or Question 2? If so, what was the mean and standard deviation for each question by racial category?

SUMMARY

Objective 1: Explain the concept of measurement.

Measurement is the process by which rules and guidelines are used to assign numbers to represent characteristics of respondents, brands, or other objects.

Objective 2: Describe the characteristics and give examples of nominal scales.

Nominal scales provide only limited information and are useful when the purpose of a question is to classify objects or respondents as having a certain characteristic (or not) or belonging to a particular group (or not). The numbers used to represent each category have no inherent meaning other than to separate those who share a characteristic from those who do not. For this reason, it is critical that the response options in nominal scales be mutually exclusive and categorically exhaustive. Data analysis options for nominal data are limited to frequency counts and percentages. Many demographic questions, such as gender, education, and ethnicity, are examples of nominal scales.

Objective 3: Describe the characteristics and give examples of ordinal scales.

Ordinal scales are those in which the response categories are ordered, or which allow the respondent to rank items on the basis of some factor, such as preference. Ordinal scales maintain the classification properties of nominal scales, but also allow subjects to show that a certain category of response is greater than or less than another. Frequency counts, percentages, and modes can be computed using ordinal data. However, as there is no guarantee that the interval between ordered item choices is the same, means and standard deviations cannot be computed for this type of data. Questions that provide categories for income or age in ascending order are examples of ordinal questions, as are those that provide categories related to frequency of use, frequency of purchase, or amount spent.

Objective 4: Describe the characteristics and give examples of interval scales.

Although interval scales contain the classification and order characteristics of lower-level scales, the data provided are more valuable because the interval between choices is equal. This allows the researcher to compute means and standard deviations and to run more advanced statistical analyses to compare the differences in means between groups using t-tests, z-tests, and ANOVA. The majority of questions devised to measure attitudes use interval scales.

Objective 5: Describe the characteristics and give examples of ratio scales.

Ratio scales are the most powerful, as they contain an absolute zero point in addition to all the scale properties discussed for lower-level scales. The numbers recorded represent actual quantities of the variable in question. While means and standard deviations can be computed, ratio-level data can also be subjected to basic empirical operations, such as division, multiplication, subtraction, and addition. Ratio scale questions are typically asked in an open-ended format so that respondents can enter the exact number that best describes their answer. The year an individual was born, the number of children living at home, frequency of patronage, weight, and a variety of other questions can be formulated as ratio scales. Generally speaking, higher-level scales should be used when possible due to the richness of the data provided.

Objective 6: Discuss methods for assessing reliability.

It is important that measurement instruments be reliable, and thus free from error, so that consistent results can be achieved over time. The degree to which a measure is reliable can be assessed using the test-retest method, the equivalent forms technique, and the internal consistency method. Problems inherent in the test-retest and equivalent forms techniques have influenced the popularity of the internal consistency method. While three methods of measuring internal consistency exist, the Cronbach's alpha method is used most frequently.

Objective 7: Elaborate on methods of evaluating validity.

Valid measurement instruments measure what they are designed to measure and are relatively free of systematic and random error. Four methods of validity assessment exist. The weakest form of validity, and the form that is simplest to assess, is known as face validity. Measures with face validity appear to measure what they are supposed to in the opinion of the researcher or experts. Content validity ensures that a concept or construct is accurately measured via a four-step process that ultimately evaluates the quality and completeness of the items used to measure the construct. Predictive validity is demonstrated by showing how well the measure predicts future actions or behavior. Construct validity assesses how well the measure captures the construct and its relationship to theory. This is the most difficult form to achieve as it requires that the researcher demonstrate two validity subtypes: convergent validity and discriminant validity. Convergent validity is exemplified when a measure correlates with another construct to which it is theoretically related. Conversely, discriminant validity ensures that a measure does not vary, or correlate with constructs to which it has no theoretical relationship.

GLOSSARY OF KEY TERMS

Absolute zero point: measurement designation of 0 indicates a total absence of the property being measured

Categorically exhaustive: all possible responses on a scale are included in the answer categories

Collectively exhaustive: responses fit into either one category or another but cannot belong to multiple categories

Construct validity: method of evaluating validity by assessing how well the measurement captures the construct or concept under consideration and how well it logically connects to underlying theories

Content validity: systematic process to evaluate validity by assessing the adequacy of the items used to measure a concept or construct

Convergent validity: refers to the degree of correlation among constructs, and tests whether constructs that should be related are related

Cronbach's alpha: internal consistency reliability method that produces a reliability coefficient for all possible combinations of a set of items within a scale

Discriminant validity: items designed to measure one construct have a low correlation with items that measure a different construct

Equivalent form reliability: method to evaluate reliability in which a second measurement instrument is developed that is equivalent to the first and then administered to the same subjects

Face validity: opinion of the researcher or experts that an instrument measures what it is intended to measure

Internal consistency reliability: method to evaluate reliability that involves using one measuring instrument and assessing its reliability through using different samples or different items within each scale

Interval scale: scale in which numbers are assigned for the purpose of identification, the numbers indicate order, and the distance between the numbers assigned is considered to be equal

Measurement: process of assigning numbers or labels to phenomena or characteristics

Mutually exclusive: each response is uniquely different from other possible responses

Nominal scale: scale in which numbers are assigned to objects or sets of objects for the purpose of identification

Ordinal scale: scale in which numbers are assigned for the purpose of identification, but also have the property of being arranged in some type of array or order

Point: interval in a scale

Predictive validity: measure of validity that assesses how well a measurement can predict future actions or behavior

Ratio scale: scale in which numbers are assigned for the purpose of identification, the numbers indicate order, the distance between the numbers is equal, and the scale has an absolute zero point

Reliability: the degree to which a measurement is free from error and provides consistent results over time

Split-half technique: method to evaluate reliability through randomly splitting items designed to measure a construct into two groups and then measuring the correlation between the two groups

Test-retest reliability: method to evaluate reliability by repeating the measurement process with the same instrument with the same set of subjects

Validity: ability of a measurement instrument to measure what it proposes to measure and be free of both systematic and random error

CRITICAL THINKING EXERCISES

1. Your firm is conducting a study in which the key dependent variable is annual sales. The firm plans to compare sales among different types of customers with whom the firm does business. What type of scale should be used to measure annual sales? Why?

2. Identify the type of scale shown below. Then critique the scale in terms of whether or not the response options are mutually exclusive and categorically exhaustive. Be specific in pointing out any flaws that exist.

   What is your household annual income from all sources?

   (1) Less than $25,000 (2) $25,000–$50,000 (3) $50,000–$75,000

   (4) $75,000–$100,000 (5) $100,000 and above

3. Identify the type of scale shown below. Then critique the scale in terms of whether or not the response options are mutually exclusive and categorically exhaustive. Be specific in pointing out any flaws that exist.

   Which of the following mass merchandise stores have you shopped at in the past week (check all that apply)?

   ___ Walmart ___ Kmart ____ Target ____ Sam's Club ____ Costco

4. Identify the type of scale shown below. Justify your answer. What type of analyses could be performed with these data?

   Please rate your university's financial aid office on the following items using a scale ranging from poor to outstanding.

	Poor	**Fair**	**Good**	**Excellent**	**Outstanding**
Friendliness of staff	1	2	3	4	5
Helpfulness of staff	1	2	3	4	5
Speed of service	1	2	3	4	5

5. Suppose a pet store is interested in surveying its customers and learning more about customers' pet ownership, attitudes toward various types of pets and pet products, basic demographic information, and spending habits. Develop a measurement instrument, in which at least one example of the different types of measurement instruments (nominal, ordinal, interval, and ratio) can be found. At a minimum, your survey will contain 4 questions. Restrict your survey to no more than 10 questions. Make certain that the questions you create are your own work, and do not duplicate questions found in this chapter. Where appropriate, check to be certain that response choices are mutually exclusive and categorically exhaustive.

6. Refer back to the measurement instrument you developed in Question 5.
   a) Critique each question. Was the type of data collected optimal, or would it have been better to collect information using a question with a higher level of measurement? Why or why not?
   b) What type of descriptive statistics would be obtained for each question?
   c) What type of analyses would you recommend for each question?
   d) How should the data be presented to the client?

7. In reading the executive summary of a research report, you note that the researcher concluded that men are twice as likely to watch sports on television as are women. With respect to sports viewership on TV, were the data collected nominal, ratio, interval, or ordinal? Justify your answer.

8. You have been asked to develop a measurement instrument capable of assessing people's attitudes toward Betty Crocker cake mixes. Construct a multi-item measure that has face validity. Justify why you feel the items you selected capture people's attitudes toward Betty Crocker cake mixes.

9. A researcher has attempted to create a measurement instrument capable of assessing college students' attitudes toward 100% online classes. Review the following items, and determine if they have face validity. Are any items missing that you recommend be added? Justify your decision.

Indicate your level of agreement or disagreement with each of the statements shown below using the following scale: 1 = Strongly Disagree (SD); 2 = Disagree (D); 3 = Neither Agree Nor Disagree (N); 4 = Agree (A); 5 = Strongly Agree (SA).

	SD	D	N	A	SA
Online classes are easy.	1	2	3	4	5
It takes less time to complete a face-to-face class than it does one that is offered in a 100% online format.	1	2	3	4	5
I like online classes because it frees up my time so that I can work more hours.	1	2	3	4	5
Online classes let me do school work when it is convenient for me to do so.	1	2	3	4	5

10. A friend of yours has just completed a one-group pretest-posttest experiment. (Refer back to Chapter 7 if you need to refresh your memory on the types of experimental designs.) He told you that he plans to assess the reliability of the key dependent measure using the test-retest method, since he was able to collect interval-level data for the measure using the same sample at two different points in time. Would you recommend that he follow through with this plan? Why or why not? If not, how would you suggest he evaluate the reliability of his key dependent variable? Justify your decision.

CONTINUING CASE STUDY: LAKESIDE GRILL

Figure 9.21 shows the demographic measures the team developed. Brooke had unsuccessfully argued that two additional demographic questions should be added that would ask how far the person lived and worked from Lakeside Grill. While the other students understood why such a question would be beneficial, they didn't believe it would yield any additional information that could be used in developing recommendations and action plans for the restaurant since any marketing tactic developed could not be restricted to a specific distance from the restaurant.

Figure 9.22 shows the patronage measures developed by the student team. The item that generated considerable discussion and disagreement was Question 4. Some students argued the information was not necessary since it asked for percentages for overall dining out and wasn't specific to Lakeside Grill. Others argued since Lakeside Grill didn't serve breakfast, including it in the question was not a good idea.

The scale used to evaluate Lakeside Grill is shown in Figure 9.23. Discussion generated by this scale centered on two concerns: the 4-point scale and whether the data were interval or ordinal. Some of the students thought it should be a 7-point scale. In terms of type of data, the group was split between the question yielding interval or ordinal data.

In terms of measuring reliability, Zach suggested they use Cronbach's alpha. While this could be used for items that had scales, it would not work for the nonscaled items. So the team decided a test-retest with a sample of students could measure the entire questionnaire's reliability. For validity, the team discussed using either face validity or content validity. Zach argued for content validity, saying, "We don't have the experience and knowledge to do construct validity, and we are not trying to predict anything, so that method is out. Besides, I think content validity is the best anyway."

Figure 9.21   Demographic Measures

Scale	Question Item
Nominal	Gender: Female _____ Male _____
Ordinal	Age: 18–22 _____ 23–29 _____ 30–39 _____ 40–49_____ 50+_____
Ordinal	Income: $0–$19,999_____ $20,000–$39,999_____ $40,000–$59,999_____ $60,000–$79,999_____ $80,000+_____
Nominal	Ethnicity: African American_____ Caucasian_____ Asian American _____ Hispanic _____ Other_____
Ordinal	Education: High school_____ Some college_____ 2-year college degree_____ 4-year college degree_____ Postgraduate_____

Figure 9.22   Patronage Measures

Scale	Question Item
Ratio	1. How many times have you eaten at Lakeside Grill during the last month? _____
Ordinal	2. On the average, how much do you spend per month dining out? $0–$49_____ $50–$99_____ $100–$149_____ $150–$199_____ $200+_____
Interval	3. In terms of your total eating out, how frequently do you eat at each of the following? Fast-food restaurant .... Never____|____|____|____|____ Always Delivery or pickup............... Never____|____|____|____|____ Always Casual dine-in restaurant... Never____|____|____|____|____ Always
Ratio	4. In terms of eating out, what percentage of your expenditures fall into each of the following categories? (The percentages should add to 100.) Breakfast _____Lunch_____ Dinner_____ Other_____

(Continued)

(Continued)

Figure 9.23   Restaurant Evaluation Measures

Scale	Question Item				
	Please rate Lakeside Grill on each of the following items using a scale from poor to excellent.				
		Poor	Fair	Good	Excellent
	Food Quality	1	2	3	4
	Food Quantity	1	2	3	4
	Food Taste	1	2	3	4
	Value for the Money	1	2	3	4
	Food Presentation	1	2	3	4
Interval	Speed of Service	1	2	3	4
	Customer Satisfaction	1	2	3	4
	Restaurant Appearance	1	2	3	4
	Restaurant Atmosphere	1	2	3	4
	Location	1	2	3	4
	Parking	1	2	3	4
	Overall Rating	**1**	**2**	**3**	**4**

Critique Questions:

1. Evaluate the demographic, patronage, and restaurant evaluation measures in terms of types of scales. Has the group used the best scales? Why or why not? What changes would you suggest? Why?

2. Zach had argued instead of using a scale for age the group should just ask respondents their age. By so doing, the students could obtain ratio data instead of ordinal data. Is this a good idea? Why or why not?

3. Should a question about distance from Lakeside Grill be added to the demographics? Why or why not?

4. Discuss Question 4 of the patronage measures (Figure 9.22). Should it be included? Why or why not? Should it be modified or a different question asked? Why?

5. As they are written now, are the restaurant evaluation measures (Figure 9.23) truly an interval scale? Why or why not?

6. Is the 4-point scale optimal for this research project, or should it be a 7-point scale? Why or why not? What other options does the team have in terms of number of points in the scale?

7. Discuss each of the methods of assessing reliability as it relates to the Lakeside Grill project.

8. Which method do you think is the best for assessing reliability for the Lakeside Grill project: test-retest or internal consistency using Cronbach's alpha? Why?

9. Discuss each of the methods of assessing validity as it relates to the Lakeside Grill project.

10. Do you agree with Zach's statement about validity—"We don't have the experience and knowledge to do construct validity, and we are not trying to predict anything, so that method is out. Besides, I think content validity is the best anyway." Why or why not?

MARKETING RESEARCH PORTFOLIO

A sample questionnaire is provided online at www.sagepub.com/clowess as part of the Chapter 9 Marketing Research Portfolio mini-case. The first task reinforces the chapter material by requiring that students identify the type of measurement scale used in each question. Critical thinking skills are challenged by the second task, which asks students to consider each question asked and whether it can be rephrased in a way that would yield higher-level data. Students are then instructed to recommend and justify changes to the questionnaire.

STUDENT STUDY SITE

Visit the Student Study Site at www.sagepub.com/clowess to access the following additional materials:

- eFlashcards
- Web Quizzes
- SAGE Journal Articles
- Web Resources

Marketing Scales

After reading this chapter, you should be able to

1. Discuss the concept of attitude measurement.

2. Explain the concept of using scales for attitude measurement.

3. Identify and describe the various comparative scales.

4. Identify and describe the various noncomparative scales.

5. Identify and describe scales that can be either comparative or noncomparative.

6. Discuss the considerations involved in selecting marketing scales.

7. Explain ways researchers can ensure the reliability and validity of scales.

INTRODUCTION

Marketing scales are used extensively by marketing researchers to measure a wide array of beliefs, attitudes, and behaviors. They can be used to measure beliefs individuals may have about brands, people, or objects. They can be used to measure people's feelings. They can also be used to measure past or current behavior as well as future intentions. Figure 10.1 shows the result of a single-item marketing scale that was used to measure how often individuals do or would open e-mails sent from coupon websites. Out of the sample of 646 respondents, 45% said they do or would open the e-mails daily, and another 31% said they do or would open the e-mails several times a week. Only 3% claimed they would never open them.

Figure 10.1   Graph of a Behavioral Marketing Scale

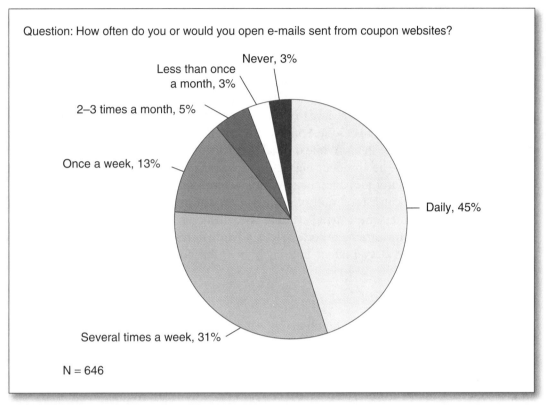

Source: Author-created with data from ReRez (**www.rerez.com**), December 2, 2011.

While scales can be used to measure behavior, they are especially important in the measurement of consumer attitudes, since attitudes cannot be observed. Various types of scales are presented in this chapter. Some scales ask individuals to make comparisons, while other scales do not. The chapter concludes with a discussion of how to ensure reliability and validity of marketing scales.

— ⚬⃝⃟ —

MEASURING ATTITUDES

Attitudes are relatively enduring predispositions to respond to an object—such as a brand, a spokesperson, an ad, an event, or a store—in a consistent fashion. You may recall from a study of consumer behavior that an attitude consists of three components: cognitive, affective (liking), and behavioral. The cognitive component represents the belief and knowledge part of attitude. Examples of items designed to measure beliefs or knowledge may be "The Ford Fusion was rated *Motor Trend*'s midsize car of the year" or "Pepsi has a sweeter taste than Coke." The affective component of attitude is the feelings and emotions. Statements such as "I love my new

■ Objective 10.1: Discuss the concept of attitude measurement.

Dell computer" or "I hate the taste of grapefruit" reflect the affective or feeling component of attitude. The behavioral component is the action or intentions aspect of attitude. It may involve measuring the intent to purchase a pair of Guess jeans at a retail store or the actual purchase of a Mounds candy bar.

Counting the number of candy bars sold from a point-of-purchase (POP) display is rather easy to do. So is comparing sales from different types of displays, different POP locations, and among stores using different types and locations of POP displays. Measuring consumer attitudes that influence those purchase decisions is more problematic. Since attitudes cannot be seen and exist only in the minds of consumers, researchers have to look at alternative methods of measurement. A common method is to use some type of scale. Some scales contain a single item, as in Figure 10.1, while others may contain multiple items. While ordinal scales are often used, researchers would prefer using interval scales since they produce higher-order data that can be subjected to more robust statistical tests. However, attitude scales that produce interval data are more difficult to construct.

Because an attitude consists of multiple dimensions, is abstract, is nonobservable, and rests in the minds of consumers, measuring attitude is challenging. To do so, researchers develop attitude constructs and measurement scales. How individuals respond to the items or questions making up the scale provides an understanding of their attitude.

SCALE DEVELOPMENT

■ Objective 10.2: Explain the concept of using scales for attitude measurement.

Since consumer attitudes cannot be observed, researchers develop scales to measure them. **Scaling** is the process of assigning numerical values or properties to subjective or abstract concepts. Attitude might be measured along a continuum using a 7-point scale with 7 indicating a very positive attitude and 1 indicating a very negative attitude. Thus, a value of 5 would indicate a more positive attitude than a value of 4, 3, 2, or 1. Alternatively, customer satisfaction attitudes might be assessed by selecting from among "Very Dissatisfied," "Dissatisfied," "Neutral," "Satisfied," and "Very Satisfied" scaled response categories.

Scales can be unidimensional or multidimensional. **Unidimensional scales** measure only one attribute or concept, such as a general attitude toward an advertisement. A researcher may use several items to measure the construct, but all of the items in a unidimensional scale measure a single concept. **Multidimensional scales** are designed to measure multiple dimensions or facets of a concept, an idea, or an attitude. Measuring store image involves multiple dimensions, such as atmospherics, aesthetics, product selection, and price.

Characteristics of a Good Scale

Developing or using good existing scales is important if a concept, such as attitude or satisfaction, is going to be measured with any degree of precision. Figure 10.2 identifies some of the characteristics of a good scale.

Scales should be relatively easy for respondents to understand. Wording is important. It is advisable to use language that is used by respondents, but also important to ensure the scale items are clear and concise. Clarity and language familiarity are important, because these factors help to ensure that respondents understand the question, and interpret it correctly, thus minimizing measurement error. The scale needs to provide useful data, so in addition to being clear and concise, the items need to discriminate well among different attitudes held by respondents. If a 5-point scale is used to measure attitude toward a brand, and if 95% of the respondents check the same response category, then the question does not discriminate adequately because it doesn't identify differences in attitudes. Scale items can be developed or borrowed from existing scales that produce a wide range of responses. In rare cases when a given scale does not discriminate well among respondents, the problem may be not with the scale but with the sample selected. If avid Apple users are surveyed, they are very likely to rate the Apple brand as a 5 on a 5-point rating scale.

Figure 10.2   Characteristics of a Good Scale

- Relatively easy for respondents to understand
- Clear and concise
- Provides useful data
- Discriminates well
- Limited response bias
- Valid and reliable

Good scales limit response bias. Asking individuals to evaluate fast-food restaurants in terms of food quality may produce response bias because respondents know the food is not the healthiest, even though they really like eating at fast-food restaurants. Thus, they may provide answers that are not completely honest. The reverse can also occur. If the survey is being taken in Japan and the respondents think the interviewer or survey sponsor wants to show the positive side of American food served in Japan, they may respond with a more positive attitude than they really believe.

Lastly, scales need to be valid and reliable. The validity and reliability tests discussed in Chapter 9 can be used to ensure a scale is valid and reliable. Alternatively, researchers can use scales that have already been established by prior researchers and that have been validated through proper research methods. It must be kept in mind, however, that if well-established scales are modified, used with a unique sample that is different from the general population, or used in a context that is significantly different, it may not produce valid and reliable results.

MARKETING SCALES

Scales can be divided into two primary categories: comparative scales and noncomparative scales. With **comparative scales** respondents are asked to evaluate or rate a brand, a product, an object, a concept, or a person relative to other brands, products, objects, concepts, or individuals or to an ideal item. **Noncomparative scales** involve respondents making judgments about a brand, a product, an object, a concept, or a person without reference to another item or an ideal item. Figure 10.3 identifies the most common scales used by marketing researchers. Typical comparative scales include rank-order, Q-sort, paired comparison, and constant sum. Common noncomparative scales are graphical rating and itemized rating. The semantic differential, Stapel, and Likert scales can be either comparative or noncomparative depending on how the question is worded.

Rank-Order Scales

When researchers want to evaluate brands in relation to competing brands, rank-order scales are often used. **Rank-order scales** involve respondents comparing two or more objects, concepts, or persons and ranking them in some type of order sequence. Because respondents are asked to make comparisons, rank-order scales are classified as comparative scales. They are relatively easy for respondents to answer and tend to mimic reality somewhat because consumers often will rank brands, products, or attributes mentally when faced with purchase decisions. Figure 10.4 illustrates a typical rank-order question.

While rank-order scales are relatively easy to administer, they do have some disadvantages (see Figure 10.5). First, the list of alternatives may not be categorically all-inclusive. In the case

■ Objective 10.3: Identify and describe the various comparative scales.

Figure 10.3   Frequently Used Marketing Scales

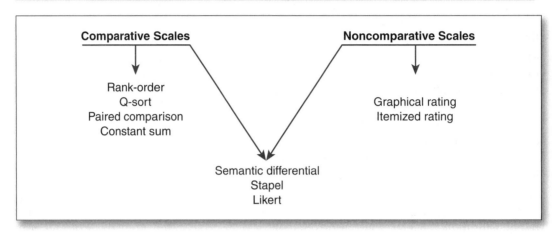

Figure 10.4   Sample Rank-Order Questions

All of the following restaurants are located in the Oakview Mall area. Please rank the restaurants in terms of your personal preference from 1 being your most preferred, to 2 being your second most preferred, and so forth, to 7 being your least preferred. Each number can only be used once, and each restaurant listed below must be ranked.

_____ Chili's

_____ Jade Garden

_____ LongHorn Steakhouse

_____ O'Charley's

_____ Olive Garden

_____ Pueblo Viejo

_____ Red Lobster

of the sample question shown in Figure 10.4, a researcher can identify all of the restaurants in the Oakview Mall area fairly easily, so this is not a problem. But, if respondents are asked instead to rank computers, a brand that a consumer prefers may not be on the list as it is much more difficult to identify all brands of computers. Ranking attributes or criteria used in making purchase decisions is even more difficult in terms of including all possible items. If the key criteria used by a consumer in making a decision are not listed, and thus not ranked, the resulting data are biased. It is also important to understand that for ranking data to be meaningful, all respondents must rank the exact same items relative to one another. This means that an "other" option with a fill-in-the-blank next to it cannot be used in a ranking question.

A second disadvantage is that a consumer may have no experience with one or more items in the list to be ranked, and as a result may be unable to make meaningful evaluations. With the sample scale shown, a respondent may have no experience with Jade Garden or Pueblo Viejo and may only have eaten at an Olive Garden in another town. Thus, ranking those three restaurants may produce meaningless data.

A third disadvantage occurs when individuals are asked to rank a long list of items. The longer the list, the more difficult it is for individuals to distinguish between the items "in the middle." Consumers know what they love, and they know what they hate, but differentiating between ranked items toward which they are relatively neutral in a meaningful way is difficult.

Fourth, ranking data is often of limited value because researchers do not have any knowledge of why the restaurants were ranked in a specific order. It could be based on price, on personal experiences, or on

Figure 10.5   Disadvantages of Rank-Order Questions

- List may not be categorically exhaustive
- Respondent may not have knowledge or experience with all items listed
- Difficult to rank middle items in a long list
- Criteria used in the ranking may not be clear
- Produces ordinal data, not interval

what someone told the respondents about a particular restaurant. Thus, rank-order questions may result in large amounts of measurement error. More importantly, the reason behind the rankings may provide more insight than the rankings themselves.

The last disadvantage relates to the type of data produced by rank-order scales—ordinal data. While ordinal data indicate an order, they do not indicate the distance between the rankings. Suppose both Maria and Josh ranked Red Lobster as 1 and Olive Garden as 2. Suppose, for Maria, the two were very close, and she had a difficult time deciding which to rank 1 and which to rank 2. But, for Josh, the decision was easy. In his mind there was a large gap between Red Lobster and Olive Garden. The magnitude of this difference in preference is not captured by ordinal data. Similarly, ranking questions forces individuals to rank items they may not consider to be viable alternatives. Thus, while Josh may have ranked Jade Garden as 5, he may have no intention of ever eating at any of the restaurants ranked 5 through 7. The forced nature of ranking questions can be misleading in terms of gauging preferences.

Rank-order questions are best used in situations in which the consumer is highly familiar with all items to be ranked and when the number of items to be ranked is relatively low. While questions featuring five items to be ranked are optimal, ultimately, there should be fewer than ten. In many cases, an itemized rating question or constant sum scale may yield more useful information and should be considered as a viable alternative.

In terms of reporting results of a rank-order scale, Figure 10.6 shows the rankings for Olive Garden for a survey of 180 respondents. Notice that the highest percentage, 25%, ranked Olive Garden as their second most preferred. It was ranked either first or second by a combined 46.7% of the respondents, indicating it is a popular choice for dining in the Oakview Mall area. Very few ranked Olive Garden near the bottom at sixth or seventh.

Another way the researcher may want to report the findings is to identify the top choice. Based on the graph in Figure 10.6, it would be easy to conclude that Olive Garden is the second most preferred restaurant in the Oakview Mall area. The manager of Olive Garden would likely be interested in which restaurant ranked first. Figure 10.7 shows the percent of respondents who ranked each of the restaurants as their "most preferred." Surprisingly, Olive Garden was ranked as the most preferred by the highest number of individuals, 21.7%. Red Lobster was second at 19.4%, and LongHorn Steakhouse was third at 18.3%. In examining results of rank-order scales and ordinal data, it is important for researchers to analyze the data in multiple ways. Frequencies, percentages, mode, and median can be used.

Figure 10.6   Results for Olive Garden

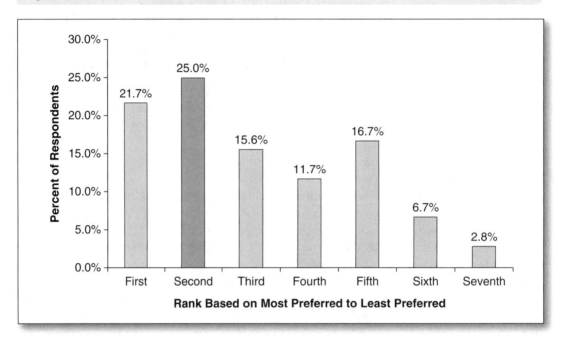

Figure 10.7   Most Preferred Brands

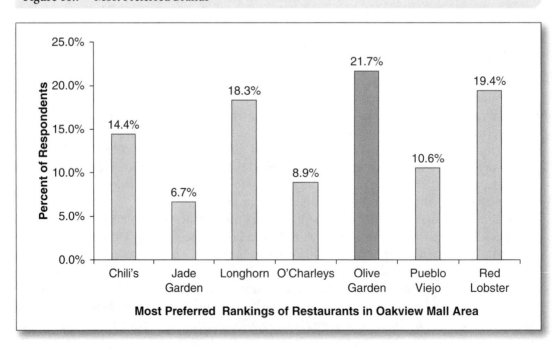

Q-Sort

Q-sorting is a comparative technique whereby respondents rank a set of objects into a prespecified number of categories along a particular attribute or criterion. Rank-order scales are good for a small number of items while Q-sorting works better for a large group of items, such as 50 to 100. Ranking 50 items using rank-ordering would be impossible for an individual to do, but can be done using Q-sorting. With this method individuals are asked to place the items in piles based on some criteria.

Suppose Oscar Mayer wanted to test three new print ads that have been designed by its advertising agency. It gathers a large number of print ads from recent issues of magazines that fit the Oscar Mayer target market. The three new Oscar Mayer ads are placed in a stack randomly with 57 other ads, making 60 ads total. Respondents are asked not to study the ad, but just to look at it as if they were thumbing through a magazine. In the first sorting round, they would begin by picking the top 5—the "great" ads. Next, they would be instructed to select the 5 "poorest" ads from the remaining pile. In the second stage, respondents would first select the 10 next best ads and place them in the "good" ad pile, then identify the 10 "next worst" ads, which would be placed in the "not so good" pile. The 30 ads that remain after the second stage sort would be left in a fifth "OK ad" pile. Switching from one extreme to the other makes the sorting task easier and faster than sorting great, good, OK, not so good, and poor ads in order. It is likely that the ads placed in the "great" pile would be ads that caused the respondents to stop and look closer. The ads in the "worst" pile would be those that were quickly ignored or were offensive in some fashion. The stacks between the two extremes would indicate some degree of interest. Using this method, a respondent could quickly evaluate 60 ads. Researchers with Oscar Mayer would be able to see how their test ads ranked compared to ads currently in circulated magazines.

Like rank-order scales, Q-sort scales produce ordinal data. The results of the Oscar Mayer Q-sort are shown in Figure 10.8. Test Ad 1 was placed in the first stack by 28.4% of the respondents and in the second stack by 35.1%. So about 63% of the respondents saw Test Ad 1 as either great or good, compared to the other 59 print ads they sorted. Notice Test Ads 2 and 3 did not produce as good of results as Test Ad 1. Less than 50% of the respondents placed the ads in the great or good groups. Clearly, Test Ad 1 is the one that Oscar Mayer should use based on this research, though other ad pretesting measures may be appropriate before making the final decision.

With a Q-sort, the results tend to display a normal distribution curve. However, instructions given by the researcher, the types of items being sorted, and the category specifications can alter the data distribution. For example, respondents in the Oscar Mayer test could have been instructed to select all of the "great" ads—regardless of the number—and so on, rather than being forced to fill preset quotas for great, good, OK, not so good, and poor categories. Had this been the case, the total distribution of ads for the Oscar Mayer Q-sort experiment could be similar to that shown in Figure 10.9, in which the distribution is skewed slightly positive. This information is beneficial to researchers since it tells them that as a group the respondents ranked more ads in the great and good categories than would be typical for a normal distribution curve.

Paired Comparisons

Rather than ask individuals to rank order a set of items, researchers may use a series of paired comparisons. With the **paired comparison scale**, respondents choose one of two items in a set based on a specific criterion or attribute. Figure 10.10 illustrates a paired comparison scale

Figure 10.8   Q-Sort Results of Oscar Mayer Test Ads

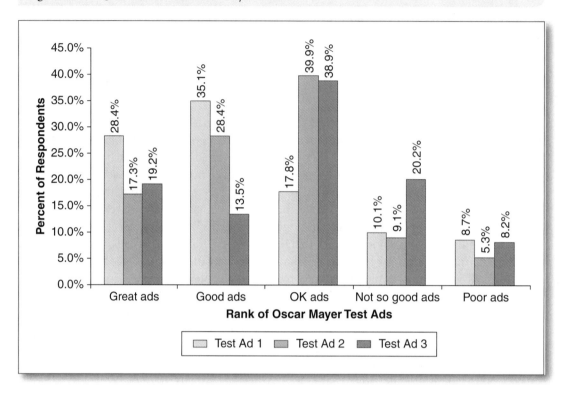

Figure 10.9   Data Q-Sort Distribution

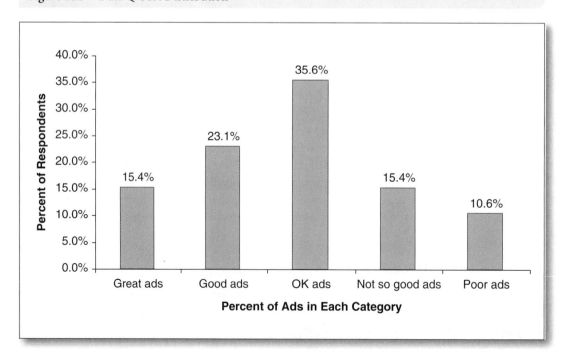

examining four criteria consumers use in purchasing a laptop computer. The key advantage of the paired comparison scale is that it is typically easier for respondents to choose between two items than it is to rank a series of items. The paired comparison scale also tends to overcome order bias that may be created in listing the items for a rank-order scale. Respondents may be influenced by the order in which items are listed in the rank-order scale, even if the list is alphabetical.

A major problem with the paired comparison scale is that all possible combinations must be listed. For a small set of items, such as the four used in Figure 10.10, only six paired combinations are needed. But, as the number of items to be evaluated increases, the number of paired combinations increases geometrically according to the following formula:

$$(n)\,(n-1)\,/\,2$$

For instance, for five items it would take 10 pairs, for six items it would take 15 pairs, and for seven items it would take 21 pairs. Asking someone to evaluate 15 or 21 pairs of items can be quite taxing, producing respondent fatigue. By the end of the exercise, respondents may start checking responses and not spend much time thinking about the paired items being evaluated.

While ordinal data are produced from a paired comparison scale, reporting the results can be challenging. Figure 10.11 provides the results of the sample comparison scale on the four purchase criteria for laptop computers. Of the 240 respondents who completed the exercise, 80% said that price was more important than the size of the computer, 65% said price was more important than the physical appearance of the computer, and 76.7% indicated that price was more important than technical specifications. Clearly, price is important. The size of the computer may be the least important since it was selected less than the other three comparison alternatives. Physical appearance was more important than either size or technical specifications. Lastly, technical specifications were more important than size.

Constant Sum

With the rank-order, Q-sort, and paired comparisons, relative distance between rankings cannot be determined and can vary substantially among respondents. To overcome this disadvantage,

Figure 10.10   Sample Paired Comparison Scale

For each of the following pairs of criteria in purchasing a laptop computer, indicate which item in each pair is most important to you by placing a checkmark on the appropriate line.

_____ Price or Size of computer _____

_____ Physical appearance or Technical specifications _____

_____ Price or Physical appearance _____

_____ Physical appearance or Size of computer _____

_____ Technical specifications or Price _____

_____ Size of computer or Technical specifications

researchers can use a constant sum comparative scale. The **constant sum scale** asks respondents to allocate points among various attributes or brands to indicate their importance or preference relative to one another. Typically, researchers will ask respondents to divide 100 points, but any number of points can be used, such as 10 or 20. Because the total points must add to 100 (or another specified number), the number of items to be ranked must remain small, usually under 10. Figure 10.12 illustrates a constant sum scale for evaluating the set of restaurants in the Oakview Mall area.

The primary advantage of the constant sum scale over rank-order and the other comparative scales is that the relative distance between rankings can be determined. Refer back to the example of both Maria and Josh ranking Red Lobster and Olive Garden 1 and 2 using the

Figure 10.11   Results From a Paired Comparison Scale

Purchase Criteria*	Price	Size	Appearance	Specs
Price		80.0%	65.0%	76.7%
Size of computer	24.2%		42.9%	38.8%
Physical appearance	35.0%	57.1%		60.4%
Technical specifications	23.3%	61.3%	39.6%	

* Percentages indicate percent of sample that chose the row criterion over the column criterion.

Figure 10.12   Example of a Constant Sum Scale

Listed below are the restaurants located in the Oakview Mall area. Please allocate 100 points among the seven restaurants based on your overall preference for each restaurant. The more points you assign to a restaurant, the higher the overall preference. The lower the number of points you assign, the lower the overall preference. A restaurant that is preferred twice as much as another restaurant should have twice as many points. It is possible to assign zero points to a restaurant if it is not at all preferred. The total number of points should add to 100.

Chili's	_____
Jade Garden	_____
LongHorn Steakhouse	_____
O'Charley's	_____
Olive Garden	_____
Pueblo Viejo	_____
Red Lobster	_____
Total number of points	100

rank-order scale. Recall that for Maria the two restaurants were very close while for Josh they were not. Using the constant sum scale, Maria may give Red Lobster a rating of 30 and Olive Garden a 28. Josh, on the other hand, may give Red Lobster a 35 and Olive Garden a 20. With the constant sum it is even possible to give the same number to two items. If Maria really could not decide between Red Lobster and Olive Garden, she could give them both the same score.

Another advantage of constant sum scales is that they produce ratio data, which are the highest order of data. In addition to rankings, researchers can compare the relative magnitude of the rankings. Suppose instead of using a rank-order scale researchers had used a constant sum scale to evaluate the seven restaurants in the Oakview Mall area. Figure 10.13 shows the results.

Results are very similar to the rank-order scale in Figure 10.7, but now relative magnitude can be compared. Notice that Olive Garden is still rated the highest, but using the constant sum scale, LongHorn Steakhouse is second and Red Lobster third. Because ratio data are produced, it is possible to say that the respondents' overall evaluation of Olive Garden is about twice as high as that for Chili's (23.14 compared to 12.41). The overall evaluation of Olive Garden is about seven times greater than for Jade Garden, a local Chinese restaurant. The low ranking for Jade Garden reflects the fact that constant sum scales allow respondents to assign a zero to items that are not at all preferred. Similarly, if asked to evaluate the relative importance of factors influencing a purchase decision, the constant sum scale would allow consumers to indicate which if any factors were not at all influential.

Figure 10.13   Results of Using a Constant Sum Scale

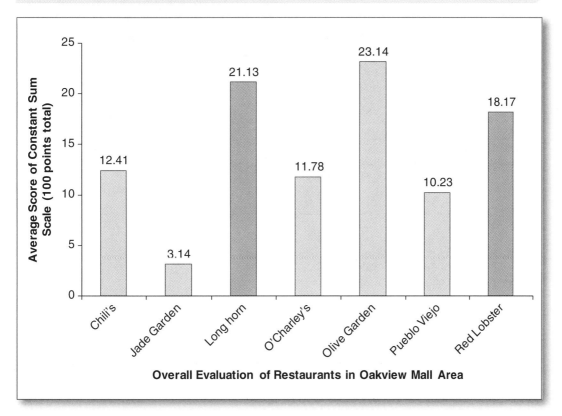

While the constant sum scale offers the advantage of producing ratio data and allows researchers to see relative distances between rankings, its primary disadvantage is the proper allocation of the points. Respondents may find it difficult to allocate 100 points among seven different choices. Unless the exercise is done on a computer that automatically adds the scores, respondents can easily make a mistake resulting in a total that does not add to 100. Using a smaller scale, such as 10, is easier for respondents to add the values, but a scale of 10 does not allow as much discrimination among choices as would 100.

Graphical Rating Scales

■ Objective 10.4: Identify and describe the various noncomparative scales.

Graphical rating scales are noncomparative scales that allow respondents to place a response anywhere on a continuous line. Respondents are not making any comparisons, but are asked to make a judgment or an evaluation. The scale is normally anchored at each end with antonyms or words with highly different meanings, such as *poor* and *excellent* or *friendly* and *unfriendly*. Figure 10.14 illustrates two different types of graphical rating scales. In the first example respondents can place an X anywhere on the line that they feel corresponds to their evaluation of service quality. The second scale has numbers, but respondents do not have to place their X on the line that corresponds to a number. They can place it between numbers if they want.

Graphical rating scales have the advantage of allowing respondents to provide a response along a continuum. The challenge is in converting the response to a number. If the line is 6 inches long, researchers may equate each inch with a number, thus a scale of 1 to 6. Alternatively, they could divide the line into 12 parts and have a scale of 1 to 12. Because of the continuous nature of a graphical scale, it will produce interval data. It cannot be ratio data since there is no absolute zero. Descriptive results would be reported in terms of a mean and standard deviation. Thus, for the graphical scales in Figure 10.14, the mean for the top scale using a 6-point scale may be 4.2, and for the bottom using a 10-point scale it may be 7.1.

Figure 10.14   Examples of Graphical Rating Scales

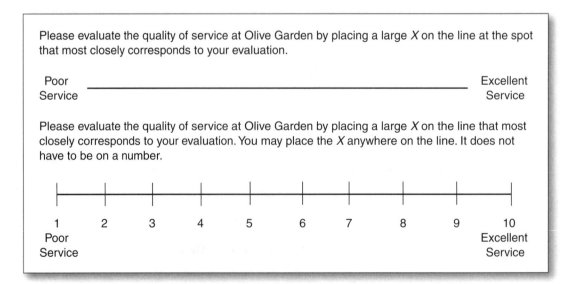

Itemized Rating Scales

With an **itemized rating scale,** respondents choose a response from a select number of items or categories. It is also a noncomparative rating scale. Figure 10.15 illustrates three possible itemized rating scales. In the first question, respondents are asked how likely they are to purchase a Dell computer. They have five different possible answers they can check from "extremely unlikely" to "extremely likely." In the second example, rather than have a 5-point scale with two extreme anchors, it has six categories, each with a distinctive label.

Itemized rating scales may also use picture-based response options instead of words, as shown in the third example. This type of graphic itemized rating scale is commonly used in the medical profession for measuring patient pain, especially in emergency situations when patients may not be able to articulate how they feel. In marketing research, the use of the smiley/sad face scale may be perceived as insulting when administered to literate adults. Yet the same scale could be very appropriate for young children or mentally disadvantaged adults who can easily point to the face that best describes how they feel about the question as read by an interviewer.

The primary advantages of the itemized rating scale are it is easy for respondents to understand and easy for researchers to code. No subjective judgment is needed to identify what number should be given to a person's response. As a result, itemized rating scales are used extensively in marketing research. They can be used in all types of survey methods from telephone surveys to online surveys.

Figure 10.15 Examples of Itemized Rating Scales

How likely are you to purchase a Dell computer?

Extremely Unlikely   ○   ○   ○   ○   ○   Extremely Likely
                 1   2   3   4   5

How likely are you to purchase a Dell computer?

_____ Extremely likely

_____ Very likely

_____ Somewhat likely

_____ Somewhat unlikely

_____ Very unlikely

_____ Extremely unlikely

Please choose the face that best describes how you feel about Rock Star Mickey.

Most itemized rating scales produce interval data because it is assumed there is equal distance between each of the categories or items in the response. In the examples given in Figure 10.15, researchers assume the distance between a 2 response and a 3 response is the same as the distance between a 4 and a 5. Therefore, the appropriate descriptive statistics would be a mean and standard deviation. For the first question, the mean may be 3.72 with a standard deviation of 1.04. For the second the mean may be 4.25 with a standard deviation of 0.96. Researchers may also want to know how many individuals checked each response, especially if the question was in response to an e-mail offer or a direct response offer.

Some itemized rating scales produce ordinal-level data (not interval), because the distance between response options cannot assumed to be equal. Figure 10.16 lists several examples. Importance, satisfaction, and other key attitudes can be assessed using itemized rating scales, but the manner in which the response categories are labeled will influence whether the resulting data are ordinal or interval in nature. When ordinal data are collected, means cannot be computed. Instead, data analysis should be limited to reporting frequencies and percents and, when appropriate, the mode or median.

- Objective 10.5: Identify and describe scales that can be either comparative or noncomparative.

Semantic Differential Scales

A semantic differential scale can be either comparative or noncomparative depending on how the question is worded. The **semantic differential scale** involves a finite number of choices anchored by dichotomous words or phrases. Most semantic differential scales have 5 or 7 points, which allows for a neutral position. In some cases the neutral position is eliminated, and a 4- or 6-point scale is used to force respondents to choose one side or the other of the scale. The key to good semantic differential scales is choosing the anchor phrases or words that will produce discriminate answers among respondents. Scale anchors should be bipolar, meaning that the anchors are perceived as "opposites" by respondents. Figure 10.17 provides an example of semantic differential scales for Home Depot.

When properly constructed, a major advantage of the semantic differential scale is its ability to discriminate differences in the direction and intensity of attitudes.[1] The key is choosing

Figure 10.16   Examples of Ordinal Itemized Scale Categories

Scales Assessing Frequency:

Very often	Often	Sometimes	Rarely	Never
All of the time	Most of the time	Some of the time	Just now and then	
All of the time	Very often	Often	Sometimes	Hardly ever

Scales Assessing Quality:

Excellent	Good	Fair	Poor	
Very good	Fairly good	Neither good nor bad	Not very good	Not good at all

Scale Assessing Uniqueness:

Extremely unique	Very unique	Somewhat unique	Slightly unique	Not at all unique
Very different	Somewhat different		Slightly different	Not at all different

Figure 10.17   Examples of a Semantic Differential Scale

Please evaluate the last purchase you made at Home Depot and the experience you had at the retail store.

Unfriendly staff	○	○	○	○	○	Friendly staff
Staff not very helpful	○	○	○	○	○	Staff very helpful
Poor selection	○	○	○	○	○	Excellent selection
Store unclean	○	○	○	○	○	Store clean
Poor value	○	○	○	○	○	Excellent value
Slow checkout	○	○	○	○	○	Fast checkout
Unsuccessful trip	○	○	○	○	○	Successful trip

anchor phrases or words that reflect opposite meanings. This isn't always an easy task. For example, most people would agree that *love* and *hate* are bipolar opposites. But, what would be the appropriate opposite of *angry*? If you answered *happy*, then what word would you choose as the opposite of *sad*? If the anchors are chosen well, the semantic differential is relatively easy for respondents to understand and therefore easy to answer. If the anchors are not chosen well, it will lead to respondent confusion and scores that tend to drift to the midpoint. Also, if anchors are too strong, then the majority of responses will tend to be in the middle. However, if anchors are too weak, then all of the answers will be at one extreme or the other.

Semantic differential scales are excellent for assessing brand personality or image, and can be quickly answered by respondents. The results tend to be reliable. They eliminate problems that can occur with question phrasing when using itemized or Likert scales.[2] Semantic differential scales are also used frequently to assess attitudes toward an advertisement, a celebrity endorser, or a retail store.

A danger with using the semantic differential scale is the **halo effect,** which occurs when respondents have an overall feeling about the topic being surveyed and that overall perception influences their response to individual items so that all of the answers are relatively close to the same. Little or no discrimination among individual items occurs. For instance, if Carla's overall experience at Home Depot was positive, she may just go through and mark the fourth circle on each item. While it is possible that those responses may reflect her actual experience, it is also highly likely she did not think about each item sufficiently. It is unlikely that her experience would be a 4 for every single item. Past research using semantic differentials has shown that halo effect is more likely to occur when all favorable evaluations are placed on the left-hand side of the scale.[3]

The semantic differential scale shown in Figure 10.17 is a noncomparative scale because survey respondents are asked to evaluate their experience with Home Depot. No comparisons are made. If researchers want to compare Home Depot to Lowe's along the seven dimensions, then the scale can be modified asking respondents to evaluate Home Depot in comparison to Lowe's. In addition, the anchors can be modified. For instance, the first item can have anchors "friendlier staff than at Lowe's" and "less friendly staff than at Lowe's."

Semantic differential scales produce interval data. Researchers assume there is equal distance between each of the points on the scale. Therefore, the appropriate descriptive measures would be a mean and standard deviation. Figure 10.18 shows the results of the semantic differential scale about Home Depot. The two lowest ratings in this particular survey were for friendly staff and helpful staff.

Semantic differentials are often used to develop brand and image profiles. Figure 10.19 shows an image profile for Williamson Hardware, a local retailer, compared to the national chain Home Depot. Instead of comparing a brand or business to a particular competitor, respondents can be asked to compare Williamson Hardware to other hardware stores in general—that is, against the industry. But, for this survey, individuals evaluated Williamson Hardware along nine dimensions and also Home Depot along the same nine dimensions. The mean scores on each item for each brand were then plotted and connected to provide a visual representation of the resulting brand image profiles. A review of the results shows Williamson Hardware was evaluated higher on the dimensions of helpfulness, fast service, pleasantness, reliability, quality, and friendliness. On the negative side, Williamson Hardware was seen as being more expensive and not as clean. A paired sample t-test could be used to test whether the differences in the perceptions of cleanliness between Home Depot and Williamson Hardware are significant, meaning that they are not due to random sampling error. Should significant differences be found, the store manager can take steps to improve the cleanliness of the store, and thereby enhance the store's image.

Figure 10.18   Results of Home Depot Semantic Differential

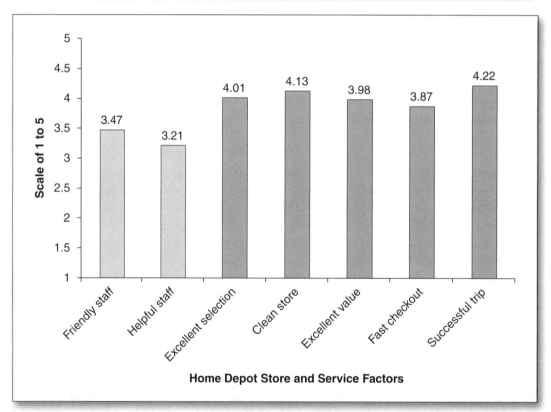

When multi-item measures are used to assess an individual's attitude toward an advertisement or a brand, the common practice is to create an overall average by summing the mean scores for each item. This summed score is then divided by the number of items in the scale to find the mean attitude score of the entire measure. This overall mean score for the scale or attitude dimension is then used in subsequent data analyses.

Stapel Scales

The **Stapel scale** is similar to the semantic differential, but uses only one anchor and both a positive and a negative numeric scale. Sample Stapel scales are shown in Figure 10.20. In this survey respondents are asked to evaluate Mel's Diner along the four dimensions. As it is currently worded, it is a noncomparative scale. It can be converted to a comparative scale by asking respondents to compare Mel's Diner to another restaurant, to restaurants in general, or to the ideal restaurant.

Figure 10.19   Image Profile of Williamson Hardware

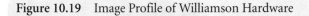

Figure 10.20   Examples of Stapel Scales

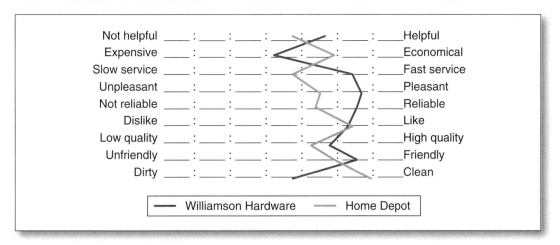

One of the challenges of the semantic differential scale is choosing bipolar anchors. The advantage of the Stapel scale is that only one anchor is needed. By using both positive and negative numbers, the scale produces both positive and negative evaluations. It is easy for respondents to use since they can signify negative evaluations by circling or checking a negative response.

The major disadvantage is the impact the one-word anchor can have. The word or phrase used as an anchor can be expressed in positive terms, in neutral terms, or in a negative format. Whichever format is used will impact the results. Using the anchor "value" produces different results than using anchors such as "poor value" or "good value." An additional disadvantage of the Stapel scale is that some respondents find it difficult to understand, and may circle the anchor itself, rather than the positive or negative number that expresses the degree to which the anchor reflects their positive or negative opinion. Misunderstandings of this nature are more likely to occur when non-neutral anchors are used. Finally, Stapel scales may take up more space on self-administered surveys, and thus be less desirable than semantic differentials. In practice, Stapel scales are not frequently used by marketing research practitioners.

Stapel scales generate interval data, and thus descriptive measures such as means and standard deviations are appropriate. Results for the Stapel scale are shown in Figure 10.21. The interior décor was rated negatively, at a −1.85. But, the restaurant provides a high level of service quality, 2.01, and food quality, 1.56. Value also had a positive evaluation. So despite the poor interior décor, Mel's Diner stays in business because of the high level of customer service and to some extent good food quality and good value for the money paid.

Figure 10.21   Results From Stapel Scale

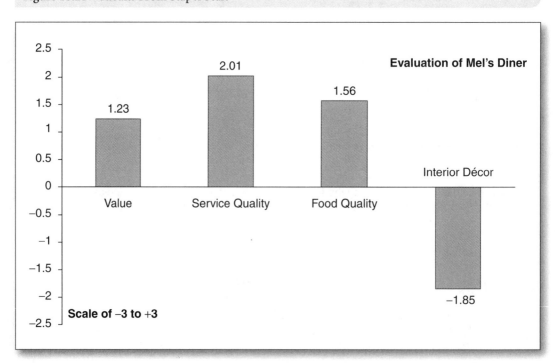

Likert Scales

Likert scales are among the most popular for marketing research. **Likert scales** list a series of statements, and respondents are asked to indicate their level of agreement or disagreement with each statement. One reason Likert scales are used frequently is their ease of construction. Likert scales avoid the difficulty of finding the right anchor words or phrases that are commonly encountered when creating a semantic differential or Stapel scale. Likert scales are easy for respondents to read and understand. They are also easy to answer as subjects can respond to a whole series of statements that utilize the same scale. Figure 10.22 contains some Likert statements about fashion.

Likert scales can be either comparative or noncomparative. The scale shown in Figure 10.22 is noncomparative. A comparative Likert scale may ask individuals to respond to a series of statements about a particular retail store, such as the Gap, as it compares to other clothing retail stores or a specific store such as rue21. An example of a comparative Likert statement would be "rue21 offers higher-quality clothing than the Gap."

Likert scales tend to be either 5-point or 7-point scales, with the 5-point scale being the most common. Because Likert scales produce interval data, means and standard deviations are the appropriate descriptive measures. This allows the researcher to conduct various tests for differences in attitudes based on demographic factors such as age, gender, or race, as well as other classification variables. Figure 10.23 graphs the results of the Likert scale about fashion. However, when multi-item Likert scales are used to assess an individual's attitude, the common practice is to sum or average the scores of all item means composing the attitude, and use this summated or average measure in data analyses rather than individual items.

Likert scales often include both reversed (negatively phrased) and nonreversed (positively phrased) items. Doing so is thought to reduce response bias due to acquiescent respondents who are likely to be agreeable and rate everything positively.[4] Mixing positive and negative items is also important because some argue it helps to alert lazy or less attentive respondents that the question content varies.[5] Unfortunately, reversing scale items has been found to diminish the reliability of scales and may result in respondents selecting the exact opposite of their true attitude.[6]

Figure 10.22   Example of a Likert Scale

Please indicate your level of agreement or disagreement with each of the following statements.

	Strongly Disagree	Disagree	Neutral	Agree	Strongly Agree
1. Wearing the latest fashion is important to me.	○	○	○	○	○
2. The brand name is important to me. ....:	○	○	○	○	○
3. I watch what celebrities wear.	○	○	○	○	○
4. I read magazines such as *Glamour* regularly.	○	○	○	○	○
5. In purchasing clothes, price is not a critical factor. ..	○	○	○	○	○
6. I am concerned about what others think of me.	○	○	○	○	○

Figure 10.23   Results of Likert Scale About Fashion

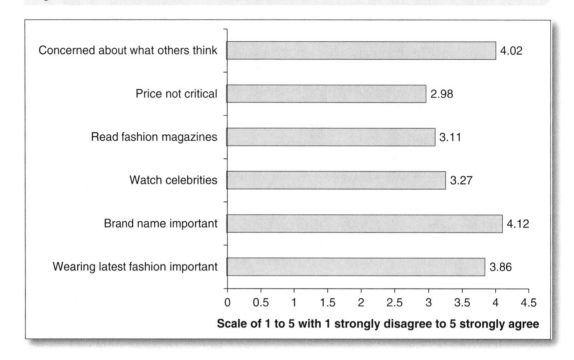

Scale of 1 to 5 with 1 strongly disagree to 5 strongly agree

SCALE CATEGORY CONSIDERATIONS

■ Objective 10.6: Discuss the considerations involved in selecting marketing scales.

Choosing the best scale for a research project requires an understanding of the research objective, target market, information needs, and mode of administration. If the objective involves comparisons with other brands or products, then one of the comparative scales should be used, or semantic differential, Stapel, or Likert scales should be used to assess multiple brands or products. The education level and reading ability of the target audience should also be considered. Some scales, such as the constant sum scale, require a higher level of education and math skills than do some of the other scales. To encourage respondents to complete the survey and to provide honest, beneficial answers, the scales need to be easy for the respondents to read, understand, and complete, a factor that often works against the Stapel scale. Researchers must also consider the information needs of the research study, especially in terms of the data that each scale will produce. Ordinal data may be sufficient for some research studies, while others may need interval or ratio data. Mode of administration has an impact on scale selection. Some scales are easier to use with telephone surveys than others. If the respondents can see the scale, as with a web or paper survey, then more complicated scales can be used than if they can only hear the scale as it is read to them.

When it comes to actually creating the marketing scale, researchers must think about the number of categories, the use of balanced versus unbalanced scales, "no opinion" and "don't know" options, forced versus nonforced choices, and the extent of category description (see Figure 10.24).

Figure 10.24   Considerations in Creating Marketing Scales

- Number of categories
- Balanced versus unbalanced scales
- "No opinion" and "don't know" options
- Forced versus nonforced choices
- Type of category description

These decisions can have a significant impact on how respondents answer questions and the usefulness of the data that are produced.

Number of Categories

In developing scales, researchers must decide on the number of categories. A 2-point or 3-point scale lacks discrimination ability. Respondents tend to feel uncomfortable when using such a scale as it limits their freedom of expression. A Likert scale that has only three categories of "disagree," "neutral," and "agree" will not provide the researcher with a great deal of information. While it may technically be an interval scale, the mean will not be of much value. Frequency counts of how many agree and how many disagree may be more useful. By expanding the number of categories to 5, 7, or 10, greater detail is obtained, and the scale increases in discriminatory power. While 5- and 7-point scales produce comparable means, 10-point scales have been shown to result in slightly lower means.[7]

As the number of categories increases from 3 to 9, the reliability of the measure improves.[8] Thus, differences in responses are more likely to be found as the number of categories increases. But, having a scale with 10 or more points may be too many for some respondents. It may be difficult for them to distinguish between values, such as 6 and 7 or 7 and 8. Reliability may also suffer as scales with a large number of categories have been found to be less reliable than those with fewer categories.[9] As a result, most marketing researchers recommend scales with 5 to 7 points as being optimal.[10] Often the decision on how many scale points comes down to researcher preference and the importance of the decision that needs to be made.

Another consideration in terms of number of categories is whether the scale should have an even or odd number of choices. When an odd number is used, such as 5 or 7, respondents can choose a neutral or middle position. With an even number of choices, respondents do not have that option. They must make a choice on one side or the other of the scale. It is a difficult decision. In some cases, individuals may not have an opinion, and so having a neutral position is valid. Forcing them to choose one side or the other may distort the data. However, the downside of having an odd number of choices is that it provides an easy escape for individuals who do not want to state an opinion.

Balanced Versus Unbalanced Scales

In addition to the number of categories, researchers must decide on whether to use a balanced or an unbalanced scale. A **balanced scale** will have the same number of positive choices as negative choices, and the phrasing of each negative choice typically mirrors the phrasing of each positive choice. An **unbalanced scale** is weighted toward one of the anchors, either positive or negative. Figure 10.25 illustrates each of the scales in relation to an individual's attitude toward wearing the latest fashions.

In the first example, the itemized rating scale has two negative response categories, a neutral position, and two positive response categories. It is balanced. In the second example, there are two negative response categories, no neutral position, and three positive response categories. It is unbalanced. The researcher could still use a neutral position in the unbalanced category if he or she desires. In most cases, a balanced scale is preferred to an unbalanced. But, if past research shows that most people lean toward a negative or positive position, then an unbalanced scale may be a better choice because it will provide greater discrimination.

Figure 10.25   Examples of Balanced and Unbalanced Scales

Balanced scale

How important is it to you to wear the latest fashions?

_____ very unimportant _____ somewhat unimportant _____ neutral _____ somewhat important _____ very important

Unbalanced scale

How important is it to you to wear the latest fashions?

_____ very unimportant _____ somewhat unimportant _____ somewhat important _____ very important _____ extremely important

There are also situations where the target audience may dictate which scale is used. If the fashion question was asked of the general population, the balanced scale would be appropriate, and expanding the number of categories to a 7-point scale may produce even better results. If the population being studied is teenage girls, then an unbalanced scale may be better since most female teenagers are concerned about personal appearance and fashions.

"No Opinion" and "Don't Know" Options

Another decision that must be made is whether to include a "no opinion" or "don't know" option. As stated earlier, if an odd number of points is used in a scale, respondents tend to think of the center point as being neutral. They may also see it as a "don't know" or "no opinion" choice if none is provided. This is problematic, as researchers are not really sure if the respondent is neutral about the issue or doesn't really have an opinion. To avoid this situation and reduce measurement error, a "no opinion" or "don't know" option can be placed to the right of the scale. By placing it on the right side, respondents are first encouraged to express an opinion. Usually just one of the options is included, but both options can be used if researchers feel that there is a significant difference between someone who doesn't want to express an opinion and someone who truly has no experience or knowledge with which to answer the question.

The downside of including a "no opinion" or "don't know" option is that its presence often encourages respondents to use it. If a "no opinion" option is used on the Likert questions in Figure 10.22, a number of respondents may check it rather than indicate a level of agreement or disagreement with the statement. This is more likely to occur if an even-numbered scale is used in which a neutral position is not available. The same situation can occur with the semantic differential scales in Figure 10.17, if a "no opinion" option is available, though most semantic differentials do not include this category.

In surveys where respondents may not have any experience with the brand or product being studied, a "don't know" option is valuable. Suppose the respondent completing the questions about fashions (see Figure 10.22) was from France or another country and was not familiar with *Glamour* magazine. The respondent has to make a decision. She could skip the question and not answer it. She could answer it in terms of magazines in general, or guess what is meant by the question since she has no familiarity with *Glamour*. She might assume it is a magazine that features celebrities, tying it in with the previous item. By having a "don't know" option, the respondent can check it, and the researcher is not left with biased data.

Forced Versus Nonforced Choices

With semantic differential and Likert scales that use an odd number of response categories, respondents can check the middle option and not have to take a stand on an issue. On the Likert scales about fashions shown in Figure 10.22, an individual can choose "neutral." While individuals can certainly be neutral about the importance of fashion, brand names of clothes, pricing, and so forth, it is also likely that they do have an opinion. They may just choose the easy route of checking "neutral," or if the researcher has a "no opinion" category, they may check it.

To force individuals to take a stand on issues, such as fashions, researchers can use an even number of points such as the 6-point scale in Figure 10.26 that does not have a neutral point. If there are no other options such as "no opinion," the respondents must make a stand, either negative or positive. Thus, they have to either disagree or agree with the statement "I like wearing brand-name clothing." The only other option open to the respondent is to refuse to answer the question and leave it blank. Most individuals, however, when forced to make a stand on an issue or a statement, will do so. Thus, by eliminating "neutral," "no opinion," and "don't know" options, researchers force respondents to either the positive or negative side of the statement or question.

Figure 10.26   Likert Scale Using Even Number of Points

For each of the following statements, indicate your level of agreement or disagreement by placing an *X* in the open box that most closely represents your feelings.

I like wearing brand-name clothing.	Strongly Disagree_|_|_|_|_|_Strongly Agree
I prefer to purchase clothes that are on sale.	Strongly Disagree_|_|_|_|_|_Strongly Agree
Wearing name-brand clothing makes me feel accepted by others.	Strongly Disagree_|_|_|_|_|_Strongly Agree
Advertising influences my decision on what brand to purchase.	Strongly Disagree_|_|_|_|_|_Strongly Agree
I use coupons when I buy clothes.	Strongly Disagree_|_|_|_|_|_Strongly Agree
I follow clothing trends so I can purchase the latest styles.	Strongly Disagree_|_|_|_|_|_Strongly Agree
I normally buy clothes that are on a sales rack.	Strongly Disagree_|_|_|_|_|_Strongly Agree
Price is important to me when selecting clothes.	Strongly Disagree_|_|_|_|_|_Strongly Agree
The brand name is important in my selection of clothes.	Strongly Disagree_|_|_|_|_|_Strongly Agree

Type of Category Description

Researchers must also decide whether each category in a scale should be labeled with a verbal description or a number, or whether only the scale anchors should be labeled. Figure 10.26 illustrates the latter situation. Alternatively, a Likert scale could be composed as shown in Figure 10.22 in which each category is labeled. A final example that combines both verbal and numerical category descriptions is shown in Figure 10.27.

Using numbers to represent categories precodes the questionnaire and saves the researcher valuable time once the data have been collected, because the results of each survey can be immediately entered into the data file. Thus, manual coding of each survey item is avoided. Interestingly, the numbers chosen for scales can significantly influence the resulting ratings. Multiple studies have compared scales containing all positive numbers, such 0–10, 1–9, or 1–5 with scales in which numbers were negatively and positively balanced (−5 to +5, −4 to +4, −2 to +2). In each instance, scales using negatively and positively balanced numeric response categories produced more positive evaluations.[11]

Limiting the use of verbal labels to anchors is desirable when the researcher wants to be certain that interval-level data are collected. However, describing each category can be helpful when the goal is to better explain the options available to respondents. Obviously, the education level of respondents should be considered when making this decision. Respondents with lower levels of education are more likely to benefit from category descriptions that are applied to every option.

Figure 10.27 Verbal and Numerical Descriptions in a Likert Scale

Please indicate your level of agreement or disagreement with each of the following statements by circling the number that best corresponds with your attitude. 1 = strongly disagree, 2 = disagree, 3 = neutral, 4 = agree, and 5 = strongly agree.

	SD	D	N	A	SA
1. Wearing the latest fashion is important to me.	1	2	3	4	5

An additional consideration when choosing category descriptions relates to the strength of the anchors chosen when only anchors appear, and individual category descriptors are not provided. Suppose a question asked consumers to "Indicate your satisfaction level with your current cell phone service provider." How should the anchors be phrased? Satisfied versus dissatisfied? Very satisfied versus very dissatisfied? Extremely satisfied versus extremely dissatisfied? While the choice may be influenced somewhat by the number of categories used in the scale, it is also important to understand that the adjectives chosen to accompany a category descriptor can influence respondents' choices. For instance, respondents would be less inclined to choose the first or last category when "extremely satisfied/dissatisfied" anchors exist than they would when the "very satisfied/dissatisfied" or "satisfied/dissatisfied" anchors are used.

VALIDITY AND RELIABILITY MEASUREMENT

In developing marketing scales, researchers have three basic options. First, they can use scales that have already been established by other researchers. The *Marketing Scales Handbook* by Bruner, Hensel, and James is an excellent source of scales that have already been established. Additional scales can be found at http://marketingscales.com. A major advantage of using these scales is that many have already gone through rigorous validity and reliability tests. Thus, results from these scales are likely to have a high level of validity and reliability.

A second option is to use established scales, but modify them to fit the product or situation being studied. By starting with scales that have gone through validity and reliability tests, it is likely that the new, revised scales will also have a higher level of validity and reliability.

The final option is for researchers to develop their own scales. Scale development is difficult and time consuming, and a great deal of academic research has been devoted to the scale development process, so those wishing to develop their own scales are best served by following established procedures.[12] Whether existing scales are modified or new scales are developed from scratch, researchers need to check the validity and reliability of their scales. Chapter 9 presented various methods of measuring reliability and ensuring validity.

Multiple items (or indicators) are often used to measure consumer attitudes or other marketing-related variables (or constructs), such as brand image or attitude toward an ad. Using more than one item to measure a single construct provides a more accurate picture than using just one-item indicators. Consider the Likert statements shown in Figure 10.26 that were taken from a survey about purchasing clothes. Researchers who developed the survey believe the nine statements selected measure two constructs: branding and price. To check if this is true, researchers can use two statistical methods: correlation analysis and factor analysis.

■ Objective 10.7: Explain ways researchers can ensure the reliability and validity of scales.

Correlation Analysis

Correlation is the degree to which one variable changes with another. If the correlation involves only two variables, it is called bivariate correlation. A common statistical test to measure bivariate correlation is the Pearson product-moment correlation. The Pearson test examines the two variables to see the amount of change in one variable compared to the amount of change in the other variable. Pearson correlations can vary from +1 to −1. A +1 score would mean an identical change. If variable *A* increased by 2, then variable *B* would increase by 2. If variable *A* declined by 4, variable *B* declined by 4. On the Likert scales shown in Figure 10.26, if two statements had a perfect +1 correlation, then the answers to both questions would always be the same.

A score of −1 would indicate an inverse relationship. If variable *A* increased by 2, then variable *B* would decline by 2 units. If variable *A* declined by 4, then variable *B* would increase by 4. A score of 0 would indicate no correlation at all. Changes in variable *A* had no relationship to the change in variable *B*. Scores of +1, −1, or 0 are extremely unlikely with a valid sample of respondents.

Referring back to the Likert statements about purchasing clothes, Pearson correlations that are positive indicate respondents tended to give the same answers to two different questions. The higher the value (i.e., the closer to 1 the correlation), the more often the same response was given to the two questions. A Pearson correlation that is negative indicates that respondents tended to give opposite answers. Thus, if the respondents strongly agreed with Statement A and it had a negative correlation with Statement B, they would tend to disagree with Statement B.

For simplification purposes, the Pearson correlation and significance level of the first two Likert statements are shown with all of the statements for a sample of 194 respondents in Figure 10.28. The values shown in the first "Correlation" column indicate how well the statement in each row is correlated with the statement "I like wearing brand-name clothing." The significance level of the correlation is reported next. The last two columns contain the Pearson correlation and significance level with the statement "I prefer to purchase clothes that are on sale."

Notice the Pearson correlation between "I like wearing brand-name clothing" and "I prefer to purchase clothes that are on sale" is –0.310, which indicates an inverse correlation. The more the respondents liked wearing brand-name clothing, the less they preferred purchasing clothes off of the sales rack. The p-value of .000 indicates that this is a significant inverse relationship that is unlikely to have been found by chance. Thus, we can be confident that the results indicate a true inverse relationship in the population since it was true for this sample. The correlation between the first and third statements is 0.712, indicating a strong positive correlation between the statements "I like wearing brand-name clothing" and "Wearing name-brand clothing makes me feel accepted by others." The 0.712 can be thought of as a percent of common answers. Thus, 71.2% of the respondents checked the same spot on the Likert scale for those two questions. In terms of the first and second statement correlations, it would indicate that 31% of the time respondents checked just the opposite answer. If they checked "strongly agree" for "I like wearing

Figure 10.28   Partial Bivariate Correlation Matrix

Likert statements	I like wearing brand-name clothing.		I prefer to purchase clothes that are on sale.	
	Correlation	P-value	Correlation	P-value
Like wearing brand-name clothes	1		–0.310	0.000
Shop clothes on sale	–0.310	0.000	1	
Wearing brands, feel accepted	0.712	0.000	–0.276	0.000
Advertising influences	0.359	0.000	–0.317	0.000
Use coupons	–0.222	0.002	0.497	0.000
Wearing latest fashions important	0.379	0.000	–0.342	0.000
Purchase from sales racks	–0.072	0.321	0.545	0.000
Price is important	–0.084	0.243	0.570	0.000
Brand name important	0.687	0.000	–0.468	0.000

brand-name clothing," then 31% of the time they checked "strongly disagree" for "I prefer to purchase clothes that are on sale."

A review of the Pearson correlation matrix shows that the first item is highly correlated with the third statement and the last statement, "The brand name is important in my selection of clothes." It is positively related to the statements about advertising and importance of wearing the latest fashions, but the correlations are not as strong. It is inversely correlated to the statements about purchasing clothes on sale and using coupons. This would indicate that individuals who felt brand names were important tended to put less emphasis on sales and coupons. But, notice that for the statements "I normally buy clothes that are on a sales rack" and "Price is important to me when selecting clothes" the correlation is negative. But neither correlation is significant, which indicates very little correlation between these two statements and "I like wearing brand-name clothing" in the sample under study. So, from the correlation analysis, the researcher can say there is no correlation between individuals who like wearing brand names and their desire to shop from sales racks and the importance of price to them.

A check of the final two columns shows just the opposite for the statement about shopping for clothes that are on sale. That statement is positively correlated with other statements about pricing and inversely correlated with statements about branding and fashions. All are significant.

Factor Analysis

A statistical procedure that is often used by researchers with multi-item attitude scales that are meant to represent multiple facets of an individual's attitude is factor analysis. A **factor analysis** involves analyzing a set of indicators (items) to determine underlying constructs dimensions) by reducing a larger number of items into a smaller subset of factors. Through factor analysis a researcher can determine which questions are measuring facets of the same component, or attitudinal dimension. For example, a researcher may start with 30 items that measure retail store image. Through factor analysis, these 30 items may be reduced to just 3 or 4 factors that measure different aspect of store image, such as atmospherics, layout, image, pricing, and product selection. The correlation matrix discussed in the previous section provides some information, but a factor analysis is a more comprehensive, statistical method that provides better information. A discussion of factor analysis can be found at the textbook's website along with instructions on how to conduct a factor analysis in SPSS.

Global Concerns

In developing scales to be used in other countries, researchers must be cognizant of differences in culture. A literal translation from English (or whatever language the original questionnaire was developed in) can yield scales that may actually have a different meaning, or at least not carry the same connotation. Engaging translators who understand the nuances of the language and culture can be extremely valuable. Double translation, in which one person translates the survey into the foreign language and another translates this survey back into English, is often used to verify that the meaning between surveys is consistent.

Still, translation is a costly and time-consuming process. Researchers studying international populations that are bilingual (in English) are often tempted to use surveys written in English rather than in the native language of the population being studied. While doing so eliminates translation costs and saves time, recent research has shown that the quality of data suffers due to an anchor contraction effect. The **anchor contraction effect** (**ACE**) is best defined as a systematic form of response bias in which international subjects "report more intense emotions" when answering questions in English, as opposed to when they answer the same questions in their native language. Thus, ACE introduces bias into the data.[13] Given the growing number of multilingual individuals worldwide, the increasingly global focus of the business environment, and the widespread influence of the Internet, this is of serious concern. ACE could artificially inflate product or business ratings in a significant fashion.

People do not always respond to scales in the same manner. Culture can impact the types of responses that are given. For instance, many individuals believe that the Likert scale is universal and easily understood by people of any language and culture. Such is not the case. A Likert scale can yield different results depending on the culture context where it is used. Research has shown that using scales with numbers anchored only by "strongly agree" and "strongly disagree" can yield different results than using verbal words for each point on the scale.[14] The problem is that there is no conclusive evidence on which Likert scale is best because results were highly dependent on the topic being studied. With some topics, the numeric Likert scale performed better, but for other topics the verbal Likert scale was better. It is important for market researchers to carefully compare results across multiple countries since the scale used may impact results. It's possible that differences found may be due to the scale rather than true differences in attitudes or opinions. To avoid this problem, researchers will often use numerical scales that have only anchors at each end. This approach appears to present the least problems in comparing results across cultures.[15]

As an alternative, researchers may benefit from using more semantic differential scales in international research. Semantic differential scales are less prone to response bias, when compared with Likert scales. A study of U.S. and South Korean respondents found no statistically significant differences in extreme responses when the semantic differential was used, while both U.S. and South Korean respondents exhibited greater levels of extreme responses when Likert scales were employed.[16]

Another concern is with Hispanic cultures. In measuring attribute importance and brand performance, Hispanics have a tendency to rate both on the upper, positive side of the scale. With a 5-point scale, nearly all responses are in the 3 to 5 range. With a 10-point scale, almost all responses are in the 6 to 10 range. These ratings tend to be higher than those of the general population. A study by Jeffry Savitz found that on the average Hispanics rate products about 6% higher than non-Hispanics. So comparing Hispanic populations to the general population or non-Hispanic cultures may be interpreted incorrectly. Researchers may see a significant difference, but that difference may be due to a cultural trend of Hispanics to rate more positively, rather than due to an actual difference in evaluation.[17] One approach that can be used with Hispanics to obtain more useful information is to use an unbalanced scale that has more positive points than negative. This will allow for greater discrimination in answers. It does not, however, allow for more accurate comparisons to non-Hispanics.

STATISTICS REVIEW

Working with established scales improves the reliability and validity of the construct being measured. However, it is always a good idea to measure the reliability of the scale being used since the sample respondents and survey conditions vary. The best statistical tool to measure a scale's reliability is Cronbach's alpha.[18]

A survey was developed to examine the source credibility of models used in print advertisements. One of the scales used measured the model's perceived expertise to endorse the product being advertised. A 5-item scale was used. The results of the Cronbach's alpha statistical test are shown in Figure 10.29. The Cronbach's alpha score for the 5-item scale is .837. Typically, Cronbach's alpha reliability scores above .700 are considered good scales.

Figure 10.29   Initial Cronbach Alpha Reliability Measures

Reliability Statistics

Cronbach's Alpha	N of Items
.837	5

Item–Total Statistics

	Scale Mean if Item Deleted	Scale Variance if Item Deleted	Corrected Item-Total Correlation	Cronbach's Alpha if Item Deleted
Source Expertise 1: Experience	14.13	18.447	.753	.770
Source Expertise 2: Qualifications	13.79	19.799	.729	.779
Source Expertise 3: Expert	14.40	21.530	.626	.808
Source Expertise 4: Skills	13.93	24.525	.404	.862
Source Expertise 5: Knowledgeability	13.75	20.687	.697	.789

The fourth column of the bottom table shows the correlation of each question with the overall correlation with the other items. Notice the correlation of the fourth question is only .404, which indicates only about 40% of the time do respondents give the same answer to this question as the others. If the fourth question was deleted from the scale, the overall Cronbach's alpha score would improve to .862. This number is given in the last column of the table. If the Cronbach's alpha reliability test was

(Continued)

(Continued)

run again in SPSS with Question 4 deleted, the Cronbach's alpha score would be .862. This second SPSS analysis with Question 4 deleted is shown in Figure 10.30.

The four items are a reliable measure of the expertise construct. An examination of the last column of the output shows the scale's reliability cannot be improved by dropping any additional questions. The Cronbach's alpha score of .862 shows that approximately 86% of the time, the responses to the four questions are the same indicating the questions are measuring the same construct or dimension.

Figure 10.30   Cronbach Alpha Score With Question 4 Deleted

Reliability Statistics

Cronbach's Alpha	N of Items
.862	4

Item -Total Statistics

	Scale Mean if Item Deleted	Scale Variance if Item Deleted	Corrected Item-Total Correlation	Cronbach's Alpha if Item Deleted
Source Expertise 1: Experience	10.55	13.036	.760	.803
Source Expertise 2: Qualifications	10.22	14.129	.743	.810
Source Expertise 3: Expert	10.83	15.682	.629	.855
Source Expertise 5: Knowledgeability	10.18	14.878	.712	.823

DEALING WITH DATA

Source credibility of models in advertisements consists of five different dimensions. The "Statistics Review" examined one of the dimensions—expertise. The other dimensions are perceived trustworthiness of the model in the ad, attractiveness, similarity, and liking. Trustworthiness involves honesty and dependability. Attractiveness consists of the model's perceived physical beauty, elegance, and sex appeal. Similarity measures if the model is perceived to have similar values, tastes, and preferences as the respondent. Liking refers to the degree to which the model appears friendly, approachable, and likeable to the respondent.

Access the SPPS data file "Chapter 10 Dealing with Data" at www.sagepub.com/clowess. The variables for each of the remaining four source credibility dimensions are provided. Use SPSS to obtain a Cronbach's alpha score for each of the following dimensions: Final Source Trust, Final Source Attractiveness, Final Source Similarity, and Final Source Liking. When you are finished, answer the following questions.

1. What is the Cronbach's alpha score for the "trustworthiness" dimension? Can the scale be improved by deleting a question? If so, which question? Based on this initial printout, what would be the Cronbach's alpha if the item was deleted? Run a new Cronbach's alpha with the item deleted. What was the new Cronbach's alpha score?

2. What is the Cronbach's alpha score for the "attractiveness" dimension? Can the scale be improved by deleting a question? If so, which question? Based on this initial printout, what would be the Cronbach's alpha if the item was deleted? Run a new Cronbach's alpha with the item deleted. What was the new Cronbach's alpha score? Can the reliability measure be improved by dropping a second question? Why or why not?

3. What is the Cronbach's alpha score for the "similarity" dimension? Can the scale be improved by deleting a question? If so, which question? Based on this initial printout, what would be the Cronbach's alpha if the item was deleted?

4. What is the Cronbach's alpha score for the "liking" dimension? Can the scale be improved by deleting a question? If so, which question? Based on this initial printout, what would be the Cronbach's alpha if the item was deleted? Run a new Cronbach's alpha with the item deleted. What was the new Cronbach's alpha score?

SUMMARY

Objective 1: Discuss the concept of attitude measurement.

Measuring consumer attitudes that influence purchase decisions is challenging because it is not visible and only exists in the minds of consumers. Attitude consists of three components: cognitive, affective, and behavioral. The cognitive component represents the belief and knowledge part of attitude. The affective component of attitude is the feelings and emotions. The behavioral component of attitude is the action or intentions aspect of attitude. Because attitude consists of multiple dimensions, is abstract, and is in the minds of consumers, researchers typically develop multi item scales to measure it.

Objective 2: Explain the concept of using scales for attitude measurement.

Scaling is the process of assigning numerical values or properties to subjective or abstract concepts. Scales can be unidimensional or multidimensional. Unidimensional scales measure only one attribute or concept, such as attitude toward an advertisement. Multidimensional scales are designed to measure multiple dimensions or facets of a concept, an idea, or an attitude. Developing good scales is important if a concept is going to be measured with any degree of precision. Scales should be relatively easy for respondents to understand, making it advisable to use language that is used by respondents. Scale items should be developed that produce a wide range of responses yet limit response bias. Lastly, scales need to be valid and reliable. Researchers can use scales that have already been established by prior researchers and that have been validated through proper research methods. Scales can be divided into two primary categories: comparative scales and noncomparative scales.

Objective 3: Identify and describe the various comparative scales.

With comparative scales respondents are asked to evaluate or rate a brand, a product, an object, a concept, or a person relative to other brands, products, objects, concepts, or individuals or to an ideal item. Typical comparative scales include rank-order, Q-sort, paired comparison, and constant sum. Rank-order scales involve respondents comparing two or more objects, concepts, or persons in some type of sequential order. They are relatively easy for respondents and tend to mimic reality. Q-sorting has respondents rank a set of objects into a prespecified number of categories. Q-sorting works well for a large number of items. With a paired comparison scale, respondents are asked to choose one of two items based on some criteria specified by the researcher. The number of comparisons grows quickly since all possible pairs must be evaluated. The constant sum scale has respondents allocating points (often 100) among various alternatives based on some prespecified criteria.

Objective 4: Identify and describe the various noncomparative scales.

Noncomparative scales involve respondents making judgments about a brand, a product, an object, a concept, or a person without reference to another or an ideal item. Common noncomparative scales are graphical rating and itemized rating. Graphical rating scales allow respondents to place a response anywhere on a continuum. It may or may not have numbers. With itemized rating scales, respondents choose from a set of alternatives.

Objective 5: Identify and describe scales that can be either comparative or noncomparative.

The semantic differential, Stapel, and Likert scales can be either comparative or noncomparative depending upon how the question is worded. Semantic differential scales involve a finite number of choices anchored by bipolar words or phrases. Semantic differential scales are easy for respondents to understand. The challenge, however, is choosing words or phrases that are opposites. Stapel scales have only one anchor, and respondents can indicate a negative or positive possession of the trait or characteristic being examined. Likert scales are commonly used in marketing and involve respondents indicating the degree to which they agree or disagree with statements. Likert scales are easy to understand and relatively easy to construct.

Objective 6: Discuss the considerations involved in selecting marketing scales.

Choosing the best scale for a marketing study requires an understanding of the research objective, target market, information needs, and mode of administration. When it comes to actually creating the marketing scale, researchers need to consider the number of category responses, balanced versus unbalanced scales, "no opinion" and "don't know" options, forced versus non-forced choices, and the type of category description. Scales can have as few as 2 choices and as many as 10, or even more. However, typically marketers use from 5-point to 7-point scales. A balanced scale will have the same number of positive choices as negative, while an unbalanced scale will be weighted in one direction. Researchers have to decide if they want to include a "no opinion" or "don't know" option. Allowing respondents to choose this option may encourage them to select it rather than state a view. Using an even number of categories forces individuals to choose either the negative or positive side since no neutral position exists. The last consideration is whether to use verbal descriptors for every category, verbal descriptors at the anchor points only, and/or numeric descriptors for categories. The choice made can influence respondents' answers.

Objective 7: Explain ways researchers can ensure the reliability and validity of scales.

In using scales, researchers have three options: use a scale that has already been developed, adapt a scale that has already been developed, or create a new scale. With the last two options it is important to ensure reliability and validity of the scale. One method of doing this is through a correlation analysis. Items that have a high correlation are measuring the same construct and therefore fit together in a scale. Another option is a factor analysis. This procedure will examine data to determine underlying constructs by reducing a large number of items into smaller subsets of factors. Items that are related will be placed together within the same factor.

GLOSSARY OF KEY TERMS

Anchor contraction effect (ACE): systematic form of response bias in which international subjects report more intense emotions when answering questions in English, as opposed to when they answer the same questions in their native language

Attitudes: relatively enduring predispositions to respond to an object in a consistent fashion

Balanced scale: has the same number of positive response choices as negative choices

Comparative scale: respondents are asked to evaluate or rate a brand, a product, an object, a concept, or a person relative to other brands, products, objects, concepts, or individuals or to an ideal item

Constant sum scale: respondents allocate points among various alternatives so the total sums to a specified amount designated by the researcher

Correlation: the degree to which one variable changes with another

Factor analysis: analysis that reduces a larger number of items into a smaller subset of factors based on similarity

Graphical rating scale: noncomparative scale that allows respondents to place a response anywhere on a continuous line

Halo effect: when respondents have an overall feeling about the topic being surveyed and that overall perception influences their response so that all of the answers are relatively close to the same

Itemized rating scale: respondents choose a response from a select number of items or categories

Likert scale: series of statements to which respondents indicate their level of agreement or disagreement with the statement

Multidimensional scale: measures multiple dimensions or facets of a concept, an idea, or an attitude

Noncomparative scale: respondents make judgments about a brand, a product, an object, a concept, or a person without reference to another item or an ideal item

Paired comparison scale: respondents choose one of two items in a set based on a specific criterion or attribute

Q-sort: comparative technique whereby respondents rank a set of objects into a prespecified number of categories along a particular attribute or criterion

Rank-order scale: respondents compare two or more objects, concepts, or persons by ranking them in some type of ordered sequence

Scaling: process of assigning numerical values or properties to subjective or abstract concepts

Semantic differential scale: involves a finite number of choices anchored by dichotomous words or phrases

Stapel scale: uses only one anchor and both positive and negative options

Unbalanced scale: response categories are weighted toward one of the anchors, either positive or negative

Unidimensional scale: measures only one attribute or concept

CRITICAL THINKING EXERCISES

1. Suppose you worked for a firm that sold products to other businesses over the Internet as well as through an external sales force. What types of attitudes might be important to assess if you surveyed your customers? Identify at least five separate attitudes that would be relevant to your firm.

2. Using the five attitude constructs you developed in response to Question 1, identify whether each attitude would likely be unidimensional or multidimensional. If multidimensional, what dimensions might be part of the overall attitude? Think carefully about the attitude in question as you do so, and justify your recommendations.

3. Critique the following scale in terms of the characteristics of a good scale that were discussed in the chapter. Make certain that you evaluate both the scale item and its response categories. Is a unidimensional scale appropriate to assess the beauty salon? Why or why not?

Please rate Debbie's Beauty Salon using the following scale:

Outstanding	Excellent	Very Good	Good	Fair	Poor	The Worst

4. Compare and contrast rank-order scales with itemized rating scales. What are the advantages and disadvantages of each type of scale relative to one another?

5. Using examples other than those described in the text, identify two specific research scenarios in which a Q-sort could be used. Explain what objects would be sorted and what labels would be assigned to each category. How could the results of the research be used by marketers? Should respondents be allowed to select as many items for each category as they want? Why or why not?

6. You have been asked to develop a scale that assesses the relative importance of factors that influence the purchase of a smartphone. Begin by listing the product attributes or other factors that you believe could be influential. If the choice was between a ranking scale, a paired comparison scale, and a constant sum scale, which would you use and why? If the choice was between an itemized rating scale, a Likert scale, and a semantic differential scale, which would you use and why? Develop the scale type you ultimately would select given all possibilities, and defend your recommendation.

7. A sample of 200 individuals completed a series of paired comparison statements to assess preference for four national fast-food chain restaurants specializing in hamburgers. Interpret the results shown below and present them in a table, using percentages. Then create a graph with the percentages. The number of individuals selecting each restaurant for a paired comparison is shown in parentheses.

(160) Sonic	(40) McDonald's
(84) Wendy's	(116) McDonald's
(94) Sonic	(106) Burger King
(78) Wendy's	(122) Burger King
(134) Sonic	(66) Wendy's
(92) Burger King	(108) McDonald's

8. If a key research objective sought to develop brand image profiles for a local bank and a key competitor, what type of scale should be used? Why? Create a multi-item scale that measures a bank's brand image. Defend the scale category choices you made in terms of number of categories, balanced versus unbalanced scales, "no opinion" and "don't know" options, forced versus nonforced choices, and type of category description.

9. Create a Likert scale or an itemized rating scale to determine student attitudes toward the university bookstore. Defend the scale category choices you made in terms of number of categories, balanced versus unbalanced scales, "no opinion" and "don't know" options, forced versus nonforced choices, and type of category description.

10. Given the relative advantages and disadvantages associated with providing a "don't know" response option, would you recommend its inclusion in a question that asks people who live within a given zip code to rate the effectiveness of the local school board? Why or why not?

CONTINUING CASE STUDY: LAKESIDE GRILL

Rather than develop their own questions to measure the quality of service at Lakeside Grill, the student group wanted to see if there was a scale that had already been established. The students were ecstatic when Brooke found a scale called SERVQUAL, which was developed by Leonard Berry and his associates.[19] After examining the scale, the team chose 12 questions they thought would be good measures of service at Lakeside Grill. The scales measured empathy, reliability, and tangibles. Empathy is the degree to which employees give attention to customers and understand their needs; reliability measures the degree to which Lakeside Grill is responsible and can be depended to perform as promised; and the tangible aspect relates to the degree to which the facilities and employees are visually appealing. The questions are listed in Figure 10.31. The students pretested the scale using college students.

The students used SPSS to run a Cronbach's alpha test for the three scales. Complete results are located at www.sagepub.com/clowess in the PDF file "Chapter 10 Lakeside Grill Output." The raw data are titled "Chapter 10 Lakeside Grill Data." The empathy scale had an initial Cronbach's alpha score of .743. Dropping the fourth question, which dealt with convenient hours, improved the Cronbach's alpha score to .806. The initial Cronbach's alpha score for the tangible scale was .868. The initial score for the reliability scale was .765. The score could not be improved by dropping any questions. So the group decided to keep all of the questions in that scale.

Figure 10.31   Lakeside Grill Pretest Questions

- Employees of Lakeside Grill give you individual attention. (E1)
- Lakeside Grill's facility is visually appealing. (T1)
- Lakeside Grill gets your order right the first time. (R1)
- Employees of Lakeside Grill understand your specific needs. (E2)
- Lakeside Grill insists on error-free customer service. (R2)
- Lakeside Grill's employees are well dressed and appear neat. (T2)
- Lakeside Grill has employees who give you personal attention. (E3)
- Tables and place settings are visually appealing at Lakeside Grill. (T3)
- Lakeside Grill has convenient hours for all of its customers. (E4)
- When Lakeside Grill promises to have food ready by a certain time, it does so. (R3)
- The exterior appearance of Lakeside Grill is attractive and inviting. (T4)
- When you have a problem, Lakeside Grill shows an interest in correcting it. (R4)

Scales ⟶   Empathy (E)
Reliability (R)
Tangibles (T)

Critique Questions:

1. Was the decision to use students to pretest the questions dealing with service quality a good decision? Why or why not?

2. How would you evaluate the Cronbach's alpha scores for each of the three scales? Would you agree with the final decision to drop the question about convenient hours? Why or why not?

3. What are the advantages and disadvantages of using these scales on the group's survey of Lakeside Grill versus the students creating their own questions?

MARKETING RESEARCH PORTFOLIO

The "Marketing Research Portfolio" for Chapter 10 requires that students first download a questionnaire and data set from www.sagepub.com/clowess. Using the questionnaire, students are asked to identify the specific type of comparative and noncomparative scales used in the survey. Next, they are asked to critically evaluate the scales used in the survey against the factors used when selecting a scale. Finally, students use SPSS to run scale reliabilities on the data set, and check to see whether any scale's reliability can be improved by dropping one or more items.

STUDENT STUDY SITE

Visit the Student Study Site at www.sagepub.com/clowess to access the following additional materials:

- eFlashcards
- Web Quizzes
- SAGE Journal Articles
- Web Resources

Questionnaire Design

After reading this chapter, you should be able to

1. Outline the questionnaire design process.

2. Discuss the two primary question formats that can be used in questionnaire design.

3. Elaborate on the three different types of closed-ended questions.

4. Identify and describe the categories of questions used in questionnaires.

5. Discuss the issues relating to the phrasing of questions.

6. Identify and explain the contents of each section of a questionnaire.

7. Describe the negative consequences of long questionnaires and the benefit of using a split-questionnaire design.

8. Discuss the steps in evaluating a questionnaire.

INTRODUCTION

For many, designing the questionnaire is the fun part of marketing research. Creating a good questionnaire produces data that can be used for making smart business decisions. Consider the data obtained from a survey sent to customers and marketing managers shown in Figure 11.1 that compare methods of communication used by companies and those desired by customers.[1] Customers prefer less face-to-face communication and more e-mail communication. They also would like to see greater use of instant messaging, mail, and social media than companies are using. This type of information obtained through questionnaire surveys can be valuable to companies in planning their customer communication strategies.

Figure 11.1   Customer/Company Communications

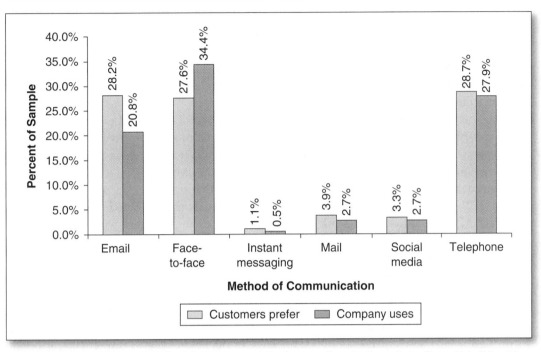

Source: Author-created with data from "Redefining Customer Value," a report from the *Economist Intelligence Unit*, SAS, p. 19.

Some would argue that questionnaire design is really an art—some people are good at it; others are not. This chapter covers some basic principles that if followed will increase the probability that useful information will result from the questionnaire. The chapter begins with a discussion of the questionnaire design process. Next will be an examination of the primary question types that are used in survey questionnaires and the pros and cons of each type. Phrasing of questions is important, so a discussion of some common pitfalls is presented. The chapter concludes with material on how a questionnaire is composed and then how it is evaluated.

THE QUESTIONNAIRE DESIGN PROCESS

- Objective 11.1: Outline the questionnaire design process.

Survey research relies on some type of questionnaire to solicit information from a sample or census of respondents. The **questionnaire** is a set of questions used to generate data that meet specific research and survey objectives. The quality of the data obtained is directly related to the quality of the questionnaire designed. While there is not a perfect format for a questionnaire, there are principles that can enhance the quality of a questionnaire, thereby increasing the usefulness of the data generated. Questionnaires standardize the data collection process and ensure all respondents are asked the same questions in the same manner. This process is especially important for telephone surveys and other situations where the interviewer is reading the question to the respondent.

Figure 11.2 outlines the steps in developing a questionnaire. The process begins with the research questions or objectives. Quite often the research objectives are provided by upper management or a client and given to the marketing department or marketing research firm. It is important to understand the research objectives before designing a questionnaire. It is also imperative to limit the research objectives to a manageable number to ensure that questionnaire length does not negatively impact the response rate. Finally, discussing the decisions that will result from the data obtained through the questionnaire will increase the chances the right data are collected.

The first step in the questionnaire design process is to determine the survey objectives. These survey objectives are derived from the research questions or objectives and clearly spell out the data that the questionnaire should generate. The survey objectives guide the process of selecting types of questions asked and the way questions are worded.

Consider the case of the video game manufacturer that wants to prepare a new product launch for the personal computer (PC). The video game will be distributed on DVD in stores, on Amazon.com, and by other online retailers. However, there is concern within the company that limiting the new product to PC distribution only may be a mistake. Industry trends show a growing preference for online gaming via social network sites, smartphones, tablets, and consoles (such as Nintendo and Xbox). Secondary research confirms that there is cause for concern, as sales of the firm's most recently released product were lower than expected, and the PC gaming market in general is no longer growing. Some individuals believe that this decline may be due to a pirating problem rather than a changing preference for gaming platforms. The decision management faces is whether the game should be released for the PC market only or whether it should be released in multiple platforms suitable for smartphones, tablets, consoles, and online use.[2] With this background information, specific research objectives can be written. These research objectives, shown in Figure 11.3, highlight what the researcher wants to accomplish.

It is tempting to skip directly from the research objectives to writing survey questions. But in doing so, incomplete information is often obtained. Using research objectives as the basis

Figure 11.2   Questionnaire Design Process

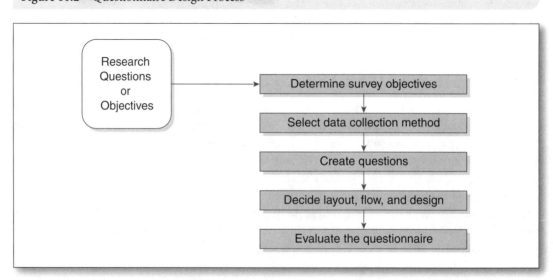

for writing survey objectives ensures that the right questions are asked and that the purpose of the study is achieved. Figure 11.4 identifies survey objectives for each of the research objectives. Notice that for the first research objective, three survey objectives have been written. In order to determine the preference of gamers for the various platforms, it is necessary to (1) solicit the preference for each of the various gaming platforms, (2) determine the usage level of each gaming platform, and (3) identify which gaming platforms gamers most prefer.

Once the survey objectives have been written, the second step in the questionnaire design process is to decide on the data collection methodology. How questionnaires are designed varies

Figure 11.3 Sample Research Objectives

- Determine the preference of gamers for the various gaming platforms (social networks, gaming consoles, PCs, smartphones, and tablets).
- Determine if gamers prefer online games to PC-based games and if there is a preference for games that can be played across multiple platforms.
- Investigate gamers' attitude toward in-game marketing efforts.
- Determine the characteristics of successful in-game promotions.
- Develop profiles of gamers based on demographic, lifestyle, and behavioral traits.

Figure 11.4 Sample Survey Objectives

1. Determine the preference of gamers for the various gaming platforms (social networks, gaming consoles, PCs, smartphones, and tablets).
   - Solicit the preference for each of the various gaming platforms.
   - Determine the usage level of each gaming platform.
   - Identify which gaming platforms gamers most prefer.

2. Determine if gamers prefer online games to PC-based games and if there is a preference for games that can be played across multiple platforms.
   - Determine if gamers prefer online games to PC-based games.
   - Ascertain if gamers want games that can be played across multiple platforms.
   - If so, identify which platforms are the most desirable.

3. Determine gamers' attitude toward in-game marketing efforts.
   - Measure attitudes toward in-game advertisements.
   - Measure attitudes toward in-game promotions.

4. Determine the characteristics of successful in-game promotions.
   - Identify past actions for in-game advertising and promotions.
   - Solicit intention to action for in-game advertising promotions.

5. Develop profiles of gamers based on demographic, lifestyle, and behavioral traits.
   - Identify demographic characteristics of sample.
   - Solicit key lifestyle measures of sample.
   - Measure behavioral traits of sample.

based on how data are collected. Questions for a telephone survey will be written differently than will questions for an online survey or a questionnaire that is handed to a respondent to answer. At times researchers may decide on the data collection method and survey objectives simultaneously because the data collection methodology may impact questionnaire design. For instance, if an online questionnaire is used, then respondents can be shown a product, an advertisement, or other material to evaluate. These types of visuals would not be possible with a telephone survey.

Once the data collection method is determined, researchers are ready to create the survey that will be used to measure the survey objectives. Key considerations include determining the question format, the types of scales to use, and the best way to phrase questions to minimize measurement error.

■ Objective 11.2: Discuss the two primary question formats that can be used in questionnaire design.

QUESTION FORMAT

The primary decision researchers make in terms of question format is whether to use open-ended questions, closed-ended questions, or a combination of both. Recall that Chapter 9 discussed the various levels of measurement: nominal, ordinal, interval, and ratio. The general rule of thumb in deciding question format is that the higher-order scales are better than the lower-order scales because they provide more valuable data and higher forms of data analysis. Thus, if an interval scale can be used, it is better than using an ordinal or a nominal scale.

However, two cautions must be mentioned. First, while ratio-level data may meet the survey objective, a lower-order scale may capture the data in a way that is more usable by the decision maker and may even be more accurate. For example, respondents in a survey about Super Bowl ads were asked what they thought a 30-second television ad cost. A blank was provided for their response. The question yielded ratio data with answers ranging from $10,000 to $50 million. What to do with the data is problematic because of these extreme answers. Neither extreme is close to the actual cost of $3.5 million to $4.0 million. It may be better to use an ordinal scale that has categories that the person checks.

A second caution deals with a respondent's ability and willingness to provide information, especially in relationship to sensitive questions. Requesting the specific dollar amount of a person's household income is very likely to result in a large number of nonresponses. Using an ordinal question with response categories increases the probability the respondent will respond. Also, there may be an inability to accurately recall information, such as when a person is asked how many soft drinks were purchased during the last 30 days. The respondent may not really know if it was 20 or 22 or 27 or 30. A category that says 20 to 30 may be just as accurate and result in more people answering the question. It is best to limit questions requesting ratio data— actual amounts—to instances in which knowing the specific number is of critical importance to accomplishing the survey objectives.

Chapter 10 provided information about the various scales, including rank-order, constant sum, Likert, and semantic differential. In examining the survey objective, a researcher must decide which type of scale would best capture the data needed. In almost all cases, more than one type of scale can be used. Consider the survey objective in Figure 11.4 that states, "Solicit the preference for each of the various gaming platforms." This objective could be measured using a semantic differential scale or a Likert scale. Although the data quality may not be as strong, graphical rating or itemized rating scales could also be used. In deciding the appropriate scale, the researcher will want to consider the target audience. Which scale would be the easiest for the respondent to use and yet obtain the most accurate responses? The researcher will also want to consider the data collection method. For instance, a graphical rating scale would not be possible with a telephone survey while a semantic differential would be difficult and time-consuming to administer over the phone. The Likert scale may be easier for respondents to answer in a phone survey and also easier for the interviewer to administer.

Open-Ended Questions

Open-ended questions allow respondents to answer in their own words. The questions can be simple, such as "What is your favorite brand of shampoo?" or "In a typical month how many times do you go out to a nightclub?" both of which would be followed by an answer blank. Open-ended questions of this type are also valuable in soliciting recall information when researchers do not want to bias an answer by listing alternative choices. Open-ended questions are used in survey pretests to help identify possible response category options when the researcher is unable to anticipate the range of responses that may exist.

However, open-ended questions can also be phrased in a more challenging and thought-provoking fashion and, as such, require detailed answers. Examples include "Describe the decision-making process you used to purchase your vehicle" or "How do you feel about the use of advertising to children?" Questions of this nature are far less suited to survey research than are those that simply require the respondent to input a number or to list one or more brand names.

Open-ended questions requiring detailed answers are best used for exploratory research when researchers want a better understanding of a problem or are seeking information to develop hypotheses. Regrettably, when incorporated into questionnaires, such questions are rarely successful in practice.[3] Figure 11.5 identifies the major advantages and disadvantages of open-ended questions.

Advantages of Open-Ended Questions

A major advantage of open-ended questions is that the answers are in the respondents' own words. They use their own language and terms, which may be different from terminology used by the marketing researcher. Open-ended answers can provide researchers with information about the thought processes behind decisions and attitudes and often provide new or different insights. Sometimes researchers go into a research study with biased views, or feel they already know what people think and want based on past research studies. Open-ended questions may yield new information that taps into attitudinal changes among the target market, or provide a new way of looking at a situation that researchers never considered.

Figure 11.5 Advantages and Disadvantages of Open-Ended Questions

- Advantages
  - Answer is in respondent's own words
  - Can provide new or different insight
  - Can provide additional alternatives
  - Allows for probing
- Disadvantages
  - Can be difficult to interpret answer
  - Editing and coding can be challenging
  - Potential for interviewer bias
  - Answer may be shallow and insufficient
  - Lower response rates

Open-ended questions can provide additional alternatives. For instance, in looking at factors consumers may consider in the purchase of resort vacation packages, an open-ended question may produce additional alternatives researchers had not identified. These can then be used later in a closed-ended question if desired. Finally, open-ended questions allow the researcher to probe and understand why people responded in a certain fashion. For example, a closed-ended question on a survey may ask respondents to identify their preferred retail store for purchasing formal wear. An open-ended question may then ask the individuals to explain why that store is their favorite. The responses may be helpful in identifying the store's competitive advantage, as perceived by customers.

Disadvantages of Open-Ended Questions

Open-ended questions have a number of disadvantages. Major problems involve the difficulty researchers have interpreting, editing, and coding answers. Suppose a survey placed in consumers' shopping bags asked, "How was your shopping experience at [name of retail store] today?" Three responses may be:

"It was a hassle."

"It was slightly better than last week."

"It would have been great if my son hadn't gotten sick."

The first response is negative, but nonspecific. There is no additional information to help the researcher understand what the respondent meant by "hassle." The second statement is also problematic to interpret and code. The researcher would need to understand the respondent's frame of reference. If last's week shopping experience was terrible, "slightly better" is by no means a positive endorsement. Lastly, the final statement also presents difficulties because the response is phrased in a conditional fashion. It would be incorrect to label this as a positive shopping experience as "would have been great if" implies that the shopping experience, in fact, was *not* great, though the circumstances that made for a negative experience were external to anything under the control of the store.

This process of reading, interpreting, and coding responses normally involves a considerable amount of time, which makes the process expensive. The time, the expense, and the questionable value of the resulting data provide strong incentives to avoid open-ended questions of an exploratory nature in most survey research.[4]

Open-ended questions pose the risk of interviewer bias. Although interviewers are trained to reduce the chances of interview bias occurring, the possibility increases when open-ended questions are used. If the interviewer is recording answers given verbally from a respondent, the way the answers are recorded is important. Ideally, answers should be verbatim. But, often the respondent talks too fast and says too much for the researcher to record every word. Therefore, the general idea of what is said is recorded. But in so doing, the response may be biased by the perceptions of the interviewer and what he or she perceived the respondent said or meant by the response.

A second way interviewer bias occurs is with the use of probing questions. While probing questions are normally written in advance, there are situations where the researcher must ask respondents to clarify a response, or probe deeper to ensure the response is understood correctly.

The manner and tone of voice that are used can influence the response given in a manner similar to that which occurs when the original questions are asked verbally by the researcher.

The last disadvantage occurs when an interviewer is not present. As demonstrated earlier by the retail shopping survey situation, the answer to open-ended questions in a self-administered survey may be shallow or insufficient. Without an interviewer, there is no opportunity to ask for clarification or additional information. The response may be a short one-sentence statement when the researcher was looking for a paragraph explaining the respondent's thinking process. To minimize this problem, the researcher can provide clear instructions in the question. A phrase such as "Please provide a detailed answer" can be used. Alternatively, instructions may ask that the response be "50 or more words."

Before including open-ended questions in a survey, researchers should consider how the data will be analyzed and used. It is possible that one or more closed-ended questions can obtain the same information. However, if open-ended questions are used, then interviewers must have the training, experience, and motivation to elicit high-quality data from the responses provided.[5]

Closed-Ended Questions

The disadvantages of open-ended questions can largely be overcome by using closed-ended questions. With **closed-ended questions** respondents are given a finite number of responses from which to choose. The respondent can be asked to choose one response from the alternatives list or all of the alternatives in the list that apply. Figure 11.6 lists the advantages and disadvantages of using closed-ended questions.

Advantages of Closed-Ended Questions

Coding and entering the data into a spreadsheet are easier and more accurate for closed-ended questions, as the respondent's answer is limited to response options listed by the researcher. Each question has a specific set of response choices. A question may have four response choices and so can be coded 1 through 4. If the survey is taken on a computer, the response is automatically entered into a spreadsheet, saving a great deal of time, and preventing possible process errors.

For paper surveys, a data coder must first physically write the number associated with each survey item's answer on the survey itself, then transcribe the data into a spreadsheet. Errors can

Figure 11.6   Advantages and Disadvantages of Closed-Ended Questions

- Advantages
  - Easy and accurate data coding and entry
  - Limited number of responses
  - Alternative list may help respondent recall
  - Limited interviewer bias
- Disadvantages
  - Researchers must generate alternatives
  - Respondents must select from given alternatives
  - No freedom for respondent in answer

occur in one of three ways. First, the person coding the paper survey may write down the wrong number, perhaps writing 1 for a male respondent when in fact males should be coded as 2. Second, the respondent may mark his or her response in such a way that it is unclear which answer was checked. The line or X may be between answers or cover two different responses, and the coder may arbitrarily choose one or the other as the answer. Establishing rules that clearly tell the coder what to do in these cases is essential if measurement error is to be avoided. The adage "When in doubt, throw it out" often applies. Finally, process error may occur when the individual inaccurately transcribes the data by entering a number different from the true answer. As mentioned in Chapter 6, double data entry and frequency tables can help to identify these errors.

Another advantage is that responses to a closed-ended question may jog a respondent's memory and generate a more accurate response. For instance, with the gaming study mentioned earlier, a question may ask respondents to identify each of the platforms on which they have played games. A respondent may have forgotten she played a game at a social network site she often visits until she saw the response category in the question. Similarly, respondents may recognize brand names from a list that they would be unable to recall from memory.

Interviewer bias is greatly reduced with closed-ended questions since the respondent selects from a list of possible responses. Interviewer bias can only occur when questions and responses are read verbally to respondents, and when interviewers or researchers code an "other" fill-in-the-blank response to a question. In the first situation, tone of voice and body language can influence which answer the respondent selects. In the second situation, coding of other responses should be left to the researcher, rather than assigned to the individual interviewers.

The researcher is best able to decide whether to add a new category based on the "other" response, pool all of the "other" responses into a single category called "other," or recode the item into an existing category that matches closely. Interviewer bias can occur due to the subjective nature of interpretation. Pooling all "other" responses into a category called "other" eliminates interviewer bias in how the response is handled, and when performed consistently by a single person, recoding responses into new categories minimizes interviewer bias. Recoding the "other" response into an existing category will certainly produce a greater level of interviewer bias since it involves interpretation.

Disadvantages of Closed-Ended Questions

Closed-ended questions have three primary disadvantages. First, researchers must generate the list of alternative answers for the question. The ideal list of response categories is mutually exclusive and collectively exhaustive. Recall from Chapter 9 that mutually exclusive means that each response category is uniquely different from the other response categories and that no overlap occurs between any of the categories. If responses are collectively exhaustive, then the categories listed for a question contain all possible answers. Having mutually exclusive response categories is easier to achieve than having a list that is collectively exhaustive.

Suppose a researcher has the question "What brand of jeans did you last purchase?" followed by a series of brands. While the list of brand names would be mutually exclusive, it would be virtually impossible to list all of the various brands. If such a list could be created, it would be so long that respondents would be challenged to find the brand they last purchased, and seeing a large number of brands may even cloud their memory in terms of which brand was really purchased. Researchers can overcome this problem by listing the major brands followed by an "other" category with a fill-in-the-blank for brands not shown on the list.

A second disadvantage is that respondents are restricted to the answers given, especially if an "other" category is not available. In such cases respondents have to either choose the item from the list that is most closely associated with their response or not answer the question at all. Either response produces inaccurate data. This disadvantage can be particularly troublesome when researchers do not have a "don't know" option for questions related to topics that respondents legitimately may know nothing about. Forcing them to select an answer introduces substantial error into the data by mixing the opinions of those who truly are knowledgeable with the opinions of those who should not even be answering the question.

Suppose "What is the most important factor in purchasing textbooks for your classes?" was asked as a closed-ended question. Perhaps the primary factor for a particular student is whether her friend is in the same class. If she is, then the two of them purchase one book and share it. If that response is not available from the list provided, the student will either have to choose one of the other answers or just leave it blank. The drawback of closed-ended questions is that respondents have no freedom in how they answer the question. They must select from the list of alternatives.

TYPES OF CLOSED-ENDED QUESTIONS

Closed-ended questions can be dichotomous, multiple-choice, or scaled-response. The researcher should choose the type that best fits the survey objectives to yield the results needed and at the same time provide the highest-quality data.

■ Objective 11.3:
Elaborate
on the three
different types
of closed-ended
questions.

Dichotomous Questions

A **dichotomous question** is a closed-ended question with two response options. Figure 11.7 shows four different dichotomous questions. Each has two response choices. Because each question has only two alternatives, it can be answered easily and quickly by respondents. Coding and entering the data into a spreadsheet for analysis is straightforward.

The first two questions are clear and easy to answer. The respondents are either female or male, and either they have played a video game on a smartphone or they have not. But, the last two questions illustrate some of the problems with dichotomous questions. The third question is clear and straightforward in terms of yes, they like playing games on their smartphone, or no, they do not. However, having respondents reply yes or no does not provide insight about intensity. The individuals may be ambivalent about playing games on a smartphone. Or they may have never played a game on their smartphone, and thus have no knowledge of whether

Figure 11.7   Examples of Dichotomous Questions

1. What is your gender?   ☐ Female   ☐ Male
2. Have you played video games on your smartphone?   ☐ Yes   ☐ No
3. Do you like playing video games on your smartphone?   ☐ Yes   ☐ No
4. Which platform do you prefer for playing video games?   ☐ Online   ☐ Computer

or not they like doing so. The dichotomous option does not allow for a neutral position. More importantly, some individuals may have strong positive feelings about it while others have rather weak positive feelings. The simple yes or no response option does not allow respondents to indicate this intensity. The same criticism is true for the last question. Some may have only a slight preference for one of the options while someone else may feel more strongly. Scaled-response questions would elicit more useful data.

Multiple-Choice Questions

With **multiple-choice questions** individuals have multiple (three or more) answers from which to choose. Figure 11.8 shows two possible multiple-choice questions. In the first question, individuals are to choose one of the platforms listed. The responses appear to be mutually exclusive and collectively exhaustive. A response would clearly indicate which platform the individual prefers. But, it would not provide any measurement of the degree of intensity. Individuals who prefer games at online websites may differ greatly in how strongly they feel about that preference. Some may have only a slight preference over the other alternative platforms while others may have a strong preference. Multiple-choice questions are often used for demographic or other classification variables, but may not be the best choice for preference.

The second question is actually a better multiple-choice question, and is often referred to as a **multiple-response question,** in which respondents are instructed to check all response options—in this case games—that apply. The response options are mutually exclusive and collectively exhaustive, and each response option is treated as a separate variable in the spreadsheet. Not only is the question easy for individuals to answer, but the results can be quickly tabulated.

An additional challenge faced by researchers when generating response categories is the length of the list or number of items listed. If the list is too long, a respondent may not take the time to look at all of the responses and may just check the first one that applies. This phenomenon is known as **position bias.** Asking individuals to identify the best brand in a list of 30 brands is likely to produce position bias. So would a question that asks respondents to check all of the reasons why they chose to do cosmetic surgery from among 15 different choices. One way to alleviate position bias is to randomize the list of responses by creating different versions of the questionnaire. This can be done easily with online surveys. It is more difficult with paper surveys since multiple copies would have to be printed.

Figure 11.8   Examples of Multiple-Choice Questions

1. Of the following platforms for video games, which do you most prefer?

   ☐ Online website
   ☐ Social network sites
   ☐ Gaming console
   ☐ Computer
   ☐ Smartphone or tablet

2. Of the following gaming platforms, which ones have you used to play video games? (Check all that apply)

   ☐ Online website
   ☐ Social network sites
   ☐ Gaming console
   ☐ Computer
   ☐ Smartphone or tablet

Scaled-Response Questions

To capture the intensity of response, researchers will often use **scaled-response questions.** Figure 11.9

is an itemized rating scale assessing the likelihood of using different gaming platforms, with response categories ranging from "highly unlikely" to "highly likely." By using a 7-point scale, researchers can solicit the degree of intensity, or likelihood of usage that each respondent has toward a particular gaming platform. In addition, the question should yield interval data that can be analyzed using more powerful statistical tests. Rather than just frequency counts, means and standard deviations can be obtained. The means can be compared across the different gaming platforms or based on other factors, such as the respondent's demographics.

Figure 11.9 Example of a Scaled-Response Question

For each of the following gaming platforms, please indicate how likely you would be to use it, ranging from "highly unlikely" to "highly likely."

	highly unlikely	unlikely	somewhat unlikely	neutral	somewhat likely	likely	highly likely
Online website	○	○	○	○	○	○	○
Social network site	○	○	○	○	○	○	○
Gaming console	○	○	○	○	○	○	○
Computer	○	○	○	○	○	○	○
Smartphone or tablet	○	○	○	○	○	○	○

In terms of drawbacks, the scaled-response question takes more time for individuals to answer. It requires thought. They can't just check a box or boxes. With the question shown in Figure 11.9, individuals must think about each platform and the degree to which they are likely to use it. The answer may be clear for some of the platforms, but for others it may not be easy to decide.

The number of categories provided influences responses. If the scale in Figure 11.9 had been designed with only five categories instead of seven, respondents would likely have found it to be more difficult to decide between responses. The elimination of the "somewhat likely/somewhat unlikely" option forces respondents to choose "likely" or "unlikely" if they have even the slightest leaning toward either direction. Individuals may mark the "likely" category for online websites on a 5-point scale. But, in their mind they may feel that they are slightly more likely to use social network sites, but not to the degree that they are comfortable selecting the "highly likely" answer. From the researcher's perspective if both answers are marked "likely," the researcher would assume there is equal preference for the two platforms. In reality, such may not be the case. Increasing the number of scale points from 5 to 7 can help determine finer distinctions in attitudinal differences, as it would allow the respondent in this example to choose "somewhat likely" for online websites, and "likely" for social networks.

■ Objective 11.4:
Identify and
describe the
categories
of questions
used in
questionnaires.

QUESTIONNAIRE DEVELOPMENT

In developing the questionnaire, it is helpful to think about the various categories of questions that can be used. Figure 11.10 identifies the six most common categories used in marketing research.[6] It is not critical to have questions from each category, but the categories can serve as a guide to determining the best way to word questions. The categories can also be beneficial in ensuring questions are asked in such a way that they will provide the information management needs to make the decision being faced.

Figure 11.10   Categories of Questions Used in Questionnaire Development

- Demographic or classification
- Knowledge
- Attitudes
- Preferences
- Intentions
- Behaviors

Source: Author-created from David M. Ambrose and John R. Anstey, "Questionnaire Development: Demystifying the Process," *International Management Review*, Vol. 6, No. 1 (2010), pp. 83–90.

Demographic or Classification

Practically all questionnaires will ask for respondent demographic information, such as gender, age, income, race, and education. The respondent just checks the appropriate category. In addition, questionnaires will often contain classification-type questions that apply to a situation. It might be a question relating to the last brand of hiking boots purchased, the store where it was purchased, or when it was purchased.

Demographic and classification questions are often used at the beginning of a questionnaire as screening questions. For instance, a question may ask if an individual has purchased an automobile within the last year. If the person has, the survey continues. If not, it is terminated since the survey deals with the purchase process. Researchers may also want to fill certain demographic quotas such as 300 males, 200 individuals ages 20–29, and so forth. When the quota of 300 males or 200 individuals ages 20–29 has been reached, then anyone falling into that category is terminated and not allowed to complete the questionnaire. When demographic questions do not function as screening questions, they are placed at the end of the survey.

Classification and demographic questions typically utilize nominal or ordinal scales. As such, the appropriate descriptive statistic would be a frequency count, and data may be presented in tables or charts that display percentages. Mode may also be of importance for nominal questions, and median may be used with questions that collect ordinal data. Researchers are limited in the data analyses they can do with demographic and classification questions. While they are needed in surveys, it is important to realize they produce lower-order data.

Knowledge

At times it is beneficial to assess the knowledge consumers may have of a topic. At the basic level would be a measure of awareness and recognition. Do consumers know the brand exists? Do they recognize the brand or logo? More in-depth knowledge can be measured to see what consumers know about a particular brand and if that knowledge is correct.

Knowledge measures can be used in advertising to measure recall of ads and comprehension of ad content. It is not uncommon for individuals to recall seeing an advertisement for vehicles while watching television but mistakenly say it was a Toyota ad when it was actually for Nissan. In addition to recall, advertisers want to see if the ad content was comprehended. Did they get the message, or did they focus on a peripheral cue such as the ad model instead? Knowledge-based questions typically provide nominal or ordinal data, though questions assessing the degree to which a respondent is knowledgeable about a topic will use a scaled-response format providing interval data.

Attitudes

Questionnaires are often used to measure feelings and attitudes. In fact, a study could be focused entirely on measuring attitude. It can be attitudes toward a product category, specific brands, attributes of a brand, or the purchase process. It might include the service component and the interaction with the company whether in person or online. Attitudes are important because attitude formation typically precedes behavior. Before consumers purchase a particular brand, they will develop a positive attitude toward it.

With attitude measures, level of intensity is important; therefore, using some type of scaled-response question works best. It might be a series of Likert statements in which respondents can indicate their level of agreement or disagreement. It might be a semantic differential that uses bipolar adjectives. It could even be a graphical scale. Whichever scale is used, it is important that the respondent is able to indicate a level of attitude beyond yes and no.

Most attitudinal measures will yield interval-type data. Since it is one of the higher-order scales, it allows researchers to obtain means and standard deviations. It allows for comparisons across other variables through higher-order data analysis techniques. A researcher can see if the respondents' demographics have an impact on how they feel about a particular brand of snow skis or advertising of Nabisco products.

Preferences

When measuring attitudes toward various brands, consumers may provide similar ratings on a 5-point or 7-point scale for multiple brands. It may then be difficult to determine for which brands consumers have the strongest feelings. To gather this information, surveys can include preference questions. It can be done by asking which brand is preferred from among a list of brands. Alternatively, individuals may be asked to rank various brands from most preferred to least preferred. Finally, the intensity of preference may be assessed via an itemized scaled-response question. The best method used to measure preference is impacted by the information needs of management, the target audience of the survey, and the type of preferences that are being requested.

The target audience of a survey influences the best way to measure a consumer's preferences.

If managers want to see where their brand falls among the primary competitors, then a ranking type of survey question may work the best as long as the number of brands in the list is relatively small. When the list becomes long, then asking individuals to rank them becomes problematic. Ranking 3 to 5 brands is easy; ranking 12 to 15 brands is virtually impossible. In the latter case, it might be best to ask from the list of 12 to 15 brands which 3 or 4 brands the respondents most prefer, or even just ask them to indicate their top and second choice. Itemized scaled-response questions can be used in situations in which understanding the intensity of brand preference is of primary importance, or in instances when researchers want to know whether preferences differ significantly among demographic groupings or by some classification variable.

Intentions

Researchers will often want to know consumer intentions. Will they purchase a particular brand in the future? It can be asked as a dichotomous question—yes or no. While helpful, it might be better to ask it using some type of scale that has 4 or 5 points ranging from "not at all likely" to "will definitely purchase." The scaled-response question provides higher-order data and indicates the degree of purchase intentions.

Past research has indicated a significant difference between purchase intentions and actual purchase behavior. The percentage of respondents who indicate intentions to purchase a product at the end of a survey is always higher than the percent who actually make a purchase. While intentions may be good, a number of extraneous variables can affect the final decision, such as promotions by other brands, advertising, product placement in the store, and even consumer moods.

Behaviors

Behavioral questions are important in surveys since the ultimate goal of marketing is to sell products. While it is important to measure knowledge and even attitudes toward ads and brands, did it result in a purchase? Asking people when, where, and how they purchased products seems to be fairly straightforward. Unfortunately, it is not because of the limited ability of humans to accurately recall past behaviors.

If consumers were asked what brand of dish detergent they last purchased, the brand-loyal consumer who always purchases the same brand would be able to recall the information accurately. But, the price-sensitive and the promotion-sensitive consumer who purchases different brands may not remember which brand was purchased last. If given a list of brands, individuals may choose a brand they know they have purchased in the past. It may not necessarily be the last one purchased or even the one they purchase most often. But, if researchers ask about the purchase of a high-ticket item such as an automobile, a computer, or furniture, purchase knowledge will tend to be more accurate. As the price and social visibility of a product increase, so does the ability to accurately recall purchase information. Also, the shorter the time period involved, the greater the chance that the individual will recall the answer accurately.

In addition to purchase behavior, researchers may want to examine other behaviors such as media consumption, store patronage, and word-of-mouth engagement. In determining how to spend advertising dollars, it is important to know what media individuals use and how much time they spend with each. Even information about the television shows watched and websites accessed is important. Store patronage is important to retail outlets, but it is also important to manufacturers. They will want to place their brands in stores that are patronized by shoppers that fit their target market. With the rise of the Internet, understanding how consumers communicate brand information has become more important. Where do they post information—good or bad? Do they read product reviews before making a purchase decision? If so, where do they read these?

QUESTION PHRASING

■ Objective 11.5: Discuss the issues relating to the phrasing of questions.

Writing the actual questions is one of the most challenging aspects of creating a survey. Good questions will yield useful data that can be analyzed and interpreted to provide beneficial information for management decisions. Poor questions will not only produce poor data, but may lead to poor decisions that cost a company thousands or millions of dollars. Good survey questions are those in which the respondent is both able and willing to answer truthfully. Properly phrased questions will be (1) clear, (2) concise, (3) understandable to the respondent, and (4) written in such a way that the respondent's answer is not biased. A well-phrased questionnaire will maintain the interest and cooperation of respondents. Figure 11.11 provides some suggestions for writing good questions.

Ambiguity, Jargon, and Clarity

Ambiguity in survey questions is a frequent problem. The researcher knows what the question is asking, but sometimes it is not clear to the respondent. Consider the following question, which appeared on a retail sale's gun application form: "Are you a nonimmigrant alien?" Despite appearances, the question is not asking about the applicant's planetary status but rather refers to foreigners traveling or studying in the United States who retain a residence in another country.

It is easy to slip jargon or language into a question that the researcher understands but the respondent does not. Marketing terms such as *cognitive dissonance, attribute evaluation, evoked set,* and *information search* are understood by marketing experts, but may not be understood by the individual who is taking the survey.

Certain words may not be clear, because they are interpreted differently by respondents. "Where did you eat dinner last night?" may seem fairly straightforward. Yet the word *dinner* is problematic, because in the South "dinner" often refers to the noon meal while Northerners consider "dinner" to be the evening meal. It is also critical that researchers write questions in a

Figure 11.11   Suggestions for Writing Good Questions

- Questions should be clearly written, free of jargon and ambiguity
- Questions should be applicable to respondents
- Questions should use vocabulary of respondents
- Questions should be in conversational style
- Questionnaire should have logical flow
- Scales should be easy to understand and use
- Understand limitations of human memory
- Avoid using either/or questions
- Questions should not be double-barreled
- Questions should not be leading

way that ensures different respondents will respond by using the same frame of reference. The question "What is your annual income?" could be interpreted from multiple frames of reference. Does "your" mean you, personally, or your household? What type of money should be included in calculations of income? Is it salary only, or should money earned from investments, property management, oil/natural gas leases, gifts, grants, loans, child support, or welfare be included? To be able to make meaningful classifications on the basis of income, the question must be phrased in a manner such that respondents understand exactly what does and does not constitute income.

Words such as *often, some, occasionally,* or *usually* are also ambiguous and likely to be interpreted differently among respondents. Failing to account for differing interpretations of words, or the potential for questions being answered from multiple frames of reference, will result in substantial measurement error and detract from the quality of data.

Because the person writing the question knows what information is being sought, ambiguity and the potential for interpretational differences may not be recognized. To ensure questions are clear and free of jargon and ambiguity, and that they are interpreted properly by respondents, researchers can do three things. First, they can leave the questionnaire for a couple of days, then come back to it. Ambiguity that was present when the question was written may be evident at a later time. Second, the questionnaire can be given to other individuals who do not have the marketing background to see if the questions make sense and how they interpret what is being asked. Third, the questionnaire can be administered to a few individuals who fit the profile of the survey's target audience. Pretesting of this nature also involves a debriefing session where the participants point out ambiguous wording, or explain how they interpreted certain questions.

Substantial measurement error can also be avoided by making certain that the questions asked are applicable to the respondent. Qualifying questions such as "Are you the primary individual responsible for grocery shopping?" can be used to skip respondents who are not the primary grocery shopper. Measurement error often occurs when respondents don't really know the answer to a question, but answer it anyway. Providing a "don't know" response category can minimize this form of error. Questions such as "How frequently do you consume energy drinks?" assumes that the respondent does in fact drink energy drinks. To accommodate this assumption, one of the response categories should be "Do not drink energy drinks."

Vocabulary and Scales

It is important to use the vocabulary of the respondents, not the vocabulary of the individual writing the questions. Usually the individuals involved in questionnaire design have a college degree, and many will have postgraduate degrees. The respondents for the survey may have only a high school education. In addition to using the vocabulary of the target audience, it is helpful to write the questions in conversational style as people would talk. This makes it much easier for them to understand what is being asked. This is especially true for telephone or personal surveys where the questions are being read to the respondent by the interviewer. But, even for self-administered questionnaires, conversation-style wording is advised.

The questionnaire should have a logical flow that makes sense to the respondent and that provides the information that is needed without biasing responses. Asking individuals a recall question, such as the last brand of toothpaste purchased, should precede a recognition question that may list various brands of toothpaste. More information about questionnaire layout and flow is given in a following section.

If scales are used, they should be easy to understand. It is important to use descriptors that fit with the subject matter and are relevant to the target audience. For instance, if you want to ask individuals how they feel about advertisements shown during the Super Bowl, *like* and *dislike* would be better descriptors to use than *good* and *bad* or *satisfied* and *dissatisfied* since most people if asked verbally about how they felt would reply with various degrees of like or dislike such as "I really liked them."

Consistency in using scales can aid in obtaining good data. This means using similar scales, similar formats, and similar arrangements. If a semantic differential scale is being used, switching to paired comparison, then to a Stapel scale, may be confusing. However, using a Likert scale with semantic differential is an easier transition. It is helpful if formats are similar. If a 7-point scale is used

When writing survey questions, it is important to use the vocabulary of the target audience.

on the first semantic differential, it makes it easier if other scales use a 7-point format. Switching from 7-point to 5-point to 3-point may be confusing to some of the respondents. Also, if some scales have an even number of points and others have an odd number of points, it can make the questionnaire more difficult for respondents. Lastly, the arrangement of the scales should be consistent because individuals become quickly accustomed to a particular format. If one set of questions has "strongly agree" on the left and "strongly disagree" on the right, but the next set has the scale reversed, individuals may never notice the change and answer an entire sequence of questions incorrectly. The more consistency that is present among the various scales, the easier it is for the respondent to answer the questions, and the greater the probability that good data are obtained.

Limitations of Human Memory and Either/Or Questions

It is important to understand the limitations of human memory. While measures of human behavior are important, researchers must understand the limitations of memory and word questions that will yield useful data, not just a guess. As stated earlier, individuals' recall of information is not always accurate, especially with low-cost items or matters that are not very important to them. Asking a respondent to indicate how many tubes of toothpaste were purchased in the previous year is a useless question—the respondent won't be able to accurately recall the answer. While unusual events, such as purchasing carpet, are more memorable, a different memory error occurs as individuals typically remember events as happening more recently than they actually did. The best way to avoid memory errors is to keep the recall period short. For example, a panel used to track information related to restaurant dining first asks respondents to indicate what day of the week they are answering the survey, then frames all questions regarding their restaurant dining behavior in terms of the previous day.

Beware of using either/or questions. While they seem a good way to obtain comparative information, they are not. For instance, asking respondents if they prefer coffee black or with cream and sugar seems straightforward. But, suppose they don't like it either way. Maybe they like to put honey in their coffee or want cream but not sugar. An either/or question eliminates other possibilities and forces respondents to choose from the two alternatives when an optimal answer may be something else. The only place an either/or question is assured to work well is with the paired comparison scale where every possible combination of pairs is evaluated.

Double-Barreled and Leading Questions

In a **double-barreled question,** respondents are asked two questions in one. For instance, they may be asked to indicate their level of agreement or disagreement with the statement "The prices at Walmart are reasonable and provide shoppers with a good value." The respondent may feel prices are reasonable but not a good value, or vice versa. Although researchers and most people may associate the two concepts, they should never be placed together in the same question. It forces respondents to accept both or neither.

Another problem that can occur is **leading questions** where the survey question leads the respondent to the desired answer. A questionnaire may ask, "Because of the harmful impact of secondhand cigarette smoke, are you in favor of banning smoking on our college campus?" The wording of this question is leading to an affirmative answer by pointing out that secondhand cigarette smoke is harmful. Another leading question is one that appeared as a Likert statement on green marketing. It stated, "Consumers are switching to brands that use biodegradable packaging because of the large amount of plastics now filling our landfills." Respondents were to indicate their level of agreement or disagreement on a 7-point scale. While the statement does not specifically say the plastics are not biodegradable, it is implied, and further it is implied that our landfills are full of plastic that is not degradable.

■ Objective 11.6: Identify and explain the contents of each section of a questionnaire.

QUESTIONNAIRE LAYOUT

Figure 11.12 identifies the primary sections of a questionnaire and the typical order in which the sections appear. For more complex surveys or questionnaires dealing with potentially sensitive information, the screening questions may precede the instructions. This allows for the exclusion of individuals who do not meet the survey participant criteria before time is spent on providing instructions.

Figure 11.12   Questionnaire Layout

- Instructions
- Screening questions
- Survey questions
- Demographic information
- Closing

Instructions

Clear instructions are essential! Respondents need to know before starting the survey what they will be doing and what is expected of them. In today's busy world, most questionnaires provide an estimate of how long it will take to complete the questionnaire. It is helpful in the instructions to provide information on who is collecting the data, why it is being collected, how it will be used, and who to contact for more information. While complete information may not be given to prevent biasing the responses, sufficient information should be provided so the respondent feels comfortable answering the questions. This becomes especially important if respondents are being asked personal and/or potentially sensitive questions. However, the less detail that is given regarding the topic of the survey, the better, since it is important that respondents not reply based on interests. If only those interested in a topic complete the survey, then it will provide biased results. What often occurs in these situations is that those who really like a topic or brand respond, as do those who have strong negative feelings. So the data are bipolar with the two extreme views, and as such may not adequately represent the population.

Instructions should include any information about incentives that are being offered. When the universe of potential respondents is large enough, incentives do not need to be used. If incentives are needed to motivate respondents to participate, realistic options are the best. A 1-in-10 chance of winning $25 cash or a prize equivalent is a better motivator than a chance to win $10,000. If incentives are used, researchers need to be careful that the incentive does not encourage people to lie or provide bogus answers in order to receive the incentive.[7] In self-administered surveys, the initial instructions should also indicate the date and method by which the survey should be returned.

Screening Questions

Not everyone in the universe is a candidate for a particular questionnaire. Before administering the questionnaire, the target audience for the survey needs to be identified along with the purpose of the research. This information allows researchers to developing screening questions to determine if someone fits the profile needed. For instance, a company that manufactures lawn equipment wants to survey individuals who purchase and use lawn equipment. It is not always the same person, and individuals' insights can be quite different. Thus, the screening question may involve asking if the individuals mow and trim their own lawn. Another question may ask if they have purchased lawn equipment in the past month. This second question is an important screening question if the company wants to investigate the purchase decision process. If someone uses lawn equipment but never makes the actual purchase, then he or she would not be a good person to participate in a survey about purchasing equipment since he or she is not involved in the purchase process. However, if the manufacturer wants to study features of lawn equipment to gather information on the development of new products, then a user can provide valuable information.

Good screening questions save researchers considerable time and money by eliminating individuals who cannot answer the questions or who should not be involved in the study. In the previous example, someone who uses lawn equipment cannot provide useful information pertaining to the purchase process. In fact, this respondent's answers may lead to erroneous results and poor decisions by management. A similar situation is sometimes found in the health care industry. While the person who is sick may provide some useful information, it may be the caregiver who should be surveyed since he or she is making the decision on medical equipment and supplies.

Screening questions are used to ensure the respondent is a good candidate for the marketing study.

When it comes to business surveys, good screening questions are even more important. The title of a person in a company does not always indicate the individuals who should participate in a study. The higher a person is in a company, in terms of title and rank, the less likely he or she is to evaluate or offer insight into purchase and usage situations of products and services. However, these higher-ranking individuals could be good candidates for surveys dealing with larger, strategic issues.

Survey Questions

After the instructions comes the body of the questionnaire. Generally, the survey should begin with broad questions and proceed to more focused questions. Most importantly, it should have a logical flow. If scales are used, placing similar scales together makes it easier for the respondent. Changing scale formats too often can be confusing and may even become frustrating. Scaled-response questions are normally found in the middle of the survey, along with other questions that require thought or effort. This may include open-ended questions. If open-ended questions are used, it is important that the researcher allow adequate room for answers. A one-line blank cues the respondent to provide a limited response; several lines' worth of open space indicates that a lengthier response is desired.

If a questionnaire has sensitive or potentially embarrassing questions, they should be near the end of the question sequence. If asked too early, it may cause individuals to quit the survey. If asked properly and at the right time, respondents are more likely to answer the sensitive questions. The goal is to gain the confidence of the respondent by the time the sensitive questions are asked. Prefacing sensitive questions with the reasoning why the information is needed, or a reassurance as to how the data will be used or reported, can help increase response rates to these questions.

To prevent the questionnaire from becoming too long, only questions that pertain to the research and survey objectives should be asked. It is tempting to tack on additional questions that a researcher or someone with the client feels would be nice to ask, but they may not relate to any survey objective.

Another approach is to use branching where additional questions are asked based on the respondent's responses to specific questions. Branching can be done easily with online and electronic surveys. For instance, suppose respondents are asked if they purchased an energy bar within the last week. If they say yes, then they see additional questions about the energy bar. If they say no, then the next question in the survey is seen.

Demographic Information

Demographic questions should be at the end of the questionnaire, unless they are used as a screening question. In that case, the appropriate demographics are asked at the beginning to determine if the person continues taking the survey or is terminated. For demographic questions at the end of the survey, a sentence explaining the importance of the demographic questions will increase the likelihood that this section will be completed.

Closing

The closing provides an opportunity to thank the respondent. It can also be used to debrief the respondent with more information on how the data will be used and the purpose of the study. Making the respondent feel he or she has contributed useful information that will be used for management decisions increases the likelihood the respondent will participate in future research studies.

It is advantageous to prepare respondents for additional research by adding a question in the closing that says, "Additional research may be required. Would you be interested in participating in future research?" If they respond yes, you can then ask for their e-mail address or another mode of contact. In some cases, the respondent may be willing to provide a phone number that will allow the researcher to make a phone call for a personal interview.

Design Considerations

Providing adequate "white space" in the form of margins and empty space between questions can make the questionnaire easier to read, and reduce refusal rates. Question instructions should be distinguished from the question itself. Choices include (1) bold text, (2) bold italic text, and (3) using a different font. Using all caps to display instructions or underlining instructions is not recommended. Both tactics reduce the readability of the information. Furthermore, in an online world, underlining is often associated with links, while all caps is considered poor etiquette and equated to "shouting."

Invitation or Cover Letter

While not an actual component of the questionnaire, the invitation (or cover letter) is important. Cover letters are typically used for mail surveys and in some cases personal interview surveys that involve giving respondents a questionnaire and asking them to complete it. But, as survey research shifts to online and mobile phones, cover letters are being replaced by an e-mail invitation. Whether a cover letter or an invitation, the purpose is to obtain the person's cooperation and willingness to participate in the research study. Figure 11.13 highlights what should be contained in an invitation or a cover letter.

In addition to identifying the organization conducting the study and it purpose, it is important to state if the responses will be anonymous or confidential. **Anonymity** means the responses given by a particular respondent can never be identified or tied to that particular person. **Confidentiality** means that although the researcher can identify who completed a particular survey, the researcher pledges to keep that information confidential and never reveal the identity of the respondent.

Figure 11.13   Content of Invitation (Cover Letter)

- Organization/company conducting the study
- Purpose of study
- Statement of anonymity or confidentiality
- Importance of participation and incentive (if appropriate)
- Time frame for completing and returning questionnaire
- Advance thank-you for participating

The invitation/cover letter should reinforce the importance of completing the study, and incentives for participation should be described. Two time frames should be given. The first one is the time to complete the actual survey. The second is the date by which the survey should be returned. In the first case, the invitation may say it will take approximately 20 minutes to complete the survey. In the second case, the individual is asked to return the completed survey by a specific date. The invitation should then close with a thank-you for participating.

SPLIT-QUESTIONNAIRE DESIGN

■ Objective 11.7: Describe the negative consequences of long questionnaires and the benefit of using a split-questionnaire design.

A major problem that often creeps into survey research is designing questionnaires that become too long. When this happens, it results in negative consequences that are not always easily seen by the researcher. The most common are declining cooperation rates, higher break-off rates, increasing item nonresponses, reduced data quality, and panel attrition (see Figure 11.14).[8]

If respondents feel that a questionnaire is too long and thus will take too much time to complete, they may opt not to take the survey. This can affect the validity of a research study because the researcher does not know if the refusal to participate is due to the topic being investigated or the length of the questionnaire. Higher nonresponse rates will cause researchers to question if those who did respond are in some way different from those who did not.

The longer the survey, the higher will be the **break-off rate,** which is the percentage of individuals who start a survey but do not complete it. With mail surveys or surveys handed to a respondent, the individual can easily see how long the survey is and approximate how long it will take to complete. If it is viewed as being too long, the individual is not likely to even start. But, with online surveys, the respondent cannot really tell how long it will take, which is why the invitation to participate should accurately state the approximate length of the survey or the time involved in completing it. Some surveys will also have an indicator on each page showing what percent of the survey has been completed. But, this can be misleading because some components may take 30 seconds to complete while others may take several minutes. If respondents feel the survey is too long or taking too much time to complete, they may just quit answering questions and leave the survey. Fortunately, many online survey software packages now allow for the respondents to leave a survey and pick up where they left off at a later time. This technology reduces the break-off rate.

Figure 11.14   Negative Consequences of Long Questionnaires

- Lower cooperation rates
- Higher break-off rates
- Higher item nonresponses
- Reduced data quality
- Higher panel attrition

Instead of quitting, respondents may just skip questions, especially questions that look like they will take too much time or too much thought. Open-ended questions are the most likely to be skipped since they require more time and thought than closed-ended questions. Questions that have multiple or long responses that the respondent has to read suffer a similar fate. Questions nearer the end of a survey are more likely to be skipped than are questions located near the beginning. Individuals will often be diligent in answering questions at the beginning, but then when they start feeling the questionnaire is too long, they will begin skipping questions. Of course, the problem researchers face is not knowing why a question was not answered. Was it due to the respondent not knowing the answer, being uncomfortable answering, not having the knowledge to answer, or perceiving the instrument as too long?

Reduced data quality is the most serious problem stemming from long questionnaires, though specific instances can be difficult to detect. Respondents will answer the questions, but not spend time thinking about the best response. They may mark any response. If a scale is being used, they often just mark the center response item. So what researchers see is a greater number of answers toward the center of a scale and fewer answers toward the extremes of the scale. Sometimes respondents may select "strongly agree" or another non-neutral response to every Likert statement. Either way, the responses are not genuine.

For companies that utilize online panels, consistently long questionnaires may result in frustration by panel members. This frustration is likely to lead to some of the members quitting the panel or being more selective in which questionnaires they complete.

The most obvious solution to long questionnaires is to shorten them. But, if it is not possible to do so and still meet the research objectives, then researchers can use a split-questionnaire design. A **split-questionnaire design** involves splitting a questionnaire into one core component and multiple subcomponents. All respondents complete the core component of the questionnaire. Each respondent is then randomly given one of the subcomponents.

Consider Figure 11.15. Respondent 1 answers the core component questions and the items in Component A. Respondent 2 answers the core questions and the items in Component B. Respondent 3 does the core and Component C, and Respondent 4 does the core with Component D. The subcomponents should be randomly assigned among respondents. But, approximately 25% of the total sample will respond to each of the subcomponents. To achieve a sufficient sample size it will be necessary to survey more individuals since only a quarter of the sample is answering the questions in each of the subcomponents. So if a research study requires a sample of 300, then 1,200 would have to be interviewed to ensure 300 people answered each of the components.

A recent study examining the validity and reliability of using the split-questionnaire design showed that the quality of data obtained was superior to that of data collected using a long, single questionnaire.[9] The reason: Respondents were able to answer the core questions and one component without the negative consequences of a long questionnaire occurring. The key to using a split-questionnaire design is the development of the core component and then each of the subcomponents. They must be developed in such a way that when respondents do not answer questions in all but one of the subcomponents, it does not impact the results.

With online surveys, an alternative to using split-questionnaire design is to provide an option that allows the respondent to leave a questionnaire and return at a later time. Online

Figure 11.15   Illustration of Split-Questionnaire Design

	Respondent 1	Respondent 2	Respondent 3	Respondent 4
Core Component	X	X	X	X
Component A	X			
Component B		X		
Component C			X	
Component D				X

survey technology makes it possible for respondents to log back into the survey and continue at the point where they had stopped. This can make a long survey seem shorter. It can also allow for unplanned interruptions that may occur.

EVALUATING THE QUESTIONNAIRE

■ Objective 11.8: Discuss the steps in evaluating a questionnaire.

Before administering the questionnaire, it is important for it to be evaluated. Figure 11.16 identifies typical steps used in the evaluation process. The evaluation should begin by comparing the questions in the survey to the survey objectives. Was each survey objective addressed adequately? Are there questions in the survey that do not meet one of the survey objectives? If so, they should be deleted.

A very beneficial second step is to have colleagues evaluate the questionnaire. These may be individuals who work in the same office, but are working on other projects. It may be individuals who work outside the organization, but understand marketing research and wouldn't mind contributing some time in evaluating a questionnaire. Sometimes these individuals can catch wording that is not quite clear, jargon, or problematic phrasing.

Figure 11.16   Steps in Evaluating a Questionnaire

- Check questions against survey objectives
- Colleagues review
- Client review
- Pretest
- Revise questionnaire
- Pretest again if necessary

Once the researcher is comfortable with the questionnaire, it should be shown to the client. The purpose of showing it to the client is to ensure the data that are being collected meet the information needs. It is not to inspect the wording of each question. Most clients are not marketing researchers and may want to rewrite questions that will confuse respondents or not produce the level of data needed. Their role is to make sure the questionnaire meets the objectives of the research study and that the results produced from the questionnaire will provide useful information to make the management decision for which the data are being collected.

Once these reviews are finished, it is time for a pretest. Typically, 20–40 individuals are chosen who mirror the target audience for the research study. They are given the questionnaire and asked to take the survey. Their input can be obtained in two different ways. The first is to have them complete the entire questionnaire just as the sample respondent will be doing. Once it is complete, then the researcher will ask the individual doing the pretest to discuss any questions that were not clear or difficult to answer. The researchers can also ask about the length of the questionnaire, the sequencing of questions, terminology, jargon, and any signs of boredom or tiring. The second approach is for the person doing the pretest to talk out loud as he or she takes the survey rather than wait until the end. The idea behind this approach is that it will help the researcher to see the thought processes that are being used in answering the questions. It may reveal information that waiting until the end would not.

In most cases the pretest will indicate revisions that should be made to the questionnaire. If these are minor, then the revisions can be made and the questionnaire is ready to launch. If major changes are made, then another pretest should be conducted. It may also be worthwhile to go through the entire process again. Time spent on questionnaire evaluation is time well spent. It will result in better data and will aid in the reduction of errors.

Global Concerns

In the last five years, online research has become prevalent internationally. The larger countries have a higher Internet penetration rate, which makes it possible to complete online surveys. However, companies sometimes try to conduct research in smaller countries and fail to consider the large number of people who may not have Internet access. This becomes an issue if the input from those who are not online is important to fulfilling the survey objectives.

Another challenge globally is the thought that to save money the survey should be offered in English only, or only in the native language where the study is being conducted. With business surveys, offering surveys only in English may be permissible. But, in doing so, a researcher may be missing valuable input. For example, suppose a survey is conducted in France, and the survey is in French only. Not everyone who works in businesses in France is fluent in French. Asians, Hispanics, and even Americans may be able to converse in French but not feel comfortable answering a survey in French. If the survey were offered in both French and English, then more respondents could respond, and better data would be obtained.

 STATISTICS REVIEW

Scales are an important part of marketing research. To ensure individuals read a series of statements within a scale, researchers often reverse questions. Some will be positively stated; others will be negatively worded. Consider the scale shown in Figure 11.17 that measures an individual's loyalty to local retail stores.

Notice Items 2, 7, and 10 are worded so that "strongly agree" response measures a more favorable attitude toward shopping outside the local area. For individuals who are loyal to the local retail stores, their responses would be a low value. To make the scale consistent and to measure loyalty to local retail stores, these three items need to be recoded, reversing the scale. In SPSS this can be done with the recode command. The coding of the original scale shows "strongly disagree" was coded a 1, "disagree" a 2, "agree" a 3, and "strongly agree" a 4. To recode Items 2, 7, and 10, the 1 is changed to a 4, the 2 is changed to a 3, the 3 is changed to a 2, and the 4 is changed to a 1. Recoding these three items makes the responses consistent with the other seven items that together compose the scale. Following recoding, the higher the value, the greater the loyalty the respondent displays to local retail stores.

It is always a good idea to recode data into a new variable. If recoding is done with the original variable, it is easy to forget whether or not it has been recoded, especially a month, six months, or a year later. It is further recommended that new variables be created for every item in the scale even though some will be identical to the original scale, as this allows you to keep the original data in case they are ever needed, and makes it easier to select the variables to be used in a particular analysis. For example, the new set of store loyalty items might be named FinalSL1 through FinalSL10, though only Items 2, 7, and 10 would differ from the original data.

In examining local retail store loyalty using this scale, researchers have two options. Either they can sum the responses to obtain a total score for the 10 items, or they can average the responses for the measure as a whole. Which method is used depends on how the results will be used and which will be the easiest for reporting to management. If the scale items are summed, then the mean value

(Continued)

(Continued)

Figure 11.17   Scale to Measure Loyalty to Local Retail Stores

1. I will pay slightly more for products if I can buy them locally...............................	Strongly Disagree	Disagree	Agree	Strongly Agree
2. I shop outside my local retail area before looking to see what is offered locally.	Strongly Disagree	Disagree	Agree	Strongly Agree
3. I shop at local stores because it is important to help my community.	Strongly Disagree	Disagree	Agree	Strongly Agree
4. I shop locally because the convenience outweighs the other advantages of shopping outside the community.	Strongly Disagree	Disagree	Agree	Strongly Agree
5. I shop locally to support the local merchants and business district.	Strongly Disagree	Disagree	Agree	Strongly Agree
6. Shopping at local stores is an enjoyable experience.	Strongly Disagree	Disagree	Agree	Strongly Agree
7. Local stores have inferior products/ services, so I prefer shopping out of town	Strongly Disagree	Disagree	Agree	Strongly Agree
8. Because I am more familiar with the local stores, I prefer shopping locally than out of town.	Strongly Disagree	Disagree	Agree	Strongly Agree
9. I shop locally even when the selection/ variety of goods is poor...........................	Strongly Disagree	Disagree	Agree	Strongly Agree
10. I am not loyal to my local shopping area. ...	Strongly Disagree	Disagree	Agree	Strongly Agree

for the 10 items is 25.32 with a standard deviation of 4.55. If an average score is used for 10 items, it is 2.53 with a standard deviation of 0.45.

Summing or averaging the items in the scale allows researchers to make comparisons with other variables. With the local retail store loyalty measures, responses between males and females were compared, which indicated a significant difference. Females tended to have a higher level of local store loyalty than males. The average level of loyalty for females was 2.53, and it was 2.48 for males, based on a sample of 492 respondents.

DEALING WITH DATA

The loyalty to local retail stores shown in the previous section was part of a larger study that also examined skepticism toward advertising, buying impulsiveness, and materialist attitude. The questionnaire for this study is titled "Chapter 11 Dealing with Data Survey," and the SPSS data file is titled "Chapter 11 Dealing with Data." Both files are located at www.sagepub.com/clowess.

Access the data and questionnaire. Start by reading through the items and noting which items are reversed and need to be recoded. For the local shopping loyalty scale, the previous "Statistics Review" section already identified Items 2, 7, and 10 as those to be reverse coded. Once you have identified the items in need of recoding for the "skepticism to advertising," "buying impulsiveness," and "materialistic attitude" scales, answer the following questions.

1. For each of the scales, which items need to be reverse coded?

2. What is the mean of these scale items (before recoding)?

3. Recode these items. What is the mean of each of these items after being recoded?

Using SPSS, sum the responses for each of the scales by creating a new variable for each scale. Repeat the same process, but average the scores for each of the scales. You will create a total of eight new variables. When finished, answer the questions below.

4. What is the sum for each of the four scales?

5. What is the average for each of the four scales?

7. If a researcher wanted to compare the overall responses from the four scales, which would be easier to understand—comparing the summated scale scores or the average scale scores? Why?

SUMMARY

Objective 1: Outline the questionnaire design process.

Questionnaire design begins with the research questions or objectives, from which survey objectives are developed. The next step is to select the data collection method since it influences how questions are written. Questions are carefully written for each survey objective. Then the layout and design of the questionnaire is determined. Once the questionnaire is complete, it is evaluated. The last step is to develop an invitation or a cover letter.

Objective 2: Discuss the two primary question formats that can be used in questionnaire design.

The two primary question formats are open-ended questions and closed-ended questions. Open-ended questions allow respondents to answer in their own words, and can provide new or different insights for researchers, as well as additional alternatives for closed-ended questions. Open-ended questions in surveys administered by interviewers allow for additional probing for understanding. The problems with open-ended questions include difficulty in interpreting the answer, challenges in editing and coding the responses, potential for interviewer bias, and insufficient and shallow answers. In contrast, closed-ended questions are easy to code, and the possibility of interviewer bias is limited. Also, the response categories can jog respondents' memories, enhancing recall. However, generating the list of alternative answers to closed-ended questions is challenging for researchers, and individuals must select from the list provided, so respondents have no freedom in how they answer a question.

Objective 3: Elaborate on the three different types of closed-ended questions.

The three types of closed-ended questions include dichotomous questions, multiple-choice questions, and scaled-response questions. Dichotomous questions have only two options. Multiple-choice questions offer multiple (three or more) options. Neither dichotomous nor multiple-choice questions allow respondents to indicate a degree of intensity. To capture intensity, researchers often use scaled-response questions, such as Likert or semantic differential scales.

Objective 4: Identify and describe the categories of questions used in questionnaires.

Survey questions can be classified into one of six categories. Demographic or classification questions ask respondents for demographic information or to identify one or more responses that apply to a situation. Knowledge questions are designed to assess the level of knowledge respondents have about a topic. Attitude questions involve measuring feelings toward a brand, an object, or a concept. Attitude measurement is important because attitude often precedes actions. Preference questions involve asking consumers to rate or rank objects or ideas. While intentions do not always equate to actions, measuring intentions can provide valuable information. Behavior questions involve past actions, such as purchases or media consumption.

Objective 5: Discuss the issues relating to the phrasing of questions.

Questions should be clearly written, free of jargon and ambiguity, and should be interpreted as meaning the same thing by different respondents. They should use the respondents' vocabulary in a conversational style. The questionnaire should have a logical flow. If scales are used, they should be easy for respondents to understand and use. In wording questions, it is important to keep recall periods short and avoid either/or and double-barreled questions. Leading questions do not provide honest responses since respondents may feel uncomfortable providing an answer other than what is suggested, and thus should be avoided. Care should be taken to ensure that the questions asked are applicable to the respondents.

Objective 6: Identify and explain the contents of each section of a questionnaire.

The questionnaire should begin with instructions, which explain not only how to complete the questionnaire but why it is important. A screening question or questions should then be used to see if the person meets the target audience criteria. In some cases, the screening question may be asked before instructions are given. The body of the questionnaire, containing the survey questions, then follows. Questions should follow a logical order and funnel from more general questions to more specific ones. Scaled-response questions should be toward the middle. If sensitive questions are asked, they should be near the end of the survey. After all of the questions have been asked, respondents should be asked demographic information. The questionnaire should end with a closing that thanks the respondent for participating and, if possible, more information about the purpose of the research.

Objective 7: Describe the negative consequences of long questionnaires and the benefit of using a split-questionnaire design.

Negative consequences of long questionnaires include lower cooperation rates from respondents, more individuals breaking off from answering questions after they started but before finishing, higher item nonresponse rates where questions are left blank, reduced data quality from respondents either just randomly answering or not taking time to provide good answers, and for panels a higher attrition rate. The split-questionnaire design avoids the problems of long questionnaires because each respondent answers a core component of the survey and only one subcomponent.

Objective 8: Discuss the steps in evaluating a questionnaire.

Questionnaire evaluation has six steps. First is checking questions against the survey objectives to be sure all survey objectives have been adequately met and that no superfluous questions have been asked. Second, colleagues should be asked to review the questions to make sure they are clear and concise. Third, clients should be asked to evaluate the questions, not for wording, but to make sure the data provided will provide the information needed to make management decisions. Fourth is a pretest with 20 to 30 individuals who mirror the target audience for the study. The fifth step is to revise the questionnaire based on the pretest information. The last step is to pretest again, if major changes were made to the questionnaire.

GLOSSARY OF KEY TERMS

Anonymity: responses given by a particular respondent can never be identified or tied to that particular person

Break-off rate: percentage of individuals who start a survey but do not complete it

Closed-ended question: question that gives respondents a finite number of responses from which to choose

Confidentiality: although a researcher can identify who completed a particular survey, the researcher pledges to keep that information confidential and never reveal who the individual was that completed the survey

Dichotomous question: closed-ended question with two options

Double-barreled question: question that involves asking respondents two questions in one

Leading question: survey question that leads the respondent to the desired answer

Multiple-choice question: question with multiple (three or more) answers from which to choose

Multiple-response question: form of multiple-choice question in which respondents are instructed to check all response options that apply

Open-ended question: question that allows a respondent to answer in his or her own words

Position bias: in a long list of response items individuals may not take time to look at all of the possible choices but simply check the first one that applies

Questionnaire: set of questions or items used to generate data that meet specific research and survey objectives

Scaled-response question: question that allows respondents to indicate a level or degree of intensity

Split-questionnaire design: involves splitting a questionnaire into one core component that all respondents answer and multiple subcomponents with respondents answering only one subcomponent

CRITICAL THINKING EXERCISES

1. Suppose that a key research objective is "to understand how different consumer segments use and share social media content." Create a minimum of three survey objectives for this research objective.

2. Your client believes that attitudes toward the firm's brand should be assessed using a semantic differential or a Stapel scale. How will the scale chosen impact the choice of data collection method? Which scale and data collection technique would you recommend and why? If the research objectives did not require comparing attitudes between subgroups, would you still use this scale and data collection method? Why or why not?

3. The use of open-ended questions in quantitative research studies is appropriate only in certain circumstances. Explain.

4. For each of the following, identify the type of closed-ended question being asked and the question category each represents.

   a. In the last week, have you visited a hair salon or barber? _____ Yes _____ No
   b. How did you hear about our salon (check all that apply)?

      _____ Radio ad _____ TV ad _____ Newspaper ad ___ Online search

      _____ Website _____ Friend _____ Other (please specify): _____

   c. Please indicate your level of agreement or disagreement with the following statements, where 1 = strongly disagree to 7 = strongly agree:

      In general, the higher the price of a product,

the higher the quality. 1 2 3 4 5 6 7

The old saying, "You get what you pay for"

is generally true. 1 2 3 4 5 6 7

You always have to pay a bit more for the best. 1 2 3 4 5 6 7

5. Select one of the survey objectives developed in response to Question 1. Write at least three complete questions for an online survey that will help to obtain the necessary information.

6. Itemized rating questions, paired comparisons, and rank-order questions are the most common methods of determining preference. Create survey questions of each type in the context of fast-food restaurants. Under what circumstances would you recommend using each and why?

7. Suppose you were tasked with developing separate questionnaires targeting (1) individuals who have immigrated to the United States from Mexico in the past 90 days, (2) welfare recipients, and (3) physicians. Explain how the respondent characteristics could influence the questionnaire development and question phrasing process.

8. Critique the following questions and response options:

How much do you normally pay for milk?

____ $3.00–$3.50 ____ $3.50–$3.99 ____ $4.00–$4.50 ____ More than $4.50

Please indicate your level of satisfaction with the quality tools made by Craftsman.

____ Very satisfied ____ Satisfied ____ Somewhat satisfied ____ Dissatisfied

How old are you, and how much do you make in a year? _____

Do you have soda with your mixed drinks? ____ Yes ____ No

Please rate the Recreation Center's natatorium using the following scale:

Clean :____:____:____:____:____:____:____: Dirty

       1   2   3   4   5   6   7

Too warm :____:____:____:____:____:____:____: Too cold

        1   2   3   4   5   6   7

Crowded :____:____:____:____:____:____:____: Just right

        1   2   3   4   5   6   7

9. A 50-item survey regarding attitudes toward used cars, salespersons, and dealerships will be conducted online. Compose (1) a survey invitation and (2) instructions that will appear at the beginning of the survey. You may make any reasonable assumptions that you would like when creating instructions or phrasing your invitation.

10. Describe a specific research study in which a split-questionnaire design might be appropriate. What types of questions would compose the core component of the survey? How many subcomponents would you recommend, and what would be the primary focus of each?

CONTINUING CASE STUDY: LAKESIDE GRILL

Alexa, Brooke, Destiny, Juan, and Zach went back to their notes and found the research questions the team had developed previously. Based on these research questions, the team created the following survey objectives.

1. What is the current level of customer satisfaction and patronage with the various aspects of Lakeside Grill?
   a. Identify level of satisfaction with customer service, food, aesthetics, and atmosphere.
   b. Request frequency of patronage of Lakeside Grill.
   c. Solicit likes and dislikes with Lakeside Grill.

2. Why have individuals not patronized Lakeside Grill?
   a. Determine reasons for not patronizing Lakeside Grill.

3. How has the addition of a new competitor down the street impacted Lakeside Grill's customer base?
   a. Determine attitude toward new competitor in relation to Lakeside Grill.
   b. Determine if frequency of patronage of Lakeside Grill declined.

4. Would changing Lakeside Grill's menu, advertising, and/or promotional practices increase sales?
   a. Solicit attitude toward new menu items.
   b. Determine impact of advertising on patronage decision.
   c. Identify promotions that may influence patronage decisions.

Using these survey objectives, the team next developed the questionnaire titled "Chapter 11 Lakeside Grill Survey" (www.sagepub.com/clowess). Almost every question resulted in some level of discussion among the team members. But, the questions that raised the most controversy were Questions 2, 4, and 5. Brooke argued that they should not use open-ended questions at all because they would get too many different answers. The other team members felt the open-ended questions were important because respondents could provide their thoughts in their own words. Juan commented that "by asking for the one thing they like and dislike about Lakeside Grill, it would provide valuable insight into what individuals are thinking."

While Alexa thought that the SERVQUAL instrument should have been used in place of the items in Question 6, others disagreed, arguing that not all of the items were relevant, and that doing so would make the survey too long. When it came to Question 10, Destiny felt the way it was worded was like an either/or question because changes in eating at Lakeside Grill may not have been caused by Fisherman's Paradise. But, Zach argued that it was clearly stated that the respondent was to answer how Fisherman's Paradise impacted eating at Lakeside Grill.

Critique Questions:

1. Review the research questions. Do they appear to be adequate for this study?

2. Evaluate the survey objectives. Are each of the research objectives covered adequately by survey objectives? Are there any survey objectives that are not clear? Are there any survey objectives that will solicit unnecessary information?

3. Match each survey question with its appropriate survey objective. What is your evaluation of the questionnaire in terms of meeting the survey objectives?

4. Using Figure 11.10, classify each question. Do you think the team used the best question type, or could a different category of questions be used that would provide better data?

5. What do you think about Questions 2, 4, and 5? Would you agree with the team or with Brooke?

6. Do you agree with Alexa that the SERVQUAL instrument should have been used in place of Question 6? Why or why not?

7. What do you think about Questions 7 through 10 about Fisherman's Paradise and its impact on Lakeside Grill? Are these good questions? Why or why not?

8. Evaluate the total questionnaire. What changes would you make in the questionnaire? Why?

MARKETING RESEARCH PORTFOLIO

The "Marketing Research Portfolio" mini-case for Chapter 11 can be used to help students apply the information from Chapters 9, 10, and 11, or can be used in an even more integrative fashion. In its simplest form, students would begin by identifying one or more survey objectives for each research question provided in the case. The survey objectives would then guide the creation of a questionnaire.

A more comprehensive application would challenge students to find and report relevant secondary data. Next, students would select and justify a data collection method and a sampling plan. Finally, survey objectives and the actual questionnaire would be developed. If used in this fashion, substantial time for completion should be allowed. The assignment instructions and case information can be found at www.sagepub.com/clowess.

STUDENT STUDY SITE

Visit the Student Study Site at www.sagepub.com/clowess to access the following additional materials:

- eFlashcards
- Web Quizzes
- SAGE Journal Articles
- Web Resources

SECTION 4

Analyzing and Reporting Marketing Research

CHAPTER 12

Fundamental Data Analysis

LEARNING OBJECTIVES

After reading this chapter, you should be able to

1. Identify the steps in the data preparation process.

2. Discuss the processes of validating and coding data.

3. Describe the processes of data entry and data cleaning.

4. Discuss the advantages of precoding questionnaires.

5. Describe the various ways of tabulating data.

6. Explain the descriptive statistics that should be used with each type of scale.

7. Discuss the principles involved in creating good graphs.

INTRODUCTION

Preparing data for analysis is important. It requires validating the data collected, coding responses to questions, entering the data into a data file, and cleaning the data. Each of these steps is necessary to minimize errors before the data are ever analyzed. Once the data have been properly prepared, it is time to tabulate the results of each question in the survey and the demographic information that was requested. This information can be presented in tables or graphs. If graphs are used, it is important to prepare graphs that contain complete information and are easy to read and properly labeled, such as the one in Figure 12.1. This graph shows the four most popular sides at casual dine-in restaurants.[1] It is easy to see that garden salads are the most popular and were chosen by 23% of the sample. Of the four sides shown, the least popular was vegetables, chosen by only 14% of the sample.

Figure 12.1   Graph Showing Most Popular Sides of Casual Diners

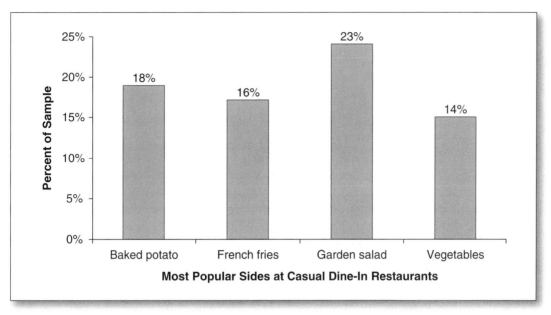

Source: "NC SBTC Restaurant Industry Study," Small Business Technology Development Center, Raleigh, North Carolina, 2005.

In discussing fundamental data analysis, it is important to understand the difference between the terms *parameter* and *statistic*. A **parameter** refers to a characteristic of an entire population, such as the mean or mode for the age of the population. A **statistic** describes a characteristic of the sample, such as the mean or mode for the age or gender of the sample respondents, and is used as an estimator for the population parameter. If collected properly, the sample should be representative of the population, and thus a statistic obtained from the sample should be a good estimation of the population parameter. In Figure 12.1, the statistics obtained from the sample are used to estimate the most popular sides for the population of casual diners.

PREPARING DATA FOR ANALYSIS

The purpose of collecting data is to gather information to make marketing decisions. The quality of those decisions is dependent on the quality of data obtained. To ensure high-quality data, it is important to follow a methodical process that will help in detecting and reducing errors. These steps are highlighted in Figure 12.2.

    The data preparation process starts as soon as the data are collected. The data may be collected through an online panel, from a mail survey, from an observation, or as a result of an experiment. Regardless of how the data are collected, data preparation begins with a validation process. Then editing and coding of the data take place. The next step is to actually enter the data into a computer spreadsheet or statistics program such SAS or SPSS. Once the data are in a data file, they can be cleaned. Only after all of these steps have been completed can the

■ Objective 12.1: Identify the steps in the data preparation process.

results be tabulated and statistical data analyses performed. The next chapter will discuss the most frequently used data analyses, many of which have already been presented in the "Statistics Review" and "Dealing With Data" sections of previous chapters.

■ Objective 12.2: Discuss the processes of validating and coding data.

DATA VALIDATION

The purpose of **data validation** is to ensure the data were collected properly and are as free of error and bias as possible. As discussed in Chapter 8, error will always occur in the process of collecting data. Random error cannot be eliminated, but can be reduced by increasing the sample size. Despite a researcher's best efforts, systematic error will occur, so the purpose of data validation is to check for any recognizable systematic error. Figure 12.3 highlights the areas that are checked in the data validation step. The first three checks occur in the field where the data are collected, and the last two are the responsibility of the research firm or research department where the data are being tabulated and analyzed.

Figure 12.2 Data Preparation Process

- Validation
- Coding
- Data entry
- Data cleaning

Data Collection Process

Data validation begins by thoroughly examining the data collection process in the field where it occurred. When interviewers are involved, this validation often occurs while the interviews are taking place. It is important for interviewers and individuals collecting the data to follow the process that has been outlined. If not, the results can be affected. For example, if a mall intercept study is being conducted and interviewers are requested to stop every 15th person and read the questions to the respondent, then it is important every interviewer follow that procedure. Sample selection error can occur if some interviewers stop every 15th person while others stop individuals around the 15th person who they think will take time to complete the survey. It might be the 13th person, the 18th person, or some other number.

Interviewer error is also of concern. If some of the interviewers read the questions while others hand the questionnaire to the respondent, then it is very possible that the answers will vary. Interviewer error can also occur when interviewers don't give respondents proper instructions or when they fail to follow skip patterns. Insufficient probing of open-ended questions also may result in interviewer error. For instance, a respondent may be asked why he or she chose to purchase a certain brand of dog food. Taking an answer such as "Because of the price" at face value and failing to probe further may lead to erroneous conclusions. While it would be natural to assume that the answer reflects the respondent's preference for low price, further probing may reveal that the respondent purchased a higher-priced brand because he or she felt price signaled a higher-quality food with superior nutrition.[2]

Field supervisors should be on the alert for these problems, and may observe interviewers' behavior either directly or remotely via camera. Confederates who pose as potential interviewees can also be used to

Figure 12.3 Areas to Check During Data Validation

- Field Validation
  - Data collection process
  - Proper screening
  - Fraud
- Primary Research Firm
  - Data completeness
  - Data usability

evaluate the interviewers' data collection procedure. Should it be determined that a particular interviewer systematically conducts the data collection process in a manner different than all other interviewers, the data collected by the problem interviewer should be discarded, and the interviewer should be dismissed or sent for retraining. Field supervisors should also check to make certain that written responses to open-ended questions are legible and that they have been sufficiently probed. Closed-ended question survey answers should be clearly marked in a single category and checked to make certain that no marks exist on lines between categories or spanning categories, which would make the correct answer difficult to determine. Surveys that lack answers to key questions, or that are only partially complete, should be eliminated from the data pool, though sometimes field service firms that specialize in data collection will forward incomplete surveys back to the research firm that employed their services.

Proper Screening

Almost all survey research has some type of screening question or questions to ensure the respondent fits the criteria stipulated by the study design. It is important that all interviewers and individuals involved in collecting the data ask the screening questions and use only respondents who pass all of the questions. In the quest to obtain a quota, data collectors may be tempted to allow individuals who do not meet all of the criteria to complete the survey. This is especially true in situations where the incidence rate is very low, meaning that only a low percentage of the population is qualified to be part of the study. It is also more common when interviewers are paid on the basis of the number of surveys completed. Again, field supervisors can randomly talk with interviewees after they have finished the questionnaire to determine whether or not they really qualified. It is very common to randomly contact about 10% of individuals who completed a survey to validate that they passed the screening criteria and to investigate whether or not the interviewer was in any way guilty of fraud, which is discussed in more detail in the next section.

Detecting those who fail screening questions can be easier in online research, especially in studies that use panel members. Each panel member fills out a complete demographic

Screening questions are used to ensure the respondent meets the criteria stipulated by the research design.

and psychographic profile before joining a panel. If a screening question is based on gender or participation in some type of lifestyle activity, such as fishing, the respondent's answer to the screening question can be easily compared against the respondent's profile to determine whether or not he or she really qualifies. Often panel members will be prescreened so that only those who meet the criteria are invited to complete the survey, resulting in a superior sample.

Fraud

The third area to be checked in the field may be the most difficult to detect, and that is fraud. With fraud, interviewers or data collectors falsify the data by completing the questionnaire themselves, or they may fill in questions the respondent left blank in order to complete the questionnaire. The latter fraudulent situation can occur when individuals are paid for completed surveys. It is easier and faster to fill in a few missing questions than to discard the questionnaire and find a new respondent. The former situation may occur when individuals responsible for data collection are under time and cost constraints. To ensure deadlines are met at the quoted price, it may be tempting to falsify the data rather than go back to the client and either admit they did not collect the number of surveys promised, or ask for additional time. Contacting alleged respondents and asking questions to help verify whether or not (1) they answered the survey at all, (2) they answered all questions in the study, and (3) their answers to key questions were accurately recorded can help to detect fraud. Also, requiring that telephone interviews be conducted from a central location under the supervision of a field supervisor will result in less fraud than if individuals are allowed to conduct telephone surveys from their home with no supervision.

Data Completeness

Data collection duties are often outsourced to firms that specialize in this process. Once the data are returned to the central office, an additional editing phase is typically undertaken. During this phase, the completeness and the usefulness of the data are examined.

Surveys may contain incomplete information. Sometimes individuals unknowingly skip a question, while other times people refuse to answer one or more questions. Surveys missing answers to entire sections or pages are likely to be of little value to the firm, and are typically eliminated at this stage on the basis of incompleteness. For example, if one of the survey objectives sought to determine whether significant differences in attitudes existed on the basis of gender, age, and education, then a survey lacking answers to these demographic questions is of no value. However, it also must be remembered that skip patterns often direct individuals away from answering questions that are not relevant. In this case, what appears to be at first glance an incomplete survey may in fact contain all the relevant information for that subject.

It is best if one individual undertakes the decision of which incomplete surveys can be retained, and which should be thrown out, as this ensures consistency in how the data are treated. Only someone with an intimate knowledge of the survey objectives and the design of the questionnaire should be given this task. Deciding which questions or how many questions must be answered in order for a survey to be included in a data set can be highly subjective.

Data Usability

The usability of the data must also be considered. Illegibly written answers, bizarre abbreviations, or responses that are understandable only to the original interviewer can hinder the coding process of open-ended responses or questions. If the original interviewer cannot be reached for clarification, the responses to these questions may be eliminated from the data, or if the questions are central to the research purpose, the entire survey may be eliminated.

Obvious patterns that indicate response bias are also identified at this stage. For example, the heart of the survey may consist of many different Likert or semantic differential "grid" questions. Two types of patterns may indicate problematic responses that could lead to elimination of surveys from the data pool: (1) straight-lining answers, and (2) zigzagging, or entering responses that create a visual pattern on that page of the questionnaire.[3]

Straight-lining occurs when a respondent selects the same response category for all or the majority of responses to "grid"-based questions such as Likert or semantic differential. If an individual selects all neutral responses for multiple scale items, it is likely that the subject either didn't read the question, or doesn't have the knowledge or experience necessary to answer the question. Straight-lining of neutral responses is particularly likely to occur in cases in which a "don't know" option is not available, or when a skip pattern was not used to determine relevancy of the topic to the individual before asking the scaled-response questions. College students who are required to participate in research studies may not read questions and may straight-line neutral responses in order to finish their task as quickly as possible. It is often in the best interest of the researcher to eliminate these questionnaires from the data pool when the attitude questions are central to the study purpose.

Individuals who select "strongly agree" or "strongly disagree" for every question or who otherwise straight-line their answers may be demonstrating one of three things. First, they may have a very strong opinion, which they wish to express quite forcibly. Responses could be legitimate if no reversed items were included in the set of scaled questions. Second, if the scale being answered is a semantic differential, responses could be a manifestation of the halo effect discussed in Chapter 10. Third, this response pattern could again be indicative of a respondent who is not really reading and considering the questions carefully, but rather speeding through the questionnaire in order to finish quickly.

One advantage of collecting data online is that "speeders" can be easily identified as the amount of time taken to complete a survey, as well as the time to complete various sections of the survey, can be determined. This information can be forwarded to the client, along with the data, so that it can be used to determine which respondents can be eliminated. The data-collecting entity may also use this information as part of its internal quality control, and eliminate certain respondents from the data pool before forwarding the data to the research client.[4] Pattern recognition algorithms can also be used with online data to identify the percent of responses that appear to be straight-lined.[5]

Also, in rare circumstances, the responses to a series of questions with scaled-response categories may be marked in a fashion that creates a visual design. This type of response bias can be caught using pattern recognition algorithms with online surveys, and respondents who attempt such behaviors are not allowed to complete the survey and are usually removed from the online panel.[6] However, this behavior is also easy to identify in mail or other self-administered paper-based surveys by simply examining the responses. Some patterns experienced by the

Online technology makes it easier to identify straight-liners and speeders.

authors of this text include perfect zigzag lines, in which a respondent may start by selecting 1 for the first question, then 2, 3, 4, 5, 4, 3, 2, 1, 2, 3, 4, 5, and so on for additional questions. Alternatively, some respondents will "X" multiple categories for each semantic differential item in order to create pictures of circles, or alphabet letters such as *N* or *Y*. Any surveys exhibiting these characteristics should be immediately discarded.

The individual tasked with determining the usability of the data should look carefully at the questions asked, to see whether answers seem to be consistent. Some researchers examine data consistency during the data cleaning stage instead of during validation. Others prefer to weed out inconsistent data before they are entered into the data file. Two scale items may read, "The ad held my attention" and "The ad was boring." An individual who marks "strongly agree" to both questions is probably not paying attention to the question content. Often researchers will eliminate a survey on the basis of such inconsistencies[7]; others may require multiple problems to be present before eliminating the survey from the data pool.

Bruzzone Research tested eight factors thought to negatively impact the quality of data. Using a study of the 2008 Super Bowl ads, Bruzzone and its research partners sought to identify whether these factors actually influenced the answers to ad-tracking questions. Straight-lining answers, speeding through the survey, and failing trap questions involving specific instructions were found to have a noticeable effect on data quality, while inconsistent answers to conflicting questions such as those outlined in the previous paragraph did not. Specifically, 3% of the survey respondents finished the survey in less than half the normal time, 3% straight-lined answers to 60% or more of the grid-based questions, and 10% failed to follow the instruction to select the "slightly disagree" category for the trap question. Overall, though, only 2% of the respondents engaged in two or more of these behaviors. Bruzzone chose only to eliminate this 2%, rationalizing that a respondent could inadvertently engage in any of the questionable behaviors without "evil intent."[8] It is up to the researcher to decide how fast is "too fast" (especially when skip patterns are present), the percentage of straight-lining that is permissible, and whether or not data from those who fail trap questions or who provide inconsistent answers are usable.

DATA CODING

After the data are validated, it is time to begin the coding process. **Coding** involves assigning numerical values to each response on the questionnaire. For written questionnaires the coding process typically occurs after the surveys are completed. However, the codes can be built into the questions at the time the questionnaire is developed. Thus, a Likert scale that uses the anchors "strongly disagree" and "strongly agree" may also have numbers under each of the possible answers ranging from 1 to 5. This makes it easy for the person recording the data from the survey response sheet.

With most quantitative research now shifting to online or electronic mechanisms, the majority of coding will be done before the data are collected. This is necessary since the data from the online or electronic mechanism are automatically placed into some type of spreadsheet. While the spreadsheet can collect the actual words used by respondents, it makes the process simpler and reduces errors if the numerical code is placed into the spreadsheet when the questionnaire is completed. However, open-ended questions, and open-ended responses associated with the "other" category, can only be coded once the data have been collected. In these cases, the words typed by the respondent will be listed in the spreadsheet verbatim.

The coding process begins by assigning a unique identifying number to each questionnaire. This facilitates the process of checking the accuracy of data coding and data entry errors. In coding surveys, every question, and every response, needs to be coded. For closed-ended questions and scales, this process is rather simple. Each response can be given a numerical code. To aid in understanding the results, higher values are typically coded with higher numbers and lower values with lower numbers. Thus "very satisfied" would be assigned a value of 7 on a 7-point scale ranging from 1 to 7. In addition, positive responses tend to be coded with higher numbers than negative responses. Figures 12.4 through 12.10 illustrate various ways questions can be coded.

Coding Closed-Ended Questions

The coding of dichotomous questions is shown in Figure 12.4. Most are coded with either a 1 or 2 or a 0 and 1. The number chosen really does not matter as long as each response is coded in the same manner. In Figure 12.4 gender was coded 1 for females and 2 for males. When questions ask for a yes or no response, the most common coding is to use a 1 for yes and a 0 for no. The numbers chosen for Question 4 can be anything, but it is easier and usually creates fewer errors if the first response is given a code of 1 and the second response a code of 2 (or 0 and 1 could also be used).

Figure 12.4   Coding of Dichotomous Questions

1. What is your gender?   ☐ Female (1)   ☐ Male (2)

2. Have you played video games on your smartphone?   ☐ Yes (1)   ☐ No (0)

3. Do you like playing video games on your smartphone?   ☐ Yes (1)   ☐ No (0)

4. Which platform do you prefer for playing video games?   ☐ Online (1)   ☐ Computer (2)

Figure 12.5 illustrates two different ways multiple-choice questions can be coded. In the first question about income, codes of 1 to 5 are used. The responses are coded such that the higher a person's income, the higher the code number. Thus, someone with an income of $80,000 would be coded a 4 while someone with an income of $33,000 would be coded a 2. Only one income category can be selected by each respondent.

The second question presents a unique coding situation because respondents can choose all the answers that apply. That means that the individual may check one answer, three different answers, or even all five answers. So coding the responses as a single variable ranging from 1 to 5 will not work. With questions of this type, a process called dummy coding is used. With **dummy coding** responses are coded with a 0 or a 1. If the respondent checks an item, such as "online website" or "gaming console," then each of these responses would be coded as a 1, and separate variables would be created to represent each. The items not checked would be coded as a 0. Thus, the question is listed in the data file as five different variables, one for each response item. In contrast, Question 1 about income is only one variable with codes ranging from 1 to 5.

Most scaled-response questions are relatively straightforward to code with the caveat that higher numbers should represent more positive responses while lower numbers are used for negative responses or less desirable responses. For the question in Figure 12.6, a code of 1 to 5 is used with the 1 representing "very unlikely to use" and the 5 representing "very likely to use." With this coding the lower numbers indicate a gaming platform that the respondent is less likely to use while a higher number represents platforms the respondent is more likely to use.

With a paired comparison scale, respondents can choose between two items. An example is shown in Figure 12.7. Since either can be checked, it is necessary to list each response as a separate variable and code the responses using the dummy coding procedure. With the first pair of items, if the individual indicated that price was more important than the size of the computer, then price would be coded as a 1 and the size of the computer as a 0. However, if the individual indicated that the size of the computer was more important, it would be coded as a 1, and price would be coded as a 0. The same procedure would be used for the entire set of paired comparisons.

Figure 12.5   Coding Multiple-Choice Questions

1. Your household income from all sources (salary, investments, gifts, etc.) is:
   - ☐ Less than $24,999 (1)
   - ☐ $25,000 to $49,999 (2)
   - ☐ $50,000 to $74,999 (3)
   - ☐ $75,000 to $99,999 (4)
   - ☐ $100,000 or more (5)

2. Of the following gaming platforms, which ones have you used to play video games? *(Check all that apply)*
   - ☐ Online website (0 or 1)
   - ☐ Social networking site (0 or 1)
   - ☐ Gaming console (0 or 1)
   - ☐ Computer (0 or 1)
   - ☐ Smartphone or tablet (0 or 1)

Figure 12.6   Coding a Scaled-Response Question

For each of the following gaming platforms, please indicate your likelihood of usage ranging from "very unlikely to use" to "very likely to use."

	Very unlikely to use				Very likely to use
	1	2	3	4	5
Online website	○	○	○	○	○
Social networking site	○	○	○	○	○
Gaming console	○	○	○	○	○
Computer	○	○	○	○	○
Smartphone or tablet	○	○	○	○	○

Figure 12.7   Coding a Paired Comparison Scale

For each of the following pairs of criteria in purchasing a laptop computer, indicate which item in each pair is most important to you by placing a checkmark on the appropriate line.

0 or 1 Price or Size of computer 0 or 1

0 or 1 Physical appearance or Technical specifications 0 or 1

0 or 1 Price or Physical appearance 0 or 1

0 or 1 Physical appearance or Size of computer 0 or 1

0 or 1 Technical specifications or Price 0 or 1

0 or 1 Size of computer or Technical specifications 0 or 1

Graphical rating scales present a unique challenge because responses are not specific. Two different graphical rating scales are shown in Figure 12.8. The responses made by two different participants are displayed in this figure as X_1 and X_2. Recall from Chapter 10 that respondents can indicate a response anywhere on either line. With the first scale, no numbers are placed on the line at all. In this situation, the most common method of coding is to use a ruler or some other type of measuring device. Suppose a 6-inch line is used and X_1 falls on the 2-inch point, thus resulting in a code of 2. But suppose X_2 is at 4.75 inches; then the researcher can code it as 4.7, as 4.8, or if two decimal points are used as 4.75. With the bottom scale, X_1 is clearly on the 3. But, X_2 is between 7 and 8. The researcher will have to choose the value he or she thinks best represents the response, which in this case may be a 7.8. A metric ruler is often used in international research or in studies that have international applications, as the metric system is prevalent everywhere except in the United States.

Semantic differential scales are usually straightforward to code. As shown in Figure 12.9, the code of 1 to 5 is being used with a 1 representing the first circle, a 2 the second circle, and on to a 5 for the last or fifth circle. For most of the questions, the higher number would represent a more desirable experience at Home Depot. For instance, a 5 would indicate friendly staff while a 1 would indicate unfriendly staff. But, to make sure the respondent is reading the questions, the second, fourth, and fifth items have been reversed. The more desirable experience is on the left of the scale and the less desirable experience on the right. In recording the data, these questions would typically be coded just as they appear on the question. Then, after all of the data are recorded, the researcher can reverse the code by using the process discussed in the "Statistics Review" section of Chapter 11. By reversing the codes on those three items, the higher responses will then represent the more desirable characteristics.

A Likert scale is shown in Figure 12.10. In the top example, the codes of 1 to 5 are used such that the 1 represents the negative, or "strongly disagree," while the 5 represents the positive, or "strongly agree." The problem comes when questions are reversed, such as in Questions 2 and 3 ("The brand name is not important to me" and "I do not watch what celebrities wear"). This problem can be resolved after all the data are recorded as shown by reversing the code in SPSS or other software package using a recoding process.

In the second Likert scale, "strongly agree" is on the left side of the scale, and "strongly disagree" is on the right side of the scale. The typical code would have the 1 on the left and the 5 on the right. But, coding in this manner makes "strongly agree" a lower value and "strongly disagree" a higher value—just the opposite of what is desired. This can be corrected by either reversing the code sheet so it goes from 5 to 1 or by recoding the data after they have been entered into the data file.

If surveys are answered on paper and recorded by humans, then coding low numbers to the left and higher numbers to the right produces the fewest errors. If the list is vertical, then it should be coded from lowest at the top to highest at the bottom. But, if the survey is completed on a computer or another electronic device, then coding can be done in any fashion since the respondent will not see the codes. Reverse codes can also be done automatically, eliminating the need to do this after the data have all been recorded.

Figure 12.8   Coding Graphical Rating Scales

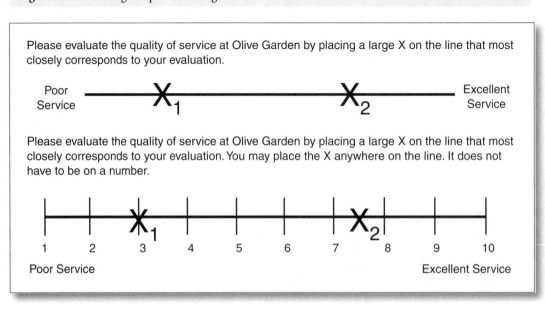

Figure 12.9   Coding a Semantic Differential Scale

Please evaluate the last purchase you made at Home Depot and the experience you had at the retail store.

Unfriendly staff	○	○	○	○	○	Friendly staff
Staff very helpful	○	○	○	○	○	Staff not very helpful
Poor selection	○	○	○	○	○	Excellent selection
Store clean	○	○	○	○	○	Store unclean
Excellent value	○	○	○	○	○	Poor value
Slow checkout	○	○	○	○	○	Fast checkout
Unsuccessful trip	○	○	○	○	○	Successful trip
Code →	1	2	3	4	5	

Figure 12.10   Coding a Likert Scale

Please indicate your level of agreement or disagreement with each of the following statements.

	Strongly Disagree	Disagree	Neutral	Agree	Strongly Agree
1. Wearing the latest fashion is important to me................................	○	○	○	○	○
2. The brand name is not important to me.…………...............................	○	○	○	○	○
3. I do not watch what celebrities wear. ……………...............................	○	○	○	○	○
Code →	1	2	3	4	5

	Strongly Agree	Agree	Neutral	Disagree	Strongly Disagree
1. I read magazines such as *Glamour* regularly.............................	○	○	○	○	○
2. In purchasing clothes, price is not a critical factor......................................	○	○	○	○	○
Code →	1	2	3	4	5
Values After Recoding or Alternative Coding→	5	4	3	2	1

A final issue involves the coding of "don't know," "no opinion," or "not applicable" responses. For purposes of the following discussion, reference will be made to the "don't know" option, though the same logic discussed can apply to the "no opinion" or "not applicable" choices. Initially, these responses are often coded with a number that breaks from the sequence used by scaled-response categories. Thus, if possible responses range from 1 for "strongly dissatisfied" to 5 for "strongly satisfied," then the "don't know" option may be coded as 9. Coding in this fashion allows the researcher to run frequency reports and to create pie charts that show the percent who responded to each scaled-response category, the percent who responded with "don't know," and even the percent who failed to respond to the question and are designated as "missing" data. Using 9 to designate the "don't know" response option helps to remind the researcher that these responses should not be included in the calculation of means and standard deviations, which are often necessary in analyzing the attitudes of individuals. After all, if they don't know or don't have an opinion, or the question is not applicable to them, then their response is not a legitimate expression of the attitude being sought and thus should not be grouped with the responses of those who do know, who do have an opinion, or to whom the question is appropriate. So prior to calculating means, standard deviations, or performing advanced statistical analyses, either the researcher will filter the data so that "don't know" responses are no longer included, or the researcher will recode the "9" values to missing system data, which automatically eliminates them from further analysis.

Coding Open-Ended Questions

Coding open-ended questions presents unique challenges that were discussed in Chapter 11. Figure 12.11 outlines a five-step process that can be used to code open-ended questions. The first step occurs prior to data collection and involves generating a list of possible answers. These responses can be obtained through past research, input from interviews with experts in the field, or even focus groups. Typically, researchers will want to code answers into a manageable set of responses, which includes an "other" category. If the number of categories is too small, the richness obtained from open-ended responses may be lost, and the percentage of responses falling into the "other" category increases. If the number of categories is too large, then tabulating and summarizing the results may not produce meaningful information that can be used by managers. Possible answers to an open-ended question related to key factors that influenced the purchase of a particular brand of sofa may initially generate the following list: price, promotional incentives/financing, quality, brand name, style, appearance, and other.

Figure 12.11   Process for Coding Open-Ended Questions

1. Generate a list of possible responses
2. Create coding rules and guides
3. Add new responses to the list
4. Consolidate related responses
5. Assign a numerical code to each response

Once the initial list has been created, a coding guide is sometimes created that defines each category and provides examples of words or phrases that are indicative of each. While a coding guide is not always developed, at a minimum the researcher will list some basic rules for coding open-ended questions. For instance, categories are generally assumed to be mutually exclusive so that the same comment does not appear in two different categories.[9] In the example cited earlier, care would have to be taken to differentiate "style"-related comments clearly from those that would be classified as "appearance." Furthermore, respondents often make multiple comments that should be separated into different categories as each represents a unique thought. Making it clear to coders whether one or more responses are acceptable for a given open-ended question is critical.

To illustrate, when asked to indicate the key factors considered when purchasing a sofa, a subject may say, "I bought an Ethan Allen sofa because the company makes a quality product. Plus, the color contrasted nicely against our new carpeting." In coding this response, the coder would have to decide whether the first portion of the comment should be coded in the "brand name" category, the "quality" category, or both. Without a coding guide or rules in place to guide the decision, one coder may classify the first sentence of the response as "brand name" related, while another may classify it as "quality" based, and yet a third may double-count the same comment by classifying it in both categories. The second portion of the comment regarding color may fall into the "appearance" category, or be treated as a new response, depending upon the coding rules that are in place.

Once the initial list has been generated, the next step is to go through the completed surveys. Each new response that is seen should be added to the list. No attempt to force it into a current response category should be made unless it is clear that it fits well with a given response category.

When all the surveys have been examined, related responses should be consolidated. This is a difficult task because it relies on the researcher's judgment. Decisions have to be made if two responses are really the same and should be consolidated into one category or should instead remain as two separate answers.

The greatest challenge in this process is interpreting an answer. While many responses will fit the codes that have been developed, some responses will not. The researcher then must decide between creating a new category or choosing a category that already exists and appears to be close to what the respondent is saying. Creating a new category for only one or two responses is not productive because those data are not very useful. Forcing such data into a category requires researcher judgment, and may not truly reflect the respondent's thoughts. Consider the following response that was provided to the question "What is the most important factor in purchasing textbooks for your classes?"

> Price is really the most important, but also convenience is too. So I always go for the lowest price, but it depends too. If I didn't have time to buy the book online before class starts, then I will go to the campus bookstore and just get it there even though it costs more.

In terms of coding this response, three possible categories that could be used are price, convenience, and time. Into which category should it be coded? While this respondent is saying price is the most important factor, the respondent is also saying convenience is important, and is willing to pay more if he or she doesn't have time to get the book online before classes begin. A case could also be made that time is most important, as when a textbook is purchased influences the decision more than price. The response could fit into all three categories, or it could be discarded since the coder is not sure what to do. While predetermined rules can help guide the coder, whatever decision is made, it represents the judgment of the coder and may not truly reflect the opinion of the respondent since the respondent's view is not clear.

The last step is to assign a numerical code to each response, using a process similar to that discussed when coding closed-ended questions. If the question asks for the single most important factor, then a single variable is created, and responses are coded from 1 to X, where X is equal to the number of response categories. If a respondent is allowed multiple answers, each response category would represent a separate variable in the data set, and dummy coding would be used.

Within the marketing research industry, a common practice is to code only 20% to 30% of the responses to open-ended questions. Research companies have found that this practice will actually yield the same results as coding 100% of the open-ended responses. It can be the first 20% to 30% of the items, or it can be a random selection of items. Either process will tend to yield the same results as long as the methodology in collecting the data is the same throughout the entire data set. However, it is critical that at least 50 open-ended responses be coded.[10]

A marketing researcher coding open-ended questions.

■ Objective 12.3: Describe the processes of data entry and data cleaning.

DATA ENTRY

Data entry is the process of entering data into a computer spreadsheet such as SPSS or Excel that can be used for data tabulation and analysis. With the increased use of online surveys, the need for manual data entry has been reduced substantially. With electronic surveys, responses from individuals taking the survey are automatically placed into a spreadsheet based on the coding that was programmed into the questionnaire.

When questionnaires are completed on paper, researchers have two options. The first is to have someone manually enter the data into a computer spreadsheet. The data being entered may have been manually coded on each paper survey, or transferred to a coding sheet in which the correct numerical response for each variable is listed on a subject-by-subject basis. The second is to use a scanning device that can read the answers. If a scanning device is used, then usually responses are recorded on answer sheets or within a designated area on the survey that will allow for electronic scanning.

DATA CLEANING

Data cleaning occurs once all of the data are entered into a spreadsheet and before results are tabulated and analyzed. **Data cleaning** is the process of checking the data for inconsistency and involves three steps:

- Examine data for values out of the coded range.
- Examine data for values that are extreme.
- Compare responses that show inconsistency.

The first step is to look for values outside of the accepted range for each question. This can be done easily by running a frequency count for each question using SPSS or Excel. For instance, in Figure 12.4, responses for Questions 1 and 4 must be either a 1 or a 2. If a 0, a 3, or any other number is found, then there has been an error in data entry. If the data were manually entered or scanned, the questionnaire could be located through the questionnaire number and then checked to see what number should have been recorded. In Figure 12.5, responses should be from 1 to 5 for Question 1. Any other response is out of this range and is an error. Values outside of the accepted range are relatively easy to detect and correct. With online and electronic questionnaires, any value out of the accepted range is almost always due to a coding error in the computer program since the individual taking the survey can only select the options that appear on the screen.

The second step in data cleaning is checking for extreme values that may occur with open-ended questions. For instance, respondents may be asked how many energy drinks they have purchased in the last month. Suppose someone has written 220. That is over 7 energy drinks a day, which is extremely unlikely. But, did the person intend to write 22 or was it 20, or could it even have been just a 2? If the respondent can be contacted again, then the correct answer can be obtained. But, the cost of doing so is probably not worth the effort since one survey among 200 or 300 is not going to change the results. Therefore, either the response is deleted, or the entire survey is discarded depending on the quality of the remaining answers on the questionnaire.

The third situation is the most difficult, checking for answer inconsistencies. It is not an outlier like the first two situations. Researchers will often put a couple of questions in a survey to make sure the respondent is reading the questions and answering thoughtfully. Suppose a respondent has said he or she does not like playing video games on a smartphone (checking the "no" response). Suppose this same person later in the survey checked "highly preferred" to the question about his or her level of preference for playing games on a smartphone. So in one question the respondent says he or she does not like playing video games on a smartphone, but then later in the survey says the smartphone or tablet is highly preferred for playing video games. Because of this inconsistency, the questionnaire may be discarded. The person either did not read the questions, intentionally provided random responses, or provided answers that did not show thought and sincerity.

PRECODING QUESTIONNAIRES

Precoding questionnaires involves putting the code number on the survey instrument prior to individuals filling it out. If the questions in Figures 12.4 and 12.6 had the codes already printed on the survey question as indicated in the figures, then they would be precoded. It is very easy

■ Objective 12.4: Discuss the advantages of precoding questionnaires.

for the individual recording the data to see what code number should be placed in the computer spreadsheet. Precoding in this fashion reduces transcription errors (also called data processing errors). One disadvantage to precoding is that some researchers feel it may influence or affect respondents' answers to questions if they see how a question will be coded in the computer. As mentioned in Chapter 10, studies have compared scales containing all positive precoded numbers (e.g., 1 to 5) with those in which precoded numbers for scales were negatively and positively balanced (e.g., −2 to +2). Scales using negatively and positively balanced numeric response categories produced more positive evaluations.[11] Others argue that no bias or influence would occur if the codes were seen by the respondents. A second disadvantage is that precoding can take up more space on a survey, reducing its readability and potentially negatively influencing perceptions of survey length.

Of course, only closed-ended questions can be precoded for surveys that a respondent sees. Precoding open-ended questions where a respondent would see possible answers would certainly bias the person's answer. But, if the question is administered by telephone or in person and read to the respondent, then having precoded answers allows the interviewer to check the person's response. If it is not in the list of possible answers, then it can be added. Suppose a question asks individuals what their favorite platform is for playing video games. The list of possible answers can be on the interviewer's list, and the response given by the individual can then be checked.

With online surveys and other electronic-type surveys, questions can be coded in advance. This allows the computer to enter the respondent's answer into a spreadsheet, saving labor costs and time spent in the data validation, data entry, and data checking stages. These time savings ultimately translate into cost savings for the firm, and allow research projects to be completed more quickly. This works well for closed-ended and scale-type questions. For open-ended questions, whatever the person enters into the survey will be transcribed into the spreadsheet. Researchers can then code those responses once the survey collection is complete.

■ Objective 12.5: Describe the various ways of tabulating data.

TABULATION

Tabulations involve counting the number of responses in each answer category of a question. While the raw number of counts can be used, more often researchers are concerned about percentages. The two types of tabulations used are one-way tabulations and cross-tabulations. **One-way tabulations** involve counting the number of responses for each answer category within one question. **Cross-tabulations** involve counting the number of responses in two or more categories simultaneously.

One-Way Tabulations

One-way tabulation involves obtaining the frequency and percentage of responses to a question. Figure 12.12 contains the SPSS output for the question "Have you played video games on your smartphone?" Responses were yes and no. "Yes" responses were coded a 1 while "no" responses were coded a 0. The total number of completed surveys was 688.

The first column of the output identifies the possible responses to the question. The second column shows the frequency. For this question, 417 respondents said "no" to the question, 263 said "yes," and 8 individuals did not answer the question. The third column provides the percent of responses for each category. Out of the sample of 688 respondents, 60.6% indicated "no,"

38.2% indicated "yes," and 1.2% did not answer the question. The fourth column titled "Valid Percent" shows the percent of responses for each category of those who answered the question. In this case, of those who answered this question, 61.3% said "no," and 38.7% said "yes."

Since there are only two answers to this question, the cumulative percentage is not a relevant statistic. It may be more relevant for the question that asked respondents their level of preference for each of the gaming platforms, shown in Figure 12.13. The output shows how likely respondents are to use video games on social networking sites. In looking at the last column, 26.3% of the respondents said they are "very unlikely" to play games on a social networking website. In the next row, a total of 53.8% said they are "very unlikely to use" or "somewhat unlikely to use" social networking sites for video games. Taken one step further, a researcher could say 76.1% are not likely to play or neutral about playing games at a social networking site. Subtracting 76.1% from 100%, the researcher could also state that only 23.9% of those who answered the question indicated any type of positive likelihood of playing games on social networking sites.

Figure 12.12   Example of SPSS Output for Dichotomous Question

Have you played video games on your smartphone?

		Frequency	Percent	Valid Percent	Cumulative Percent
Valid	No	417	60.6	61.3	61.3
	Yes	263	38.2	38.7	100.0
	Total	680	98.8	100.0	
Missing	System	8	1.2		
Total		688	100.0		

Figure 12.13   Example of SPSS Output for Likelihood Usage Question

Usage likelihood for social network site

		Frequency	Percent	Valid Percent	Cumulative Percent
Valid	Very unlikely to use	172	25.0	26.3	26.3
	Somewhat unlikely to use	179	26.0	27.4	53.8
	Neither likely nor unlikely to use	146	21.2	22.4	76.1
	Somewhat likely to use	98	14.2	15.0	91.1
	Very likely to use	58	8.4	8.9	100.0
	Total	653	94.9	100.0	
Missing	System	35	5.1		
Total		688	100.0		

In many questions, the value of the missing data is not relevant. It just tells the researchers how many did not answer the question. Usually, it is a very small percentage. But, occasionally the missing value number (or percentage) is important to a researcher. Notice the results in Figure 12.14, which asks respondents where they purchased their last video game. In looking at the third column, 27.3% purchased their last game from a retail store, 43.9% purchased it online, 2.9% rented the game, and 25.9% did not answer the question. Sometimes a large number of nonresponses are due to the sensitive nature of the question and a respondent's desire to protect his or her privacy. In this case, the large percent of missing data is likely due to the fact that the response options are not categorically exhaustive. This brings up the interesting question that if the game was not purchased online or from a retail store, and was not rented, then where/how was it obtained? At this point, the researcher can only speculate. Identifying other sources for video game purchases would require additional investigation, which could be accomplished via personal interviews, a focus group, asking an open-ended question, or offering an "other" with a fill-in-the-blank option to the existing question.

Cross-Tabulations

Cross-tabulations analyze relationships and involve comparing data across two different variables, at least one of which is measured at the nominal level. Figure 12.15 is the SPSS output of the question "Have you played video games on social networking sites?" by the respondent's gender. It shows the frequency count for the "yes" and "no" responses as well as the column percentages. In respect to females, 85.4% said "no" to the question, and 14.6% responded "yes" that they had played games on social networking sites. For the males in the sample, 93.7% said "no," and only 6.3% indicated "yes."

Three-way cross-tabs are occasionally used when researchers believe two different variables may be impacting a response. For example, with video games a researcher may think that both gender and income drive attitude toward the various gaming platforms. Using SPSS, a three-way cross-tab table can be produced, as shown in Figure 12.16. Thus, two- and

Figure 12.14   Example of SPSS Output With a Relevant Missing Value

Where did you purchase your last video game?		Frequency	Percent	Valid Percent	Cumulative Percent
Valid	Retail store	188	27.3	36.9	36.9
	Online	302	43.9	59.2	96.1
	Rented—did not purchase	20	2.9	3.9	100.0
	Total	510	74.1	100.0	
Missing	System	178	25.9		
Total		688	100.0		

Figure 12.15   Example of Cross-Tabulation SPSS Output

Have you played video games on social networking sites? * Gender Cross-tabulation

| | | | Gender | | |
			Female	Male	Total
Played video games on social networking sites	No	Count	223	385	608
		% within gender	85.4%	93.7%	90.5%
	Yes	Count	38	26	64
		% within gender	14.6%	6.3%	9.5%
Total		Count	261	411	672
		% within gender	100.0%	100.0%	100.0%

Figure 12.16   Example of a Three-Way SPSS Cross-Tab Output

Have you played video games on social networking sites? * Gender * Income Cross-tabulation

| | | | | | Gender | | |
					Female	Male	Total
Lessthan $24,999	Played video games on social networking sites	No		Count	37	63	100
				% within gender	88.1%	90.0%	89.3%
		Yes		Count	5	7	12
				% within gender	11.9%	10.0%	10.7%
$25,000– $49,999	Played video games on social networking sites	No		Count	53	84	137
				% within gender	93.0%	93.3%	93.2%
		Yes		Count	4	6	10
				% within gender	7.0%	6.7%	6.8%
$50,000– $74,999	Played video games on social networking sites	No		Count	45	79	124
				% within gender	84.9%	94.0%	90.5%
		Yes		Count	8	5	13
				% within gender	15.1%	6.0%	9.5%
$75,000– $99,999	Played video games on social networking sites	No		Count	43	68	111
				% within gender	82.7%	91.9%	88.1%
		Yes		Count	9	6	15
				% within gender	17.3%	8.1%	11.9%
$100,000+	Played video games on social networking sites	No		Count	34	68	102
				% within gender	75.6%	97.1%	88.7%
		Yes		Count	11	2	13
				% within gender	24.4%	2.9%	11.3%

three-way cross-tabulations divide the sample into subgroups in order to better understand how the dependent variable is related to and varies by the different subgroups.

Of concern to researchers is the percentage for each gender in each income group. For the first two income groups (less than $24,999 and $25,000–$49,999), the percentages of females and males who indicated they had played video games ("yes" responses) on social networking sites are relatively equal. But, beginning with the $50,000–$79,999 income bracket, differences appear. Of females, 15.1% said "yes," compared to only 6% of males who said "yes." Differences are also present in the $75,000–$99,999 income group. The most drastic differences are in the $100,000-plus income bracket where 24.4% of females have played video games on social networking sites compared to only 2.9% of males.

Basic Descriptive Statistics

■ Objective 12.6: Explain the descriptive statistics that should be used with each type of scale.

Reporting the results of every question in a survey, including the demographic profile of the sample, is basic descriptive statistics. It provides researchers with an overview of the data that were obtained through the questionnaire. The type of descriptive statistics obtained is dictated by the type of scale within each question. Figure 12.17 provides an overview of the type of data and appropriate descriptive statistic. For nominal and ordinal data, the appropriate descriptive statistic would be a frequency count. For interval and ratio data, the key appropriate descriptive statistics are the mean, a measure of central tendency, and standard deviation, a measure of dispersion.

Figure 12.18 provides the SPSS output for usage likelihood for various gaming platforms. Means and standard deviations are appropriate because this variable represents interval-level data, based on the assumption that the distances between categories will be perceived by respondents as being equal. With regard to the mean, the platform with the lowest likelihood of usage is social networking sites (2.53), and the platforms with the highest likelihood of usage are smartphones (3.52) and the computer (3.44).

The standard deviation provides an indication of the degree of variation in the responses. Of the five variables listed in Figure 12.18, the likelihood of playing games on online websites has the highest standard deviation while preference for games on social networking sites has the lowest. This would indicate that responses in reference to online websites are spread out or dispersed more than are the responses for social networking sites, and suggest that tests for differences should be performed on the basis of gender, income, age, or other factors that might help to account for the differences, or dispersion in responses.

Respondents in the gaming platform study were asked how many games they purchased in the last year, which generates ratio data. The SPSS analysis provided a mean of 3.73 with a standard deviation of 2.98. Although the mean and standard deviation are appropriate descriptive statistics for ratio data, it sometimes is helpful to obtain the mode and median as well. The frequency count for the various responses is shown in Figure 12.19.

The mode is the most frequent response, which according to the SPSS output is 2 video games (114, or 16.6%). It would also be important to note that 1 game is also high with 100 responses, or 14.5%. The median is the midpoint of the data, below which 50% of the observations fall. In examining the cumulative percentage, the 50% point is within the response 3 games. This is useful information because the researcher can say that 53.9% of the respondents purchase 3 or fewer games a year.

Figure 12.17   Type of Scale and Descriptive Statistics

Type of Scale	Descriptive Measure
Nominal	Frequency
Ordinal	Frequency
Interval	Mean Standard Deviation
Ratio	Mean Standard Deviation

Figure 12.18 Descriptive Statistics for Interval Data

Descriptive Statistics

	N	Minimum	Maximum	Mean	Std. Deviation
Usage likelihood for online website	662	1	5	3.03	1.528
Usage likelihood for social networking site	653	1	5	2.53	1.269
Usage likelihood for gaming console	653	1	5	2.89	1.351
Usage likelihood for computer	666	1	5	3.44	1.313
Usage likelihood for smartphone	648	1	5	3.52	1.279
Valid *N* (listwise)	616				

Figure 12.19 Frequency Count of Ratio Data

Number of games purchased in last year

		Frequency	Percent	Valid Percent	Cumulative Percent
Valid	0	87	12.6	12.7	12.7
	1	100	14.5	14.6	27.4
	2	114	16.6	16.7	44.1
	3	67	9.7	9.8	53.9
	4	68	9.9	10.0	63.8
	5	59	8.6	8.6	72.5
	6	55	8.0	8.1	80.5
	7	47	6.8	6.9	87.4
	8	33	4.8	4.8	92.2
	9	28	4.1	4.1	96.3
	10	12	1.7	1.8	98.1
	11	6	.9	.9	99.0
	12	3	.4	.4	99.4
	14	2	.3	.3	99.7
	15	2	.3	.3	100.0
	Total	683	99.3	100.0	
Missing	System	5	.7		
Total		688	100.0		

With the array of numbers shown in Figure 12.19, researchers may want to collapse the data into categories so the information can be presented either in a table or graphically. In doing so the researcher will look at the data array three ways. First, are there any natural breaks in the data? Second, approximately how many categories are desirable? Third, what would be logical groupings of the data?

Figure 12.20 illustrates one possible grouping of the data. It makes sense to have a category for zero since this indicates the number of individuals who did not make any purchases in the last year. Such individuals should be separated from those who did make purchases. Then using groupings of three provides five total categories and makes logical sense. Thus, the groups are 0 games, 1–3 games, 4–6 games, 7–9 games, and 10-plus games.

The mode and median may be even more useful now. Recall that the mean was 3.73. The mode for the grouped data is 1–3 games, which has a frequency of 281. Most individuals, 41.1%, purchase 1–3 games. The median is also at this point with approximately half purchasing 3 or fewer games and approximately half purchasing 4 or more games.

Figure 12.20   Ratio Data Reported in Groups

Number of games purchased (categories)					
		Frequency	Percent	Valid Percent	Cumulative Percent
Valid	0 games	87	12.6	12.7	12.7
	1–3 games	281	40.8	41.1	53.9
	4–6 games	182	26.5	26.6	80.5
	7–9 games	108	15.7	15.8	96.3
	10+ games	25	3.6	3.7	100.0
	Total	683	99.3	100.0	
Missing	System	5	.7		
Total		688	100.0		

GRAPHING DATA

■ Objective 12.7: Discuss the principles involved in creating good graphs.

Graphs are an effective way of presenting basic descriptive statistical results. They are easy to read, and if done properly the viewer can quickly see the results as well as any differences that may exist. The basic principle behind a good graph is that it be able to stand alone. The title, the labeling of each axis, the legend, and the way the data are graphed must provide enough information that the viewer understands the data being presented. If the viewer has to ask questions or read comments in a paper to understand the graph, then inadequate information has been provided in the graph, or information has not been conveyed effectively. Detailed information concerning how to create effective charts and graphs will be presented in Chapter 14. The purpose of the following section is simply to demonstrate how various results can be incorporated into a chart or graph.

Data can be presented in a variety of graphical formats. Often the selection of a particular type is based on the personal preference of the individual graphing the data. But, in making that selection, it is important to choose the type of graph that will present the data in a clear, understandable way.

Bar charts are quite flexible and can be used with many types of data, while pie charts, line graphs, and area charts are more restrictive. Line graphs and area charts should be reserved for continuous data. **Continuous data** is simply another name for ratio-level data that can take any value, and may include both integers and decimal points. Some examples of continuous data are height, weight, miles per gallon, sales, and number of meals eaten at a particular restaurant.

Figure 12.21 illustrates one way nominal data can be presented. Recall from the earlier discussion that the missing responses were important for understanding the results of this question. Thus, the basis for this pie chart is all sample respondents, rather than simply those individuals who answered the question. Someone viewing the graph can quickly see that the highest percentage of individuals purchase video games online, followed by at retail stores. It can also be seen that a large percentage, 25.9%, did not answer the question. Notice the total percentage for the four categories equals 100%. If it was less or more than 100%, a pie chart could not be used (with the exception of decimal rounding errors).

A bar chart/column graph works well for ordinal data as illustrated in Figure 12.22. The graph shows the number of video games that were purchased during the last year by the respondents. By placing the value labels above each column, it is easy for the reader to see what percentages correspond with each category. While the height of the columns is an indicator of magnitude, it helps when the reader can see 41.1% of the individuals purchased 1 to 3 games during the last year, 26.6% purchased 4 to 6 games, and so forth. With a column (or bar) graph, it is important to label both the x-axis and the y-axis. Simple bar charts can also be used to present the results of questions that gather nominal- and interval-level data for a single variable.

Graphing data generated from a cross-tab analysis can be more challenging. Figure 12.23 shows one way to graph the data presented earlier, which looked at who played video games on social networking sites by gender and income (see Figure 12.16 for the data). Note that the researcher is only concerned about the "yes" responses since the purpose of the graph is to illustrate the percentage of individuals within each income bracket and gender who have played video games on social networking sites. The graph presents a

Figure 12.21   Pie Chart Graph of Nominal Data

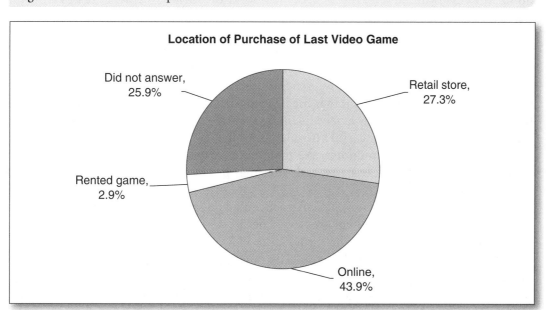

Figure 12.22   Simple Bar Chart Graph of Ordinal Data

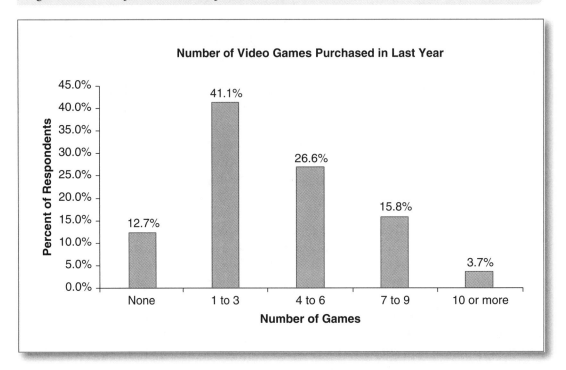

clear picture of the differences between males and females based on income that would be more difficult to see if the data were instead displayed only in a table. Except for the drop in the $25,000–$49,999 income bracket, the percentage of females playing games on social networking sites increases with income. While the decline in usage by income is not as pure, or perfect, there is a tendency for males to play games on social networking sites less as income rises.

With interval data, researchers often obtain a mean. This makes comparisons easier, and using a bar/column chart provides an excellent picture of the various means of multiple variables. Figure 12.24 shows the preference for the various gaming platforms. Since a scale of 1 to 5 was used, it is important that the label for the y-axis has markings from 1 to 5 and that a note is made on the axis label explaining the scale that was used. Again, the value on top of each column provides useful information by listing the actual mean for each gaming platform. From a visual standpoint, the preferences for computer and smartphone platforms look to be equal. While statistically they may be equal, it is helpful to see the actual numerical mean of both.

Graphing ratio data can be a challenge depending on the range. If the range of variables to be graphed is similar and there are few or no breaks between the category values, then an area graph or a line chart can be used. Figure 12.25 shows an area graph for the number of games purchased during the last year. The range for the number of games is from 0 to 15 with values for each category except 13. The area graph presents a vivid picture of how many games individuals purchase each year. The percentage increases from 0 and peaks at 2 games, then starts declining.

Figure 12.23   Graph of Cross-Tab Data Using a Clustered Bar Chart

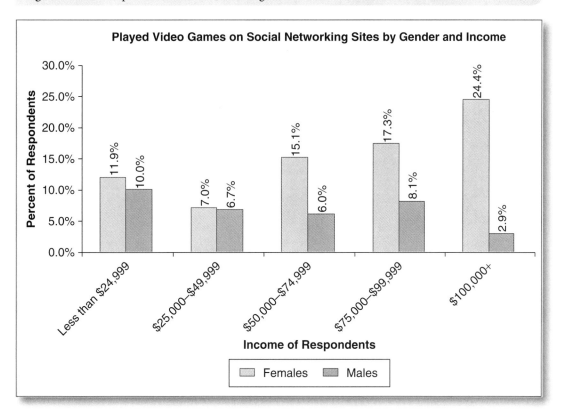

Figure 12.24   Graph of Interval Data

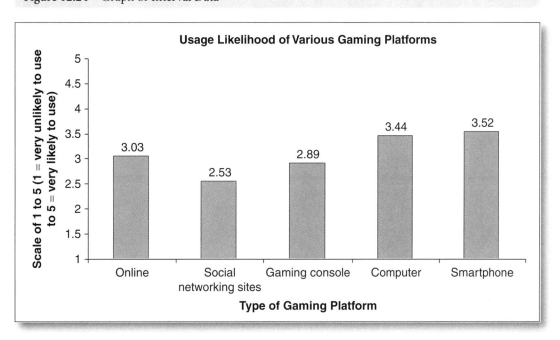

Figure 12.25   Graph of Ratio Data

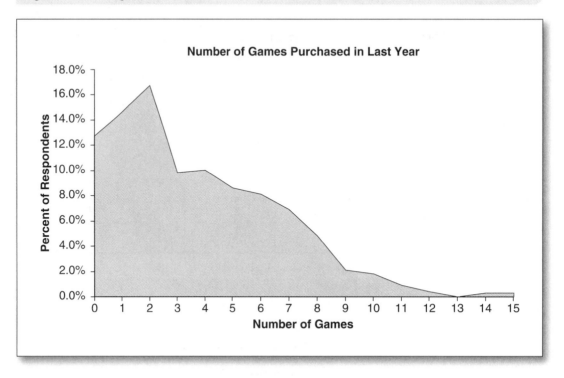

 Global Concerns

Many U.S. client firms and research providers are outsourcing international survey design, data collection, and validation tasks to international firms specializing in these areas. Outsourcing of international research is predicted to increase as a result of several factors. Cost-savings help research firms to remain profitable in today's demanding economic climate, which continually expects research firms to cut costs while producing results more quickly. By outsourcing tasks, research firms are also able to engage in more projects, increasing their capacity to do business. Finally, disaggregation is becoming more and more prevalent in the marketing research industry as a whole; the international research community is no exception.[12]

To ensure that the validation process is relatively trouble-free, U.S. client firms or their U.S. research partners must take care when selecting their primary international outsourcing firm. Only those firms with strong references who can provide evidence of having completed similar projects in the country(ies) in question should be considered.[13]

Once the primary outsourcing firm has been selected, careful thought must be put into creating playbooks. "Playbooks establish clear standards, protocols, and processes to be followed by all parties to ensure error-free deliverables and success. They are meant to ensure every process and quality step is followed. The playbook should identify clear detailed roles and responsibilities, timeliness, process flows and quality-control procedures."[14]

Playbooks are particularly important as many international partners in turn subcontract work at the country, region, and even local level. This means that client firms or U.S. research partners may be working with data that have passed through as many as four levels of subcontractors.

Consistency in performance and adherence to the playbook standards are of critical importance. Data accuracy and completeness should be stressed, not only within the playbook, but during the negotiation process. Costs related to ensuring that complete and accurate data are delivered should be built into the price of the primary outsourcing firm's services. The playbook should require the primary outsourcing firm to fully disclose its hiring and training procedures for interviewers, to describe upfront how interviewers will be compensated, and to ensure that all interviewers (regardless of whether employed by the outsourcing firm or a subcontractor) adhere to a standard training process and use standardized training materials. The primary outsourcing firm should also be required to provide a list of all subcontractors, and agree upon and fully disclose the quality control process used to validate data at the field level.

Furthermore, the primary outsourcing firm should be required to deliver evidence of validation activities as part of its deliverables. The contract should specify that subcontractors clarify ambiguous data in the field and that they provide both the original information and the validated information as part of their deliverables. This is important as cost, local custom, and language barriers make validating information by the primary outsourcing agency virtually impossible. If the primary outsourcing firm or a subcontractor is responsible for cleaning the data, the original and cleaned data files should also be required as part of the deliverables. While many factors impacting the validation process vary by country, adhering to this process can help to maximize the accuracy and completeness of data collected in an international setting.[15]

 STATISTICS REVIEW

As discussed in the chapter, data cleaning is the process of checking the data for inconsistencies. Figure 12.26 shows the SPSS output for a scaled-response question with inconsistencies. The question asked respondents to indicate their level of preference for video games on smartphones. It is a 5-point scale from "would not use" to "highly prefer." Notice in the output there is a "0" response and two "6" responses. Neither can be correct.

To locate the questionnaires with these three incorrect responses, the data can be sorted by this question. If using Excel, make certain that all fields are selected as part of the sort, or only data in the selected column will be sorted and will not match up with the original questionnaires. For SPSS, the variable related to this question is selected for the sorting. Depending on whether the data are sorted in ascending or descending order, the "0" response and "6" responses will be at the top and bottom of the data file. Once these are located on the spreadsheet, the questionnaire number can be identified. The questionnaire can then be checked to see if there was an entry error or some other mistake that resulted in the incorrect responses. In most cases, the incorrect value can be replaced with the correct value.

Open-ended questions that produce ratio data are more challenging. Figure 12.27 shows the SPSS printout for the number of games individuals purchased last year. Notice the last two items, the "77" response and the "115" response. Both seem highly unlikely since the nearest response is 15. If the researcher has the paper survey, then it is possible that the correct answer can be found.

But, what if this survey was completed online and there is no paper questionnaire to examine? Is it possible the person meant "7" and just accidentally typed in "77," or perhaps this person was not being serious and just typed it in to throw off the results? For the former, there is no way of knowing. In the latter situation, the researcher could check all of the person's other answers to see if they make sense and if they

(Continued)

(Continued)

Figure 12.26 Data Cleaning for a Scaled-Response Question

Preference for smartphone		Frequency	Percent	Valid Percent	Cumulative Percent
Valid	0	1	.1	.2	.2
	Very unlikely to use	54	7.8	8.3	8.5
	Somewhat unlikely to use	95	13.8	14.7	23.1
	Neither unlikely nor likely to use	152	22.1	23.5	46.6
	Somewhat likely to use	155	22.5	23.9	70.5
	Very likely to use	189	27.5	29.2	99.7
	6	2	.3	.3	100.0
	Total	648	94.2	100.0	
Missing	System	40	5.8		
Total		688	100.0		

appear to be consistent. If not, then the questionnaire can be discarded. The same process can be used for the "115." Here it is more difficult because there is no way of knowing if the person meant "11" or "15" as both would be legitimate answers. Regardless, the researcher must decide whether or not to keep extreme data points that cannot be validated, or whether they should be deleted. Most researchers would opt to remove the data points since their inclusion would significantly influence the mean number of games purchased.

In data cleaning, another situation that must be considered is constant sum questions. In the questionnaire dealing with gaming platforms, a constant sum question asked respondents what percent of the games they played across four platforms: game consoles, online, computer, and smartphone. The total of the four should add to 100%. While this can be automatically checked in online surveys, self-administered surveys rely on the user to correctly complete the question. Sometimes respondents make mistakes, and their answers do not add to the necessary 100%. Since the researcher cannot really know what the respondent meant to answer, the constant sum scale should be deleted from the analysis and values changed to missing data. Failure to add properly does not necessarily mean that the rest of the questionnaire data is bad, so unless multiple validation problems exist within the survey, the rest of the data can be retained.

To check if the four responses did indeed add to 100%, a new variable can be created that sums the answers to the four categories (each represented by a separate variable). Results of the gaming platform study for the constant sum question are shown in Figure 12.28. Notice out of the 617 individuals who answered this question, 603 or 97.7% did so correctly. That means 14 responses did not sum to 100. Totals ranged from 80 to 200. Some were close, such as the 95 and the 105, but the researcher cannot know what happened and cannot arbitrarily subtract or add 5 percentage points from one of the four platform responses. Neither can the response of the individual whose total came to 200 be halved for each category. The same is true for the other cases where the constant sum did not equal 100.

In examining data, sometimes researchers want to know how a specific segment of the sample, rather than the entire group, responded to questions. For instance, in developing video games it may

Figure 12.27   Data Cleaning for an Open-Ended Ratio Scale

Number of games purchased in last year

		Frequency	Percent	Valid Percent	Cumulative Percent
Valid	.00	87	12.6	12.7	12.7
	1.00	100	14.5	14.6	27.4
	2.00	114	16.6	16.7	44.1
	3.00	66	9.6	9.7	53.7
	4.00	68	9.9	10.0	63.7
	5.00	59	8.6	8.6	72.3
	6.00	55	8.0	8.1	80.4
	7.00	47	6.8	6.9	87.3
	8.00	32	4.7	4.7	91.9
	9.00	28	4.1	4.1	96.0
	10.00	12	1.7	1.8	97.8
	11.00	6	.9	.9	98.7
	12.00	3	.4	.4	99.1
	14.00	2	.3	.3	99.4
	15.00	2	.3	.3	99.7
	77.00	1	.1	.1	99.9
	115.00	1	.1	.1	100.0
	Total	683	99.3	100.0	
Missing	System	5	.7		
Total		688	100.0		

be important to know what heavy purchasers think. Instead of looking at all individuals, it may be a good idea to look only at those who purchased 5 or more video games during the last year. This would be approximately one third of the sample. Researchers can do this by filtering or selecting only those who purchased 5 or more games. Out of the original sample of 688 respondents, 247 indicated they had purchased 5 or more video games during the last year.

The view of these individuals can be important in terms of developing an application for smartphones. When asked if they like playing video games on smartphones, the percentage of "yes" responses for the entire sample was 38.7%, but for those who had purchased 5 or more video games in the last year it was 53.1%. Clearly, those who are heavy purchasers of video games like playing video games on smartphones more than the sample as a whole.

Figure 12.29 shows the difference in usage likelihood for video games played on the computer and smartphones for the entire sample compared to heavy users. By using filtering, researchers can advise the video game producer that providing games on both platforms is important in reaching the heavy purchasers of video games.

(Continued)

(Continued)

Figure 12.28   Totals for a Constant Sum Questions

Sum Constant Sum

		Frequency	Percent	Valid Percent	Cumulative Percent
Valid	80.00	1	.1	.2	.2
	90.00	2	.3	.3	.5
	95.00	1	.1	.2	.6
	100.00	603	87.6	97.7	98.4
	105.00	3	.4	.5	98.9
	115.00	1	.1	.2	99.0
	125.00	1	.1	.2	99.2
	130.00	1	.1	.2	99.4
	132.00	1	.1	.2	99.5
	160.00	1	.1	.2	99.7
	200.00	2	.3	.3	100.0
	Total	617	89.7	100.0	
Missing	System	71	10.3		
Total		688	100.0		

Figure 12.29   Example of Results With Filtering

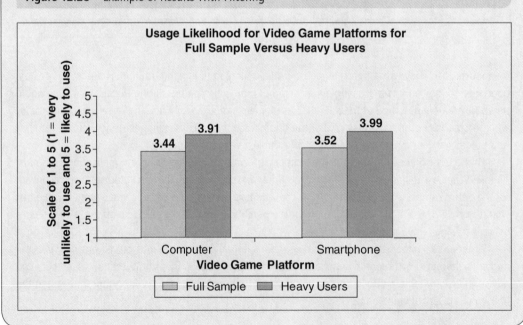

DEALING WITH DATA

A study was conducted with 180 respondents concerning criteria in selecting a retail clothing store. The questionnaire is titled "Chapter 12 Dealing with Data Survey," and the data are titled "Chapter 12 Dealing with Data." Both files are located on the textbook website, www.sagepub.com/clowess. Respondents were asked to indicate how important nine different criteria were in selecting a retail clothing store. A 5-point scale was used from "very unimportant" to "very important." Another question asked respondents to indicate what percent of clothing they purchased in discount stores, department stores, specialty stores, and online.

The first step in cleaning the data is to run a frequency count of every question to make sure no responses are outside the accepted range from very unimportant to very important. For those that fall outside the range, it is important to identify the specific questionnaire or "case" number of the invalid data so it can be fixed. This can be done by sorting the data on that variable.

The second step in the data cleaning is to create a new variable that is the sum of the constant sum categories. The total should add to 100%. Again, the specific case number where problems occur must be identified. After completing these steps, answer the following questions.

1. Of the nine criteria individuals use to select retail clothing stores, which ones have answers outside the 5-point scale? Identify the question and the response that was incorrect, as well as the specific case number that corresponds with each error. (This can also be done by running a cross-tab with Case ID as the row variable and the criteria question as the column variable.)

2. Looking at the summed total for the constant sum question, how many individuals were identified as "missing system"?

3. Looking at the summed total for the constant sum question, what percent of the answers add to the correct 100%? What other totals are seen in the output? Link the case number to each incorrect constant sum total. (Again, this can be done by using the cross-tab function, or sorting the data by the sum variable.)

4. Do any of the questionnaires indicate multiple validation problems? If so, which specific cases (questionnaires) would you recommend eliminating entirely from the data pool, and why?

SUMMARY

Objective 1: Identify the steps in the data preparation process.

The data preparation process involves four steps: validation, coding, data entry, and data cleaning. Data validation is a process used by researchers to ensure data were collected properly and are free of error and bias. The next step is data entry, which is actually entering data into a computer spreadsheet such as SPSS or Excel that can be used for data tabulation and analysis. The last step is data cleaning, which is the process of checking the data for inconsistencies.

Objective 2: Discuss the processes of validating and coding data.

Validation starts by checking the data collection process to make sure procedures were followed and data were collected properly. If multiple interviewers were used, data must have been collected the same way. The data are then checked to make sure only qualified respondents passed the screening questions and unqualified respondents were not interviewed or did not complete questionnaires. The next validation step is checking the data for fraud. While extremely difficult to detect, the researcher can check for signs that it may have occurred. Finally, the completeness and usability of the data must be checked by someone with excellent knowledge of the study purpose and survey objectives. The second step in the validation process is coding, which is assigning numerical values to each response on the questionnaire. Coding closed-ended questions and scaled questions tends to be rather easy. Open-ended questions, however, require some level of interpretation and classification of responses, a time-consuming and expensive process.

Objective 3: Describe the processes of data entry and data cleaning.

Data entry involves entering the data into a computer spreadsheet. With online surveys the data are automatically entered into a spreadsheet through the programming of the online survey. If entered manually, the person doing the data entry must be given a code sheet that specifies the code to be used for each response. Double-data entry may be used. Data cleaning involves checking the data for inconsistencies and involves three steps. First, the data are examined for values out of the range for a particular response. Second, the data are checked for extreme values that appear to be incorrect and not feasible. Third, the data are checked for responses that show inconsistency and lack of reading the question or attention on the part of the respondent. Correlation analysis helps identify data entry errors when double entry is used.

Objective 4: Discuss the advantages of precoding questionnaires.

Precoding involves putting the code numbers on the questionnaire prior to administering the survey. For online and computerized surveys, precoding automatically occurs in writing the program because the computer needs to know what numerical value to give to each response. Paper surveys can also be precoded. This makes it easier for the person entering the data into a computer, and most researchers feel it does not bias responses.

Objective 5: Describe the various ways of tabulating data.

Tabulation is counting the number of responses in each answer category of a question. One-way tabulation involves counting the number of responses for each answer category within one question. Cross-tabulation is counting the number of responses in two or more categories simultaneously. In tabulating responses, researchers must be cognizant of the number of missing items (individuals who left the question blank). In most cases it is small and insignificant to understanding the data. In other instances, nonresponses are important and need to be considered in the tabulation.

Objective 6: Explain the descriptive statistics that should be used with each type of scale.

Descriptive statistics is the reporting of every question in a survey, including sample demographics. If the type of scale is nominal or ordinal, the appropriate descriptive statistic is a frequency count. If the type of scale is interval or ratio, then the appropriate descriptive statistic is the mean and standard deviation.

Objective 7: Discuss the principles involved in creating good graphs.

Graphs are an effective means of presenting descriptive statistics. In creating graphs, it is important to have a title that clearly explains the data. Also important is the labeling of the x-axis and y-axis. If a pie chart is used, then the percentages need to add to 100%. Pie graphs, bar graphs, and column graphs work well for nominal and ordinal data. For interval data, bar and column graphs tend to work well. For ratio data, line and area charts can be used. In selecting the type of graph, the critical criteria are which type of graph will show the results clearly and be the easiest for the viewer to understand.

GLOSSARY OF KEY TERMS

Coding: assigning numerical values to each response on the questionnaire

Continuous data: another name for ratio-level data that can take any value and may include both integers and decimal points

Cross-tabulation: counting the number of responses in two or more categories simultaneously

Data cleaning: process of checking data for inconsistency

Data entry: process of entering data into a computer spreadsheet such as SPSS or Excel that can be used for data tabulation and analysis

Data validation: process to ensure data were collected properly and are as free of error and bias as possible

Dummy coding: responses are coded 1 if a response option is selected and 0 if it is not selected

One-way tabulation: counting the number of responses for each answer category within one question

Parameter: characteristic of a population, such as the mean or mode

Statistic: characteristic of a sample used as an estimator for the population parameter

Straight-lining: occurs when a respondent selects the same response category for all or the majority of responses to "grid"-based questions

Tabulation: counting the number of responses in each answer category of a question

CRITICAL THINKING EXERCISES

1. In validating a mall intercept survey, a field supervisor asked a recent interviewee what she answered when asked, "What is the one thing you dislike most about Fashion Lu's retail store?" The respondent answered, "Fashion Lu's doesn't carry the top clothing brands that are most popular among people my age." The response written by the interviewer read, "Carries low-quality brands." Is the interviewer's recorded response an accurate representation of the interviewee's opinion? Why or why not?

2. An open-ended question asked, "What is your favorite thing about football?" Critique the phrasing of the question, create a list of possible response categories, and code the following responses into categories. Justify your decisions.
   a. "High-scoring games are exciting."
   b. "Men in tight pants."
   c. "There's nothing better than being with friends in the stands, watching your college team beat up on a rival, especially if you sneak a flask into the game. I love close games."
   d. "I hate football."
   e. "Watching an NFL game on TV is the perfect way to spend a rainy Sunday afternoon."
   f. "It's fun."
   g. "I love playing football on nice fall days, but I really don't like playing when it rains."
   h. "Tim Tebow is so cute and such a nice guy! I wish he was a better player, though."
   i. "I like watching well-matched defenses play against one another."
   j. "Tailgating is great! I love visiting with friends, eating lots of food, and getting drunk. The game is OK, I guess."

3. Identify whether the data below are nominal, ordinal, interval, or ratio data. What type of chart or graph would you recommend to present the results of this table? Should data from other brands be included as well? Why or why not? What additional information would be needed in order to create a chart that is clear and easily understood?

Rank Walmart		Frequency	Percent	Valid Percent	Cumulative Percent
Valid	Least desirable	139	69.5	69.5	69.5
	4th most desirable	26	13.0	13.0	82.5
	3rd most desirable	20	10.0	10.0	92.5
	2nd most desirable	10	5.0	5.0	97.5
	Most desirable	5	2.5	2.5	100.0
	Total	200	100.0	100.0	

4. Suppose you developed a Likert scale to assess the degree to which attracting new customers was given priority in the marketing plan. Which of the following items need to be reversed so that more positive responses are expressed by higher numbers? Assume that respondents will use a scale ranging from 1 (*strongly disagree*) to 5 (*strongly agree*).

   1. Formal strategies are in place to attract new clients.

   2. We do not give enough attention to attracting new clients.

   3. Our employees are not motivated to sell our services to potential customers.

   The following questions require you to access the textbook's website at www.sagepub.com/ clowess. The SPSS data file is named "Chapter 12 Critical Thinking Data," and the Word file "Chapter 12 Critical Thinking Survey" has the survey questions.

5. Review the survey questions that accompany the data file, and think about whether they represent nominal-, ordinal-, interval-, or ratio-level data. Open the SPSS data file, and look at the column titled "MEASURE." For each variable, change the measure from "SCALE" to either "ORDINAL" or "NOMINAL" if appropriate. Remember, interval- and ratio-level measures are designated by "SCALE" in SPSS. String characters (such as responses to open-ended questions) by default are classified as "NOMINAL" data.

6. Except for the first variable "IDNO" (the survey number corresponding to each respondent), run frequencies for each of the variables contained in the data file. Create a table based on this output, which lists the variable name, incorrect value, and "IDNO" for each problem found.

7. Variables "4aCSRunning" through "4aCSSwimming" represent the results of a constant sum scale. Validate the data by creating a new variable that sums the constant sum variables. Run a frequency for the new variable, then create a table listing this variable's name, the incorrect percentages, and the "IDNO" for each problem case.

8. Question 6 of the survey asks individuals why they joined a health club. Code the open-ended responses into categories. Justify why you chose the categories that you did. For each category, create a table that lists the category name, and the verbatim responses that fall into that category. Should any of the open-ended remarks be thrown out? Why or why not? Next, create a new variable in SPSS containing these classifications, and code each case. Save your data file.

9. Examine the items in Question 3. Which need to be recoded so that the more positive attitudes are represented by higher numbers? Recode these into new variables. Be sure to keep the old variables. When you are finished, run descriptive statistics (frequencies, means, range, and standard deviations) for each of the Question 3 variables. If you were to present this information visually, what type of graph or chart would you recommend? Why? What portion of the data would you graph, the frequency count, percentage, mean, or standard deviation? Justify your answer.

10. Create a chart or graph that accurately displays a cross-tabulation of "Q6WhyJoin" by "Q7Gender." Comment on the results. What other variables might make good candidates for cross-tabulations? List your recommendations.

11. Which of the variables in the data set would be good candidates for pie charts? Why? Which would be better represented by some type of bar/column chart? Why? Are any variables in this data set suitable for area chart or line graphs? Why or why not?

CONTINUING CASE STUDY: LAKESIDE GRILL

The student team collected data using four different methods. First, they passed the questionnaire out to patrons at Lakeside Grill and asked them to fill it out while waiting for their food. Second, they sent e-mails to businesses that were members of the Chamber of Commerce and asked that the e-mail be circulated among the business's employees. The e-mail directed respondents to an online version of the survey. Third, the team used a mall intercept approach asking individuals to fill out the questionnaire. The fourth approach was e-mail sent by students in three different marketing classes to family and friends who lived in the area. These approaches produced 247 completed surveys.

Located on the textbook website (www.sagepub.com/clowess) is the final questionnaire used for the study, "Chapter 12 Lakeside Grill Survey." The data that were collected are in an SPSS file called "Chapter 12 Lakeside Grill Data." The data were validated, coded, and entered into the SPSS spreadsheet. During the data cleaning process, several errors were detected. The original questionnaires were obtained to determine the cause of the error. Several items were corrected, and eight questionnaires were discarded because of inconsistencies in answers.

Upon completion of the data preparation process, descriptive statistics for each question were run. This output file is titled "Chapter 12 Lakeside Descriptive Output." From the data, the team developed graphs for each question and placed them in a PowerPoint file. The title of this file is "Chapter 12 Lakeside Descriptive Graphs." All of these files can be found at the website (www.sagepub.com/clowess).

Access all of these files and then answer the questions below.

Critique Questions:

1. Critique the four methods the team used to collect the data. Should they have identified the source (data collection method) of each response? Why or why not?

2. Critique the final questionnaire. Look carefully at the responses to Questions 2, 4, and 5 in the SPSS data file. Evaluate how these open-ended questions were coded.

3. Open the output file titled "Chapter 12 Lakeside Descriptive Output." Compare the output file to the questionnaire. Did the team run the correct descriptive statistics? If not, what descriptive statistics should have been run? Are there any other statistics that should be obtained using SPSS?

4. Open the "Chapter 12 Lakeside Descriptive Graphs" file. Examine each graph. Is it clear, understandable, and properly labeled? What are some of the problems that can occur when graphing in SPSS? Compare each graph with the SPSS output file. Discuss each graph in terms of being appropriate for its descriptive statistic.

MARKETING RESEARCH PORTFOLIO

Using a data set and questionnaire found at www.sagepub.com/clowess, this chapter's "Marketing Research Portfolio" mini-case provides practice in data validation, running descriptive statistics, and reverse coding of items. Finally students are challenged to note problems in the questionnaire that could influence the quality of data collected.

STUDENT STUDY SITE

Visit the Student Study Site at www.sagepub.com/clowess to access the following additional materials:

- eFlashcards
- Web Quizzes
- SAGE Journal Articles
- Web Resources

CHAPTER 13

Analysis of Differences and Regression Analysis

LEARNING OBJECTIVES

After reading this chapter, you should be able to

1. Identify and explain the steps in hypothesis testing.

2. Understand the misuses of statistical significance and how statistically significant results may differ from those with practical importance.

3. Explain the difference between Type I and Type II errors.

4. Explain how the chi-square test is used.

5. Identify and describe the various tests for differences in means.

6. Demonstrate an understanding of regression analysis.

INTRODUCTION

The reason companies collect data is to provide information to make better decisions. Once data are collected and have been validated, it is time for more intensive analysis that will reveal significant differences that can be used by management. Recently, Lightspeed Research conducted a consumer study concerning the Super Bowl. The study investigated who watches, why, and how they interact with smartphones and the Internet before, during, and after the game. The survey yielded 2,001 usable responses.[1] One question on the survey asked respondents why they watched the Super Bowl. Part of the analysis was to see if the reason individuals watch the game varies by age. The results are shown in Figure 13.1.

Figure 13.1   Primary Reason Individuals Watch the Super Bowl

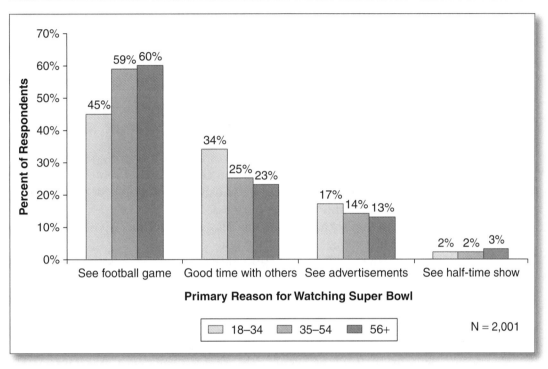

Source: Author-created with data from "Super Bowl Sunday Consumer Survey," *Lightspeed Research*, January 2011, www.light speedresearch.com.

A couple of conclusions can be drawn from the graph. Clearly, the primary reason individuals watch the Super Bowl is to see the game. But, the percentage who indicated this reason was higher for individuals 35 and older than it was for the 18–34 age category. Younger consumers like to watch the game with friends and relatives and see it as an opportunity to have a good time to a greater extent than do older consumers. Watching to see the new commercials was cited more by younger consumers than older consumers. Few indicated that seeing the half-time show was the primary reason they watched the Super Bowl.

This chapter first reviews hypothesis testing and how data analysis can be used to support and reject the null hypothesis. The second part of the chapter examines various tests that are often used in marketing research. These include goodness-of-fit tests and various tests for measuring differences in means between populations or components of a sample.

HYPOTHESIS TESTING

In Chapter 2, the concept of a research hypothesis was briefly introduced in the text and reviewed in the "Statistics Review" section of the chapter. Understanding the research hypothesis concept is important because marketers want to know if conditions or situations constitute a change in

■ Objective 13.1: Identify and explain the steps in hypothesis testing.

Figure 13.2   Steps in Hypothesis Testing

1. State the hypothesis
2. Select the statistical test
3. Determine the decision rule
4. Calculate the test statistic
5. State the conclusion

the marketing strategy that is being used. While differences may exist, more important to researchers is whether the difference is significant. Furthermore, does that significant difference warrant a change in a firm's marketing strategy or the development of a separate marketing campaign? Figure 13.2 identifies five steps involved in testing a hypothesis.

Step 1: State the Hypothesis

Hypothesis testing involves writing a null hypothesis (H_0) and an alternative hypothesis (H_A). The null hypothesis is a statement or claim that can be statistically tested. It is derived from the research questions or objectives of the study. It can be based on past research, the current situation, or a supposition on what may be the situation. The purpose of the hypothesis is to state the claim in such a way that it can be measured and tested.

If the subject of a hypothesis is a single variable, then the null hypothesis is usually stated in terms of equality. For instance, a manufacturer of computers may have as a hypothesis "Individuals purchase a new laptop computer on average every 3 years." A firm that is testing a newly designed coupon may have a null hypothesis that states, "The coupon redemption rate is 0.85%." The 0.85% is based on an average of previous coupon issuances and the percent of coupons redeemed.

The alternative hypothesis (H_A) states what must be true if the null hypothesis (H_0) is false. For the null hypothesis about computer purchases, the alternative hypothesis would be "Individuals do not purchase a new laptop computer on average every 3 years." For the coupon redemption, the alternative hypothesis would be "The coupon redemption rate is not equal to 0.85%."

In situations when comparisons are made between groups or variables, the null hypothesis is usually stated as the status quo situation or in terms of no differences between the groups being tested. For instance, in examining the loyalty toward local stores versus shopping at regional malls or stores outside the area where a person lives, a null hypothesis may state, "Loyalty toward local retail stores does not vary by a person's gender." The alternative hypothesis would then state the opposite, or that there is a difference. For the local store loyalty hypothesis, the alternative would be "Loyalty toward local retail stores does vary by a person's gender." The null hypothesis and the alternative hypothesis do not have to be limited to two groups in the comparison. Local store loyalty could be examined based on a person's age or ethnicity, but each hypothesis should specify only one test variable. Thus, age and ethnicity should not be listed together in a single hypothesis. Possible null and alternative hypotheses for age could be

H_0: Loyalty toward local retail stores does not vary based on a person's age.

H_A: Loyalty toward local retail stores does vary based on a person's age.

Step 2: Select the Statistical Test

Once the null and alternative hypotheses have been stated, the researcher can choose the appropriate statistical test. As Figure 13.3 illustrates, the correct statistical test depends upon the nature of data, the number of variables, and the nature and size of the sample. You may recall from your statistics course that **parametric procedures** are statistically more robust, but can only be used with interval- or ratio-level data (metric data). **Nonparametric procedures** are appropriate for tests in which at least one variable is nominal and ordinal in nature (nonmetric). For nominal and ordinal data, the primary statistical test that is used is a chi-square goodness-of-fit test. With the chi-square test, actual frequency counts are compared to what would be expected based on the researcher's null hypothesis. For interval and ratio data, the most common statistical tests are t-tests

Figure 13.3   Types of Statistical Tests

Statistical Test	Number of Variables	Nature of Data	Nature of Sample
Chi-square	1	Nonmetric	1 sample, independent
	2+	At least one nonmetric	2 or more samples, independent
t/z-tests *			
One-sample	1	Metric: means or proportions	1 sample, independent
Independent	2	DV = metric, IV = nonmetric **	2 samples, independent *(e.g., DV limited to 2 categories)*
Paired comparison	2	Metric	2 samples, dependent
One-way ANOVA	2	DV = metric, IV = nonmetric	3 or more samples, independent *(e.g., DV has 3 or more categories)*

*t-tests are used when $n < 30$; z-tests are used when $n > 30$.

**DV = dependent variable (test variable); IV = independent variable (grouping or factor variable).

and ANOVA. Z-tests or t-tests are used when comparing two groups, and ANOVA tests are used when comparing three or more groups.

Step 3: Determine the Decision Rule

It is important to state the decision rule prior to conducting the data analysis to prevent the results from affecting whether the null hypothesis should be accepted or rejected. The decision rule is a measure of certainty in the conclusion that is drawn. Most marketers use a significance level of .05, which means the researcher is willing to accept a 5% chance he or she is wrong, but a 95% chance that the conclusion is correct. For decisions involving millions of dollars, marketing managers may want a lower significance level of .02 or even .01, which would mean the probability of being wrong is 2% and 1%, respectively. For minor decisions, a significance level of .10 may be adequate.

Step 4: Calculate the Test Statistic

Using the sample data that have been collected, the researcher can calculate the test statistic using the appropriate statistical test. The test statistic is then compared to the decision rule. If a significance level of .05 is chosen, then the null hypothesis is rejected if the test statistic has a significance level of .05 or lower. It is accepted if the significance level of the test statistic is above .05.

Figure 13.4 shows the null hypothesis, the alternative hypothesis, the decision rule, and the output from SPSS with the test results. The null hypothesis stated that the importance of service in selecting a clothing store does not vary based on the respondent's gender. Service importance was measured on a scale of 1 to 5, where 1 was "very unimportant" and 5 was "very important." The alternative hypothesis would then state there is a difference based on gender. The decision rule chosen by the researcher was a significance (or alpha) level of .05.

The SPSS procedure used to test this hypothesis was an independent t-test, which will be explained in more detail later in the chapter. The mean for males was 3.78, and the mean for females was 3.99. The sample had a total of 218 individuals respond to this question, 73 of whom were male. Is the difference between the mean for males and the mean for females significant at the decision rule of α (alpha) = .05? The last table in Figure 13.4 shows the SPSS output from the t-test. The t-value is -1.351 with a significance level, or p-value, of .178.

Figure 13.4   Example of Hypothesis Test for Importance of Service

H_0:   The importance of service in selecting a clothing store does not vary based on a person's gender.

H_A: The importance of service in selecting a clothing store does vary based on a person's gender.

Decision rule: significance level of .05

Group Statistics

	Q8. What is your gender?	N	Mean	Std. Deviation	Std. Error Mean
Q5d. Service	Male	73	3.78	1.003	.117
	Female	145	3.99	1.086	.090

			t-test for Equality of Means				
						95% Confidence Interval of the Difference	
	t	df	Sig. (2-tailed)	Mean Difference	Std. Error Difference	Lower	Upper
Q5d. Service	−1.351	216	.178	−.205	.152	−.505	.094

Scale: 1 = very unimportant; 2 = unimportant; 3 = neither important nor unimportant; 4 = important; 5 = very important

Figure 13.5 shows the null hypothesis, the alternative hypothesis, the decision rule, and the SPSS results for the importance of offering amenities such as gift wrapping and alterations to selecting a retail clothing store. The null hypothesis states there is no difference in importance of amenities on the basis of gender while the alternative states there is a difference. The decision rule of $\alpha = .05$ is again used. The mean for males is 2.30, and for females it is 2.65. The results of the t-test show a t-value of -2.219 and a significance level of .028.

Figure 13.5   Example of Hypothesis Test Showing Significant Difference

H_0:   In selecting a clothing store, the importance of offering amenities (e.g., gift wrapping and alterations) does not vary based on a person's gender.

H_A: In selecting a clothing store, the importance of offering amenities (e.g., gift wrapping and alterations) does vary based on a person's gender.

Decision rule: significance level of .05

Group Statistics

	Q8. What is your gender?	N	Mean	Std. Deviation	Std. Error Mean
Q5i. Amenities (e.g., gift wrapping, alterations)	Male	73	2.30	1.009	.118
	Female	145	2.65	1.128	.094

			t-test for Equality of Means			95% Confidence Interval of the Difference	
	t	df	Sig. (2-tailed)	Mean Difference	Std. Error Difference	Lower	Upper
Q5i. Amenities (e.g., gift wrapping, alterations)	−2.219	216	.028	−.347	.156	−.655	−.039

Scale: 1 = very unimportant; 2 = unimportant; 3 = neither important nor unimportant; 4 = important; 5 = very important

Step 5: State the Conclusion

The conclusion is based on the statistical test in comparison to the decision rule. Researchers will often maintain a list of research hypotheses for their own internal use, which they update to indicate whether the null hypothesis was rejected, or whether they failed to reject the null hypothesis. While one may wonder why the researcher simply doesn't "accept" the null hypothesis as having been proven true, "failing to reject the null hypothesis" is more accurate, as it reflects that the researcher is drawing conclusions about a population based on sample data. While the results may seem to indicate that there are no differences in the population, one can never be 100% certain. There is always that 1-alpha (the decision rule) chance that the researcher is wrong in stating his or her conclusion about the null hypothesis.

When dealing with clients, the conclusion should be stated in the context of the research question or objective it addresses, and provide the manager with information that is needed to make a decision. Suppose the manager of a boutique retail clothing store wanted information on whether she should increase the number of retail employees working in the female departments of her stores compared to the male departments. The results of the first hypothesis test shown in Figure 13.4 indicate that there is insufficient evidence to reject the null hypothesis, as the two-tailed significance level of .178 exceeds the decision rule, or cutoff value, of .05. So the researcher can conclude with 95% confidence that there is no difference between males and females concerning the importance of service in selecting a retail clothing store. In practice, researchers typically do not mention confidence levels or the term *significant differences* when discussing the results with clients unless the client is well versed in statistics. Instead, the researcher might state the conclusion as "The study found no meaningful differences between men and women in terms of their perceptions of the importance of service when selecting a retail clothing store."

In the second situation shown in Figure 13.5, one would conclude that the null hypothesis should be rejected as the significance value of .028 is less than the .05 decision rule. The researcher would conclude on the basis of this evidence that amenities such as gift wrapping and alterations are more important to females than they are to males. As we will see in the next section, and in more detail in Chapter 14, conclusions must be interpreted beyond examining results for significance, and should ultimately influence recommendations made to the client.

■ Objective 13.2: Understand the misuses of statistical significance and how statistically significant results may differ from those with practical importance.

STATISTICAL SIGNIFICANCE VERSUS PRACTICAL IMPORTANCE

Professionals associated with commercial market research firms have long argued that the concept of statistical significance has been misused in industry by some individuals and overrelied upon by others. For those in management positions who must make decisions based on marketing research, statistical significance is not always the same as practical importance.

Misuses of Statistical Significance

Some researchers have been guilty of interpreting highly significant results (such as statistical test significance levels, or p-values that are $\leq .01$, or $\leq .001$) as providing insight into the magnitude of differences found.[2] Actually, the significance level has nothing to do with how much the mean of Group A differs from the mean of Group B. The significance level simply states the probability of finding these results in the sample, when the differences noted are not true in the population. Thus, it is important to understand that the significance level indicates the probability that random (sampling) error has occurred and does not indicate magnitude of the difference.

Another misperception is that statistical significance can be used to gauge the validity of the data. This is false. The significance level assesses only the probability that random error is present in the sample data (due to the fact that the entire population has not been studied). The significance level implies nothing about the presence or absence of systematic error due to other problems. Measurement error stemming from the phrasing of or interpretation of questions is a major factor in determining data validity. Issues such as nonresponse bias, response bias, interviewer error, sample selection error, and process error will all influence the validity of the data collected.[3] Significance levels do not reflect the extent to which any of these factors are present or absent from the data.

Relevancy and Statistical Significance

Statistical significance can also be misused when researchers turn a blind eye to any results that are not significant, or when they form recommendations on the basis of statistically significant results that have little practical value to managers.[4] Consider the previous discussion of Figures 13.4 and 13.5. The results displayed in Figure 13.4 are not significant at the .05 level. In forming recommendations back to the client, researchers who seek only "significant results" would ignore the data regarding the importance of service in selecting a clothing store because the results suggest that importance does not vary by gender. However, this overreliance on significance tests may cause researchers to develop recommendations that miss key insights of importance to the client. Good researchers rarely rely on tests of statistical significance alone.

To illustrate, when interpreting the data for an independent t-test, it is also important to compare the mean scores for each gender against the scale used. Comparing the mean scores in Figure 13.4 to the 5-point scale used indicates that both men and women rated service as important even though their attitudes did not differ significantly from one another. The mean scores are greater than the neutral point of 3, and actually fall much closer to 4. Thus, service is important to both genders, and the researcher should recommend that the manager offer the same, fairly high level of service in both the men's and women's departments.

Figure 13.5 illustrates an example in which the null hypothesis is rejected. This means that the sample data suggest women place a higher level of importance on amenities than do men. Yet are these differences important enough to generate actionable recommendations? The researcher again needs to consider the overall mean values before determining whether gift wrapping and alteration services should really be recommended to the client. Although gift wrapping and alterations were found to be significantly more important to females, the mean scores for both genders fall between "unimportant" and "neutral," which leads one to wonder whether offering the amenities is truly worth the cost it would entail.

A second instance in which the meaningfulness of statistically significant results must be considered relates to sample size. The larger the sample size, the easier it is to find statistically significant differences in the data. The theory behind this idea is that larger sample sizes better represent the population and thus reduce random error. According to Doug Berdie, senior business manager at Maritz Research, "Large enough samples almost always lead to statistically significant results and very small samples rarely do."[5]

Commercial researchers argue that that the real question to be asked is not whether results are significant, but instead whether or not the significant differences found have practical importance to managers. Suppose a national survey of 20,000 soft drink consumers found that Brand A was preferred to its direct competitor Brand B, on the basis of sweetness of taste. It would be foolish to immediately assume that Brand B needs to change its formula, or introduce a sweeter-tasting brand spinoff, without first examining the effect size, or magnitude of the difference between the mean scores for each brand.

With such a large sample, it is very likely that the difference between mean scores could be as little as one tenth of a point (.1). Thus, if the mean for Brand A was 6.8 while the mean for Brand B was 6.7 on a 7-point scale, rational individuals would reason that investing millions of dollars in research and development to introduce a new brand, or improve the "sweetness" of Brand B, would not be a wise investment. Though significant, the results in this scenario would have little practical value to managers.

Furthermore, in the grander scheme of things, this difference—though real in the population—may have little practical value in terms of marketing application. Understanding the market and environment must come into play. Do factors other than sweetness of taste influence which brand is purchased? If so, the differential in taste preference may be moot when compared to preferences based on brand image, availability, promotions, price, or some other marketing factor.

In summary, more practical considerations must be brought to bear when considering whether or not a given result has practical relevance for management. Clearly the absolute value of the difference (effect size) must be considered. On a 7-point scale, a difference in mean scores of 2 points warrants more attention than does a 0.1 difference. The cost-to-benefit ratio of taking a prescribed course of action must be evaluated,[6] as must existing marketing objectives and strategies.[7]

■ Objective 13.3: Explain the difference between Type I and Type II errors.

TYPES OF ERROR

Figure 13.6 illustrates the correct and incorrect decisions that can be made in regard to hypothesis testing. It is important to keep in mind that in most situations researchers are using a sample to make inferences to a population. If the state of the population is actually known, there is no need to conduct research. But, since it is not known, researchers will use a sample to draw conclusions about the entire population being studied. If the researcher does not reject the null hypothesis on the basis of the study, and indeed the null hypothesis is correct in the population, then a correct decision has been made. Conversely, if the researcher rejects the null hypothesis when the null hypothesis is in fact false among the population, then the correct decision has also been made.

In either failing to reject or rejecting the null hypothesis, researchers can make two types of error. **Type I error** occurs when the null hypothesis is rejected, when it is actually true. In

Figure 13.6   Types of Errors With Hypothesis Testing

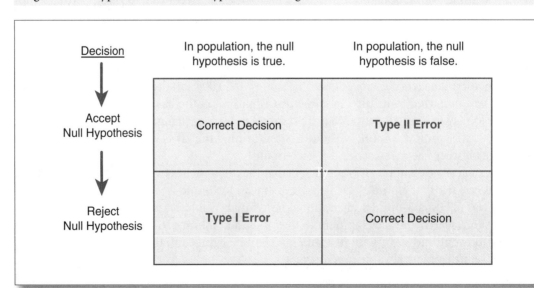

statistical terms, Type I error is referred to as *alpha* with the Greek symbol α. Type I error, or α, as mentioned earlier, is used to determine the decision rule that guides statistical tests. If the decision rule is set at .05, it means that $\alpha = .05$ and the researcher is comfortable with a 5% chance of a Type I error occurring. For the null hypotheses shown previously, the researcher feels comfortable with making a conclusion about the results of the study when there is a 5% chance that an incorrect decision has been made. Of course, this also means that recommendations implemented on the basis of these data may fail, if the premise on which they are based is incorrect.

Type II error occurs if a null hypothesis is not rejected on the basis of the sample data, even though it is actually false in the population. Type II errors are important, because of the potential opportunity costs they represent. For example, a study might have consumers evaluate the attributes and benefits of a new product concept versus those of a competitor's brand. A Type II error can lead to a recommendation that a marketer drop the product concept from the new product development process, or send it back for revision. This represents an opportunity cost, because the product concept is actually preferred to the competitor's product by the population.

The nomenclature for Type II error is *beta* or the Greek symbol β. While the level of α is set by the researcher in deciding the decision rule, the level of β can be calculated but is rather complicated and beyond the scope of this textbook. The level of β cannot be set in advance. It can only be calculated after data are collected and the analysis performed, because it is influenced by the final sample size used in a particular statistical test.[8]

But, the value of β is inversely related to the value of α. As α decreases, β increases, and the reverse is also true; as α increases, β decreases. So, to decrease the chances of retaining a false null hypothesis (and not finding differences when they exist in the population), then the value of β needs to be reduced. This is accomplished by increasing the value of α, which in effect makes significant differences easier to find. If the value of α is increased from .05 to .10, the researcher increases the chances of a Type I error occurring by 5%, but decreases the value of β and thus reduces the chances of a Type II error. Therefore, in setting the significance level (α), the researcher needs to decide which error is more serious, Type I or Type II, in light of the decision that is to be made from the data.

Academic researchers strive to minimize Type I errors, especially when testing theoretical models. Rarely will academic researchers use an α greater than .05. Medical researchers studying the impact of new drugs often use double-blind studies based on very small samples. Due to the large potential for random error in small samples, medical research tends toward very stringent decision rules using small alphas, such as .01 or even lower. Given the negative consequences, making a Type I error—for example, developing and marketing a drug (which costs millions of dollars) that ultimately proves to be ineffective—is a waste of corporate resources. Throw in the potential lawsuits, which might be initiated by patients or their survivors, and it is no wonder that medical researchers stress Type I error over Type II error. Lives could be at stake. It also explains why new drugs require such a long approval process by the Food and Drug Administration. Multiple studies must be conducted to help demonstrate that the results are "real," and that Type I error is not responsible for the drug's alleged efficacy.

In some situations, commercial practitioners of market research may be more comfortable with alphas of .10, so as to reduce the possibility that a Type II error occurs. If the cost of a proposed course of action is minimal while the potential returns are large, then such actions are warranted. As mentioned previously, commercial firms also evaluate factors other than significance levels when drawing conclusions. Their focus is to find results that have practical relevance to managers. Even though a decision rule may use .05, results showing a significance of .061 may be deemed "close enough" by commercial researchers to be actionable, depending upon the magnitude of the finding (effect size) and other factors.

CHI-SQUARE TEST

Marketing researchers often want to examine if there are significant differences in the frequency counts of nominal and ordinal data. It may involve a one-way frequency count or a cross-tabulation. With one-way frequencies researchers may be looking to see if the frequencies are equal across the various categories or if they follow a specific pattern determined by the researcher prior to collecting the data. With cross-tabulations researchers are interested in knowing if the frequency counts differ across multiple categories. The chi-square test compares the actual frequency counts from a data sample to what would be expected if the null hypothesis were true.

Researchers often call the single variable chi-square test a goodness-of-fit test because the procedure evaluates how well the actual frequencies "fit" the expected frequencies. When the differences between the actual and expected frequencies are large, then there is not a good fit. If the null hypothesis states that there is no significant difference between the expected and the actual values observed, then the null hypothesis is rejected. When differences are small, the chi-square value is small, and therefore there is a good fit between the expected and the actual frequency counts.

Certain assumptions and conditions must be met for the chi-square test to yield useful results. In using the chi-square test, it is important that each cell has a minimum expected count of 5. Also, if more than 20% of the cells have actual counts lower than 5, then results will not be reliable. Finally, if any cell has an expected value of 0, the results will not be reliable. For this reason, a researcher may "collapse" categories that border on one another by recoding the variable to contain fewer categories, and thereby increasing the number of observations falling into each cell before running a chi-square analysis.

One-Way Frequency

A common use of the chi-square test is to see if a sample represents a particular target audience that is being studied. A small clothing boutique store chain collected data from a sample of 221 respondents. Before analyzing the data, the researcher in charge of data collection wanted to see if the sample represented the firm's current target base. Using the retailers' database, the researcher was able to identify that 70% of its customers were female and 30% were male. In terms of age, 50% of the customers were 18 to 29, 30% were 30 to 49, and 20% were 50 or older. Figure 13.7 shows the chi-square tests for both gender and age.

The left side of Figure 13.7 shows the chi-square test results for gender. The sample consisted of 74 males and 146 females. If 30% of the customers are male, then a sample of 220 individuals should have 66 males (220 * 30%). The sample should have 154 females (220 * 70%). The sample size of 220 is used because one person in the overall sample did not indicate his or her gender. Comparing the actual frequency count to the expected count, the chi-square value is 1.385 with a significance level of .239. At the 95% confidence level, there is no significant difference between the actual gender count and the expected values, which means the sample is representative of the customer base for this retail chain.

Figure 13.7   Chi-Square Test of a Single Frequency Count

Q8. What is your gender?			
	Observed N	Expected N	Residual
Male	74	66.0	8.0
Female	146	154.0	–8.0
Total	220		

Q8. What is your age?			
	Observed N	Expected N	Residual
18–29	114	110.5	3.5
30–49	40	66.3	–26.3
50+	67	44.2	22.8
Total	221		

Test Statistics	
	Q8. What is your gender?
Chi-square	1.385[a]
df	1
Asymp. Sig.	.239

a. 0 cells (.0%) have expected frequencies less than 5. The minimum expected cell frequency is 66.0.

Test Statistics	
	Q8. What is your gender?
Chi-square	22.305[a]
df	2
Asymp. Sig.	.000

a. 0 cells (.0%) have expected frequencies less than 5. The minimum expected cell frequency is 44.2.

For age, the sample had 3.5 too many individuals in the 18–29 age category and 22.8 too many in the 50-plus category. But, in the 30–49 age group, the sample was short 26.3 individuals. If the decision rule is at the 95% level, then the conclusion is that there is a significant difference between the sample's age breakdown and the ages of the firm's customers. Thus, the sample is not representative of the customer base in terms of age.

Cross-Tabulations

A second common use of the chi-square test is with cross-tabulation tables to see if differences are present in responses across multiple categories. Suppose the clothing boutique store wanted to see if there was a difference in the age composition of its customers among three of its stores. Respondents were asked which of the three stores they patronized the most. The null hypothesis would be that there is no difference in the ages of its customers in the three stores. The alternative hypothesis would be there is a significant difference in the age composition of the customer base of the three stores. The hypothesis was tested at the 95% confidence level, which means a significance level of .05 or lower. Results of the SPSS chi-square test are shown in Figure 13.8.

To understand the top table in Figure 13.8, start with the last column. Out of the sample of 220 respondents, 69 (31.4%) indicated they shopped at the Walnut Street store the most, 87 (39.5%) indicated they shopped at the Highland Boutique store the most, and 64 (29.1%) said they shopped at the Riverwalk Mall store the most. These percentages are then used to calculate the expected values seen in the table. The assumption with the chi-square test is that the percentages of each age group within a row should be the same. Thus, the chi-square will test for the Walnut Street store if the percentage of individuals 18–29, 30–49, and 50+ are the same. Based on the last column, there should be 31.4% for each column. For the Highland Boutique store, the chi-square will compare the actual counts to the 39.5% expected. For the Riverwalk Mall store, the expected is 29.1%.

Figure 13.8   Chi-Square Test With Cross-Tabulation

Q17. Which store do you patronize the most? * Q7. What is your age? Cross-tabulation

			Q7. What is your age?			
			18–29	30–49	50+	Total
Q17. Which store do you patronize the most?	Walnut Street store	Count	23	18	28	69
		Expected Count	35.8	12.5	20.7	69.0
		% within Q7. What is your age?	20.2%	45.0%	42.4%	31.4%
	Highland Boutique store	Count	70	11	6	87
		Expected Count	45.1	15.8	26.1	87.0
		% within Q7. What is your age?	61.4%	27.5%	9.1%	39.5%
	Riverwalk Mall store	Count	21	11	32	64
		Expected Count	33.2	11.6	19.2	64.0
		% within Q7. What is your age?	18.4%	27.5%	48.5%	29.1%
Total		Count	114	40	66	220
		Expected Count	114.0	40.0	66.0	220.0
		% within Q7. What is your age?	100.0%	100.0%	100.0%	100.0%

Chi-Square Tests

	Value	df	Asymp. Sig. (2-sided)
Pearson Chi-Square	53.245ᵃ	4	.000
Likelihood Ratio	57.851	4	.000
Linear-by-Linear Association	.234	1	.628
N of Valid Cases	220		

a. 0 cells (.0%) have expected count less than 5. The minimum expected count is 11.64.

Comparing the actual count for each store and age group against the expected values yields a Pearson chi-square value of 53.245 with a .000 significance level. Since the test was at the 95% confidence level and the significance level is below .05, the conclusion is that there is a significant difference in the age composition of the patrons of each store. This information is helpful to the managers of the stores because they can merchandise the store with fashions appropriate for the ages of their primary shoppers. These differences can be seen more clearly in the graph in Figure 13.9. With 61% of the 18- to 29-year-olds shopping in the Highland Boutique store, it should have a large collection of clothes that cater to younger shoppers. Similar merchandise decisions can be made for the other store locations.

■ Objective 13.5: Identify and describe the various tests for differences in means.

TESTING FOR DIFFERENCES IN MEANS

Researchers often want to compare two or more means. The means can be from the same sample or from different samples. For instance, in the first case (same sample), researchers may want to compare the average or mean number of meals eaten at quick-service restaurants, dine-in restaurants, and pickup or carryout for male respondents. If the researcher wanted to compare the means for those three variables between males and females, then it would be a comparison of two different samples.

The two primary statistical tests used by researchers are t-tests (or z-tests) and ANOVA (analysis of variance). T-tests (or z-tests) are used when comparing two means. The one-way ANOVA test is used when comparing three or more means. With both tests, the data being analyzed must be either interval or ratio.

Figure 13.9   Graphical Results of Cross-Tab Chi-Square

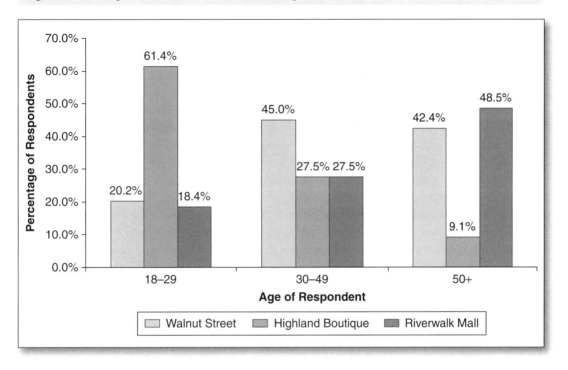

t-Tests and z-Tests

As stated, t-tests and z-tests are used to compare the means of two groups. T-tests are used with samples containing fewer than 30 subjects per cell. Z-tests are used for larger samples of 30 or more per cell. SPSS and most statistics programs automatically compute the correct test, though both are uniformly referred to as t-tests by the software. The groups compared by t-tests can be from the same sample or different samples. The formula for the t-test is not provided in this text. It can be obtained from most statistics books as well as a number of websites. The goal of this discussion is to explain (1) how to use t-tests and (2) how to interpret the results.

The t-test is used with interval and ratio data. It is especially useful with small samples ($n < 30$), but is commonly used by researchers with samples of any size. It is a good test for situations where the population standard deviation is not known, which occurs in almost all research conducted by companies and marketing research firms. In order to use the t-test, researchers assume the sample is drawn from populations with normal distributions and the variances of the populations are equal. Three types of t-tests will be discussed: one-sample t-tests, independent-sample t-tests, and paired-sample t-tests.

One-Sample T-Test

A one-sample t-test is used to test if the mean of a sample distribution is different from a specified or test mean. For the clothing boutique stores, the manager would like to see if the e-mail campaign conducted this year yielded significantly better results than the direct mail campaign that was used last year. Both campaigns were conducted using the firm's database of customers that was obtained from individuals filling out loyalty cards. The results of the one-sample t-test are shown in Figure 13.10.

The top table shows the sample size was 221 respondents, and the mean number of purchases made in the 90 days following the e-mail marketing campaign was 5.10 with a standard deviation of 3.13. The mean for the direct mail campaign last year was 4.23. Using SPSS, the number of purchases this year in the last 90 days was compared to the test value of 4.23. The one-sample t-test produced a t-value of 4.120 with 220 degrees of freedom and a significance level of .000. The difference between the current sample mean (5.0995) and the test mean (4.23) is 0.86955. Using a confidence level of 95%, the mean difference's confidence interval is between 0.4536 and 1.2855. Thus, the manager conducting this research can be 95% confident that the mean difference between the two campaigns is somewhere between 0.45 and 1.28. The t-test shows there was a significant increase in the number of purchases using the e-mail campaign versus the direct mail campaign.

While the one-sample t-test showed the e-mail campaign yielded a significantly higher number of purchases than the direct mail campaign, the manager must be aware that other factors could have created the differences. Since the two campaigns were a year apart, economic conditions may have changed. The fashions being sold in the stores would certainly be different. The customer base may have even shifted. So, from a managerial perspective, it is important to examine the entire situation before concluding that the e-mail marketing campaign was significantly superior to the direct mail campaign.

Independent-Sample T-Test

Quite often managers want to know if there is a significant difference between two groups. The appropriate SPSS test to use is the independent-sample t-test. This test requires the dependent variable is an interval- or ratio-level variable that is being tested for differences. The grouping,

Figure 13.10   Results of One Sample T-Test

One–Sample Statistics

	N	Mean	Std. Deviation	Std. Error Mean
Q14. Number of purchases in last 90 days	221	5.0995	3.13761	.21106

One–Sample Test

	Test Value = 4.23					
					95% Confidence Interval of the Difference	
	t	df	Sig. (2-tailed)	Mean Difference	Lower	Upper
Q14. Number of purchases in last 90 days	4.120	220	.000	.86955	.4536	1.2855

or factor, variable must contain mutually exclusive categories that are usually nominal or ordinal in nature. In the clothing store study, the manager of the three stores wanted to see if there was a significant difference in the purchases made by males and female customers exposed to the e-mail marketing campaign. Gender serves as the grouping variable, while purchases made is the dependent variable being tested. The results of the study can aid in advertising efforts and influence how future e-mail messages are designed. The researcher found that the mean for females was 5.13 while the mean for males was 4.97, a mean difference, or effect, of .16. But, is this significant at the 95% confidence level? The results of the independent-sample t-test are shown in Figure 13.11.

The top table in Figure 13.11 shows the sample size, mean, and standard deviation for the two genders. The standard error is calculated from the standard deviation and sample size. It identifies the precision of the mean for each of the two samples. The smaller the standard error, the more likely the sample mean equals the true population mean. So, for this sample, the standard error for the female portion of the sample is lower than that for the males, 0.253 compared to .381. The primary reason for the lower standard error for females is the larger sample size. Since the denominator used in calculating the standard error is the square root of the sample size, the standard error can be reduced by increasing the sample size.

SPSS will calculate two t-values, one assuming the variance of the two populations is equal and the other assuming the variances of the two populations is not equal. In most cases, the same significant or not-significant results will be obtained with both methods of calculating the t-value. But, to ensure the correct values are used, SPSS will produce a Levene's test for equality of variances. For the independent-sample t-test that was run, the F-value for the Levene's test was .578 with a p-value of .448. If the same 95% confidence level is used, the researcher can

Figure 13.11   Results of an Independent Sample T-Test

Group Statistics					
Q8. What is your gender?		N	Mean	Std. Deviation	Std. Error Mean
Q14. Number of purchases in last 90 days	Male	74	4.9730	3.28122	.38143
	Female	146	5.1370	3.06623	.25376

		t-test for Equality of Means						
							95% Confidence Interval of the Difference	
		t	df	Sig. (2-tailed)	Mean Difference	Std. Error Difference	Lower	Upper
Q14. Number of purchases in last 90 days	Equal variances assumed	−.366	218	.715	−.16401	.44805	−1.04708	.71906
	Equal variances not assumed	−.358	138.283	.721	−.16401	.45813	−1.06987	.74184

Levene's Test for Equality of Variances
F-Value = .578
Sig. = .448

assume the variances of the male and female samples are the same, as .448 is greater than the decision rule of .05. To assume the variances are different, the significance level would have to be .05 or below.

Using the top row (equal variances assumed), the t-test for equality of means is −0.366 with a significance level of .715. The negative value of the t-test is not important. It can be either negative or positive depending on how the mean difference between the two samples is calculated. In this case, it was done by subtracting 5.13 from 4.97, thus producing a negative number −0.16401. Because the significance level is .715, the conclusion of the t-test is that there is no significant difference in the mean purchases of males and females. The last two columns show the confidence level of the differences. The researcher can be 95% confident that the mean difference between males and females in terms of purchases is between −1.04 and 0.71.

Paired-Sample T-Test

Paired-sample t-tests are used when a researcher wants to compare two different responses from an individual respondent. With the clothing store study, the manager wanted to know if the e-mail campaign produced immediate results. Through the company's database, it was able to identify the number of purchases individuals made in the 90 days prior to the e-mail campaign and the number of purchases that were made in the 90 days following the campaign. To see if there is a significant difference between pre- and postcampaign sales, a paired t-test is used. With the paired-sample approach, the computer will compare for each individual the number of purchases made during the 90 days prior to the campaign and the number of purchases made in the 90 days after the campaign. Results of this paired-sample t-test are shown in Figure 13.12.

Figure 13.12   Results of a Paired Sample T-Test

Paired-Sample Statistics

		Mean	N	Std. Deviation	Std. Error Mean
Pair 1	Q16.Number of purchases in 90 days after campaign	6.2534	221	3.70860	.24947
	Q15.Number of purchases in 90 days prior to campaign	4.9321	221	3.16370	.21281

Paired-Sample Correlations

	N	Correlation	Sig.
Pair 1 Q16. Number of purchases in 90 days after campaign; Q15. Number of purchases in 90 days prior to campaign	221	.677	.000

Paired-Sample Test

	Paired Differences							Sig. (2-tailed)
	Mean	Std. Deviation	Std. Error Mean	95% Confidence Interval of the Difference Lower	95% Confidence Interval of the Difference Upper	t	df	
Pair 1 Q16.Number of purchases in 90 days after campaign; Q15. Number of purchases in 90 days prior to campaign	1.32127	2.80761	.18886	.94906	1.69347	6.996	220	.000

From the top table, the manager can see the mean number of purchases made after the e-mail campaign was 6.25, and the number before was 4.93. The second table measures the correlation between each person's first response and the person's second response. If a person made a high number of purchases before the campaign, then it would be expected that the individual will make a high number of purchases after the campaign. Similarly, individuals who made a low number of purchases before the campaign are likely to make few purchases after the campaign. A high correlation value shows this pattern exists. A low correlation value shows the relationship between the two values is random. With this study, the correlation of .677 is relatively high indicating there is a high level of correlation between the purchases before and after the campaign.

The bottom table provides the t-test statistical values. The mean difference between pre- and postmeasures is 1.32, which indicates that, on the average, customers made 1.32 more purchases in the 90 days after the campaign than in the 90 days prior to the campaign. The t-value for this mean difference is 8.996 with a significance level of .000. The researcher can conclude the campaign was successful since on the average purchases increased by 1.32. Further, the researcher can be 95% confident that the mean increase was somewhere between 0.94 purchases and 1.69 purchase.

Analysis of Variance

For situations involving the comparison of three or more means, researchers use analysis of variance (ANOVA) tests. As with the t-test, the formula for calculating ANOVA is not provided, but students are referred to statistics textbooks. The ANOVA procedure tests if the means of the groups are equal. An ANOVA test comparing the number of purchases by the respondent's age is shown in Figure 13.13.

Figure 13.13   Results of an ANOVA test

Descriptives

Q14. Number of purchases in last 90 days

	N	Mean	Std. Deviation	Std. Error	95% Confidence Interval for Mean Lower Bound	95% Confidence Interval for Mean Upper Bound	Minimum	Maximum
18–29	114	5.0702	3.29580	.30868	4.4586	5.6817	.00	10.00
30–49	40	3.8250	1.93334	.30569	3.2067	4.4433	.00	8.00
50+	67	2.0448	1.22391	.14952	1.7462	2.3433	.00	5.00
Total	221	3.9276	2.90676	.19553	3.5422	4.3130	.00	10.00

ANOVA

Q14. Number of purchases in last 90 days

	Sum of Squares	df	Mean Square	F	Sig.
Between Groups	386.762	2	193.381	28.638	.000
Within Groups	1472.079	218	6.753		
Total	1858.842	220			

The mean number of purchases for individuals 18 to 29 years of age is 5.07, for individuals 30 to 49 it is 3.82, and for individuals 50 and older it is 2.04. In addition to the mean, SPSS provides calculations for the standard deviation, the standard error, the confidence interval for the mean at 95% confidence level, and the minimum and maximum values.

The second table provides the statistical information from the ANOVA test. The test statistic is an F-value. For an understanding of the F-statistic and how it is calculated, a basic statistics book or the Internet can be accessed. For this situation, the resulting F-value is 28.638 with a significance level of .000. The ANOVA test shows there is a significant difference in the number of purchases made by the three age groups. The results are graphically displayed in Figure 13.14.

The results of the basic ANOVA test indicate that significant differences exist somewhere in the data, meaning that the differences in the means for at least two categories of the factor variable (age) differ significantly from one another. Determining which age categories differ requires multiple "pairwise comparisons" be performed. Pairwise comparisons test the mean of each subgroup against the mean of each other subgroup to determine whether the numerical difference between the two mean scores is significant. Thus a comparison for the basic ANOVA test shown in Figure 13.13 would first compare the mean of the 18- to 29-year-old group (5.07) against the mean of the 30- to 49-year-old group (3.82) to determine if the difference between the two means is significant. Pairwise comparisons would also be performed for the 18- to 29-year-old and 50+ groups, and for the 30- to 49-year-old group and 50+-year-old groups.

Various methods can be used to calculate post hoc comparisons, such as these, since it occurs after the initial analysis. Most statistical programs offer several options. The correct choice depends first upon whether equal variances can be assumed for the means within each category. Duncan's, Tukey's, Tukey's-b, and Scheffé's tests are common forms of post hoc comparison tests when equal variances are assumed. Of these, many researchers prefer to use

Figure 13.14   Graph of ANOVA test results

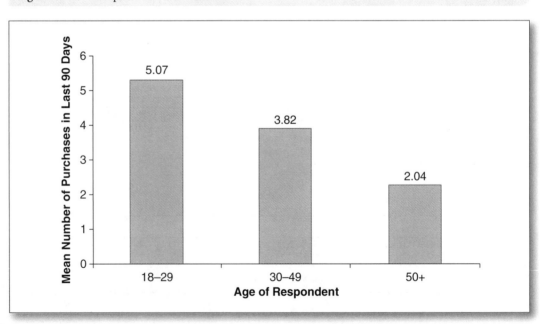

Scheffé's test because it is the most conservative, meaning that significant results for Scheffé's test require larger differences between subgroup mean scores than do most other methods.[9] The implication, then, is that Scheffé's test minimizes Type I error when making pairwise comparisons. The results of the Scheffé's post hoc comparison tests are illustrated in Figure 13.15.

The top table shows the individual t-tests for each age group when contrasted with the other two groups. The results are interpreted as previously explained when discussing independent t-tests. In this case, the age groups differ significantly from one another. The bottom table lists the mean and sample size for each age subgroup. The fact that every mean is shown in its own unique column visually demonstrates that the results differ significantly from one another. If the means of two groups were numerically different, but appeared in the same column, it would indicate that the means were not significantly different at the alpha level chosen for the decision rule.

A note of caution is appropriate at this juncture. Scheffé's test should only be performed after the basic one-way ANOVA has been found to be significant. Some researchers may select an ad hoc test when specifying the initial run of an ANOVA. While this saves some time and is more convenient for the researcher, it is inappropriate to make use of ad hoc test results if the overall ANOVA test result is not significant.

Figure 13.15   Scheffé Ad-Hoc ANOVA Test Results

Post Hoc Tests

Multiple Comparisons

Dependent Variable: Q14. Number of purchases in last 90 days
Scheffé

(I) Q7. What is your age?	(J) Q7. What is your age?	Mean Difference (I–J)	Std. Error	Sig.	95% Confidence Interval Lower Bound	95% Confidence Interval Upper Bound
18–29	30–49	1.24518*	.47755	.035	.0682	2.4222
	50+	3.02540*	.40002	.000	2.0395	4.0113
30–49	18–29	−1.24518*	.47755	.035	−2.4222	−.0682
	50+	1.78022*	.51923	.003	.5005	3.0600
50+	18–29	−3.02540*	.40002	.000	−4.0113	−2.0395
	30–49	−1.78022*	.51923	.003	−3.0600	−.5005

* The mean difference is significant at the .05 level.

Homogeneous Subsets

Q14. Number of purchases in last 90 days

Scheffé[a,b]

Q7. What is your age?	N	Subset for alpha = .05 1	Subset for alpha = .05 2	Subset for alpha = .05 3
50+	67	2.0448		
30–49	40		3.8250	
18–29	114			5.0702
Sig.		1.000	1.000	1.000

Means for groups in homogeneous subsets are displayed.
  a. Uses Harmonic Mean Sample Size = 61.605.
  b. The group sizes are unequal. The harmonic mean of the group sizes is used. Type I error levels are not guaranteed.

■ Objective 13.6:
Demonstrate
an
understanding
of regression
analysis.

REGRESSION ANALYSIS

Regression analysis provides a test for measuring the relationship or correlation among two or more variables. If the number of variables being examined is two, then it is simple regression. If more than two variables are being examined, it is called multiple regression. With both simple and multiple regression, the researcher has one dependent (or outcome) variable that is being examined. With **simple regression,** the researcher is examining the relationship of one independent or predictor variable to the outcome variable. With **multiple regression,** multiple independent or predictor variables are being examined to determine which ones are good predictors of the outcome variable.

It is extremely important to understand that mathematical relationships do not prove cause and effect. Just because one variable is highly correlated with another a researcher cannot say that one causes the other to occur. A researcher may see a high level of correlation between temperature and the sales of snow shovels and other snow removal equipment. But, it is not the cold weather that causes the sales to increase. It is the snow that comes with the cold weather. Thus, in building regression equations, researchers should select variables that logically can influence the dependent or outcome variable.

Simple Regression

The manager of the clothing boutique stores noticed that age appeared to be related to the number of purchases made at the three stores. Before deciding if she should enlarge her young women's fashions, she thought it would be good to run a simple regression. The dependent variable would be the number of purchases made in the last 90 days. The independent or predictor variable would be the respondent's age. The SPSS outcome of this analysis is shown in Figure 13.16.

The top table in Figure 13.16 provides model summary information on how well the model fits the data, and how well the predictor variable, the person's age, is able to predict the number of purchases made in the last 90 days. The first value shown is R, which is a measure of how well the predictor variable predicts the outcome. But, to obtain a more accurate measure, it is necessary to square the R value, which is the third column, "R-Square." R-square values range between 0 and 1. A "0" score indicates no predictive ability at all and that the two numbers are just random. A "1" score would indicate a perfect predictor. The .207 shown in this table says that 20.7% of the variance in the number of purchases in the last 90 days is based on the person's age. That is a fairly low level of predictability. While 20% is explained by age, the other 80% is caused by other factors not present in the regression equation.

The second table measures if the regression is significant or not. Since the F-value is 57.104 with a significance level of .000, it is a significant predictor of purchases in the last 90 days. Although the regression model is significant, keep in mind that the R-square is only .207 indicating it has a low level of predictability.

The bottom table in Figure 13.16 provides the coefficients. The constant is where the regression line crosses the y-axis. The unstandardized coefficient (B) for the age variable is −1.499, which indicates an inverse relationship. This means that as the customer's age increases, the number of purchases made decreases, which confirms what the manager suspected. The

Figure 13.16   Results of Simple Regression Analysis

Model Summary

Model	R	R-Square	Adjusted R-Square	Std. Error of the Estimate
1	.455[a]	.207	.203	2.59469

a. Predictors: (Constant), Q7. What is your age?

ANOVA[b]

Model		Sum of Squares	df	Mean Square	F	Sig.
1	Regression	384.448	1	384.448	57.104	.000[a]
	Residual	1474.394	219	6.732		
	Total	1858.842	220			

a. Predictors: (Constant), Q7. What is your age?
b. Dependent Variable: Q14. Number of purchases in last 90 days

Coefficients[a]

Model		Unstandardized Coefficients		Standardized Coefficients		
		B	Std. Error	Beta	t	Sig.
1	(Constant)	6.608	.395		16.717	.000
	Q7. What is your age?	−1.499	.198	−.455	−7.557	.000

a. Dependent Variable: Q14. Number of purchases in last 90 days

unstandardized coefficient shows the amount of change in the outcome variable based on an increase or decrease of 1 unit in the predictor variable. Recall that the age variable consists of three categories: 18–29, 30–49, and 50+. So if the age category is increased by 1 unit to the next category, the number of purchases declines by 1.499. Based on the unstandardized coefficient, the regression equation can be written in the following manner:

$$Y = 6.608 + (-1.499 * X)$$

$$\text{Purchases in last 90 days} = 6.608 + (-1.499 * \text{age category})$$

Using this equation, the number of purchases can be predicted for each of the three age categories. The results are shown in Figure 13.17. If a customer is between 18 and 29, the predicted number of purchases would be 5.11. If the individual is 30 to 49, then it would be 3.61, and if 50 and over, it would be 2.11. When the means of these three groups are obtained from SPSS, they are very close to the purchases made for each category, which are listed in the last column in the table.

The standardized coefficient will be discussed in the section on multiple regression since it really only has meaning when multiple independent variables are in the equation. The t-value and corresponding significance level shows if the variable being considered is significant. With this simple regression, both the constant and age variables are significant and therefore should be part of the regression equation.

Figure 13.17   Outcome of Simple Regression Equation

Purchases in last 90 days = 6.608 + (−1.499 * age category)

Age Category	Code	Regression Equation		Predicted # of Purchases	Sample Mean
		Constant	Age Beta		
18–29	1	6.608	−1.499	5.11	5.07
30–49	2	6.608	−1.499	3.61	3.82
50+	3	6.608	−1.499	2.11	2.04

Multiple Regression

With the simple regression explaining only 20.7% of the variance in the number of purchases, the manager of the boutique stores decided to run a multiple regression analysis with additional variables in the model. Each respondent was asked to evaluate the clothing store along eight dimensions. In addition to these eight and the age variable, the person's household income was added to the model. The model summary and fit statistics are shown in Figure 13.18.

According to the ANOVA table, the multiple regression equation is a significant fit with the data. The R-square has improved, .568 compared to .207 with the simple regression. Approximately 56.8% of the outcome variable is explained by the multiple regression equation. The beta coefficients for the multiple regression are shown in Figure 13.19.

Figure 13.18   Model Summary for Multiple Regression

Model Summary

Model	R	R-Square	Adjusted R-Square	Std. Error of the Estimate
1	.754[a]	.568	.547	1.93932

a. Predictors: (Constant), Q12. What is your family income?, Q5a. Product selection, Q5i. Amenities (such as gift wrapping, alterations), Q7. What is your age?, Q5b. Price, Q5d. Service, Q5h. Parking, Q5g. Store image, Q5f. Location, Q5c. Convenience

ANOVA[b]

Model		Sum of Squares	df	Mean Square	F	Sig.
1	Regression	1000.905	10	100.090	26.613	.000[a]
	Residual	759.715	202	3.761		
	Total	1760.620	212			

a. Predictors: (Constant), Q12. What is your family income?, Q5b. Price, Q7. What is your age?, Q5a. Product selection, Q5h. Parking, Q5d. Service, Q5g. Store image, Q5f. Location, Q5e. Store atmosphere, Q5c. Convenience b. Dependent Variable: Q14. Number of purchases in last 90 days

Figure 13.19 Multiple Regression Coefficients

Coefficients[a]

Model	Unstandardized Coefficients		Standardized Coefficients	t	Sig.
	B	Std. Error	Beta		
1 (Constant)	−.804	.969		−.829	.408
Q5a. Product selection	.380	.153	.132	2.492	.014
Q5b. Price	−.009	.176	−.003	−.052	.958
Q5c. Convenience	−.139	.200	−.048	−.699	.485
Q5d. Service	.799	.140	.320	5.704	.000
Q5e. Store atmosphere	364	.176	134	2.064	.040
Q5f. Location	−.056	.193	−.019	−.289	.772
Q5g. Store image	.428	.140	.172	3.047	.003
Q5h. Parking	−.116	.129	−.047	−.902	.368
Q7. What is your age?	−.689	.169	−.210	−4.064	.000
Q12. What is your household income?	.928	.140	.336	6.644	.000

a. Dependent Variable: Q14. Number of purchases in last 90 days

It is helpful to look first at the t-value and significance level for each of the independent variables. At the 95% confidence level, any variable that has a significance level of .05 or lower would be considered a significant predictor of the outcome variable, or the number of purchases made in the last 90 days. According to the SPSS analysis, significant predictors of the number of purchases made by customers are product selection, level of service, store atmosphere, store image, the person's age, and household income. These are the variables the researcher and store manager will want to address since they drive purchase behavior.

The standardized beta coefficient can help the researcher and store manager understand which significant variables are the most important and the relative magnitude of importance. The standardized coefficients convert all of the variables to a 0-to-1 scale so they can be compared. With this process, the beta weights gain ratio properties. For example, in reviewing the standardized betas in Figure 13.20, household income and service have the highest values at .336 and .320, respectively. While the manager has no control over the household income of her customers, she can control the level of service customers receive. When the .320 beta weight for service is compared to the .132 for product selection, .172 for store image, and .134 for store atmosphere, the manager can make the assumption that the level of service is approximately twice as important as the other three variables (.32/.132 = 2.42; .32/.172 = 1.86; .32/.134 = 2.39).

To spend money on training and motivating employees to provide high-quality service appears to be a wise decision, at least according to the regression analysis. Notice that price, convenience, location, and parking do not have a significant impact on purchases. To say they have none is incorrect. But, their impact is minimal. Resource allocations should focus on service, product selection, store image, and store atmosphere.

As was found with the simple regression, age is inversely related to the number of purchases. It would make good management sense to focus on fashions for the younger consumers.

To understand the predictive ability of a regression model, consider Figure 13.20. On the left is a good customer. This customer evaluates each of the store attributes as a 4 on the 5-point scale, is in the youngest age category, and is in the highest income bracket. The regression model predicts this customer would purchase 8.82 items over a 90-day period. Now consider the poor customer who rates each of the store's attributes as a 2 out of 5, is in the oldest age category, and is in the lowest income bracket. This customer would generate only 1.36 purchases in the same time period.

Figure 13.20   Comparison of Good/Poor Customers

Good Customer:

1) Evaluate items as 4 out of 5

2) Youngest age group

3) Highest income bracket

Poor Customer:

1) Evaluate items as 2 out of 5

2) Oldest age group

3) Lowest income bracket

Good Customer	Value	Beta	Value*Beta
Constant		−0.804	−0.804
Product selection	4	0.380	1.520
Price	4	−0.009	−0.036
Convenience	4	−0.139	−0.556
Service	4	0.799	3.196
Store atmosphere	4	0.364	1.456
Location	4	−0.056	−0.224
Store image	4	0.428	1.712
Parking	4	−0.116	−0.464
Age	1	−0.689	−0.689
Income	4	0.928	3.712
Summed Total (Number of Purchases)			8.82

Poor Customer	Value	Beta	Value*Beta
Constant			
Product selection	2	0.380	0.760
Price	2	−0.009	−0.018
Convenience	2	−0.139	−0.278
Service	2	0.799	1.598
Store atmosphere	2	0.364	0.728
Location	2	−0.056	−0.112
Store image	2	0.428	0.856
Parking	2	−0.116	−0.232
Age	3	−0.689	−2.067
Income	1	0.928	0.928
Summed Total (Number of Purchases)			1.36

Just like the simple regression, the unstandardized beta weights provide useful information. It shows the change in the outcome variable, the number of purchases, with a 1-unit increase in that particular variable. Suppose the poor customer shown in the right table in Figure 13.20 marked a 3 on service instead of a 2. Just that one change would increase the outcome variable by 0.799 from 1.36 to 2.16. If the customer rated service a 4 instead of a 2, it would jump to 2.96. This change in the number of purchases reinforces the idea that service is extremely important.

Global Concerns

Mathematics, statistics, and the process of analyzing quantitative data using traditional statistical tests and software packages are well accepted throughout the world. The primary concern for the global researcher is making certain that all parties have access to the same version of the software as this facilitates collaboration during data analysis, as well as the sharing of findings.

Specialized software packages also exist to assist in the analysis of qualitative data. While a variety of software packages are available, collectively they are referred to as computer-assisted qualitative data analysis software, or simply by the acronym CAQDAS. The growth of qualitative research in an international context has recently spurred renewed interest in CAQDAS.[10]

CAQDAS programs such as NVivo (http://www.qsrinternational.com/) allow users to organize, synthesize, and integrate qualitative data from interview transcripts, secondary data from articles, videos, photos, survey data, and more. Characteristics of those interviewed or the internal data pertinent to the firms they work for can also be stored. NVivo works in just about any language, and the software allows for qualitative data to be retained in multiple languages concurrently. The software saves the user time by helping to identify themes or categories in the data, and users can write notes on insights found at any point in the process. As NVivo is multiuser compatible, different researchers can analyze the same data from their unique perspective concurrently, or can choose to work collaboratively. Finally, the software assists in creating visual displays of information, including models, charts, and more.[11]

Despite the apparent sophistication and usefulness of CAQDAS, a study published in 2008 demonstrated that the programs are not frequently used in Britain. In fact, only 9% of the research industry professionals surveyed used the software to assist with qualitative data analysis.[12] As the marketing research industry in the United Kingdom is second in size only to that of the United States, this finding is somewhat surprising. The use of CAQDAS among research practitioners in Spain was also found to be low, and typically reserved for projects requiring large volumes of data to be analyzed, or a team-based analysis approach. Barriers to usage in Spain appear to be related to a lack of knowledge on how to use the software, as well as attitudinal perceptions that suggest researchers are skeptical of the software's benefits.[13] Only time will tell if advances in technology and the benefits of CAQDAS eventually result in increased usage in the context of global marketing research.

DEALING WITH DATA

A marketing research firm that specializes in social media marketing conducted a study about social media usage by consumers. Data were collected from 502 respondents. The data set is titled "Chapter 13 Dealing with Data." After accessing the data at www.sagepub.com/clowess, perform the following analyses. In a Word document, highlight all of the significant and/or managerially relevant findings from the analysis. The questionnaire and additional data collected are found in the document called "Chapter 13 Dealing with Data Survey."

1. Run a descriptive analysis of the data obtaining frequency counts of nominal and ordinal data and means for interval and ratio data.

(Continued)

(Continued)

2. Run a chi-square test of the following variables by the demographics of gender, age, and race using the cross-tab function.

   a.   Visited a social media site within last 30 days.
   b.   Have a Facebook profile page.
   c.   Type of site visited after leaving the social media page.
   d.   Uploaded photos or video within the last 30 days.

3. Run a one-sample t-test for the following variables against the test variable indicated in parentheses.

   a.   Number of Facebook visits within the last 30 days (mean for the same month last year was 14.83).
   b.   Percentage of purchases made online (mean in prior 60 days was 6.88).

4. Run an independent-sample t-test of the following variables based on gender.

   a.   Number of Facebook visits within the last 30 days.
   b.   Average time of each visit on Facebook.
   c.   Number of online purchases in last 60 days.
   d.   Percentage of purchases made online.
   e.   Percent of online communications with friends, siblings, children/parents, significant other, and colleagues.
   f.   Semantic differential statements about branding.

5. Run an ANOVA test of the following variables based on age and race.

   a.   Number of Facebook visits within the last 30 days.
   b.   Average time of each visit on Facebook.
   c.   Number of online purchases in last 60 days.
   d.   Percentage of purchases made online in last 60 days.
   e.   Percent of online communications with friends, siblings, children/parents, significant other, and colleagues.
   f.   Likert statements about branding.

SUMMARY

Objective 1: Identify and explain the steps in hypothesis testing.

Hypothesis testing involves five steps: (1) state the hypothesis, (2) select the statistical test, (3) determine the decision rule, (4) calculate the test statistic, and (5) state the conclusion. The hypothesis should have both a null and an alternative hypothesis with the null hypothesis typically assuming equality or no effect. The statistical test appropriate for nominal and ordinal data is the chi-square test. For interval and ratio data, the appropriate tests are the t-test (z-test) and

ANOVA. The decision rule is the level of confidence the researcher desires. The test statistic is calculated from the sample using SPSS or another appropriate statistical software. Based on the test statistic and decision rule, the null hypothesis is either accepted or rejected.

Objective 2: Understand the misuses of statistical significance and how statistically significant results may differ from those with practical importance.

Statistical significance is not a proxy for effect size. It is incorrect to assume that more highly significant results indicate a greater magnitude of difference. Statistical significance also cannot be used to assess the validity of the data, as significance only assesses random error. When evaluating tests of differences, the mean score must be considered in addition to whether or not results are significant in order to determine if results have practical value for managers. Larger sample sizes increase the likelihood that significant differences will be found for small effect sizes; before recommending action, cost-to-benefit ratio, marketing objectives, and strategy must be considered.

Objective 3: Explain the difference between Type I and Type II errors.

Type I error occurs when the researcher rejects the null hypothesis when it is actually true. Type I error is set by the researcher in selecting the decision rule. For instance, if a 95% confidence level is chosen, then there is a 5% chance of Type I error occurring. Type II error occurs when the null hypothesis is accepted when it is actually false. While the level of Type II error can be calculated, it is beyond the scope of this text. It is important to know there is an inverse relationship between Type I and Type II errors. When a researcher decreases the chances of a Type I error occurring by increasing the level of desired confidence, the probability of a Type II error occurring will increase. To decrease the probability of Type II error occurring requires an increase in the probability of a Type I error.

Objective 4: Explain how the chi-square test is used.

Chi-square is used to test for significant differences in the frequency counts of nominal and ordinal data. The test compares the actual frequency count of the sample with the expected count. The chi-square test can be used for a single variable, or it can be used with cross-tabs. With a single variable, the frequency count of the sample is tested against an expected frequency count supplied by the researcher. With cross-tabs, chi-square tests for equality across specified categories based on the sample characteristics for the test variable.

Objective 5: Identify and describe the various tests for differences in means.

To test for differences in means with interval and ratio data, researchers utilize either t-tests (z-tests) or an ANOVA test. The t-test is used when comparing two categories, and ANOVA is used when comparing three or more categories. Common t-tests include one-sample t-test, independent-sample t-test, and paired-sample t-test. The one-sample t-test is used when comparing the mean of a sample variable to a test mean. The independent-sample t-test involves comparing the mean of two different groups, such as males and females. The paired-sample t-test looks at before and after (or related) scores for each individual case.

Objective 6: Demonstrate an understanding of regression analysis.

Regression analysis provides a test for measuring the relationship or correlation among two or more variables. If the number of variables being measured is two, then it is simple regression. If more than two variables are involved, it is multiple regression. With both types of regression, there is one outcome or dependent variable that the researcher wants to predict. Simple regression involves one predictor or independent variable while multiple regression involves two or more independent or predictor variables. How well the regression model predicts the outcome variable is measured by R-square. The t-value and corresponding significance level of each predictor variable determines if it is a significant predictor of the outcome variable.

GLOSSARY OF KEY TERMS

Multiple regression: examination of the relationship of multiple independent or predictor variables and one dependent or outcome variable

Nonparametric procedures: statistical tests that are appropriate for nominal and ordinal data

Parametric procedures: statistical tests that can only be used with interval- or ratio-level data

Simple regression: examination of the relationship of one independent or predictor variable and one dependent or outcome variable

Type I error: occurs when the null hypothesis is rejected when it is actually true

Type II error: occurs when the null hypothesis is accepted when it is actually false

CRITICAL THINKING EXERCISES

1. Critique the following null and alternative hypotheses. If not appropriate, rewrite them using acceptable language.

   H_0: No differences will be found on the basis of income.

   H_A: Higher incomes will be as likely to purchase as will low incomes.

2. A retailer is interested in investigating whether doubling the value of manufacturer coupons will (a) increase the number of shoppers and (b) increase store profits. "Doubling" means that the store would give consumers a discount equal to twice the coupon face value, with the retailer absorbing the cost of the extra discount. The retailer would also like to know whether the redemption percentage of doubled coupons varies by gender, income, or age. Write the null and alternative hypotheses

associated with each test that would need to be performed in order to provide this information. For each null hypothesis, indicate the type of data that should be collected to best test the hypothesis, and the type of statistical test that would need to be performed.

3. In speaking with a friend, Lauren, you learn that she is performing community service by analyzing the attitude data collected on behalf of a not-for-profit organization. Lauren tells you, "I'm just going to run the analyses and find the most statistically significant results and base my recommendations off of that. After all, the more statistically significant the result, the bigger the difference in attitudes." What do you think of Lauren's data analysis strategy? Should she ignore all non–statistically significant results? Why or why not? Is her assumption regarding the degree of statistical significance and the size of the attitude difference correct? What factors influence the ease with which statistical differences are found in a sample?

4. A study was conducted to assess undergraduate college students' attitudes toward the student bookstore. Since many students attend a local junior college before transferring to the university, the classification of those responding to the study is a key demographic. Is the sample representative of the population according to the chi-square test shown in Figure 13.21, given that the student body is composed of 7% freshmen, 6% sophomores, 42% juniors, and 35% seniors? Why or why not? If the sample is not representative, what action(s) would you suggest that the researcher take?

5. Suppose Nike commissioned a study to better understand factors that influence men and women when purchasing sneakers, as the firm believes different factors are important to each gender. The results of key independent-sample t-tests based on gender are shown in Figure 13.22. What

Figure 13.21   Chi-square Results for Critical Thinking Question 4

Frequencies

	Category	Observed N	Expected N	Residual
1	freshman	18	14.2	3.8
2	sophmore	21	12.1	8.9
3	junior	76	84.9	−8.9
4	senior	67	70.8	−3.8
Total		182		

Test Statistics

	Classification
Chi-Square [a]	8.665
df	3
Asymp. Sig.	.034

a. 0 cells (.0%) have expected frequencies less than 5. The minimum expected cell frequency is 12.1.

conclusions can you draw regarding key differences between male and female attitudes? (1 to 5 scale with 1 = strongly disagree to 5 = strongly agree) Now interpret this information. What findings are meaningful for Nike, and how can the firm make use of the information?

Figure 13.22   Independent Sample T-test Results for Critical Thinking Question 5

Group Statistics

	Gender	N	Mean	Std. Deviation	Std. Error Mean
The brand name of a sneaker influences my purchase decision	Female	104	3.8462	1.27538	.12506
	Male	96	3.8750	.93189	.09511
I prefer to buy sneakers when they are on sale	Female	104	3.5865	1.56174	.15314
	Male	96	4.2083	1.05548	.10772
Advertising Influences which sneaker brand I purchase	Female	104	3.3942	1.21014	.11866
	Male	96	2.7292	1.37251	.14008
Price is important to me when selecting sneakers	Female	104	4.0288	1.24211	.12180
	Male	96	4.1563	.87453	.08926
I choose style over comfort when buying sneakers	Female	104	2.1442	1.32503	.12993
	Male	96	2.8021	1.64553	.16795
I prefer to shop online	Female	104	2.6250	1.43593	.14080
	Male	96	3.2292	1.44717	.14770
Athlete endorsements affect my sneaker purchase decision	Female	104	2.0096	1.22669	.12029
	Male	96	2.5729	1.49909	.15300

Independent Sample Test

		Levene's Test for Equality of Variances		t–test for Equality of Means						95% Confidence Interval of the Difference	
		F	Sig.	t	df	Sig. (2–tailed)	Mean Difference	Std. Error Difference		Lower	Upper
The brand name of a sneaker influences my purchase decision	Equal variances assumed	14.700	.000	−.181	198	.856	−.02885	.15905		−.34250	.28480
	Equal variances not assumed			−.184	188.305	.855	−.02885	.15712		−.33879	.28109
I prefer to buy sneakers when they are on sale	Equal variances assumed	41.910	.000	−3.272	198	.001	−.62179	.19006		−.99660	−.24699
	Equal variances not assumed			−3.321	181.871	.001	−.62179	.18723		−.99123	−.25236
Advertising Influences which sneaker brand I purchase	Equal variances assumed	7.978	.005	3.641	198	.000	.66506	.18266		.30485	1.02528
	Equal variances not assumed			3.623	190.015	.000	.66506	.18359		.30294	1.02719
Price is important to me when selecting sneakers	Equal variances assumed	4.116	.044	−.832	198	.406	−.12740	.15306		−.42925	.17444
	Equal variances not assumed			−.844	185.369	.400	−.12740	.15100		−.42531	.17050
I choose style over comfort when buying sneakers	Equal variances assumed	31.971	.000	−3.125	198	.002	−.65785	.21053		−1.073	−.24269
	Equal variances not assumed			−3.098	182.463	.002	−.65785	.21234		−1.077	−.23890
I prefer to shop online	Equal variances assumed	.376	.541	−2.962	198	.003	−.60417	.20400		−1.006	−.20188
	Equal variances not assumed			−2.961	196.470	.003	−.60417	.20406		−1.007	−.20173
Athlete endorsements affect my sneaker purchase decision	Equal variances assumed	14.111	.000	−2.917	198	.004	−.56330	.19308		−.94406	−.18254
	Equal variances not assumed			−2.894	183.923	.004	−.56330	.19462		−.94728	−.17932

6. A local credit union is interested in creating a Visa card product that would appeal to graduating college seniors. A marketing research class conducted a study of 72 graduating seniors in which their attitudes were assessed toward various credit card features. For each of the paired comparison t-tests shown in Figure 13.23, state the null hypothesis, and your conclusion based on the findings. Do you have any reservations about the study? Explain. What would you recommend the credit union do? Justify your decisions.

Figure 13.23   Paired Samples T-test Results for Critical Thinking Question 6

Paired-Sample Statistics

		Mean	N	Std. Deviation	Std. Error Mean
Pair 1	Prefer 0% interest promotion for 12 months	1.67	72	.475	.056
	Prefer $0 balance transfer fee	4.68	72	.470	.055
Pair 2	Prefer cash back reward program	4.40	72	.522	.061
	Prefer points rewards program for Amazon.com	4.54	72	.502	.059
Pair 3	Prefer higher credit limit with higher standard interest rate	4.51	72	.503	.059
	Prefer lower credit limit with lower standard interest rate	3.64	72	1.079	.127

Paired-Sample Correlations

		N	Correlation	Sig.
Pair 1	Prefer 0% interest promotion for 12 months Prefer $0 balance transfer fee	72	.337	.004
Pair 2	Prefer cash back reward program & Prefer points rewards program for Amazon.com	72	.123	.302
Pair 3	Prefer higher credit limit with higher standard interest rate & Prefer lower credit limit with lower standard interest rate	72	.113	.344

Paired-Sample Test

| | | Paired Differences | | | | | | | |
		Mean	Std. Deviation	Std. Error Mean	95% Confidence Interval of the Difference Lower	Upper	t	df	Sig. (2-tailed)
Pair 1	Prefer 0% interest promotion for 12 months Prefer $0 balance transfer fee	-3.014	.544	.064	-3.142	-2.886	-47.039	71	.000
Pair 2	Prefer cash back reward program - Prefer points rewards program for Amazon.com	-.139	.678	.080	-.298	.020	-1.739	71	.086
Pair 3	Prefer higher credit limit with higher standard interest rate - Prefer lower credit limit with lower standard interest rate	.875	1.138	.134	.608	1.142	6.527	71	.000

Scale: 1 = Not strongly prefer to 5 = Strongly prefer

7. Exit surveys from the previous year indicated that visitors to a theme park spent, on average, $217 on food, mementos, and merchandise per family during their stay. The theme park's general manager is wondering if the economic downturn has negatively impacted sales for these items in the current year. The results of a one-sample t-test comparing last year's average sales to the current year's average sales, as determined by the most recent exit survey, are shown in Figure 13.24. State the null hypothesis being tested, and your conclusion. Now interpret these findings. Is the general manager correct in his assumption?

8. Women who live in the South participate more frequently in hunting and fishing activities than do women in other parts of the country, and thus represent a market of interest to sporting goods stores. A national sporting goods chain conducted a study of Texans who hunt and fish regularly, which, among other questions, asked participants to rank their store preferences for purchasing hunting

Figure 13.24   One Sample T-test Results for Critical Thinking Question 7

One-Sample Statistics

	N	Mean	Std. Deviation	Std. Error Mean
How much did you spend on other expenses (food, merchandise, etc.)?	88	187.8409	132.31101	14.10440

One-Sample Test

	Test Value = 217					
					95% Confidence Interval of the Difference	
	t	df	Sig. (2-tailed)	Mean Difference	Lower	Upper
How much did you spend on other expenses (food, merchandise, etc.)?	-2.067	87	.042	-29.15909	-57.1931	-1.1251

and fishing equipment. The CEO of the sporting goods chain was curious to see if men and women differed in their store preferences. Five national store brands were ranked, and a cross-tabulation and chi-square analysis was performed by gender for each store. The results for Brand A are shown in Figure 13.25. Do men's and women's preferences differ for the store? If so, how do they differ? What recommendations would you make to the CEO?

Figure 13.25   Cross-Tabulation and Chi-Square Results for Critical Thinking Question 8

			Cross-Tab				
			Rank Brand A				
			4th most desirable	3rd most desirable	2nd most desirable	Most desirable	Total
Gender	Female	Count	21	10	20	53	104
		% Within Gender	20.2%	9.6%	19.2%	51.0%	100.0%
		% of Total	10.5%	5.0%	10.0%	26.5%	52.0%
	Male	Count	16	15	45	20	96
		% Within Gender	16.7%	15.6%	46.9%	20.8%	100.0%
		% of Total	8.0%	7.5%	22.5%	10.0%	48.0%
Total		Count	37	25	65	73	200
		% Within Gender	18.5%	12.5%	32.5%	36.5%	100.0%
		% of Total	18.5%	12.5%	32.5%	36.5%	100.0%

Chi-Square Tests			
	Value	df	Asymp. Sig. (2-sided)
Pearson Chi-Square	14.659[a]	4	.005
Likelihood Ratio	18.538	4	.001
Linear-by-Linear Association	1.419	1	.234
N of Valid Cases	200		

a. 4 cells (40.0%) have expected count less than 5. The minimum expected count is 2.40.

The following questions require that you access the textbook's website at www.sagepub .com/clowess. Open the SPSS data file titled "Chapter 13 Critical Thinking Data" and the questionnaire that accompanies the data file titled "Chapter 13 Critical Thinking Survey."

9. Is gender associated with playing intramural basketball (Question 5)? Is gender associated with playing basketball in high school (Question 4)? Run the appropriate analyses, state your conclusion, and interpret the findings.

10. Do males and females hold similar attitudes toward the statements assessed in Question 3 of the survey? State the null hypothesis, perform the appropriate statistical test, explain your conclusions, and interpret the findings.

11. Do people spend as much money on other expenses associated with attending an NBA game (parking, food, merchandise, etc.) as they do on the price of the ticket itself (Questions 8 and 10)? State the null hypothesis, perform the appropriate statistical test, explain your conclusions, and interpret the findings.

12. Does the number of professional basketball games attended vary by income (Question 2)? State the null hypothesis, run the appropriate test, explain your conclusion, and interpret the finding.

13. Your friend believes that the average price paid for a single NBA ticket is $95 a game (Question 8). Run the appropriate statistical test, explain your conclusion, and interpret the finding. What is the confidence interval for the average price paid for a single NBA game ticket?

CONTINUING CASE STUDY: LAKESIDE GRILL

The student team had looked forward to this part of their project. The questionnaire had been created, data were collected, and now it was time to focus on the analysis. After validating and cleaning the data, the team divided the analyses among the team members.

However, the first task was to code the open-ended questions and create a few new variables. This task was given to Alexa. She added the number of noon meals eaten at

(Continued)

(Continued)

Lakeside Grill to the number of evening meals eaten to create a new ratio variable that represented the total meals eaten at Lakeside. She then used this information to create a variable containing three categories called light users, moderate users, and heavy users. Light users were defined as those who ate 6 or fewer meals, moderate users consumed 7 to 10 meals, and heavy users ate 11 or more meals per month at Lakeside Grill. Another new variable created used categories to classify if the respondent ate at Lakeside Grill primarily for lunch, primarily for dinner, or a combination of both. To determine the correct classification, Alexa subtracted the number of evening meals from the number of lunch meals. If the result was −2 or below, then the person was labeled as an evening diner; if the result was from −1 to +1, the label was both meals; and if the result was 2 or greater, the person was labeled as a lunch diner. The last two variables created related to the distance that respondents (a) lived from Lakeside Grill and (b) worked from Lakeside Grill. For each of these variables, the two categories with the largest distances were collapsed into a single category using the recoding process.

After this work was done, Destiny ran the descriptive analysis of every question. The SPSS data file used in this and subsequent analysis is titled "Chapter 13 Lakeside Grill Data Coded." The questionnaire is titled "Chapter 13 Lakeside Grill Survey." With each part of the analysis, the team decided to write down significant or interesting findings. This document is titled "Chapter 13 Analyses Findings." All of the files for this exercise are located at the textbook website, www.sagepub.com/clowess.

Using independent t-tests, Brooke compared answers to Questions 6, 11, and 12 based on the respondent's gender and whether the person ate primarily at noon or in the evening. Using ANOVA tests, Brooke analyzed responses to Question 6, Question 11, and Question 12. To see if the new restaurant, Fisherman's Paradise, had an impact on Lakeside Grill, Destiny analyzed the evaluation of the food at Fisherman's Paradise compared to the Lakeside Grill (Question 9) and the impact on dining at Lakeside (Question 10). The last part of the analysis included chi-square tests. Brooke examined the ranking of Lakeside Grill, and Zach examined the change in dining at Lakeside Grill since Fisherman's Paradise opened. For this last test, Zach collapsed the first two categories, quit eating and eating less, into a single category.

Critique Questions:

1. Evaluate the work Alexa did on the original data set in terms of coding the three open-ended questions and the creation of the new variables.

2. Access the "Significant and Interesting Findings" for the Lakeside Grill analyses. For each of the following sections, evaluate the work of the team. The output file's name is given in the parentheses following the analysis technique. Open each and compare the output results to the findings indicated by the team.

   a. Descriptive analysis (Chapter 13 Lakeside Grill Descriptives)
   b. Independent-Sample T-Tests (Chapter 13 Lakeside Grill Independent T-Tests)
   c. ANOVA Tests for Question 6 (Chapter 13 Lakeside Grill ANOVA Question 6)

    d. ANOVA Test for Question 10 (Chapter 13 Lakeside Grill ANOVA Question 10)

    e. ANOVA Tests for Question 11 (Chapter 13 Lakeside Grill ANOVA Question 11)

    f. ANOVA Tests for Question 12 (Chapter 13 Lakeside Grill ANOVA Question 12)

    g. Chi-Square of Ranking of Lakeside Grill (Chapter 13 Lakeside Grill Chi-Square Ranking)

    h. Chi-Square of Changes in Eating at Lakeside Grill Because of New Competitor (Chapter 13 Lakeside Grill Chi-Square Competitor)

3. Based on the findings from the SPSS analysis, what recommendations would you make to the owner of Lakeside Grill?

MARKETING RESEARCH PORTFOLIO

The assignment instructions, data set, and questionnaire for the Chapter 13 "Marketing Research Portfolio" can be found at www.sagepub.com/clowess. The client in this case is considering investing in marketing communications targeting female bloggers. Data were collected to fulfill six research objectives, which are stated in the case. Students are tasked with deciding which statistical analyses should be run on the data set in order to fulfill the study's research objectives, and are encouraged to write null hypotheses to guide the analysis.

STUDENT STUDY SITE

Visit the Student Study Site at www.sagepub.com/clowess to access the following additional materials:

- eFlashcards
- Web Quizzes
- SAGE Journal Articles
- Web Resources

CHAPTER 14

Research Reports and Presentations

LEARNING OBJECTIVES

After reading this chapter, you should be able to

1. Identify the goals of preparing marketing research reports and presentations.
2. Describe the various components of a marketing research report.
3. Explain the four principles of an executive-ready report.
4. Discuss the use of oral presentations in marketing research reporting.
5. Explain how to use graphs and charts effectively.

INTRODUCTION

While the descriptive information obtained from a study's data is interesting and the significant results obtained through t-tests, ANOVA, and chi-square tests are important, companies want to know what it all means. What are the conclusions? What are the marketing implications? How can the findings be used to make management and marketing decisions?

A recent study by Lyris Inc., a global digital marketing firm, took findings from the analysis of survey data to identify eight digital trends relating to e-mail marketing.[1] These trends are listed in Figure 14.1. The ultimate goal of marketing research is to turn data into information that can be used by individuals and companies making decisions. The trends identified by Lyris can guide marketing managers in developing digital marketing plans. It can also be helpful in developing a marketing budget and how much is going to be allocated for the digital component of marketing.

Figure 14.1   Trends in E-mail Marketing

1) Increased use of mobile communication.

2) Potential for word-of-mouth multiplier effect with social media.

3) Integration of social media and e-mail.

4) Social media marketing can earn brands social currency.

5) Potential for location-based marketing via smartphones.

6) Understanding how consumers shop online and off so relevant, integrated communications can be targeted.

7) Millennials are at the cutting edge of technology.

8) Increased social gaming.

Source: Author-created from "The Future of Email: 8 Trends to Watch in 2012," *Lyris Marketing Guide*, Lyris Inc., www.lyris.com, December 2011.

This chapter takes the data analysis discussed in the previous chapters and outlines how those conclusions are to be presented. While most reports are written, some are oral. In the past, all reporting was done in person by the marketing research agency or marketing research personnel within a company. Today, other alternatives exist. Formal reports may not even be written. It may just be a presentation that is given via Skype, attached to an e-mail, or delivered through a website.

GOALS OF REPORTS AND PRESENTATIONS

- Objective 14.1: Identify the goals of preparing marketing research reports and presentations.

The quality of a marketing research report is directly related to the effort put into it by the research staff. It is tempting to spend all of the time doing the research, then throw the report together at the last minute. Such an approach may leave a lasting negative impression and waste the valuable research that was performed. To ensure quality, it is important to consider the goals of preparing reports and making presentations shown in Figure 14.2.

Effectively Communicate Findings

The first and ultimate goal is to effectively communicate the findings. If the results cannot be communicated in an effective manner, then it doesn't matter how well the research was conducted or what was learned. The recipients of the research will not be able to make informed management decisions if they don't understand the results.

Writing effective research reports begins with understanding the different groups of individuals who will be reading the report or listening to the presentation. There will be individuals

Figure 14.2   Goals of Reports and Presentations

1. Effectively communicate findings
2. Provide interpretations of findings
3. Draw conclusions
4. Provide insight
5. Make recommendations
6. Discuss limitations

who are only interested in the executive summary, and who only want to hear the conclusions and recommendations. They don't want to bother with anything else or get bogged down in a discussion of the research methodology. Another type of individual will want to read or hear the findings from the marketing research, in addition to learning the conclusions and listening to recommendations. These people are interested in how the findings tie into the conclusions and how the recommendations are then derived. The third group is composed of those people who have some expertise in marketing research, or at least believe they do. This group wants to gain a detailed understanding of how data were collected, how they were analyzed, and how the findings were drawn. However, most individuals involved in reading or listening to a marketing research report or presentation fall into the first two categories.

In addition to understanding the type or types of individuals who will be involved, it is important to understand that most individuals have extremely limited knowledge of research. They do not know what a t-test, ANOVA, or chi-square analysis is, and their knowledge of the meaning of "statistical significance" is very low. Even those who have heard of various statistical tests typically have no idea of how the test was performed and how the results are read, much less what they mean. As a result, the report and presentation need to be free of marketing research jargon and terminology. Definitions, detailed explanations, and statistical test printouts can be placed in the appendices where the individual who is interested can go for in-depth information. Still, in most cases, even the appendices often contain few actual statistical analyses or tables. However, quality research providers should be willing and able to make this information available to the client upon request in a timely manner.

Provide Interpretations of the Findings

It is important to focus on the fact that the marketing research was conducted because of some research objectives stated at the beginning of the project. The findings and corresponding interpretations of the research must relate to these research objectives. More importantly, the interpretations of the findings need to be written or presented in a nontechnical manner that can be easily understood by someone without any marketing research knowledge. This can be a challenge for individuals trained in marketing research because research terminology has become such a critical part of their vocabulary. More difficult is discussing results of the research without using research terminology such as *t-value*, *level of significance*, and *confidence interval*.

At this juncture it is important to distinguish between findings and interpretations. **Findings** are the results of the data analysis. Findings include the data analysis output, frequency tables, descriptive statistics, cross-tabulations, chi-square analyses, factor analysis, scale reliability, tests for differences in means, and regression analysis. **Interpretations** put these findings into a context that the listener or reader can more easily understand. For example, findings related to descriptive statistics may be placed into summary tables that show the key attitude questions that were asked, the number of subjects who expressed an opinion (n), and the means and standard deviations for each question. Normally, a small note would appear under this table explaining the scale. The notation might say, "Subjects answered each question by selecting a response ranging from 1 = strongly disagree to 5 = strongly agree."

Discussion in the report may interpret this finding by pointing out that a mean of 4.5 on an item assessing satisfaction with customer service is very strong. Data from the frequency chart can be cited to expand on this finding to report the percent of total respondents who answered either "agree" or "strongly agree" in response to the question.

Alternatively, the report discussion for a different question assessing satisfaction with the company's pricing may point out that while a mean score of 3.5 is positive (as 3 indicates a neutral position), the large standard deviation of 1.57 indicates that pricing satisfaction varies widely from individual to individual. This interpretation can then provide a lead-in for additional analyses, which may test for differences in satisfaction, perhaps on the basis of gender, age, education, income, buyer loyalty, or some other key variable being investigated.

As will be discussed later, charts and graphs help to visually interpret and display information. Thus, if significant differences in terms of pricing satisfaction were found on the basis of age categories, a clustered bar chart could be used to help individuals visualize the differences in satisfaction levels between people of different age groups.

Sometimes researchers will discover findings that to them are interesting, but do not relate to the research objectives in any way. In such situations, they must avoid the temptation to put them in the main body of the report. Findings that don't relate to the research objectives can be placed in the appendices if the researcher feels they are important or will be of interest to the client. Furthermore, not all findings have to be reported. If a variety of cross-tabulation analyses revealed that no relationships were present between the variables being tested, the researcher may choose to limit discussion of these tests to a single sentence stating that no relationships were found, include the cross-tabulation analyses in the appendices but not discuss them in the report, or eliminate any reference to these findings at all. Which approach is taken depends upon the degree to which the findings relate to specific research objectives.

Drawing Conclusions

The third goal of reports and presentations is to draw conclusions based on the findings and interpretations. Conclusions expand upon the interpretation and attempt to explain to the reader or listener what the results of the study actually mean. It is critical that the conclusions tie into the research objectives. Specifically, conclusions should be explicitly stated for each research objective. After all, that is why the research agency was contracted to conduct the study. In drawing these conclusions, the researcher needs to have an understanding of the client's business, customers, and marketing strategy.

For instance, if the firm under study had recently implemented a customer service training program for its personnel, the high satisfaction scores pertaining to customer service provide strong evidence to conclude that the training program was most likely a success. The conclusion could be further bolstered if current satisfaction scores could be compared against satisfaction scores achieved by the firm prior to implementing its training program. In phrasing the conclusion, the researcher would need to be careful in the claims made. "The training program appears to have been successful. The differences in customer satisfaction scores from before and after the training program were implemented indicate a large improvement. Slightly more than 93% of the respondents to our recent survey indicated that they agreed or strongly agreed with the question, compared to only 72% who expressed these same levels of agreement before the training program was implemented."

As the example above illustrates, it is important that every conclusion drawn is based on solid interpretations of the research. If the study does not provide sufficient information or evidence to state a conclusion for a particular research objective, then this fact must be made clear. Drawing evidence-based conclusions is especially important if a conclusion is different from what the client expected. In such cases, the client may question the credibility of the conclusion. The researcher needs to be prepared to present analytical evidence that provides justification.

Conclusions regarding causation can be especially misleading. Researchers should be wary of concluding that one variable definitively "caused" another variable to change. In most circumstances, a conclusion of this nature will be inconsistent with the research methodology used in the market research study. You may recall from Chapter 7 that experiments under highly controlled conditions are used for proving causation. Marketing research studies performed outside of an academic setting are rarely experimental in nature, and thus lack the necessary control over other variables that could have an influence on the dependent variable. Finally, remember that correlation analysis alone is grossly insufficient to prove causation. High correlations between two variables does not provide sufficient evidence to indicate that one variable caused the other variable to change.

Provide Insight
· Kraft mac + cheese (blue box)
· 10% price markup.

In the past, marketing research companies went from the third goal of drawing conclusions directly to the fifth goal of making recommendations (as listed in Figure 14.2). With increased global competition and tighter marketing research budgets, companies now want more than conclusions and recommendations. They want to know how the conclusions derived from the research apply to their business and how they can use these conclusions to make more intelligent marketing decisions. They want **insights** that will lead to a competitive advantage for their company or brand.

In addition to research conclusions, companies are looking for insights that will lead to competitive advantages.

Generating insights is a complex, challenging, and labor-intensive process. It requires thinking beyond numbers. It involves using analytical and creative skills and an in-depth knowledge of the firm's operation and especially its customers. It involves spending time with the client to gain a better understanding of the situation the firm is facing. In our example, the researcher would need to gain a detailed understanding of how the customer service training program was implemented and exactly what customer service standards were set. Additional changes to business policies, processes, and procedures that could impact customer service should also be learned through discussions with the client. Finally, pending client approval, the researcher may also conduct additional focus group interviews to better understand why customers feel so strongly satisfied with customer service and what factors influenced their ratings.

A key insight gained from this process might be that multiple customer service and information access options should exist to satisfy every type of patron. Thus, in person or over the phone, older adults can "speak to a human" who graciously helps them in a warm, friendly, and positive fashion. On the other hand, those who desire self-service are satisfied because they are able to find needed information on the company's website using the FAQ section, technical support manuals, or company blog. Those who fall in between the two extremes may be satisfied because they can mostly find what they need online, but can e-mail a technical support person directly and receive a response within 24 hours. These insights can provide a competitive advantage when generalized to other aspects of the business, such as designing, ordering, and returning products.

Make Recommendations   *Actionable*

The fifth goal of research reports and presentations is to make recommendations. **Recommendations** are courses of action that should be taken by the firm based on the results of the study. The recommendations need to be based on the insights that were gained from the data analysis and the conclusions that were drawn. They also need to be tied into the objectives of the research. Making recommendations is typically the most difficult part of the report since many marketing researchers are not marketing strategists. They often are venturing into areas where they have limited knowledge. So consultations with the client may occur prior to writing the recommendations to ensure the recommendations are appropriate. However, researchers must be careful doing this. It is easy to offer recommendations the client wants, and not recommendations based on the research findings and conclusions.

Recommendations must be actionable. "Investing in additional research" would be a poor recommendation if unaccompanied by specific details outlining the research objectives, proposed methodology, cost, timeline, and expected value of the study. A well-presented recommendation section will provide support for the proposed actions, and justify why these actions should be implemented.

In the example cited previously, it would be particularly important to offer recommendations for action given the disparate results related to satisfaction with the company's pricing policies. Depending upon the conclusions and insights generated, the recommendations could fall into the area of customer relationship management. Strategically, the recommendation might be to "fire" a particularly unprofitable or hard-to-please segment. Specific actions to be taken may include recommending the removal of specific customers from the firm's direct marketing database to prevent future marketing communications from reaching those individuals.

Alternatively, depending upon the conclusions or insights that are relevant, recommendations may suggest that promotional incentives be targeted toward price-conscious consumers. More specific suggestions regarding the type of promotional incentive, the timing, and how the promotion should be communicated to the target audience would provide an actionable plan, as long as they are based on consumer insights, interpretations, and conclusions drawn.

Discuss Limitations

The last goal of reports and presentations is to discuss any limitations of the study. **Limitations include any potential problems that may have arisen during the data collection process, or assumptions that were made during the research study.** The most frequently cited limitation is the sample used for the study. Nonprobability samples, such as convenience samples, yield results that cannot be generalized to the larger population. Even when probability sampling is attempted and every effort is made to ensure the sample is representative of the target market, it may not be an identical match in terms of important demographic, geographic, or psychographic characteristics. To a certain extent, this can be compensated for by weighting the data, and if such techniques are used, they should be mentioned. The size of the sample may also be of concern.

Other limitations may involve the manner in which the data were collected, or the analytical tools used to interpret the data. The use of self-reported data in marketing research is often criticized due to memory errors or perceptual differences that may not be relevant to the questions being asked, but that introduce response error into the results. Both overall nonresponse and item nonresponse levels should also be discussed. Thus, if only 5% of the sample answered an open-ended question that was critical to fulfilling a key research objective, the client must be informed, as this calls into question the validity of the interpretation, conclusion, insights, and recommendations related to the research objective.

■ Objective 14.2: Describe the various components of a marketing research report.

PREPARING RESEARCH REPORTS

The typical format of the marketing research report is shown in Figure 14.3. The terminology and section headings may differ depending on the industry, the client, and the marketing research firm. But, most will cover the basic elements shown. This section will cover the typical or long version of the marketing research report. In the next section, a newer, shorter version will be presented.

Title Page

The **title page**, or front cover, of the report should have four basic pieces of information. The first is the title of the report or study. Titles do not have to be complete sentences, but should convey the essence of the topic contained in the report. Next should be the name of the person to whom the report is directed and/or the name of the organization for which the report is prepared. The third piece of necessary information is the date of the report. The last informational segment should relate to the individual and company that prepared the report. This typically includes the name of the firm, the primary contact person's name within the firm, and contact information such as phone number, address, e-mail, and corporate URL.

Table of Contents

The **table of contents** lists the different sections of the report in sequential order. Usually the first page of each section of the report is identified along with the corresponding page number. Some reports will have a separate listing of the figures and tables. This is handy for those who are looking for a specific piece of information, or for those who want to see a table that was used as the basis for a chart or graph presented on a slide during the oral presentation. In addition to the regular sections, the table of contents will contain a listing of the appendices, if relevant.

Figure 14.3 Format of the Marketing Research Report

1. Title page
2. Table of contents
3. Executive summary
4. Introduction
5. Research methodology
6. Data analysis findings
7. Conclusions and recommendations
8. Appendices

Executive Summary *+ critical*

The executive summary is a key component of the report. The **executive summary** presents a summary of the entire research report including the purpose of the research, key findings, conclusions, and recommendations. Although the summary is placed at the beginning of the research report, it is the very last portion of the report to be written, as it summarizes what is in the report.

It is important to remember that this will be the only section some individuals will read. It must be written concisely. These individuals are not interested in research methodologies used, type of analyses that were performed, and the individual significant results. They want to know why the research was conducted, the method of sampling, and the sample size. It should contain the key findings—not all of the findings—just those that are the most critical and that support the conclusions, insights, and recommendations. It is these latter topics, conclusions, insights, and particularly recommendations that are the most important to an executive. They need to be identified clearly, but concisely. If the executive wants further information, he or she can refer to other sections of the report.

Introduction

The introduction contains background information for the study. Background information may contain secondary information, or summaries of other studies that were conducted on the topic that relate to the current study. Events or factors that led to the study will be explained. For instance, declining market share over the last year may have triggered a need to look for alternative methods of reaching consumers or a revision of the current marketing plan. As a result, the current study may have been commissioned.

The introduction will contain the specific research objectives or questions that the study addresses. If hypotheses were developed, they will be stated. Usually the hypotheses are not stated in formal null and alternative fashion. Instead, the research hypotheses will be summarized in layman's terms. In fact, the word *hypothesis* is seldom used. A hypothesis written in layman's words might read, "We expected no differences between the rate of responses for males and females."

Research Methodology

This section is often difficult for a marketing researcher to write. The reader just wants to know what and how it was done. The researcher, on the other hand, often wants to provide specific step-by-step details of the entire project from sample selection to questionnaire design to data analysis. When writing this section, it is important to remember that readers do not really care about details; they just want enough information to understand what research was conducted and how it was done. Information that should be contained in this section is listed in Figure 14.4.

Figure 14.4 Information in the Research Methodology Section

1. Research design
2. Secondary data used
3. Procedure for collecting primary data
4. Sampling plan
5. Sampling procedure
6. Data collection process
7. Analytical techniques

The research design is the plan that was used for conducting the research. At a minimum, the research design specifies whether qualitative, quantitative, or both types of research were implemented. The use of descriptive, observational, or causal research techniques should also be specified. In discussing the research design, reference should be made back to the research objectives or questions by showing how the research that was conducted was appropriate for answering these questions or objectives.

Conciseness
Readibility
Adaptability
Balance
S

If secondary data were incorporated into the study beyond the data that were already identified in the introduction, details should be provided. It is especially important to identify the source of the secondary data and how they were utilized in the study.

Most research reports involve primary data collection. The procedure for collecting this data should be outlined in the report. The sampling plan must be thoroughly explained since sampling is a critical component of any research study. The client needs to be shown that the sample is representative of the population being studied and, as such, provides accurate information for the problem being addressed. The procedure that was used to obtain the sample needs to be discussed to assure the reader that it was a quality sample.

The researcher next should explain the data collection process. Some processes such as online surveys need little explanatory information. Other methods such as observation research, experimentation, mixed-method research, or a focus group will need more details.

The last component in the methodology section is a brief explanation of the analytical techniques used. This information is there if someone wants to know, but it is seldom reviewed. But, in case it is reviewed, it is important to describe the analytical methods accurately, yet without overusing confusing statistical terms. For example, instead of saying a t-test was used to test for differences based on gender, the researcher can say the analysis examined purchase behavior to see if there was a difference between males and females.

Data Analysis Findings

This will be the largest section of the report. It contains the findings from the data analysis as well as a description of the sample respondents. How to organize the section can be a challenge. A common method of organization is to begin by describing the characteristics of the sample and then arrange the findings by research objectives or questions. The analysis and findings for each research objective would be shown under a heading listing that specific research objective. Care must be taken when presenting findings so that undue emphasis is not placed on findings that lack statistical significance. A major advantage of this type of organization is that it discourages researchers from adding findings that do not pertain to a particular objective.

A second approach is to organize the report in the order of the questionnaire. This approach allows an individual reading the report or listening to the presentation to follow along with the questionnaire and understand how each question or item has been analyzed and the corresponding findings. If this organizational method is used, some distinction must be made to explain that while some comparisons between groups may appear to indicate that differences exist, they likely would not represent a real difference in the population. The issue of statistical significance again is at the heart of this challenge; explaining why two results that are numerically different in the sample aren't really different at all without getting into statistical language can be quite challenging. Another disadvantage is that because most questionnaires leave demographics until the end of the survey, the discussion of the nature of the sample takes place last, and will seem out of place. Modifying the presentation of information so that the sample characteristics are presented before the rest of the questionnaire can help to reduce confusion and frustration on the part of the reader.

Throughout this process, the key challenge for the marketing researcher is to present the findings in a way that is understood by the audience. Using statistical terminology tends to confuse, rather than clarify, and thus should be avoided unless the audience is well versed in statistical knowledge. The researcher should instead rely on graphs, charts, and tables to present the results. Graphs and charts especially are easier to understand and allow the findings to be grasped rather quickly. In addition to graphs, charts, and tables, the researcher needs to write about the results. This is important in case the reader wants additional information. It also can provide details that may not be easily recognizable in the graph or figure. Furthermore, not all information warrants a chart, graph, or table.

Conclusions and Recommendations

The conclusions and recommendations are obtained from the data analysis and corresponding findings. The conclusions should be specific, clear, and concise. Each conclusion should be tied with a specific research objective. The number of conclusions will vary depending on the type of research conducted and the findings that were found from the analysis. Some objectives may have only one conclusion while others may have more conclusions. It is also possible that no conclusions can be drawn for a specific research objective.

The recommendations are clear statements of action. They are derived from the conclusion. They are the result of critical thinking and application of the conclusions to the research problem that was the catalyst for the research study.

When citing conclusions and making recommendations, it is also a good idea to identify any limitations associated with the research. Although researchers strive to conduct errorless research, it is impossible to eliminate all error. As was discussed in previous chapters, the goal is to reduce or eliminate systematic error and reduce the level of random error. But, even the best designed studies are likely to have some error, and therefore limitations that affect the conclusions and recommendations that are made should be addressed. The most common limitations cited include sampling bias and measurement error. The researcher may also want to cite time limitations or budget constraints if either or both impacted the quality of the data.

Appendices

The content of the appendices and the number of appendices will vary greatly. Almost all studies will put a copy of the questionnaire or survey instrument in an appendix for referral. Tables and information that is technical may be put in an appendix and referred to in the text of the report. Some reports will put copies of pertinent or specific data analysis output in an appendix. It would be extremely rare to include all of the analysis because it may be 100 to 200 pages long. More likely is the enclosure of data analyses that deal with a specific issue that the researcher feels the client may want to see. This is often the case if a finding is contrary to what the client expected. Having the analysis available in an appendix can be valuable to assure the client the correct interpretation was made.

EXECUTIVE-READY REPORT

■ Objective 14.3: Explain the four principles of an executive-ready report.

In the past, marketing research executives as well as executives of client firms considered a long, detailed marketing research report to be the norm. Clients and marketing managers wanted all of the details. They wanted every possible piece of information and analysis that was conducted. Marketing research agencies believed that by providing length and details they were producing quality research. But times have changed. E-mail, smartphones, and instant messaging have changed the way people communicate and even the way executives communicate. Today's executives want a shorter, more readable version that can be read on a BlackBerry, dissected on the plane, in an airport, or in a taxi on the way to a business meeting. As a result, a newer, trimmer version of the marketing research report is being used by many companies. This **executive-ready report** is based on four principles: conciseness, adaptability, readability, and balance.[2]

Smartphones and email have changed the way business executives communicate and have resulted in executive-ready research reports.

A concise report eliminates all of the unnecessary words, figures, tables, and charts. While there is written content, bullet points, headlines, and subheads are used frequently to provide emphasis and conciseness. The idea is if it can be said in 5 words, why use 15? The goal is to allow the reader the opportunity to quickly grasp the point or idea without reading an entire paragraph. Additional information can be provided in appendices or a supporting document.

In making the executive-ready report concise, it is important to realize this does not simply refer to the elimination of word content. It also does not dictate that all information be presented in bullet points. While bullet points are used, some may need further explanation. Thus, some written content is needed. Conciseness does not imply that only major points or conclusions should be addressed while minor ones should be left out. Conciseness does require full reporting, but looks for ways of doing it more efficiently and succinctly.

Adaptability refers to the ability of the report to be adapted by different individuals within an organization. Some members of the executive team may read only headlines and subheads and by means of this process should be able to grasp the research findings, conclusions, and recommendations. By reading the executive summary, the executive will know the stated research objectives, how the study met those objectives, and the future strategic or management decisions that need to be made. The marketing director and other midlevel managers will likely read the bullet points and examine the figures, graphs, tables, and charts. But, this can be done rather quickly. The executive-ready report is not 200 pages long. Further, the report should be provided in a format such as PDF, so that reviewing can be done on a smartphone, wherever the executive may be.

While the executive-ready report is condensed, it is important for it to be readable. The report should tell a story. One point should lead to the next. To be readable, the report needs to be visually appealing. This involves spatial placement of headlines, subheads, bullet points, and content. But, it also involves the use of visuals. Tables, charts, and graphs are helpful. But, a report that is full of tables, graphs, and figures quickly becomes boring and tedious to read. Other visuals can be used, such as photographs, line drawings, and even cartoons. The idea is to create a report that is visually appealing and draws the reader into the report.

Balance is the last principle of an executive-ready report. Balance is important from two perspectives. First, is the balance between visual interest and professional presentation. While visuals add interest to the report, if overdone, they can make the report look cartoonish and unprofessional. However, a lack of visuals makes the report boring and tedious to read. Second, balance is required between brevity and being too wordy. Using headlines, subheads, and bullet points makes the report smaller and easier to scan but, if overdone, can leave out critical information. The reader should never be left wondering what was meant by a bullet point, subhead, or head. Because of the abbreviated nature of the executive-ready report, every word is important and should be carefully considered.

ORAL PRESENTATIONS

■ Objective 14.4: Discuss the use of oral presentations in marketing research reporting.

In addition to a formal written report, clients may want an oral presentation. An oral presentation allows for a personal meeting between the client and the research firm or the research specialist within a company research department. It allows for two-way communication. Clients are able to ask questions and seek clarification. The research firm not only has the opportunity to respond, but the researchers can also check to make sure the points they are making are clearly understood.

With current technology, oral presentations can be presented virtually. It may be a live video conference over the web or a recorded presentation that is viewed at the convenience of the client. The high cost of travel is the primary driving force behind virtual presentations although time savings of high corporate executives are often another factor behind the decision to use the digital approach.

If an oral presentation is requested, it is extremely important that the presentation be done well. It is very likely that top management will attend to hear the results. These are individuals who are not likely to read the written report, so the oral presentation will be their only exposure to the study. If they do access the written report, it will be either just to read the executive summary or to check for more details about some aspect of the oral presentation.

Creating Effective Presentations

A recent conversation with the president of a Fortune 500 company and communications consultant Gary A. Schmidt resulted in what Gary termed "The Five Things Top Management Wants to Tell Research—But Just Can't."[3] These five things were based on attending hundreds of meetings and listening to multiple marketing research presentations. They are

1. You're boring us to tears.

2. Enough with all the numbers already—what do we do?

3. I don't have all day to listen to you—how about 10 pages next time instead of 50?

4. I don't care about fancy methodology—what's the bottom line?

5. Take a position. I don't care about "confidence levels" or "statistical significance."

These statements reinforce the need for firms to embrace the executive-ready marketing research reporting style. It also highlights that during the oral presentation, listeners want the same type of approach. Long, boring presentations loaded with facts are out; short, to-the-point, concise presentations are desired.

Data, analysis, and significant findings are the core of marketing research. But, when it comes to making the presentation, these should be left in the marketing research lab. Attendees at the presentation want to know what it all means for their business or their brand. The purpose of the presentation is not to showcase marketing research and the methodologies that were used, but to provide insight that can help managers make good decisions. To accomplish this purpose, Gary Schmidt suggests presenters adhere to the "Fab Five Principles" shown in Figure 14.5.

The first principle, "keep it right," refers to the idea of keeping the findings of the research brief on point and, most importantly,

Figure 14.5   "Fab Five Principles" in Effective Research Presentations

- Keep it right
- Keep it simple
- Focus on the audience's needs (not yours)
- Be engaged and engaging
- Take a risk

Source: Author-created from Gary A. Schmidt, "Take a Risk, Keep It Simple," *Quirk's Marketing Research Review*, April 2007, Article ID 20070404.

focused on insights. To relay there is a significant difference based on age is presenting the findings. Managers want to know what this means for their business. How does this difference impact marketing strategy and marketing decisions? The answer to that question provides valuable insight.

Marketing research is very complex and to most managers is filled with statistical jargon they don't really understand, although they often pretend that they do. The second principle, "keep it simple," means taking the complex marketing research analysis and making it simple so that managers can really comprehend it and do not have to pretend they understand when in fact they may not. The key is to tell the audience what is important, no more or no less, in terminology the managers understand.

Keeping it right and keeping it simple help with the next principle—"focus on the audience's needs." The research presentation is not about showing how skilled a researcher is or how knowledgeable he or she is about marketing research techniques. It is about the audience and the business or brand each individual represents. The audience does not care how difficult it was to get the data or how many hours were spent interviewing respondents; these managers want to know what was learned and how will it help them to make better marketing decisions.

Focusing on the audience's needs will necessitate that presenters "be engaged and engaging," which is Principle 4. No one wants to attend a boring meeting, and if that meeting is also long, it becomes unbearable. The t-test, the significance level, or the sampling design may be exciting to the researcher; it is not exciting to the audience. What gets the audience engaged are results, conclusions, recommendations, and insights into what has happened and what needs to be done. To engage the audience requires the right message be delivered in an exciting tone and with enthusiasm. Excitement and enthusiasm are contagious. If the presenter is excited about the finding and the corresponding insights, it will infect the audience.

The last principle cited by Gary Schmidt is to "take a risk." Marketing researchers tend to want to play it safe. They want significant results. They want to stay within the confidence interval. They want to hide behind potential systematic and random error. But, to make a presentation that is effective requires taking a risk. It means suggesting a strategy, proposing a course of action, and then supporting it with research. It is very unlikely that research can eliminate all risk. But, it can provide insight to the "better" decision. Managers make decisions every day without perfect information, so they understand that insights and recommendations from research contain risk. Their goal is to reduce that risk and choose the path that has the highest probability of success. The marketing research presentation should not only direct the client or management to that path, but provide support for why it is a better decision.

Creating Effective Visuals

In terms of format, the oral presentation is usually similar to the written report except it begins with the introduction, and then proceeds through the other steps of the research methodology, description of sample respondents, data analysis findings, conclusions, and recommendations. To engage the audience, oral presentations need to be accompanied by visuals. The most commonly used visual is PowerPoint, although handouts and flip charts can be used. However, PowerPoint allows for much greater creativity in making the presentation. Changes can be made at the last minute. Graphs, figures, and tables can be easily embedded into the slide. Multiple people can be involved in preparing the PowerPoint as long as someone coordinates the final version so it is uniform and fits together.

The keys to effective visuals are visibility, simplicity, and legibility (see Figure 14.6).[4] Whatever visuals are used, they must be easily seen by everyone in the audience. They should be colorful and simple and, most importantly, illustrate or convey only one point. They should be legible and easy to understand. If the audience is staring at a visual trying to figure out what it says or what it means, these attendees are not listening to the speaker. The visual should assist the speaker, not be a distraction from what is being said. Thus, animated visuals are usually not recommended. Experts on presentations suggest that no more than one visual for every 30–60 seconds should be used. Changing visuals too frequently can be distracting.

Figure 14.6   Keys to Effective Visuals

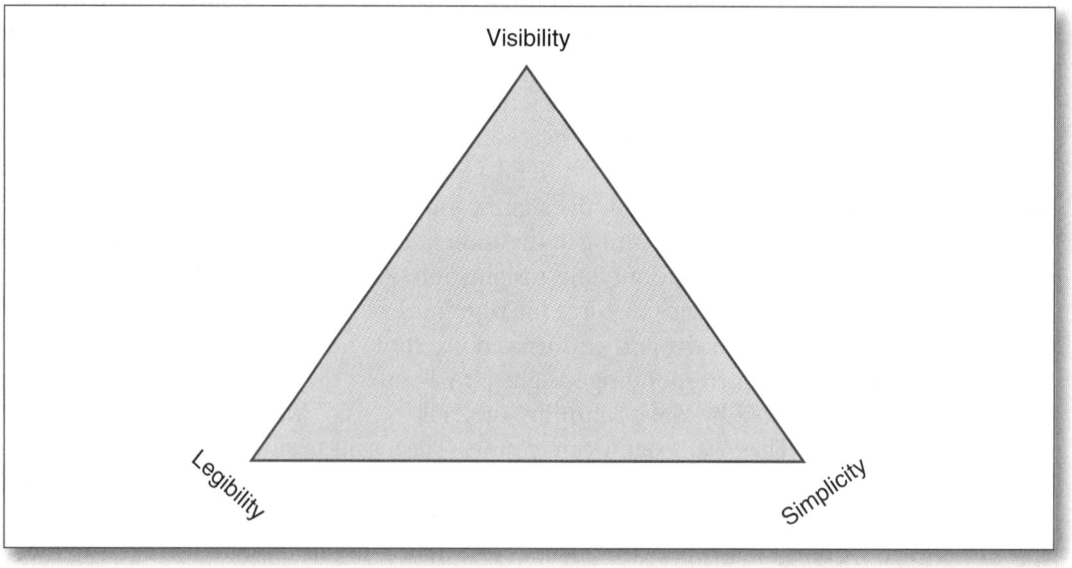

Source: Author-created with data from N. Carroll Mohn, "How to Effectively Present Marketing Research Results," *Quirk's Marketing Research Review*, January 1989, Article ID 19890104.

Making PowerPoint Presentations Come Alive

PowerPoint has almost become the standard for presentations of all kinds, including marketing research presentations. Unfortunately, PowerPoint is often used improperly and ineffectively. Figure 14.7 provides a list of some common mistakes that have been made with PowerPoint slides.[5] It ranges from using too many slides to placing too much information on each slide to ineffective use of visuals or no visuals at all. Too much variance with colors, fonts, font sizes, and slide formats and cluttered slides are also problematic. Bullet points should be restricted to a few key words and not be excessive in length; nor should bullet points be phrased as long sentences.

In contrast to the list in Figure 14.7 of poor and ineffective PowerPoint slides, Figure 14.8 highlights five ways to make PowerPoint presentations come alive.[6] The first step is to start strong. Think about the audience and the purpose of the PowerPoint presentation. Choose fonts and colors that are appropriate considering who will be viewing the slides and what the presenter wants to accomplish. Select a slide background, body text style, heading placement, fonts, and accent colors that fit, and apply these in the master slide for consistency. This will ensure every slide in the presentation utilizes the same stylistic elements.

The amount of text on each slide should be minimal. The purpose of the text or bullet points is to highlight the main ideas or thoughts. The text serves as an aid to keep the presenter on track and gives the audience an idea of what will be covered. Slides with too much text can easily become a distraction as the audience reads the slide instead of listening to the presenter.

Consistency is important and makes a PowerPoint presentation look professional. The best way to ensure consistency is to utilize pre-made templates. The ones provided by Microsoft within PowerPoint are used frequently by many types of businesses, so it is a good idea to either create a new template or access one of the hundreds of templates that are now online. While some variance among the slides is good, too much variance can be distracting and make the presentation look amateurish.

In terms of fonts, it is a good idea to use no more than two font families. If the presentation will make use of the client's computer, care should be taken to select font families that are commonly installed on all PCs, such as Arial, Calibri, Times New Roman, or Tahoma. There's nothing more embarrassing than opening a presentation, only to find that the font substituted for the one you had chosen has altered the displayed information, perhaps by forcing words off the slide, or creating a "look" that is

Figure 14.7   Poor and Ineffective PowerPoint Presentations

- Too many slides
- Slides with all text—no graphics or white space
- Cluttered slides with clip art, visuals, or animation
- No visuals
- Too much variance in colors, fonts, font sizes, and slide formats
- Excessive bullet points
- Long sentences
- Too much information on one slide

Source: Author-created from Melissa Murray, "Making the Results Come Alive," *Quirk's Marketing Research Review*, October 2006, Article ID 20061005.

Figure 14.8   Making PowerPoint Presentations Come Alive

- Start strong
- Minimize text
- Be consistent
- Be visually engaging
- Use technology to add life

Source: Author-created from Melissa Murray, "Making the Results Come Alive," *Quirk's Marketing Research Review*, October 2006, Article ID 20061005.

inconsistent with the image promoted by the rest of the template. Fonts can be varied by using bold and italics, even shadowing. But by using only two font families, consistency is maintained. It is also a good idea to add the company's name or the client's name or logo on each slide, along with a copyright symbol. This can be done through the master slide. This addition will make the presentation look more credible, as well as professional. Lastly, slide transitions can improve the presentation. But, if used, the same transition should be used throughout the entire presentation.

As has already been discussed, visuals are critical to engaging an audience. Photographs, clip art, line drawings, tables, figures, and charts can be easily embedded into a slide. Typically, only one visual should be used per slide. However, there are instances where a photograph may be included with a table, graph, or chart to reinforce the data being shown or to illustrate the impact of the result. Photographs are more professional and persuasive than line art or clip art. Clip art tends to be negatively viewed by many, and often detracts from the professionalism of the presentation. While visuals can help engage the audience, too many can be distracting. It is a matter of creating a balance between text and visuals.

Expanding the PowerPoint to include videos and audio recordings can further enhance a presentation and make it come alive. It provides variety to the presentation, but also can provide support for research findings. A short video of actual customers talking about a product or making points that reinforce a conclusion, an insight, or a recommendation can be powerful. The goal of using videos and audio is not just to break up a presentation and simply add variety; it is to present information in a unique way that communicates effectively. A story told in a short video can make an impression on a client or marketing executive that is difficult to do in a PowerPoint slide or from the lips of the presenter.

■ Objective 14.5: Explain how to use graphs and charts effectively.

CREATING CHARTS AND GRAPHS

Charts and graphs are an essential component of conveying the results of marketing research. They provide a visual picture of data, which is easier for someone to grasp than numbers in a paragraph or even in a table. It is important that all charts and graphs be properly labeled with a title. The vertical axis, the horizontal axis, and every other component of a graph or chart must also be labeled. It is also a good idea to provide value labels for data so the viewer can quickly see the value for each component. Creating effective graphs and charts takes time, but is well worth the effort.

Prior to graphing results, the researcher must decide what "base" will be used when presenting data. The researcher can choose to use (1) the entire sample, (2) only respondents who were asked the question, or (3) only those respondents who answered the question. The choice is important, because the percentages calculated and reflected in the graph will be influenced by the selected base. Most of the time researchers select Option 2 or 3, though there are exceptions. Selecting the appropriate base to use for charting data is particularly important when skip patterns are present, as some respondents may not have been eligible to answer a particular question. In these cases, only the responses of those who were asked the question should be graphed.

Similarly, when graphing responses to questions such as product ownership, preference, level of agreement or disagreement with a statement, or likelihood of usage, the graphed data are often restricted to those who were asked the question. However, some researchers may choose to display the results from only those who answered the question, particularly when the scaled-response question being graphed is part of a multi-item measure. In such cases, subjects who do not answer one question within a multi-item measure are dropped from subsequent analyses. Also, when questions are meant to express an attitude, those who did not answer, or who answered but checked the "don't know" or "not applicable" response category, are typically not included in data on which the graph is based.

Pie Charts

Pie charts are used frequently in presentations and are excellent for conveying nominal and ordinal data. With pie charts, the data are limited to a single variable containing typically a minimum of 3 and generally no more than 10 mutually exclusive categories. The pie chart itself consists of a 360-degree circle, sliced into segments, where each segment represents a category within the variable. Ideally, each category should be large enough in size so that each pie slice is easily identified in the chart.

Pie chart data should be presented in terms of percentages rather than raw numbers, as using raw numbers will visually exaggerate the results and may cause the reader to believe that differences are more extreme than is truly the case. Using percentages also makes the data much easier for people to understand and puts the information into perspective, particularly when large samples are used. As a whole, the slices in a pie chart should add up to 100%. If the total is 65%, then a pie chart cannot be used unless the remaining 35% is labeled as "other" or using some other nondescriptive name. Another inappropriate use of a pie chart would be one in which the combined percentages exceed 100%. Pie charts can be used to graph interval data associated with a single variable, but should never be used for ratio data.

Pie charts are commonly used to display the demographics of the sample, such as race, income, and education. When describing sample respondents, most researchers will include a category for those who did not answer the question. The point is to represent all participants in the study, regardless of whether they answered a particular demographic question or not. Gender is rarely displayed as a pie chart due to the small number of categories, and is typically not graphically displayed unless used in combination with another variable when presenting cross-tabulation data. Exceptions might be made for surveys that allow respondents to mark "transgender" and/or "prefer not to respond" options.

Because pie charts are visual representations of data, the way the pie is created is important. Consider the pie chart at the upper left corner in Figure 14.9. Most people will look first in the upper right hand corner of a pie chart, then move clockwise around the pie. Thus, the first

Figure 14.9   Rotating a Pie Chart to Change Perception

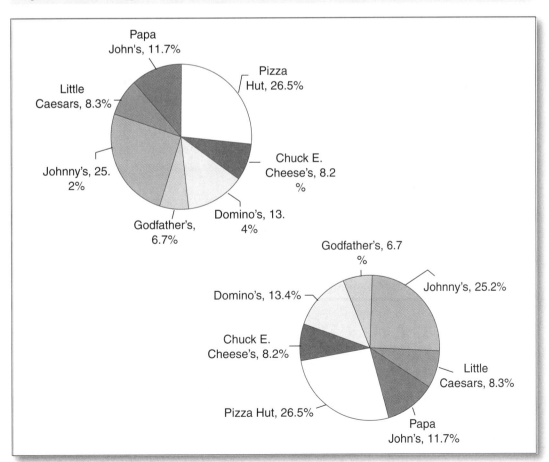

Figure 14.10   Cutting a Slice to Provide Emphasis

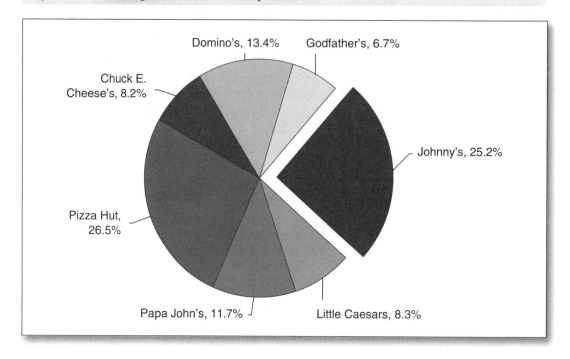

slice that is seen is Pizza Hut. The eyes then move to Chuck E. Cheese's, Domino's, Godfather's, and on around to Johnny's. Very little attention will be paid to the last two brands. Simply by the way it is designed the pie appears to emphasize Pizza Hut. At least that is the perception.

Suppose the marketing research study was done for a local pizza chain called Johnny's Pizza. The perception of the pie chart can be changed by simply rotating it to the right, in this case by 250 degrees. Now Johnny's is on the upper right and would be the first part of the pie that is noticed. This fits with the perception the research agency wants to create since the study was conducted for Johnny's.

To create even a stronger perception, the slice for Johnny's can be cut and pulled from the rest of the pie (see Figure 14.10). Now, it clearly becomes the immediate focus of the pie chart. Another more subtle change was putting two smaller pieces of the pie on each side of Johnny's. This gives the impression that the Johnny's share is even larger. Also, the names of the two pieces for Godfather's and Little Caesars were moved slightly away from Johnny's. Again, these actions create the perception that the central focus of the pie chart is Johnny's Pizza.

Line and Area Charts

Line and area charts are used to graph ratio data. These charts cannot be used to graph nominal, ordinal, or interval data because line charts imply a continuous variable. Line charts are often used to express patterns in variables over time, such as sales, gross margins, or market share percentages. Line charts allow flexibility in that multiple sales variables representing different regions or different sales representatives can be graphed concurrently for the same time period and compared against one another. In line charts, the data shown for each data point in each line are the actual amount of sales for that region (or person) at a particular point in time. However, for line charts or area charts to be used effectively, the range of values to be graphed should be similar and there should be no breaks, or only a very few breaks, between the category values. When creating a line or area chart, most individuals think of the horizontal axis as being time and the vertical axis as being values of whatever variable is being graphed.

Figure 14.11 shows a line chart of the number of complaints at a tanning salon over the last year. It is easy to see that the number of complaints spiked in March and was considerably higher that month for some reason than during the rest of the year. It is also evident that the number of complaints increased in the spring and summer months presumably because a tanning salon's business increases during those months.

Multiple lines can be shown on one graph, or a stacked area graph can be used. While stacked area charts look good, their usage sometimes makes it difficult for the viewer to decipher the information being represented. The key to understanding stacked charts is to realize that each additional level represents incremental values. Consider the sales figures at the tanning salon from four different types of tanning products. Because there are four different shaded areas for each tanning bed's sales data, it is necessary to have a legend. **Legends** provide a key for understanding the data, and in this case differentiate the types of tanning products on the basis of their relative sales. The stacked area chart in Figure 14.12 provides an excellent visualization

Figure 14.11   Line Chart Showing the Number of Complaints (see artwork file)

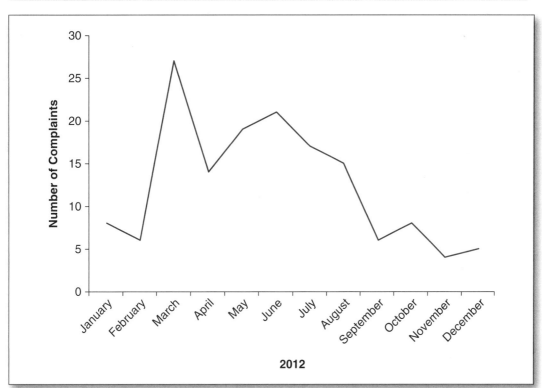

Figure 14.12   Stacked Area Chart Showing Sales

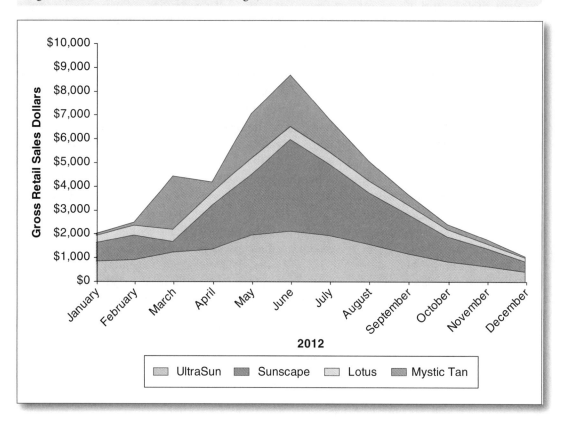

of the changes in sales between the four different brands of tanning products. Sales from using the UltraSun tanning beds tend to stay rather stable all year, as do sales for Lotus. But, use of the Sunscape tanning beds increases sharply from April through September and represents a high percentage of total sales. The Mystic Tan is a spray-on product that can give the skin the appearance of a tan. It is quick and easy and provides an even tan. Notice sales of Mystic Tan shoot up in March around spring break, then again in May and June for the summer months.

Remember, the width of the color band represents the amount of incremental sales attributed to each product. In the case of Lotus, incremental sales contributed by the brand range from $318 in January to a high of $692 in May, and a low of $177 in December. This one graph can convey considerably more information visually than a table or an explanation by a presenter.

Bar/Column Charts

Bar charts (called column charts in Excel) allow for the highest level of flexibility when presenting data and will fit almost all types of data. Simple bar charts can be used to display responses to nominal-, ordinal-, or interval-based questions. Clustered bar charts are excellent for visually presenting the results of cross-tabulations. Stacked bar charts serve as an alternative to pie charts, and show the cumulative percent of respondents who selected each response option for a particular variable, with the final percentage equaling 100%.

Bar charts are also excellent ways to show the results of paired t-tests and ANOVA, since multiple columns of data can be shown. Figure 14.13 is a graph showing the percentage of online purchases compared to a person's total purchases in six different categories for males versus females. It is easy to see that females purchase a higher percentage of apparel, books, videos, and shoes online while males purchase a higher percentage of electronics, home/garden items, and sporting goods. When creating bar or column charts, label both the y-axis and the x-axis, and make certain that the legend clearly identifies each column and the values for each column.

While bar charts provide excellent visual representations of data, they can be created to deceive or at least give a false impression. Examine the graph in Figure 14.14 of the level of satisfaction at Tony's Diner across six categories. Food is rated the highest at 4.89. The menu and appearance of the facility also appear to be rated relatively high. The only real concern for Tony's is level of service, which shows a mean value of 3.12. But, it appears not to be dangerously low, maybe midway on the scale.

However, when you examine the graph more diligently you notice the y-axis labeling is incomplete, as all it says is "level of satisfaction," and the x-axis labeling is missing. The viewer of the graph has no idea what scale was used. Was it a 5-point scale, a 6-point scale, or even a higher level of scale? Most will assume that it is a 5-point scale, based on the manner in which the data are presented. However, this may be misleading.

Figure 14.13   Online Purchases as a Percent of Total Purchases

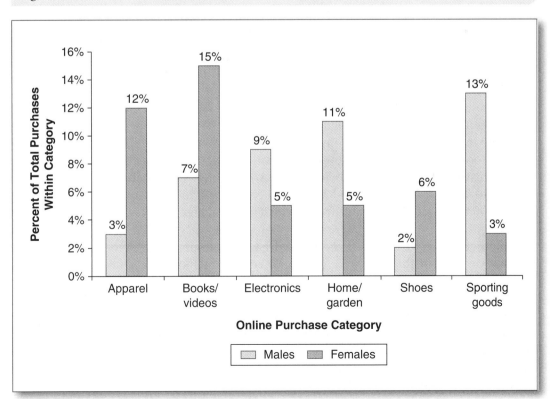

Figure 14.14   Level of Satisfaction at Tony's Diner

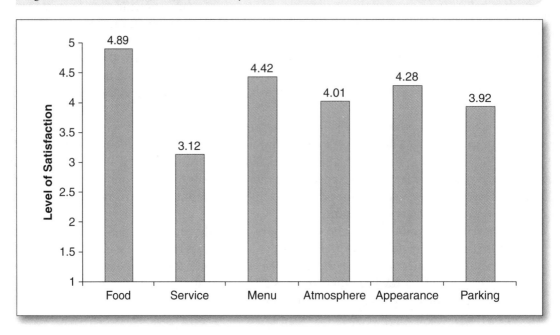

Figure 14.15 shows the results from Tony's Diner with the true vertical scale indicated, which was a 7-point scale ranging from 1 = very unsatisfied to 7 = very satisfied. When the data are viewed from this perspective, the picture of satisfaction with Tony's changes drastically. Now the food rating, which looked good before, is just barely above the midpoint on the scale, and the service score is now extremely low. The other categories that were evaluated also appear to be low. By just adjusting the scale that is used for the vertical column, the perception of satisfaction with Tony's Diner can be altered.

To present an even more accurate picture of Tony's Diner, it is beneficial to compare it to other restaurants in the area. Figure 14.16 does this. The first thing a person will notice when looking at the graph is that Tony's was evaluated lower across all six dimensions. But, in terms of food, it is not that far below the competitors' average. Neither is parking. However, service is extremely low, and it is obvious that is where Tony's Diner needs to invest resources and improve if it wants to stay in business. The visual picture and resulting perception of Tony's Diner changed considerably from the first graph in Figure 14.14 to the last one shown in Figure 14.16.

Another bar chart option is the stacked bar or column chart. Figure 14.17 shows a stacked bar chart of the four types of suntan beds or methods for a local tanning salon. The stacked chart provides a relative picture of total sales for each method. Total sales are highest for the Sunscape tanning bed while lowest for the Lotus bed. The individual bars can be examined to see, in this case, which age group is using which bed or method. The Mystic Tan appeals the most to the 20- to 29-year-old age group and the least to individuals 40 and older. Sales of the UltraSun and Sunscape are highest for the two middle-age categories. While the Lotus bed has the lowest sales, it appeals to the older customers more than the younger customers.

Figure 14.15   Level of Satisfaction at Tony's Using the True Scale

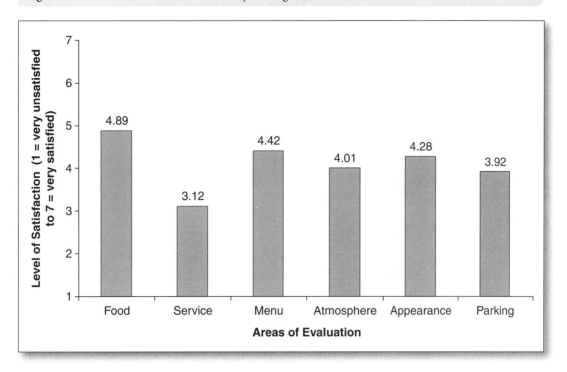

Figure 14.16   Competitive Comparison of the Level of Satisfaction with Tony's Diner

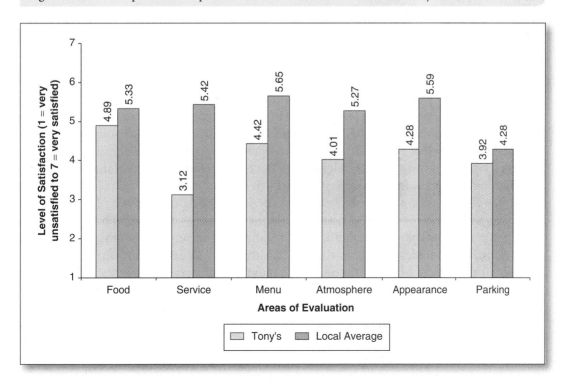

Figure 14.17   Example of Stacked Bar Chart

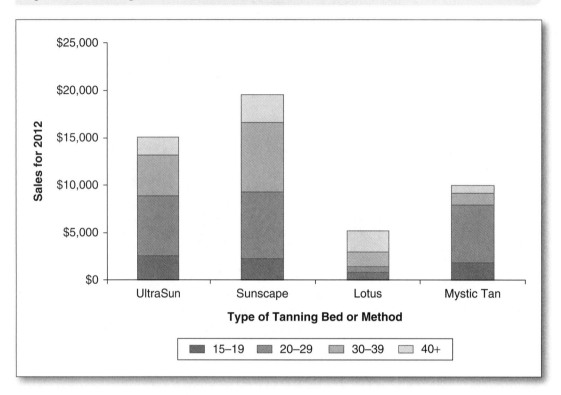

Global Concerns

Reporting the results of a global research study can be particularly challenging. Effectively communicating results can be difficult when the audience is composed of people from different countries. While English is typically used for oral presentations as it tends to be the language that audience members are most likely to have in common, comprehension may suffer among those who consider English to be their second language. Misinterpretation can even occur among those who speak English in the United Kingdom versus America. For example, a report given by a researcher from England might state, "It is recommended that the planned expansion into Eastern Europe be tabled." To an American, this recommendation would seem to indicate that expansion plans be abandoned or shelved. Yet in England the word *tabled* means to put forth for approval, which is the exact opposite of the meaning as understood by Americans.[7]

Interpreting data collected in another country and then drawing conclusions from that data can be difficult and fraught with risk. Reineke Reitsma, research director at Forrester Research, has over 20 years of experience with conducting international research projects. "It's really hard to understand the real drivers of behavior in different regions. Just looking at the results and comparing them with those of other countries might result in the wrong conclusions."[8]

Reitsma believes it is essential that research firms collaborate with local teams in the country under study. She strongly recommends that local teams serve as a resource for gaining additional insights into the data and brainstorming potential recommendations. Local teams help to provide perspectives that may be lacking on the part of a researcher who is not as familiar with cultural nuances. "One of the challenges is that our brain translates new information into concepts with which it is familiar . . . But is it true?"[9]

In the past, marketers have ignored cultural norms to their detriment. "These norms are very influential forces, and can represent the difference between successful production introduction and failure. Unfortunately, cultural norms are usually very subtle rather than blatant or obvious, which makes them hard to discern and detect."[10] Thus understanding cultural norms is a key area in which local teams can be particularly helpful, especially when developing insights, and brainstorming potential recommendations.

SUMMARY

Objective 1: Identify the goals of preparing marketing research reports and presentations.

The goals of marketing research reports and presentations are to effectively communicate research findings, provide interpretations of the findings, draw conclusions, provide insight, make recommendations, and highlight limitations of the research. Effective research reports begin with understanding the different types of individuals who will read the report or listen to the presentation. These individuals are looking for insights and information to make a business decision.

Objective 2: Describe the various components of a marketing research report.

The components of a research report include the title page, table of contents, executive summary, introduction, research methodology, data analysis findings, conclusions and recommendations, and appendices. The title page indicates who the report is for and who prepared it. The executive summary is written last and should provide an overall summary of the report's content. The introduction lays the foundation for the report by providing background information and the original research objectives. The research methodology discusses the research design, secondary data used, procedure for collecting primary data, sampling plan, sampling procedure, data collection process, and analytical techniques. The largest section of the paper is the findings from the data analyses. Each finding should be tied to a specific research objective. The conclusions and recommendations should be derived from the findings of the data analysis and insights gained from the research. The appendices will contain any supporting documents.

Objective 3: Explain the four principles of an executive-ready report.

A newer, trimmer version of the research report is the executive-ready report. It is based on the four principles of conciseness, adaptability, readability, and balance. Conciseness refers to eliminating all unnecessary words, figures, tables, and charts. Adaptability refers to a report that can be adapted by different people within an organization, from high-level executives to marketing personnel. Readability means the report tells a story, is visually appealing, and engages the reader. Balance involves obtaining a balance between visual interest and professional content. It also refers to a balance between being too wordy and too brief.

Objective 4: Discuss the use of oral presentations in marketing research reporting.

Oral reports are often part of research reports. Creating effective oral presentations involves five principles: keep it right, keep it simple, focus on the audience's needs, engage the audience, and take a risk. Keeping it right involves providing insights, not just reporting findings. Keeping it simple means not using research terminology. Focusing on the audience's needs refers to presenting information the audience wants, which primarily provides insights into how to solve the problem at hand. Such an approach will engage the audience. Lastly, the presenter needs to take some risk and take a stand on what should be done.

Objective 5: Explain how to use graphs and charts effectively.

Charts and graphs are an essential component of reports and provide visual appeal. It is important to make sure they are well prepared, are properly labeled, and provide the correct perception. With pie charts, individuals look at the upper right corner first, so the pie needs to be rotated so the correct piece is displayed. Pie charts are excellent for nominal and ordinal data. For ratio data, line or area charts can be used. In creating line or area graphs, it is important to label both axes. Column and bar charts can be used for graphing nominal, ordinal, or interval data. They are excellent for tests that involve differences of means or percentages, such as chi-square, t-test, and ANOVA.

GLOSSARY OF KEY TERMS

Conclusions: expanding of the interpretation to explain what the results of a research study actually mean

Executive summary: presents a summary of the entire research report including the purpose of the research, key findings, conclusions, and recommendations

Executive-ready report: shorter marketing research report based on principles of conciseness, adaptability, readability, and balance

Findings: results of the data analysis

Insights: conclusions derived from research that help firms to make more intelligent marketing decisions, which result in a competitive advantage for their company or brand

Interpretations: presentation of findings in a context that the listener or reader can more easily understand

Legend: explains what each different color-coded portion of the graph or chart represents

Limitations: any potential problems that may have arisen during the data collection process or because of assumptions that were made during the research study

Recommendations: courses of action that should be taken by the firm based on the results of the study

Table of contents: lists the different sections of the report in sequential order

Title page: front cover of the research report

CRITICAL THINKING EXERCISES

1. Critique the bar chart shown in Figure 14.18. What problems need to be addressed? Is any information missing that would aid in interpretation? Explain.

Figure 14.18   Critical Thinking Question

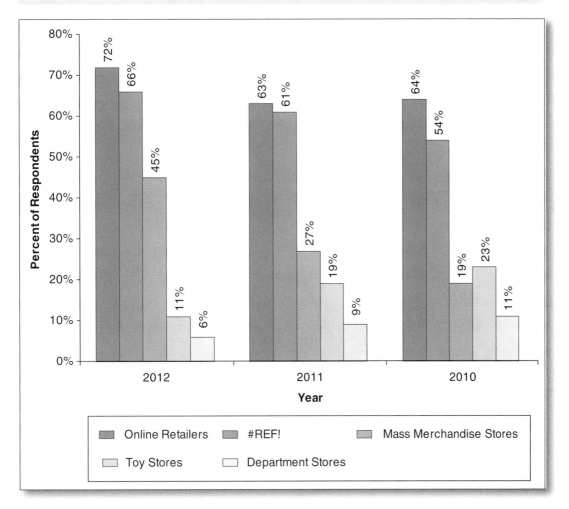

2. Critique the pie chart shown in Figure 14.19. What problems need to be addressed? Is any information missing that would aid in interpretation? Explain.

Figure 14.19   Critical Thinking Question 2

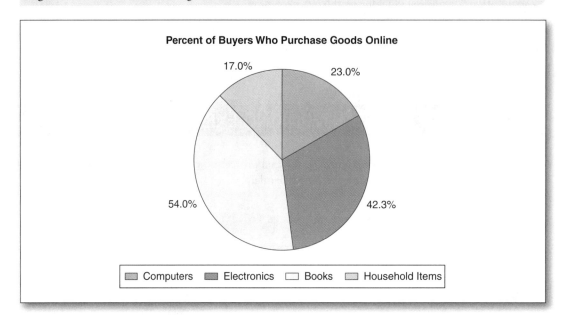

3. Critique the stacked area chart shown in Figure 14.20. What problems need to be addressed? Is any information missing that would aid in interpretation? Explain.

Figure 14.20   Critical Thinking Question 3

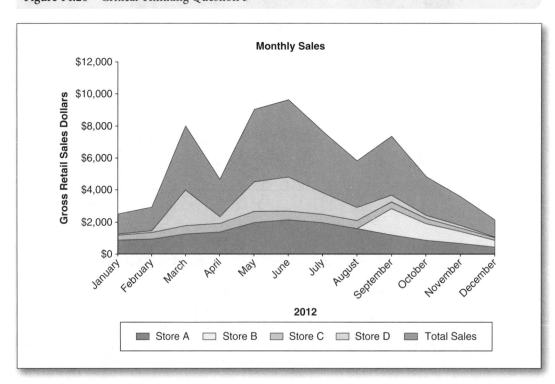

4. Critique the line chart shown in Figure 14.21. What problems need to be addressed? Is any information missing that would aid in interpretation? Explain.

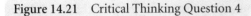

Figure 14.21   Critical Thinking Question 4

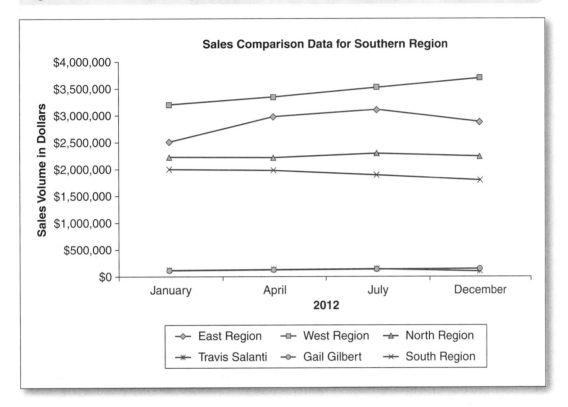

5. In reporting the nature of the sample, should the percent of individuals who failed to pass the screening criteria be mentioned in the report? Why or why not?

6. Compare and contrast the nature of findings, conclusions, insights, and recommendations in your own words. In what ways are they related? How do they differ? Use an example to illustrate your discussion.

7. A Nielsen research study found that 60% of social media users generate product or service ratings/reviews online. Only 5% and 7% of those who engaged in online reviewing rated baby care, or toys, respectively. However, an additional 16% and 22% of social media users read reviews related to baby care and toys, respectively. These findings contributed to Nielsen's insight that "creation of content about toys, jewelry and baby care is concentrated—far more people consume this content vs. creating."[11] How could you use this insight to help create actionable recommendations for the marketing of either toys or baby care items?

The following questions require that you access the SPSS data file titled "Chapter14 Critical Thinking Data," as well as the files titled "Chapter 14 Critical Thinking Analysis" and "Chapter 14 Critical Thinking Survey" (located at www.sagepub.com/clowess).

8. Assume you have been tasked with creating the visuals for a PowerPoint presentation related to this study. As part of the planning process, your manager has requested that you create a table listing the following information: chart title, name(s) of variable(s) to be charted, level of data corresponding to each variable (nominal, ordinal, interval, and ratio), type of chart recommended, base to be used, and special instructions. Be specific in making recommendations. Specify whether a bar chart should be a simple bar chart, clustered bar chart, or stacked bar chart. For pie charts, note if an exploding slice is desired. Area charts can be plain or stacked. Indicate whether the base to be used should be all members of the sample, only those who were asked the question, or just those who answered. Special instructions may include directions to eliminate those who chose "don't know," "no opinion," or "not applicable" response categories.

9. Create a pie chart, a bar chart, and a stacked bar chart for Question 1 and for Question 3 of the questionnaire. Which chart would you recommend using to display the answers to each question, and why?

10. Review the independent t-test results for Question 2 of the survey. Create one or more charts or graphs to display the results of these tests. Should your charts be limited to displaying only those variables for which significant differences were found? Why or why not?

11. Devise a table, chart, or graph to display the results to Question 4 of the questionnaire. Justify your choice for presenting the data in this fashion.

12. Create a clustered bar chart to display the cross-tabulations between Questions 3 and 5, Questions 3 and 6, and Question 3 and 7. Would you recommend including all of these charts in the final report? Why or why not?

CONTINUING CASE STUDY: LAKESIDE GRILL

With the analysis finished, the team of Alexa, Juan, Destiny, Brooke, and Zach jumped into discussing insights they gained from the research. Using their analysis as well as discussions with their marketing professors and the owner of Lakeside Grill, the team drew some conclusions. Based on these conclusions, they generated some recommendations.

The team debated on the best approach for the report and presentation. After talking it over with their marketing advisor and the owner of Lakeside Grill, the team decided to create a PowerPoint presentation since there would be an oral presentation. They developed two versions of the presentation. The first was a PowerPoint with all of the findings, conclusions, insights, and recommendations. They would give this to the owner in case he wanted additional information or wanted to see everything they learned. The second PowerPoint had only the findings that were relevant to the conclusions, insights, and recommendations. It was this second one that was used for the actual oral presentation.

In the process of preparing the report, the team realized that "wait time" for food and service was an issue. So they went back and pulled the data from the restaurant relating to sales and costs, especially labor costs. This information was then added to the primary research that was conducted through the survey.

Access the report and PowerPoint presentation at the textbook website, www.sagepub. com/clowess. The first PowerPoint is titled "Chapter 14 Lakeside Grill Full Report" and the second is titled "Chapter 14 Lakeside Grill Presentation."

Critique Questions:

1. Review the full PowerPoint presentation in terms of factors that are commonly associated with poor and ineffective PowerPoint presentations (see Figure 14.7). How well did the students avoid these pitfalls?

2. Now review the full PowerPoint presentation in terms of the factors presented in Figure 14.8, how to make a presentation come alive. How well did the team do?

3. Examine the conclusions, insights, and recommendations. Do these fit the findings? Do you see any additions, deletions, or modifications that should be made? Justify your thoughts.

4. Evaluate the "Chapter 14 Lakeside Grill Presentation" PowerPoint that was used for the formal presentation to the owner of Lakeside Grill. What is your evaluation of the conclusions, insights, and recommendations? Evaluate the merits of each recommendation.

5. Now compare the presentation (second PowerPoint) to the full PowerPoint. Do you agree or disagree with the slides that were not included? Why? Are there slides in the final presentation that should not have been included? If so, which ones? Why?

6. Overall, how well did the team do with the presentation?

MARKETING RESEARCH PORTFOLIO

The Chapter 14 "Marketing Research Portfolio" assignment offers students the opportunity to prepare an executive-ready report. It is recommended that an instructor first assign the Chapter 13 "Marketing Research Portfolio" assignment, as the executive-ready report will be built off of the data analyses assigned in this chapter. Students will also prepare charts, graphs, and appendices to accompany the written report. The assignment instructions and case information can be found at www.sagepub.com/clowess.

STUDENT STUDY SITE

Visit the Student Study Site at www.sagepub.com/clowess to access the following additional materials:

- eFlashcards
- Web Quizzes
- SAGE Journal Articles
- Web Resources

Appendix

Careers in Marketing Research

T hinking about a career in marketing research? If not, perhaps you should be, as the research industry is booming. According to the U.S. *Occupational Outlook Handbook* (http://www.bls.gov/ooh/), faster-than-average growth is being experienced in many marketing research positions. For example, the number of marketing research analyst positions is expected to grow by 41% between 2010 and 2020.[1] Check the U.S. *Occupational Outlook Handbook* for the most current information regarding median pay, the work environment, and several other factors of interest.

SKILLS NEEDED

A career in marketing research is not for everyone. Virtually every professional position requires strong analytical skills. The ability to communicate well, both verbally and in writing, is also important. As global business initiatives continue to grow, being successful in the research industry will require an increasingly global outlook. Furthermore, it is very important that individuals entering the industry thoroughly comprehend how social networking and the Internet have changed data collection. An integrative understanding of how qualitative and quantitative data can be used together to provide insights and the ability to work well with others are also necessary ingredients for success. The majority of professional research positions require at least a bachelor's degree while some require advanced degrees. Job prospects in more senior positions are better for candidates who have both advanced degrees and several years of experience in the industry.

INDUSTRIES EMPLOYING MARKETING RESEARCHERS

The field of marketing research is quite diverse as the need for information is prevalent in almost every industry. Research positions often exist within major corporations, such as consumer goods firms like General Mills. These firms use marketing research information internally to understand their target markets, develop new products, gauge customer satisfaction, and develop and evaluate marketing mix options. Some major business-to-business firms employ researchers in a similar capacity, though their focus is on understanding the needs of the business end user and developing and marketing products or services to meet business firms' needs.

A variety of firms exist solely for the purpose of conducting, packaging, and selling marketing research services. Research suppliers range from major syndicated research firms such as the Nielsen Company and Millward Brown to smaller full-service or boutique consulting practices, and even include firms that specialize in sample provision or data collection. Research providers are probably the most common employer of individuals who work in the marketing research industry. It is also typical for major advertising agencies to have a research department that assists in the development of creative advertising campaigns, by providing targeted research that allows the account managers and creative staff to better understand their clients' products and services.

TYPES OF MARKETING RESEARCH POSITIONS

While there are some positions in the research industry that require little education and experience, such as interviewers who read questions on telephone surveys or administer surveys in a face-to-face setting, professional research positions are the focus of this section. Brief descriptions of major career options in the marketing research industry are provided. Specialized positions, such as focus group moderator or statistician, which typically require degrees in areas other than business, are not discussed.

Project Director

Many individuals begin their careers as research project directors. Project directors work one-on-one with the client to develop the research purpose and questions, project schedule, qualitative and quantitative data collection instrument(s), and analysis plan. They then supervise the project as it is executed and report to a senior project director. Project directors manage internal resources as well as any outsourcing tasks, and are responsible for verifying the quality of data. Project directors are typically required to manage multiple research studies at the same time and thus must possess strong organizational, communication, and computer skills. Salaries range from $30,000 to $50,000.[2]

Senior Project Director

Senior project directors typically have a minimum of 3–5 years of experience in the research industry as well as a bachelor's degree in business, math, or science. Senior project directors train, supervise, and mentor project directors. Unlike their junior counterparts, senior project directors often deal directly with more sophisticated research studies, especially those that involve strategic business and marketing challenges, which they manage from inception to completion. It is not uncommon for senior project directors to conduct data analyses. Senior project directors are often involved in soliciting new business for their firm, as generating research proposals is a key function of this position. They are also responsible for managing and building relationships with existing clients. Typical salaries for senior project directors range from $40,000 to $60,000.[3]

Market/Marketing Research Analyst

Market(ing) research analysts interpret data, draw insights, and report research findings to the client. Most importantly, research analysts use the results of the research study to make and justify actionable recommendations that are in line with their clients' business goals and strategies. The heavy emphasis on client interaction and the presentation of information requires exceptional oral and written communication skills, as well as an excellent understanding of marketing tactics and overall business strategy. Strong analytical skills are necessary, as research analysts often perform complex data analyses in their search for insights. Analysts are often consulted in the development of data collection instruments, to ensure that the proper information is collected. Many positions require master's degrees in business, statistics, or math and at least 3 years of experience in the custom research industry. Salaries typically range from $50,000 to $80,000.[4]

Market Research Manager/Director

Market research managers/directors interact with clients in order to understand their needs and business objectives and then plan the research methodology, including the specific qualitative and quantitative research techniques to be used. While research managers may design questionnaires or moderator guides, they also work closely with either external research suppliers or internal project directors to ensure that the devised research plan is properly implemented. Similar to a research analyst, research managers are often required to interpret data, report findings, and make actionable recommendations. Strong analytical skills, often with advanced statistical modeling techniques, may be required. However, positions as research managers are often specific to a particular industry or sector, requiring 1–3 years of experience within that industry and 5–7 years of experience in the field of custom market research. Advanced degrees may also be required. Salaries for research managers typically range from $50,000 to $70,000.[5]

Senior Research Manager/Director

Senior research managers/directors work closely with clients who face more complex situations and assist in defining the challenges that face the client's business. Senior research managers then develop research plans and select the appropriate qualitative and quantitative research techniques to address the client's research needs. Similar to senior project managers, senior research managers train, supervise, and mentor research managers. Senior project managers review data analyses and reports created by others for accuracy, and critique as necessary to maximize the value of the deliverables. Senior research management positions require 5–7 years of industry or sector experience and a minimum of 7–10 years of experience in the field of custom market research. Master's level or doctoral degrees are required. Salaries for senior research managers typically range from $60,000 to $90,000.[6]

Market Research Account Executive

Account executives, sometimes called account managers, differ from the positions discussed thus far in that they are rarely, if ever, involved in the execution of research tasks, data analysis, or reporting. Rather, account executives' primary responsibility is to sell the services of the syndicated, boutique, or custom research firm. As such, they are responsible for meeting sales goals, developing research proposals in response to requests for proposal, delivering creative sales presentations, and working with project managers and research managers to develop the desired deliverables. Much of their effort may be geared toward building customer relationships and gaining incremental business among current customers via cross-selling of the firm's products. Account executive positions require recent sales experience in a position that provides service to clients. Travel is often required. The typical salary for a market research account executive ranges from $50,000 to $70,000 (exclusive of bonuses and commissions), and a bachelor's degree is required.

Senior Market Research Account Executive

Senior account executives have many of the same responsibilities as an account executive, with a few key differences. Senior account executives are responsible for managing and mentoring account executives. Prospecting and finding new customers is a key job function. Thus, senior account executives must be creative in developing proposals that are innovative and that make research recommendations (often related to new or revised product opportunities) of value to the potential client firm. As senior account executives are heavily involved in the contract development for new clients, negotiation skills are critical. Strong industry contacts are helpful, and frequent travel is typically part of the job. Senior account executives need 5–7 years of market research sales experience; salaries range from $70,000 to $100,000 (exclusive of bonuses and commissions).[7]

Market Research Vice President

At the pinnacle of the research profession is the vice president of market research. Positions of this nature are primarily found in research suppliers, such as syndicated or custom research firms. Generally, vice presidents have 10–15 years of marketing research sales experience as well as experience in the planning and implementation of both qualitative and quantitative research methods. An MBA or advanced degree is required. Vice presidents are primarily responsible for all research efforts pertaining to a geographic region, specific industry, or sector. Duties include strategic planning to meet sales and profitability goals; identifying opportunities to exploit, which could grow sales or market share; providing leadership to and staffing/managing positions within the research department; and ensuring customer satisfaction and quality deliverables. Salaries for vice presidents of market research begin at approximately $125,000 and can be much higher.[8]

Notes

Chapter 1

1. "Social Media 2011—Updated Version," March 25, 2011, http://www.youtube.com/watch?v=QSQrNUrGFr0 (accessed January 18, 2012).

2. "The Social Break-up," Report #8, *ExactTarget CoTweet,* 2011, http://www.exacttarget.com/Resources/SFF8.pdf (accessed June 9, 2012).

3. Shar VanBoskirk, "US Interactive Marketing Forecast, 2009 to 2014," *Forrester Research, Inc.,* July 6, 2009 (updated July 20, 2009).

4. "Super Bowl Sunday Consumer Survey," Super Bowl XLV (January 2011), *Lightspeed Research,* p. 17.

5. Klaus M. Miller, Reto Hofstetter, Harley Krohmer, and Zhand Z. John, "How Should Consumers' Willingness to Pay Be Measured? An Empirical Comparison of State-of-the-Art Approaches," *Journal of Marketing Research,* Vol. 48, No. 1 (February 2011), pp. 172–184.

6. Section based on Earl R. Babbie, *Survey Research Methods* (Belmont, CA: Wadworth, 1973), pp. 10–19.

7. David W. Stewart, "From Methods and Projects to Systems and Processes: The Evolution of Marketing Research Techniques," *Marketing Research,* Vol. 3, No. 3 (September 1991), pp. 25–36.

8. Scott Christofferson and Beverly Chu, "The Client-Side Researcher 2.0," http://rwconnect.esomar.org/2011/05/10/the-client-side-researcher-2.0 (accessed January 20, 2012).

9. Interview with Debbie Peternana and Carrie Bellerive, ReRez (February 25, 2011).

10. Brett Hagins, "Getting to the Big Picture—the Pros and Cons of In-House vs. Outsourced Research," *Quirk's Marketing Research Review,* May 24, 2011, http://www.quirks.com/articles/2011/20110526–1.aspx?searchID=203333123&sort=5&pg=1 (accessed June 9, 2012).

11. Section-based interview with Leonard Murphy, BrandScan 360 (April 14, 2011); Jack Neff, "Will Social Media Replace Surveys as a Research Tool?" *Advertising Age,* March 21, 2011, http://adage.com/print/149509 (accessed June 9, 2012).

12. Jack Neff, "Will Social Media Replace Surveys as a Research Tool?" *Advertising Age,* March 21, 2011, http://adage.com/print/149509 (accessed June 9, 2012).

13. Interview with Michael Patterson, Probit Research (April 14, 2011).

Chapter 2

1. Laurie Sullivan, "Millennials Remain Difficult to Reach," *Online Media Daily,* January 24, 2012, www.mediapost.com/publications/article/166427 (accessed June 15, 2012).

2. Ibid.

3. "Online Shoppers Value Reviews, Ratings, Search," April 23, 2010, http://www.market ingprofs.com/charts/2010/3563/online-shoppers-value-reviews-ratings-search (accessed June 15, 2012).

4. Ibid.

5. Interview with Dave Snell, The Richards Group (May 11, 2010).

6. Wayne Friedman, "Online Ads Surpass TV Ads in Recall, Likability," *Media Daily News,* April 22, 2010, http://www.mediapost.com/publications/article/126671/online-ads-surpass-tv-ads-in-recall-likability.html (accessed June 15, 2012).

7. Ibid.

8. This section based on Brian Morrissey, "Social Media Use Becomes Pervasive," *Adweek,* April 15, 2010, http://www.adweek.com/news/technology/social-media-use-becomes-perva sive-102092 (accessed June 15, 2012); "2010 Social Media Matters Study," http://www.blogher .com/files/Social_Media_Matters_2010.pdf (accessed April 19, 2010).

9. "ICC/ESOMAR International Code on Market and Social Research," http://www .esomar.org/uploads/public/knowledge-and-standards/codes-and-guidelines/ICCESOMAR_ Code_English_.pdf (accessed June 15, 2012).

10. Ibid.

11. Danuta Babinska and Aleksandra Nizielska, "International Marketing Research on the Markets of Central and Eastern Europe," *Journal of Economics & Management,* Vol. 6 (2009), pp. 5–19.

12. Adapted from Fred Pyrczak and Randall R. Bruce, *Writing Empirical Research Reports: A Basic Guide for Students of the Social and Behavioral Sciences,* 6th ed. (Glendale, CA: Pyrczak), 2007.

Chapter 3

1. "NPD Reports on E-Commerce: A Look at Consumers' Cross-Category Online Shopping Behavior," NPD Group Press Release, January 24, 2012, https://www.npd.com/wps/ portal/npd/us/news/pressreleases/pr_120124#.UAc1zzFSRDQ (accessed July 18, 2012).

2. Bette Marston, "Mobile Marketing: Only 9% of Mobile Users Ready for Ads," *Marketing News Exclusives*, April 15, 2010.

3. Michael Malone, "Study: Vast Majority of Live TV Viewers Sit Through Commercials," *Broadcasting & Cable*, May 10, 2010, http://www.broadcastingcable.com/article/452428-Study_ Vast_Majority_of_Live_TV_Viewers_Sit_Through_Commercials.php (accessed July 18, 2012).

4. NC SBTCD Restaurant Industry Study (Small Business & Technology Development Center, 2005).

5. Ciji A. Tlapa, Richard K. Miller, and Kelli Washington, "Restaurant & Hotel Food Trends," *Restaurant, Food & Beverage Market Research Handbook* (2010), pp. 1–73.

6. "My Best Segment: American Dreams," www.claritas.com/MyBestSegments (accessed June 15, 2010).

7. Ed Lee, "Effectiveness of Email and Direct Marketing: The Importance of Integrated Marketing Campaigns," May 7, 2008, http://edlee.ca/2008/05/07/effectiveness-of-email-and-direct-marketing–the-importance-of-integrated-marketing-campaigns.html (accessed June 20, 2010).

8. "E-mail Effectiveness UP: Study," DIRECT, November 25, 2003, http://chiefmarketer.com/news/e-mail-effectiveness-study (accessed July 18, 2012).

9. Michael Learmonth, "Study: Most Brands Still Irrelevant on Twitter," *Advertising Age*, July 27, 2010, http://adage.com/digital/article?article_id=145107 (accessed July 18, 2012).

10. Emily Steel, "Marketers Find Web Chat Can Be Inspiring," *The Wall Street Journal*, November 23, 2009, http://online.wsj.com/article/SB10001424052748703819904574551562382557556.html (accessed July 18, 2012).

11. <endnote id="ch09en35" label="35"><inst></inst><para>"Problem Solved," <emphasis>BtoB</emphasis> 92, No. 15 (November 12, 2007), p. 21.</para></endnote>

12. Kim McLynn, "Lowest Prices, Guarantees, and Brand Variety Are the Top Customer Satisfaction Drivers in the DIY Market, Reports NPD," June 7, 2010, http://www.npd.com/press/releases/press_100607.html (accessed July 18, 2012).

13. R. Lucas, "Issues to Consider Before Starting Your Market Research Project in Eastern Europe and/or Russia," *PMR Publications*, September 2006, http://www.research-pmr.com/userfiles/file/wp/issues_to_consider_before_starting_your_market_research_project_in_eastern_europe_russia.pdf (accessed December 15, 2010).

14. Danuta Babinska and Aleksandra Nizielska, "International Marketing Research on the Markets of Central and Eastern Europe," *Journal of Economics & Management*, Vol. 6 (2009), pp. 5–19.

15. "Using Basic Statistical Techniques," http://www.statcan.gc.ca/pub/11–533-x/2005001/using-utiliser/4072242-eng.htm#indexes (accessed July 16, 2010).

Chapter 4

1. Kelly Hancock, "Finding the Right Frequency," *Quirk's Marketing Research Review* (www.quirks.com), February 2012, Article ID 20120205, pp. 32–34.

2. Interview with Dave Snell, The Richards Group (May 11, 2010).

3. Carey V. Azzara, "Qualitatively Speaking: The Focus Group vs. In-Depth Interview Debate," *Quirks Marketing Research Review* (www.quirks.com), June 2010, Article ID 20100601, p. 16.

4. Based on an interview with Stan Richards, The Richards Group (February 5, 2010).

5. Raúl Pérez, "What Effect Does Tabletop Shape Have on Focus Group Dynamics and Client Viewing?" *Quirk's Marketing Research Review* (www.quirks.com), May 2010, Article ID 20100505, pp. 34, 36–40.

6. Barbara Lippert, "Domino's Delivers," *MediaWeek,* Vol. 20, No. 21 (May 24, 2010), p. 22.

7. Mark Goodin, "No More Mr. Nice Guy: Professional Respondents in Qualitative Research," *Quirk's Marketing Research Review* (www.quirks.com), December 2009, Article ID: 20091225-2.

8. Rhoda Schild, "Qualitatively Speaking: Communication Keeps Focus Groups Divine Not Dreadful," *Quirk's Marketing Research Review* (www.quirks.com), May 2009, Article ID: 20090501, pp. 20, 22–23.

9. Naomi Henderson, "Invisible Gold Mines: Unseen Opportunities Exist Just Outside the Focus Group," *Marketing Research,* Vol. 21, No. 3 (Fall 2009), pp. 26–27.

10. Piet Levy, "In With the Old, In Spite of the New," *Marketing News,* Vol. 43, No. 9 (May 30, 2009), p. 19.

11. Andrew Adam Newman, "Yes, the Diner's Open. How About a Seat at the Counter?" *The New York Times,* February 1, 2011, http://www.nytimes.com/2011/02/02/business/media/02adco.html (accessed July 23, 2012).

12. Naomi Henderson, "Hot Notes: Capture What Shouts Loudest," *Marketing Research,* Vol. 21, No. 4 (Winter 2009), pp. 28–29.

13. Michael Arndt, "Damn! Torpedoes Get Quiznos Back on Track," *Business Week,* No. 4164 (January 25, 2010), pp. 54–55.

14. Ibid.

15. "Aramark Launches Student-Created Burger Studio on College Campuses," *Foodservice Equipment & Supplies,* Vol. 62, No. 11 (November 2009), p. 8.

16. Katie Harris, "Qualitative Research: Quo Vadis?" *B&T Magazine,* Vol. 56, No. 2660 (May 30, 2008), p. 15.

17. http://www.decisionanalyst.com/Services/OnlineQualitative.dai (retrieved September 20, 2010).

18. Nikki Hopewell, "Online Group Messaging," *Marketing News,* Vol. 41, No. 14 (September 1, 2007), p. 22.

19. Lindsay E. Sammon, "Roxy Lady," *Footwear News,* Vol. 65, No. 6 (February 9, 2009), p. 84.

20. Interview with Kerri Martin, brand manager for BMW Motorcycles USA (October 12, 2002).

21. Interview with Sarah Stanley, University of Wisconsin—Oshkosh (July 28, 2010).

22. Carlos Flavian and Raquel Gurrea, "Digital Versus Traditional Newspapers," *International Journal of Market Research,* Vol. 51, No. 5 (2009), pp. 635–657.

23. http://www.decisionanalyst.com/Services/OnlineQualitative.dai (accessed September 16, 2010).

24. Emily Eakin, "Penetrating the Mind by Metaphor," *New York Times,* February 23, 2002, p. B11.

25. Catheryn Khoo-Lattimore, Maree Thyne, and Kirsten Robertson, "The ZMET Method: Using Projective Technique to Understand Consumer Home Choice," *The Marketing Review,* Vol. 9, No. 2 (2009), pp. 139–154.

Chapter 5

1. "Pharmaceutical Marketing," Ad Age Insights, White Paper (October 17, 2011), p. 10.

2. John Karelefski, "Simulated Supermarket Helps Frito-Lay Understand Shopper Behavior," *Shopper Insights,* August 2008, http://www.cpgmatters.com/ShopperInsights0808.html (accessed September 29, 2010).

3. Todd Wasserman, "Virtual Shopping, Real Results," *Brandweek,* April 16, 2009, http://www.brandweek.com/bw/content_display/news-and-features/direct/e3i27945265e8c954251e65ca9f07388ca1 (accessed September 29, 2010).

4. Moniek Buijzen and Patti M. Valkenburg, "Observing Purchase-Related Parent-Child Communication in Retail Environments: A Development and Socialization Perspective," *Human Communications Research,* Vol. 34, No. 1 (January 2008), pp. 50–69.

5. Paula Andruss, "The Case of the Missing Research Insights," www.marketingpower.com (accessed June 23, 2010).

6. Steve Hawter, Mae Nutley, and John F. Cindric, "An Employee, a Guest and a Mystery Shopper Walk Into a Restaurant . . . How CiCi's Pizza Used Mystery Shopping to Set Company-wide Standards/Evaluation Metrics," *Quirk's Marketing Research Review* (www.quirks.com), March 2010, Article ID: 2010032, pp. 24–28.

7. "93% of Banks Fail to Treat Incoming Prospect Inquiries as Sales Opportunities, Claims Report," *Credit Control*, Vol. 26, No. 3 (2005), p. 48.

8. Michael Carlon, "Qualitatively Speaking: Evolving Ethnography," *Quirks Marketing Research Review* (www.quirks.com), April 2008, Article ID: 20080408, pp. 18, 20.

9. Paul Skaggs, "Ethnography in Product Design: Looking for Compensatory Behaviors," *Journal of Management & Marketing Research*, Vol. 3 (January 2010), pp. 1–6.

10. Maren Elwood, "Of Stovetops and Laptops: Ethnography Tracks the Migration of Technology Into the American Kitchen," *Quirk's Marketing Research Review* (www.quirks.com), May 2010, Article ID: 20100506, pp. 42, 44–45.

11. Bill Abrams, "The Irreplaceable On-Site Ethnographer," *Quirk's Marketing Research Review* (www.quirks.com), February 2012, Article ID: 20120202, pp. 20–22.

12. Michael Carlon, "Qualitatively Speaking: Evolving Ethnography," *Quirks Marketing Research Review* (www.quirks.com), April 2008, Article ID: 20080408, pp. 18, 20.

13. Jiyao Xun and Jonathan Reynolds, "Applying Netnography to Market Research: The Case of the Online Forum," *Journal of Targeting, Measurement, and Analysis for Marketing*, Vol. 18, No. 1 (March 2010), pp. 17–31; Nikhilesh Dholakia and Dong Zhang, "Online Qualitative Research in the Age of E-Commerce: Data Sources and Approaches," *Forum Qualitative Sozialforshung/Forum: Qualitative Social Research*, Vol. 5, No. 2, Article 29 (May 2004).

14. "BrandBowl 2010 Presented by Mullen and Radian6," http://brandbow12010.com (accessed October 2, 2010).

15. Michael Bush, "Text Mining Provides Marketers With the 'Why' Behind Demand," *Advertising Age*, Vol. 80, No. 26 (July 27, 2009), p. 14.

16. Weiguo Fan, Linda Wallace, Stephanie Rich, and Zhonju Zhang, "Tapping the Power of Text Mining," *Communications of the ACM*, Vol. 49, No. 9 (September 2006), pp. 77–82.

17. Matt Schroder, "Watch Me as I Buy: How Online Observational Techniques Help Qualitative Researchers Keep Pace With the Speed of Consumers," *Quirk's Marketing Research Review* (www.quirks.com), February 2010, Article ID: 2010024, pp. 32, 34–35.

18. Eric Ward, "How Search Engines Use Link Analysis," http://searchenginewatch.com/2158431 (accessed December 19, 2001).

19. "New Age for Radio—Electronic Audience Measurement With the Portable People Meter™ System," www.arbitron.com/portable_people_meters/ppm_service.htm (accessed October 3, 2010).

20. Ibid.

21. "Television: How the Numbers Come to Life," http://en-us.nielsen.com/content/nielsen/en_us/measurement/tv_research/panels.html (accessed October 3, 2010).

22. Jon Puleston, "They Watch, You Learn," *Quirk's Marketing Research Review* (www.quirks.com), April 2008, Article ID: 20080406, pp. 64, 66–67.

23. "Eye Tracking: Case Study," *Marketing Week*, Vol. 32, No. 34 (2009), p. 23.

24. Bruce F. Hall, "On Measuring the Power of Communications," *Journal of Advertising Research*, Vol. 44, No. 2 (June 2004), pp. 181–188.

25. Ibid.

26. John Capone, "Microsoft and Initiative Strive for Better Advertising Through Neuroscience," *Online Media Daily,* December 9, 2009, www.mediapost.com/publications/?fa=Articles.printFriendly&art_aid=118835 (accessed July 25, 2012); Steve McClellan, "Mind Over Matter: New Tools Put Brands in Touch With Feelings," *Adweek,* February 18, 2008, http://www.adweek.com/news/television/mind-over-matter-94955 (accessed July 25, 2012).

27. Laurie Burkitt, "Battle for the Brain," *Forbes,* Vol. 184, No. 9 (November 16, 2009), pp. 76–78.

28. http://www.channelm2.com/M2VoiceAnalysis%20-%20Considerations.html (accessed October 3, 2010).

29. Pablo Flores and Jennifer Karsh, "Getting to Know You," *Quirk's Marketing Research Review* (www.quirks.com), February 2012, Article ID 20120206, pp. 36–39.

Chapter 6

1. Interview with Shama Kabani, Marketing Zen Group (February 20, 2010).

2. Diana Alison, "Email Beats Social Media for Grabbing Consumers' Attention," *InformationWeek,* July 30, 2010, www.informationweek.com/story/showArticle.jhtml?articleID=226400046 (accessed July 28, 2012).

3. Reba L. Kieke, "Report Shows Americans Do Not Do Their Homework When It Comes to Health Care," *Managed Care Outlook,* Vol. 19, No. 16 (August 15, 2006), pp. 1–6.

4. Edith DeLeeuw, Mario Callegaro, Joop Hox, and Gerty Lensvelt-Mulders, "The Influence of Advance Letters on Response Rates in Telephone Surveys," *Public Opinion Quarterly,* Vol. 71, No. 3 (Fall 2007), pp. 413–443.

5. Paula Vicente, Elizabeth Reis, and Maria Santos, "Using Mobile Phones for Survey Research," *International Journal of Market Research,* Vol. 51, No. 5 (2009), pp. 613–633; Paul J. Lavraksa, Charles D. Shuttles, Charlotte Steeh, and Howard Fienberg, "The State of Surveying Cell Phone Numbers in the United States," *Public Opinion Quarterly,* Vol. 71, No. 5 (2007), pp. 840–854.

6. Tanja Pferdekaemper, "Mobile Research Offers Speed, Immediacy," *Quirk's Marketing Research Review* (www.quirks.com), June 2010, Article #20100607, pp. 52, 54, 56, 58–59.

7. Ibid.

8. Ibid.

9. Gordon Freeman and Homer Moser, "How the Public Views Optometrists' Advertising: An Empirical Study," *Journal of Medical Marketing,* Vol. 9, No. 3 (July 2009), pp. 255–267.

10. "Internet Usage and Population in North America," http://www.internetworldstats.com/stats14.htm (accessed June 15, 2011).

11. Chris Gwinner, "By the Numbers: Protecting Online Survey Data Integrity," *Quirk's Marketing Research Review* (www.quirks.com), July 2008, Article #20080708, pp. 20–22; Michael Hesser, "Each Has Its Strengths and Weaknesses," *Quirk's Marketing Research Review* (www.quirks.com), January 2008, Article 20080101, pp. 26–28.

12. Andrew O'Connell, "Reading the Public Mind," *Harvard Business Review* (October 2010), pp. 27–29.

13. Interview with Debbie Peternana, ReRez Research (February 25, 2011).

14. Ibid.

15. Francois Coderre, Natalie St. Laurent, and Anne Mathieu, "Comparison of the Quality of Qualitative Data through Telephone, Postal and Email Surveys," *International Journal of Marketing Research*, Vol. 46, No. 3, Quarter 3 (2004), pp. 347–357.

16. Michael Hesser, "Each Has Its Strengths and Weaknesses," *Quirk's Marketing Research Review* (www.quirks.com), January 2008, Article 20080101, pp. 26–28.

17. Interview with Debbie Peternana, ReRez Research (November 13, 2011).

18. Pam Bruns, "By the Numbers: Make Your International Phone Interviews Successful in any Language," *Quirk's Marketing Research Review* (www.quirks.com), December 2009, Article #20091202, pp. 20, 22.

19. Jeffrey M. Jones, "Obama Approval Rally Largely Over," June 15, 2011, http://www.gallup.com/poll/148046/Obama-Approval-Rally-Largely.aspx (accessed July 15, 2012).

20. Ibid.

Chapter 7

1. "Case Study: DTech," www.hepcommunications.com/our-work/case-studies (accessed February 10, 2012).

2. Information in this section is based on Donald T. Campbell and Julian C. Stanley, *Experimental and Quasi-Experimental Designs for Research* (Boston: Houghton Mifflin, 1963), pp. 5–12.

3. Paul E. Spector, *Research Designs* (Beverly Hills: CA: Sage, 1981), pp. 16–17.

4. Marla B. Royne, "Cautions and Concerns in Experimental Research on the Consumer Interest," *The Journal of Consumer Affairs*, Vol. 42, No. 3 (2008), pp. 478–483.

5. Komal Nagar, "Effect of Deceptive Advertising on Claim Recall: An Experimental Research," *Journal of Services Research*, Vol. 9, No. 2 (October 2009), pp. 105–122.

6. Keith Chrzan, "Data Use: An Overview of Pricing Research," *Quirk's Marketing Research Review* (www.quirks.com), July/August 2006, Article ID 20060711, pp. 24, 26–29.

7. Milford Prewitt, "R&D Executives Find Testing New Products, Designs Costly but Necessary," *National's Restaurant Business*, Vol. 40, No. 49 (December 4, 2006), pp. 1, 46.

8. Karen Dillon, "I Think of My Failures as Gifts," *Harvard Business Review*, Vol. 89, Issue 4 (April, 2011), pp. 86–89.

9. Milford Prewitt, "R&D Executives Find Testing New Products, Designs Costly but Necessary," *National's Restaurant Business*, Vol. 40, No. 49 (December 4, 2006), pp. 1, 46.

10. Robert Zimmerman, "Problems Inherent in Using a Test Market," *Quirk's Marketing Research Review* (www.quirks.com), August 1988, Article ID: 19880804, p. 12.

11. Jerry Mullman, "The Next Hot Spot for U.S. Test Market is in Canada," *Advertising Age*, Vol. 80, Issue 38 (November 9, 2009), pp. 4, 33.

12. "Coca-Cola Soft Drink—Raspberry," *MarketWatch: Drinks*, Vol. 4, No. 9 (September 2005), p. 6.

Chapter 8

1. "HipCricket: 2011 Mobile Marketing Survey Research Brief," www.hipcricket.com (accessed February 12, 2012).

2. Rieva Lesonsky, "Survey Says: Why Women Love Facebook and Twitter More Than Shoes," aol.original, July 28, 2010, http://smallbusiness.aol.com/2010/07/28/survey-says-why-women-may-love-facebook-and-twitter-more-than-s/ (accessed August 5, 2012).

3. "Travel and Hospitality Study Reveals Top Email Marketing Challenges and Priorities," Yahoo! Finance, May 6, 2010, http://www.strongmail.com/company/news-and-events/press-releases/2010/press_050610 (accessed August 5, 2012)

4. Richard P. Vioksy and Todd F. Shupe, "Manufacturers' Perceptions About Using Treated Wood in Children's Playground Equipment," *Forest Products Journal*, Vol. 55, No. 12 (December 2005), pp. 190–193.

5. Mansour Fahimi and Dale Kulp, "Address-Based Sampling May Provide Alternatives for Surveys That Require Contacts with Representative Samples of Households," Quirk's Marketing Research Service (www.quirks.com), May 2009, Article ID: 20090508, pp. 66, 68–70, 72.

6. Bonnie W. Eisenfeld, "Qualitatively Speaking: Sampling for Qualitative Researchers," *Quirk's Marketing Research Review* (www.quirks.com), March 2007, Article ID: 20070308, pp. 18, 20.

7. Joe DeCosmo, "Nth-ing to Consider," *Direct*, Vol. 15, No. 7 (May 15, 2003), pp. 29–31.

8. Andrew Zelin and Roger Stubbs, "Cluster Sampling: A False Economy?" *International Journal of Market Research*, Vol. 47, No. 5 (2005), pp. 503–524.

9. "Use of Social Media Explodes—Almost Half of Americans Have Profiles, Says New Arbitron/Edison Research Study," April 8, 2010, www.smartbrief/news/AAAA/inudstryPR-details.jsp (accessed April 13, 2010); "Online Shoppers Value Reviews, Ratings, Search," April 23, 2010, www.marketingprofs.com/charts/2010/3563/online-shoppers-value-reviews-ratings-search (accessed August 3, 2012); Brian Morrissey, "Social Media Use Becomes Pervasive," *Adweek*, April 15, 2010, http://www.adweek.com/news/technology/social-media-use-becomes-pervasive-102092 (accessed August 3, 2012).

10. "Global Panel Sizes," www.researchnow.com (accessed January 16, 2011).

11. Thomas F. Stafford and Dennis Gonier, "The Online Research Bubble," *Communications of the ACM*, Vol. 50, No. 9 (September 2007), pp. 109–112.

12. Interview with Debbie Peternana and Carrie Bellerive, ReRez (February 25, 2011).

13. Craig Stevens, Terry Sweeney, and Ben Hogg, "Methods Matter," *Marketing Week*, Vol. 32, No. 8 (February 19, 2009), p. 41.

14. "Internet Usage Statistics: The Internet Big Picture. World Internet Users and Population Stats," http://www.internetworldstats.com/stats.htm (accessed June 14, 2011).

15. "Internet Usage and Population Statistics for North America," http://www.internet worldstats.com/stats14.htm#north (accessed June 14, 2011).

16. Chuck Miller and Suresh Subbiah, "Methods of Ensuring Online Sample Quality Around the World," *Quirk's Marketing Research Review* (www.quirks.com), January 2011, Article #20110104, pp. 34, 36, 38.

Chapter 9

1. Carl Marcucci, "Mobile Advertising Up Dramatically," *Radio & Television Business Report,* November 28, 2011, http://rbr.com/mobile-advertising-up-dramatically/ (accessed August 6, 2012).

2. A. Parasuraman, Valerie A. Zeithaml, and Leonard L. Berry, "SERVQUAL: A Multiple-Item Scale for Measuring Customer Perceptions of Service Quality," *Journal of Retailing,* Vol. 67 (Winter 1998), pp. 420–450.

3. Gordon C. Bruner II, Karen E. James, and Paul J. Hensel, *Marketing Scales Handbook: A Compilation of Multi-Item Measures,* Vol. III (Chicago: American Marketing Association, 2001); Gordon C. Bruner II, Paul J. Hensel, and Karen E. James, *Marketing Scales Handbook:*

A Compilation of Multi-Item Measures for Consumer Behavior & Advertising, 1998–2001, Vol. IV (Mason, OH: Texere, an imprint of Thomson/South-Western, 2005).

    4. Julia Lin, "Does the Rating Scale Make a Difference in Factor Analysis?" *Quirk's Marketing Research Review* (April 2008), p. 22, http://www.quirks.com/articles/2008/20080409.aspx?searchID=186762791&sort=4&pg=2 (accessed June 13, 2011).

Chapter 10

    1. William A. Mindak, "Fitting the Semantic Differential to the Marketing Problem," *Journal of Marketing*, Vol. 25, No. 4 (1961), pp. 28–33.

    2. Ibid.

    3. Hershey H. Friedman, Linda Weiser Friedman, and Beth Gluck, "The Effects of Scale-Checking Styles on Responses to a Semantic Differential Scale," *Journal of the Market Research Society*, Vol. 30, No. 4 (1988), pp. 477–481.

    4. John J. Ray, "Reviving the Problem of Acquiescent Response Bias," *Journal of Social Psychology*, Vol. 121, No. 3 (1983), pp. 81–96.

    5. Aimee L. Drolet and Donald G. Morrison, "Do We Really Need Multiple-Item Measures in Service Research?" *Journal of Service Research*, Vol. 3, No. 2 (2001), pp. 196–204; Jum C. Numally, *Psychometric Theory* (New York: McGraw-Hill, 1978).

    6. Scott D. Swain, Danny Weathers, and Ronald W. Niedrich, "Assessing Three Sources of Misresponse to Reversed Likert Items," *Journal of Marketing Research*, Vol. 45, No. 1 (2008), pp. 116–131.

    7. J. Dawes, "Do Data Characteristics Change According to the Number of Points Used? An Experiment Using 5-Point, 7-Point, and 10-Point Scales," *International Journal of Market Research*, Vol. 50, No. 1 (2008), pp. 61–77.

    8. A. W. Bendig, "The Reliability of Self-Ratings as a Function of the Amount of Verbal Anchoring and the Number of Categories on the Scale," *Journal of Applied Psychology*, Vol. 37, No. 1 (1953), pp. 38–41.

    9. Ibid.

    10. Eli P. Cox, "The Optimal Number of Response Alternatives for a Scale: A Review," *Journal of Marketing Research*, Vol. 17, No. 4 (1980), pp. 407–422.

    11. T. Amoo and H. H. Friedman, "Do Numeric Values Influence Subjects' Responses to Rating Scales," *Journal of International Marketing Research*, Vol. 26 (2001), pp. 41–46; C. Armitage and C. Deeprose, "Changing Student Evaluations by Means of the Numeric Values of Rating Scales," *Psychology of Learning and Teaching*, Vol. 3, No. 2 (2003), pp. 122–125; N. Schwartz et al., "Rating Scales: Numeric Values May Change the Meanings of Scale Labels," *Public Opinion Quarterly*, Vol. 55, No. 4 (1991), pp. 570–582.

    12. Gilbert A. Churchill, "A Paradigm for Developing Better Measures of Marketing Constructs," *Journal of Marketing Research*, Vol. 16, No. 1 (February 1979), pp. 64–73; Robert F. DeVellis, *Scale Development: Theory and Applications*, 3rd ed. (Thousand Oaks, CA: Sage, 2012); David W. Gerbing and James C. Anderson, "An Updated Paradigm for Scale Development Incorporating Unidimensionality and Its Assessment," *Journal of Marketing Research*, Vol. 25 (May 1988), pp. 186–192.

    13. Bart De Langhe, Stefano Puntoni, Daniel Fernandes, and Stijn M. J. Van Osselaer, "The Anchor Contraction Effect in International Marketing Research," *Journal of Marketing Research*, Vol. 48, No. 2 (April 2011), pp. 366–380.

14. Kristin Cavallaro, "Data Use: Are Global Scales As Easy as 1–2-3 or A-B-C?" *Quirks Marketing Research Review* (www.quirks.com), January 2011, Article 20110101, pp. 18, 20–22.

15. Keith Chrzan and Joey Michaud, "Response Scales for Customer Satisfaction Research," *Quirk's Marketing Research Review,* Article 20041004 (October 2004), p. 50.

16. Joseph F. Rocereto, Marina Puzakova, Rolph E. Anderson, and Hyokjin Kwak, "The Role of Response Formats on Extreme Response Style: A Case of Likert-Type vs. Semantic Differential Scales," *Advances in International Marketing,* Vol. 10, No. 22 (2011), pp. 53–71.

17. Patrick Elms, "Using Decision Criteria Anchors to Measure Importance Among Hispanics," *Quirk's Marketing Research Review,* Article 200101401 (April 2001); Jeffry N. Savitz, "Reconciling Hispanic Product Evaluation Ratings," *Quirk's Marketing Research Review,* Article 20111203 (December 2011), pp. 26, 28–32.

18. Gilbert A. Churchill, "A Paradigm for Developing Better Measures of Marketing Constructs," *Journal of Marketing Research,* Vol. 16, No. 1 (February 1979), pp. 64–73.

19. A. Parasuraman, Valarie A. Zeithaml, and Leonard L. Berry, "SERVQUAL: A Multiple-Item Scale for Measuring Consumer Perceptions of Service Quality," *Journal of Retailing,* Vol. 64 (Spring 1988), pp. 12–40.

Chapter 11

1. "Redefining Customer Value," a report from the Economist Intelligence Unit, SAS, p. 19.

2. Based on www.emarketer.com/reports/all/emarketer_2000815.aspx (accessed September 27, 2011).

3. Jonathan E. Brill, "The Exploratory Open-Ended Survey Question," *Quirk's Marketing Research Review* (www.quirks.com), March 1995, Article ID: 19950301.

4. Ibid.

5. Ibid.

6. David M. Ambrose and John R. Anstey, "Questionnaire Development: Demystifying the Process," *International Management Review,* Vol. 6, No. 1 (2010), pp. 83–90.

7. Interview with Debbie Peternana, ReRez (December 1, 2011).

8. Marco Vriens, Michael Wedel, and Zsolt Sandor, "Split-Questionnaire Designs: A New Tool in Survey Design and Panel Management", *Market Research* (American Marketing Association, Summer 2001), pp. 14–19.

9. Feray Adiguzel and Michel Wedel, "Split Questionnaire Design for Massive Surveys," *Journal of Marketing Research,* Vol. 45, No. 5 (October 2008), pp. 608–617.

Chapter 12

1. "NC SBTC Restaurant Industry Study," Small Business Technology Development Center, Raleigh, North Carolina, 2005.

2. Jonathan E. Brill, "The Exploratory Open-Ended Survey Question," *Quirk's Marketing Research Review* (www.quirks.com), March, 1995, Article ID: 19950301.

3. Bill MacElroy, "How to Catch a Cheat," *Quirk's Marketing Research Review* (www .quirks.com), July 2004, Article ID: 20040704, p. 46.

4. Shawna Fisher, "How to Spot a Fake," *Quirk's Marketing Research Review* (www.quirks .com), January 2007, p. 44.

5. Bill MacElroy, "How to Catch a Cheat," *Quirk's Marketing Research Review* (www .quirks.com), July 2004, Article ID: 20040704, p. 46.

6. Ibid.

7. Ibid.

8. Don Bruzzone, "Sampling the Impact: How Do Respondent Behaviors and Online Sample Quality Affect Measures of Ad Performance?" *Quirk's Marketing Research Review* (www .quirks.com), April 2009, Article ID: 20090404, pp. 32, 34–37.

9. Stephen J. Hellebusch, "By the Numbers: To Double-Code or Single-Code?" *Quirk's Marketing Research Review* (www.quirks.com), December 2003, Article 20031210.

10. Interview with Debbie Peternana, ReRez (December 1, 2011).

11. T. Amoo and H. H. Friedman, "Do Numeric Values Influence Subjects' Responses to Rating Scales," *Journal of International Marketing Research,* Vol. 26 (2001), pp. 41–46; C. Armitage and C. Deeprose, "Changing Student Evaluations by Means of the Numeric Values of Rating Scales," *Psychology of Learning and Teaching,* Vol. 3, No. 2 (2003), pp. 122–125; N. Schwartz et al., "Rating Scales: Numeric Values May Change the Meanings of Scale Labels," *Public Opinion Quarterly,* Vol. 55 (1991), pp. 570–582.

12. Kumar Mehta, "Best Practices in Managing Offshore Research Processes," *Quirk's Marketing Research E-Newsletter* (www.quirks.com), July 25, 2011, Article ID: 20110726-2.

13. Karl Field, "Do You Know Where Your Data Came From?" *Quirk's Marketing Research Review* (www.quirks.com), November 2007, Article 20071101, p. 24.

14. Kumar Mehta, "Best Practices in Managing Offshore Research Processes," *Quirk's Marketing Research E-Newsletter* (www.quirks.com), July 25, 2011, Article ID: 20110726-2.

15. Karl Field, "Do You Know Where Your Data Came From?" *Quirk's Marketing Research Review* (www.quirks.com), November 2007, Article 20071101, p. 24.

Chapter 13

1. "Super Bowl Sunday Consumer Survey," *Lightspeed Research,* January 2011, www .lightspeedresearch.com.

2. Patrick Baldasara and Vikas Mittel, "The Use, Misuse, and Abuse of Significance," *Quirk's Marketing Research Review* (www.quirks.com), November 1994, Article ID: 19941101.

3. Terry Grapentine, "Data Use: Statistical Significance Revisited," *Quirk's Marketing Research Review* (www.quirks.com), April 2011, Article ID: 20010401, pp. 18, 20–23.

4. Patrick Baldasara and Vikas Mittel, "The Use, Misuse, and Abuse of Significance," *Quirk's Marketing Research Review,* November 1994, Article ID: 19941101; Terry Grapentine, "Data Use: Statistical Significance Revisited," *Quirk's Marketing Research Review* (www.quirks .com), April 2011, Article ID: 20010401, pp. 18, 20–23; Doug Berdie, "Significant Differences," *Quirk's Marketing Research Review* (www.quirks.com), January 2012, pp. 30, 32–35.

5. Doug Berdie, "Significant Differences," *Quirk's Marketing Research Review* (www .quirks.com), January 2012, pp. 30, 32–35.

6. Doug Berdie, "Significant Differences," *Quirk's Marketing Research Review,* January 2012, p. 33.

7. Patrick Baldasara and Vikas Mittel, "The Use, Misuse, and Abuse of Significance," *Quirk's Marketing Research Review* (www.quirks.com), November 1994, Article ID: 19941101.

8. Gary M. Mullet, "The Statistics of Missed Opportunities (or) You Better Beware of Beta," *Quirk's Marketing Research* (www.quirks.com), December 1991, Article ID: 19911208.

9. Marija Norusis, *SPSS Base System User's Guide* (Chicago: SPSS Inc., 1990).

10. Rudolph R. Sinkovics and Elfriede Penz, "Multilingual Elite-Interviews and Software-Based Analysis: Problems and Solutions Based on CAQDAS," *International Journal of Market Research,* Vol. 53, No. 5 (2011), pp. 705–724.

11. Jesús Cambra-Fierro and Alan Wilson, "Qualitative Data Analysis Software: Will It Ever Become Mainstream?" *International Journal of Market Research,* Vol. 53, No. 1 (2011), pp. 17–24.

12. Ruth Rettie, Helen Robinson, Anja Radke, and Xiajiao Ye, "CAQDAS: A Supplementary Tool for Qualitative Market Research," *Qualitative Market Research: An International Journal,* Vol. 11, No. 1 (2008), pp. 76–88.

13. Jesús Cambra-Fierro and Alan Wilson, "Qualitative Data Analysis Software: Will It Ever Become Mainstream?" *International Journal of Market Research,* Vol. 53, No. 1 (2011), pp. 17–24.

Chapter 14

1. "The Future of Email: 8 Trends to Watch in 2012," *Lyris Marketing Guide,* Lyris Inc., www.lyris.com, December 2011.

2. Carla Penel and Will Leskin, "Mixing Art With Science: A Guide to Executive-Ready Reporting," *Quirk's Marketing Research Review* (www.quirks.com), May 2006, Article 20060504, pp. 48, 50–51.

3. Gary A. Schmidt, "Take a Risk, Keep It Simple," *Quirk's Marketing Research Review,* (www.quirks.com), April 2007, Article 20070404, pp. 52, 54–55.

4. N. Carroll Mohn, "How to Effectively Present Marketing Research Results," *Quirk's Marketing Research Review* (www.quirks.com), January 1989, Article 19890104.

5. Melissa Murray, "Making the Results Come Alive," *Quirk's Marketing Research Review* (www.quirks.com), October 2006, Article 20061005, pp. 58, 60–62, 64, 66.

6. Melissa Murray, "Making the Results Come Alive," *Quirk's Marketing Research Review,* October 2006, Article 20061005.

7. Robert B. Young and Rajshekhar G. Javalgi, "International Marketing Research: A Global Project Management Approach," *Business Horizons,* Vol. 50 (2007), pp. 113–122.

8. ESOMAR, "Running Global Research Projects," *RW Connect,* December 2, 2011, http://rwconnect.esomar.org/2011/12/02/the-challenges-of-running-global-research-projects/ (accessed January 3, 2012).

9. Ibid.

10. Robert B. Young and Rajshekhar G. Javalgi, "International Marketing Research: A Global Project Management Approach," *Business Horizons,* Vol. 50 (2007), pp. 113–122.

11. Radha Subramanyam, "Television Gets Social," *NM Incite—The State of Social Media Survey 2011* (The Nielsen Company, 2011).

Appendix

1. http://www.bls.gov/ooh/business-and-financial/market-research-analysts.htm (retrieved May 20, 2012).

2. http://www.marketresearchcareers.com/jobsandtrends.aspx (retrieved May 20, 2012); http://www.marketresearchcareers.com/jdprojectdirector.aspx (retrieved May 20, 2012).

3. http://www.marketresearchcareers.com/jobsandtrends.aspx (retrieved May 20, 2012); http://www.marketresearchcareers.com/jdseniorprojectdirector.aspx (retrieved May 20, 2012).

4. http://www.marketresearchcareers.com/jobsandtrends.aspx (retrieved May 20, 2012); http://www.marketresearchcareers.com/jdmarketresearchanalyst.aspx (retrieved May 20, 2012).

5. http://www.marketresearchcareers.com/jobsandtrends.aspx (retrieved May 20, 2012); http://www.marketresearchcareers.com/jdresearchmanager.aspx (retrieved May 20, 2012).

6. http://www.marketresearchcareers.com/jobsandtrends.aspx (retrieved May 20, 2012); http://www.marketresearchcareers.com/jdseniorresearchmanager.aspx (retrieved May 20, 2012).

7. http://www.marketresearchcareers.com/jobsandtrends.aspx (retrieved May 20, 2012); http://www.marketresearchcareers.com/jdsenioraccountexecutive.aspx (retrieved May 20, 2012).

8. http://www.marketresearchcareers.com/jobsandtrends.aspx (retrieved May 20, 2012); http://www.marketresearchcareers.com/jdvicepresident.aspx (retrieved May 20, 2012).

Photo Credits

Index

About the Authors

Kenneth Clow, PhD, is a professor of marketing and holds the Biedenharn Endowed Chair of Business in the College of Business Administration at the University of Louisiana at Monroe. Previously, he served as dean at both the University of Louisiana at Monroe and the University of North Carolina at Pembroke. His teaching career began at Pittsburg State University where he also served as the MBA director. He obtained his PhD from the University of Arkansas in 1992.

Dr. Clow has published over 220 articles in academic journals, proceedings, and textbooks. He has published articles in journals such as *Journal of Services Marketing; Services Marketing Quarterly; Journal of Business Research; Marketing Management Journal; Journal of Economics and Finance Education; International Journal of Business, Marketing, and Decision Sciences; Journal of Internet Commerce; Health Marketing Quarterly;* and *Journal of Restaurant and Foodservice Marketing.*

Books coauthored by Dr. Clow include *Integrated Advertising, Promotion, and Marketing Communications,* 6th edition (Prentice Hall); *Concise Encyclopedia of Advertising* (Haworth); *Essentials of Marketing,* 4th edition (Textbook Media); *Sports Marketing,* 1st edition (Prentice Hall); *Concise Encyclopedia of Professional Services Marketing* (Routledge, Taylor and Francis Group); and *Marketing Management* (SAGE).

Karen E. James, DBA, is a professor of marketing and chair of the Department of Management and Marketing at LSU Shreveport, where she holds the Joe and Abby Averett Professorship in Business. Dr. James earned both her DBA (1994) and MBA (1987) degrees from Southern Illinois University in Carbondale. She also received a BA in mass communication from Purdue University after completing a double major in public relations and radio and television production. Prior to joining the faculty at LSUS, Dr. James was employed in a full-time capacity as a marketing coordinator. Dr. James has consulted in health care marketing and focus group moderation, and has created numerous educational supplements for various publishers. She teaches marketing research on a regular basis, and has been published in *Business Communication Quarterly, Marketing Management Journal, Services Marketing Quarterly, Journal of Higher Education Management and Policy,* and *Journal of Education for Business,* among others.

SAGE researchmethods

The essential online tool for researchers from the world's leading methods publisher

Find exactly what you are looking for, from basic explanations to advanced discussion

More content and new features added this year!

"I have never really seen anything like this product before, and I think it is really valuable."

John Creswell, University of Nebraska–Lincoln

Discover **Methods Lists**—methods readings suggested by other users

Watch video interviews with leading methodologists

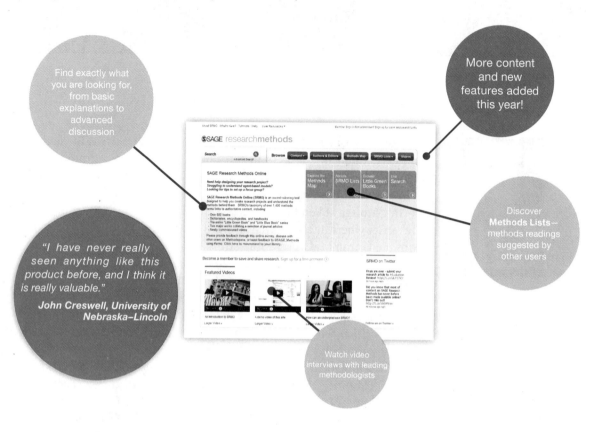

Explore the **Methods Map** to discover links between methods

Search a custom-designed taxonomy with more than 1,400 qualitative, quantitative, and mixed methods terms

Uncover more than 120,000 pages of book, journal, and reference content to support your learning

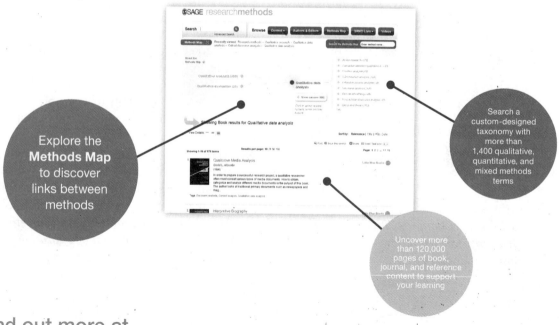

Find out more at
www.sageresearchmethods.com